4283

THE IDEA OF POVERTY

THE IDEA OF POVERTY

ENGLAND IN THE
EARLY INDUSTRIAL AGE

Gertrude Himmelfarb

ALFRED A. KNOPF

New York 1984

THIS IS A BORZOI BOOK
PUBLISHED BY ALFRED A. KNOPF, INC.

———————————

Copyright © 1983 by Gertrude Himmelfarb
All rights reserved under International and Pan-American Copyright
Conventions. Published in the United States by Alfred A. Knopf,
Inc., New York, and simultaneously in Canada by Random House
of Canada Limited, Toronto. Distributed by Random House, Inc.,
New York.

Library of Congress Cataloging in Publication Data

Himmelfarb, Gertrude.
The idea of poverty, England in the early industrial age.

Includes index.
1. Poor—England—History—19th century.
2. Poor—England—History—18th century. 3. Great
Britain—Economic conditions—1760–1860. I. Title.
HV4086.A3H55   1983   362.5'0942   83–47964
ISBN 0–394–53062–4

Manufactured in the United States of America
First Edition

To my husband

CONTENTS

PART THREE

"THE UNDISCOVERED COUNTRY OF THE POOR"

PART FOUR

THE FICTIONAL POOR

Photographic inserts will be found following pages 180 and 340

ACKNOWLEDGMENTS

This study grew—and grew—out of two essays written a dozen years ago. The first, on Jeremy Bentham's "Pauper Management" scheme (a pauper "utopia," as he called it), revealed so bizarre an experiment in "reform," and the second, on Henry Mayhew's *London Labour and the London Poor,* so strange a case of mistaken identity (the "labour" and "poor" of the title being strikingly at variance with the contents), that I was led to inquire further into a subject that could produce such anomalies. I soon discovered that it was not in fact a recognized subject of historical research—that while much had been written about poor laws and social reforms, about conditions of work and standards of living, there was little or no discussion, and certainly no systematic study, of the idea of poverty underlying either the reforms or the conditions. Because the subject had no accepted structure, no established boundaries, I found it expanding as I worked on it, so that what was originally meant to be a small monograph is now an inordinately large volume, with yet another to follow.

In the course of these years, I have incurred many obligations. I am grateful to the Woodrow Wilson International Center for the opportunity to devote the academic year of 1976–77 to research and writing and for the intellectual stimulation provided by the other fellows and the staff. A Rockefeller Foundation Humanities Fellowship in 1980–81 permitted me to complete this volume (and a fair part of the next) undistracted by teaching and administrative duties. The librarians of the Graduate School of the City University of New York and my research assistants over the years have all been more resourceful and helpful than I had any reason to expect. I want especially to thank Helga Feder, Myrna Chase, Gail Benicke, Ellen Jacobs, Sanford Hamilton, Barbara Leopold, Louise Forsyth, and Reinhard Igler.

An all too brief visit at Christ's College, Cambridge, in the winter of 1981 gave me the opportunity to discuss some of the themes of this book with historians, philosophers, and economists. If I did not avail myself of all their suggestions (a structuralist analysis of Adam Smith or a Freudian analysis of Malthus), I was stimulated and provoked by them. Those who read parts of this manuscript in an earlier draft—Lewis Feuer, Myron Magnet, John Osborne, Bernard Semmel, and Joel Wiener—will recognize my debt to them in the final product. And those who were burdened with the whole of it, the historian Robert K. Webb, my editors, Ashbel Green and Melvin Rosenthal, and above all my husband, Irving Kristol, cannot be sufficiently thanked, not only for their invaluable criticism and advice but for a vote of confidence in the book at a time when I had been too long with it and could no longer take the measure of it.

G.H.

THE IDEA OF POVERTY

INTRODUCTION

A decent provision for the poor is the true test of
civilization. . . . The condition of the lower orders, the
poor especially, was the true mark of national discrimination.
—Samuel Johnson, 1770[1]*

There is no touchstone, except the treatment of childhood, which reveals the true character of a social philosophy more clearly than the spirit in which it regards the
misfortunes of those of its members who fall by the way.
—R. H. Tawney, 1926[2]

It says a good deal about the history of modern England that the eighteenth
century Tory and the twentieth century Socialist should agree about this if
about little else—that the condition of the poor is the "touchstone" of a
civilization, a nation, a philosophy. They disagreed, to be sure, about what
constituted a "decent provision" for the poor, a disagreement that reflected
not only the ideological differences between Tory and Socialist but a
century and a half of economic, technological, social, and cultural changes
which profoundly transformed the very idea of poverty as much as the
condition of the poor. Yet it is surely significant that on the eve of that
transformation, from the heart of that "old society," there should have issued
sentiments which could so readily have been endorsed by one of the most
progressive thinkers of our own time. Whatever else changed during this
period, in this respect at least the end was in the beginning.

The "beginning" can, of course, be taken back to the very beginning
when it was first discovered that "ye have the poor always with you." That
thought came echoing down through the centuries with the authority of
Scripture and the practical wisdom of the ages. And with it came a complicated—ambivalent, we would now think it—conception of poverty, which
made it at the same time a blessing to be devoutly sought and a misfortune
to be piously endured. The "holy poor" embraced poverty as a sacred vow,
the better to do God's will; the "unholy poor" tolerated it (or railed against
it) as an unhappy fact of life, a cross to be borne with Christian fortitude

*Notes to chapters begin on p. 535.

3

or resisted with unchristian defiance. Those who were blessed not with poverty but with riches had the sacred duty of charity, the obligation to sustain the holy poor and to relieve the misery of the unholy. With every aspect of poverty and charity penetrated by religious meaning, the church inevitably became the instrument both of social amelioration and of spiritual salvation; indeed the one was a function of the other.

By Samuel Johnson's time, the conception of poverty had become largely secularized, so that it came to mean, in common usage, the involuntary, ignoble poverty of the "lower orders." This is not to say that there was anything impious in this conception. Johnson himself, a man of the firmest religious convictions, had no doubt that poverty had its source and justification in the primeval Fall, which condemned man to toil all the days of his life and to eat his bread by the sweat of his brow. But neither had he any romantic illusions about the ennobling nature of that poverty.

> In the prospect of poverty there is nothing but gloom and melancholy; the mind and body suffer together; its miseries bring no alleviations; it is a state in which every virtue is obscured, and in which no conduct can avoid reproach; a state of which cheerfulness is insensibility, and dejection sullenness, of which the hardships are without honour, and the labours without reward.[3]

This was no radical maverick, no professional philanthropist or reformer, but a notably unsentimental high Tory and high churchman who gave expression to a view of poverty that had become common in his time: the idea that while poverty was a natural condition, it was an unfortunate one, to be alleviated if possible, and that society had some responsibility for that alleviation. It was in this sense that a "decent provision" for the poor was the "true test of civilization," the "true mark of national discrimination."

As the idea of poverty became secularized, the poor tended to become (in some circumstances and for some purposes) the charge of the state. So it was, at any rate, in England. And it was partly because the English state assumed this responsibility that Johnson (and most of his contemporaries, Whig and Tory) judged England to have passed the "test of civilization" with the highest marks. The Elizabethan poor laws, dating from the late sixteenth century, had not only established the principle of a legal, compulsory, secular, national system of relief; they had also given England the reputation of a country where compassion had become public policy. Whatever the actual effect of those laws, however much they varied in practice from one area to another and from one time to the next, however much they were criticized or defended, amended or supplemented, that principle remained. And the laws themselves remained for three and a half centuries, until they were finally replaced by the welfare state after the Second World War. During the whole of that time (which is to say, a good part of the history of the modern world), England served as a social laboratory for other countries. The debates in Parliament and in the press, Royal Commission and Select Committee reports, social tracts and statistical surveys, were regularly cited and studied abroad. At least until the end of the nineteenth century, England was generally thought to be in the vanguard of social philosophy and social policy, in thinking about the problem of poverty and in trying to ameliorate it.

Just as America was the exemplar of democracy, so England was the exemplar of social welfare—and in both cases, for both good and ill. Visiting England in 1766, Benjamin Franklin paid tribute to the country which tried to do so much for the relief of the poor—and in the process, he believed, unwittingly exacerbated the problem of poverty.

> There is no country in the world where so many provisions are established for them; so many hospitals to receive them when they are sick and lame, founded and maintained by voluntary charities; so many almshouses for the aged of both sexes, together with a solemn law made by the rich to subject their estates to a heavy tax for the support of the poor. . . . In short, you offered a premium for the encouragement of idleness, and you should not now wonder that it has had its effect in the increase of poverty.

A quarter of a century later, Franklin reported that his own nation, now independent, had unfortunately followed the example of the mother country, but "we begin now to see our error, and, I hope, shall reform it."[4] Several years later England herself was caught up in the agitation for the reform of the poor laws, which became one of the most dramatic and divisive issues of the early nineteenth century. While many, abroad as well as at home (Tocqueville and Hegel were among those who followed the English debates with fascination), deplored the practical effects of a system of relief that seemed to create as many problems as it solved—created, some claimed, the very problem it sought to solve—even they conceded the moral impulse behind that system.

During the whole of this time, private charity continued to flourish in England. Indeed, it flourished most when public relief was most generous, thus belying the familiar prediction that the assumption of responsibility by the state would diminish the sense of private responsibility; clearly the same moral impulse that expressed itself in charity also expressed itself in parish relief. Yet the locus of moral responsibility had shifted, the state having become, symbolically at least, the repositor of the national conscience. This is what made the debate over the poor laws so agonizing. Even those who were persuaded that the poor laws were counterproductive, that they did a disservice to the poor themselves, were troubled by the implication that a retreat from the poor laws might be construed as a failure of morality. For both sides in that debate, the moral issue was paramount. For both, the question was not whether the public had a moral commitment to the poor but how that commitment could best be discharged.

The period covered by this volume is the century during which England emerged as the "first industrial nation," roughly 1750 to 1850, a time not only of intensive economic and social change but of those social experiments, ideologies, and policies designed to cope, as Tawney put it, with "those of its members who fall by the way." Because of the crucial role of legislation in this national effort—the climactic reform of the poor law in 1834, factory and mine acts regulating the hours and conditions of work of children and women, sanitation and public health acts, education and prison acts—much of the social history of England has been written as a history of social reforms. This kind of history, as Asa Briggs has pointed out, is especially prone to the "Whig interpretation of history," the tendency to read the past as a progressive movement toward a more enlightened future. In this reading of history, the nineteenth century reforms become the "origins" of the welfare state, the first stage in its "evolution" and "development."[5]

A longer historical perspective suggests the inadequacy of this interpretation. If ever there was a corrective to the Whig fallacy, it can be found in the history of social policies going back to Elizabethan times. So far from falling into a linear pattern, an ineluctable line of development culminating in the welfare state (or beyond that, in a socialist state, as some would have it), this history more often resembles a pendulum oscillating between extremes of regression and progression, of punitive, repressive policies and generous, melioratory ones. Even this image distorts the reality, for it assumes that policies can be clearly identified as regressive or progressive, negative or positive. In fact most policies, if they were not ambivalent in intention, were ambiguous in their effects. Contemporaries were well aware of the "unintended consequences" of their actions, of reforms conceived in the most positive, benevolent spirit which turned out to have the most unfortunate negative results. "Ambiguity" and "ambivalence" also lend themselves to a Whig interpretation, if they express the historian's sense of what was consistent and fitting rather than the contemporary's. The Elizabethans were not "ambivalent" toward the poor when they proposed to punish the able-bodied vagrant and at the same time to give relief to the disabled and the aged; they were deliberately distinguishing between two kinds of poor and devising policies which, as they saw it, dealt appropriately with each. Nor were the nineteenth century reforms all of a piece. From a later perspective they can be made to fit a pattern of increasing governmental control over every aspect of social life. At the time, the process was much more differentiated and the outcome more problematic.

Another approach to the subject of poverty avoids the Whig fallacy by coming to it not from the "solution" side of the equation—policies, reforms, laws, institutions, administrative agencies—but from the "problem" side. The emphasis here is on the economic, technological, social, demographic, urban, and other conditions which helped determine the nature and incidence of poverty at any particular time and place. Intensive archival research and econometric analysis have yielded valuable information about costs and standards of living, wages and employment, infant mortality and life expectancy, housing and literacy, drink and crime, income differentials and social mobility, the opportunities and "disamenities" of urban life compared with those of rural life. If the implications of some of these findings are still being hotly debated, the debate itself has elevated the discussion to a new level of sophistication, making the old standard-of-living question seem primitive and coarse.

Confronted with these "problems" and "solutions," the historian is tempted to look for correlations between the two, for solutions appropriate to the problems. Often what he finds are disjunctions. And not only because of the familiar "social lag," the sheer passage of time required to cope with a problem, so that the solution is always somewhat "out of sync" with the problem (the familiar phenomenon of the general staff fighting the last war), but also because of all the other circumstances which mediate between the perception of a problem and the proposal of a solution. The problem had first to be recognized as a problem requiring solution; different formulations of the problem, reflecting different interests and ideologies, lent themselves to different solutions; and what may now seem to be an obvious, rational solution might have been precluded by any one of a number of economic, legal, administrative, political, or cultural factors.[6]

One of the mediating facts that intervened between problem and solution and played a crucial part in this history was the set of ideas contemporaries brought to it—ideas about how to mitigate or "solve" the problem of poverty, and ideas about what constituted poverty and what made it a problem requiring remedy or solution. This raises a host of questions that are somewhat different from the conventional concerns of the social historian. What was the idea or conception of poverty that elevated it to the status of a problem? How did one conception give way to another, so that the "natural," unproblematic poverty of one age became the urgent social problem of another? Which of the poor were regarded as problematic, and how did the popular image of that group affect the proposals for reform? How were the "unworthy," "undeserving" poor distinguished from the "worthy" and "deserving," and why was it that first the former and then the latter became the primary focus of the social problem? How did the concept of the "deserving poor" become redefined so as to make them eligible for public assistance, when earlier they were thought deserving precisely because they were self-sustaining, hence not in need of assistance? How did the largely undifferentiated poor of earlier times ("the poor" equated with the "lower orders") become highly differentiated, the "dependent" poor being sharply distinguished from the "independent," the "pauper" from the "laboring poor," the "residuum" from the "respectable poor"? How were these essentially moral categories integrated with the later "objective" definitions of poverty based on income and subsistence? And how did these conceptions, definitions, and categories relate to the prevailing social ethos, the moral and intellectual climate that affected the condition of the poor as well as the disposition of those reformers who took it upon themselves to improve that condition?

None of these questions can be divorced from the familiar issues of "problems" and "solutions." Yet they are a different order of questions and require a different treatment. Even when they draw upon the same materials for their answers, they use those materials in a different way, eliciting from them different kinds of information and meanings. To ask these questions, to address oneself to the "idea" of poverty in this sense, is not to belittle either the problem of poverty or the policies designed to ameliorate it. It is rather an effort to elucidate both by adding another dimension to the social reality.

Nor does a concern with the "idea" of poverty imply any priority or determinacy for ideas in general or for this idea in particular. I would not say, as did R. G. Collingwood, that "all history is the history of thought," or even that the history of thought determines all of history.[7] I do believe, however, that there is a history of thought in all of history, and that the two are often intertwined and interdependent. Even the "hard facts" about poverty—about wages and prices, employment and unemployment, living and working conditions—appeared to contemporaries as facts and functioned as such only as they were mediated by a structure of ideas, values, opinions, beliefs, attitudes, perceptions, and images. This does not mean that nothing was real unless contemporaries thought it to be so. Late eighteenth century reformers, seeking to alleviate the poverty of agricultural laborers, had no clear idea of the extent to which their distress was caused by "underemployment," as we would now say, rather than unemployment, or by structural rather than cyclical changes. If they were ignorant of these distinctions (it may be argued that they were familiar with them under other terms), that itself is a fact of some consequence in shaping the social reality.

History is full of discrepancies between what historians believe to be fact and what contemporaries thought to be such. The famous standard-of-living question is one such instance. The latest econometric evidence may demonstrate that the standard of living was rising at a time when most contemporaries were convinced that it was falling. It is vitally important to have that evidence. But it would distort the historical reality, indeed make much of it unintelligible, if this fact were permitted to displace others—if in the zeal to correct the historical record, the ideas of contemporaries were expunged from the record for no other reason than that they have since been exposed as mistaken. Historians on both sides of this controversy have been at fault: the "optimists," as they are known, who argue so strenuously that the standard of living was rising that they pay little heed to contemporaries who believed otherwise and acted on that belief; and the "pessimists" who maintain that whatever the truth about the material standard of living, the important fact was the decline of the "quality" of life, and who define that quality in terms more appropriate to the sensibilities of a late twentieth century professor than of an early nineteenth century laborer. This is not to disparage the efforts to determine either the material standard of living or the quality of life. It does suggest that an essential part of the reality was what contemporaries took it to be, what they thought was happening to them, how they felt about it, and what they did about it.

John Stuart Mill once rebuked Bentham for being interested only in the question "Is it true?" The more significant question, he said, was that posed by Coleridge: "What is the meaning of it?"

> The one [Bentham] took his stand *outside* the received opinion, and surveyed it as an entire stranger to it: the other [Coleridge] looked at it from within, and endeavoured to see it with the eyes of a believer in it; to discover by what apparent facts it was at first suggested, and by what appearance it has ever since been rendered credible—has seemed, to a succession of persons, to be a faithful interpretation of their experience.[8]

The "idea of poverty" is responsive to Coleridge's question. It obliges the historian to take his stand with contemporaries, to look at history from their point of view, to attend to the facts available to them and in the form in which they were available, to find the meanings they attached to those facts, and to try to reconstruct their own "interpretation of their experience." Most historians pride themselves, like Bentham, on standing "outside the received opinion," as if this were a warrant of objectivity and superior insight. But the "received opinion" of contemporaries is a vital part of the historical reality, and the historian's sensitivity to that opinion is the best security for objectivity.

The Coleridgean question "What is the meaning of it?" also alerts us to the danger of taking contemporary documents at face value—taking them as facts rather than meanings, as truth rather than opinion or interpretation. This has been the case with the two major sources for the study of nineteenth century poverty: Henry Mayhew's *London Labour and the London Poor,* published in the middle of the century, and Charles Booth's *Life and Labour of the People in London,* at the end. The latter has been especially seductive, with its carefully delineated classes of "poor" and "very poor," its estimates of the number of people falling into each of these classes, its statistics about earnings and expenditures, employment and housing, drinking habits and religious affiliations. While being critical of Booth's moral judgments and practical recommendations, historians have been insufficiently skeptical about his classifications and statistics. The point is not whether his figures were accurate but how they were ordered and arranged; what conceptions, definitions, and assumptions produced those particular classes and thus the numbers that fell within them; what configuration of classes and numbers led him to focus upon a particular class of the poor and a particular kind of poverty; and how that delineation of the "social problem" suggested a particular kind of social policy.

For the purposes of this study, sources such as Mayhew or Booth are less interesting for their manifest content—facts about the conditions of life and work, the incidence and degree of poverty—than for their latent content, the ideas lurking behind the facts. Some of these ideas do appear on the surface, in the form of judgments and opinions voiced by the author or attributed by him to his subjects. Other ideas are implicit in the facts themselves, "facts" that are, in effect, intellectual constructs. In this sense a social document may be read as a literary text to elicit meanings that are not overt—on the condition, however, that it is read in its contemporary context, that the words are given their contemporary connotation, and that the ideas deduced from them reflect the sensibility and consciousness of contemporaries rather than of the historian.

The "idea of poverty" is obviously a hybrid subject, a cross between two distinct species, social history and intellectual history. If the social historian finds the "idea" in the title obtrusive, an unnecessary complication and distraction from the "real" subject of poverty, the intellectual historian may object to an "idea" that is vague and amorphous, more often implicit than explicit—not at all the respectable kind of idea he is accustomed to. It is not an idea which lends itself to rigorous philosophical analysis. Nor can it be found in philosophical texts; there were, in fact, no treatises on "the idea of poverty." Nor, for that matter, have there been any histories of the subject (on the order, for example, of histories on the idea of progress). Embedded in the social milieu, the idea can only be extracted from that milieu, from the behavior of people as well as from their writings, from legislation and debates, popular movements and public issues, economic treatises and religious tracts, novels and "penny dreadfuls." "Idea" in this sense is a shorthand expression for a complex of concepts, attitudes, values, beliefs, perceptions, images.

Another shorthand term that may be thought equivalent to "idea," and that has recently acquired a great vogue, is *"mentalité collective."* Originating with the Annales school in France (it goes back at least to Lucien Lévy-Bruhl's *La Mentalité primitive* in 1922), it is today associated with such social historians as Emmanuel Le Roy Ladurie, Philippe Ariès, and Lawrence Stone, and has close fraternal connections with cultural anthropologists like Clifford Geertz and Mary Douglas. If the term is still not quite naturalized in the English-speaking world—it generally appears in the French form— it is perhaps because the usual translations, "collective mentality" or "mental structure," are not only graceless but have overtones that may be uncongenial, suggesting a more impersonal, uniform, collectivistic, deterministic "structure" than such familiar words as ideas, values, attitudes, beliefs. A more important objection is the anti-intellectual bias often evident in discussions of this subject, a bias against ideas in the more formal sense, ideas that had been consciously worked out by serious thinkers and presented to the world in the form of systematic treatises. The inclination of the *mentalité* historian is to regard such ideas as irrelevant or suspect, irrelevant because he sees them as suspended in the rarefied atmosphere of philosophical discourse, or suspect because he regards them as "rationalizations" (in the invidious sense) of interests, passions, and prejudices.

In retaining "idea," I propose to give that word its largest latitude without depriving it of its more literal, formal meaning. If the present volume attends to the ideas of poverty implicit in the radical movements of the 1830s or in the fiction of the 1840s, it also takes seriously the text of the *Wealth of Nations* and of the *Essay on Population.* Thus, while parts of this study resemble *mentalité* history, other parts fall within the traditional discipline of intellectual history (the history of ideas, as it is commonly known in England), a discipline that has a high regard for "high ideas" and pays them the compliment of seeing them as an essential, integral part of the social reality. To give "idea" this wide extension is not to subscribe to a principle all too fashionable today, which was best expressed by Charles

Peirce almost a century ago: "It is the beliefs men betray and not that which they parade which has to be studied."[9] This statement itself betrays, one might say, a low opinion both of men and of their beliefs, a distrust of reflection and conviction, as if people habitually lie to others or deceive themselves about those matters they think about most earnestly. One does not have to demean the beliefs men consciously "parade" (itself a pejorative word) in order to attend also to those they unconsciously "betray."

In tracing the history of the idea of poverty during this period, one is startled to find how rapidly it changes, how quickly, for example, the "optimism" of Adam Smith gave way to the "pessimism" of Malthus and Ricardo, the bitterness of the 1830s to the social consciousness of the 1840s and to the spirit of reconciliation and "equipoise" of the 1850s. (This rapid change of social climate should not be altogether surprising to the present-day reader, for whom the 1950s convey a quite different image from the 1960s, or the 1960s from the 1970s.) This is not to say that the eighteenth and nineteenth centuries (any more than recent times) exhibited a tidy, decade-by-decade progression from one *Zeitgeist,* one *mentalité collective,* to the next. On the contrary, there were heated debates at each point about what could or should be done about, for, with, or to the poor. Yet even as the ideological battles were being most vigorously waged—over Malthusianism, or the New Poor Law, or Chartism—there were significant respects in which most of the parties in the disputes (and there were generally more than two sides to any one question) were in agreement, sharing the same moral and intellectual assumptions about poverty, making the same distinctions among the poor, focusing on the same group of poor as "the social problem," and using the same vocabulary to describe that group and that problem.

In this sense there was something like a moral consensus, a common view of what was moral and what immoral, and, more important, of the primacy of morality in the formulation of the social problem and in the making of social policy. This was true even when the dominant ideology (never quite as dominant as is sometimes thought) presumed to "de-moral-ize" political economy, to convert the old "moral philosophy" into an economic science and the old "moral economy" into a market economy. Thomas Carlyle had the greatest contempt for the "pig philosophers" and "rat-catchers" who wanted to reform the poor law on the principle that if paupers, like rats, were made miserable enough, they would soon disappear. But he himself was as committed as the reformers to the "work ethic" and as averse as they were to any "indiscriminate" system of poor relief. And radicals as well as reformers agreed with him that the main objective of public policy was to enhance the moral integrity of the independent laborer by preserving his independence and preventing his pauperization.

This ethos emerges more clearly by contrast to the latter part of the century, when the moral categories began to lose their primacy, when "social responsibility" began to replace "moral responsibility" as the basic category of thought, and when the causes of poverty came to be defined increasingly (although never entirely) in nonmoral terms. "Unemployment," for example, entering the vocabulary in the 1880s, signified an abstract, impersonal, amoral condition, in contrast to the older word "unemployed," which conjured up a multitude of individuals having distinctive characters, virtues, and vices. Even then, however, poverty had a large moral component, and the poor retained their moral identity.

It is unfortunate that these later developments must await the second volume of this work. It had originally been my intention to deal with the whole of what is sometimes called "modern England," from the industrial revolution to the welfare state, in a single volume so as to highlight precisely this contrast. But the earlier period turned out to be so complex—the idea of poverty implicit in Adam Smith so different from that in Malthus, or the Old Poor Law from the New—that it came to occupy a volume in itself. The material also proved to be richer than I had suspected. Fiction is usually represented by the great social novels of Charles Dickens, Benjamin Disraeli, and Mrs. Gaskell. Other novels, however, now barely known, rivaled them in popularity, and provided a dramatically different image of the poor and a radically different view of the popular culture. The most successful of these, *Mysteries of London* by G. W. M. Reynolds, portrayed the poor as so brutal and degraded that it seemed to make of them not so much a lower class as a lower species of being—and this in spite of the fact that Reynolds was a militant Chartist who periodically interrupted his tales to plead the cause of the oppressed poor.

Only a careful examination of a variety of sources can begin to do justice to these complexities. Each section of this book utilizes a different kind of source—economic, political, sociological, and literary; and in each case the sources are those which were regarded as important by contemporaries and had a significant impact at the time. (One notable exception is Engels's *Condition of the Working Class in England*, which was not published in England until late in the century but which is now so influential as to warrant inclusion here.) The sources are thus public rather than private, except insofar as a private letter, memoir, or unpublished manuscript might cast light upon the intention or effect of a public document. Most of them are analyzed at some length, so that the idea of poverty may be deduced not from an occasional, isolated comment but from the larger context of an economic doctrine or radical movement, a popular novel or social commentary. This is not to say that the sources I have selected are the only

ones or even the best ones. One can obviously come to a subject like this
in many ways and from many directions—from an analysis of the Ten
Hours Bill as well as the New Poor Law, from art or poetry as well as
fiction.[10] All one can do, especially if one has the dubious distinction of
trying to define a subject that has so far not been defined, is to select sources
that are significant and to use them responsibly.

This approach is designed to avoid the usual pitfalls of impressionism:
the random citations, the bits and pieces of evidence taken out of context,
the trivia and esoterica that testify more to the industry and ingenuity of
the historian than to the realities of the historical situation. If the evidence
cannot be quantified (as it cannot be for this subject), it can be used
rigorously enough to preserve its integrity and complexity. And used in this
fashion, it may serve to elucidate not only the idea of poverty but the larger
scheme of thought in which that idea was located—the political economy
of Adam Smith in contrast to that of Malthus, or the "old" radicalism of
Cobbett in contrast to the "new" radicalism of the *Poor Man's Guardian*. In
this sense the history of the idea of poverty is a microcosm of the history
of ideas in general.

There is one kind of source the historian would dearly love to have:
the direct testimony of the poor themselves. Almost a century and a half
ago Carlyle put the question that still remains with us, the question not only
of the "condition of the working people" but of "their disposition, their
own thoughts, beliefs and feelings."[11] Unfortunately we have all too little
direct evidence of that "disposition." What we do have, by way of working
class sources, are documents more often addressed to the working classes than
originating with them. While the radical, often illegal newspapers of the
1830s spoke in the name of the poor and on their behalf, the actual voices
were those of their reporters and editors, most of whom were as middle-class
as their colleagues on *The Times;* what distinguished them was their ideas
and beliefs, not their class status. The Chartist papers probably had more
working class contributors, who generally came from the artisan class, the
"labor aristocracy," as it has been called. Historians who find these artisans
insufficiently militant or "class conscious" sometimes attribute that failing
to their "middle class values." But this is an ideological judgment, not a class
description. If we are careful not to identify the "respectable," comfortable,
upwardly mobile artisans with the bulk of the working classes, we must also
be careful to apply the same caution to the radicals and militants among
them—those energetic, assertive, articulate individuals who delivered
speeches and organized movements, wrote articles and memoirs, and otherwise left behind the kinds of records available to the historian, all of which
made them, by definition, atypical.[12]

In a sense the issue itself is false; there was no typical, representative, "authentic" voice of the working class, if only because there was not, in this period, a single working class. Nor was there any widespread conception of a single working class. While the "language of class" became increasingly common—"inferior sorts" and "lower orders" giving way to "lower classes" and "working classes"—that language was almost always couched in the plural; even the radical press habitually spoke of "working classes" rather than "the working class." Even by the middle of the nineteenth century, the language of individuals—"workmen," "workers," "labourers," "labouring people"—was more common than the language of class. And throughout the period "the poor" remained the constant of social discourse, for all parties and classes.

The multiplicity of groups and types among the poor emerges most dramatically in Mayhew's *London Labour and the London Poor*. While Mayhew himself was sympathetic to his subjects, he hardly pretended to be one of them—his stance was that of the professional, objective reporter and commentator. Nor was his work intended primarily for a lower class or working class audience. Yet he did write about them with an intimacy and empathy that were unique at the time. Reviewers spoke of his work as a "revelation" of the true lives and experiences of the poor. And so it seemed, in part because much of it was related in the first person, often in dialect, as if transcribed literally from his interviews—"oral history," as we would now say. If his work too must be taken with some reserve, it is not so much because of its political or ideological bias (although there is a good deal of that), as because of a natural journalistic tendency to dramatize and sensationalize, to present as firsthand what may have been secondhand, and, more important, to represent as typical what may have been an extreme case. Indeed, the whole of the work was, in a sense, a compilation of extreme cases, dealing with a relatively small, highly visible, and distinctive class of the poor—the "street-folk," as Mayhew called them. Yet it remains a source of incalculable value, both for its descriptions of the many varieties of street-folk, and for its revelation of attitudes, assumptions, and images which sometimes belied his own professed opinions and unwittingly gave credence to modes of thought (Malthusianism, for example) for which he had profound contempt.

Another source that is still more challenging, because it made no pretense of literal truth and yet infused the public consciousness (and the consciousness of the poor) in ways that are not easily demonstrated, is fiction. If the poor were not given to writing, they were given to reading (or, if they could not read, being read to), and a good part of the publishing industry was geared to providing the penny and twopenny installments of fiction that made up their favorite reading matter. The range of this fiction, from the works of Dickens to the tawdriest melodramas, from "silver-fork" novels (about the very rich) to "Newgate" novels (about criminals), is itself an interesting commentary on the sensibility and imagination of their audiences. It is also interesting to speculate about what the poor made of all those fictional characters who purported to be like them, who appeared in the guise of artisans, laborers, servants, beggars, paupers, and criminals. If it is reasonable to suppose that the widely read Chartist paper, the *Northern Star,* to some degree affected and even reflected the political ideas of its readers, it is also plausible to think that the fiction read by the poor, however sentimentalized and sensationalized, to some extent shaped their images of themselves and of their world—intensifying, perhaps, their anxieties about a poverty that so often, in life as in fiction, verged on criminality, or fostering the hope that virtue and respectability would be rewarded, again in life as in fiction, by happiness and prosperity.

If the ideas of the poor themselves continue to evade us, it is no small matter to know something about the ideas and attitudes of others toward the poor. It is commonplace today to deplore the fact that so much of the history of the mass of the people has been made for them, as if they had been passive spectators rather than actors in their own history. The point is well taken, and historians have been much occupied in repairing this fault, in writing history "from below," as is said. But it is also easy to err in the opposite direction, to discredit or belittle the history that was made from above. The fact is that during all of the eighteenth century and well into the nineteenth, an important part of the history of the poor was in fact made by the "higher orders," by landlords and employers most obviously, but also by reformers, philanthropists, politicians, government officials, writers, economists, social critics, teachers, clergymen, doctors, magistrates, justices of the peace, and guardians of the poor. All of these impinged in myriad and momentous ways upon the lives of the poor, by administering the laws and institutions of the country, by trying to reform those laws and institutions, or by trying to reform the poor themselves. It is surely important to know what conceptions of poverty inspired their efforts and what perceptions of the poor made them think that the poor (or particular groups of the poor) could or should be reformed.

Even two volumes (the sequel covers the latter half of the nineteenth and the early part of the twentieth century) can hardly do justice to this subject. Ideally one should go much further back in time, at least to the Tudor period when the poor laws established a system of relief and a set of categories which helped define the poor for centuries to come, or beyond that to the feudal period when a different conception of the poor made them the natural charges of the church and the manor. One should also like to venture beyond England to the rest of the world—to France, where attitudes toward poverty reflected a social and intellectual history as different from that of England as was its political history, and where the question of poverty was complicated by an ideology committed to "liberty, equality and fraternity"; or to America, which took over the principles of the English poor laws but administered them in an atmosphere that was at the same time more egalitarian and more intolerant of poverty than England; or to the industrially backward areas of Europe and of the non-European world, where poverty was infinitely greater than in England but was not perceived as such, certainly not regarded as a social problem that society, still less the state, was obliged to relieve.

In this volume the comparative perspective appears only intermittently, when Tocqueville, for example, visited England during the height of the debate over the poor laws and came away with his usual perceptive and paradoxical analysis, anticipating such later sociological "discoveries" as the "theory of relative deprivation," the "revolution of rising expectations" (or "entitlements," in its latest guise), and the "law of unintended consequences"; or when other Frenchmen compared their "dangerous classes" with those in England, the consensus being that the French variety were more dangerous than the English; or when the Young Hegelians introduced the concept of the *Lumpen* (made famous by Marx under the title of *Lumpenproletariat*), thus unwittingly reinforcing the "bourgeois" distinction between the "respectable" and "unrespectable" poor. Even in these instances, where the experiences of other countries were most relevant to England, the national differences were more striking than the similarities, and to pay proper regard to both would require at least another volume of this size. At best comparative history is a difficult enterprise. In this case, where the subject itself, the idea of poverty, has been so little examined, the difficulties are even more formidable. Only now are there beginning to appear the kinds of monographic studies which will eventually make possible a serious comparative history.[13]

In the meantime, within the confines of England and within this critical period of social change, there is matter enough to occupy the historian. It was in 1750 that Thomas Gray penned that memorable line, "The short and simple annals of the poor"—a line he surely meant ironically. His "Elegy Written in a Country Churchyard" has a deceptive calm, almost a bucolic quality. But just beneath the surface is a seething passion at the thought of "some village Hampden," "some mute inglorious Milton," stilled not only by the death that awaits us all but by the poverty that, even in life, made these unfortunates mute and inglorious. "Chill Penury repress'd their noble rage, / And froze the genial current of the soul." That is hardly the tone of a man insensible to the tragedy of poverty. But the tragedy Gray confronted in that country churchyard was the natural, eternal condition of poverty, which was as much a fact of life as death was. Measured by the timeless rhythm of nature, of all eternity, the "annals of the poor" were all too "short and simple."

In this sense, 1760—the somewhat arbitrary date assigned to the somewhat hyperbolic event known as the industrial revolution—marked a decisive turning point. For it was then that poverty was removed from nature and brought into the forefront of history. That had happened on occasion before, when the decline of feudalism "liberated" the poor and threw them upon the mercies, not of a free economy but of a freer one; or when the enclosure movement of the sixteenth century disrupted age-old conventions of land tenure and created new conditions, and opportunities, of life and work; or, on a smaller scale, at all times and places when social changes loomed larger for contemporaries than they do in historical retrospect. On each of these occasions the new condition was soon assimilated into the old, made to seem eminently natural, yet another variation on the eternal phenomenon of the poor who are "always with you."

After the middle of the eighteenth century it became increasingly difficult to take refuge in that timeless maxim. If the poor were as omnipresent as ever—indeed, more plentiful than ever, given the rapid increase of population and thus the vastly increased numbers of poor—they were also more problematic than ever. All the changes coming to a head at this time —technological, economic, demographic, political, ideological—affected the poor to a greater degree than any other class and made their poverty more conspicuous, more controversial, and in a sense less "natural" than it had ever been before. And this in spite of notable attempts to "naturalize" poverty, to subject it, as Adam Smith did, to the natural laws of political economy, or, as Malthus did, to the biological laws of food and sex. Malthus complained that previous histories had been exclusively histories of the "higher classes," that they had ignored that large part of mankind, the poor, who had borne the brunt of the pressure of population and food. After Malthus, no one could make that complaint. The poor, if they were not the subject of written histories, were visibly, consciously the subject of history itself.

It was thus that the "annals of the poor" ceased to be "short and simple" and became long and complicated. In the period of only a century, circumstances conspired to create a highly differentiated poor, with different groups, at different times, in different conditions, with different characteristics, emerging as "the social problem." This was not a matter, as a later generation was to think, of raising or lowering the "poverty level" so that more or fewer of the poor were included in that rubric. The changes affecting the poor were changes in kind as well as degree, in quality as well as quantity, in ideas, attitudes, beliefs, perceptions, values. They were changes in what may be called the "moral imagination," the imagination that makes sense of reality, not by being imposed on reality (as ideology is) but by so thoroughly penetrating it that the reality has no form or shape apart from it.

PART ONE

THE REDEFINITION
OF POVERTY:
FROM MORAL PHILOSOPHY
TO POLITICAL ECONOMY

I

PROLOGUE:

BEFORE THE "REVOLUTION"

> There is a moral and religious, as well as material, environment, which sets its stamp on the individual, even when he is least conscious of it. . . . Between the conception of society as a community of unequal classes with varying functions, organized for a common end, and that which regards it as a mechanism adjusting itself through the play of economic motives to the supply of economic needs; between the idea that a man must not take advantage of his neighbor's necessity, and the doctrine that "man's self-love is God's providence"; between the attitude which appeals to a religious standard to repress economic appetites and that which regards expediency as the final criterion—there is a chasm which no theory of the permanence and ubiquity of economic interests can bridge, and which deserves at least to be explored.[1]

The "chasm" described so memorably by R. H. Tawney has haunted philosophers and historians. The vision of a society devoted to the common end, valuing communal and spiritual rather than private and material goods, is a standing reproach to modern society, which is presumed to have no higher aspiration than the gratification of economic appetites and no higher principle than self-love and expediency. The contrast is between a moral society and an amoral one—an immoral one, not to put too fine a point on it.

One may quarrel with Tawney's image of the chasm. One may suspect that it was never as wide and deep as he made it out to be, or that it did not make its appearance when he said it did. Yet to deny it entirely is, in a sense, to affirm it. To insist that society is and always has been nothing more than the sum of individuals, that the common end can only be achieved by maximizing individual interests, that the economy is, by definition, a mechanism governed by economic motives for the satisfaction of economic needs, that religious standards are at best irrelevant to the economic enterprise, at worst detrimental—this mode of reasoning is itself a confirmation of Tawney's thesis. For it is a peculiarly modern way of thinking, patently at variance with the beliefs most people lived with for most of history.

Tawney associated the new ethic with the commercialization of agriculture in England in the sixteenth century and the growth of capitalist industry in the following centuries. Derived from Puritanism, that ethic had the effect, as he described it, of sanctifying riches, degrading poverty, subverting the traditional system of social obligations, and providing the rationale for an individualist, competitive, acquisitive capitalist society. It was the ethic Adam Smith was to promulgate in the *Wealth of Nations* and Marx was to criticize in a memorable passage of the *Communist Manifesto:* "The bourgeoisie, wherever it got the upper hand, put an end to all feudal, patriarchal, idyllic relations, and pitilessly tore asunder the motley feudal ties that bound man to his 'natural superiors,' and left remaining no other bond between man and man than naked self-interest and callous cash payment."[2] According to Tawney, that ethic had become the informal, spontaneous "rule of English public life" a century before Smith. It was reflected in an attitude toward the "new industrial proletariat" (as he, anachronistically some might say, called it) that was harsher than anything that had preceded it—indeed that had "no modern parallel except in the behavior of the less reputable of white colonists towards colored labor"—and in a "new medicine for poverty," a medicine designed not to cure poverty but to punish it.[3]

The "Tawney thesis" (like the "Weber thesis" before it) has been endlessly analyzed, criticized, qualified, and revised in the half-century since it was formulated, and few historians today would accept it in its original form. The Puritan ethic no longer seems as unequivocally, uniformly, pervasively capitalistic as it once did. The disembodied spirit of Adam Smith is no longer seen hovering over English society a century or more before the *Wealth of Nations.* The wicked landlord (as Lawrence Stone has said) has been replaced by demography as the *diabolus ex machina* of the agrarian revolution, and similar impersonal causes are threatening to replace the wicked capitalist as the *diaboli ex machina* of the industrial revolution.[4] But if Tawney's account of the new ethic is dubious, he has called attention to a real problem. By locating its origins in the sixteenth and seventeenth centuries and finding its harshest manifestation in the early eighteenth, he has obliged us to look more closely at the period preceding those two epochal events: the industrial revolution commonly attributed to the latter half of the eighteenth century and the ideological revolution commonly associated with Adam Smith.

Whatever the subsequent effects of the Puritan ethic, the rise of Puritanism itself coincided with the introduction of a national, legal, compulsory, public system of relief, the first such in modern history. The Elizabethan poor laws, an amalgam of earlier laws and practices, were codified in 1597–98 and reenacted in 1601. The latter, the famous 43 Elizabeth, established the principles of the "old poor law" as it later became known: the parish as the basic unit of administration, a compulsory poor rate levied on householders by overseers appointed by the local justices (the overseers obliged to serve under penalty of a fine), and various types of relief for various kinds of needy—alms and almshouses for the aged and infirm, apprenticeship for children, and work for the able-bodied (and punishment or confinement for the "sturdy beggar"). The system flourished under the watchful eye of the Privy Council in the reigns of the early Stuarts, and was much weakened (in practice although not in law) during the Civil War and Interregnum when control reverted to the local authorities. Soon after the Restoration an Act of Settlement was passed authorizing justices to return to his previous parish within forty days anyone moving into a new parish and renting a house with an annual value of less than £10. While the principle of settlement was not new, this precise and uniform definition of settlement was new; and while it was often ignored or evaded, and even modified by law, it remained a major feature of the old poor law and a major source of dissatisfaction, contention, and litigation.

The Act of Settlement together with other legislation of the late seventeenth and early eighteenth centuries—an act requiring paupers to wear the letter P on their coats, and another permitting parishes to build workhouses for both the able-bodied and the infirm—earned this period the reputation of being harsh and repressive.[5] Some highly publicized voluntary schemes, designed to combine employment with relief, contributed to the same impression. John Locke, then a Commissioner of Trade, devised a plan for "pauper schools," in which the children would be put to work as well as taught, and in which their mothers would also be employed—this as part of a larger proposal for the suppression of "debauchery" and "sloth" by means of forced labor, impressment, whipping, and other disciplinary measures.[6] In spite of Locke's eminence, the scheme was rejected, apparently because it was regarded as excessively harsh. A more popular and generous plan was advanced by Josiah Child, whose *New Discourse of Trade* went through five editions between 1668 and 1699. Child proposed to create a body of officials to be known as the "Fathers of the Poor" who would be authorized to buy land, build workhouses and hospitals, and set the poor to work, on the principle that it was man's "Duty to God and Nature to provide for and employ the poor, whose condition is sad and wretched, diseased, impotent, and useless."[7]

This period, which Tawney saw as an anticipation of Smith, is better known today under the label of mercantilism. And it was Smith himself who invented the term "mercantile system" to characterize a philosophy and a policy that was the antithesis of his own "system of natural liberty." To the mercantilist the idle poor represented a drain upon the nation; unproductive in themselves, they used up precious resources in the form of poor relief and charity. It was to convert this national liability into something like an asset that the mercantilists devised plans for workhouses, schools of industry, and labor camps which would have the dual function of reducing the poor rates and enhancing the productive power of the nation by putting the poor to work. When Daniel Defoe argued against these schemes, he did so on the mercantilist ground that they did not achieve their ostensible purpose. Since they created no new industry and no new consumption, they succeeded only in "giving to one what you take away from another, enriching one poor man to starve another, putting a vagabond into an honest man's employment."[8] Defoe's pamphlet, published in 1704 under the memorable title *Giving Alms No Charity, and Employing the Poor a Grievance to the Nation,* may have contributed to the defeat of a bill authorizing the overseers of the poor to put the unemployed to work upon any trade that might seem suitable. It did not, however, put an end to such proposals, nor to the principle of "employing the poor."

Some of these proposals are surely deserving of the familiar adjectives, harsh, punitive, and negative—deserving of them not by present-day standards but by those of many contemporaries who objected to them for just these reasons. But these judgments do not exhaust the matter. If the Act of Settlement was restrictive and punitive compared with the earlier rules of settlement, it did reaffirm the principle of public responsibility for the poor. At no time in the discussion of this act was any serious consideration given to the possibility of repealing the poor law itself. Indeed the act was titled "An Act for the Better Relief of the Poor of this Kingdom," and the preamble explained that stricter rules of settlement were required to prevent "the perishing of any of the poor, whether young or old, for want of such supplies as are necessary."[9] And the Workhouse Act of 1723, requiring that relief be given to the able-bodied in the workhouse, was itself a permissive act; parishes, or unions of parishes, were empowered, not obligated, to build workhouses, and only if there were such workhouses did the restrictive aspect of the law take effect. Moreover, the workhouses were only one of many forms of relief available, in varying amounts, under varying conditions, and at different times and places: food, rent, fuel, medical services, funeral expenses, and, of course, the dole.

The "great Debate of the Poor," as one historian has described it, raged at a time when the poor rates (the taxes levied specifically for relief) rose from £665,000 in 1685 to £900,000 in 1701. In the course of the following decade the expenditure for poor relief and charity combined rose to over £2,000,000—this for a population of under 6,000,000.[10] It is little wonder that mercantilists, intent upon maximizing the productivity and power of the nation, should try to devise more "positive," as they thought it, means of relief. More surprising is the fact that Defoe's strictures on relief were not widely accepted, and that others continued to urge that the poor law remain what it had always been: a means of providing, as one pamphlet put it, "work for those that will labour, punishment for those that will not, and bread for those who cannot."[11]

There was no anomaly in this combination of punitive and positive measures. Here, as in the original Elizabethan laws, the two were complementary. If idleness was castigated, it was because labor was so highly valued— "the chiefest, most fundamental and precious commodity," William Petty wrote, the source of all "value," as Locke had it.[12] At a time when "labor" and the "poor" were virtually synonymous, when a laboring man might be employed one day and unemployed the next, it was difficult to sustain a consistently punitive attitude toward the "able-bodied pauper." Locke and Defoe might suspect that most of the unemployed were so by intent, that they did not work because they did not want to work. But that was by no means the universal view, and in any case it would have been difficult to implement so long as one-fourth of the nation was in that dubious condition.

It was not only the magnitude of poor relief that made for this amorphous conception of the poor. In 1696 Gregory King drew up an estimate of the size and income of the various classes of the population. That exercise in "political arithmetic," as it was then called ("social statistics," as it was later renamed), is now thought to be remarkably accurate. As revealing as the numbers is the image of society conjured up by King's table of classes. The 5,500,000 people in England were divided roughly in half, the top half (or something less than half) subdivided into twenty-one classes ranging from temporal lords through shopkeepers and artisans, and the bottom half into five classes: common seamen, labouring people and outservants, cottagers and paupers, common soldiers, and vagrants. It is interesting to observe the extreme refinement of distinctions at the top (freeholders of the "better sort" being distinguished from those of the "lesser sort," "merchants and traders by sea" from "merchants and traders by land"), in contrast to the marked lack of differentiation at the bottom, with cottagers and paupers combined in a single huge class (1,300,000) and laborers and outservants in another (1,275,000)—the latter class including agricultural and industrial workers, miners, fishermen, weavers, and others.* As striking as the classes themselves is the sharp line separating the top half from the bottom, the former characterized as "increasing the wealth of the kingdom," the latter as "decreasing the wealth of the kingdom."[13]

---

*"Cottagers" were agricultural laborers with little or no land. Since they were irregularly employed and had no land to supplement their earnings, they were among the poorest classes, often dependent upon relief or charity. "Outservants" were laborers who did not live in the household of their employers.

Perhaps at no other time in history could society have been divided in just this way—not so much in terms of the wealth of the various classes as their contribution to the "wealth of the kingdom." It is in this light that policies and attitudes toward the poor in the late seventeenth and early eighteenth centuries have to be regarded. If there was no firm distinction between pauper and poor, between the independent and dependent poor, between the deserving and undeserving poor, between those who should be punished and those who should be helped, it was because most of the laboring population (with the exception of artisans) were regarded as "poor." They were poor in the traditional sense in which those who depended on their labor for their livelihood were poor; these were Mandeville's poor, "forced to get their daily bread by their daily labour."[14] They were also poor in the sense that their earnings were insufficient (because too irregular or too meager) for subsistence, so that most of them, at one time or another, to one degree or another, in old age if not earlier, were dependent upon private charity or public relief.

The mercantilist ethic thus superimposed upon the Puritan ethic what might be called an ethic of productivity. To the mercantilist the Puritan virtues—hard work, temperance, prudence, self-discipline—might be sufficient for the salvation of the individual. But they were not sufficient for the salvation of society, since even those who had these virtues belonged to that large mass of the population which, for one reason or another, diminished the wealth of the nation. In this respect the mercantilist ethic was less moralistic than the Puritan ethic, less concerned with the moral failings of the poor than with the objective effects of their idleness and unproductivity, less vindictive in spirit, however more harsh and coercive it may have been in practice.

If one had to select a single work to exemplify the amoral, asocial ethic decried by Tawney, it would be *The Fable of the Bees* by the philosopher (and physician) Bernard Mandeville.[15] Published originally in 1714 and in an expanded version in 1723, the *Fable* is a repository of quotations designed to confirm Tawney's worst suspicions. Its subtitle, "Private Vices, Public Benefits," aptly conveys its message: society is based neither on the "friendly qualities and kind affections" of man's nature nor on the virtues acquired by "reason and self-denial," but rather on "what we call evil in this world, moral as well as natural." Evil is "the grand principle that makes us sociable creatures, the solid basis, the life and support of all trades and employments without exception." If ever evil were to cease, "society must be spoiled if not totally dissolved." With a fine display of impartiality and irreverence, Mandeville applied this jaundiced view of human nature to rich and poor alike, to lawyers, doctors, clergymen, officials, merchants—and laborers.

> Everybody knows that there is a vast number of journeymen weavers, tailors, clothworkers, and twenty other handicrafts, who, if by four days labour in a week they can maintain themselves, will hardly be persuaded to work the fifth; and that there are thousands of labouring men of all sorts, who will, though they can hardly subsist, put themselves to fifty inconveniences, disoblige their masters, pinch their bellies, and run in debt, to make holidays. When men show such an extraordinary proclivity to idleness and pleasure, what reason have we to think that they would ever work, unless they were obliged to it by immediate necessity?[16]

Whatever satirical intent might have been read into the original *Fable*—the inversion, in effect, of vice and virtue—the second edition, which included an essay on charity and charity schools, precluded any such interpretation. In exposing the vanity, pride, self-love, and hypocrisy which often passed as charity, and even more, in attacking the charity schools, Mandeville made his intentions perfectly clear—and utterly offensive to prevailing opinion. For the charity schools, as he said, enjoyed an "uncommon vogue" at the time, being "unanimously approved of and admired among all sorts and conditions of people."[17] First appearing in England toward the end of the seventeenth century, the schools proliferated rapidly in the first quarter of the eighteenth. They catered to pauper and orphan children between the ages of seven and fourteen, fed and clothed them, taught them to read the Bible and to write sufficiently to copy passages from it, and then sent them out to work as apprentices or servants. Later historians may take a dim view of an education that was overtly devotional and moralistic, designed as a form of "social control."[18] Most contemporaries saw nothing amiss in this, nothing improper in the attempt to "better" the poor, as they said—to "moralize" and "socialize" them, as we might say.

Mandeville's objection was that education had no such moralizing and socializing effect, either upon the poor or upon the rich. Alluding to the notorious South Sea Bubble, the speculative boom and crash of 1720, he cited that year as one "prolific in deep villainy, and remarkable for selfish crimes and premeditated mischief"—crimes committed not by "poor ignorant rogues that could neither read nor write," but by the "better sort of people as to wealth and education," people who were "great masters in arithmetic, and lived in reputation and splendor."[19] If education was of so little moral avail to the rich, it was of still less use to the poor, incapacitating their children for the life of poverty and hard work that was in their own best interest and in the best interest of society at large.

> In a free nation where slaves are not allowed of, the surest wealth consists in a multitude of laborious poor; for besides that they are the never failing nursery of fleets and armies, without them there could be no enjoyment, and no product of any country could be valuable. To make the society happy and people easy under the meanest circumstances, it is requisite that great numbers of them should be ignorant as well as poor. Knowledge both enlarges and multiplies our desires, and the fewer things a man wishes for, the more easily his necessities may be supplied.

> Going to school in comparison to working is idleness, and the longer boys continue in this easy sort of life, the more unfit they'll be when grown up for downright labour, both as to strength and inclination. Men who are to remain and end their days in a labourious, tiresome and painful station of life, the sooner they are put upon it at first, the more patiently they'll submit to it for ever after.[20]

Mandeville knew just how provocative his argument was. How "perverse," he predicted, people would think him for preferring ignorance to education, dirty linen to clean, "oaths and imprecations" to the Bible and catechism.[21] And so they did, the defenders of the schools insisting that the poor, so far from being corrupted by education, were taught to bear their poverty with greater fortitude, were deterred from a life of dissipation and crime, and were provided with virtues and skills that made them better workers and better people. Some went further than this, actually welcoming the prospect that Mandeville feared, pleased to think that schooling would encourage the poor to "better" themselves, to improve their conditions and their rank, to become, as we would put it today, "upwardly mobile." It is significant that so many people approved of this prospect, and that others who were made uneasy by it were nonetheless willing to take that risk.

The fact is that the *Fable,* so far from being representative of its time, profoundly shocked contemporaries, provoked a frenzy of attacks, and resulted in a presentment handed down by the grand jury of Middlesex condemning it as a "public nuisance." Mandeville's replies to this first wave of criticism only compounded the affront, and the chorus of abuse continued long after his death in 1733. Among his critics were divines and philosophers, men of letters and men of affairs—William Law, Francis Hutcheson, George Berkeley, Edward Gibbon, Lord Shaftesbury, Adam Smith—a roster of eighteenth century greats. And they attacked him as much for his attitude toward the poor as for his views on morality. Mandeville is as close as one can come to Tawney's moral "chasm," a new ethic subversive of traditional morality and utterly hostile to the poor. But it was a profoundly unpopular ethic, a "wholly pernicious one," Smith described it.[22]*

It is curious that Tawney, having made so much of Puritanism, should have done so little with its counterpart in the eighteenth century—Wesleyanism, or, as it came to be known, Methodism.† The only mention of Wesley in *Religion and the Rise of Capitalism* is a passing reference to one of his sermons as a "conspicuous exception that only served to heighten the impression of the general acquiescence in the conventional [Puritan or capitalist] ethics."[24] This is all the more curious in view of the fact that Tawney had been provoked to write his book by Max Weber's famous essay *The Protestant Ethic and the Spirit of Capitalism,* in which Methodism appears as one of the forms of "ascetic Protestantism" that helped shape the Puritan ethic.[25]

In retrospect, it may seem anomalous that Methodism should have preserved so many features of a pre-capitalist or anti-capitalist ethic—the prohibition of usury and pawnbroking, and the appeal to a just or natural price—while advocating a Puritan ethic often associated with capitalism: thrift, prudence, diligence, temperance, honesty, hard work. But it was precisely this conjunction of principles that constituted the distinctive Wesleyan ethic. This is not to say that there was no tension within it. Wesley himself was acutely aware of that tension, aware of it not only in its implications for social behavior but in its effect on religion. One of the purposes of religion, he ardently believed, was the inculcation of morality, which in turn was conducive to industry and the acquisition of wealth. But wealth, he suspected, was all too likely to subvert religion.

> I fear, wherever riches have increased, the essence of religion has decreased in the same proportion. Therefore I do not see how it is possible, in the nature of things, for any revival of true religion to continue long. For religion must necessarily produce both industry and frugality, and these cannot but produce riches. But as riches increase, so will pride, anger, and love of the world in all its branches. How then is it possible that Methodism, that is, a religion of the heart, though it flourishes now as a green bay tree, should continue in this state?[26]

*It was Mandeville's moral (or amoral) philosophy that Smith thought so pernicious. He might have been equally critical of his economic theories. Although Mandeville is generally placed within the tradition of laissez-faire (indeed, is often cited as the main progenitor of Adam Smith), Jacob Viner has made out a good case for regarding him as a mercantilist. Certainly on matters of foreign trade and the necessity for government regulation of trade he was an orthodox mercantilist.[23]

†Like so many labels—Tory and Whig, for example—Methodism was originally a pejorative term until it was adopted by the Wesleyans themselves.

Wesley tried to resolve this paradox by propounding a new trinity: "Gain all you can," "Save all you can," and "Give all you can." This trinity constituted the moral life on earth and the assurance of salvation hereafter —"laying up in store for yourselves a good foundation against the time to come, that ye may attain eternal life." In his famous sermon "The Use of Money," he elaborated upon these precepts in such a way as to endow each with an ethical quality and to make of the whole a comprehensive social ethic. Thus the prescription "to gain" was qualified by the injunction against gaining at the expense of one's own or one's neighbor's bodily or mental health, or at the expense of another's "substance"—the last interpreted as a prohibition of interest and unfair competition.[27] Moreover, this was not meant to be an entirely private, individual ethic. The process of giving and helping was institutionalized and publicly encouraged, sometimes even pre-scribed. Collections following the sermon were conducted by stewards appointed for that purpose and the money (as well as food and clothing) were distributed to the poor; loan funds were set up and in some instances work projects for the unemployed; Methodists were enjoined to pay "visita-tions" to the sick and to prisoners in jail; meetinghouses were used as schools, poorhouses, and clinics. It is not surprising to find that Methodists were prominent in the founding of orphanages, schools, hospitals, friendly soci-eties, benevolent associations, and philanthropic enterprises of every kind.

By later standards—the standards of the late nineteenth century Char-ity Organization Society, which prided itself on its "scientific" social work, or of the twentieth century welfare state with its national system of relief —the local, voluntary nature of Methodist charity may seem trivial. But it was not trivial in fact (especially considered as a supplement to poor relief), still less in principle. If there was much of the self-help ethic in Methodism, there was also a social ethic of some significance. Both derived from the same source: the idea of individual moral responsibility which held every human being, rich or poor, responsible to God, to his fellow human beings, and to himself. That ethic was neither as condescending nor as insensitive as might be thought. Those who were in a position to help their brethren were instructed to do so in such a way as to consider the feelings of those they were helping. "Put yourself in the place of every poor man," Wesley advised the stewards, "and deal with him as you would God should deal with you."[28]*

Today, when the very idea of preaching is suspect, the word itself

---

*Wesley was notably less sensitive in regard to children. By Tawney's other test—the "touchstone" of a social philosophy being the attitude to childhood as well as to poverty—Wesley fails abysmally. In the school he established for the children of miners, the regulations governing their work and conduct were harsh even by the standards of his time. This attitude was carried over into the Evangelical movement of the early nineteenth century. It was all the more conspicuous because in other respects the culture was becoming more lenient and humane, children being catered to as they had not been before with books, toys, games, amusements, and clothing designed especially for them.[29]

pejorative, Methodist sermons evoke the familiar charges of paternalism and social control, the imposition upon the poor of alien values designed to domesticate and manipulate them. In earlier times, when church-going (or chapel-going) was a natural activity and the sermon a familiar part of the service, there was nothing invidious in being preached to. What was invidious was not being preached to, not having access to the kinds of moral, religious, and communal experiences that were a normal part of life for those not so poor as to be deprived of them. For Wesley no one was so poor. In this sense the Methodist ethos was eminently democratic. The poor were not only objects of solicitude; they were the sect's main constituency. From the beginning Wesley declared it his mission to "preach the Gospel to the poor." When the Anglican churches were closed to him, he made a virtue out of necessity by making it a principle to preach in the open in order to reach the largest number of the poor. He assured the other clergymen that they need fear no competition from him: "The rich, the honourable, the great, we are thoroughly willing . . . to leave to you. Only let us alone among the poor." His poor, moreover, were not only the "deserving," "respectable" poor who were the obvious candidates for conversion. In the early years especially, he made a point of seeking out the least likely prospects, the "outcasts of men," the "forlorn ones," the "most flagrant, hardened, desperate sinner."[30] To save a sinner otherwise doomed to eternal perdition was deemed a higher spiritual mission than to cater to those who were already in a state of grace. It was an article of his faith that no one was beyond salvation, no one too poor, benighted, or uncivilized to attain the spiritual and moral level deserving of the name Christian.

A religion that proudly proclaimed, "The poor are the Christians," could hardly regard poverty, as some earlier Puritans did, as demeaning or disreputable, the evidence of a personal failure of character or grace. Wesley himself denounced as "wickedly, devilishly false" the insinuation that poverty was the product of idleness.[31] Politically, to be sure, at least as long as he was alive, his movement was staunchly conservative, firmly committed to Church, King, and Country, implacably opposed to sedition and revolution. And socially it was conservative in its insistence upon the principle of authority. "Do you honor and obey all in authority? All your governors, spiritual pastors, and masters? Do you behave lowly and reverently to all your betters?"[32] But if Wesley so often and so vigorously affirmed his loyalty to established authorities, it was partly because his teachings were insidiously subversive in other respects. By beseeching the poor to behave, work hard, and save, he was enjoining them to improve their conditions and stations. It has often been observed that the Methodists produced a disproportionate number of people who rose out of the lowest ranks to become skilled artisans, masters, even men of wealth. The ethos was, in fact, a powerful stimulus to social mobility, an affirmation of the right and duty to better oneself—morally and spiritually in the first instance, but also materially and socially. If the poor were enjoined to obey their masters, this did not preclude them from themselves becoming masters, and being obeyed, as such, in turn. (Wesley's respect for authority and property, moreover, did not extend to slave owners; he was prominent in the antislavery movement and the author of an influential tract condemning slavery.)

"Christianity," Wesley said in one of his sermons, "is essentially a social religion."[33] This was true not only in the sense that it prescribed a set of social virtues but also that it provided a social community in which those virtues could be exercised. The historian Bernard Semmel has aptly described this communal aspect of Methodism as the equivalent of the French ideal of *fraternité*. "In the century of Voltaire's *sauve qui peut* and Smith's *laissez-faire*, when the paternalism of the traditional hierarchical society was breaking down, Methodism sought to endow the lower classes with a sense of their own worth, and to revive traditional religion as a source of warmth and solace, of comfort and joy."[34] The religious experience itself was inseparable from the religious community. Excluded from the polity, occupying the lowest rank in society, the poor found themselves, in this one area of their lives (and a not unimportant one), members of a fellowship in which they shared a common faith, purpose, and destiny.

The Methodist system of organization encouraged this sense of fellowship. Although the movement was large, the units were small, so that each member felt himself part of an intimate group. The basic unit, the "class," had between five and twelve members and met at least once a week under the direction of a class leader. It was this class that imposed and enforced all the regulations for which the Methodists were famous, regulations about charity, dress, deportment, drink, visitations. This is not to say that the Methodists were a democratic organization. Wesley himself, and the Conference controlled by him, selected the class leaders, preachers, and stewards. "We are no republicans," he declared, "and never intend to be"—no more republican in their internal organization than in their political principles.[35] Wesley assumed for himself the divine right to lead his order, in much the same way that he granted to the king the divine right to lead the country. Within the classes, and even in the larger "bands" and "societies," the members constituted a "family," in which the leader was the father and the others were (and called themselves) "brothers" and "sisters." Later the classes were to serve as a model for the Chartists and other radical movements. In this early period they were radical in more subtle ways. While changes in agriculture and industry were uprooting the poor, depriving them of their traditional trades and ways of work, dissolving the conventional bonds of masters and men, Methodism mitigated the shock of change by creating new roots and ties, new forms of community and fraternity, new opportunities and prospects.

While the Methodists were preaching morality to the poor, the philosophers were propounding a moral philosophy for the "middling" and upper classes. To Wesley those philosophers were nothing less than atheists; to the philosophers Wesley was a primitive zealot. Yet there was a curiously symbiotic relationship between the two. In the following century the moral equivalent of Wesleyanism was to make itself felt among the upper classes in the form of Evangelicalism. At this time it was secular thought that unwittingly conspired with religion to sustain a social ethic.

In his attack on charity and the charity schools, Mandeville had identified the main culprit as that "noble writer," Lord Shaftesbury, who "fancies that as man is made for society, so he ought to be born with a kind of affection to the whole of which he is a part, and a propensity to seek the welfare of it."[36] Next to Locke, the third Earl of Shaftesbury was probably the most influential philosopher of his time—and after his time as well, his books going through numerous editions following his death in 1713, and his theory of "social affections" appearing in one or another guise throughout the century, as "moral sense," "benevolence," "sympathy," or "humanity." Adam Smith, Joseph Butler, Francis Hutcheson, and others, reasoning from either utilitarian or theological premises (or both), agreed that while self-interest—self-love, as it was more commonly called—was a basic fact of human nature, that fact had to accommodate itself to the higher virtue of the love of others, the public good. Hutcheson (who may have coined the expression "the greatest happiness of the greatest number") thought it fortunate that the individual generally found his own "enjoyment" in the disposition to promote the general good; but it was this social disposition, not his private pleasure, that constituted the moral sense.* Even Hume, whose conception of human nature and behavior was notably unsentimental, paid obeisance to the prevailing view. "It appears that a tendency to public good, and to the promoting of peace, harmony, and order in society does, always, by affecting the benevolent principles of our frame, engage us on the side of the social virtues."[38]

If Mandeville had been writing only a decade or two later, he would have had more reason to deplore the insidious philosophy that attributed to man an "affection" for society and a "propensity to seek the welfare of it."

---

*Hutcheson's version was "the greatest happiness for the greatest numbers." Jeremy Bentham is probably responsible for the fact that the expression is generally attributed to Joseph Priestley. In his memoirs, Bentham said that he had borrowed the expression from Priestley, although he once gave Beccaria as another source.[37]

The social virtues Hume spoke of took the form of an extraordinary profusion and variety of "philanthropy," as it was called at the time—literally, "love to mankind." The term "philanthropist" was usually reserved for those who made a profession, a full-time occupation, of it: John Howard, Jonas Hanway, Thomas Gilbert, and the like. It might also be applied to the thousands of people of modest means who contributed to the scores of philanthropic enterprises and societies founded at the time. Mandeville had complained of the popularity of the charity schools among "all sorts and conditions of people." And so they were, the charity schools (like the later Sunday schools and night schools) being supported neither by the state nor large private endowments but by thousands of subscribers of modest means; guinea subscriptions were typical. Schools were only a small part of their efforts. In the second quarter of the century, five new hospitals were founded in London alone and another nine in the country, all intended primarily or exclusively for the poor. After the middle of the century, there was a proliferation of societies for every kind of worthy purpose: the Society for Promoting Christian Knowledge (the coordinating agency for the charity schools), the Society for the Abolition of the Slave Trade, the Society for Bettering the Condition and Increasing the Comforts of the Poor, and a multitude of other societies for deserted infants, sick and maimed seamen, orphans of clergymen, penitent prostitutes, the deaf, dumb, and blind. Even those who might be thought hostile to the principle of philanthropy found some cause to elicit their sympathy: Defoe wrote a tract in favor of foundling hospitals, and Mandeville approved of poor relief for the aged and sick.

One of the most important chroniclers of this period, William Maitland, included in his *History of London* a detailed account of the schools, hospitals, almshouses, and charitable societies that testified to the greatness of the metropolis and that were a natural consequence of its commercial preeminence. "As opulency and riches are the result of commerce, so are learning, hospitality and charity the effects thereof." He reminded his readers that while the English were raising vast sums of money to support their poor, "according to their several necessities and stations," foreigners, having no legal provision for their poor, were leaving them "to starve at the discretion of the rich."[39] This was written in 1739. In 1756, when the second edition appeared, the section on hospitals, schools, and charities had to be greatly expanded to take account of the many new institutions that had been founded in the interim. Maitland then had even more reason to commend his countrymen for the "truly Christian spirit of Benevolence, which at this time so generally prevails amongst us, to the great honour of this Age and Nation."[40]

"The Age of Benevolence," Hannah More later called it—not altogether in praise.[41] But while she and others like her deplored the infatuation with the idea of benevolence, they did so in the knowledge that they were mavericks, out of tune with their times—and sometimes, as in the case of

More, while themselves founding schools and engaging in "good works" that were suspiciously benevolent. One London magistrate rebuked Shaftesbury for inventing the "cant phrase, goodness of heart," and Henry Fielding for making of virtue little more than "good affections." "We live in an age," he complained, "when humanity is in fashion."[42]

Rousseau is often credited with originating this sentiment, with making a concern for others a passion rather than a duty (as it was for the Christian) or a matter of self-preservation and self-interest (as it was for Hobbes and Locke). Only Rousseau, this argument goes, grounded that passion—compassion—in the feeling of common suffering that was the great social equalizer, that made the poor the equal of the rich and gave the poor a claim on the hearts of the rich.[43] One hesitates to put Shaftesbury or the other English moral philosophers on a par with Rousseau, even in this one respect. Yet there may be some warrant for it in the prominence they gave to benevolence, humanity, philanthropy, sympathy, the social affections; they even used the word "compassion" in the same sense. Like Rousseau they located that sentiment at the heart of human nature, made it the distinctive and preeminent attribute of mankind, and found evidence of it in every sphere of life, in the relations of individuals, families, orders, and nations. "To compassionate, i.e., to join with in passion. . . . To commiserate, i.e., to join with in misery. . . . This in one order of life is right and good; nothing more harmonious; and to be without this, or not to feel this, is unnatural, horrid, immane."[44] It was Shaftesbury, not Rousseau, who wrote that. Shaftesbury went on to add that such compassion must not be permitted to degenerate into "temper," that the natural affection for mankind must be "disinterested," seeking nothing for the self—a bit of stoicism Rousseau might have spurned. But the compassion that was a joining in passion, the commiseration that was a joining in misery, was surely as much a principle for the English moral philosopher as it was for Rousseau.*

The "Age of Benevolence" in England, like the "Age of Enlightenment" in France, had its "underside." If it produced a great generation of reformers

---

*Burke's criticism of the French *philosophes,* who substituted "humanity or benevolence" for "principle," could as well have been directed against the English (and Scottish) moral philosophers.

> But I have observed that the philosophers, in order to insinuate their polluted atheism into young minds, systematically flatter all their passions, natural and unnatural. They explode, or render odious or contemptible, that class of virtues which restrain the appetite. . . . In place of all this, they substitute a virtue which they call humanity or benevolence. By these means their morality has no idea in it of restraint, or indeed of a distinct settled principle of any kind. When their disciples are thus left free, and guided only by present feeling, they are no longer to be depended upon for good or evil. The men who, today, snatch the worst criminals from justice, will murder the most innocent persons tomorrow.[45]

and humanitarians, it was partly because there was so much to reform, so much to offend the sensibilities of a humane person. The system of justice, contemporaries were beginning to suspect, was redeemed from sheer barbarity only because the prescribed penalties were so often evaded. Conditions in the prisons and poorhouses were such as to warrant the most heroic efforts of philanthropists and reformers. The act of 1769 requiring pauper infants to be sent to the country for nursing was a response to the appalling rate of infant mortality in the poorhouses. The chimney sweep act of 1788 addressed itself to only one aspect of the problem of child labor, a problem that had always been with the poor but that became onerous when more and more children were employed in factories and mines. If the inscription over the doorway of the ginshop in Hogarth's "Gin Lane"—"Drunk for a Penny, Dead Drunk for Twopence, Clean straw for nothing"—was not a literal representation of a real sign, it did represent a real problem and had a real effect: the cartoon and others like it contributed to the passage of the Gin Act of 1751, a turning point, it has been said, in the social history of London.[46]* So it was with the other causes that occupied the reformers. Every reform was a response to an evil crying out for reform; every expression of compassion and revulsion was provoked by the unmistakable evidence of misery and vice.

This double-sided reality has given rise to an unfortunate distinction between "optimistic" and "pessimistic" historians—unfortunate because of the moral overtones of these terms, as if the historian presenting the evidence of humanitarianism and reformism is more complacent, insensitive, and ideological than the historian presenting the evidence of hardship and suffering. To say that social ills or evils were generally exposed by the reformers themselves, that some of these conditions were no worse at this time than they had been in the past (or than they were in other countries), and that they appeared intolerable in part because the spirit of the age made them seem so, is not to deny or belittle their reality but only to point to another aspect of that reality. Yet if the labels "optimist" and "pessimist" are misleading, they do point to a real division among historians, a division of subject as much as attitude, so that their histories sometimes read as if they were accounts of different countries at different times. Where one historian draws his material from preachers, politicians, reformers, and writers, another draws his from the lower classes, especially

---

*The cartoons were just that, not literal representations of reality, and certainly not of the reality of the mass of the poor. An otherwise thoughtful commentary on Hogarth says of one of the more grotesque scenes in his "Industry and Idleness" series that it "probably gives a fair picture of the conditions in which poor people lived at the time"—this of the scene of the "idle apprentice" in bed with a prostitute, in a room in a state of total decay and filth, with a cat tumbling down the chimney in pursuit of a rat.[47] (See illustration #1 in the insert following page 180.)

those who have left evidence of their lives in criminal records—rioters, poachers, arsonists, anonymous threatening-letter writers. Thus where one historian finds 1766 noteworthy as the date of publication of Jonas Hanway's *Earnest Appeal of Mercy to the Children of the Poor,* a tract which publicized infant mortality rates in the poorhouses and prepared the way for the boarding-out law, another cites that year as a time of an unprecedented number of food riots—sixty in a three-month period, by one count.[48]

The subjects of this populist history—a "counter-history," it may be called—are often not so much the poor as the "mob" or "rabble." In contemporary usage these terms generally referred to rioters and demonstrators, so that the "mob" in the Wilkes riots of 1768 or the Gordon riots of 1780 included shopkeepers and artisans as well as the "inferior set of people" (as Wilkes himself called them). Sometimes "mob" was a pejorative term for those of the "inferior set" or "lower orders" who were obstreperous and unruly.* Recent historians, wanting to avoid any invidious connotation, have adopted the more neutral-sounding term "crowd,"[50] and have made of it something like a "vanguard" of the working classes.

If the "crowds" of the late eighteenth century are the heroes of the new history, the food riots are the principal events of that history. The immediate cause of the riots was the shortage and high price of food. But the rioters often went beyond the issue of food, E. P. Thompson and George Rudé claim, demanding a restoration of the "moral economy," an economy based upon "just prices," "just wages," and a traditional, paternalistic order. The moral economy represented a "popular consensus" about what was legitimate and what illegitimate, a consensus shared to some extent by the authorities themselves.

> While this moral economy cannot be described as "political" in any advanced sense, nevertheless it cannot be described as unpolitical either, since it supposed definite, and passionately held, notions of the common weal—notions which, indeed, found some support in the paternalist tradition of the authorities; notions which the people re-echoed so loudly in their turn that the authorities were, in some measure, the prisoners of the people. Hence this moral economy impinged very

---

*George Rudé claims that "mob" was sometimes used as an "omnibus term" for the whole of the "lower strata of society in the pre-industrial age." In support of this usage he cites a description offered by Henry Fielding in 1752: "that very large and powerful body which form the fourth estate in this community and have long been dignified by the name of the Mob." But when Fielding had used that word in *Tom Jones,* published three years earlier, he took the precaution of adding a footnote: "Wherever this word occurs in our writings, it intends persons without virtue or sense, in all stations; and many of the highest rank are often meant by it."[49]

generally upon eighteenth-century government and thought, and did
not only intrude at moments of disturbance.[51]

The moral economy, to be sure, functioned imperfectly, the "paternalist
model" repeatedly breaking down, which is why the poor were so often
driven to riots to reassert it. Nor was it only the poor who had an interest
in it. The "paternalists" themselves, the local magistrates and the Privy
Council, invoked it in times of crisis, prohibiting forestalling, for example,
toward the end of the century when food was scarce. Thus paternalism, and
the moral economy of which it was part, had not only an "ideal existence"
but a "fragmentary real existence."[52]

At this point the counter-history, "history from below," overlaps with
conventional history, "history from above." If "plebs" and "patricians" (as
Thompson elsewhere calls them) had different interests, as they assuredly did,
those interests did not necessarily translate themselves into such radically
different views of society as to make them totally irreconcilable. To the
extent to which they shared the same ethos, the same conceptions of social
rights and obligations, the same idea of a moral economy, they partook of
the same history.

No brief account of this period before the "takeoff" of industrialism (in
Walt Rostow's famous phrase) can begin to do justice to the complexities
of an "old society" that was neither old nor new.[53] But even the briefest
account suggests the inadequacy of one of the most influential theories that
have shaped our thinking about this period, the theory of a Puritan ethic
imbued with the values of capitalism and profoundly subversive of the
society and the ethos which had traditionally given sustenance to the poor.
That Puritan-*cum*-capitalist ethic may describe the philosophy of Mandeville, but not the dominant schools of moral philosophy which found
Mandeville utterly reprehensible. It may account for the harshness of the Act
of Settlement or the poor laws of the early eighteenth century, but not for
the unquestioned commitment to the principle of a poor law and to a policy
of relief which, even in its most restrictive period, placed a heavy burden
on taxpayers (who were not the poor). It may explain some aspects of
Methodism—the work ethic, perhaps (although even this was not peculiar
to capitalism)—but not the prohibition of interest, the practice of charity,
or the spirit of communality and fraternity that was later to make Methodism a seedbed of radicalism and trade unionism. Nor can it account, except
by some devious theory of "social control," for the proliferation of philanthropic enterprises throughout the century and for the more generous spirit
of legislation in the second half, so that even Tawney admitted that the harsh

attitude toward the poor abated about 1760—this at precisely the time when industrialism and capitalism began their "takeoff."* If the Age of Benevolence had its "underside," if every humanitarian enterprise was evidence of some inhumane condition, if every food riot testified to a failure of the "moral economy," this too suggests that "the world we have lost" was not wholly lost, that the "chasm" had not yet engulfed the poor.

On the eve of the industrial revolution poverty was essentially what it had always been: a natural, unfortunate, often tragic fact of life, but not necessarily a demeaning or degrading fact. At a time when no one seriously conceived of a society without poverty, when there were not even utopian fantasies of such a society (the utopianism generated by the English Civil War having been dissipated, and that inspired by the French Revolution being well in the future), the most that could be hoped for the poor was a society in which they had a legitimate and secure moral status. In such a society poverty was part of the natural order of things—of a physical nature that was precarious, an economy that was straitened, a human nature that was frail and fallible. But if poverty was natural, so was the relief of poverty: private, voluntary charity as enjoined by the sacred tenets of religion (reaffirmed by Methodism) and by the "social affections" innate in every man (reaffirmed by the moral philosophers); and public, compulsory relief as prescribed by the poor laws (and modified but also reaffirmed in the course of the century). Although both forms of relief varied enormously, from time to time, from one parish to another, from one individual or group to another, the principle remained. And that principle, more perhaps than the principle of a just wage or just price, was part of the "moral economy of the poor."

The moral economy was very much an ideal (perhaps had always been an ideal), and was as inconstant and infirm as all such ideals. If it had become much attenuated in reality, as a result of the economic, social, demographic, technological, religious, and intellectual changes of the preceding two centuries, it continued to be the ideal by which reality was judged. To that extent it continued to be part of the reality itself—not only in preindustrial England, but during the whole of the following century when a "new society" was in the making.

*The difficulty with the theory of "social control" is that it can be neither proved nor disproved, since it can account for anything and everything: the restriction of poor relief or its expansion, the provision of education for the poor or the failure to provide such education, the passage of a Ten Hours Bill or the defeat of that bill, a religious movement that catered to the poor or one that ignored the poor. In any event, whatever the presumed intention of the sponsors of such reforms and movements—the defusing of social unrest or the creation of an efficient, docile labor force—the objective effect was to improve the conditions and prospects of the poor. The claim of some recent historians that the Elizabethan poor laws, for example, were intended to "regulate" the poor, or of Fernand Braudel that they were "laws *against* the poor," would have seemed perverse to most contemporaries, certainly to those radicals who so vigorously championed these laws.[54]

II

ADAM SMITH:

POLITICAL ECONOMY

AS MORAL PHILOSOPHY

If there was a "chasm" in the history of social thought, it must surely, one would think, be attributed to Adam Smith, that "half-bred and half-witted Scotchman," John Ruskin called him, who deliberately perpetrated the blasphemy, "Thou shalt hate the Lord thy God, damn His laws, and covet thy neighbour's goods."[1] It cannot have been an accident that the publication of Smith's work coincided with two major revolutions: the American Revolution, which professed to speak in the name of a new "science of politics," and the industrial revolution, which created the material conditions for both the new political science and the new political economy.

This theory invites the obvious demurral, that the *Wealth of Nations* was not all that revolutionary, either in its ideas or in its effects. Even the distinctive terms associated with it antedated it by many years. "Political economy" made its appearance as early as 1615, in Antoyne de Mont-chrétien's *Traicté de l'oeconomie politique.* The term was introduced into England by William Petty later in that century, and received wide currency with the publication, almost a decade before the *Wealth of Nations,* of James Steuart's *Inquiry into the Principles of Political Oeconomy.* Another French import was "laissez faire," which goes back at least to the time of Louis XIV, when a merchant is reported to have pleaded with the king's minister, Colbert, *"Laissez-nous faire."* The phrase was later popularized by the French Physiocrats in their struggle against the highly regulated economy of the old regime. Petty preferred the Latin version, *Vadere sicut vult.*[2] Smith himself used neither the French nor the Latin phrase in the *Wealth of Nations.*

Nor, more surprisingly, did either Malthus or Ricardo, although "laissez faire" had come into general usage by that time. It is ironic that this doctrine, which is thought of as distinctively English, should have retained the French form and that to this day there should be no satisfactory English equivalent. (Neither "free trade" nor "individualism" expresses quite the same idea.)

The "division of labor," a term Smith did use frequently and prominently, also originated elsewhere. Both the term and the concept may have been adopted, complete with the famous pin-factory illustration (and with the same eighteen operations), from the *Encyclopédie,* the latter probably inspired by the account of the same manufacturing process (this time in twenty-five operations) in Chambers's *Cyclopaedia,* published almost three decades before the *Encyclopédie* and almost five before the *Wealth of Nations.* One historian, claiming Plato as the source of the idea, pointed out that Smith's library contained three complete sets of the Dialogues.[3] But Smith could as well have come upon the concept in Thucydides or Aristotle, or in the work of his own friend Adam Ferguson, whose *Essay on the History of Civil Society* appeared in 1767. Every manufacturer, Ferguson casually remarked, knew that "the more he can subdivide the tasks of his workmen, and the more hands he can employ on separate articles, the more are his expenses diminished, and his profits increased."[4]

The question of originality had been anticipated by Smith himself. In 1755, before the publication of the *Theory of Moral Sentiments* and long before the *Wealth of Nations,* he wrote a paper claiming priority for some of the leading ideas of both works, including the principle (although not the phrase) of laissez faire. This and other of his ideas, he pointed out, had been the subject of his lectures in 1750, his last year at the University of Edinburgh, and in the dozen years (1752–64) during which he occupied the chair of moral philosophy at the University of Glasgow. The lectures had been written out by his clerk in Edinburgh, and he could "adduce innumerable witnesses, both from that place and from this, who will ascertain them sufficiently to be mine."[5] If Smith's claim was unduly proprietary (and uncharacteristically immodest), it had objective merit. While specific ideas in the *Wealth of Nations* were not entirely novel, the implications of the work as a whole were. Walter Bagehot put the matter well when he said that the doctrine of free trade was indeed "in the air," but it was not accepted or established; "on the contrary, it was a tenet against which a respectable parent would probably caution his son;—still it was known as a tempting heresy and one against which a warning was needed."[6] What Smith did— and this was his historic achievement—was to convert a minor heresy into a new and powerful orthodoxy.*

*Joseph Schumpeter was far harsher in his judgment. The *Wealth of Nations,* he said, contained not a "single *analytic* idea, principle, or method that was entirely new in 1776," nothing that would

Another kind of priority raises more serious questions. Was it the intellectual revolution wrought by the *Wealth of Nations* (assuming there was such a revolution) that was decisive, or the industrial revolution presumably reflected in that work? What in fact was the relation between the two? It is interesting that after several decades during which the expression "industrial revolution" fell into disrepute, it has recently been revived and is now used less apologetically. The timing of the revolution, to be sure, has been somewhat changed, the preferred date today being 1780 rather than 1760, which was the date assigned it by Arnold Toynbee when he popularized the term a century ago.[8] The chronology points to the problem. According to Smith himself, the basic thesis of the *Wealth of Nations* had been conceived as early as 1750, which suggests that it anticipated the industrial revolution, at least as that revolution is commonly defined (not, to be sure, the division of labor or factories, both of which existed at the time). Most economic historians, acutely aware of the chronology of technological and economic developments, tend to minimize the connection between the industrial revolution and the new political economy. Intellectual historians, on the other hand, seeking to ground ideas in social and economic history, use such words as "insight" and "foresight" to signify some kind of connection, however tenuous.[9]

Whatever the resolution of this debate—whether it was from "ideas" or "reality" that Smith drew his inspiration, whether the *Wealth of Nations* was primarily prescriptive or descriptive—the effect of Smith's work was to give technology and industry a new and decisive role, not only in the economy but in society. The division of labor (if only the relatively primitive kind found in a pin factory) became the harbinger of a social revolution as momentous as anything dreamed of by political reformers and revolutionaries. It is in this sense that the book was genuinely revolutionary, in creating a political economy that made the wealth and welfare of the people dependent on a highly developed, expanding, industrial economy and on a self-regulating "system of natural liberty."

Perhaps it was because this revolutionary thesis emerged so naturally in the course of the book, starting with the homely illustration of the pin

---

entitle it to rank with Newton's *Principia* or Darwin's *Origin* as an "intellectual achievement." Conceding that it was a "great performance" deserving of its success, he then went on to explain that this success was, paradoxically, due to Smith's limitations:

Had he been more brilliant, he would not have been taken so seriously. Had he dug more deeply, had he unearthed more recondite truth, had he used difficult and ingenious methods, he would not have been understood. But he had no such ambitions; in fact he disliked whatever went beyond plain common sense. He never moved above the heads of even the dullest readers. . . . And it was Adam Smith's good fortune that he was thoroughly in sympathy with the humors of his time. He advocated the things that were in the offing, and he made his analysis serve them.[7]

factory, that it was accepted so readily. Some of Smith's friends were afraid that the book was too formidable to have any immediate impact. David Hume consoled Smith that while it required too close a reading to become quickly popular, eventually, by its "depth and solidity and acuteness" as well as its "curious facts," it would "at last take the public attention."[10] In fact, in spite of its forbidding appearance (two large volumes, a total of 1,100 pages), the work achieved a considerable measure of popularity, and sooner than Hume had anticipated. Within a month of its publication, the publisher reported that sales were better than might have been expected of a book requiring so much thought and reflection, qualities, he regretted, that "do not abound among modern readers."[11] The first edition sold out in six months, a second appeared early in 1778, and three others followed in the dozen years before Smith's death. It was translated into French, German, Italian, Danish, and Spanish, and received the stamp of success in the form of a lengthy abridgment. Smith's first biographer, writing three years after his death, was pleased to report that Smith had had the satisfaction of seeing his principles widely accepted during his lifetime and witnessing their application to the commercial policy of England.

There were some critics, to be sure: the economist and agriculturist Arthur Young, who thought the book full of "poisonous errors," and the Whig leader Charles James Fox, who said that he had never read it (although he cited it in a debate in Parliament) and claimed not to understand the subject, but was certain that he heartily despised it.[12] But even the radicals offered little serious objection to it, Thomas Paine and Richard Price, for example, actually declaring themselves admirers of Smith. For a short period after his death, at a time when anti-French feelings were running high, the charge was heard that his teachings were hostile to government and therefore subversive. Apart from that, however, the prevailing attitude was overwhelmingly favorable, with some of the most prominent men of the time —Hume, Burke, Gibbon, Pitt, Lansdowne, North—proudly proclaiming themselves his disciples.

The ultimate accolade, the comparison of Smith with Newton,[13] recalls the reception given to that other latter-day Newton, Charles Darwin. In fact, the *Wealth of Nations* and the *Origin of Species* had much in common: Both were classics in their own time, and for some of the same reasons. Each had been amply prepared for by the reputation of its author, by the importance he himself attached to it and the many years he devoted to it, and by tantalizing previews in the form of conversations, letters, and lectures. And each announced itself, by the boldness of its thesis, its comprehensiveness, and its imposing title, as a major intellectual event. Whatever questions might be raised about the originality or validity of Smith's work, its importance and influence are hardly in dispute. For good or ill, *An Inquiry into the Nature and Causes of the Wealth of Nations* heralded the beginning

of "political economy" as that term was generally understood at the time
—"classical economics," as a later generation was to know it.

The basic themes of the *Wealth of Nations* are too familiar to need elaboration: the division of labor making for increased productivity and thus the
increased "opulence" of all of society; the fundamental facts of human
nature—self-interest (or "self-love") and the "propensity to truck, barter,
and exchange"—which were the generating force of the economic process;
the "invisible hand" (a metaphor used only once but implied throughout)
which made the individual's interest an instrument for the general good; and
the "system of natural liberty" which was the only certain means to achieve
both the wealth of nations and the welfare of individuals.[14] The argument
was worked out in great detail under such headings as money, trade, value,
labor, capital, rent.

One subject that did not appear in the chapter titles or subheads was
poverty. Yet this was as much a theme of the book as wealth itself. Indeed,
it may be argued that if the *Wealth of Nations* was less than novel in its
theories of money, trade, or value, it was genuinely revolutionary in its view
of poverty and its attitude toward the poor.

It was not, however, revolutionary in the sense which is often supposed: the de-moralization of the economy resulting from the doctrine of
laissez faire, the de-moralization of man implied in the image of "economic
man," and the de-moralization of the poor who found themselves at the
mercy of forces over which they had no control—over which, according
to the new political economy, no one had any control.[15] This is a common
reading of the *Wealth of Nations,* but not a just one. For it supposes that
Smith's idea of a market economy was devoid of moral purpose, that his
concept of human nature was mechanistic and reductivist, and that his
attitude toward the poor was indifferent or callous. Above all, it fails to take
account of the fact that Smith was a moral philosopher, by conviction as
well as profession. As the Professor of Moral Philosophy at the University
of Glasgow and the celebrated author of *The Theory of Moral Sentiments,*
he could hardly have thought it his mission to preside over the dissolution
of moral philosophy.

Published in 1759, *The Theory of Moral Sentiments* went through four
editions before the *Wealth of Nations* appeared, and another edition a few
years later. Its three French translations made Smith almost as well known
among the *philosophes* as Hume was. Today Smith's fame rests so completely upon the *Wealth of Nations* one might be tempted to dismiss the
earlier work as just that, an early, minor work that was overshadowed and
superseded by his later, major work. In his own time, however, his reputa-

tion derived at least as much from the earlier book, and this even after the publication of the *Wealth of Nations*. (In his *Memoir* of Smith written three years after his death, Dugald Stewart devoted twenty-six pages, one-third of the whole, to *Moral Sentiments* and only seventeen pages to the *Wealth of Nations*.) Smith had always planned to revise *Moral Sentiments*, and the last year of his life was devoted entirely to that task. The new edition expanded upon, but did not substantively alter, the thesis of the original. The most important change was the addition of a chapter, the title of which testifies to his abiding concern: "Of the Corruption of Our Moral Sentiments, Which is Occasioned by this Disposition to Admire the Rich and the Great, and to Despise or Neglect Persons of Poor and Mean Condition."[16]

A major theme of controversy among Smith scholars has been *Das Adam Smith-Problem*, as a German commentator portentously labeled it— the question of the congruence of *Moral Sentiments* with the *Wealth of Nations*.[17] About the doctrine of *Moral Sentiments* itself, there is little dispute. The operative word in that book was "sympathy." Sympathy was presumed to be as much a principle of human nature as self-interest; indeed, it informed self-interest since it was one of the pleasures experienced by the individual when he contemplated or contributed to the good of another. "To feel much for others and little for ourselves, . . . to restrain our selfish, and to indulge our benevolent affections, constitutes the perfection of human nature; and can alone produce among mankind that harmony of sentiments and passions in which consists their whole grace and propriety." Smith distinguished his idea of sympathy from Hutcheson's "moral sense," which was so radically at variance with self-interest that it supposed virtue to reside in the denial of one's interest and the defiance of one's nature. But Hutcheson's doctrine, Smith argued, at least had the merit of maintaining a distinction between virtue and vice, in contrast to the "wholly pernicious," "licentious system" of Mandeville, which made no such distinction and recognized no motive, no principle of conduct, other than self-interest.[18]* Unlike Mandeville (or Bentham), Smith was able to credit such sentiments and to use unapologetically such words as sympathy, beneficence, virtue, humanity, love of others. And there were many occasions, he insisted, when the interests of the individual had to make way for the interests of others, regardless of any calculations of utility.

---

*By the same token, Smith would have rejected the kind of utilitarianism espoused by Jeremy Bentham, who said that he could not conceive of a human being "in whose instance any public interest he can have had, will not, insofar as it depends upon himself, have been sacrificed to his own personal interest." Even Bentham, however, did conceive of one such human being—himself, whom he once described as "the most philanthropic of the philanthropic: philanthropy the end and instrument of his ambition."[19]

One individual must never prefer himself so much even to any other
individual, as to hurt or injure that other, in order to benefit himself,
though the benefit to the one should be much greater than the hurt
or injury to the other.[20]

The wise and virtuous man is at all times willing that his own private
interest should be sacrificed to the public interest of his own particular
order or society. He is at all times willing, too, that the interest of this
order or society should be sacrificed to the greater interest of the state
or sovereignty, of which it is only a subordinate part. He should,
therefore, be equally willing that all those inferior interests should be
sacrificed to the greater interest of the universe.[21]

The argument of *Moral Sentiments* is subtle, complicated, and not
without difficulties, but even the barest statement of it is enough to demonstrate that Smith was hardly the ruthless individualist or amoralist he is
sometimes made out to be. Whatever difficulties there may be in the
reconciliation of *Moral Sentiments* with the *Wealth of Nations,* it is clear
enough that Smith intended both as parts of his grand "design," that he had
the *Wealth of Nations* in mind even before he wrote *Moral Sentiments,* and
that he remained committed to *Moral Sentiments,* reissuing and revising it
long after the *Wealth of Nations* was published.[22]

A close reading of the *Wealth of Nations* itself suggests that political
economy as Smith understood it was part of a larger moral philosophy, a
new kind of moral economy. Schumpeter complained that Smith was so
steeped in the tradition of moral philosophy derived from scholasticism and
natural law that he could not conceive of economics per se, an economics
divorced from ethics and politics.[23] The point is well taken, although not
necessarily in criticism. The bias and the rhetoric of the moral philosopher
crop up again and again in the *Wealth of Nations:* in the condemnation of
the "vile maxim," "All for themselves, and nothing for other people"; in
the proposition that the trade of the nation should be conducted on the same
principles that govern private affairs; in the denunciations of manufacturers
and merchants who were all too willing to sacrifice the public interest for
their private interests and were prepared to use any stratagem to achieve
their ends; in the charges of "impertinent jealousy," "mean rapacity," "mean
and malignant expedients," "sneaking arts," "interesting sophistry," "interested falsehood."[24] One of Smith's main criticisms of the mercantile system
was that it encouraged merchants and manufacturers to be selfish and du-
plicitous.

Our merchants and master-manufacturers complain much of the bad
effects of high wages in raising the price, and thereby lessening the sale
of their goods both at home and abroad. They say nothing concerning

the bad effects of high profits. They are silent with regard to the pernicious effects of their own gains. They complain only of those of other people.

The clamour and sophistry of merchants and manufacturers easily persuade them that the private interest of a part, and of a subordinate part of the society, is the general interest of the whole.

People of the same trade seldom meet together, even for merriment and diversion, but the conversation ends in a conspiracy against the public, or in some contrivance to raise prices.

The proposal of any new law or regulation of commerce which comes from this order, ought always to be listened to with great precaution, and ought never to be adopted till after having been long and carefully examined, not only with the most scrupulous, but with the most suspicious attention. It comes from an order of men, whose interest is never exactly the same with that of the public, who have generally an interest to deceive and even to oppress the public, and who accordingly have, upon many occasions, both deceived and oppressed it.

It is the industry which is carried on for the benefit of the rich and powerful, that is principally encouraged by our mercantile system. That which is carried on for the benefit of the poor and the indigent, is too often, either neglected, or oppressed.[25]

These attacks on "private interests" that were in conflict with the "general interest," especially with the interests of the "poor and indigent," may seem difficult to reconcile with the famous dictum: "It is not from the benevolence of the butcher, the brewer, or the baker, that we expect our dinner, but from their regard to their own interest."[26] But this principle of self-interest was predicated on certain conditions: that the butcher, brewer, and baker not take unfair advantage of others, that they abide by the rules of the free market, that they not "conspire," "deceive," and "oppress." Under these conditions self-interest was itself a moral principle—not as lofty as altruism, but, in the mundane affairs of life (the provision of "dinner"), more reliable and effective. Hovering over these individual interests, ensuring that they work together for the greater good of the whole, the general interest, was the benevolent, ubiquitous "invisible hand."[27]

The "invisible hand" has been much criticized. If only, it has been said, Smith had not introduced that unfortunate metaphor with its teleological overtones, if only he had confined himself to the austere language of mechanics and nature, he would have avoided much misunderstanding. There is some justice in this complaint. The invisible hand was indeed invisible; the genius of the system of "natural liberty" was that it required no "hand," no intervention, direction, or regulation to bring about the general good. But the metaphor served the important purpose of keeping the reader mindful of the purpose of that system. It was by means of the invisible hand that the individual was led "to promote an end which was no part of his intention"; "by pursuing his own interest he frequently promotes that of society more effectually than when he really intends to promote it."[28] Without that metaphor the weight of the argument might have rested with the individual's interests. The invisible hand shifted the emphasis to the general interest. If the metaphor was unfortunate, it was not for the reason that it was teleological; on the contrary, its utility and justification lay in the fact that it clearly expressed the teleological cast of the argument.

The general interest that emerged from Smith's system was "general" in the Rousseauan or Hegelian sense of a general interest more elevated than the sum of individual interests—Hegelian perhaps more than Rousseauan, the "invisible hand" resembling Hegel's "cunning of reason" which contrived to make the interests and passions of individuals serve a larger purpose of which the individuals themselves were unaware.* It was also "general" in the pedestrian, utilitarian sense of the totality of interests of all the members of society. This second sense pointed to the importance of the "people" and the "poor" in Smith's theory. The "wealth of nations" of the title referred not to the nation in the mercantilist sense—the nation-state whose wealth was a measure of the power it could exercise vis-à-vis other states—but to the people comprising the nation. And "people" not in the political sense of those having a voice and active part in the political process, but in the social and economic sense, those working and living in society, of whom the largest part were the "lower ranks" or "poor."

The concern with the people emerged early in the book in the discussion of the division of labor, when it appeared that the great advantage of that mode of production was the "universal opulence which extends itself to the lowest ranks of the people . . . , a general plenty [which] diffuses itself through all the different ranks of the society."[29] Addressing the "common complaint" that since luxuries had become available to the poor they were no longer content with the humble food, clothing, and lodging that had once been their lot, Smith put the question: "Is this improvement in the

---

*There is no suggestion that the "cunning of reason," as it appeared in Hegel's *Philosophy of History*, was inspired by Smith's "invisible hand." But Hegel had read Smith (as well as other political economists, including Say and Ricardo), and there are distinct echoes of Smith's marketplace in the *Philosophy of Right*, especially in the concept of "civil society," the realm intermediate between the individual and the state in which individuals pursue their private interests.

circumstances of the lower ranks of the people to be regarded as an advantage or as an inconveniency to the society?" His answer was unequivocal.

> Servants, labourers and workmen of different kinds, make up the far greater part of every great political society. But what improves the circumstances of the greater part can never be regarded as an inconveniency to the whole. No society can surely be flourishing and happy, of which the far greater part of the members are poor and miserable. It is but equity, besides, that they who feed, clothe and lodge the whole body of the people, should have such a share of the produce of their own labour as to be themselves tolerably well fed, clothed and lodged.[30]

The condition of the poor was decisive, Smith reasoned, partly by sheer force of numbers—since they formed the largest part of society, their condition necessarily determined the condition of the whole of society—and partly as a matter of equity; as producers of the goods enjoyed by the rest of society, they were entitled to a fair share of those goods. They also had a special claim to Smith's attention by virtue of being one of the two "orders" of society—laborers and landlords—whose interests were "connected with the general interest of society," in contrast to the third, merchants and manufacturers, whose interests were often at variance with it.[31] Yet it was the laborers who were at the greatest disadvantage under mercantilism. As consumers, they were ill served by a system that promoted high prices and discouraged imports; and as producers, by a system that permitted their employers, by fair means or foul, to keep wages low and prices high. The poor, in short, were the chief victims of the existing system—and would be the chief beneficiaries of the "natural" system proposed by Smith.

Smith's critique of mercantilism is generally read as an attack on government regulation and a plea for laissez faire. But it was much more than that, as contemporaries were aware. Among other things, it was a criticism of the prevailing theory of wages. While Smith was not the first to question the expediency or desirability of low wages, he was the first to offer a systematic, comprehensive rationale for high wages. The consensus at the time was that low wages were both natural and economically necessary: natural because the poor would not work except out of dire need, and necessary if the nation were to enjoy a favorable balance of trade. This was the view of Hume, who explained that in years of scarcity when wages were low, "the poor labour more, and really live better, than in years of great plenty, when they indulge themselves in idleness and riot."[32] Arthur Young put it more succinctly: "Every one but an idiot knows, that the lower classes must be kept poor, or they will never be industrious."[33] Both admitted that excessively low wages would provide no incentive to work. "Two shillings and sixpence a day," Young remarked, "will undoubtedly tempt some to work, who would not touch a tool for one shilling."[34] But this was an argument for subsistence wages, not for high wages.

It remained for Smith to defend high wages, the "liberal reward of labour."

> The liberal reward of labour, as it encourages the propagation so it increases the industry of the common people. The wages of labour are the encouragement of industry, which, like every other human quality, improves in proportion to the encouragement it receives. A plentiful subsistence increases the bodily strength of the labourer, and the comfortable hope of bettering his condition, and of ending his days perhaps in ease and plenty, animates him to exert that strength to the utmost. Where wages are high, accordingly, we shall always find the workmen more active, diligent, and expeditious, than where they are low: in England, for example, than in Scotland; in the neighbourhood of great towns, than in remote country places.[35]

Smith granted that some workers, if they earned enough in four days to keep them for a week, would be idle the other days; but these were a minority. Most workers, he was convinced, were given to the opposite failing: if they were well paid by the piece, they would so overwork themselves as to impair their health. It may have been with Hume in mind (and out of courtesy to his friend that he did not quote him to this effect) that Smith disputed the conventional view: "That men in general should work better when they are ill fed than when they are well fed, when they are disheartened than when they are in good spirits, when they are frequently sick than when they are generally in good health, seems not very probable."[36]

The doctrine of high wages was a corollary of Smith's conception of a "progressive" economy. Since high wages were the result of increasing wealth and at the same time the cause of increasing population, only in an expanding economy, where the demand for labor kept abreast of the supply, could real wages remain high. "It is in the progressive state, while the society is advancing to the further acquisition, rather than when it has acquired its full complement of riches, that the condition of the labouring poor, of the great body of the people, seems to be the happiest and the most comfortable." In a "stationary" state, on the other hand, the condition of the poor was "dull" and "hard," and in a "declining" state it was "miserable" and "melancholy."[37] The division of labor was crucial for the same reason, because it made for greater productivity and thus for an expanding, progressive economy where increased wealth could extend to the "lowest ranks of the people."[38]

The idea of a progressive economy places Smith in the ranks of the "optimists." It may also be his chief claim to originality. Unlike previous economists for whom one good could be purchased only at the expense of another —the general interest at the expense of individual interests, agriculture at the expense of industry, the power of the nation at the expense of the liberty of its citizens, the productivity of labor at the expense of the happiness of the laborer—Smith envisioned an economy in which most goods and interests were compatible and complementary. Free trade would enhance both freedom and wealth; high wages would ensure productivity and well-being; the self-interest of the individual would promote, however unwittingly, the public interest. It was a prescription for a liberating, expanding, prospering, progressive economy in which the legitimate values and interests of society supported and reinforced each other: liberty and prosperity, the individual and society, industry and agriculture, capital and labor, wealth and well-being.

This optimistic view of the economy presupposed an optimistic view of human nature. It is the French *philosophes* who are usually credited with such a view. But their optimism, based upon the supposedly transforming power of reason, was not a conspicuously democratic doctrine, at least not at a time when the mass of the people were uneducated and illiterate. Because reason was paramount, and because the ordinary people were presumed to be not yet capable of exercising the degree of reason required for a truly rational order, most of the *philosophes* looked to enlightened rulers, "benevolent despots," to do for society what the people could not do for themselves.

To Smith (and the Scottish Enlightenment in general), it was not reason that defined human nature so much as interests, passions, sentiments, sympathies. These were qualities shared by all people, not in some remote future but in the present. No enlightened despot was required to activate those interests, no Benthamite legislator to bring about a harmony of interests. All that was necessary was to free people—all people, in all ranks and callings—so that they could act on their interests. From these individually motivated, freely inspired actions, the general interest would emerge without any intervention, regulation, or coercion.

In a sense Smith's was a more modest—"lower," one might say—view of human nature, and by that token a more democratic one. If people differed, as they patently did, it was not because of any innate differences but because the qualities common to all had been developed in them in different degrees. On the nature-nurture issue, as we now know it, Smith was unequivocally on the nurture side.

The difference of natural talents in different men is, in reality, much less than we are aware of; and the very different genius which appears to distinguish men of different professions, when grown up to maturity, is not upon many occasions so much the cause, as the effect of the division of labour. The difference between the most dissimilar characters, between a philosopher and a common street porter, for example, seems to arise not so much from nature, as from habit, custom, and education. . . . By nature a philosopher is not in genius and disposition half so different from a street porter, as a mastiff is from a greyhound.[39]

The idea that differences were less the "cause" than the "effect" of the division of labor radically differentiates Smith from other philosophers—Plato, most notably—who had used the concept of the division of labor. While some of Smith's illustrations and "stages of history" were reminiscent of Plato, the heart of his thesis could not have been more dissimilar. Given Smith's respect for classical philosophy, and for Plato especially, one may even take his spirited denial of any difference in "nature" between the philosopher and the street porter as an implicit rebuke to Plato. To Plato, natural differences were precisely the "cause" rather than the "effect" of the division of labor: the division of labor reflected the innate differences among people and permitted people of essentially different natures to cooperate for the common good. The only innate quality mentioned by Smith, and the only one necessary to his system, was the "propensity to truck, barter, and exchange."[40] This propensity was shared by porter and philosopher alike; it was the common denominator that made it possible for everyone to participate in the division of labor, and for everyone to profit from that division. It was also the common denominator that united the highest and lowest ranks in a single human species, a species in which the varieties were not half so different as were mastiff and greyhound.

Just as the differences among individuals were functional rather than organic, so the differences among the "orders" of society were functional rather than hierarchic. Those three orders were defined by the nature of their income—rent, wages, and profits—not by their position in a hierarchy—upper, middle, and lower. In fact wage earners, or laborers, constituted the "second order."[41] Elsewhere Smith did use the terms current at the time, "lower ranks" or "lower classes," to describe the laborers. What was important about them, however, was not that they were of the lower classes but that they received their income in the form of wages rather than rent or profit. In this respect the laborer was a partner in the economic enterprise, the most important partner, Smith sometimes gave the impression, since it was his labor that was the source of value. And labor, like rent and profit, was a "patrimony," a form of property entitled to the same consideration as any other kind of property.

> The patrimony which every man has in his own labour, as it is the original foundation of all other property, so it is the most sacred and inviolable. The patrimony of a poor man lies in the strength and dexterity of his hands; and to hinder him from employing this strength and dexterity in what manner he thinks proper without injury to his neighbour is a plain violation of this most sacred property.[42]

. . .

There was, however, one point at which this optimistic vision failed Smith, failed him so seriously, in the opinion of some recent commentators, as to make him a prophet of doom, a critic of capitalism on the order of Marx —indeed, a precursor of Marx in exposing that fatal flaw of capitalism, the "alienation" of the working class.[43]

If Smith did anticipate something like Marx's theory of alienation, as Marx himself intimated, it must also be said that he avoided the ambiguity that appeared in Marx's own discussion of that subject as well as in recent Marxist thought.[44] For Smith clearly located the source of alienation (if it may be called that) not in capitalism as such but in industrialism, and more specifically in the division of labor that was the peculiar character and the special strength of modern industry. The poignancy of Smith's argument comes from the paradox that the division of labor, which provided the momentum for the progressive economy that was the only hope for the laboring classes, was also the probable cause of the mental, spiritual, even physical deterioration of those classes.

> In the progress of the division of labour, the employment of the far greater part of those who live by labour, that is of the great body of the people, comes to be confined to a few very simple operations, frequently to one or two. But the understandings of the greater part of men are necessarily formed by their ordinary employments. The man whose whole life is spent in performing a few simple operations, of which the effects too are, perhaps, always the same, or very nearly the same, has no occasion to exert his understanding, or to exercise his invention in finding out expedients for removing difficulties which never occur. He naturally loses, therefore, the habit of such exertions, and generally becomes as stupid and ignorant as it is possible for a human creature to become. The torpor of his mind renders him, not only incapable of relishing or bearing a part in any rational conversation, but of conceiving any general, noble, or tender sentiments, and consequently of forming any just judgment concerning many even of

the ordinary duties of private life. Of the great and extensive interests of his country he is altogether incapable of judging; and unless very particular pains have been taken to render him otherwise, he is equally incapable of defending his country in war. The uniformity of his stationary life naturally corrupts the courage of his mind, and makes him regard with abhorrence the irregular, uncertain, and adventurous life of a soldier. It corrupts even the activity of his body, and renders him incapable of exerting his strength with vigour and perseverance, in any other employment than that to which he has been bred. His dexterity at his own particular trade seems, in this manner, to be acquired at the expence of his intellectual, social, and martial virtues. But in every improved and civilized society this is the state into which the labouring poor, that is, the great body of the people, must necessarily fall, unless government takes some pains to prevent it.[45]

This passage is sufficiently powerful in itself, and sufficiently problematic in the context of Smith's work, to stand on its own without being assimilated into the Marxist idea of alienation and without taking on all the difficulties associated with that idea. There were, one might argue, two different Marxist ideas: that of the "early Marx," where alienation arose in the earliest stages of society as a result of the separation from physical nature and the division of labor in the family; and that of the "mature Marx," where it was attributed to the worker's divorce from the ownership of the means of production and from the products of his own labor. Neither of these ideas corresponds to Smith's. For Smith, the question of ownership was as irrelevant as the question of nature or the family. His only concern was the debilitating effect of the division of labor in the industrial process. In this respect the factory worker in a socialist regime, or in any other form of cooperative or public enterprise, would suffer just as grievously as the factory worker under capitalism.

That Smith held industrialism rather than capitalism at fault is apparent from the only other passage in the *Wealth of Nations* bearing upon this subject. Here Smith compared the industrial worker with the agricultural laborer, to the disadvantage of the former. Husbandry, he argued, required a greater degree of knowledge and experience, judgment and discretion than most industrial trades. The ordinary ploughman might be deficient in the arts of "social intercourse," his voice and language uncouth by the standards of the townsman, but his "understanding," sharpened by the variety of tasks which he had to perform, was superior to the mechanic occupied with one or two simple operations. "How much," Smith concluded, "the lower ranks of people in the country are really superior to those of the town, is well known to every man whom either business or curiosity has led to converse much with both."[46]

If the problem was not alienation in the Marxist sense, it was in its own terms serious enough, serious not only for Smith himself, who wrote of it with great passion, but for the reader who may find it a grave flaw in the argument of the *Wealth of Nations.* How can one reconcile this dismal portrait of the industrial worker reduced to a state of torpor, stupidity, and ignorance, lacking in judgment, initiative, courage, or any "intellectual, social, and martial virtues"—all this because of the division of labor—with the earlier image of the "hearty," "cheerful" worker who, as a result of the same division of labor, received a "plentiful subsistence," enjoyed "bodily strength," was "active, diligent, and expeditious," and looked forward to the "comfortable hope of bettering his condition" and ending his days in "ease and plenty"?[47] How can one reconcile the favorable view of the agricultural laborer, who acquired "judgment and discretion" because he had to deal with so many different tasks, with an earlier image of the same laborer who, precisely because he went from one activity to another, developed the habit of "sauntering," became "indolent," "careless," "slothful and lazy," "incapable of any vigorous application even on the most pressing occasions"? In that earlier passage Smith contrasted the dilatory farm laborer to the factory boy whose only task was the opening and shutting of a valve, and who was inspired, by boredom itself, to invent a labor-saving device which was "one of the greatest improvements" made on the steam engine.[48]

These discordant images are not reconcilable. What can be said, however, is that the dominant image, that which informs by far the largest part of the book and which bears the largest weight of the argument, is the "optimistic" one: the image of an active, intelligent, industrious worker, receiving good wages, constantly bettering himself, and sharing in the "universal opulence" created by the division of labor and the expansion of industry. It was this scenario that impressed itself on Smith's readers in his own time and for generations afterward. Although Marx, in *Capital,* quoted the passage describing the worker stupefied by the division of labor, it was not until the "early Marx" and the idea of alienation came into fashion after the Second World War that this passage became the subject of serious attention and that the vision of "another" Smith, a "pessimistic" Smith, began to emerge.*

---

*The two Smiths appear most dramatically in the work of Robert Heilbroner. His influential history of economic thought, *The Worldly Philosophers* (1953), presented the conventional optimistic Smith. His recent work introduces a "deeply pessimistic" Smith, this based not only on the so-called alienation passage, which Heilbroner now emphasizes to the point where it seems to dominate the *Wealth of Nations,* but on a reinterpretation of Smith's economic theory. So far from positing a "progressive," expanding economy, Smith is seen as predicting decline and decay: "material decline awaiting at the terminus of the economic journey, moral decay suffered by society in the course of its journeying."[49] This argument depends on ascribing to Smith something like a Malthusian theory, in which higher wages lead to an increase of population, an eventual decline of wages, and thus a stagnant and "stationary" economy. But Smith had anticipated this argument and had refuted it, at least for the foreseeable future. So long, he reasoned, as the division of labor continued (the division

. . .

It is also important to recall the context in which Smith praised the farm laborer at the expense of the industrial worker. The first passage appeared in the midst of his denunciation of the scheming merchants and manufacturers who "seldom meet together, even for merriment and diversion, but the conversation ends in a conspiracy against the public." It was then that Smith put in a good word for the agricultural classes—laborers as well as farmers —who were not in the habit of conspiring together and who deserved to be defended against those "very contemptible authors" who spoke of them so contemptuously.[52] The second passage appeared toward the end of the work in a discussion of the functions of government. Of all these functions —defense, justice, public works, the support of the sovereign—the subject to which Smith devoted by far the most space was education. After a lengthy account of the history of educational institutions, he posed the question of the state's role in education. Should the "public" (the "state," in the marginal notes) pay attention to the "education of the people," and if so, how should this be done for the "different orders of the people"? It was at this point that Smith inserted the dramatic warning about the dire effects of the division of labor. And it was to forestall those effects, to prevent the "corruption and degeneracy" of the laboring people, that he then went on to develop an elaborate scheme of public education.[53]

The proposal was simple and bold. The "common people," including those "bred to the lowest occupation," were to be required to master the essential ingredients of education: reading, writing, and arithmetic. To this end the state was to establish a school in every district, charging a fee so modest that even the common laborer could afford it, the major cost being borne by the government. Although the schools themselves would not be compulsory, some form of schooling would be. To enforce this provision, Smith suggested that an examination in the "three R's" be required before anyone could enter a guild or set up in a trade.[54]

In one sense the proposal was not remarkable. Smith was simply drawing upon the experience of Scotland, where the parish schools had taught, as he said, "almost the whole common people" to read and a great proportion of them to write and reckon.[55] In another sense, however, it was extraordinary, not only because he proposed to extend to England a state

---

of labor serving as a metaphor for the process of mechanization and invention), the economy would be able to absorb the higher wages and remain in a progressive, expanding state.[50]

When John Stuart Mill, almost three-quarters of a century later, argued for the desirability as well as the inevitability of a "stationary state," it was under the influence of Malthus and Ricardo rather than Smith, and on moral and esthetic as well as economic grounds. Finding competitiveness and material acquisitiveness disagreeable, he preferred a society in which, "while no one is poor, no one desires to be richer."[51]

system of education that had never existed there and that was bound to incur (as it did even a century later) a great deal of hostility, but because it went against the grain of his own doctrine. Having spent the better part of two volumes arguing against government regulation, he now advanced a scheme requiring a greater measure of government involvement than anything that had ever existed before. In the same chapter in which he made this proposal he criticized the principle of endowments for schools and colleges on the ground that they gave the institutions an assured income and relieved them of the necessity of proving their merit; for the same reason he opposed salaries for university teachers, preferring fees paid by individual students to individual instructors. Yet here, for the "common people," he urged the establishment of a state-administered, state-supported, state-enforced system of education with only token fees to be paid by the parents—enough to give them a stake in the education of their children but not enough to cover the cost of education. Perhaps it was to justify this large departure from his general principle that he painted so dramatic a picture of the industrial worker whose degeneracy could only be arrested by a compulsory system of education.

Having made out so strong a case for public education, Smith went on to extol the virtues of education as such. "A man without the proper use of the intellectual faculties of a man, is, if possible, more contemptible than even a coward, and seems to be mutilated and deformed in a still more essential part of the character of human nature." Even if the state were to derive no practical benefit from the education of the lower orders, that education would still warrant its active concern. In fact the state would benefit from it indirectly: a better instructed people were less inclined to the disorders that came from "delusions of enthusiasm and superstition"; they were more likely to be "decent and orderly"; feeling "respectable" themselves, they would be respected by others and be respectful of others; they would not be easily taken in by "faction and sedition"; and in a free country, where it was important that the government have the "favourable judgement" of the people, it was also important that the people should not judge the government "rashly or capriciously."[56]

One commentator has described this view of education as an "unformulated theory of 'social control.' "[57] If this is so, any idea of education which is more than purely vocational, which attributes to it any effect on character, sensibility, intelligence, and behavior, falls under the same reproach. Moreover, any alternative would be similarly suspect. What kind of education could Smith have proposed which would not have been an instrument of social control? Had he taken the obvious laissez faire position of denying to the state any role in education (as his contemporary Frederick Eden, for example, did), would this not have exposed him to the charge of being unconcerned with the plight of the lower classes, unwilling to exert himself (and the state) in an effort to improve their condition, perhaps deliberately keeping them in a state of ignorance so that they would remain docile and subservient? Or if he had recommended the kind of education Hannah More favored, reading but not writing or arithmetic, on the assumption that reading alone was necessary to inculcate the precepts of religion and the "habits of industry and virtue," was this, too, not an obvious exercise of social control?[58] And all the voluntary schools of the time— charity schools, Sunday schools, night schools, industry schools, schools connected with workhouses and poorhouses—which provided the rudiments of literacy for large numbers of people who would otherwise have been totally illiterate, were these reprehensible for the same reason, or were they in any way preferable to Smith's plan?

It might be said that it is not Smith's proposal for a comprehensive, state-supported system of education that is suspect, but the specific moral purpose he attached to it, this being all the more ominous in view of the role of the state. Or perhaps the objection is not so much to the exercise of "social control" as to the violation of the "indigenous" culture of the poor, the imposition upon them of alien "middle-class values." Again this is to ignore the contemporary context. Smith was not arguing against latter-day romantics who idealize illiteracy as part of a natural, superior, folk culture. He was arguing, at least implicitly, against those of his contemporaries who denied to the poor the capacity and opportunity to achieve those "middle-class values," who thought that no amount of education could civilize, socialize, and moralize them, or who worried that an educated populace would be restless, demanding, discontent. When Smith urged that the poor be educated so that they would become better citizens, better workers, and better human beings, he was not demeaning the poor but crediting them with the virtues ("values," in modern parlance) he himself held in such high esteem.

In a brilliant commentary on Smith, Joseph Cropsey has argued that the dual purpose of his political economy was to make freedom possible and to make of freedom a form of virtue.[59] This was also, one might say, the purpose of his system of education. Just as the laborer, by dint of his labor, was to be a free and full participant in the economy, so by dint of his education, he was to be a free and full participant in society. For Smith, freedom was itself a virtue and the precondition of all other virtues. It was this cardinal virtue that he wanted to make available to the "common people," even to those "bred to the lowest occupation."

If Smith's political economy was not the amoral, asocial doctrine it has sometimes been made out to be, neither was it as dogmatically, rigorously laissez faire as has been thought.[60] His plan of education was only one of several instances in which he departed from the strict construction of laissez faire, and not unwittingly but deliberately. He did so when he proposed a law to limit the freedom of bankers to issue notes, and when he advocated retaining the law against usury. He also did so when he implicitly sanctioned the poor laws.

Smith's position on the poor laws has been generally ignored or misunderstood. Because he was so forthright in criticizing the Act of Settlement of 1662, it is sometimes assumed that he was also opposed to the poor laws.[61] It is significant, however, that while he did attack the Settlement Act (and the Statute of Apprentices as well), he did not attack the poor laws. Moreover, his criticism of the Settlement Act had nothing to do with the giving of relief, but only with limiting the mobility of labor and violating the liberty of the poor.

> To remove a man who has committed no misdemeanour from the parish where he chooses to reside, is an evident violation of natural liberty and justice. . . . There is scarce a poor man in England of forty years of age, I will venture to say, who has not in some part of his life felt himself most cruelly oppressed by this ill-contrived law of settlements.[62]

This passage was much quoted (and disputed) at the time, and Smith was credited with helping bring about the reform of the laws of settlement in 1795. What Smith conspicuously did not do was to challenge the poor law itself, the obligation to provide relief for those who could not provide for themselves. Nor was he one of those who, in the years following the publication of the *Wealth of Nations,* expressed anxiety about the mounting costs of relief. He died before the movement to restrict relief reached its peak, but not before Joseph Townsend and others had raised the alarm and urged the drastic reform, if not the abolition, of the poor laws.

On the subject of taxation Smith exhibited the same pragmatic, humane temper and the same concern for the poor. His first principle was that taxes be levied "in proportion" to the ability to pay; and the corollary was that they be levied only on "luxuries" rather than "necessaries." He went on to define "necessaries" as "not only the commodities which are indispensably necessary for the support of life, but whatever the custom of the country renders it indecent for creditable people, even of the lowest order, to be without"—linen shirts and leather shoes, for example. In the same spirit he recommended that highway tolls on "carriages of luxury" (coaches, post chaises) should be higher than on "carriages of necessary use" (carts, wagons), so that "the indolence and vanity of the rich is made to contribute in a very easy manner to the relief of the poor."[63] Today, when it is taken for granted that necessity and luxury are relative terms, Smith's ideas on the subject may seem unremarkable. In his own time, when many of his contemporaries were bitterly complaining about the "luxuries of the poor," and when the low-wage theorists were using the evidence of such luxuries—and precisely linen shirts and leather shoes—as an argument against higher wages, Smith's views were notably progressive.

So too were his views on mercantilism. Among his other objections to mercantilist regulations was the fact that they were generally in the interests of the merchants and manufacturers and against the interests of the workers. On the few occasions when they were otherwise, he actually favored retaining them, even at the expense of free trade.

> Whenever the legislature attempts to regulate the differences between masters and their workmen, its counsellors are always the masters. When the regulation, therefore, is in favour of the workmen, it is always just and equitable; but it is sometimes otherwise when it is in favour of the masters.[64]

Thus he disapproved of the regulation of wages—which established not a minimum but a maximum rate of wages—and supported the law requiring employers to pay their workers in money rather than in goods. "This law [payment in money] is in favour of the workmen; but the 8th of George [the fixing of wages] is in favour of the masters." For the same reasons he protested against the injustice of permitting masters to combine while forbidding workers to do so.[65]

More important than the effect of this or that policy on the poor was the image of the poor implicit in those policies. These were the "creditable people, even of the lowest order," who deserved more than the bare necessities of life, the "sober and industrious poor" who were the proper beneficiaries of a proportionate system of taxation, the "lowest ranks of the people" who would become more, not less, industrious as a result of high wages and who would benefit, morally and materially, from a progressive economy. That Smith, like most of his countrymen, thought it just to devise policies that would favor the "sober and industrious poor" rather than the "dissolute and disorderly" is not surprising. What is more interesting is his confident assumption that the overwhelming number of the poor were in fact sober and industrious. It was this assumption that permitted him to "connect" the interests of the "labouring poor" with the "general interest" of society. And not only their interests but their natures. It was because the poor were presumed to have the same virtues and passions as everyone else, because there were no innate differences separating them from the other classes, that they were capable of working within the "system of natural liberty" and profiting from it as much as everyone else. These "creditable" poor were capable and desirous of bettering themselves, capable and desirous of exercis-

ing the virtues inherent in human nature, capable and desirous of the liberty
that was their right as responsible individuals.[66]

This is not the doctrine cynically described by Anatole France: "The
law, in its majestic equality, forbids the rich as well as the poor to sleep under
bridges, to beg in the streets, and to steal bread." Smith did not pretend that
the "formal" equality of the law, even the "natural" equality of the laws
of political economy, had the same effect on rich and poor alike. This is why
he devised a state system of education specifically intended for the poor, why
he proposed taxes on luxuries rather than on necessities, why he did not
object to poor relief, why he supported regulations favoring workers, why
he advocated a policy of high wages and a "progressive" economy. He did
not shrink from the fact of inequality or deny the need for correctives and
palliatives. But neither did he retreat from his basic assumption: that the
poor, as much as the rich, were free, responsible, moral agents. Later, this
idea of moral responsibility was to be turned against the poor, used to justify
the denial of poor relief and the opposition to such protective ("paternalistic," as was said pejoratively) measures as factory acts. To Smith the idea
of moral responsibility had quite another function: to establish the claim of
the poor to higher wages, a higher standard of living, a higher rank in life
—to whatever goods might accrue to them as a result of a free, expanding
economy.

Between the old "moral economy" and Smith's political economy
there was a gulf—a chasm, as some said. The former depended, at least in
principle, on a system of regulations derived from equity, tradition, and law,
a system prescribing fair prices, just wages, customary rights, corporative
rules, paternalistic obligations, hierarchical relationships—all of which were
intended to produce a structured, harmonious, stable, secure, organic order.
The "system of natural liberty," on the other hand, prided itself on being
open, mobile, changeable, individualistic, with all the risks but also all the
opportunities associated with freedom. The contrast is to a certain extent
artificial, the old moral economy having been much attenuated in the
century before Smith, and the new political economy having its own moral
imperatives and constraints. For Smith political economy was not an end
in itself but a means to an end, that end being the wealth and well-being,
moral and material, of the "people," of whom the "laboring poor" were
the largest part. And the poor themselves had a moral status in that economy
—not the special moral status they enjoyed in a fixed, hierarchic order, but
that which adhered to them as individuals in a free society sharing a common
human, which is to say, moral, nature.

III

AN ODD LOT OF DISCIPLES

Historians have long been intrigued by the fact that the "heyday" of laissez faire was so brief. The eminent jurist A. V. Dicey deplored the fact that it lasted only half a century, from 1825 to 1875, its death coinciding almost exactly with the centenary of the *Wealth of Nations;* but even during that period he found important exceptions to the doctrine.[1] Other historians, noting the growth of the state administrative apparatus as well as legislative intrusions, have whittled down the period of its dominance to a single decade, the 1830s. Even then the opposition to it was so strong and came from so many directions that the ideology seems to have been barely installed before it was being undermined by a powerful counter-ideology.

No less intriguing is the early history of laissez faire. Just when it was coming of age, being assimilated into the culture and giving every indication of becoming the dominant ideology, it suffered a dramatic setback. It had just reached maturity (literally, twenty-two years separated the *Wealth of Nations* from the *Essay on Population*), when it experienced the familiar fate of all revolutions; it was devoured by its offspring. Malthus is often thought of as the heir of Smith, and so he was in some respects. But in others he was nothing less than a usurper. Appearing in the guise of the son, promising to carry out the mandate of the father (indeed to carry it out more rigorously than the father had done), he inaugurated a new revolution in the name of the old.

In retrospect, one is inclined to look upon Malthusianism as a natural and necessary development. In good "Whig" fashion, by reading history backward with all the advantage of hindsight, one can find in the period preceding the *Essay on Population,* preceding even the *Wealth of Nations,* intimations and premonitions of Malthusianism. One can trace the origins of that doctrine, as Schumpeter did, to the late sixteenth century, when Giovanni Botero became alarmed by the discrepancy between the natural increase of population and the increase of the food supply, or to the late

64

seventeenth, when William Petty explained the discrepancy in terms of the geometrical growth of population. Malthus himself in his *Essay* cited only his immediate predecessors: Montesquieu, Benjamin Franklin, Robert Wallace, James Steuart, Arthur Young, and Joseph Townsend. Of these, only Wallace had been familiar to him before he wrote his own book; the others were brought to his attention afterwards and were properly credited in the second edition. It is interesting that Townsend's *Dissertation on the Poor Laws,* published in 1786, which most closely approximated the *Essay* both in its theory and in its proposals, was at first unknown to him, in spite of the fact that it had attracted some attention at the time (more, however, for its views on the poor laws than on population).

Any discussion of the precursors of Malthus runs the risk of making too much of them, attributing to them a more coherent body of ideas than they had and giving the impression of a movement intent upon carrying out those ideas to their logical, inevitable conclusion. In fact, the situation in this period, especially in the critical post-Smith, pre-Malthus decade of the '90s (Smith died in 1790 and Malthus's *Essay* was published in 1798), was extremely fluid, and it was by no means clear what direction social thought and social policy might take. Resisting the knowledge of hindsight and looking not for anticipations of Malthusianism but for expressions of opinion on the part of contemporaries who were blissfully unaware of what lay ahead, one can better appreciate the alternatives as they appeared at the time —dramatically different alternatives, as it happens. In the few years preceding the publication of the *Essay,* analyses and proposals were advanced which were strikingly at variance with each other. What makes the situation especially piquant is the fact that they were all by self-avowed disciples of Smith.

The timing was no accident. The bad harvest of 1795 and the hardships created by the Napoleonic Wars had aggravated the distress caused by the economic, technological, and demographic changes of the preceding decades. To cope with this problem poor relief had been vastly expanded and new modes of relief instituted. The most dramatic innovation (or so it seemed in retrospect—at the time it appeared to be only one of many devices to achieve the same end) was the "Speenhamland system," as it has come to be known.[2] At a meeting in Speenhamland in 1795, the justices of the peace of Berkshire decreed that "every poor and industrious man" whose earnings fell below a given standard, determined by the price of bread and the size of his family, would receive a subsidy from the parish to bring his income up to that minimum subsistence level. Following that precedent, a similar policy was adopted by other counties, especially in the depressed rural areas of the south, with the result that a considerable number of agricultural laborers became dependent, entirely or in part, upon the parish. These allowances, or "rates in aid of wages," were only one of several kinds of relief available: relief in money and kind, employment wholly or partially subsidized by the parish, and "indoor relief" in the workhouse or poorhouse. The full significance of Speenhamland—the fact that the employed as well as the unemployed were being supported out of the poor rates and that everyone below a given standard of subsistence was assumed to have a legitimate claim on the parish—did not emerge until much later. Indeed, its significance, as well as its actual effects, are still being debated today.[3] What was clear at the time was that the problem of poverty had attained a new urgency and, more important, that the solutions themselves were becoming problematic, if only because the costs had become so burdensome.

One of the many curiosities of this much debated subject, and one which has not received the attention it deserves, is the fact that the work of Adam Smith, in spite of its considerable influence and authority, did not provide the guidance that might have been expected at this critical time. Had Smith been alive, he might well have given a different direction to social thought and social policy, forestalling the acrimonious debate over the New Poor Law of 1834 and the still more virulent animosities generated by that law. The question of Smith's attitude toward either Speenhamland or the New Poor Law is, of course, moot; it may be that he could not have stemmed the tide had he wanted to, or that he himself would have been swept along with it. It is useful to raise the question if only to be reminded that there were real alternatives at the time and that his disciples could, in good conscience, have quite different views of the social problem and propose quite different remedies for that problem.

1. Edmund Burke

Edmund Burke is not normally remembered as a disciple of Adam Smith. Or if that fact is recalled, it is in passing, as a matter of biographical interest but of no great consequence for an understanding either of Burke himself or of political economy.[4] Yet he proudly proclaimed himself a disciple, Smith was pleased to accept him as such, and their friends were well aware of that relationship and attached some importance to it. One contemporary, if dubious, account has Smith consulting Burke while writing the *Wealth of Nations;* another, more reliable one has Smith telling Burke, after a discussion about economics, that Burke was "the only man, who, without communication, thought on these topics exactly as he [Smith] did."[5] Burke himself, toward the end of his life, boasted of having been a student of political economy from his "very early youth," while the discipline was still in its infancy in England and long before it had engaged the minds of "speculative men" on the Continent.[6]

Nor is Burke commonly thought of as a social critic, still less as a commentator on poverty or the poor—except perhaps to recall his much publicized, and generally misquoted, epithet, "swinish multitude."* Yet he wrote an important essay on political economy and poverty, which is interesting as an expression of his own views and as an anticipation of a mode of thought that was to become common, even dominant, in the decades to follow.

"Thoughts and Details on Scarcity," written in November 1795, shortly after the Speenhamland ordinance, opened with an unequivocal affirmation of the principle of free trade. "Of all things, an indiscreet tampering with the trade of provisions is the most dangerous, and it is always worst in the time when men are most disposed to it; that is, in the time of scarcity." At such a time, as at all times, the proper role of government was noninvolvement. "To provide for us in our necessities is not in the power of government. . . . It is in the power of government to prevent much evil; it can do very little positive good in this, or perhaps in anything else." In any event, Burke was convinced, the recent hardships were temporary and exceptional. The material condition of laborers had been much improved in recent years, and this was true of all descriptions and gradations of laborers, from the highest to the lowest. The rate of wages had kept up with the increase of prices, laborers were working more and reaping the advantage of their labors, and many were finding it possible to save as well as spend more. If there was no assurance that the "moral or philosophical happiness" of the laboring classes increased with the improvement of their material condition, there was a presumption of some such connection, of some relationship between the "happiness of the animal man" and the "happiness of the rational man."[8]

So far Burke seemed to be following the example of Smith. But his essay soon took a very different direction and tone. Because labor was a "commodity," he argued, an "article of trade" subject to the "laws of trade" and the "rules of commerce," it was not a fit subject for government regulation. This principle allowed no exception; it could not be suspended in "calamitous seasons," nor for reasons of illness, old age, or the needs of a large family. If in any of these circumstances the laborer could not be governed by the rules of commerce, he came within the "jurisdiction of mercy," which is to say, charity. "Charity to the poor is a direct and obligatory duty upon all Christians, next in order after the payment of debts, full as strong, and by nature made infinitely more delightful to us." By

---

*Conor Cruise O'Brien has pointed out that Burke spoke of "a swinish multitude," meaning *a* particular multitude on *a* particular occasion, not "the swinish multitude," which would imply that *the* multitude was by nature swinish. In this interpretation, "a swinish multitude" was the equivalent of "mob" rather than "people" or "populace."[7] The misquotation and misinterpretation started in Burke's time with a slew of pamphlets, such as *An Address to the Hon. Edmund Burke from the Swinish Multitude, The Rights of Swine,* and others which featured in their titles "Hog's Wash," "Pig's Meat," and the like, and it became part of the radical litany in the 1830s and '40s.

means of private charity, and only by such means, could the suffering of the poor properly be alleviated, since charity involved no violation of economic laws and no illegitimate intrusion of the government. "My opinion," Burke firmly declared, "is against an over-doing of any sort of administration, and more especially against this most momentous of all meddling on the part of authority; the meddling with the subsistence of the people."[9]

Burke may well have thought that in denying to the government the right to "meddle" with relief, he was carrying out the mandate of Smith. His very words were Smith's as he paid tribute to "the benign and wise Disposer of all things, who obliges men, whether they will or not, in pursuing their own selfish interests, to connect the general good with their own individual success."[10] In fact Smith never carried out that principle as rigorously as Burke did.* Certainly Smith was never so restrictive about the limits of government. He would never have said that government can do no good in this, "or perhaps in anything else"; his plea for a state system of education belies this. Nor did Smith preclude any form of government relief; his only objection to the poor laws was to the law of settlement.

A more interesting departure from Smith, and a momentous portent of the future, was Burke's deliberate, insistent attempt to establish a distinction between the "labourer" and the "poor." This redefinition of terms may be the most significant part of his essay. He first alluded to it in a passing reference to "those who labour, and are miscalled the poor," and he repeated it more forcefully a few paragraphs later: "Nothing can be so base and so wicked as the political canting language, 'the labouring *poor.*'" His objection was to the amalgam of "labouring people" and "poor," which implied that the condition of the laborers was so lamentable, so unfortunate, as to warrant the appellation "poor"—and the further implication that society or the state was obligated to relieve that intolerable condition. "The labouring people are only poor because they are numerous. Numbers in their nature imply poverty."[12]

Two years later, in the course of an essay on quite another subject, Burke again took the occasion to expose the "puling jargon" of the "labouring poor."

> We have heard many plans for the relief of the *"labouring poor."* This
> puling jargon is not as innocent as it is foolish. . . . Hitherto the name

---

*Toward the end of the essay, evidently uncomfortable with his extremely negative comments on the role of the state, Burke raised the general question of what could rightly be done by the state and what should be left to the individual. He then laid down the principle that the state should confine itself to "what regards the state, or the creatures of the state"—religion, the magistracy, revenue, military force, and corporations—"in a word, to everything that is *truly and properly* public, to the public peace, to the public safety, to the public order, to the public prosperity." But he allowed no qualification of his earlier prohibition of any "meddling" with subsistence, even on the occasions of famine or great distress.[11]

of poor (in the sense in which it is used to excite compassion) has not been used for those who can, but for those who cannot, labour—for the sick and infirm, for orphan infancy, for languishing and decrepit age; but when we affect to pity, as poor, those who must labour or the world cannot exist, we are trifling with the condition of mankind. It is the common doom of man that he must eat his bread by the sweat of his brow, that is, by the sweat of his body, or the sweat of his mind. . . . I do not call a healthy young man, cheerful in his mind, and vigorous in his arms, I cannot call such a man, *poor;* I cannot pity my kind as a kind, merely because they are men. This affected pity only tends to dissatisfy them with their condition, and to teach them to seek resources where no resources are to be found, in something else than their own industry, and frugality, and sobriety.[13]

The only "poor" were those who could not work—the sick and the infirm, orphan infants and the decrepit aged; they alone were the proper objects of "pity" and thus the proper recipients of charity. Burke did not say explicitly here, as he did in his earlier essay, that the remedy for this kind of poverty was charity rather than poor relief, but since this essay was written only a few months after the other, it may be presumed that this was his intention. In any case the message was unambiguous: the laborer was not "poor," not to be pitied, and above all not to be deluded into thinking that he could depend upon anything other than his own "industry, and frugality, and sobriety."

Burke's immediate object, in both essays, was to discredit the policy represented by Speenhamland which would have brought all laborers within the province of the poor law by categorizing them all as "poor." But the implications of his argument went well beyond this, illegitimizing not only the Speenhamland system but the original Elizabethan laws as well. Those laws had used the word "poor" in precisely the generic sense Burke deplored, the sense of the "laboring poor." It was in keeping with this usage that they provided not only for Burke's "poor"—the sick and infirm, infants and aged—but for the "able-bodied" who were able to work and could not find work. Even those reformers who sought to make relief to the able-bodied available only in the workhouse did not presume to exclude the able-bodied from the mandate of the poor laws. Still less did they propose to remove from the aegis of the poor laws the sick, the young, and the old by making them the responsibility of private charity alone.

It is interesting that Burke should have gone so far beyond Smith in so many respects: in rejecting the poor laws in principle, in allowing the government so little power to do "positive good," in reducing labor to a "commodity" governed strictly by the "rules of commerce," and in making so sharp a

distinction between "laboring people" and the "poor." That he should have
gone to such extremes is all the more noteworthy because one might have
expected quite the opposite. Even in its more moderate form the doctrine
of laissez faire was something of an anomaly for Burke. How could he
reconcile the liberty adhering to each individual as an individual with the
historic liberties he himself acclaimed, liberties transmitted from generation
to generation as a "patrimony," an "entailed inheritance"? Where, in such
an individualistic system, could he find room for the established institutions
and traditions, the corpus of manners and morals, the ties binding the present
to the past, which constituted the "wisdom of our ancestors"? How could
he have been so solicitous of the "rules of commerce," after decrying those
"sophisters, oeconomists, and calculators" who signaled the end of the "age
of chivalry," and after advising that most enlightened emperor, Leopold II,
"to forget, once for all, the *Encyclopédie* and the whole body of economists,
and to revert to those old rules and principles which have hitherto made
princes great, and nations happy"? Most important, how could he accommodate Smith's minimal state with his own conception of the state: a state
which "ought not to be considered as nothing better than a partnership
agreement in a trade of pepper and coffee, callico or tobacco, or some other
such low concern," but which was to be looked on with reverence because
it was a "partnership in all science; a partnership in all art; a partnership in
every virtue, and in all perfection"?[14]

If the moderate form of laissez faire espoused by Smith seems ill suited
to Burke's philosophy, all the more unsuitable, one would think, was the
extreme form advanced by Burke himself to justify his critique of poor
relief. In his *Reflections on the Revolution in France* he had made the lower
classes an integral part of that "great primeval contract" which bound
together God and man, rulers and ruled, in an organic order, an order in
which rights and duties were determined not by "abstract," "geometric"
principles but by the natural, historic realities of laws, traditions, and institutions. Yet in considering poor relief Burke was prepared to negate two
centuries of history, to nullify laws, traditions, and institutions which had
given the poor an assured place in that natural, organic order. In a private
letter written at the same time as the *Reflections,* Burke enunciated the
principle of "prescription" which was to play so large a part in his attack
on the French Revolution: "That which might be wrong in the beginning,
is consecrated by time and becomes lawful."[15] In this context the principle
was meant to defend the landed estates and church property against the
familiar charge that they had been acquired by force and fraud and had
therefore no legal or moral claim upon posterity. But the principle applied
as well, indeed even more cogently, to the poor laws, which, however ill
conceived, had been entirely lawful in origin and had been consecrated by
two centuries of law and practice.

Ten years earlier, Burke had confronted a similar problem when he proposed an elaborate plan to reorganize and economize the business of government. After defending the need for such a radical measure—"When the reason of old establishments is gone, it is absurd to preserve nothing but the burthen of them"—he proceeded to argue for the "reformation" rather than the abolition of those "old establishments." Lifetime sinecures, however unjust and wasteful, had become the basis of property settlements, security for creditors, and thus part of the structure of the law. And the law itself was "sacred." "If the barriers of law should be broken down, upon ideas of convenience, even of public convenience, we shall have no longer anything certain among us." No reform, no consideration of expediency, was worth that sacrifice. It was always preferable to "reconcile our economy with our laws, than to set them at variance; a quarrel which in the end must be destructive to both."[16] On the same ground Burke might have been expected to argue for the reformation rather than the abolition of that other "old establishment," the poor laws, which were also part of the structure of law, and to try to reconcile economy with those laws rather than setting them "at variance."

It is disconcerting to find Burke, so sensitive to the rhetoric of politics, so critical of the *philosophes* for attempting to transform the substance of politics by altering the terms of discourse, himself proposing a radical change in conventional usage. However logical his distinction between "labouring people" and "poor," it was as unhistorical and as unrooted in reality as any of the "metaphysical distinctions" and "delusive plausibilities" expounded by the theorists of natural right.[17] To discard the familiar expression "labouring poor," to speak of "labour" as a "commodity" or "article of trade" whose price was determined not by the "necessity of the vender" (otherwise known as "subsistence") but by the "necessity of the purchaser," was to indulge in precisely the kind of abstractions he deplored on the part of the *philosophes.* [18] The rhetoric and reasoning were of a piece—but not of a piece with Burke's normal mode of rhetoric and reasoning.

There are several ways of reconciling the inconsistencies in Burke. The most obvious is to deny him any pretense of consistency, to think of him as a politician or publicist who had no firm philosophical principles and who was all too ready to accommodate his reasoning to the exigencies of the occasion. The difficulty with this explanation is that it requires us to ignore most of Burke's writings and to dismiss the counsel of eminent thinkers who took him seriously and found in him principles of enduring value.[19] Another interpretation would separate his economic theories from his social and political ones, permitting Burke to apply the principles of political economy, as he understood them, to the economic realm, and the principles of prescription and tradition to the social and political realm. Unfortunately this disjunction is itself a violation of his basic principle, which made of society an organic whole, a seamless web, and the state a partner in all science, art, virtue, and "perfection." Moreover, even if the two realms could be divorced and the economy (or "civil society," in Hegel's sense) put under the autonomous rule of political economy, this does not account for the fact that Burke adopted a more dogmatic and extreme form of laissez faire than Smith himself, or, for that matter, than Smith's other disciples who were addressing the same problem at much the same time with very different results.

Another explanation is the chronological one: an "early" Burke who was more liberal, humane, and progressive than the "late" Burke. Or, perhaps, an early Burke who confronted problems that were more amenable to liberal, humane, progressive solutions—a moderate American Revolution rather than a violent French Revolution, or a poverty that had not yet been exacerbated by industrial and agricultural changes, bad harvests and wars, and the excessively generous policy, as he saw it, of poor relief. One of the documents that might be quoted in favor of this early, liberal Burke is an essay written in 1756, "A Vindication of Natural Society," the subtitle of which spelled out the ostensible thesis: "A View of the Miseries and Evils Arising to Mankind from Every Species of Artificial Society." Among the miseries and evils caused by that "artificial society" was poverty, a peculiarly artificial poverty, since the sole purpose of the poor was to minister to the "idleness, folly, and luxury" of the rich, and the chief occupation of the rich (when they were not indulging in idleness, folly, and luxury) was to look for ways of "confirming the slavery and increasing the burdens of the poor." It was in such a society that hundreds of thousands of innocent people were condemned to utter misery and abject slavery.[20]

That early essay, one might think, was the aboriginal Burke, compassionate toward the poor and passionate in denouncing the inhuman, artificial society cultivated by the rich. In fact, however, the whole of the "Vindication" was an elaborate spoof. In the preface to the second edition Burke was obliged to make explicit what had evidently escaped the notice of some of his readers: that his essay was intended as a parody of Bolingbroke's critique of "artificial religion."* By extending that critique to "artificial society," by portraying the miseries and evils of society in such extreme terms, and by representing poverty as artificial and unnatural, Burke thought to expose

---

*The portrait in the "Vindication" of the "miseries and evils" of society was evidently more memorable than the preface explaining that it was a satire. Or perhaps later commentators read editions that did not contain the preface. In any event, the essay continued to be quoted as if Burke had intended it literally. In his *Enquiry Concerning Political Justice* published three years after the *Reflections,* William Godwin, no great admirer of Burke, praised the "Vindication" as an eloquent attack on the evils of existing society. More than a century later, Elie Halévy, perhaps under the influence of Godwin's comments, described Burke's essay as a "defence of natural society."[21]

the absurdity of Bolingbroke's argument—the absurdity of any form of utopianism that postulated a "natural" religion or society in contrast to the established, "artificial" one—and by the same token the absurdity of a view of poverty that regarded it as unnatural, degrading, and enslaving.

Whatever the explanation for Burke's conception of poverty, there is no doubt that that conception was to become prevalent in the decades after his death and was to play a large part in the movement to abolish or reform the poor laws. And the tension in his own thinking was to be reflected in later generations of conservatives—the "paternalists" of the 1840s, for example, who cherished a vision of a traditional social order and who, at the same time, were persuaded of the virtues of an individualistic, competitive economy; or conservatives of the present day who are still trying to reconcile the legacies of Edmund Burke and Adam Smith.*

2. William Pitt and Frederick Eden

When Burke presented the Prime Minister with his "Thoughts and Details on Scarcity," he might have expected a sympathetic reading, since they both professed to be guided in these matters by Adam Smith. William Pitt, in fact, was even more effusive in his admiration of Smith than Burke was. The story has it that when Smith arrived late to a party, the host, Lord

---

*C. B. Macpherson resolves the "Burke-Smith problem" by making Burke (and, by implication, conservatism in general) an apologist for laissez faire capitalism. If Burke posed as a "traditionalist," Macpherson maintains, it was only because by his time "the capitalist order *had in fact been* the traditional order in England for a whole century." Thus in defending history, tradition, convention, the hierarchy, and the establishment, he was simply defending capitalism and the market economy. When he invoked natural or divine law, it was only to maintain the pretense that the existing order was just in order to ensure the submissiveness of the working class and thus an orderly process of capitalist accumulation. And when he attacked the French Revolution, it was only because he did not realize that it was a "bourgeois revolution."[22] This interpretation depends not only on a selective and tendentious reading of Burke, in which the vast bulk of his writings becomes an elaborate subterfuge, but also on a dubious reading of history, in which capitalism is ushered in (as it was for Tawney) a full century or more before the *Wealth of Nations.* (In his earlier book, *The Political Theory of Possessive Individualism,* Macpherson applied much the same theory to Hobbes and Locke, making them both the spokesmen of the bourgeois revolution, of an England that was already, by the middle of the seventeenth century, an almost fully developed market society.)[23]

An equally ingenious and dubious interpretation of Burke has been advanced by Conor Cruise O'Brien. In this case the esoteric Burke, the real Burke, is an Irish Catholic (or crypto-Catholic) whose attitude to the French Revolution, as to all political and social questions, was determined by his basic commitment to an oppressed and potentially revolutionary Ireland. If he seemed to be counter-revolutionary, it was because only thus could he express a "suppressed revolutionary part of his own personality." Even those writings which read like a defense of the established order were an insidious attack on that order, since to defend the old regime in France was implicitly to attack the Protestant ascendancy in Ireland, which was based on the same revolutionary usurpation he condemned in France. "Thus, where Burke is at his most extravagantly counter-revolutionary, in relation to France and Europe, he is most subtly subversive in relation to the existing order in his own country."[24]

Dundas, and his distinguished guests (Pitt, Henry Addington, William Wilberforce, William Grenville) spontaneously rose, and when Smith asked them to be seated, Pitt said, "No, we will stand till you are seated, for we are all your scholars." Smith's tribute to Pitt recalls a similar compliment to Burke: "What an extraordinary man Pitt is; he makes me understand my own ideas better than before."[25]

In public as in private, Pitt repeatedly paid homage to Smith, invoking his authority in a debate on finances in 1792 and again four years later in opposing a bill for the regulation of wages. Introducing the wages bill (in effect a proposal to establish minimum wages), Samuel Whitbread explained that while he himself believed in free trade, regulation in this instance was justified as an emergency measure in an exceptional situation. In reply Pitt agreed that the principle of free trade admitted exceptions—not to allow for them would be the "most absurd bigotry"—but insisted that in this case, as in most others, trade and industry should go their own way unimpeded by regulations which "violated their natural operation and deranged their proper effect." A wiser reform, he suggested (echoing Smith), would be the abolition of the law of settlement, which interfered with the circulation of labor and thus kept wages below their natural level.[26] Pitt's speech easily carried the day and Whitbread's bill was voted down. Some historians have made much of the defeat of this attempt at wage regulation.[27] But perhaps as important was the principle enunciated by Pitt in its stead:

> Let us . . . make relief in cases where there are a number of children, a matter of right and an honour, instead of a ground for opprobrium and contempt. This will make a large family a blessing, and not a curse; and this will draw a proper line of distinction between those who are able to provide for themselves by their labour, and those who, after having enriched their country with a number of children, have a claim upon its assistance for their support.[28]

If Burke had any illusions about Pitt's views on poverty or poor relief, this speech would have disabused him. Professing the highest regard for Smith and the most earnest devotion to free trade, Pitt managed to arrive at a position diametrically opposed to Burke's. Indeed, it may well have been Pitt's reference in this speech to the "labouring poor" that provoked Burke to denounce that "puling jargon." Or perhaps it was Pitt's poor relief bill that incurred Burke's wrath.[29]

In rejecting Whitbread's proposal for the regulation of wages, Pitt had promised to introduce an alternative measure that would restore the poor law to its "original purity" and establish relief as a "right and an honour." His bill, drawn up late in 1796, was a compendium of every variety of relief currently in effect, plus some novelties devised by Pitt himself. It included rates in aid of wages, family allowances, money for the purchase of a cow or some other worthy purpose, schools of industry for the children of the poor, wastelands to be reclaimed and reserved for the poor, insurance against sickness and old age, a further relaxation of the law of settlement, and an annual poor law budget to be submitted to Parliament. In committee the bill was expanded still further, until the multiplicity of provisions (some of them conflicting) and of administrative agents (wardens, visitors, guardians, and justices of the peace) exposed the bill to ridicule, and it was finally withdrawn without being debated or voted.

Bentham later claimed that it was his criticisms of the bill that doomed it, and that it had been withdrawn in favor of his own plan. Neither assertion seems warranted. He had written a long critique which he had circulated in manuscript (it was published only posthumously), but there was little contemporary reference to it and no mention of it by Pitt; nor has a copy been found among Pitt's papers. Bentham's main objection to the bill was that it would have put "the *idle* and *negligent* exactly upon a footing in point of prosperity and reward with the *diligent* and *industrious*"—a variation on the "less-eligibility" principle he was to enunciate in *Pauper Management*. [30] But this point was almost lost in the laborious analysis of each provision of the bill and the exposure of all its inconsistencies and imprecisions.

There were other, better known and more cogent critiques of the bill. One of these was by the political economist and social critic Frederick Eden, whose three-volume *State of the Poor* appeared early in 1797. Like most of Smith's disciples, Eden bore his discipleship lightly, not hesitating to take issue with him on the subject, for example, of the law of settlement, the practical effect of which he thought Smith had much exaggerated. In general, however, Eden was closer to Smith than many who spoke in his name. If he was, as Marx said, "the only disciple of Adam Smith during the eighteenth century that produced any work of importance," it is all the more interesting that that work should have been an extensive treatise on the poor.[31]

Like Smith, Eden believed it to be one of the functions of government to "check the progress of vice and immorality, by pointing out and encouraging the instruction of the rising generation in the social and religious duties." But in economic affairs he held (again like Smith) that individuals should be free to pursue their own interests, and that the interference of the state was generally undesirable. Thus he criticized Whitbread's wage regulation bill and Pitt's relief bill on the same grounds: that they undermined individual exertion, encouraged idleness, and usurped the proper role of charity. More interesting were his remarks on Burke, because it was here that he showed himself to be a true disciple of Smith and a better Burkean than Burke himself. He agreed with Burke that the only "right" to the fruit of labor was that which the individual could claim as the result of his own exertions, that the legislature should not attempt to establish any right to employment or maintenance, and that any legal provision for the poor was a deterrent to industriousness. But he went on to argue that however inadvisable it might have been to create a "national establishment for the poor," it was even more inadvisable to abolish such an establishment after it had been long in existence. Quoting Burke's *Reflections,* he applied to the poor law the same principles Burke had used to justify religious and political establishments. Like any institution of long standing, Eden reasoned, the poor law must be presumed to have some utility; if it was faulty, the fault should be remedied by reforming the law rather than abolishing it. In this case Eden recommended that the poor law be limited to the "removal of extreme wants, in cases of most urgent necessity," leaving all other needs to be filled by voluntary charity.[32]

The full title of Eden's work, *The State of the Poor: or, An History of the Labouring Classes in England,* suggests another disagreement with Burke, the apparent equation of "poor" and "labouring classes" violating Burke's injunction against just that confusion of terms. In the text itself, however, Eden made occasional halfhearted attempts to conform to Burke's usage: in the preface he promised to describe "the present state of the Labouring part of the community, as well as the actual Poor"; and a few pages later he explained that the "actual Poor" were those receiving relief, in contrast to the "labouring part of the community . . . whose daily subsistence absolutely depends on the daily unremitting exertion of manual labour."[33] Later still he gave an account of the historical origin of "the poor" which supported the Burkean sense of that word. Before the introduction of manufacturing, he explained, there had been no "poor." It was manufacturing that liberated an entire class of people from bondage to the soil, and liberated them at the same time from the territorial lords who had assumed responsibility for them in times of drought or war. In that earlier condition of servitude there had been no "poor," only "slaves." The poor were thus a "new class," a product of emancipation.

> I ascribe the introduction of a new class of men, henceforward described by the Legislature under the denomination of *Poor;* by which term, I conceive, they meant to signify freemen, who, being either incapacitated by sickness, or old age, or prevented by other causes from getting work, were obliged to have recourse to the assistance of the charitable for subsistence.[34]

It was for this class of "poor" that the poor laws were intended.*

Eden was not, however, as vigorous or consistent in applying this distinction as Burke had been, just as he was not as thoroughgoing in condemning the poor law, and in both cases because he was more sensitive to the prevailing climate of opinion. That even Burke was not entirely impervious to that climate is suggested by his choice of words. A more pointed way of expressing the distinction he thought so important would have been to contrast "pauper" to "laborer" or "laboring poor." If instead he (and Eden as well, although less consistently) preferred to speak of those receiving relief—those who came under the province of the "poor law"—as "poor," it was perhaps because, at a time when relief was so extensive, it would have been unseemly to stigmatize so large a part of the population with the invidious term "pauper."†

Burke's distinction did not take hold in general discourse. "Laborers" and "poor" continued to be used interchangeably, and were often amalgamated in the term "laboring poor." The poor thus remained what they had always been: a generalized, undifferentiated, heterogeneous body of people subject to all the vicissitudes that befell those who had no other resources than their unremitting labor, vicissitudes that might at any time require them to seek relief of some kind or other, from some source or other. They were Smith's poor, the "lowest ranks," the "common people." They were Samuel Johnson's poor: "not rich; indigent; necessitous; oppressed with want."[37] They were Henry Fielding's poor, who had "no estate of their own to support them, without industry; nor any profession or trade, by which, with industry, they may be capable of gaining a comfortable subsistence."[38] They were the poor who were so numerous that Arthur Young estimated them at 8,000,000—out of a total population of 9,000,000.[39]

Only later, when Malthusianism had created a new sense of the social problem and a new image of poverty, was the continuum of the "laboring poor" effectively broken. It is significant that the distinction that then came into general use was not Burke's "poor" versus "laboring people," but "pauper" (or "indigent") versus "poor." Patrick Colquhoun gave the classic formulation to this distinction in a tract published in 1799, *The State of*

---

*In the 1880s, Arnold Toynbee was to make the same connection between free men and paupers —the latter meaning exactly what Burke and Eden meant by "poor." "It is a great law of social development that the movement from slavery to freedom is also a movement from security to insecurity of maintenance. There is a close connection between the growth of freedom and the growth of pauperism; it is scarcely too much to say that the latter is the price we pay for the former." The economist Alfred Marshall made the same point in the course of his controversy with Henry George in 1883, when he said that "pauperism is the product of freedom."[35]

†Contemporaries (including Burke and Eden) did occasionally use the word "pauper" of someone receiving relief or charity, but they did so casually, in passing, not as part of any formal or systematic analysis. In Samuel Johnson's *Dictionary* "pauper" was briefly defined as "a poor person; one who receives alms."[36]

Indigence, and the Situation of the Casual Poor in the Metropolis Explained, and again in his more influential *Treatise on Indigence* of 1806:

> In contemplating the affairs of the poor, it is necessary in the first instance to have a clear conception of the distinction between *Indigence* and *Poverty*.

> *Poverty* is that state and condition in society where the individual has no surplus labour in store, and, consequently, no property but what is derived from the constant exercise of industry in the various occupations of life; or in other words, it is the state of every one who must labour for subsistence. . . .

> *Indigence* therefore, and not *poverty*, is the evil. It is that condition in society which implies *want, misery,* and *distress*. It is the state of any one who is destitute of the means of subsistence, and is unable to labour to procure it to the extent nature requires. The natural source of subsistence is the labour of the individual; while that remains with him he is denominated *poor;* when it fails in whole or in part he becomes *indigent.* [40]

In his earlier work, *Treatise on the Police of the Metropolis,* which predated Malthus's *Essay* by four years, Colquhoun had not made this distinction; he did introduce it, however, in the edition published two years after the *Essay.*

3. Jeremy Bentham

If Burke had an ambiguous relationship to Smith, Jeremy Bentham's was more ambiguous still. Bentham too professed to be a disciple of Smith. He even criticized Smith for not carrying his principles far enough—for not advocating, for example, the abolition of the usury laws. Yet Bentham himself, while declaring the usury laws an intolerable infringement on free trade, had a penchant for schemes involving a considerable degree of regimentation and for monopolistic establishments of unprecedented size. One such scheme was his plan for the reform of poor relief. This resembled nothing so much as the mercantilist projects popular a century earlier which by this time had been largely discredited, partly because they had proved ineffectual, partly because they had come to be seen as unduly onerous.

Bentham's *Pauper Management Improved,* published in 1798, was a companion piece to his *Panopticon,* the plan of a model prison which had appeared several years earlier.[41] In that earlier work Bentham had explained that the model would serve for a variety of institutions: "houses of industry, work-houses, poor-houses, manufactories, mad-houses, lazarettos, hospitals, and schools." It would also realize the highest purposes: "Morals reformed, health preserved, industry invigorated, instruction diffused, public burthens lightened, Economy seated, as it were upon a rock, the gordian knot of the Poor-Laws not cut but untied—all by a simple idea of Architecture!" That simple architectural idea, a circular structure with the inspector's lodge in the center, would permit total visibility of the cells and thus total control over the life and work of the prisoners. The arrangement, Bentham prided himself, had the virtue of combining "the *apparent omnipresence* of the inspector (if divines will allow me the expression), . . . with the extreme facility of his real presence."[42]

Bentham's pauper plan was even more ambitious than his prison plan, if only because the potential pauper population was so enormous. It called for the establishment of a National Charity Company organized on the model of the East India Company, a joint-stock company privately owned and partially subsidized by the government. The company would have "undivided authority" over the "whole body of the burdensome poor." Starting with 250 industry-houses accommodating 500,000 people, the enterprise would expand until by the end of two decades it would comprise 500 houses and 1,000,000 people. Each of these houses would contain living and working quarters for 2,000 people, and every one of those people, Bentham boasted, would be under the constant supervision and "absolute" authority of the governor—a claim as startling as the thought of 500 such houses run by a privately owned company with an exclusive contract for the support and employment of over 10 percent of the population of England.[43]

More remarkable still was the premise upon which the enterprise was based: "No relief but upon the terms of coming into the *house*." It was this principle that made it necessary for the institution to be so large—and it was this that constituted the truly radical nature of the plan. Only by eliminating every other source of relief, for young and old, able-bodied and infirm, could the plan have the comprehensive, uniform, absolute, monopolistic character implied in the opening sentence of the book: "The management of the concerns of the poor, throughout South Britain, to be vested in *one* authority, and the expense charged upon *one* fund."[44]

The easy transition, in the course of the very first page, from "pauper" in the title to "burdensome poor" and "poor" in the text suggests that Bentham was doing exactly what Burke had protested against—taking the current loose usage of "poor" to enlarge the area of dependency, making all the poor potentially paupers.* Bentham went even further than Speen-

---

*That Bentham was aware of the stricter construction of these terms is apparent from an unpublished manuscript, "Essay on the Poor Laws," dated 1796. Bentham there made the distinction between "poverty" and "indigence" that Patrick Colquhoun and others were later to popularize.

> Poverty is the state of everyone who, in order to obtain *subsistence,* is forced to have recourse to *labour.* Indigence is the state of him who, being destitute of property

hamland in this respect. For he proposed to bring within the purview of
the National Charity Company, and thus within the confines of the industry-houses, not only those who applied to the parish (in effect, the company)
for relief, but many who did not seek relief and were forced to accept it
on the company's terms. Adults without visible means of support, children
who were not being educated, insolvent fathers of bastards, unwed mothers,
beggars, "depredators" ("proved" or "suspected"), the wives, and children
of depredators, "unruly" apprentices, wives, and children, and "victimized"
apprentices, wives, and children—all of these were to be sought out by the
company, apprehended, and consigned to the houses.

There was one more group of inmates for whom Bentham made
elaborate provision: the "indigenous class," those who were born in the
house or who entered it as minors and were obliged to remain as apprentices.
Under this provision males would remain in the house until the age of
twenty-one or twenty-three, females until nineteen or twenty-one, this
regardless of whether they were married. This class, Bentham explained, was
the heart of his plan; it was the largest single group and the main cause of
the growth of the enterprise, the doubling of the number of houses and the
pauper population in a single generation. It was also the largest source of
profit since it included those who were at the height of their productive (and
reproductive) powers. All the others—the aged and sick, beggars and depredators, "unruly" and "victimized" wives, children, and apprentices—
were the "refuse of the population." And the company would make good
use of that refuse: "So many industry-houses, so many crucibles, in which
dross of this kind is converted into sterling."[46] But the apprentices were pure
sterling.

"Dross" into "sterling"—Bentham meant this literally. Every variety
of "refuse," including the sick and the aged, was to be put to some kind
of gainful labor and made to yield some profit above the cost of board; a
200 percent profit, Bentham calculated, for men and 100 percent for women.
(The apprentices would yield a "still more advantageous" return.) These
profits were possible because of the strict regimen of life and work, the
unremitting supervision and discipline, the ingenious economies of diet,
dress, and lodging, the prolonged hours of labor, the enforced stay of
apprentices during the years of greatest productivity, and the requirement
that the condition of the inmates be "less desirable" than that of the poorest
person outside. (Less desirable, too, Bentham pointed out, than the condition
of paupers in the existing poorhouses, who enjoyed such "luxurious and

---

... is at the same time, either *unable to labour*, or unable, even *for* labour, to procure the supply
of which he happens thus to be in want.[45]

It is interesting that this distinction does not appear in *Pauper Management* or in any other of
Bentham's writings published at this time.

expensive" amenities as three meals a day, an occasional serving of meat, conventional attire, and little or no labor.)[47]

The plan involved, Bentham acknowledged, a large restriction of liberty, for the public as well as the inmates. In order to apprehend "suspected depredators" (suspected because they were without visible means of support), Bentham proposed to establish a "Universal Register of names, abodes and occupations." In his unpublished notes he anticipated the obvious objection to such a register:

> Objection—liberty infringed. Answer—liberty of doing mischief. As security is increased, liberty is diminished. . . . That it [the register] would be an infringement upon liberty is not to be denied: for in proportion as security is established, liberty is restricted. To one branch of liberty—the liberty of doing mischief—it would be, not prejudicial only, but destructive. . . . Public security commands it. Justice does not forbid it.[48]

It was not only the "security" of the public that would be promoted by this "infringement upon liberty." Those whose liberty was to be infringed would themselves be benefited, since they were no more capable of liberty, of governing themselves, than unruly children. "The persons in question are a sort of forward children—a set of persons not altogether sound in mind, not altogether possessed of that moral sanity without which a man cannot in justice to himself any more than to the community be intrusted with the uncontrolled management of his own conduct and affairs."[49]

The provision Bentham was most proud of concerned the apprentices —the "children of the public," children who could not be properly cared for by their own parents and who were as much the "property of the public" as other children were of their parents. These apprentices, he claimed, would enjoy advantages not available to ordinary children. Put to work at the age of four rather than at the conventional age of fourteen, they would be spared the loss of those "ten precious years in which nothing is done! nothing for industry! nothing for improvement, moral or intellectual!"* To those who might object to putting four-year-olds to work in a factory, he had a ready answer. "There is a degree of cruelty, I have heard it said, in shutting up children in a manufactory, especially at a tender age. But unless by the

---

*In fact pauper apprenticeship often started before the age of fourteen. Perhaps Bentham used that figure under the impression that it strengthened his case, ten wasted years sounding better than seven or eight. It should also be pointed out that the published plan, detailed as it was in all other respects, did not specify the age he proposed for beginning apprenticeship, perhaps because the public was not sufficiently enlightened to appreciate the advantages of putting four-year-olds to work. But the manuscript versions of the plan are unambiguous on this point, and all his calculations depended on a starting age of four.

expression shutting up is meant unnecessary confinement, there is no cruelty in the case; the cruelty would be in not doing it."[50]

So it went, each feature of the plan which might offend the sensibility of the reader, which might be thought illiberal or inhuman, was declared to be eminently rational and enlightened. If the children were deprived of meat or the few pennies of pocket money allotted to them in other poorhouses, it was for their own good, to protect them against corrupting habits and tastes. If their hours of work left little time for exercise or sleep, it was because the best form of exercise was that "infused" into work itself, and the optimum amount of sleep was "the least that can be made sufficient for health and strength." If their education was strictly utilitarian, it was to spare them "intellectual exercise of the most painful kind." If they were separated from their families and permitted to speak with their fathers only in the presence of company officials, it was so that they might enjoy the rational government of an "appointed Father" whose attribute was "perfectibility," rather than the "arbitrary" and "variable" government of their natural fathers.[51]

The plan reached the acme of perfection, as Bentham saw it, with the provision for matrimony "at the earliest period compatible with health." This "privilege," hitherto reserved for royalty, would be the happy lot of every pauper child. With all their financial, material, even psychological needs provided for—and those of their children as well—they would be free to marry at the earliest age and propagate without limit. The only conceivable restraint was the possibility that a "too early sexual indulgence" might lead to a "premature termination" of the sexual faculty, but even this problem could be solved by experiments designed to establish the optimum period of sexuality. This "gentlest of all revolutions," the sexual revolution, would be as salutary for the country as for the youths of the house, because it would contribute to the increase of population which was so desirable. And, unlike ordinary infants who were "worse than worthless," the infants raised in the industry-house were "endowed with an indubitable and universal value." "In this way, so long as land lasts, you may go increasing population without end and without expense. . . . Give them [children] a value and you may have them without end."[52] So, too, the National Charity Company would have them without end—the apprentice's children, born in the house, becoming apprentices in turn, and so on ad infinitum.*

*One of the intriguing aspects of this work is the blithe assumption that a large population was eminently desirable. Unfortunately, the plan was published just before Malthus's *Essay*. Later Bentham was sufficiently embarrassed by this paean to early marriage and large families to delete the final section on the "gentlest of all revolutions," the sexual revolution. He did so without mentioning the deletion and without altering the plan itself, which could only have had the effect of increasing population. In the 1812 edition the deletion was all the more disingenuous because Bentham described this version as a reprint from the original, and in all other respects (including a footnote referring to a section that was never written) it did seem to be that. In the posthumous edition of his *Works*, the last section was restored, again without mentioning the earlier deletion.

It was almost as an anticlimax that Bentham disclosed the ultimate virtue of his plan: the psychological security that came from being spared the desires and temptations lurking in the outside world. In the industry-house there would be "no unsatisfied longings, no repinings, nothing within knowledge that is not within reach." The constriction of desire was yet another incentive to propagation: "It is by diminishing wants, not by multiplying them that the capacity of population is increased." All of this —the satisfaction of material needs, the opportunity for unlimited sexual gratification, the happiness of blissful ignorance—made his plan, Bentham boasted, a veritable "Utopia," a Utopia not in the sense that it was too good to be realized but that it was as practicable as it was "excellent."[53]

Unfortunately, there is no record of any response to this Utopia, except Bentham's own bitter tirades against the king for preventing its adoption. "But for George the Third," he wrote in his memoirs, "all the paupers in the country would, long ago, have been under my management." He even invented a title for the position that had been denied him: "Sub-Regulus of the Poor."[54] Written toward the end of his life, these comments testify to his enduring commitment to this scheme. He reprinted *Pauper Management* twice, in 1802 and 1812, and made plans to reissue it in 1828 and again in 1831, a year before his death, so that it can hardly be attributed to a momentary aberration, a youthful excess of zeal. (When it was first published, in 1798, Bentham was fifty years old and an established author.)

That the plan attracted no attention, so far as is known, and this in spite of the fact that Bentham had access to people of considerable influence, suggests how alien it was to the spirit of the time—alien to the spirit of Adam Smith, who would have been appalled by this gargantuan institution, a parody of the mercantilist monopoly (one can hear him inveighing against those scheming, self-serving merchants), and also to the prevailing spirit of reform. While Bentham was proposing to bring together into a single institution young and old, able and infirm, criminals and noncriminals (with only the apprentices to be separated from the rest so that they would not be contaminated by paupers used to the "luxurious" ways of other poorhouses), other reformers were protesting against just such "mixed," "promiscuous" workhouses. The preferred mode of reform was to create institutions for the specific needs of specific groups: orphanages or the "boarding out" system for infants, hospitals and clinics for the sick, a Marine Society for indigent sailors, a Magdalen Asylum for "penitent prostitutes." When Frederick Eden protested against any "general, unexceptionable, and complete system for the management of the Poor," he might well have had Bentham's plan in mind.[55]

At every point Bentham's scheme went counter to the current mode of thought and practice. While he vigorously defended the idea of a privately owned and managed company, arguing that the profit incentive was "the strongest stimulation to what is good in management and the strongest check to what is bad," and that such a profit system was the "only shape which genuine and *efficient* humanity can take,"[56] other reformers, reacting against the much publicized abuses of the "private contracting" or "farming" system, urged that poorhouses be owned by the parish or a union of parishes and managed by salaried officials. And while Bentham justified his elaborate system of workhouses on the ground that security was preferable to liberty, others condemned the workhouse as an intolerable infringement of liberty—a "gaol without guilt," it was commonly said. This was Eden's main objection to the workhouse. "A prisoner under the custody of his keeper may perhaps be confident of receiving his bread and his water daily; yet, I believe, there are few who would not, even with the contingent possibility of starving, prefer a precarious chance of subsistence, from their own industry, to the certainty of regular meals in a gaol."[57] Eden was only echoing the often quoted statement by Joseph Townsend a decade earlier: "The terror of being sent to a workhouse acts like an abolition of the poor's tax on all who dread the loss of liberty."[58] Sentiments such as these had led to the passage of the act of 1795 which offered relief "to any industrious poor person or persons . . . at his, her, or their homes," and to the Speenhamland system, which extended this principle of "outdoor" relief to laborers as well as paupers.[59]

Bentham's plan was the exact obverse of these. If Speenhamland was the ultimate form of outdoor relief, Bentham's was the *reductio* of the workhouse system. Yet in one sense both had the same effect: Both blurred the distinction between the independent and the dependent poor—between the "labouring people" and the "poor," as Burke had put it. It was later claimed that Speenhamland, by extending outdoor relief to those employed at inadequate wages, reduced the independent laborer to the status of the pauper, thus "pauperizing" the poor. But its more immediate result, as was said at the time, was to make relief respectable, to grant it as a "right" rather than a "stigma," thus elevating the pauper to the status of the laborer. Bentham similarly confused the categories by extending the jurisdiction of the company far beyond the normal limits of the workhouse, reducing to dependency, by fiat so to speak, a considerable body of people who would not otherwise be dependent. In his case, however, the immediate effect would have been to degrade and stigmatize all those who came within the purview of the company—by confining them within the house for prolonged periods (often the better part of their lives and the lives of their children), by subjecting them to an unprecedentedly austere and authoritarian regimen, by treating them like "forward children" who were not sufficiently "sound in mind" or possessed of the "moral sanity" required to manage their own affairs. The final act of degradation was to include in their ranks those who did not qualify for ordinary prisons (because they were not "proved" depredators) but who in his opinion deserved to be confined somewhere, on the grounds that they were "suspected" depredators or "unruly" (or even "victimized") apprentices, wives, and children.

All of this was to be done in the name of *Pauper Management Improved.* If "improved" in that title seems dubious, the other words were appropriate and even prophetic, the concept of "pauper" and the idea of "management" emerging as basic principles of the poor law reform of 1834. Bentham's idea of pauperism, however, was very different from that of the reformers. Where he enlarged the scope of the term by extending it to the considerable number of laboring poor who would be confined in his industry-houses, they deliberately narrowed it precisely to exclude the laboring poor from the compass of the New Poor Law. And where his plan of management provided for a system of workhouses owned and managed by a private company (of which he was to be a major shareholder), theirs was a publicly owned system supervised by a central board of commissioners appointed by the government.

If Bentham was, as is so often said, the father of the New Poor Law, it was neither because of his ideas of poverty and pauperism nor because of his proposal of reform, but because of a rationalistic temper that encouraged a radical break with the past, with traditional ways of thinking about poverty and traditional ways of dealing with the poor.*

*The claim that Bentham was the father of the New Poor Law is largely based on the principle of "less-eligibility" and the use of the workhouse. But the workhouses established by the New Poor Law, unlike Bentham's, were publicly owned and managed; and they were intended, by means of the "workhouse test," to reduce the pauper population rather than, like Bentham's, to increase it. Similarly, the less-eligibility principle under the New Poor Law was meant to discourage the poor from applying for relief, whereas its main function for Bentham was to make the industry-houses more profitable by reducing the cost of upkeep of a considerably larger body of paupers.

Bentham's *Constitutional Code* is often cited as the inspiration for the Central Board established under the New Poor Law. The *Code,* however, provided for an "Indigence Relief Minister" whose functions were far more limited than the Board—"inspective, statistic, and melioration-suggestive" —i.e., inspecting the workhouses and providing information and advice to the various agencies (private contractors as well as parish authorities) who actually owned and managed the houses.[60] Written in the late 1820s, the *Code* was published posthumously, after the enactment of the New Poor Law, and while it was probably known in manuscript to Edwin Chadwick, Bentham's secretary and one of the leading figures in the drafting of the law, it was probably not known to Nassau Senior and others responsible for the law.

It has also been suggested that Colquhoun borrowed the distinction between "poverty" and "indigence" from Bentham's unpublished essay of 1796.[61] But Bentham himself conspicuously violated this distinction in *Pauper Management Improved,* his only published work on the subject, whereas Colquhoun made it prominent in his own work and introduced it into the public domain. Since Bentham and Colquhoun are so often linked together, it should be noted how different Colquhoun's practical proposals were from Bentham's. Opposed in principle to the idea of workhouses, Colquhoun tried to prevent the worst of the abuses associated with them by bringing them under the authority of the central government. Long before Bentham's *Constitutional Code,* he recommended the establishment of a board responsible to the Home Office to supervise the local

4. Thomas Paine

The last of this odd lot of disciples, in some ways the oddest of all, was Thomas Paine. It is one of the ironies of history that those two great antagonists, Burke and Paine, should have paid not merely lip service but genuine homage to the same master. The Burke-Paine debate defined, for their own time and for posterity, diametrically opposed ways of thinking about man, nature, God, history, morality, law, authority, society, the polity. On the subject of the economy, however, they both professed adherence to Smith's "system of natural liberty." It is a measure of the latitude allowed within that system that they could agree on this and on nothing else. Yet for Paine as for Burke there was an undeniable tension between their economic principles and their political and philosophical ones. If the doctrine of laissez faire is not easily reconciled with the traditionalist Burke, neither is it with the radical Paine, the Paine who has been celebrated as the progenitor of a "state system of social security," of the "welfare state," and of "social democracy."[63]

These claims derive from two proposals, the first and better known appearing toward the end of *Rights of Man*, Paine's famous rebuttal to Burke's *Reflections*. A major theme of the book was the evils of taxation, and at this point Paine was urging the abolition of what he regarded as the most onerous of the taxes, the poor rates. (This, it should be noted, was in the spring of 1792, before the war with France and a series of bad harvests had driven the poor rates to that much higher level which provoked Burke's essay on "Scarcity" and, later still, Malthus's *Essay on Population*.) Since the abolition of the poor rates would have meant the abolition of the poor law, Paine was moved to propose an alternative mode of relief and an alternative means of financing it.

Paine's proposal—a social budget, in effect—was worked out in precise bookkeeping terms, each item stipulating the number of people affected by it and the amount of money required to finance it. A sum of £4,000,000 (double the current poor rates) was to be allocated to "that class of poor which need support"—one-fifth of the population, Paine estimated. The largest items in the budget were allowances for children (£4 a year for needy children under the age of fourteen) and for the aged (£6 a year for needy persons between the ages of fifty and sixty and £10 over the age of sixty). Since large families and old age were the two major causes of poverty, these

---

authorities. He also urged that where workhouses were in use, separate buildings be reserved for different groups: one for pauper infants, another for the "virtuous, aged, and infirm," and a third for the "vicious and depraved." For the relief of the agricultural poor he favored cottages and gardens rather than workhouses. And in general he warned (as Frederick Eden had) against any attempt to establish "fixed and detailed rules, applicable to a pauper system, or suitable to every particular case."[62]

allowances alone would obviate the need for the conventional forms of relief. Smaller sums were specified for other purposes: education allowances of 10 shillings a year for those children who were "not properly of the class of poor" but who could not afford schooling; birth and marriage allowances of 20 shillings for those needy couples who applied for them; funeral expenses for those who died while working away from home; and the cost of constructing workhouses in the metropolis to employ and if necessary house and feed the "casual poor." These measures, Paine was confident, would go far toward alleviating the miseries afflicting the poor, and at the same time make it possible to abolish the poor laws, "those instruments of civil torture."

> Widows will have maintenance for their children, and will not be carted away, on the death of their husbands, like culprits and criminals: and children will no longer be considered as increasing the distress of their parents. The haunts of the wretched will be known, because it will be to their advantage; and the number of petty crimes, the offspring of distress and poverty, will be lessened. The poor, as well as the rich, will then be interested in the support of government, and the cause and apprehension of riots and tumults will cease.[64]

The other part of the proposal was a major reform of taxation, starting with the abolition of the poor rates and the taxes on houses and windows. (Eventually some of the excise taxes were also to be reduced or eliminated.) The reduction of revenue would be partially offset by reductions in expenses: most of the army and navy would be dismantled, many officeholders would be discharged, and the government debt, and thus the interest on the debt, would be reduced. The additional revenue needed to finance the program for the poor was to be provided by a new tax on landed estates. The tax would start at the rate of 3 pence in the pound on small estates and would rise to 20 shillings in the pound at the £23,000 level. (Thus an estate producing £1,000 a year would pay a tax of £20, and an estate of £23,000 a tax of over £10,000.) "The object," Paine explained, "is not so much the produce of the tax as the justice of the measures." The justice lay in the principle of progressive taxation—"rendering taxes more equal than they are"—as well as the effect of the new tax in subverting the "unnatural law of primogeniture."[65] Since the landlord would obviously find it advantageous to distribute to his younger children and other relatives that part of his estate which would be subject to a very large tax, primogeniture would be discouraged if not actually nullified.

It was an impressive scheme, but perhaps not quite as impressive as it is often represented. For it was not a "social security," "social democracy," or "welfare state" program in the usual meaning of those terms—a program providing for the entire population as a matter of right rather than need. It was, in fact, another version of the poor law, the "class of poor which need support" comprising one-fifth of the population below the age of fifty and one-third over that age—hardly the entire body of the laboring poor, still less the entire population. Nor was it much more generous than the bill proposed by Pitt only a few years later; in one respect it was actually less generous, for in giving relief mainly in the form of child and old-age allowances (both of which Pitt also provided for), it made no provision, except the workhouse, for the non-aged poor who did not have children but who were nonetheless needy. The principle, however, was the same. When Paine insisted that relief to the aged should be "not of the nature of charity, but of a right," he did not mean it to be a right regardless of need.[66] He meant it in the same sense that Pitt did when he defended children's allowances as a "matter of right and an honour," or that Cobbett later did when he defended the old poor law as a legal and moral commitment to the poor in times of need.

It was not by chance that Paine's program for the poor emerged in the course of his attack on the existing system of taxation. A recurrent theme in *Rights of Man,* a principal item in his indictment of the British government and of monarchy in general, was the "excess and inequality of taxation." From the Norman Conquest on, Paine charged, the object of all tyrannical, monarchical, hereditary government was the extortion of money from the many for the benefit of the few. "The real object of all despotism is revenue"; monarchy is "a mere court artifice to procure money"; the English Constitution is "the most productive machine for taxation that was ever invented." War itself, for such governments, was only the "pretense" for the raising of money. "Taxes were not raised to carry on wars, but . . . wars were raised to carry on taxes." "All the monarchical governments are military. War is their trade, plunder and revenue their objects."[67]

Poverty and unrest were similarly a function of misgovernment and taxation. In America, where the people were not overtaxed, they were not discontented. "Their taxes are few, because their government is just; and as there is nothing to render them wretched, there is nothing to engender riots and tumults." In England, on the other hand, taxes kept the people "constantly on the brink of commotion," "easily heated to outrage." The excessive poor rates were the result of excessive taxation; in the past when taxes were low, the people were able to maintain themselves so that there was no need for poor rates. It was the increase of taxes that had caused an increase in the number and wretchedness of the poor and thus the dramatic rise in the poor rates.[68]

The poor were not the only or even the chief victims of this system of taxation. While they bore a disproportionate burden of the taxes on consumption, they did not, Paine pointed out, pay either the poor rates or the bulk of the house and window taxes, both of which fell most heavily on the "middle class of people." These were the two taxes Paine proposed to abolish immediately, leaving the taxes on consumption (including the tax on malt and hops which was most resented by the poor) to be reduced gradually. The substitution of a progressive tax on landed estates for the poor rates and window and house taxes would have had the effect of shifting the burden of taxes not from the poor to the rich but from the "middle class" to the landed aristocracy.

Paine was not alone in seeking some measure of tax relief for both the poor and the middle classes. In his opening address to the new session of Parliament, on January 31, 1791, Pitt proposed a series of tax reforms. Paine thereupon hastily added an appendix to *Rights of Man* charging that the government had deliberately held up the publication of the second part of his book so that the Prime Minister could take credit for Paine's proposal. It was "extraordinary," he sarcastically observed, that such an "unprecedented" act as the abolition of taxes, and of these specific taxes, should have occurred to Pitt at just this time.[69] In fact it was neither extraordinary nor unprecedented, Pitt having repeatedly reduced taxes since taking office in 1784, and without prompting by Paine. Nor were Pitt's specific proposals identical with Paine's. Nor was Pitt alone in favoring tax reforms. Such a notorious "reactionary" (as Paine would have regarded him) as Blackstone vigorously opposed the excise taxes. And it was Burke who drew up and eloquently defended one of the most comprehensive economy bills of the time, and sought to introduce the principle that no new taxes be levied without corresponding economies in government.*

On the subject of taxes, Pitt, Burke, and Paine were all disciples of Adam Smith. When Paine proposed abolishing the poor rates and taxes on houses and windows, he explained that since these taxes were not "confounded with trade," their abolition would not "embarrass" trade; the

---

*There was a large consensus, in principle at least, that taxes on the poor were undesirable and that as far as possible excise taxes should be levied only on luxuries. Most of the taxes retained or instituted by Pitt were on such items as drink and tobacco, fruit and sugar, china, silver, and glass, ladies' ribbons and men's hats. Although there was no progressive estate tax such as Paine proposed, there was a land tax; and the taxes on houses and windows, carriages and coaches, servants and legal documents, obviously weighed more heavily on the middle and upper classes than on the poor. The demand for the reduction of taxes became more widespread when it was discovered that such a reduction actually had the effect of increasing government revenues by stimulating trade and productivity and discouraging smuggling (of tea, for example). (A generation taught by Adam Smith was obviously receptive to "supply-side" theories.)

customs duties and excise taxes, on the other hand, which had the closest connection with trade, were to be reduced gradually.[70] And when he defended the landed estate tax on the ground that it would render taxes "more equal than they are," he was restating the first of Smith's principles governing taxation, the principle of "equality," according to which individuals would contribute toward the support of the government "in proportion to their respective abilities; that is in proportion to the revenue which they respectively enjoy under the protection of the state."[71] It was this principle of "equality," or "proportion," that led Smith to advocate taxes on luxuries rather than necessities, a land tax but not a window tax, a tax on the salaries of higher officials but not on the wages of ordinary workers.

More important than the principles of taxation were those principles of political economy which bore upon the relationship of the individual and society, self-interest and the common interest, commerce and the polity, society and government. Here the resemblance between Paine and Smith was even more striking, so striking that passages of the *Rights of Man* could well have appeared in the *Wealth of Nations*.

> I have been an advocate for commerce, because I am a friend to its effects. It is a pacific system, operating to unite mankind by rendering nations, as well as individuals, useful to each other. . . . The most effectual process is that of improving the condition of man by means of his own interest; and it is on this ground that I take my stand.
>
> The mutual dependence and reciprocal interest which man has upon man, and all parts of a civilized community upon each other, create that great chain of connection which holds it together. The landholder, the farmer, the manufacturer, the merchant, the tradesman, and every occupation, prospers by the aid which each receives from the other, and from the whole. Common interest regulates their concerns, and forms their laws; and the laws which common usage ordains, have a greater influence than the laws of government.
>
> All the great laws of society are laws of nature. Those of trade and commerce, whether with respect to the intercourse of individuals, or of nations, are laws of mutual and reciprocal interest. They are followed and obeyed because it is the interest of the parties so to do, and not on account of any formal laws their governments may impose or interpose.[72]

The animus against government in the second part of *Rights of Man* was exacerbated by Paine's hatred of the monarchy, but it had its roots in a conception of man and society reminiscent of Smith. It might have been Smith discoursing on the "enterprise and industry" of individuals which were responsible for all improvements in society; or the "diversity of wants" which could be satisfied only by "reciprocal aid"; or the "social affections" necessary to the individual's happiness; or the "unceasing circulation of interest, which, passing through its million channels, invigorates the whole mass of civilized man"; or the individual who owed so little to government that all he could hope for was that government would "let him alone." Paine went even further than Smith in making that "reciprocally accommodating" society so self-sufficient and all-sufficient as almost to obviate the need for any government.

> Society performs for itself almost everything which is ascribed to government.
>
> Government is no farther necessary than to supply the few cases to which society and civilization are not conveniently competent. . . . Every thing which government can usefully add thereto, has been performed by the common consent of society, without government.
>
> It is but few general laws that civilized life requires, and those of such common usefulness, that whether they are enforced by the forms of government or not, the effect will be nearly the same.[73]

There was an obvious contradiction between the minimal government Paine argued for so passionately in the beginning of Part Two of *Rights of Man,* and the intrusive government that would have been required to carry out his social program at the end of that book.* Even in the latter case, however, the government was to intrude into the affairs of only a relatively small, well defined class, the needy poor. The ordinary laboring poor, Paine made it clear, were to be neither hindered nor assisted by the government. He opposed the regulation of wages partly because it would unjustly limit wages at a time of rising prices, and also because workers should be "as free to make their own bargains" as landlords were to make theirs. Similarly he insisted that all combinations were illegal, whether for the purpose of raising wages, prices, or taxes. "If the one be illegal, it will be difficult to show that the other ought to exist."[74]

One might have expected that a man so enamored of reason would have embraced Smith's plan of education or some other comprehensive plan. In fact Paine's hostility to the state made him as suspicious of the govern-

---

*For that matter, there was a contradiction between this minimal government and the strong national government he had advocated in America at the time of the revolution. But his American policies, it might be argued, antedated his reading of the *Wealth of Nations.*

ment's involvement in education as in the economy. Although his social program stipulated that every child receiving an allowance have some schooling and provided a small sum for that purpose, he rejected the kind of state-subsidized, state-supervised system Smith had recommended. "Public schools," he said, "do not answer the general purpose of the poor"—this because they were likely to be in towns some distance from the poor. But instead of satisfying that objection by proposing the establishment of village schools, he recommended giving the education allowance directly to the parents and making them responsible for finding teachers for their children. "Distressed clergymen's widows," he suggested, were ideal for that purpose.[75]*

In his diatribes against taxes and the national debt, Paine often sounded like an agrarian populist resentful of industry, technology, and political economy. But while there was a populist streak in him, a faith in the common sense of the common man, there was no animus against industry or commerce and no nostalgia for the simple rural life. On the contrary, his social imagination, like that of Benjamin Franklin or Adam Smith, was rooted in the modern, enterprising, inventive, expansive world. When he returned to England after a dozen years in America, it was not to carry the message of revolution from the New World to the Old (although he did that as well), but more immediately to carry out his plans for the construction of an iron bridge. The essay by Paine which converted William Cobbett to radicalism, "The Decline and Fall of the English System of Finance," repeatedly cited Adam Smith as the preeminent authority on the subject of finance as on economics in general. In predicting the collapse of that financial system under the weight of the debt, Paine failed to take into account the ability of an expanding economy to absorb and accommodate a growing debt. But he was nonetheless appreciative of an economy committed to technological innovation, industrial expansion, and commercial prosperity.

Even Paine's obsession with taxes ("there are two distinct classes of men in the nation, those who pay taxes, and those who receive and live upon the taxes")[76] was motivated in large part by his concern for the welfare of industry, commerce, and agriculture, since taxes were as burdensome to the economy as to the poor. When he complained of the "greedy hand of government thrusting itself into every corner and crevice of industry, and grasping the spoil of the multitude," the "multitude" that was being despoiled was everyone engaged in productive enterprise, the whole body of the "industrious classes." And the tax he proposed to levy

---

*If Paine cannot be said to have anticipated the welfare state, he can be credited with devising what is now known as the "voucher system," payments to parents to be spent on schools of their choice.

on landed estates was meant to limit not "property acquired by industry" but only that which could not have been so acquired.[77]*

The most radical statement of Paine's views of property and poverty appeared in *Agrarian Justice Opposed to Agrarian Law and to Agrarian Monopoly*, a pamphlet written while he was in exile in France and published there in 1797. "Agrarian Law" in the title referred to the demand for the abolition of private ownership of land, a doctrine associated with the "Conspiracy of the Equals" led by "Gracchus" Babeuf, which had recently been suppressed by the French Revolutionary Government.[79] Against that "agrarian law" on the one hand, and the existing "agrarian monopoly" on the other, Paine affirmed the basic principle of private property while calling for some measure of redistribution. This double strategy was reflected in his distinction between two kinds of property: the "natural property" that was a product of the original creation, the natural right to earth, air, and water; and the "artificial or acquired property" that was the "invention of man." The first was the "common property of the human race," the second the rightful domain of "individual property."[80]

The distinction between "natural" and "artificial" property gave rise to a distinctive view of poverty. Instead of attributing poverty, as he had earlier done, to taxation and misgovernment, Paine now attributed it to the inequitable distribution of property that came with civilization. Poverty did not exist in the "natural state"; it arose only in "civilized life." But the latter also brought with it all the advantages of agriculture, manufactures, arts, and science. Civilization thus had the effect of making "one part of society more affluent, and the other more wretched, than would have been the lot of either in a natural state."[81] Implicit in this theory of poverty was the solution: the restoration to the poor of the property that rightfully belonged to them as their natural heritage, and the confirmation of the property of individuals that rightfully belonged to them as a result of their "inventions." If the system of "agrarian monopoly" was unjust because it created an artificial condition of poverty, an "agrarian law" would be unjust because it took

---

*Today some of Paine's admirers confess to their disappointment with his "economic conservatism," his preference for a market economy rather than a "moral economy." One has gone so far as to suggest that his economics "would not dismay someone like Enoch Powell"—the latter embodying, presumably, the most doctrinaire kind of laissez-faireism. These critics cite his opposition to price controls in America during a period of inflation when others were advocating such controls; his spirited defense of the privately owned Bank of America against those who criticized the large dividends it was paying its shareholders and sought the revocation of its charter; his program for relief in *Rights of Man* which fell far short of economic or social equality; and his failure to develop a theory of economic oppression as the cause of poverty or to propose any serious plan for the redistribution of property.[78]

no account of the value added to the land by invention and cultivation—
the value that could legitimately be passed on in the form of property by
inheritance or purchase.[82]

The details of Paine's new proposal were worked out with the same
bookkeeping precision that had characterized his program in *Rights of Man*.
As compensation for the property that had been theirs in the state of nature, all
adults would receive at the age of twenty-one a sum of £15, and at the age of
fifty an annuity of £10 for the rest of their lives. These sums were to be paid
out of a "national fund" created by an inheritance tax: a 10 percent tax for
direct heirs and 20 percent for collateral and other heirs. The tax was to be
levied on "personal property" (derived from industry, trade, and finance) as
well as landed property, on the ground that personal property, although not
originally owned in common, was the "effect of society," so that some part of
it should rightfully be returned to society.[83] The inclusion of personal property (which may have been an afterthought—it was belied by the emphasis on
"agrarian" in the title) was one important difference between this plan and
that in *Rights of Man*. More significant was the fact that this plan was truly
based on right rather than need. "It is not charity but a right, not bounty but
justice, that I am pleading for."[84] Because it was a right, the payments both at
maturity and old age were to go to everyone, rich and poor alike. Most of the
rich, Paine was confident, would not accept these sums; in fact his calculations
assumed that 10 percent of those entitled to them would decline them. The
principle, however, required that everyone be offered them since everyone
had lost something by the transition from nature to civilization.

It was a fine line Paine was treading, between a partial redistribution
of property and a reaffirmation of the right of private property. That dual
purpose was reflected in his rhetoric, which alternated, often in successive
sentences or within a single sentence, between a passionate appeal for justice
for the poor and a principled defense of private property and the accumulation of wealth (including inherited wealth).

> While, therefore, I advocate the right, and interest myself in the hard
> case of all those who have been thrown out of their natural inheritance
> by the introduction of the system of landed property, I equally defend
> the right of the possessor to the part which is his.
>
> The contrast of affluence and wretchedness continually meeting and
> offending the eye, is like dead and living bodies chained together.
> Though I care as little about riches as any man, I am a friend to riches
> because they are capable of good.
>
> I care not how affluent some may be, provided that none be miserable
> in consequence of it.[85]

This ambivalence was revealed even more strikingly in the scheme itself. For the fact is that the sums to be distributed were relatively small: a single payment of £15 at maturity and £10 annually in old age. And the "national fund" from which they were to be paid consisted not of the entire fund of property in the nation, not even of the fund of landed property, but of the revenue from a 10 or 20 percent inheritance tax (which was not, incidentally, a progressive tax). Paine said nothing here of the program for the needy developed in *Rights of Man*. But if, as is probable, the present plan was meant to supersede the earlier one, it was more radical in principle but possibly less generous in the actual sums to be distributed to the poor in the course of their lifetime.

"A revolution in the state of civilization is the necessary companion of revolutions in the system of government."[86] So Paine described the purpose of *Agrarian Justice:* to bring about a social revolution that would complement the political revolution heralded by *Rights of Man.* Had he wanted to call attention to the discrepancy between those works, he could not have done so more effectively than by suggesting that parallel. Nor could he have chosen a more revealing title. The political revolution called for in *Rights of Man* was a genuine revolution requiring the abolition of the entire heritage of the past, including the monarchy and aristocracy, and inaugurating something like a "permanent revolution" with each generation creating its own laws and institutions. An equivalent social revolution would have entailed a comparable degree of economic and social equality —not "Agrarian Justice" as Paine described it, but precisely that "Agrarian Law" which he repudiated. "Man has no property in man; neither has any generation a property in the generations which are to follow";[87] in *Rights of Man* this had a purely political connotation—indeed one of the "rights of man" was the right to property. But the principle could obviously be taken literally, as a denial not only of "property in man" but of property in things.

This was, in fact, how it was taken by some of Paine's contemporaries in England as well as France. Seventeen years before Paine's *Rights of Man,* Thomas Spence published a pamphlet under the identical title advocating the abolition of private property in land and the vesting of ownership in the parish for the use of the cultivators of the land. Five years later William Ogilvie published *An Essay on the Right of Property in Land* which differed from Spence's plan in detail but not in principle. Reissuing his pamphlet after Paine's *Rights of Man* was published and again after *Agrarian Justice,* Spence made a point of criticizing the "poor beggarly stipends" Paine proposed to give the poor—contemptible substitutes for the "lordly and just pretensions to the soil of our birth."[88]

It was not only by contrast to land nationalization (or communitarian or egalitarian) schemes that Paine's "stipends" appeared to be less than revolutionary. If *Agrarian Justice* invited comparison with proposals for an agrarian law, it also evoked echoes, even in its title, of the more substantial and influential work by his friend William Godwin, whose *Enquiry Concerning Political Justice* was published in 1793 and issued in a new edition in 1796, a year before *Agrarian Justice*. Godwin did not put forward any specific economic or social program, but he did enunciate a theory of property that was far more radical than Paine's. By limiting rightful property to that which originated in either utility or labor, Godwin effectively illegitimized most existing forms of property, including inherited property. When Elie Halévy said that *Political Justice* was the "inspiration" for *Agrarian Justice,* he could only have meant that Godwin called Paine's attention to the problem of property, not that Paine adopted Godwin's theory of property.[89] Only by ignoring the contemporary context—the writings and activities of Spence and Ogilvie, Godwin and Babeuf—can one of Paine's biographers acclaim *Agrarian Justice* as a "heroic remedy" for the problem of poverty.[90]

If *Agrarian Justice* seems somewhat less than "heroic," it is because social criticism and reform were not Paine's forte. What made him famous in his own day and for generations to come were his political and philosophical views, his defense of revolution in *Common Sense* and *Rights of Man,* and his attack on Christianity in *The Age of Reason*. *Agrarian Justice* was not widely known in his time or later. *Rights of Man,* of course, caused a sensation when it first appeared and remained an inspiration to radicals for generations to come. But it was not the social program in that book that made it famous. That program appeared in Part Two, published in February 1792. The previous March, Part One had sold 50,000 copies within a few weeks of publication—this at the not inconsiderable price of three shillings.* If Part Two had a still more spectacular sale, it was because of the publication of a sixpence edition and the enormous publicity given the book by the indictment of Paine on the charge of seditious libel.

What made Part Two so provocative for the public, and so seditious for the government, was the argument that the English political system was unconstitutional and tyrannical, that only a republican form of government was in accord with the rights of man, and, by implication, that revolution was morally and politically defensible, indeed necessary. "All hereditary

*Burke's *Reflections,* which was also regarded as enormously successful, sold 12,000 copies in the first month and over 19,000 within the year—this, too, at the price of three shillings.

The sales of *Rights of Man* are impressive enough without being inflated, as they often are. It was said at the time that 200,000 copies of both parts were in circulation within a year, and Paine himself claimed 400,000 to 500,000 in 1802. Other estimates give the sale of Part Two alone as 1,500,000 by the time Paine died in 1809. Richard Altick has pointed out that this would have been one copy for every ten people—man, woman, and child—in the United Kingdom.[91]

government is in its nature tyranny."[92] There was no escaping the clear message of that statement and of innumerable others to the same effect. Nor was there any mistaking the refrain of "revolution" which ran through Part Two, and not in reference to France or America but to England. It was as if Paine were deliberately waving a red flag and inviting the charge of sedition. But it was a political, not a social, revolution he was inciting. When he published the sixpence edition in August 1792, he deleted the passages cited by the government as "seditious libel," none of which came from the social program. In a sense it was precisely because *Rights of Man* was so revolutionary a political document that it was not a revolutionary or even a particularly radical social document. Paine's passions and commitments were political. To the extent to which he raised other issues, they tended to be subsumed under the political. This was the clear implication of one of his most impassioned and often-quoted comments on poverty: "When in countries that are called civilized, we see age going to the work-house, and youth to the gallows, something must be wrong in the system of government"[93]—the system of government, not of property.

If poverty was not Paine's primary concern, neither were the poor his special constituency. In attacking taxes he said he was defending "the cause of the poor, of the manufacturers, of the tradesmen, of the farmers, and of all those on whom the real burden of taxes fall—but above all, I defend the cause of humanity." And in condemning the monarchy he professed to speak for "the farmer, the manufacturer, the merchant, the tradesman, and down through all the occupations of life to the common labourer."[94] This amalgam of classes may now seem primitive or naïve, but at the time the idea of a continuum of lower and "middling" classes was commonplace among radicals and conservatives alike. (The word "manufacturer" was itself significant; in contemporary usage it applied to both employer and employee, or, as was often the case, to the self-employed worker.) Malthus complained that *Rights of Man* had done "great mischief among the lower and middling classes of people in this country."[95] And a friend of Burke reported that the book was circulating "among the middling Class of People, who peruse it with the greatest avidity, and communicate and inculcate its political tenets among the lower orders of Men."[96] The Constitutional Societies which did so much to popularize it (until they became disaffected by the overt republicanism of Part Two) were predominantly of the middling classes, while the more militant London Corresponding Society was described by its founder (himself a shoemaker, which is to say, a "respectable" artisan) as consisting of "tradesmen, shopkeepers, and mechanics."[97]

Paine's constituency was socially heterogeneous, in part because contemporaries commonly linked together those classes and groups, in part because the issue on which he appealed to his readers was political and in this respect they had a shared interest. Paine was hardly unaware of the social and economic differences separating the "common labourer" from "the farmer, the manufacturer, the merchant, the tradesman." But it was precisely his point that these differences—differences of birth, condition, and occupation—were irrelevant to the question of political rights, that in this regard all men were equal, and that this equality could be assured by a proper system of government.

On those occasions when Paine seemed to imply something like a class war, the enemy was the "landed interest": "a combination of aristocratical land-holders, opposing their own pecuniary interest to that of the farmer, and every branch of trade, commerce, and manufacture."[98] Even then it was a political war he was waging, his assumption being that the aristocracy was able to assert its "pecuniary interest" over the rest of society because of the political power it wielded, the power to make laws and declare wars, to tax others and to take the proceeds of those taxes for themselves. If he sometimes fell into the familiar antithesis of rich and poor, he was clearly using "rich" as a shorthand term for the "aristocratical land-holders." More often he resisted that antithesis. Even in *Agrarian Justice,* his most radical social tract, he made a point of saying that he was a "friend to riches because they are capable of good," and that he did not care "how affluent some may be, provided that none be miserable in consequence of it."[99] Earlier he had associated the rights of the poor with the property of the rich so that each had a stake in the other: "When the rich plunder the poor of his rights, it becomes an example to the poor to plunder the rich of his property. ... When the rich protect the rights of the poor, the poor will protect the property of the rich."[100] While he was still living in America, he made it clear that he favored a "perfect equality" of rights, not because that would result in an equality of wealth but because it would promote "security" for rich and poor alike. "Let the rich man enjoy his riches, and the poor man comfort himself in his poverty."[101]

Paine, then, had no "heroic remedy" for poverty, because poverty was not his problem. Nor did he make a hero of the poor per se. When he protested that Burke "pities the plumage, but forgets the dying bird," that "dying bird" was not, as one might think, the poor man but the victim of political tyranny; in this context it referred specifically to the political prisoners in the Bastille, most of whom were not notably poor (some, in fact, were lesser nobility).[102]

When Paine himself became a hero to later generations of radicals, it was not because of his social programs or his views on poverty, but for a variety of other reasons. William Cobbett praised him as the first to expose the truth about taxes and the public debt; the radical journalists of the thirties as the champion of free speech and a free press; the Chartists as the advocate of political equality and universal suffrage; G. W. M. Reynolds as the forefather of republicanism; George Holyoake and Charles Bradlaugh as the apostle of rationalism, secularism, and "atheism" (the latter a free translation of Paine's "deism"). Each of these causes was sufficient in itself to make Paine the hero of one or another radical movement. But transcending them all was the image of Paine as *the* radical, the symbol of a "generic" radicalism, so to speak, the champion of the simple, natural, universal "rights of man." E. P. Thompson has said that the two texts of the "English working-class movement" were *Pilgrim's Progress* and *Rights of Man*. [103] If this is so, it suggests that Paine, like Bunyan, was the great celebrator, neither of the working class nor of the poor, but of "everyman," as Bunyan would have said—or "man," as Paine preferred.

IV

MALTHUS:

POLITICAL ECONOMY

DE-MORALIZED

In the history of ideas the *Essay on Population* is often represented as a footnote or postscript to the *Wealth of Nations*, an addendum to the doctrine of laissez faire intended to clarify one important detail that Smith had unaccountably neglected. From a later perspective, in which Adam Smith and Thomas Robert Malthus stand together as representatives of "classical economics" (in contrast to neoclassical, Keynesian, Marxist, or other schools of economics), this amalgam has some justification, provided it is based upon Malthus's *Principles of Political Economy* rather than his *Essay on Population*. [1] But it was the *Essay* that profoundly affected the historic reality long before the *Principles* appeared, and that defined "Malthusianism" for his own generation and for generations to come.

When the *Essay* was published in 1798, it gave every indication of being quite as revolutionary as the *Wealth of Nations*—indeed, more so, to judge by the passions it evoked on the part of critics and admirers alike. (The *Wealth of Nations*, by contrast, had been received with relative equanimity.) And it was revolutionary in relation to the *Wealth of Nations* itself. The one detail contributed by Malthus, the "principle of population," subverted the whole of Smith's theory, starting with his views on industrial productivity and high wages and culminating with his predictions of economic and social progress. It is hard to imagine a more thorough reversal of thought, short of a return to mercantilism. (In some respects the *Essay* represented a return to the physiocratic doctrine, which, from Smith's point of view, was almost as regressive.)

The effect of Malthusianism was immediate and dramatic. For half a century social attitudes and policies were decisively shaped by the new turn of thought. It was in this form, the form given it by Malthus and modified by Ricardo, that political economy took hold in the early part of the nineteenth century. And it was under the aegis of Malthus and Ricardo that political economy freed itself from its ties to moral philosophy and emerged in the guise of a natural science—a "natural economics," one might say, which professed to be nothing more than the application to the economy of the simple, inviolable laws of nature. This "naturalization" of economics had momentous consequences for society as a whole and for the poor in particular. For it threatened to undermine whatever remained of the "moral economy" (the poor laws, most notably), to deprive the poor of the moral status they enjoyed in Smith's market economy, and to renege on his promise of moral and material progress. At a time of acute economic distress and social tension, Malthusianism precipitated a profound moral crisis and provoked one of the most intense ideological conflicts in modern English history.

Perhaps the *Essay* had the impact it did because it professed to be based on a simple "principle" rooted in natural "laws." Smith too had invoked natural principles and laws—self-interest, the social affections, the "propensity" to trade—but in a context that made them seem part of an older philosophical tradition. Smith's doctrine, moreover, was sufficiently malleable, as his disciples amply demonstrated, to permit a variety of interpretations, modifications, and applications. Malthus's was not so accommodating. It derived, by his own account, from immutable facts of nature—physical, biological facts unaffected by human will or legislative fiat. One could not compromise with Malthusianism; one could only affirm or deny it. Nor could one compromise with its practical implications. If it was true, it required a radical change in social policies, policies legitimized by more than two centuries of English history and by a variety of institutions, laws, and traditions which had permeated every aspect of English society.

Malthus's simple, momentous contribution was the "principle of population." He was not the first, he admitted, to recognize the "obvious truth" that "population must always be kept down to the level of the means of subsistence." He did, however, claim to be the first to inquire into the "means by which this level is effected." These means, more than the principle itself, were decisive, because they constituted the "strongest obstacle in the way to any very great future improvement of society."[2]

It was this last point, the "future improvement of society," that was at the heart of the matter. Later commentators and critics, attending to the principle of population itself—the reasoning and evidence behind it, its plausibility and validity—have distracted attention from the larger issue. Contemporaries were not so easily diverted. It was not the "obvious truth" about population that aroused their passions. Nor was it the familiar attack on the poor laws. What was novel about the *Essay,* what came as a shock of recognition to some and as a shocking abomination to others, were the means by which population was reduced to the level of the food supply, means which denied the possibility not only of a "very great" improvement of society but of any significant degree of improvement, which denied, indeed, the basic assumption of modern enlightened thought—the idea of progress.

Malthus had been provoked to write his book, he explained, by a recent essay by William Godwin which raised the issue of the future improvement of society.* In that essay, "Of Avarice and Profusion," Godwin argued that since the poor and the rich had the same wants, and since the improvement and happiness of both classes were dependent on the satisfaction of those wants, it was a gross injustice to deprive the poor of the products of their labor and the necessities of life so that the rich might enjoy luxuries that were unnecessary and corrupting. This injustice could only be remedied by a "state of cultivated equality" which would be in harmony with the nature of man and would promote the "extensive diffusion of felicity."[4]

It was hardly an original thesis, Godwin himself having developed it much more elaborately in his earlier *Enquiry Concerning Political Justice.* (It was this work that Malthus cited extensively in the *Essay.*) Written in 1791–92 and published early in 1793, *Political Justice* reflected the heady experience of the early years of the French Revolution, a revolution that seemed to herald the advent of the heavenly city on earth. Even if his book did not have quite the renown Godwin claimed for it—"There was not a person almost in town or village," he wrote, who did not know of it—the literary community was sufficiently appreciative.[5] Coleridge eulogized Godwin in verse; Southey confessed that he "all but worshipped" him; and

---

*It is curious that only two years earlier, in an unpublished essay, "The Crisis, a View of the Present Interesting State of Great Britain," Malthus took an entirely conventional view both of population and of the poor laws. Commenting on a statement by William Paley, that the amount of happiness in a country could be measured by the number of its inhabitants, Malthus amended this to read that the real measure of happiness was the *increase* of population, since the absolute numbers reflected only the "happiness which is past," whereas the increase reflected the present degree of happiness. He then went on to argue that both happiness and population could be augmented by those parts of Pitt's bill which provided for outdoor relief, especially the family allowance provision.

> Though it is by no means to be wished that any dependent situation should be made so agreeable, as to tempt those who might otherwise support themselves in independence; yet as it is the duty of society to maintain such of its members as are absolutely unable to maintain themselves, it is certainly desirable that the assistance in this case should be given in the way that is most agreeable to the persons who are to receive it.[3]

It evidently took Godwin's utopianism to provoke Malthus to a diametrically opposite view of social happiness and poor relief.

Wordsworth advised a young man, "Burn your books on chemistry and read Godwin on necessity."[6] This enthusiasm did not long survive the Terror and Napoleonic Wars. Godwin himself, in the second edition published in 1796, modified some of his more extreme statements and omitted others, though he left his basic argument unchanged.[7]

That argument centered on the proposition that all the evils of society and the apparent defects of human nature were the product of civil institutions, especially the institution of private property. Were it not for those institutions mankind would enjoy the blessings of equality, justice, and reason. Uncorrupted by the passions generated by artificial society, people would be totally rational; untainted by self-interest and self-love, they would be totally benevolent; uninhibited by the state, government, law, family, organized work (involving a division of labor), or any other form of cooperative enterprise (musical concerts, theatrical performances), they would be free to express their individuality, realize their happiness, and progress toward a state of perfect virtue and wisdom. "Man is perfectible," Godwin proclaimed, "or in other words susceptible of perpetual improvement."[8]

Perfectibility brought with it, among other things, the attenuation and ultimately the elimination of sexuality, since "one tendency of a cultivated and virtuous mind is to diminish our eagerness for the gratification of the senses"; thus the fully rational, virtuous man "will probably cease to propagate." By the same token "mind will one day become omnipotent over matter"—not only the matter of external nature but the "matter of our own bodies." By the "power of intellect" all bodily defects—sickness, the frailties of old age, even sleep—would be overcome. If it was idle to speak of the "absolute immortality of man" (but only because the idea of immortality was so vague), it was entirely reasonable to anticipate an infinite prolongation of life "beyond any limits which we are able to assign." In that happy future, spared the need to reproduce and the wastefulness of death, virtue and wisdom would reign supreme.

> The whole will be a people of men, and not of children. Generation will not succeed generation, nor truth have, in a certain degree, to recommence her career every thirty years. Other improvements may be expected to keep pace with those of health and longevity. There will be no war, no crimes, no administration of justice, as it is called, and no government. Every man will seek, with ineffable ardour, the good of all.[9]

Before arriving at this point, Godwin confronted one possible objection to his system, an objection upon which another utopian scheme had foundered. Robert Wallace, in his *Various Prospects of Mankind, Nature and*

Providence, published in 1761, abandoned his egalitarian plan—"a community of goods," Godwin disapprovingly described it, "to be maintained by the vigilance of the state"—when he realized it would be undermined by the "excessive population that would ensue." Godwin quickly disposed of this problem by invoking that principle in human affairs which made everything "tend to its level" without any interference or regulation. Thus the "principle of population" saw to it that population adjusted to the level of subsistence. Where subsistence was plentiful and wages were high, men had large families; where subsistence was meager and wages were low, men delayed marriage and had fewer children. Population might also be "checked" by infanticide, abortion, sexual promiscuity, and sexual abstinence, but these were generally unnecessary because the natural regulatory principle usually proved to be "all-powerful in its operation." Even if population did not find its natural level, the problem was one for the remote future, since three-fourths of the habitable globe was still uncultivated. "Myriads of centuries of still increasing population may pass away, and the earth be yet found sufficient for the support of its inhabitants." At worst, Godwin concluded, overpopulation was a distant "contingency" rather than a serious deterrent to utopia.[10]

The same problem had occurred to another utopian, Condorcet, whose *Esquisse d'un tableau historique des progrès de l'esprit humain* was written while he was hiding from the police, and was published in 1795 after he had been executed by the revolutionary government. This was indeed a triumph of mind over matter. Watching the degeneration of the revolution in which he had had such high hopes, anticipating his own death at the hands of that revolution, Condorcet redoubled his faith in an ideal future. His last testament was a doctrine of perfectibility very like Godwin's, including the intimation of immortality. He too raised the specter of overpopulation.

> Must not there arrive a period . . . when the increase of the number of men surpassing their means of subsistence, the necessary result must be either a continual diminution of happiness and population, a movement truly retrograde, or at least, a kind of oscillation between good and evil? In societies arrived at this term, will not this oscillation be a constantly subsisting cause of periodical misery? Will it not mark the limit when all further amelioration will become impossible, and point out that term to the perfectibility of the human race which it may reach in the course of ages, but can never pass?[11]

And he too solved the problem, first by putting it off to the "very distant" future, by which time "the human race will have attained improvements, of which we can at present scarcely form a conception"; and then by a suggestion that Malthus professed not to understand: the prevention of breeding either by "promiscuous concubinage" or by "something else as unnatural."[12]

Godwin and Condorcet provided the occasion for Malthus's rebuttal and the substance of that rebuttal. All Malthus had to do was to make their "distant contingency" a clear and present danger. He turned their own arguments, their very phrases, against them. It was Godwin who formulated the "principle of population," and Condorcet who suggested that the "retrograde" movement and "oscillation" of population might result in "periodical misery." The very ideals they hoped to realize—liberty, equality, reason—would have made that distant contingency more imminent. The freedom of sexual relations resulting from the abolition of marriage (before a diminution of sexuality would have set in), the system of equality ensuring everyone's right to subsistence, the ascendancy of reason which would put an end to war, struggle, disease, even death—all of these were bound to increase population beyond the means of subsistence. Godwin had implicitly recognized this when, at the end of his book, he brought propagation itself to a halt. To Malthus, this exposed the ultimate fallacy of his system, for it violated one of the fundamental "postulata," or "fixed laws," of human nature.[13]

There were two such laws: the first, "that food is necessary to the existence of man," the second, "that the passion between the sexes is necessary and will remain nearly in its present state." The corollary of these laws was the proposition that "the power of population is indefinitely greater than the power in the earth to produce subsistence for man." The precise amount of that "indefinitely greater" was provided by the formula: "Population, when unchecked, increases in a geometrical ratio. Subsistence increases only in an arithmetical ratio." The enormous discrepancy between these ratios (as a "slight acquaintance with numbers will show") suggested that population was never, in fact, "unchecked."[14] It was the nature of the checks that belied not only Godwin's expectations of perfectibility but any theory of progress, indeed any benign view of the condition of mankind in general and of the lower classes in particular. The checks were "positive" and "preventive." The positive checks—starvation, sickness, war, infanticide—reduced the population after it came into existence (that is, reduced longevity); the preventive ones—delay of marriage, restraint of sexual passion, forms of sexual intercourse which did not result in procreation—inhibited the increase of population before it occurred (reduced fecundity). The effect of both was "misery and vice," misery being an "absolutely necessary consequence" and vice a "highly probable one."[15] By such means was population reduced to the level of the food supply.

In his preface Malthus apologized for the "melancholy hue" of this

vision of human life.[16] And well he might, "misery and vice" running as
a refrain throughout the essay, punctuating every turn of the argument,
appearing sometimes on successive pages and even paragraphs. These were
the "means" for which he claimed credit—not the principle of population
itself but the way that principle operated. What made these means so
powerful and irresistible was the fact that they derived from the basic laws
of human nature, the need for food and the sexual drive. It was because
sexuality was as peremptory as hunger that the restraint of that passion,
however voluntary, resulted in the "inextricable unhappiness" of both sexes
and thus in misery and vice.[17]

As laws of nature, hunger and sexual passion were obviously binding
on everyone equally, but as checks on population they affected different
groups to different degrees. Where the preventive check operated to some
extent in all ranks of society, the positive check operated chiefly among the
poor. In a prescient passage (anticipating the complaints of social historians
today), Malthus explained why the law of population had been so long
ignored.

> One principal reason is that the histories of mankind that we possess
> are histories only of the higher classes. We have but few accounts that
> can be depended upon of the manners and customs of that part of
> mankind, where these retrograde and progressive movements [of popu-
> lation] chiefly take place.[18]

It was among the lower classes, where the pressure of population was
most acute, that were to be found those "unhappy persons who, in the great
lottery of life, have drawn a blank." Except in extreme cases, "moral merit"
was not a factor in that lottery. Famine struck with all the force of an act
of nature, taking its toll indiscriminately among the poor. The vices of
mankind contributed to the same end, becoming the "active and able ministers of depopulation." Thus the poor conspired in their tragic fate, their
manners and customs making them peculiarly susceptible to misery and vice.
When they received wages in excess of their present needs, they spent the
surplus on "drunkenness and dissipation," unlike tradesmen and farmers who
saved it for future needs. The poor law encouraged this improvidence by
ensuring the support of their families however irresponsible their own
behavior.[19]

Even here, where the poor appeared in the least attractive light, they
exhibited aspects of human nature common to all men. The "fixed laws"
of human nature applied to people of all ranks. Unlike some of his contemporaries, Malthus did not attribute to the poor a more primitive or brutish
sexual drive than that displayed by the upper classes. Nor did he assume that
the upper classes were more given to self-restraint than the lower; his

examples of the exercise of such restraint came from the laborer, the servant, and the gentleman alike. Yet in spite of the essential uniformity of human nature and the universality of the laws of nature, the effect of those natural instincts and laws was profoundly unequal. The principle of population weighed most heavily on the lower classes, and with it the burden of misery and vice.

The same tension, between an original equality of nature and an actual inequality of condition, reappeared toward the end of the *Essay*, where Malthus proposed a theodicy to justify the "melancholy hue" of his work. Misery and vice were necessary to rouse man from the "torpor and corruption" that were the "original sin of man."* "Man as he really is, [is] inert, sluggish, and averse from labour, unless compelled by necessity." That necessity was provided by the pressures of nature. It was want that stimulated the infant to "sentient activity" and the savage to exertion, inspired industry and agriculture, gave "wings to the imagination of the poet, pointed the flowing periods of the historian, and added acuteness to the researches of the philosopher"—even created the "immortal mind of a Newton."[21] Yet it was not, Malthus conceded, poets and philosophers who were most in need of stimulation but the "mass of mankind." The implication was that the masses needed it most because they were closest to the condition of man in his "original" state. Like the infant and the savage, they were most "averse from labour" unless goaded to it by necessity; among them leisure was more likely to "produce evil rather than good" and prosperity more apt to "degrade than exalt the character." To be sure, the "middle parts" of society were also subject to the pressures of want, and those pressures were as salutary for them as for the lower classes, the possibility of being reduced to the ranks of the poor keeping them in the state of "animated exertion" that was the necessary stimulus for the intellect. "If no man could hope to rise or fear to fall, in society, if industry did not bring with it its reward and idleness its punishment, the middle parts would not certainly be what they now are."[22]

Had Godwin or Condorcet been Malthus's main target, the *Essay* would have been an exercise in "over-kill." The principle of population was not necessary to refute the doctrine of perfectibility. A modicum of common sense, some good-natured ridicule, and a liberal dose of quotations would

---

*Earlier, in criticizing Godwin, Malthus said that it was because of the "inevitable laws of nature," rather than the "original depravity of man," that any Utopia was doomed to failure. But he did not then deny the "original depravity." Having made so much of the theme of misery and vice, he had finally to reaffirm the benevolence of God and the goodness of His creation by asserting that "moral evil is absolutely necessary to the production of moral excellence."[20] To a former curate of the Church of England (even one whose early education exposed him to Unitarianism), this was a familiar and plausible theodicy.

have sufficed to expose a utopia that was to be blissfully free of passion, emotion, sexuality, interest, conflict, war, sickness, sleepiness, even death. This was all the more true at the time Malthus was writing. It might have been otherwise five years earlier when *Political Justice* first appeared and when even sensible men succumbed to the most extravagant enthusiasms. By 1798, after the Reign of Terror, Thermidor, and the Napoleonic Wars, that utopian impulse had been largely dissipated.

What was very much alive in 1798 was the spirit of Adam Smith. And it was the refutation of Smith's theory of progress, not Godwin's doctrine of perfectibility, that was the significant purpose of the *Essay*.

> This argument appears to be conclusive, not only against the perfectibility of man, in the enlarged sense in which Mr. Godwin understands the term, but against any very marked and striking change for the better, in the form and structure of general society, by which I mean, any great and decided amelioration of the condition of the lower classes of mankind, the most numerous, and, consequently, in a general view of the subject, the most important of the human race.[23]

This was the "melancholy hue" for which Malthus apologized—not that men would never attain the near-divine state which had always been the stuff of fantasy, but that they would never enjoy the improvement Smith had held out for them, that, on the contrary, the lower classes, the "most important part of the human race," were doomed to misery and vice.

If Malthus devoted so large a part of the *Essay* to Godwin and Condorcet—half a dozen chapters, better than one-third of the book—it was perhaps because they were easy targets. To take on so formidable a figure as Smith was no small matter; one can sympathize with Malthus for backing into his argument by way of the utopians, for smuggling in his criticism of Smith's modest vision of progress in the guise of an attack on Godwin's outlandish theory of perfectibility. Finally, however, Malthus did confront the real issue. Warily and respectfully, at the very end of his last chapter on Godwin he broached the subject: "I cannot avoid venturing a few remarks on a part of Dr. Adam Smith's *Wealth of Nations,* speaking at the same time with that diffidence which I ought certainly to feel in differing from a person so justly celebrated in the political world."[24]

In the following chapter Malthus proceeded (without undue diffidence) to take issue with Smith, and on a matter that went to the heart of Smith's philosophy: the idea that an increase in the wealth of the nation would result in an increase in "the happiness and comfort of the lower orders of society." It was this proposition that Malthus disputed. Manufacturing, he granted, abetted by the division of labor, did produce greater productivity and wealth, but this form of economic activity was least conducive to the well-being of the lower classes. Increased productivity in manufacturing led to an increase both of the wages of labor and of the number of laborers, and this without any commensurate increase in the food supply; indeed, to the extent to which laborers were enticed away from agriculture into manufacturing, the food supply actually diminished. So far from enjoying a greater command over the "necessaries and conveniences of life," the lower classes would actually have less by way of food and still less of other goods required for health, comfort, and happiness.[25]

On the relative merits of agriculture and manufacturing, Malthus openly sided with the French physiocrats, going so far as to suggest that manufacturing labor was "unproductive" compared with agricultural labor. Even short of that theoretical proposition, he had no doubt that in practice the lower classes were better served by a predominantly agricultural economy than a predominantly industrial one. In the former, "the poor would live in great plenty, and population would rapidly increase," the increase of population being consonant with the increase of subsistence; in the latter, "the poor would be comparatively but little benefitted and consequently population would increase slowly."[26] A manufacturing economy, in short, however favorable to the wealth of the nation as a whole, was inimical to the well-being of the lower classes, who were most at the mercy of the principle of population.

It is curious that at no point, not even while taking issue with the fundamental thesis of the *Wealth of Nations,* did Malthus allude to Smith's views on the subject of population. In the *Wealth of Nations* Smith had stated, as if beyond dispute, that "the most decisive mark of the prosperity of any country is the increase of the number of its inhabitants."[27] This sounds like the familiar mercantilist doctrine, except that Smith made the increase of population a symptom, or "mark," of wealth rather than a cause. Yet in a sense it was, even for him, a cause. The two conditions he posited for a "progressive state" were an increase of wages and an increase of population. Without a growing population to provide a larger body of consumers as well as laborers, high wages would lead to lower profits, a decline in investment, and the onset of a "stationary state." He briefly considered the possibility that a country might be "fully peopled in proportion to what either its territory could maintain or its stock employ," but was confident that no country had ever yet arrived at that condition. China, to be sure, was a stationary state, having reached a "full complement of riches" consistent with its laws and institutions; but other laws and institutions might have permitted it to exploit its resources differently, thus postponing that stationary condition.[28] Although Smith did not pursue this point, it is evident that (like Godwin and Condorcet) he projected the contingency of a "fully peopled" country to some remote future. In any event he was satisfied that the England of his own time and of the foreseeable future was enjoying and would continue to enjoy the growth of population that was the mark of the progressive state.

While Malthus did not mention Smith's views on population, he did discuss, in the chapter on Smith, the contrary views of Richard Price. In an argument with Frederick Eden, who had defended Smith's position, Price had asserted that while the population of other countries had increased, that of England had declined. This was a not uncommon opinion at the time. What was startling was Price's estimate of the extent of the decline—30 percent since the English Revolution, which would have brought the population down to 5,000,000 by 1780. This finding was disputed by Eden, Arthur Young, John Howlett, and others, who claimed that the population had risen during the whole of this period and most of all in recent years. (Howlett's estimate was almost the reverse of Price's; he had the population increasing by one-third since the revolution and one-sixth in the last decades alone.) Although Smith did not publicly intervene in this debate, his views were well known. He provided Eden with statistics bearing out his case, predicted that Price's theory would fall into the neglect it deserved, and described Price, with an acerbity that was not typical of him, as a "factious citizen, a most superficial philosopher, and by no means an able calculator."[29]

As a philosopher in the tradition of the *philosophes,* a believer in natural rights and universal reason, an admirer of the French Revolution, and something of a utopian (although not on the grand scale of Godwin), Price should have been no more congenial to Malthus than he was to Smith. At one point Malthus rebuked him for suggesting that if only people were allowed to lead lives that were entirely "natural and virtuous," there would be no disease, pain, or distemper, and "death would come upon them like a sleep, in consequence of no other cause than gradual and unavoidable decay."[30] In spite of such fantasies, Malthus professed to be more in agreement with Price than with his critics. Even if the population had not actually declined, as Price had claimed, Malthus insisted that the increase could only have been small and slow. (In later editions of the *Essay,* published after the census of 1801 and the subsequent censuses, he conceded the rise of population.)

It is ironic to find the author of the most celebrated work on population, the source of all later "Malthusian" alarms about a "population explosion," so egregiously wrong about the demographic situation in his own time. Knowing what we now do (and what some contemporaries suspected at the time) about the unprecedented increase of population in England in the latter half of the eighteenth century, we might assume that Malthus's *Essay* was a response to that situation, that he was moved to formulate a principle of population, and to put that principle at the center of his social theory, because he was impressed by the gravity of the problem confronting

England. The truth is quite the opposite. So far from appreciating what was actually happening at the time, he vigorously disputed the views of those who had a more accurate sense of the situation.

The paradox is understandable if Malthus's theory is taken to be not about population but about progress. If his main concern was to challenge Smith's predictions about the improvement of the laboring classes in an industrial society, he had to deny the increase of population which Smith (and most contemporaries) took to be one of the symptoms of improvement. By the same token, it was essential to his own theory that there be no long-term increase of population (except in an underdeveloped society such as the American colonies), since the population was always being kept down to the level of the food supply. Indeed, the very idea of a "population explosion" is incompatible with Malthusianism: long before such an explosion could have built up, population would have been reduced by one or another of the checks. Godwin himself fell into this common error when he said that the author of the *American Gazetteer,* "proceeding on the principles of Malthus," predicted that in a century the population of New York City would be 5,257,493. "Does anyone," Godwin jeered, "for himself or his posterity, expect to see this reached?"[31] Malthus certainly did not, any more than Godwin did (although Godwin could foresee an end to sickness, death, and procreation). But Smith, with his views of an expanding, "progressive" economy, could well have anticipated such an increase of population—which in fact took place in almost exactly the period of time predicted by the *Gazetteer.*

The distance between Malthus and Smith may be measured by their differences on social policy as well as theory. Where Smith criticized the corn laws and tacitly approved of the poor laws, Malthus reversed those positions, defending the corn laws and bitterly attacking the poor laws. The rationale for the corn laws was made explicit only in the second edition, although it was implied in the first. The attack on the poor laws, however, was overt and unequivocal; indeed it was so prominent that it has been taken as the primary purpose of the *Essay.*

The poor laws, Malthus conceded, had been devised with the best of intentions: they were meant to mitigate the natural checks on population and alleviate the misery of the poor. The effect, however, was just the opposite—to depress the condition of the poor by encouraging them to marry and have children with little or no prospect of support. The increase of population without any increase in the means of subsistence meant that the available food had to be divided among a larger number of people, thus reducing the share of each person and driving more and more laborers to the parish for support. In this sense the poor laws might be said to "create the poor which they maintain." They also had the unfortunate effect of diverting resources from the "more industrious and more worthy members" of society to the least industrious and least worthy. Every attempt to improve conditions in the workhouses or to increase outdoor relief depressed the conditions of the independent poor by raising the price of food. The dependent poor were thus the "enemy" of the entire class of poor.

> If men are induced to marry from a prospect of parish provision, with little or no chance of maintaining their families in independence, they are not only unjustly tempted to bring unhappiness and dependence upon themselves and their children, but are tempted, without knowing it, to injure all in the same class with themselves. A labourer who marries without being able to support a family may in some respects be considered as an enemy to all his fellow-labourers.[32]

Malthus's case against the poor laws consisted of equal parts of economics and morality: every member of the lower orders was adversely affected by the poor laws, and the most deserving poor, the independent poor, were most grievously affected. The moral cast of the argument—the encouragement of "carelessness and want of frugality," the weakening of "sobriety and industry," the incitement to "drunkenness and dissipation"— seemed to taint all the poor, independent and dependent alike. Yet this was not Malthus's intention. If he deplored the demoralizing effects of the laws, it was to plead the cause of those poor who refused the enticements of relief. "Fortunately for England, a spirit of independence still remains among the peasantry." The poor laws tended to subvert that spirit but had not yet entirely succeeded in doing so, which was why their "pernicious tendency" had been so long concealed.[33] He also objected to the poor laws for the same reason Smith had objected to the law of settlement, because they were an infringement on liberty—the liberty of those actually receiving relief as well as of the entire body of the poor. "The whole class of the common people of England is subjected to a set of grating, inconvenient, and tyrannical laws, totally inconsistent with the genuine spirit of the constitution." Like Smith he found the laws of settlement "utterly contradictory to all ideas of freedom," a "most disgraceful and disgusting tyranny."[34] But he went beyond Smith in condemning all the poor laws on the same grounds, as subversive of liberty, morality, and a sound economy.

In contrast to Pitt, who had proclaimed relief "a matter of right and an honour," Malthus put forward the principle that "dependent poverty ought to be held disgraceful."[35] And in contrast to Pitt's poor bill, he recommended the total abolition of all parish poor laws. The only concession he made was in cases of "extreme hardship," for which purpose he proposed to establish county workhouses financed by a national poor rate and open to anyone in the entire country. The fare in the house was to be "hard," and those who were able to work should be obliged to do so; in fact, part of the workhouse was to be set aside for those seeking a day's work at the prevailing market price. To increase the supply of food he suggested offering premiums for turning up fresh land, repealing those laws (of apprenticeship, for example) which tended to lower agricultural wages relative to wages in industry or commerce, and strengthening other laws (the corn laws) which directed more capital to the land. These proposals, however, were "palliative," and "palliatives are all that the nature of the case will admit." They might increase the quantity of happiness among the common people, but they could not prevent the recurrence of misery, which was "beyond the powers of man."³⁶ The checks on population would continue to operate as they always had and would continue to produce, for the mass of mankind, misery and vice.

This, finally, was Malthus's quarrel with Smith as much as with Godwin. By his standards they were both utopian. Compared with their expectations, his own were "most disheartening."³⁷ There was no complacency in his tone, only the sad conviction that to conceal the truth would be to invite even worse mischief. This melancholic message was all the more striking by contrast to the exhilarating vision that had inspired the *philosophes.* Malthus himself invited that contrast when he opened his *Essay* by recalling the bright hope of the Enlightenment: the great scientific discoveries, the diffusion of knowledge, the sense of free inquiry, the dazzling phenomenon of the French Revolution descending upon earth like a "blazing comet," all of which induced the belief that "we were touching on a period big with the most important changes, changes that would in some measures be decisive of the future fate of mankind."³⁸ The idea of perfectibility developed naturally in this climate of opinion. It was Malthus's unhappy task to expose that utopian dream by forcing men to confront the harsh reality of the truth, and, by confronting it, to avoid an even greater tragedy, the tragedy of Sisyphus.

> If we proceed without a thorough knowledge and accurate comprehension of the nature, extent, and magnitude of the difficulties we have to encounter, or if we unwisely direct our efforts towards an object, in which we cannot hope for success, we shall not only exhaust our strength in fruitless exertions and remain at as great a distance as ever from the summit of our wishes, but we shall be perpetually crushed by the recoil of this rock of Sisyphus.³⁹

· · ·

That, at any rate, was the Malthus of the first edition. In the preface he explained that the *Essay* would have been more complete had he included more facts in support of his argument, but he had been unable to do so owing to the pressure of time and other affairs. Five years later he published a second edition which was no longer an anonymous short essay but a signed, 600-page, guinea-and-a-half tome. Most of the new material consisted of accounts of primitive, ancient, and modern societies illustrating the operation of the principle of population. Occupying less space but far more significant was a revision of the thesis itself, a revision so substantial as to warrant a new title. The first edition was called *An Essay on the Principle of Population, as it affects the Future Improvement of Society, with Remarks on the Speculations of Mr. Godwin, M. Condorcet, and other Writers.* The title of the second (and all subsequent editions) was *An Essay on the Principle of Population, or, A View of its Past and Present Effects on Human Happiness; with an Inquiry into our Prospects Respecting the Future Removal or Mitigation of the Evils which it Occasions.*

In the preface to the new edition, Malthus prepared his readers for the change. It differed "in principle" from the first essay by introducing "another check to population which does not come under the head either of vice or misery." Although this had the effect of softening some of the "harshest conclusions" of the first edition, the principle of population itself remained "incontrovertible." To some readers, he predicted, the new check would make no difference at all. "To those who still think that any check to population whatever would be worse than the evils which it would relieve, the conclusions of the former Essay will remain in full force; and if we adopt this opinion we shall be compelled to acknowledge, that the poverty and misery which prevailed among the lower classes of society are absolutely irremediable."[40]

The new "check" may have been suggested by Godwin himself. Shortly after the appearance of the first edition Godwin wrote to Malthus criticizing his theory on the ground that "prudence" would act as a check on population, thus making possible the eventual perfectibility of man and society. Malthus's response at this time (only a few months after the publication of the *Essay*) was not to deny the effectiveness of prudence as a check or even to claim (as he did in the *Essay* itself) that prudence was itself conducive to misery and vice, but rather to argue that it undermined Godwin's own thesis. It would make for competition and thus inequality; it would destroy the incentive for labor and production and thus reduce the food supply; and, by placing responsibility upon the conduct of individuals, it belied Godwin's claim that public institutions were to blame for the sad state of society. Unpersuaded, Godwin restated his case in a pamphlet published in 1801, arguing that the crucial check on population, "whether virtue, prudence, or pride," was already in operation in England, and if it was not as powerful as it might be among the lower classes, this was because they were too wretched to be moved by the higher sentiments. In a just and equal society such as he was proposing, they would be more inclined to submit to the "most obvious rules of prudence."[41]

Whether in response to Godwin or to other critics who had raised the same objection, Malthus amended the edition of 1803 to take account of this check. The name he gave it, to distinguish it from the "prudence" (or "prudential restraint") that figured in his first edition, was "moral restraint." "Prudential restraint" signified a delay in marriage associated with promiscuity or some other form of misery or vice. "Moral restraint" was a delay in marriage not accompanied by "irregular gratifications," and therefore not "resolvable" into misery and vice.* Thus the earlier litany, "misery and vice," gave way to the new trinity, "moral restraint, misery, and vice." Even a careful reader of the *Essay* might be forgiven for not fully appreciating the significance of the difference between "prudential" and "moral" restraint. It was not until the third edition that Malthus clarified the distinction, and then only in a footnote.

> It will be observed that I here use the term *moral* in its most confined sense. By moral restraint I would be understood to mean a restraint from marriage from prudential motives, with a conduct strictly moral during the period of this restraint; and I have never intentionally deviated from this sense. When I have wished to consider the restraint from marriage unconnected with its consequences, I have either called it prudential restraint, or a part of the preventive check, of which indeed it forms the principal branch.[45]

That a distinction so crucial to his argument should have been introduced so belatedly and casually—and applied so inconsistently, as will be

---

*The restraint that is now known as "birth control" comes under Malthus's category of "prudential restraint"—in his view, very decidedly a form of vice. In the first edition he had professed "not to understand" Condorcet's suggestion that in the future, when the "ridiculous prejudices of superstition would . . . have ceased to throw over morals a corrupt and degrading austerity," the problem of population would be solved either by a "promiscuous concubinage" which would prevent breeding, or by "something else as unnatural." To remove the difficulty this way, Malthus protested, was to destroy the "virtue and purity of manners" that was the main purpose of Condorcet's system.[42] When one of his critics accused him of recommending the "restraints prescribed by Condorcet," Malthus hotly denied it.

> I have never adverted to the check suggested by Condorcet without the most marked disapprobation. Indeed I should always particularly reprobate any artificial and unnatural modes of checking population, both on account of their immorality and their tendency to remove a necessary stimulus to industry. If it were possible for each married couple to limit by a wish the number of their children, there is certainly reason to fear that the indolence of the human race would be very greatly increased, and that neither the population of individual countries nor of the whole earth would ever reach its natural and proper extent.[43]

In the 1820s this "artificial and unnatural" mode of restraint was publicized and recommended as a solution to the Malthusian problem by a group of radicals that included Richard Carlile, Francis Place, and John Stuart Mill. In the 1860s birth control came to be known as "Malthusianism," and later in the century it acquired the more accurate label "Neo-Malthusianism."[44]

seen—suggests Malthus's own uncertainty about the practical import of the new check, its actual and potential effectiveness. In the same footnote in which he finally clarified the distinction, he responded to the charge of having underestimated the influence of moral restraint in curbing population. Much as he would like to be mistaken, he feared that if moral restraint was understood in the "confined sense" of that term, the only truly moral sense, his judgment had been right. Later in the *Essay* he repeated his belief that moral restraint "does not at present prevail much among the male part of society." It was more prevalent, to be sure, in modern Europe than in primitive societies, and among women rather than men. The main check, however, continued to be the prudential one, the delay in marriage "without reference to consequences"—that is, without moral constraints.[46]

If the distinction remained unclear, it was partly because in common parlance "moral restraint" and "prudential restraint" (or "prudence") were used interchangeably (as Malthus's own lapses testify), and partly because he himself wavered about the practical implications of moral restraint. Having earlier been frankly skeptical about it, he later gave it enough credence to warrant a more optimistic view of the "future improvement" of society in general and of the lower classes in particular. One chapter, suggestively titled "Of the Effects which would result to Society from the prevalence of Moral Restraint," reasoned that "prudential restraint" (here used, to compound the confusion, in the sense of moral restraint) would limit the supply of labor, raise wages, and permit even a large family to be maintained "with decency." Thus "all abject poverty" would be eliminated or confined to those "very few" who had fallen into misfortune through no fault of their own.[47]

This happy prospect was followed by some equally cheerful reflections on chastity, a virtue, Malthus now found, that was not a product of "artificial society" but was grounded in "nature and reason." So far from issuing in misery and vice, it had the most agreeable effects, encouraging a "more familiar and friendly intercourse" between the sexes, so that young people could get to know each better before marriage, discover kindred dispositions, and form lasting attachments. The period of "delayed gratification" would be especially beneficial to women, who need no longer feel doomed to spinsterhood at the ripe age of twenty-five, and could look forward to a late and happy marriage. For both sexes the delay would heighten the pleasures of eventual gratification.

> The passion, instead of being extinguished, as it now too frequently is, by early sensuality, would only be repressed for a time, that it might afterwards burn with a brighter, purer, and steadier flame; and the happiness of the married state, instead of only affording the means of immediate

indulgence, would be looked forward to as the prize of industry and
virtue, and the reward of a genuine and constant attachment.[48]

Nothing more dramatically revealed the difference between the two
editions than the discussion of Christianity with which this chapter concluded. Where the first edition took two entire chapters (of a much shorter
essay) to work out a theodicy in which misery and vice were seen as part
of the providential order, the revised edition required only a few paragraphs
to justify the lesser degree of misery and vice which now seemed to be the
fate of mankind. Since each individual had it in his own power to avoid
the evil consequences of the principle of population by practicing a virtue
enjoined upon him by nature, reason, and religion alike, there was no reason
to impugn the justice or benevolence of God merely because He rewarded
those who exercised that virtue and punished those who did not. Moral
restraint thus emerged as the instrument not only of man's salvation but also
of God's justification.[49]

These, however, were "the effects which would result to society from
the prevalence of moral restraint"—the operative word being "would."[50]
In the very next chapter, indeed on the very next page, Malthus confessed
that he had little hope that moral restraint would in fact prevail to the extent
necessary to have these salutary effects. "Few of my readers can be less
sanguine than I am in their expectations of any sudden and great change in
the general conduct of man on this subject." Even after this warning against
excessive optimism, he went on to draw a picture of human nature, and
especially of the lower classes, that was far more optimistic than anything
he had allowed himself in the first edition. In entertaining the theoretical
possibility of a virtuous society, he explained, he was not being "visionary"
in the manner of a Godwin or Condorcet. His ideal society required no
radical alteration of human nature. On the contrary, it depended only on
the pursuit by each individual of his own "interest and happiness." At this
point his argument recalls Smith's "invisible hand."

> The happiness of the whole is to be the result of the happiness of
> individuals, and to begin first with them. No cooperation is required.
> Every step tells. He who performs his duty faithfully will reap the full
> fruits of it, whatever may be the number of others who fail. This duty
> is intelligible to the humblest capacity. It is merely that he is not to
> bring beings into the world for whom he cannot find the means of
> support.[51]

· · ·

Implicit in this argument was a democratic as well as a beneficent view of
human nature. The duty of every individual was identical, it was "intelli-

gible to the humblest capacity," and it was within the means of the humblest person. In the first edition "man as he really is" was the product of "original sin": "inert, sluggish, and averse from labour," sunk in "torpor and corruption," capable of being roused to "sentient activity" only by dire physical necessity.[52] In the revised edition there was no such "original sin," no such primitive, lumpish man. The two postulates of food and sex remained as the basic biological drives, but they were now less exigent since they could be restrained by the morality and reason that were also part of human nature. "The preventive check, as far as it is voluntary, is peculiar to man, and arises from that distinctive superiority in his reasoning faculties which enables him to calculate distant consequences." Because man was rational, he was capable of making that calculation, and because he was moral, he was capable of acting on it, of making those "sacrifices of temporary to permanent gratification, which it is the business of a moral agent continually to make."[53]

This newly acquired rationality and morality also brought with it a new freedom. What gave the first edition its "melancholy hue" was its determinism, the "inevitable laws of our nature" that condemned the entire class of the poor to a life of misery and vice regardless of any individual's will and efforts, that caused the industrious poor to suffer as a result of the improvidence of others, and that made every man who married imprudently the "enemy to all his fellow-labourers."[54] In the revised edition, the laws of human nature were less inevitable and the principle of population less inexorable. The principle of population now worked selectively, punishing the improvident and rewarding the provident. "He who performs his duty faithfully will reap the full fruits of it, whatever may be the number of others who fail." All that was necessary was that the poor understand that "they are themselves the cause of their poverty; that the means of redress are in their own hands and in the hands of no other persons whatever." The "moral agent" was a free and responsible individual, the master of his own fate.[55]

This elevated view of human nature made for a new conception of poverty and a new image of the poor. It was no longer torpid, corrupt, inert man who had to be roused to work by extreme poverty, the need to satisfy his most primitive needs; instead, it was precisely in that primitive state that the impulse to work was minimal. The most effective incentive came not from extreme poverty but from the desire for improvement. "It is the hope of bettering our condition, and the fear of want, rather than want itself, that is the best stimulus to industry; and its most constant and best efforts will almost invariably be found among a class of people above the class of the wretchedly poor."[56] Malthus could now "venture to indulge a hope," as he tentatively put it, that in the future "the processes for abridging labour, the progress of which has of late been so rapid, might ultimately supply all the wants of the most wealthy society with less personal effort than at present."* The result of technological progress would be to diminish either the severity of the individual's work or the number of those employed in severe toil, thus reducing the size of the lowest classes and enhancing the prospects for happiness for individuals and for society as a whole.

> If the lowest classes of society were thus diminished, and the middle classes increased, each labourer might indulge a more rational hope of rising by diligence and exertion into a better station; the rewards of industry and virtue would be increased in number; the lottery of human society would appear to consist of fewer blanks and more prizes; and the sum of social happiness would be evidently augmented.[60]

This passage is dramatic enough in itself. But it is even more striking in contrast to the "lottery of life" passage in the first edition, where a far larger part of the population was depicted as having drawn a "blank" in that lottery. It is also strikingly different from the oak metaphor in the first edition, where the "roots" or "extreme parts"—the lower classes—were seen as vital to the tree as a whole and could not be significantly diminished without impairing the flow of sap through the "middle parts."[61]

To win the prizes available in this lottery of life, the lower classes would have to learn to exercise moral restraint. If until now they had not done so, if they had not understood that they themselves were the "cause of their own poverty" and that the "means of redress" were in their own hands, it was because the rest of society had unwittingly kept them in ignorance.

*This favorable allusion to the division of labor suggests a modification of his views about industry and agriculture. While the revised editions muted or eliminated some of his earlier remarks about the "unproductive" nature of manufacturing, and conceded (out of deference to the census) that industrial growth was evidently compatible with the growth of population, these concessions were grudging and qualified. Sometimes Malthus implied that industrial workers might be better clothed and lodged but not better fed than agricultural laborers; sometimes that they might be better fed but that their happiness depended upon "conveniences and even luxuries" which they did not have; sometimes that they might enjoy more conveniences but that the conditions of work were less healthy. In one footnote he acknowledged that the "interference of the legislature"—a reference to the Factory Act of 1819—had resulted in a considerable improvement in the conditions of children.[57]

This ambivalence carried over into his other writings. In 1814, in a pamphlet on the corn laws, Malthus presented a largely favorable picture of the effects of manufacturing on the "general state of society." The very next year, however, he argued that the movement of wealth and population from country to town would be "slow, painful, and unfavorable to happiness."[58] Some commentators have found his *Principles of Political Economy* strikingly at variance with the *Essay*. As his contemporary, the French economist Jean-Baptiste Say, remarked: "Either the Author of the *Essay on Population* or the Author of the *Principles of Political Economy* must be wrong."[59] Say himself preferred the author of the *Essay*.

"Almost everything that has hitherto been done for the poor has tended, as if with solicitous care, to throw a veil of obscurity over this subject, and to hide from them the true causes of their poverty."[62] The worst thing that had been done for them, and to them, was the institution of the poor laws. Here Malthus repeated the arguments of the first edition, including the statement that the chief victims of the poor laws were not the "lowest classes," the recipients of relief, but those just above them. And here he came into contradiction with that part of the revised essay which held that "he who performs his duty faithfully will reap the full fruits of it, whatever may be the number of others who fail."[63] The idea of moral restraint had seemed to rescue the poor from the determinism which made them all the indiscriminate victims of the principle of population, of circumstances over which they had no control. Yet they were now thrust back into that fatalistic world, deprived of the prizes that had been promised them in the lottery of life. Malthus did not confront this contradiction, or others which arose from the addition of the new check.

The new edition did, however, modify the proposal for the abolition of the poor laws by providing a brief period of transition. A law declaring any child born within a year or two ineligible for relief would give the population due notice of the impending abolition. This would be more humane than any precipitous action and at the same time more forthright, since in setting a deadline for parish relief, the law would formally "disclaim the *right* of the poor to support," thus reaffirming the principle that "dependent poverty ought to be held disgraceful."[64] In this edition Malthus also raised the possibility of providing work for the unemployed on roads, bridges, railways, and canals. If the time should come when moral restraint was prevalent, he was even prepared to entertain the idea of allowances for each child in excess of five or six—not, he hastened to add, as a reward for large families, but only to alleviate a cause of distress that could not be entirely anticipated or controlled. The poor would also be helped by the retention of the corn laws, which he now defended as a necessary "exception" to the principle of free trade—"exception" being a disingenuous word to apply to the issue that Adam Smith had made a symbol of everything wrong in the protectionist system.[65]

On another subject Malthus was happy to concur with Smith: the need to educate the people. In the first edition, disputing Godwin's vision of rational man, Malthus argued that the lower classes would never be "sufficiently free from want and labour to obtain any high degree of intellectual improvement."[66] In the revised edition, having endowed them with the reason and virtue that would permit them to exercise moral restraint, he enthusiastically endorsed Smith's proposal for a state-supported system of education. In one respect he went further than Smith; in addition to the usual subjects of instruction, he wanted the poor to be taught the basic principles of political economy, including the principle of population that was so vital to their well-being.* Rejecting the "illiberal" argument that education did not come within the province of government (an argument Godwin had made in *Political Justice*), Malthus declared it a national disgrace that so much money should be spent in ways that aggravated the misery of the poor and so little in ways that might genuinely help them.[68]

The case for education suggested a still more radical proposal. If government had the power and duty to educate the lower classes, it also had the power and duty to give them the "respectability and importance" that came from "equal laws, and the possession of some influence in the framing of them." Malthus made a point of distinguishing his position from the familiar utilitarian one (held by Bentham at the time) that the only reason for giving the people a larger share in the government was to ensure better laws. His own view was that participation in the making of laws, even more than the laws themselves, was important in giving the poor "a greater personal respectability, and a greater fear of personal degradation"—the prerequisites for self-improvement.[69]

The principle underlying all these policies was the same: to raise the condition of the lower classes by providing them with "liberty, security of property, the diffusion of knowledge, and a taste for the convenience and comforts of life."[70] This was not to say that all men could ever be made equal, or even that all of the lower orders could be assimilated into those "middle parts" of society which were assumed to be the most virtuous, industrious, and talented. Differences of rank were necessary to inspire that "animated activity" which came with the hope of rising in society and the fear of falling. But the relative sizes of those ranks could change, and here Malthus found cause for optimism. "Our best-grounded expectations of an increase in the happiness of the mass of human society are founded in the prospect of an increase in the relative proportions of the middle parts."[71]

By the end of the revised *Essay* Malthus was able to see a ray of light in the future. It was hardly a dazzling beacon, nothing like the brilliant radiance cast by Godwin, Condorcet, or the *philosophes,* but something like the mellow glow imparted by Smith.

> On the whole, therefore, though our future prospects respecting the mitigation of the evils arising from the principle of population may not be so bright as we could wish, yet they are far from being entirely disheartening, and by no means preclude that gradual and progressive

*The idea of teaching the poor the principles of political economy was later taken up by the poor-law reformers, who wanted to persuade the poor that the New Poor Law was in their best interests. This was the purpose of many of the tracts distributed by the Society for the Diffusion of Useful Knowledge and of the "tales" written by Harriet Martineau. It is interesting to find political economists otherwise committed to laissez faire agreeing on the need for a public system of education.[67]

improvement in human society which, before the late wild speculations on this subject, was the subject of rational speculations.[72]

Hedged in by a string of negatives and qualifiers, this conclusion was an oblique, equivocal, tentative admission that Smith may have been, after all, correct.

Yet the popular impression of the *Essay* was quite otherwise. It is as if the gloom of the first edition had cast a permanent shadow upon the work which could not be dispelled even by the glad tidings of moral restraint. Malthus himself, even while delivering those tidings, was unable to throw off the "melancholy" induced by the law of population. The revision of his thesis was only partial and hypothetical. Moral restraint was an addendum to misery and vice; it supplemented but did not supersede them. And it supplemented them not in the present but in some remote and problematic future. As Godwin and Condorcet (and Smith as well) put off the problem of population to some distant time, so Malthus, even in the revised edition, put off the solution of that problem—moral restraint—to the future.

If one can cull from the revised edition a series of quotations which give it a decidedly optimistic coloration, one can also cite all those other passages which reproduce the pessimistic message of the first edition, often in the very words of that edition. The most notorious passage, cited again and again by contemporaries as evidence of Malthus's heartlessness, appeared only in the second edition. This was the parable of "nature's feast," as it was ironically called.

> A man who is born into a world already possessed, if he cannot get subsistence from his parents on whom he has a just demand, and if the society do not want his labour, has no claim of *right* to the smallest portion of food, and, in fact, has no business to be where he is. At nature's mighty feast there is no vacant cover for him. She tells him to be gone, and will quickly execute her own orders, if he does not work upon the compassion of some of her guests. If these guests get up and make room for him, other intruders immediately appear demanding the same favour. The report of a provision for all that come, fills the hall with numerous claimants. The order and harmony of the feast is disturbed, the plenty that before reigned is changed into scarcity and the happiness of the guests is destroyed by the spectacle of misery and dependence in every part of the hall, and by the clamorous importunity of those, who are justly enraged at not finding the provision which they had been taught to expect. The guests learn too late their error, in counteracting those strict orders to all intruders, issued by the great mistress of the feast, who, wishing that all her guests should have

plenty, and knowing that she could not provide for unlimited numbers, humanely refused to admit fresh comers when her table was already full.[73]

Playing with the metaphor of the "feast," Robert Southey described it as so disgusting that it could be stomached only by those with an "appetite, like the Hottentots, for garbage."[74] Although Malthus hastened to remove this passage from subsequent editions (and called attention to the deletion in the "advertisement" to the third edition), it continued to be quoted against him. If it nevertheless persisted, in impression if not in fact, it was because there was so much else in the revised edition to reinforce that impression. Almost every hopeful comment was followed by a note of caution, from the caveat in the preface that in spite of the new check the principle of population remained "incontrovertible" and "poverty and misery" continued to be an urgent problem, to the end of the volume, where Malthus ventured the "hope" of a "considerable degree of *possible* improvement" (the italics were his), but reminded his readers that he himself was "very cautious" in his expectations of "probable improvement."[75]

In view of these reservations, equivocations, and reaffirmations, it is little wonder that much of the criticism of the new edition was directed against the original thesis. Indeed, most of the critics seem to have read the revised edition as if it had been the first one. Even so sober a political economist as Nassau Senior (later a prime mover of the New Poor Law) confessed that he was responding more to the "popular opinion" of the *Essay* than to a literal reading of it when he charged Malthus with making misery and vice the principal checks on population and ignoring the desire of man to better his condition. This was in 1829, a quarter of a century after the revised edition had appeared (and after five other editions based on that revised one). Years later Senior remarked upon the fact, as if it had just come to his notice, that Malthus had evidently modified his thesis "in the course of his long and brilliant philosophical career."[76] But even the sixth edition of the *Essay,* Senior complained, left him with an overwhelming impression of the original thesis.*

The literary critics responded more passionately, and again to the original thesis. Coleridge's celebrated comments on the *Essay* were in the form of annotations of the second edition. Quite as if Malthus had never introduced the subject of moral restraint, Coleridge accused him of suggesting that "lust and hunger were alike passions of physical necessity, and the

---

*A recent biographer of Malthus deplores the attention paid to the first edition, as if, he protests, a scholar were to be judged by his master's thesis instead of by the work of his mature years.[77] But the "historic" Malthus, the Malthus who had the largest historical impact in his own time and for generations afterward, was the Malthus of the first edition, the edition which survived as an "oral tradition," so to speak, long after it had been superseded (though not entirely so) by the later editions.

one equally with the other, independent of the reason and the will." When Southey included these comments verbatim in his review of this edition of the *Essay,* he took cognizance of the revision, but with such contempt as to make the book seem utterly ridiculous as well as irredeemably vicious. Malthus, he said, had ended by confuting what he had set out to prove, thus perishing "by a stupid suicide, like the scorpion who strikes his tail into his own head."[78] So too Byron, Shelley, Hazlitt, Cobbett, Carlyle, Dickens, Disraeli, and scores of others, who made of Malthus, as his first major biographer said, the "best abused man of his age."[79] Ignoring the principle of moral restraint and the modification of the thesis to which that gave rise, or mentioning it only to say that Malthus himself ignored it, they accused him of calumniating man and God alike. He had bestialized man by making him a creature of lustful passion, and had maligned God by making Him the creator not only of that degraded species but of a universe so ill devised as to produce men and women faster than He could feed them. Engels, holding no brief for a benevolent or any other kind of God, denounced Malthusianism as "this vile, infamous theory, this revolting blasphemy against nature and mankind."[80]

Those who did refer to "moral restraint" spoke of it as cruel and coercive—an attempt to prohibit, by force or law, the most natural human function. Cobbett, confessing that he had in his life detested many men but none so heartily as Malthus, accused him of seeking an "act of parliament to prevent poor people from marrying young, and from having such lots of children."[81] Shelley decried the insolence that would compel the poor "to abstain from sexual intercourse, while the rich are to be permitted to add as many mouths to consume the products of the labours of the poor as they please."[82] This argument was often joined to a personal attack on the "Parson" (as the Reverend Malthus was derisively called) who wanted to deprive the poor of the natural satisfactions of marriage and children while himself indulging in these pleasures to an inordinate degree. One rumor was that he had eleven children, all daughters, as if this heightened the absurdity and hypocrisy of his position. (In fact he had two daughters and one son.)* Even when the uninhibited polemical style of the time is taken into account, the abuse heaped upon Malthus seems so excessive as to call for some special explanation. Perhaps it was the sexual provocativeness of his thesis, his boldness in speaking of sexual intercourse and making that as primary a need as food, that prompted comments which were almost obscene. Southey's remark to a friend, that Malthus was as great a favorite of the *British Critic* as of "other voiders of menstrual pollution," elicited

---

*Marx, on the other hand, said that Malthus had taken the "monastic vow of celibacy," in contrast to other Protestant ministers who had "shuffled off the command enjoining celibacy of the priesthood" and had contributed "to a really unbecoming extent" to the increase of population while preaching restraint to the poor.[83]

the reply that if the "cursed book" was true, its truth was so dangerous that "a man ought to be rather indicted for it than for a publication of the Grossest Obscenity."[84] (This last was from the otherwise staid civil servant and statistician who was responsible for the census of 1801.)

After three editions of the *Essay* had come and gone, William Hazlitt published a long, bitter attack on it. As if the idea of moral restraint had never been broached, he accused Malthus of regarding mankind, and the poor especially, as "so many animals *in season.*" Deriding compassion as weakness and elevating selfishness to the level of principle, Malthus made the poor a "defenceless mark" against which others could vent their malice with impunity. Like those who give a dog a bad name and hang him, he exacerbated the "natural stigma" under which the poor labored. His reputation, Hazlitt predicted, would "prove fatal to the poor of this country"; his name would be "suspended over their heads, *in terrorem,* like some baleful meteor."[85] Decades later the echoes of that impassioned indictment could be heard in the essays of Cobbett and Carlyle, whose talent for invective was as impressive as Hazlitt's, and in the novels of Dickens, whose irony was still more deadly. In one of Dickens's Christmas tales, an old man complained of the impending marriage of a young couple.

> Married! Married! The ignorance of the first principles of political economy on the part of these people. . . . A man may live to be as old as Methuselah, and may labour all his life for the benefit of such people as those; and may heap up facts on figures, facts on figures, facts on figures, mountains high and dry; and he can no more hope to persuade them that they have no right or business to be married, than he can hope to persuade 'em that they have no earthly right or business to be born. And *that* we know they haven't. We reduced it to mathematical certainty long ago.[86]

The issue became so acrimonious it was sometimes hard to know what was intended as irony and what was not. In 1838 two obscure tracts published under the pseudonym of "Marcus" proposed to solve the population problem by a systematic policy of infanticide. Reading like a parody of a parody, they might have been the work of a latter-day Swift. (More than a century earlier, Swift's *Modest Proposal,* suggesting that the infants of the poor be fattened up and served at the tables of the rich, had ostensibly been intended as an alternative to infanticide.) In fact the pamphlets were evidently written by a fanatical Malthusian, who proposed, in all seriousness, that every fourth child born to a poor family, and one-fourth of all third children (these to be chosen by lot), be gassed after birth. The project was to be overseen by an association created by Parliament, and the infants whose lives were to be so mercifully extinguished were to be buried in a park adorned with

colonnades and flowers, which would be closed and warmed in the winter
so that it might serve as a place of recreation and edification for all classes
—a veritable "infants' paradise." The pamphlets would have died in obscurity had they not been reproduced and widely distributed by the Chartists
under the title *The Book of Murder*. Attributed to the Poor Law Commissioners or their minions (the Chartist paper, the *Northern Liberator,* professed
to find in them the unmistakable style of Benthamism), they became one
of the set pieces in the anti–poor law campaign.[87]

If Malthus was the best-abused man of his time, he was also one of the most
influential. Hazlitt complained that he was "a sort of 'darling in the public
eye,' whom it was unsafe to meddle with."[88] Not unsafe, surely, in the
literary community, where attacks on Malthus were de rigueur. But the
virulence of those attacks testified to the critics' sense of frustration and
impotence, their realization that they were on the losing side in this great
battle of their generation.

    The point is not simply that Malthus made converts in high places:
among politicians (Pitt, Brougham, Mackintosh), economists (Ricardo,
McCulloch, both Mills), philosophers (Paley, Bentham), historians (Hallam,
Macaulay), and nameless and numerous journalists. (While *The Times* was
generally hostile, the radical *Westminster Review* and the Whig *Edinburgh
Review* were enthusiastic from the start, and even the Tory *Quarterly Review*
conceded, in 1817, that it was easier to "disbelieve Mr. Malthus than to refute
him.")[89] More important were the untold number of people who accepted
his thesis without making a public profession of it, sometimes without being
consciously aware of it. Even some of his bitterest critics found themselves
addressing the issue on his terms. Carlyle despised Malthusianism as much
as Benthamism and the rest of the materialistic, mechanistic "pig philosophy" of his time. But there was more than a suggestion of Malthusianism
in his own insistence that men must work if they would be fed, that idleness,
intemperance, and improvidence were the besetting sins of the lower classes,
and that the poor laws aggravated all these evils. Even Coleridge and
Southey were not immune to the virus, both of them at one time or another
denouncing relief to the idle in terms reminiscent of Malthus.

    This was the extraordinary achievement of Malthus: to have formu-
lated the terms of discourse on the subject of poverty for half a century—
and not only in respect to social policy (the debate over the poor laws, most
notably), but in the very conception of the problem. It was Malthus who
defined that problem, gave it a centrality it had not had before, made it
dramatically, urgently, insistently problematic. Whatever difficulties there
were in his theory, however faulty the logic or evidence, it gripped the

imagination of contemporaries, of all ranks, classes, callings, and persuasions, as few other books had ever done.

What was so gripping was the message of the first edition. "In its first form," Walter Bagehot later explained, "the *Essay on Population* was conclusive as an argument, only it was based on untrue facts; in its second form it was based on true facts, but it was inconclusive as an argument."[90] It was the argument, not the facts, that prevailed. And even the "untrue facts" gave weight to the argument. Critics derided the formula upon which the theory was supposedly based: the geometric increase of population and the arithmetic increase of food. John Stuart Mill, a staunch Malthusian, insisted that this unfortunate attempt to "give numerical precision to things which do not admit of it . . . is wholly superfluous to his argument."[91] But that numerical precision gave an authority, a mathematical exactitude and certitude to the theory which enhanced its appeal and was almost mesmerizing in its effect. A skeptical reader could reach for paper and pencil, perform the appropriate calculations, and find, as Malthus had predicted, that in two centuries the ratio of population to food would be 256 to 9, in three centuries 4,096 to 13, and so on to astronomical disproportions. Malthus's biographer explained the formula as the "natural liking of a Cambridge man for a mathematical simile."[92] But even university men did not always take it as a "simile." Another Cambridge man, Charles Darwin, rebuked one of Malthus's critics because, "mathematician though he may be, he cannot understand common reasoning."[93] And the Oxford historian Henry Hallam declared Malthus's thesis to be as "certain as the multiplication table."[94] Non-university men were even more likely to be impressed by the array of figures which were so indisputable and which added up to a problem of such enormity. Again, it was Bagehot who saw the force of that simple formula which gave credence to that simple theory. "He advertised his notions and fixed them among the men who understood a simple and striking exaggeration far more easily than a full and accurate truth. He created an entirely new feeling on his subject."[95]

That "new feeling" came as much from the image of the poor who constituted the social problem as from the magnitude of that problem. Malthus was accused of approving of all the checks which kept population to a tolerable limit—plagues, famines, wars, sickness, infanticide. Even those who were not inclined to blame the bearer of bad tidings, who were not even inclined to blame the subjects of those bad tidings, could not help but be repelled by the image of those doomed to such misery and vice. Nor was it only those at the lowest levels of society, on the margins of existence, who were so doomed. Malthus made it clear that all the poor shared, in some measure, the same fate. And not in the sense that some natural catastrophe or personal misfortune might cast anyone at any time into the nether depths.

Malthus's catastrophe was more pervasive and more imminent, so that even at the best of times the poor—all the poor—could only await the return of the pendulum which would bring with it the familiar saga of misery and vice. All the poor were implicated in the common disaster; all were injured by the improvidence of the few; all shared the ill effects of misguided policies; all suffered from the penury of nature which provided so little sustenance for so many mouths; all were subject to an unending, unrelenting "struggle for existence," a struggle fought with the desperation born of the knowledge that "death would be the punishment of defeat, and life the prize of victory."[96]

Later the "struggle for existence" was made memorable by Charles Darwin, who used it as the basis of his theory of "natural selection" and the "origin of species." Although Darwin himself was much criticized for that bleak view of nature and had to devise a theodicy not unlike Malthus's to justify a providence that countenanced such cruelty, he had the advantage of being able to appeal to the "grandeur" of evolution; by means of the struggle for existence, new and higher forms of life, including man, had evolved, and evolution itself was "progress towards perfection."[97] Malthus had no such justification. On the contrary, he denied the theory of evolution in exactly the same terms and for the same reasons that he denied the theories of progress and perfectibility.* When he used the idea of the struggle for existence, it was not to elevate man above the animal but, his critics complained, to reduce man to the level of the animal. And since the struggle

---

*It is ironic that Darwin should have been inspired by the *Essay* to develop the theory of evolution that later found expression in the *Origin of Species*. For one of the incidental themes of the *Essay* was a denial of the theory of evolution. When Malthus cited the experiences of plant and animal breeders, it was to disprove the theory of evolution as well as perfectibility. Although breeders, he argued, might succeed in producing sheep with small heads and small legs, they could never go beyond certain obvious limits; they could never produce a sheep with the head and legs of a rat; nor could any amount of cultivation produce a carnation the size of a large cabbage. In every case there was a "limit to improvement," a limit which belied the theory of perfectibility—and by the same token belied the theory of evolution.[98] (Malthus did not deny the evolution of variations *within* a species, but he did deny the evolution of species themselves, which was precisely the point of Darwin's theory.)

It is also ironic that in adopting Malthus's idea of the struggle for existence, Darwin unwittingly pointed up an important difficulty in Malthusianism. When Malthus enunciated the principle of population, he took it to apply to men but not to plants and animals: it was mankind that increased geometrically while the food supply (plants and animals) increased only arithmetically. Darwin described his own theory as "the doctrine of Malthus applied with manifold force to the whole animal and vegetable kingdoms; for in this case there can be no artificial increase of food, and no prudential restraint from marriage."[99] Thus plants and animals, even more than men, would increase geometrically if unchecked. Darwin himself did not realize that by applying Malthusianism "with manifold force" to animals and vegetables, he was removing the discrepancy between the rate of increase of man and that of the food supply which was the very basis of Malthusianism. Marx, however, saw this as soon as he read the *Origin*. "What amuses me in Darwin," he wrote to Engels, "is his assertion that he applied the theory of Malthus to plants and animals alike, whereas the whole joke in Malthus was that he applied the theory to men alone, with the geometrical progression, in opposition to plants and animals."[100]

for existence was most severe among the poor, it was they who were most debased and bestialized by it.

The Malthusian vision was all the more dismal by contrast not to the vision of perfectibility, about which most people had already become disenchanted, but to the modest prospect of progress which Smith had held out for the poor. Compared with Godwin, Malthus was sober and realistic; compared with Smith, he was grim and despairing. At one point Smith described a class with some of the stigmata of the Malthusian poor: a "lowest class" that was "overstocked," in imminent peril of starvation, suffering from "want, famine, and mortality." This, however, was the "lowest class," not the poor in general, and that class only in a "declining country"—Bengal or some parts of the East Indies, he specified.[101] When Malthus described the poor in similar terms, he was speaking not of the poor of India but of England. And not rural, "backward" England but precisely the most advanced industrial areas of the country, those areas which Smith regarded as in the most "progressive" state. And not the "lowest class" of the poor but the "lower classes"—all the poor.

Compared with Smith, Malthus represented not so much a lowering of expectations as a total reversal of expectations. In place of a pacific, benign society, in which an "invisible hand" ensured that individual interests would conduce to the common good and individual competition would produce social harmony, Malthus envisaged a struggle for existence that resembled nothing so much as Hobbes's "state of nature," with the poor condemned to a life that was "solitary, poor, nasty, brutish, and short." In place of an industrial economy cooperating with nature to bring about a "natural progress of opulence," he had nature and industry working at cross purposes, with industry creating more mouths to feed and nature providing less food to feed them. In place of a "progressive state" in which wages and population increased simultaneously, he postulated an inverse relationship between the two—an inverse relationship, in effect, between survival and natural passion, so that it was only by doing violence to themselves, by thwarting human nature, that the poor could exist.

In this Malthusian universe the poor were pitted not only against nature—their own nature as well as external nature—but also against society. This social struggle was even more bitter than the familiar class struggle since it took place primarily within their own class. The "enemy," Malthus implied, was themselves, their own kind, every poor child being another mouth to feed and eventually another body to work, thus driving up the price of food while forcing down the wages of labor. And everyone who tried to interfere with that struggle, however well intentioned, was also their enemy. Neither the good will of individuals nor the good offices of government could undo what nature had decreed; anything they did do would only make things worse. There was, to be sure, the one mitigating factor of moral restraint. But this was of dubious practical value, certainly in the present and probably in the future. In any case, this third check, belatedly introduced and ambivalently presented, was no match for the misery and vice produced by the principle of population, which remained, now as ever, "incontrovertible."

At any other time, Malthus's theory of population might have been just another theory to be debated by learned men in learned journals. At just this time, however, a time of acute distress and rapid change, it struck a chord that resounded and reverberated. Population became, in effect, the "objective correlative" of all the fears and misgivings of the generation, all the free-floating anxiety induced by uncertainty as much as by actual distress. If Malthus did not allay this anxiety—if in fact he intensified it—he did make sense of it. He told people what was happening to them, what they might expect, and what little they might do by way of alleviation. Once articulated, the theory acquired a momentum of its own. People began to worry about the principle of population as well as everything else they had to worry about, and they began to use it to give substance and credence to their other fears.

They also used the theory to give support and credibility to their interests. It might be said that Malthus prevailed over Smith in this critical early period of industrialism because Malthusianism was more congenial to early capitalism. It taught the poor, so this argument goes, that they were fated to remain poor and would be doing well if they managed not to become poorer than they were, that nature, not some malevolent employer, kept wages down, that poverty was a fact of life on the order of such other natural facts as food and sex, indeed, an inevitable consequence of those natural facts. It taught paternalistic, philanthropic employers that they too were bound by those natural laws, that any attempt on their part to interfere with them for the benefit of their employees would necessarily redound to the disadvantage of these workers, that true philanthropy and humanity consisted in keeping faith with nature. And, of course, it taught the government to stay out of the economic process, on the ground that wages, prices, hours, conditions of work, and all other economic factors should be determined the only way they could be naturally, efficiently, justly determined, by the free market, and that the main function of legislation was to pass such positive laws as would make the institutions of society congruent with natural laws.

Much of this rationale, however, could as well have been deduced from Smith's theory—and without stirring up the rancor that Malthus's did. Smith too predicated a free market for labor, while giving the working classes a stake in that market, making them, as well as their employers, the beneficiaries of the "system of natural liberty." He made poverty remediable, not by interfering with the operation of natural laws but by the natural expansion of the economy that was the inevitable result of the operation of those laws. Instead of pitting man against nature, labor against machine, class against class, worker against worker, he presumed an essential harmony of interests, in which everyone would benefit from the "natural progress of opulence."

What is curious about the history of this period is that the enemies of Malthusianism unwittingly contributed to its success. It was Coleridge and Southey, Cobbett and Carlyle, Chartists and radicals, who, in attacking Malthusianism, identified it with political economy per se. If one is to look for Machiavellian motives, one might find them here: in the fact that the critics of capitalism chose to present capitalism in its bleakest form, chose to interpret it in terms of a "dismal science" rather than a "moral philosophy." If political economy was de-moralized and de-socialized, it was they who helped do it by depriving political economy, and thus capitalism itself, of the moral and social roots Smith had given it—and by the same token, depriving the poor of the moral and social status Smith had given them.

James Bonar, Malthus's nineteenth century biographer, summed up the crucial difference between Malthus and Smith: "If Adam Smith had shown the power of labour as a cause of wealth, Malthus thought he had shown the power of poverty as a cause of labour."[102] For Smith the basic concept was labor, and the basic characteristic of the poor was that they were laborers. Since the primary function of labor was the creation of wealth, and since wealth itself increased in a free and progressive economy, the laboring poor would necessarily share in the wealth they created. Thus labor, the "cause of wealth," was also the source of redemption, the means by which the poor could ameliorate their poverty. For Malthus, on the other hand, the defining characteristic of the laborer was his poverty. It was poverty that was the "cause of labour," the precondition and sole motivation of labor. Without poverty the laborer would cease to labor. Hence poverty was the necessary and permanent condition of the laborer.

The distinction between "labour as a cause of wealth" and "poverty as a cause of labour" had its corollary in the distinction between relative and absolute poverty. For Smith, poverty was relative, a function of inequality. His progressive economy envisaged a continuum in which the very poor were drawn toward the poor and the less poor toward the "comfortable." As the individual's standard of living rose, so too did the standard itself. The idea of needs was as relative as the idea of poverty; "necessaries" included the goods "indispensably necessary for the support of life" as well as whatever social custom decreed to be "indecent for creditable people, even of the lowest order, to be without."[103] For Malthus, on the other hand, poverty signified not fewer of the goods of life but a want of the most essential goods, not what it was "indecent" to be without but what it was physically, biologically, impossible to be without. Nor was his poverty the intermittent kind that came from occasional misfortune; on the contrary, it was an endemic condition and a potentially fatal one. In his continuum the poor were always being pulled down toward the very poor, and the very poor toward the abyss of starvation and death. In the unrelenting struggle for existence that was the constant state of the poor, the stakes were nothing less than life and death—death the "punishment of defeat," life the "prize of victory."[104]

The economist John Maynard Keynes wrote, "If only Malthus, instead of Ricardo, had been the parent stem from which nineteenth-century economics proceeded, what a much wiser and richer place the world would be today!"[105] Keynes had in mind their respective works on political economy. The historian, sensible of the enormous impact of Malthusianism, the Malthus of the *Essay,* in this critical period of early industrialism, might be inclined to amend that statement: "If only Smith, instead of Malthus, had been the parent stem from which nineteenth-century social history proceeded, what a much wiser and richer place the world would be today!"

V

THE LEGACY

OF MALTHUSIANISM

If Malthusianism succeeded in de-moralizing political economy, and with it the image of the poor, it did not at all succeed in dulling the moral imagination or sensibility of contemporaries. On the contrary, to the extent to which they were deprived of a theory that was morally acceptable, a *Weltanschauung* that made moral sense of society and the economy, industry and commerce, poverty and wealth, their imagination and sensibility were given free rein. It is not too much to say that England in the first half of the nineteenth century was in a state of moral and intellectual turmoil, as some people tried to assimilate the message of Malthusianism, others frantically resisted it, and still others found themselves caught up in a mode of thought and feeling that seemed to be intellectually irresistible and morally repulsive.

It was in conjunction with Ricardianism that Malthusianism transformed political economy from a discipline rooted in moral philosophy to one that Carlyle baptized "the dismal science."[1] There were, to be sure, important differences between Malthus and Ricardo on such subjects as value, rent, and the "glut." These differences emerged most sharply in Ricardo's *Principles of Political Economy and Taxation* in 1817 and Malthus's *Principles of Political Economy* in 1820. By then, however, the *Essay on Population* had gone through five editions, establishing itself as one of the most famous—or infamous—works of the generation and inspiring a host of critiques and defenses, parodies and popularizations. It was the *Essay,* not the *Principles,* that defined Malthusianism in popular parlance. And it was in this sense that Ricardo was a Malthusian, the principle of population being as much an "iron law" in his schema as the principle of wages, and making him as much an opponent of the poor laws as Malthus himself. While Adam Smith continued to be quoted in Parliament and in the press, generally on issues of free trade and fiscal policy,[2] the voices of Malthus and Ricardo tended to dominate on those matters that directly and critically affected the poor: the implications of the principle of population for poor relief and wages, the effect of machinery in increasing unemployment and creating a "surplus" population, the inverse relationship between wages and profits, the incipient class struggle resulting from this conflict of interests, and above all the thoroughly pessimistic prospect induced by the principle of population and the idea of the "stationary state."* Even the powerful counter-currents generated by Malthusianism testified to the power of that doctrine, for they equated it with political economy per se, and made political economy the *fons et origo mali.*

The dramatic, even traumatic, effect of Malthusianism cannot be understood without appreciating the sheer intellectual force of that "simple and striking" thesis, as Bagehot put it. But neither can it be understood without reference to the extraordinary circumstances of the time. The doctrine itself suggests one of those circumstances: the rapid growth of population. While this played no part in the original inspiration of the *Essay* — Malthus himself first denied and then minimized the increase of population—and while it was not, strictly speaking, consonant with his theory (which assumed that population would always be kept in check), the findings of the census of 1801, and of the censuses of subsequent decades, gave credibility and prominence to any theory that made population a paramount fact of economic and social life.

An even more conspicuous fact of life were the poor rates, which grew at an even faster rate than population. In 1785 the cost of poor relief was just under £2,000,000, by 1803 it was over £4,000,000, and by 1817 almost £8,000,000—quadrupling in little more than three decades, and this without including the cost of private charity and philanthropy. The increase of the

---

*Some economists have minimized or even denied the conventional view of Ricardo as a "pessimist," by interpreting his stationary state as an analytic model rather than a description of reality, by making light of his theory that machinery was responsible for unemployment and thus for the creation of a "surplus" population, and by emphasizing one passage in the *Principles* which seemed to offer a happier prospect for the working classes:

> The friends of humanity cannot but wish that in all countries the labouring classes should have a taste for comforts and enjoyments, and that they should be stimulated by all legal means in their exertions to procure them. There cannot be a better security against a superabundant population. In those countries where the labouring classes have the fewest wants, and are contented with the cheapest food, the people are exposed to the greatest vicissitudes and miseries.[3]

But this passage was clearly hypothetical ("the friends of humanity cannot but wish . . ."); the stationary state was taken literally by contemporaries; and the chapter on machinery was widely quoted by radicals to support their case against machinery. However one may now interpret Ricardo, there is little doubt that in his own time and for generations thereafter his doctrine was regarded as "pessimistic," at least as far as the future of the working classes was concerned—which was why he was the favored economist of the socialists.[4]

poor rates naturally precipitated a growing demand for the abolition of the poor laws. The most persuasive of the early tracts on the subject, by the Nonconformist minister Joseph Townsend, was published anonymously in 1786. Townsend did not, however, base his case on the inexorable laws of physical and human nature. It remained for Malthus to do that, and the whole of the later debate was cast in Malthusian terms. Yet here too there were anomalies. Although the New Poor Law that was eventually enacted was popularly regarded as Malthusian, it provided for the reform rather than the abolition of the poor laws, and for reasons that were not strictly in accord with Malthusianism. But it was Malthus who brought the issue to the forefront of public consciousness, made it intellectually respectable (if also, his critics claimed, morally reprehensible), and gave it an urgency it had not had before.

More conspicuous, and more urgent still, were the social and economic conditions which made Malthusianism seem all too pertinent and prescient. The "dismal science" prevailed, one might say, because it conformed to the dismal realities of life in the first half of the nineteenth century. However one may qualify the idea of an agricultural or industrial "revolution," there can be no doubt of the enormity of the changes in the countryside and towns. There were fewer "deserted villages" than poets thought, but many depressed ones; fewer large cities by later standards, but many rapidly growing ones with all the problems they brought in their wake. It was not a majority of craftsmen and domestic workers but a substantial minority who languished in declining trades or were demoted to the status of factory "hands"; not an entire class of "sturdy yeomanry" that was annihilated but a good number of freeholders who were forced to become day laborers, cottagers, and even paupers. Just at this time, while the technological changes in industry and agriculture were causing a myriad of other changes in the economy and society, they were accelerated and aggravated by a number of "fortuitous" events: a series of bad harvests creating food shortages, high prices, and swollen relief rolls, and the Napoleonic Wars which disrupted trade, depressed industry, increased unemployment, and otherwise made a difficult situation even more difficult.

The impact of these changes on the poor has been a subject of much dispute. The "condition-of-England" or "condition-of-the-people" question, as it was then called—the "standard-of-living" question, as historians have come to know it—is generally discussed as if it were a question of industrialism alone, a measure of the social and economic costs and gains of mechanization and urbanization.[5] In fact, as contemporaries experienced it, and as it was reflected in prices and wages, production and consumption, living and working conditions, it was as much a product of such natural and political catastrophes as famine and war as of the industrial and agricultural revolutions. It was also the product of the "demographic revolution," which itself was partly a consequence of industrialism and partly a cause or "precondition" of it, and in either event a major factor in the condition-of-England question: the overcrowding of towns, the bad state of sanitation, the creation of a "surplus population," and the changing proportions of young and old which made for an unfavorable ratio of dependents to wage-earners.

If the condition-of-England question cannot be reduced to a calculus of the social benefits and social costs of industrialism, neither can benefits and costs be neatly demarcated as such. While some contemporaries regarded the greater availability and cheaper cost of cotton clothing, leather shoes, and tea as a boon to the poor, others were citing these very items as evidence of the degradation of the poor, the decline from the "good old days" when the poor wore woolen clothes and clogs and enjoyed the healthy, hearty drink of beer. Nor can benefits and costs, gains and losses, be added up to produce a single "bottom line" figure, or even, perhaps, entered on a single balance sheet. How can one speak of the "poor" or "working classes" in the aggregate when different groups were obviously affected in different ways, at different times, in different places, and under different conditions? How can one quantify and incorporate into a standard-of-living formula diverse factors of unequal weight and importance and, often, of contrary effect (the rising cost of rent and the declining cost of fuel, or regular low-paid work and irregular higher-paid work)? How can one add to these the different kinds of considerations involved in determining the "quality of life," the "amenities" and "disamenities" of different occupations and different modes of life? How can one measure the benefits accruing to the poor by public services and private agencies: hospitals, schools, sewers, street-lighting, police, charity, relief? How can one compare the psychological satisfaction of independence experienced by some young factory workers who took the first opportunity to leave their parents' homes, with the psychological deprivation of others torn from the bosom of their families—or the dissatisfaction of parents deprived of the company (and earnings) of their children? How can one offset the losses of one generation or one group by the gains of another? Or psychic losses by material gains? Or the same condition perceived as a loss by some and as a gain by others?

Even in its older, simpler form, involving calculations of prices and wages, physical conditions and material goods, the standard-of-living question is difficult enough, involving historians in still unresolved disputes about appropriate periods of time (base lines and terminal dates), the reliability and adequacy of the data, the interpretation of the data, and deductions and generalizations that can be summed up in terms of a rise or fall in "the" standard of living. For the most part, taking the whole of the period of early industrialism, from about 1780 to 1850, and taking the working classes in the aggregate and on an average, the "optimists" have had the better of the debate—which has obliged the "pessimists" to retreat to the "quality of life" argument. Often, however, both the optimists and the pessimists have applied standards that are not always pertinent to the contemporary experience of reality, and have ignored large aspects of the existential reality which do not fit into their formulations and calculations.

That reality included the phenomenon now known as "cultural lag," which in this case amounted to something like a cultural trauma. Just as the "Depression mentality" was to retain its hold long after the Great Depression of the 1930s had spent itself, so a century earlier the memory of the worst of times continued to haunt the working classes even after their conditions had actually improved. For some workers—the handloom weavers, most notably—the "worst of times" continued for the whole of their lives and sometimes the lives of their children.[6] Their plight cast a pall over the entire period and over all the working classes, overshadowing the very real improvement that could be measured in terms of averages and aggregates. Statistical data could not begin to compete with the graphic accounts of distress relayed by newspapers, parliamentary debates, Royal Commission and Select Committee reports, radical tracts, hortatory tales, sensationalist stories, and popular novels. These accounts, whether true or fictional, typical or untypical, were often perceived as real, and as such became incorporated into the contemporary reality.

The contemporary reality, then, was more pessimistic—more Malthusian—than the reality as historians may define and understand it. Historians, taking a longer, larger, more "objective" view of events, may find conditions improving. Contemporaries, more sensitive to dramatic instances of distress than to the undramatic, unheralded instances of relative comfort (to say nothing of the undramatic evidence of statistics, much of which did support the "optimistic" position), were inclined to take a grimmer view of things, a view which was more in accord with the grim vision of the "dismal science."

One aspect of the contemporary reality which lent itself to different interpretations, which some brave contemporaries responded to with confidence and a sense of exhilaration but which many more found ominous and fearsome, was the simple, overwhelming fact of change. Again there may be a disjunction between a historical understanding of the past and the contemporary experience of it. Historians properly dwell on the continuity that was as much a reality of the time as change.[7] But it was change that impressed itself more upon the consciousness of most contemporaries. And that sense of change was unnerving and disturbing, all the more so because there was no end in sight. Few changes are without cost, but even when the cost is minimal, temporary, or outweighed by the benefit, the anxiety generated by change, even a change for the better, is itself a considerable social cost.

Again the usual caveats are in order. The technological, economic, social, and geographical changes in this early period of industrialism were not as rapid or as thorough as may be thought. Until the middle of the century over a fifth of the population continued to be employed in agriculture and almost half continued to live in rural areas (the absolute numbers were about the same from the beginning to the middle of the century). Domestic industry actually grew during this period, so that as late as 1850 more people worked at home or in small shops than in factories. And domestic service rose steadily, by 1850 numbering over a million people; in London domestic servants constituted by far the largest single occupational group, and in the country as a whole twice as many men and women were servants as were employed in the cotton industry, the largest, most mechanized industry. But if it is important to correct the overly revolutionary impression left by the term "industrial revolution," it is also important to credit the sensibilities of contemporaries who believed themselves to be living in a revolutionary period.

This was more than the familiar lament of every generation that never had things changed so rapidly. In the early nineteenth century that rhetoric was uncomfortably close to reality. If domestic industry continued to grow, so too did factories, and at a more rapid rate. While agriculture continued to be the largest single occupation, industry as a whole bulked larger in the economy. Population continued to increase dramatically; between the first census in 1801 and the fifth in 1851 the population of England and Wales doubled (from 9,000,000 to 18,000,000), with the greatest rate of growth (17 percent) occurring between 1811 and 1821. In that same half-century, the number of cities with a population of over 20,000 increased from 15 to 63, and the population in those cities rose from 1,500,000 to 6,250,000. These figures, while impressive enough, were only the superficial indicators of change. Beneath the surface, as the historian David Landes has said, the "vital organs," the very "metabolism" of the system, were being transformed, in ways that escape the statistician but that contemporaries were quick to perceive.[8]

To contemporaries the most dramatic change—dramatic symbolically as well as in actuality—was the railway, the first radical innovation in transportation since ancient times to affect ordinary people in their ordinary lives. The first passenger line was opened in 1825; by 1851 there were 6,800 miles in operation. The economic and social effects were immediately evident, and not only the most obvious of these—the cheaper cost of transporting goods and the greater availability of perishables—but also the larger effects upon the economy and society, the stimulation of trade and industry, the widening of horizons and opportunities, the social mobility that came in the wake of geographical mobility. The impact upon the imagination and sensibility was no less momentous. Even more than the factory, the railway symbolized the advent of modernity. The speed, noise, smoke, crowds were a totally new experience, requiring, as Jacques Barzun has said, "a reeducation of the nervous system."[9] And like most new experiences, this generated the most ambivalent responses.

Even Wordsworth, "so long," he wrote (at the ripe age of twenty-eight), "a worshipper of Nature," was not impervious to the awesome, seductive power of this rival to nature.[10] In 1844, when the novelty of the railway had worn off and its disagreeable reality had become all too manifest, he weighed the "mischief with the promised gain," and found the balance on the side of the mischief.

> Hear YE that Whistle? As her long-linked Train
> Swept onwards, did the vision cross your view?
> Yes, ye were startled;—and, in balance true,
> Weighing the mischief with the promised gain,
> Mountains, and Vales, and Floods, I call on you
> To share the passion of a just disdain.[11]

In a note appended to the poem he mitigated that "just disdain": "Once for all, let me declare that it is not against railways but against the abuse of them that I am contending," in evidence of which he referred his readers to an earlier poem of his, written in 1835. Under the prosaic title "Steamboats, Viaducts, and Railways," he envisioned Nature embracing her "lawful offspring," the mechanical arts.

> Motions and Means, on land and sea at war
> With old poetic feeling, not for this,
> Shall ye, by Poets even, be judged amiss!
> Nor shall your presence, howsoe'er it mar
> The loveliness of Nature, prove a bar
> To the Mind's gaining that prophetic sense
> Of future change, that point of vision, whence
> May be discovered what in soul ye are.
> In spite of all that beauty may disown
> In your harsh features, Nature doth embrace
> Her lawful offspring in Man's art; and Time,
> Pleased with your triumphs o'er his brother Space,
> Accepts from your bold hands the proffered crown
> Of hope, and smiles on you with cheer sublime.[12]

It was "that prophetic sense of future change," the promise of time triumphing over space, that reconciled some of the poets, some of the time,

to the "harsh features" of the new conveyance, the noise, dirt, tumult, even
risk to life and limb. The inaugural trip of the Liverpool and Manchester
Railway, on September 15, 1830, was the occasion of the first railway
fatality, which was all the more memorable because the victim was William
Huskisson, President of the Board of Trade in Canning's government. When
the train stopped to take on water, Huskisson, accustomed to the more casual
ways of the horse-drawn coach, crossed the track to greet the Duke of
Wellington, and was struck down on his return by a train on the parallel
track. Tennyson was another of the distinguished guests on that maiden
voyage, and it was then that he penned the famous line which was to appear
in *Locksley Hall:* "Let the great world spin for ever down the ringing
grooves of change." When the error in this description was pointed out to
him, he explained that the night was so dark and the crowd so dense that
he could not see that the wheels did not actually run in grooves. But he
let the metaphor stand in the interest of a higher poetic truth, the vision of
progress inspired by the ceaseless rotation of wheels on those endless steel
tracks, a vision that could withstand even the tragedy of Huskisson's death.*

The ambiguous nature of the changes ushered in by the railways, and
the even more ambivalent attitude toward them, was epitomized by the

---

*The familiar pastoral animus against the railway—that "old poetic feeling" referred to by
Wordsworth—has obscured the existence of another poetic genre that enthusiastically celebrated the
railways, death and all. A tombstone in the cloister of Ely Cathedral commemorated the victims of
a railway accident in an elaborate metaphor in which the First, Second, and Third Classes of the train
corresponded to the religious virtues, and the railway itself was a direct line to heaven:

> The Line to heaven by Christ was made
> With heavenly truth the Rails are laid,
> From Earth to Heaven the Line extends
> To Life Eternal where it ends.
> Repentance is the Station then
> Where Passengers are taken in,
> No Fee for them is there to pay.
> For Jesus is himself the way.
> God's Word is the first Engineer
> It points the way to Heaven so dear,
> Through tunnels dark and dreary here
> It does the way to Glory steer.
> God's Love the Fire, his Truth the Steam,
> Which drives the Engine and the Train,
> All you who would to Glory ride,
> Must come to Christ, in him abide
> In First and Second, and Third Class,
> Repentance, Faith and Holiness,
> You must the way to Glory gain
> Or you with Christ will not remain.
> Come then poor Sinners, now's the time
> At any Station on the Line.
> If you'll repent and turn from sin
> The Train will stop and take you in.[13]

"navvies," the construction workers who laid the lines. Typically without families or homes, restless and rootless as much by nature, it was thought, as by occupation, moving from one construction site to another, they left behind them the memory of men with gargantuan appetites (their daily fare was said to have been two pounds of meat, two pounds of bread, five quarts of ale), and a capacity for hard work matched only by their capacity for hard drinking and brawling. If the textile worker seemed to be a new species of worker, the stunted, emaciated product of the confined, congested, fetid factory, the navvy was a distinctive species of another kind. Spawned by the steam engine, he resembled nothing so much as that huge, belching, roaring monster that tore through the countryside, shattering the calm, ruining the landscape, and presaging the doom of old England. To some he represented the industrial laborer at his worst; to others he was a salutary reminder of the new opportunities for employment. By the middle of the century there were 300,000 workers employed in the construction of the lines, and another 60,000 running the railroad systems. If the navvy ate, drank, and brawled so prodigiously, it was because his wages were high enough to permit him to indulge himself on that scale. The coarsest of laborers bore the title "king of the labourers."

So it was with the other changes brought about by industrialism. The employment of women and children was regarded by many as an unmitigated evil. But they were also aware that while the problem was aggravated by industrialism, it was not a new problem and not peculiar to industrialism. The women and children of the poor had always worked, in domestic industries and in fields, often at harder labor, for longer hours, and with more meager rewards, and, in the case of children, at a younger age. The historian Ivy Pinchbeck, who has written the most comprehensive works on this subject and who is by no means an "optimist" in these matters, compares child labor in the old society and in the new.

> The exploitation of child labour in the early factories has probably caused more horror and indignation, and rightly so, than any other feature of the industrial revolution; but it is not so often realised that the same sort of thing was equally characteristic of the older domestic industries. Hidden away in cottages, where they attracted no attention, thousands of children in rural areas worked factory hours every day, under conditions which were often no better than those which aroused so much feeling in the industrial centers.[14]

Formerly "hidden away in cottages," the children—and women as well—were all too visible in the factories, visible partly because the factories themselves were so visible, partly because the number of women and children employed in them was so considerable. (In the case of the children, their numbers rose absolutely with the general increase of population, and relatively as well, the accelerating growth of population resulting in a larger proportion of children and young people.)

More important than numbers, either relative or absolute, was the widespread feeling that the factory, while not always the most grueling kind of work for women and children, was the most demoralizing. It raised the specter of women abandoning the hearth, incapacitated for domestic life, coarsened, corrupted, even forced into prostitution; and of children deprived of parental supervision, regimented by the machine, brutalized and dehumanized. On the other hand, there were those who pointed out that machinery had relieved women and children (and men as well) of some of the most backbreaking, inhuman kinds of labor; that husbands and fathers could be more tyrannical and brutal than employers; that factory children had better opportunities for education than farm children (especially after the passage of the Factory Act of 1833, requiring that time be set aside for their schooling); that women and children factory workers were more intelligent, spirited, self-reliant, and independent than their counterparts on the farm; and that the labor of women and children was a boon to those families fortunate enough to have more than one wage-earner and thus the opportunity to better themselves. Against these arguments was the evidence dramatically documented in a series of reports and tracts—Richard Oastler's "Child Slavery" in 1830, for example, and the *Sadler Report* of 1832—describing cruelties and tragedies which could not be mitigated by comparisons with the past or by the promise of amelioration in the future.

The physical hardships for women and children in the factories and, more, in the mines, would have been reason enough to make them the focus of reforms—and perhaps also, as opponents of the reforms suggested (and some of the reformers admitted), to make them the thin edge of the wedge that would lead to reforms for adult males as well. Beyond these considerations was an overriding moral one, the sense that women and children were morally as well as physically vulnerable, that their vulnerability was potentially perilous to all of society, and that they were especially vulnerable in the factories and mines. The most sensational parts of the Children's Employment Commission reports on the mines, published in 1842, were descriptions (accompanied by graphic woodcuts) of naked and half-naked women and children harnessed to carts, accounts of sexual intercourse taking place in the bowels of the earth, and reports of abortions and infanticide. Contemporaries were also well aware of the prevalence of illegitimacy and infanticide in agricultural areas. But that fact was perhaps too familiar, and too bucolic in its setting, to be shocking, although numerically and socially it was obviously far more significant. (There were, we now know, no more than 5,000 or 6,000 women employed in the coal mines at this time.[15]) One of the repeated charges brought against the factory owners was that they sexually abused their female employees. The charges were as repeatedly denied; it was pointed out that women were more commonly the victims of their fellow workers than of their employers, and that the greatest incidence of prostitution was not among factory workers but among seamstresses. Yet it was the abuse, or supposed abuse, in the factory that captured the imagination and aroused the indignation of the public.

It is perhaps no accident that at the very time the condition of working class women and children was seen as most grievous, middle class women were being exalted as paragons of virtue and domesticity, and middle class children as models of decorum and obedience. With factories, mines, and slums conjuring up visions of a Hobbesian state of nature, with political economy appearing to legitimize the laws of the jungle and Malthusianism holding out the prospect of unending misery and vice, it became more than ever necessary to assert the values of decency, propriety, and chastity—to re-moralize what had been so fearfully de-moralized. If the condition of women and children slaving away in factories and mines seemed all the more appalling by comparison with these highly romanticized, mythicized middle class ideals, this itself was an invitation to reformers to make yet greater exertions, to bring about moral reformation by way of social legislation. Again, it is no accident that the major reforms—the Factory Act of 1833, the Mines Act of 1842, the Ten Hours Act of 1847—dealt exclusively with women and children, and that the most ardent, persistent reformer was the Evangelical Lord Ashley, for whom social reform was a species of moral reform, and moral reform the instrument of spiritual redemption. It was Ashley who explained, in 1842, why these reforms were so crucial.

> In the male the moral effects of the system are very sad, but in the female they are infinitely worse, not alone upon themselves, but upon their families, upon society, and, I may add, upon the country itself. It is bad enough if you corrupt the man, but if you corrupt the woman, you poison the waters of life at the very fountain.[16]

The spirit of reform, it was often said at the time, reflected the enlarged moral sensibilities of the age, an accession of compassion and humanitarianism which made people unwilling to tolerate evils that had long been tolerated. This is undeniably true. But the change of sensibility was itself a reflection of the anxiety and insecurity generated by the rapidity of change, change in the material and social conditions of life and, perhaps no less unsettling, in the ideas that traditionally gave shape and meaning to life. A stable society can tolerate a large amount of injustice, misery, and vice. An unstable one cannot. Every exposure of injustice, every admission of misery, every example of vice becomes a threat to the legitimacy of the society. And that legitimacy can only be affirmed by a renewal of moral purpose. The first half of the nineteenth century witnessed one after another attempt at such a renewal, each seeking to cope with the condition-of-England question, each trying to come to terms with the legacy of Malthusianism.

The condition-of-England question was variously interpreted—by poor law reformers and factory reformers, by Tories, Whigs, and radicals of every description, by Carlyle who invented the phrase, Disraeli who adopted it, and scores of writers, politicians, and publicists who exploited and sensationalized it. Carlyle and Disraeli jeered at the statisticians who thought the condition of the poor could be measured in wages and prices, food consumption and longevity. But even the statisticians did not confine themselves to material facts; they tried to take the moral measure of the poor by citing statistics of crime and pauperism, education and church attendance. Their moral imagination may have been impoverished, but such as it was, it gave meaning to their inquiries. Other critics, reformers, and radicals gave evidence of a more feverish imagination, a more exacerbated sensibility. Denouncing political economy as immoral, they tried to redress the condition of the poor by re-moralizing them, by restoring to them the moral status they imagined them to have had in the past, or, as in the case of the Chartists, by providing them with a new moral status appropriate to their present condition. If the social history of the early nineteenth century was so frenetic, it was because so many individuals and groups tried so desperately to fill the moral vacuum created by Malthusianism.

PART TWO

REFORM AND DISSENT

VI

THE NEW POOR LAW:

PAUPER VERSUS POOR

In 1833, Alexis de Tocqueville visited England. His little-known "Memoir on Pauperism," written two years later, opened with a typical Tocquevillian paradox.

> When one crosses the various countries of Europe, one is struck by a very extraordinary and apparently inexplicable sight. The countries appearing to be most impoverished are those which in reality account for the fewest indigents, and among the people most admired for their opulence, one part of the population is obliged to rely on the gifts of the other in order to live.[1]

The most opulent country was, of course, England, which had impressed Tocqueville, as it had so many other travelers, as the "Eden of modern civilization." At every step he found sights to make "the tourist's heart leap": magnificent roads and new houses, well-fed cattle grazing in rich meadows, healthy farmers and wealthy landowners, more material amenities than were to be found anywhere else, and a sense of universal prosperity. The parish registers, however, told quite a different story. With "indescribable astonishment," he discovered that "one-sixth of the inhabitants of this flourishing kingdom live at the expense of public charity." The astonishment was all the greater when these statistics were compared with those of other countries—of Portugal, for example, where the countryside was half cultivated and the people were ignorant and coarse, ill fed, ill clothed, and ill housed. Yet there the number of paupers was insignificant: one in twenty-five according to one estimate, one in ninety-eight according to another. Elsewhere the figures were different, but the phenomenon was the same. While "the English poor appear almost rich to the French poor; and the latter are so regarded by the Spanish poor," the number of paupers in each of these countries was in inverse relationship to the actual condition of the poor.[2]

To explain this paradox, Tocqueville ranged far back in human history: to primitive peoples living the life of savages and barely able to satisfy their most basic animal needs; to the first stages of agricultural civilization, when men could begin to entertain desires beyond their urgent needs; to feudalism, when one class was assured of its subsistence at the cost of its subordination and another enjoyed ostentatious luxuries while lacking the most elementary comforts; and so on to modernity, when the development of trade and industry permitted people to acquire new tastes and desires which became habitual and thus part of the necessities of life. In the most advanced state of civilization, as needs expanded to encompass what had once been luxuries, the satisfaction of those needs became increasingly precarious. The industrial worker, removed from the soil and dependent on the vagaries of trade, sometimes found himself without the bare subsistence that was generally available to the poorest peasant in earlier times. To make matters worse, he felt deprived of a multitude of goods he had come to think of as necessities. In a primitive state, poverty had consisted only in "not finding something to eat"; to civilized peoples, and to the English preeminently, "the lack of a multitude of things causes poverty."[3]

There was an additional paradox in this situation. For the progress of civilization brought with it not only an expansion of needs and therefore an enlargement of the definition of poverty, but also a determination to alleviate poverty as it had come to be understood.

> In a country where the majority is ill-clothed, ill-housed, ill-fed, who thinks of giving clean clothes, healthy foods, comfortable quarters to the poor? The majority of the English, having all these things, regard their absence as a frightful misfortune; society believes itself bound to come to the aid of those who lack them, and cures evils which are not even recognized elsewhere. In England, the average standard of living man can hope for in the course of his life is higher than in any other country of the world. This greatly facilitates the extension of pauperism in that kingdom.[4]

Thus pauperism was a product of the moral as well as the material advance of civilization—the increased capacity to provide material goods and an increased compassion for those who could not provide those goods for themselves.

That enlarged conception of poverty, together with the determination to relieve it, brought with it a new way of assuring the "welfare" of the poor. The old kind of charity left it to each individual to alleviate, according to his means, the suffering he saw about him. The new kind, born of Protestantism, was less instinctive, more rational and systematic. It made of charity a matter for social action rather than the exercise of a private virtue, and it transformed it from a moral obligation to a legal right. At first sight this modern form of charity seemed altogether commendable. It was a "moving and elevating sight" to contemplate a society "continually examining itself, probing its wounds, and undertaking to cure them"; Tocqueville could not but admire the effort to use the surplus of the wealthy to relieve the misery of the poor. But England, having gone further than any other country in dispensing this new kind of charity, was witnessing its most unfortunate effects. A basic fact of human nature was that man had a "natural passion for idleness." Of the two incentives that could overcome that passion and move men to work, the need to live and the desire to improve the conditions of life, only the first was effective for the majority of men. By guaranteeing to all the means of subsistence as a legal right, England had relieved the poor of the obligation to work.[5]

Was it possible to escape the "fatal consequences of a good principle"? The English had tried to do so by inquiring into the causes of each person's poverty before relieving it, and, in the case of the able-bodied, making relief conditional upon work. This effort was doomed to failure. "Nothing is so difficult to distinguish as the nuances which separate unmerited misfortune from an adversity produced by vice." Character and circumstance were too intimately related, misery and vice too much a part of each other, to lend themselves to such distinctions. What magistrate had the wisdom, or conscience, or time, to distinguish them? Even if they could be distinguished, who would let a poor man die because it was his own fault he was dying? Who would reason coolly about his vices while hearing his cries? If the personal, financial interest of a private benefactor could not resist the appeal of the heart, could the interest of the public treasury be more availing? If the heart were not engaged, would not fear have the same effect, the fear of public opinion and of the poor themselves? Even if there were the will to enforce the law and make relief conditional upon work, where would sufficient work be found for a sixth of the population of England?[6]

Apart from these practical difficulties, Tocqueville found serious flaws in the very idea of relief as a matter of right, and this in spite of the attractiveness of the idea of right in principle. "There is something great and virile in the idea of right which removes from any request its suppliant character, and places the one who claims it on the same level as the one who grants it." But this particular right, the right of the poor to public relief, had the opposite effect: so far from elevating the suppliant, it debased him. In other countries, where the poor were dependent upon individual charity, they were obliged to recognize their inferiority, but only "secretly and temporarily." In England, where they had to inscribe themselves on the poor rolls in order to receive relief, they acknowledged their inferiority publicly. "What is the achievement of this right if not a notarized manifestation of misery, of weakness, of misconduct on the part of its recipient"? Other rights testified to the superiority of those upon whom they were bestowed. This right publicized and legalized their inferiority. And the more extensive and permanent the exercise of this right, the more degrading it became.[7]

Public relief was unfortunate in other respects. Where private charity created a moral bond between giver and recipient, public relief dissolved that bond. The rich were resentful when their money was taken from them without consulting them, and the poor were ungrateful when it came to them by right and dissatisfied when it alleviated only the worst of their poverty. Thus it exacerbated the fear and loathing of one class, the despair and envy of the other, and the sense of strife between them. "It ranges each one under a banner, tallies them, and, bringing them face to face, prepares them for combat." Of the "two rival nations," the poor naturally fared worse. Demoralized by the public and legal status of dependency, the pauper could not but sink lower in his own estimation, and, as a result, in his actual condition. "What can be expected from a man whose position cannot improve, since he has lost the respect of his fellow men which is the precondition of all progress, whose lot could not become worse, since, being reduced to the satisfaction of his most pressing needs, he is assured that they will always be satisfied?" This degradation was occurring at precisely the time when other classes were bettering their condition, when education was becoming more diffuse, when morals were improving, tastes becoming more refined, and manners more polished. The effect was all the worse because the poor were deprived of their freedom as well as their self-respect. Since the parish had responsibility only for its own residents, a poor man left its boundaries at the risk of forfeiting his right to relief. He was as much bound to the earth as the medieval peasant—indeed, more so, the peasant of old being forced against his will to stay on the land, while the modern laborer was deprived even of the will to move. Nor was it only paupers who were thus immobilized; all the poor were similarly affected since they were naturally loath to abandon the assurance of relief.[8]

To illustrate the evils of this system of relief, Tocqueville cited a series of cases that had come before the justices of the peace of Wiltshire in 1833: an old man, clearly in good health, wearing a wig and fine clothes, petulantly protesting against the reduction of the sum allowed him by the parish; a pregnant woman, abandoned by her husband and bearing the visible marks of suffering, denied support by her rich father-in-law, who refused to fulfill the duties imposed on him by nature rather than by law; several vigorous, insolent young men who lodged a complaint against the parish authorities for failing to give them either work or relief; two young mothers brazenly identifying the fathers of their illegitimate children. Tocqueville's host, one of the justices, assured him that these were typical examples of the thriving state of vice brought about by the poor law. Since that time, Tocqueville noted, the law had been reformed in the hope of eliminating precisely the kinds of scenes he had witnessed. But the reform had not changed the essential situation. So long as the law continued to affirm a legal right to relief, the obligation of society to feed the poor, all the defects of the old law would persist.

Yet Tocqueville did not entirely preclude some form of public relief. Individual charity, to be sure, was almost always preferable. "It devotes itself to the greatest miseries, it seeks out misfortune without publicity, and it silently and spontaneously repairs the damage." But it was not always sufficient or responsive to every need. For some purposes, public charity was more suitable: for the relief of infants and the aged, the sick and the insane, and as a spontaneous, temporary measure in times of calamity. These kinds of public charity did not imply a legal right to relief. Nor were they suitable for the distress that so frequently accompanied industrial progress. For the latter, other means might be considered: slowing down the displacement of populations so that men did not leave the land until they could be accommodated in industry, regulating production and consumption so as to avoid depressions and crises, and promoting savings by the working classes so that they might provide for themselves in time of need. Tocqueville posed these possibilities briefly and tentatively, promising to pursue them on some later occasion (a promise he did not, in fact, carry out). What was not tentative, however, or the least bit equivocal, was his conviction that the present system was disastrous.

> But I am deeply convinced that any permanent, regular, administrative system whose aim will be to provide for the needs of the poor, will breed more miseries than it can cure, will deprave the population that it wants to help and comfort, will in time reduce the rich to being no more than the tenant-farmers of the poor, will dry up the sources of savings, will stop the accumulation of capital, will retard the development of trade, will benumb human industry and activity, and will culminate by bringing about a violent revolution in the State, when the number of those who receive alms will have become as large as those who give it, and the indigent, no longer being able to take from the impoverished rich the means of providing for his needs, will find it easier to plunder them of all their property at one stroke than to ask for their help.[9]

It is no surprise that even in this brief essay Tocqueville should have brought to the problem of poverty the same incisiveness he brought to the problem of democracy. Nor is one surprised to find him dwelling on the familiar theme of the unhappy consequences of good intentions. Yet neither this paradox nor his conception of the problem was unique to him. Today sociologists would translate his analysis into the "theory of relative deprivation," the "revolution of rising expectations," and the "principle of entitlement." At the time all of these ideas were part of the received wisdom. When Tocqueville said that of the two incentives to work, the need to live and the desire for improvement, only the first operated in the case of the majority of the people, he was reflecting the familiar Malthusian image of sluggish, slothful man impelled to work only by the direst necessity. Similarly, his assumption that private charity would disappear if public charity were available was widely held and eminently plausible; if it was later belied by the facts, it was that later phenomenon, the extraordinary outpouring of philanthropy toward the end of the century, that requires attention and explanation. Even his lesser errors were typical. We now know that the figure of one-sixth of the population on relief was much exaggerated. Contemporaries, however, did not know that, and it is useful to be reminded that the metaphor of the "sunken sixth" represented the best-informed opinion of the time.

More important was the description of the chain of events set in motion by any "permanent, regular, administrative system" of relief: the poor degraded and depraved, the rich impoverished and resentful, savings and capital discouraged, trade and industry stagnant, a good part of the population pauperized and the rest in imminent threat of becoming so, and, finally, when the sources of relief were depleted, a "violent revolution." Although it is easy now to dispute this prognosis and scoff at these fears, the fact that they came from Tocqueville should give us pause; if he thought the situation so parlous, lesser men can surely be forgiven for thinking so.*

The image of a "violent revolution" was given credence by other events which Tocqueville must have been aware of: the "Swing riots" in 1830 and the agitation over the franchise in the following years. The riots, a kind of rural Luddism, were directed primarily against the threshing machines, but they also took the form of the burning of ricks and barns and threatening letters to landlords, farmers, and parsons (often over the signature of "Cap-

---

*Several years earlier, the French economist Jean-Baptiste Say issued a similar warning to those of his countrymen who were tempted to take England as a model of humanitarianism.

> England is the country that has most havens available to the unfortunate, and it is perhaps the one where most unfortunates demand aid. Let public welfare or private associations open, a hundred, a thousand others—all—will be filled; and there will remain in society equally as many unfortunates who will request permission to enter or who will claim it as a right if one recognized it as such.

It was the English, Say pointedly noted, who had invented the term "pauperism."[10]

tain Swing," hence the name given to these episodes). Widely reported in the press, and often much exaggerated in the reporting, they seemed even more ominous against the background of the revolution in France and the tumultuous events leading to the Reform Act of 1832. The combination of rural unrest and political agitation made these two years one of the more volatile periods of modern English history. Recent scholarship suggests that the threats of revolution inspired by the controversy over the Reform Bill were part of a concerted, calculated strategy to bring about reform by playing on the fear of revolution.[11] But whatever the private intentions of those engaged in this strategy and however remote the likelihood of revolution, the threats themselves, and the fears generated by those threats, were real enough.

It is at this time that the issue of the poor laws came to a head. Yet it would be a mistake to draw too direct a connection between the social and political unrest of these years and the passage of the New Poor Law.[12] The poor laws had been under attack for at least a quarter of a century, and proposals for their abolition or reform had been as plentiful as the exposures of their evils. The Select Committee of the Lords appointed late in 1830 to inquire into the poor laws was clearly a response to the Swing riots, but it had ample precedent in earlier parliamentary committees on the same subject (there were four such between 1816 and 1820 alone) and others on such related subjects as emigration. Nor was the appointment in 1832 of the Royal Commission on the Poor Laws a direct consequence of the Reform Act of 1832, an act which, it has been said, brought to power a "new and self-conscious middle class" eager to promote its interests.[13] The Poor Law Commission was in fact appointed by the unreformed government of Lord Grey, and the law itself had the support of both parties, both houses of Parliament, and most of the landed as well as the manufacturing classes. Yet the very fact of electoral reform, quite apart from the classes or interests presumably empowered by that reform (which is itself a subject of controversy), undoubtedly emboldened the poor law reformers, just as the Swing riots undoubtedly added to the impetus for reform.

The New Poor Law is generally, and rightfully, given pride of place in any discussion of nineteenth century poverty. Certainly it was the most important piece of legislation on the subject since the passage of the original poor laws more than two centuries earlier. Yet in a sense it was obsolete almost from the time of its enactment, the abuses it was meant to correct having become less urgent by 1834. It also proved to be less effectual than the reformers would have liked, subject to so many compromises, exceptions, evasions, and regional variations that an entire literature has grown up demonstrating the gap between the law and its application. In spite of all this, in spite of the limitations built into the act and the limitations imposed upon it from outside, it exerted a powerful influence on the intellectual, moral, and social climate. Violated in practice—violated, often, by the same people who were committed to it in principle—it gave support and sanction to ideas and attitudes which decisively affected the course of social history in this critical period.

There was, to be sure, a considerable opposition to the law, in principle as well as practice. The opposition came from Tories and Radicals, from Anglican ministers and Nonconformist preachers, from squires and "agitators," as they were called. While the opponents succeeded in publicizing their dissent and impeding the operation of the law, they saw themselves, and were seen by others, as resisting the dominant "spirit of the age." It was that spirit, expressed in the principles, assumptions, and rhetoric of the New Poor Law, that prevailed until well toward the end of the century—until very different principles, assumptions, and rhetoric brought about another revolution in social sensibility and social policy.

If the ideas of the New Poor Law outlived the law itself, they also predated that law. It is difficult to think of any comparable legislative act in recent English history that was so long and so thorough in its preparation. (By comparison the Reform Acts of 1832 and 1867 extending the franchise were precipitate and improvised.) Apart from the more famous critics of the old poor laws—Townsend, Eden, Malthus, Bentham, Colquhoun, Chalmers —there were hundreds of lesser-known pamphleteers, justices of the peace, clergymen, magistrates, Members of Parliament, landowners, economists, philanthropists, and reformers, who made this one of the most hotly debated and voluminously documented subjects of contention.

Much of the criticism focused on the Speenhamland system—the supplementation, out of parish rates, of earnings which fell below a standard based upon the price of bread and the size of the laborer's family. Recent historical research, pioneered by the economist Mark Blaug, has considerably modified the conventional view of Speenhamland and of the old poor laws.[14] Allowances, or "rates in aid of wages," were neither as pervasive nor as considerable as had been thought (by 1834 the Speenhamland system had been discontinued in many counties, including Berkshire where it had originated); some of the evils associated with it can more properly be attributed to other causes; and the overall effect may have been salutary rather than detrimental. But most influential contemporaries thought otherwise. Outdoor relief in general, and the allowance system in particular, were held responsible for a vicious cycle of evils: an increase of poor rates, a decrease in wages (which were supplemented out of the rates), a decline of the yeomanry (who had to pay the rates but did not profit by the wage subsidy since they did not employ laborers), a rise in agricultural unemployment (the displaced yeomen swelling the ranks of the agricultural laborers), a fall in productivity (pauper labor being less efficient than independent labor), higher food prices (resulting from the decline of productivity), an increase of population (relief encouraging the poor to marry earlier and to have more children), still lower wages (resulting from this increase of population), and so on, all of which affected the industrial economy as much as the agricultural. The main complaint, repeated in countless pamphlets, tracts, sermons, articles, speeches, and reports, was that the poor laws were "pauperizing the poor."

This was also the main theme of the Royal Commission report issued in 1834. The familiar charge that the report was grossly biased and "wildly unhistorical" has been amply confirmed by economists and historians.[15] Whatever its faults, it was, for contemporaries as for historians, an invaluable social document, for it provided the rationale for the New Poor Law and formulated and disseminated ideas about poverty which were influential far beyond the scope of the law. In a sense, its very faults enhance its value: in pointing up the discrepancy between the reality as historians now know it and the reality as a good many contemporaries perceived it, the report demonstrates the character and power of the ideas that mediated between these two versions of reality.

Even before the report appeared, interest in it was whetted by the publication of a 400-page volume of *Extracts* consisting of preliminary reports by the assistant commissioners; 15,000 copies of this were sold at 4 shillings apiece. The following year the official report was published. This was a readable 200 page volume, of which 10,000 copies were sold and another 10,000 distributed free to parish authorities. This was followed by 15 volumes of testimony, replies to questionnaires, and other documentary evidence; if these were less commonly bought and still less often read, their very existence lent weight and credence to the report itself. Finally there was the text of the Poor Law Amendment Act of 1834. Each of these documents was reviewed, analyzed, criticized, summarized, digested, and extracted, thus augmenting the already voluminous literature on the poor laws.*

The seven-man commission responsible for this barrage of publicity and polemic has been described (in terms reminiscent of those used by Walter Bagehot of the English Constitution) as consisting of three "dignified" members and four "effective" ones, the former including bishops and a Member of Parliament, and the latter political economists and Benthamites.[16] Even the dignitaries, however, were no mere figureheads, all of them having been active in public affairs and in the poor-law debate. John

---

*The extraordinary interest in the report continued well after the immediate occasion had passed. At the end of the century, when there was renewed talk of poor law reform, the 1834 report was reprinted three times by the Stationery Office, and its influence may be seen in the deliberations of the Poor Law Commission of 1905.

Sumner, Bishop of Chester (and formerly Senior's tutor at Eton), was a prominent Evangelical, the author of a well known treatise defending Malthus—and defending also the omniscient and benevolent God who had used the law of population for His own providential purposes. Charles James Blomfield, Bishop of London (and later an influential church reformer), testified before the Committee on Emigration in 1826 in favor of government subsidies to encourage the emigration of the "surplus population." And William Sturges Bourne, a Tory member of the House of Commons, had been chairman of the Poor Law Committee of 1817 and had introduced a number of bills on the poor laws, some of which were enacted.

The leading member of the commission was the economist Nassau Senior. His only rival for preeminence was Edwin Chadwick, who was originally appointed as an assistant commissioner and was elevated to the rank of commissioner upon Senior's recommendation. Secretary to Bentham in the last year of his life (Bentham died in 1832 at the age of eighty-four, one day before the Reform Act became law and a few months after the appointment of the Poor Law Commission), Chadwick inherited his mentor's temperament as well as philosophy, an energy, zeal, arrogance, abrasiveness, and intolerance that made him seem even more domineering than he actually was (and not only on this occasion but in every enterprise in which he was engaged). His biographer has suggested that Chadwick "converted" Senior, and thus the commission as a whole, to the principles and policies embodied in the report. Yet there is good reason to suppose (as Senior's biographer maintains) that the principles, if not the administrative details of the proposals, had been arrived at by Senior independently, and that the report itself was the work of both men, with Senior writing most of the analytical section and Chadwick the "remedial measures."[17]

The most important fact about the report was the proposal to amend rather than abolish the poor laws. From a later perspective this seems so obvious as to call for little comment.[18] At the time it was no small matter, the Malthusian alternative, the case for abolition, being plausible and respectable. Malthus himself was alive and active during the whole of this period. (He died at the very end of 1834, ten months after the report was released and six months after the New Poor Law was passed.) Although he corresponded with Senior as late as January 1834, commenting politely but noncommittally on the report, he had not been involved in the work of the commission, perhaps because he was known to favor abolition. Testifying before the Select Commission on Emigration in 1827, he had repeated his earlier proposal that "those that were born after a certain time should not be allowed to have parish assistance."[19] Many still agreed with him, including, it was generally thought, Senior himself. In fact, Senior was as little a Malthusian in this respect as he was in regard to the theory of population itself.

It was Senior's recent opposition to a poor law for Ireland that made some people regard him as an abolitionist. But the pamphlet he wrote in 1831, *Letter to Lord Howick on a Legal Provision for the Irish Poor,* based its argument on the peculiar nature of poverty in Ireland, a poverty so extreme and pervasive that no poor law could begin to alleviate it. Unlike England, where distress could be publicly relieved because it was usually temporary and confined to particular groups, Ireland had a chronic condition of poverty afflicting all the laboring classes. That kind of poverty could be remedied only by an increase in the wage fund which would result in a general rise in the standard of living; and this, in turn, required an increase of productivity. To this end Senior proposed government subsidies for the building of roads, railways, harbors, docks, and canals, and measures to encourage agricultural productivity by reclaiming waste land, consolidating farms, and introducing more scientific techniques of cultivation. When he opposed the poor law, it was not on laissez faire grounds; on the contrary, he favored a large intrusion of the government into the economy of Ireland. Nor was his argument meant to apply to England, where a poor law (although not the existing one) was appropriate. Nor can his position even in the case of Ireland properly be characterized as "abolitionist," since it was a question not of abolishing an existing law but of instituting a new one, which was bound to reproduce the worst aspects of the English law. Even for Ireland, he favored some kind of relief for the blind, the insane, the maimed, the chronic invalid, and the orphan (although not the aged)—for all those who could not be made productive and for whom relief would not tend "to diminish industry or providence."[20]

The same concern for productivity inspired Senior's earlier controversy with Malthus on the subject of population. Where Malthus assumed that population tended to increase faster than subsistence, Senior posited the opposite tendency. An increase in the manufacturing population would lead to an increase of productive power, and workers, desiring to improve their lot, would voluntarily delay marriage, thus permitting subsistence to rise above the level of population. Unlike Malthus—and like Smith—Senior believed that productivity rather than population was the main factor in the determination of wages, and that the growth of productivity, combined with the aspiration for improvement, made for a progressive economy and a prospering laboring population.

> As wealth increases, what were the luxuries of one generation become the decencies of their successors. Not only a taste for additional comfort and convenience, but a feeling of degradation in their absence becomes more and more widely diffused. The increase, in many respects, of the productive powers of labour, must enable increased comforts to be enjoyed by increased numbers, and as it is the more beneficial, so it

appears to me to be the more natural course of events, that increased comfort should not only accompany, but rather precede, increase of numbers.[21]

This optimistic view of the possibilities of social progress derived from a fundamentally optimistic and progressive view of human nature. Once again, it is the echo of Smith rather than of Malthus that may be heard in Senior's description of the "normal type" of laborer, the "natural offspring of the Saxon race," who was hardworking to a fault, intent upon improving his condition even at the expense of his health; if he was imprudent, it was only because he knew that the parish would take care of his family in case of need.[22] Senior, then, was anti-Malthusian—which is to say, anti-abolitionist—on the subject of the poor laws, because he was profoundly anti-Malthusian in his economic and social philosophy. And so, in spite of his reputation and rhetoric, was Chadwick. The empirical evidence, Chadwick maintained, showed no correlation between poor relief and an increase of population.* What it did show was a correlation between relief and the decline of productivity and demoralization of the laboring classes. It was for this reason that Chadwick and Senior objected not to the relief of the impotent but only to those forms of relief for the "able-bodied" which undermined the natural, healthy impulses of the "normal type" of English laborer.

The decision to reform rather than abolish the poor laws was not a compromise forced upon a reluctant commission by memories of Swing riots or the fear of revolution, but a rational, principled position. Had it been otherwise, had it been for reasons of expediency that the commission embarked upon the course of reform, to conciliate and pacify the laboring classes, to forestall violence and social unrest, these reasons would have surfaced in the report and in the subsequent debates. Today such motives might be concealed, as if they were not quite seemly for public discussion. At the time, the argument from expediency was entirely respectable; it was this very argument, in fact, that had been used so effectively in the debate over the Reform Act. On this occasion, however, the more compelling argument was simply principle.[23] Whatever the arts of persuasion (and distortion) evident in the hearings of the commission and in the final report, the actual case for reform—and for the particular kind of reform proposed in the report—was grounded in theory and conviction. Later, to be sure, in translating the recommendations of the commission into a parliamentary

---

*The *Poor Law Report* was not consistent on the subject of population. At one point, it suggested that the reform would have the effect of arresting the increase of population caused by the old poor laws; at another that overpopulation was not a serious problem and that such as there was could easily be corrected by emigration and internal mobility (the latter resulting from a reform of the laws of settlement). More significant was the fact that the subject of population occupied so little space in the report.

bill, in amending that bill as it went through various committees and both houses, and, still later, in applying and enforcing the Poor Law Amendment Act (as it was appropriately called), other factors came into play: interest, expediency, fear, demagoguery, compassion, even intimations of contrary principles. But it is to the report that one must look for the purpose and meaning of the reform, and it is the report that set the tone and terms of the debate for a generation or more.

The Royal Commission was charged with "inquiring into the administration and practical operation of the Poor Laws"; and so its report was entitled. A fundamental part of that inquiry was the identification and definition of the poor who came within the purview of the poor laws. Without that identification and definition neither the analysis of the problem nor the proposed remedies can be understood.

The preface stated the underlying principle of the report: "Distinction between the poor and the indigent; the indigent alone within the province of the law."[24] At every point of the argument that distinction was invoked. Like Burke before them, the commissioners protested against applying the same word, "poor," to independent laborers and to those who were dependent upon the public largesse for their subsistence.* The misuse of the word confused the poor themselves. "Those who work, though receiving good wages, being called *poor,* and classed with the really indigent, think themselves entitled to a share of the 'poor funds.' "[25] The opponents of reform made the most of that confusion.

> Such persons will, no doubt, avail themselves of the mischievous ambiguity of the word *poor,* and treat all diminution of the expenditure for the relief of the poor as so much taken from the labouring classes; as if those classes were naturally pensioners on the charity of their superiors, and relief, not wages, were the proper fund for their support; as if the independent labourers themselves were not, directly or indirectly, losers by all expenditure on paupers; as if those who would be raised from pauperism to independence would not be the greatest gainers by the change; as if, to use the expression of one of the witnesses whom we have quoted, the meat of industry were worse than the bread of idleness.[26]

The complaint that the "poor" might think themselves entitled to a share of the "poor funds" implied that the ambiguity of that word, the confusion between paupers and the laboring poor, derived from the "poor

---

*Unlike Burke, however, who wanted to reserve "poor" for the sick and infirm, the commissioners, acquiescing in current usage, assigned that term to the self-sustaining laboring classes, and "pauper" or "indigent" to the recipient of relief or charity.

laws" themselves, from the name given to those laws and from their very substance. Perhaps the commissioners did not make this point explicitly because they did not want to put themselves in opposition to so venerable an institution; like all reformers (and many revolutionists) they professed to be seeking a restoration or purification of the original mandate. Thus they insisted that the Act of 1601, the famous 43rd Elizabeth, had never contemplated giving relief to "industrious persons" but had only proposed putting them to work, reserving relief for the infirm. "The engagements of the 43 Elizabeth, were perhaps dangerous engagements, but they were engagements which for 100 years were performed apparently without substantial injury to the morals and industry of the labourers, or to the general prosperity of the country." The injury came later when relief was extended to the able-bodied, a practice that was "opposed to the letter and still more to the spirit" of the original laws.[27]

While the report criticized others for violating the Elizabethan laws, it itself went against the letter and spirit of those laws. For it did not suggest putting the able-bodied to work; nor did it derive the distinction between pauper and poor from the original laws. Senior himself was well aware of this, having earlier denounced the Elizabethan laws as thoroughly "mischievous" in establishing a "right to gratuitous relief," and as "barbarous" in reducing the laboring classes to the status of "serfs."[28] The Elizabethan laws were, in fact, genuinely and unambiguously "poor" laws precisely because they did not make any sharp distinction between poor and pauper. They did distinguish various groups coming under the jurisdiction of the laws: the "able-bodied," the "impotent," the "thriftless," the young; and they made suitable provisions for each: employment, alms, houses of correction, apprenticeship. But these categories and measures were by no means as distinct as later reformers made out, and did not correspond to the demarcation between poor and pauper. Moreover, the poor laws themselves were complemented by other laws prescribing the conditions of work for "artificers, labourers, servants of husbandry, and apprentices."[29] These laws were part of a continuum with the poor laws because the poor themselves, independent and dependent alike, were part of a single continuum, an undifferentiated body of "laboring poor." They were enacted at a time of great economic dislocation, when a good many able-bodied, "industrious" poor found themselves in the condition of "sturdy beggars." It was also a time when society assumed responsibility, in theory at least, for "poorer folke," when it was thought natural and proper not only to relieve distress but to set wages and prices, terms of apprenticeship, and conditions of work.

It was this undifferentiated idea of poverty that the report objected to when it complained of the "mischievous ambiguity of the word *poor.*" The purpose of the reform was to establish, in law and in practice, the distinctions that would remove that ambiguity. To do that it was not necessary to abolish the poor laws and eliminate all public relief, but only to amend the laws and provide relief in such a way as to reinforce those distinctions.

Thus the commission had no objection in principle to relief given to the "impotent"—the aged and the sick—nor to the kinds of relief currently given to them. It proposed no change in their status or in their treatment. They would continue to receive outdoor relief in whatever form was convenient—money, food, medical services, housing; and if they did choose to enter a workhouse, that would be entirely voluntary on their part. "The aged and impotent," Senior assured Lord Lansdowne, "the true poor as they are called in the 18th Eliz., are excluded"[30]—excluded from the reform, that is, because they were not a problem requiring reform. The problem was the able-bodied pauper. But even the able-bodied could receive relief, in certain cases and under certain conditions. Anything else would be "repugnant to the common sentiments of mankind." All civilized communities recognized the need for some kind of relief, public or private, compulsory or voluntary, in cases of "extreme necessity." Everywhere except in England, however, such relief was confined to the "relief of *indigence,* the state of a person unable to obtain, in return for his labour, the means of subsistence." Only in England did it extend also to the "relief of *poverty;* that is, the state of one, who in order to obtain a mere subsistence, is forced to have recourse to labour."[31]

The definition of "indigence" thus included the able-bodied pauper unable to support himself, as well as the aged and sick. Both could be given relief "safely and even beneficially," not, as the Malthusian would have it, by means of private charity, but as part of a compulsory, public, legal system of relief.[32] And not merely to placate the "humanity mongers" or pacify the poor. One could argue that it was precisely to sharpen the distinction between pauper and poor, to give that distinction all the force of law, that the commission chose the course of reform rather than abolition. By providing for the pauper, even the able-bodied pauper, not outside the law (by private charity) but within it—within the framework of what would be, in effect, a pauper law—the commission proposed to legislate and institutionalize the distinction itself.

It was, then, a matter of definition and distinction—of separating the able-bodied pauper from the laboring poor. The difficulty came from the ambiguity of "poor," which gave the laboring poor the illusion that they were entitled to a share of the "poor funds." And the problem was compounded by the allowance system, which first blurred the distinction between relief and wages and then raised expectations that were unrealistic and insatiable. "Whatever addition is made to allowances under these circumstances, excites the expectation of still further allowances; increases the conception of the extent of the right, and ensures proportionate disappointment and hatred if that expectation is not satisfied." The frustration was all the worse because the "right" was couched in language that was so vague, all those denominated "poor" being told that they had a "right to a 'reasonable' subsistence,' or 'a fair subsistence,' or 'an adequate subsistence.' " When authorities used such empty words, the claimants "filled" them with their own desires and imaginations. As a result, discontent and violence were often greatest in those districts where relief was most generous.[33]

The alternative to this vacuous notion of right was the idea of "contract." The laborer had no "right" to a "reasonable" or "fair" or "adequate" subsistence; but he did have a contract in the form of wages which determined the level of his subsistence and the limits of his expectations. Wherever wages for the performance of work had been substituted for relief, "employment has again produced content, and kindness became again a source of gratitude." Wages also brought a sense of responsibility and independence. Knowing the terms of his employment, the laborer knew that he was responsible for his and his family's welfare, that any increase in their numbers would entail a decrease of their comforts, that their subsistence depended on his own efforts and prudence rather than on the benefactions of a magistrate. As soon as subsistence became dependent upon relief rather than contractual wages, that sense of responsibility was undermined.[34]

The suspension of the idea of contract also entailed a suspension of the laws of nature. The effect of the poor laws was "to repeal pro tanto the law of nature by which the effects of each man's improvidence or misconduct are borne by himself and his family," and by the same token "to repeal pro tanto the law by which each man and his family enjoy the benefit of his own prudence and virtue."[35] The employer, as well as the pauper, took advantage of this suspension of natural law; knowing that the parish would make up the difference, he could pay wages below the subsistence level and dismiss or hire laborers at will. Even the apparent beneficiaries of the system suffered when nature was flouted. Employers soon discovered that cheap labor was inferior labor, since paupers did not have the same incentive to work as independent laborers. And the paupers were ill served by allowances in lieu of wages. Because their subsistence did not depend on their labor, they lost respect for their work and for themselves, doing what little they had to do "with the reluctance of a slave." Nor did they husband their earnings, as they would have had they worked hard for them. Instead they became, in the recurrent words of the report, idle, indolent, ignorant, lazy, dishonest, fraudulent, worthless, dissolute, degraded, and, finally, "callous to their own degradation."[36]

The worst of the system was that it demoralized even those among the poor who were not by nature dissolute, who were pauperized and degraded in spite of themselves. The independent laborer, however much he cherished his independence, might find his wages depressed by the allowance system to the point where he too had to have recourse to the parish. With that loss of independence came the familiar train of evils: the loss of self-respect, responsibility, prudence, temperance, hard work, and the other virtues that had once sustained him. It was this degradation of character, more than material impoverishment, that defined the pauper. The pauper might actually receive more money than the laborer, and yet exhibit the typical symptoms of pauperism. "In every district," the commission found, "the condition of this class [the independent labourer] is found to be strikingly distinguishable from that of the pauper, and superior to it, though the independent labourers are commonly maintained upon less money."[37] The main purpose of the reform was not so much to redeem the pauper as to rescue the poor from the fate of pauperism, to prevent the independent laborer from succumbing to the dependency that brought with it all the vices of pauperism.

To this end, the "dispauperizing" of the poor, the commission sought to create a "broad line of distinction between the class of independent labourers and the class of paupers."[38] The whole of the report was, in effect, an exercise in definition and distinction, an attempt to establish that line theoretically and to maintain it institutionally. Each of the "remedial measures" was intended to make the social reality accord with the principle, to separate pauper and poor in practice just as they were separated by definition. Contemporaries quarreled about the justice and wisdom of these measures, and historians have quarreled about the evidence upon which the theory was based. To a certain extent both issues are beside the point. The heart of the matter was in the distinction between pauper and poor. Once that was conceded, the rest fell into place.

The "first and most essential" principle of reform, the primary means of establishing that "broad line of distinction" between pauper and poor, was the requirement that the condition of the able-bodied pauper be less "eligible"—desirable, agreeable, favorable—than that of the "lowest class" of independent laborer. The commission did not claim originality for this principle, which was "universally admitted" even by those who most frequently violated it.[39] What it did try to do was to apply that principle rigorously and systematically, to make it the foundation of a new poor law.

One aspect of the principle of less-eligibility is so obvious it is rarely commented on. This is its thoroughly relativistic character: it was the condition of the pauper relative to the independent laborer that was decisive. In this respect, as in others, it was diametrically opposed to Speenhamland, which tried to create an objective standard of need, a minimum level of subsistence, determined by such objective measures as the price of bread and the size of the family. The only standard implied in the principle of less-eligibility was that the relief given to the pauper be of such a kind as to make his condition inferior to that of the poorest independent laborer. The relativity of the principle assured the distinction of pauper and poor both as individuals and as classes. Under Speenhamland the single standard of subsistence, whether achieved through wages or relief or a combination of both, had the effect of amalgamating pauper and poor under the name of the "laboring poor." The principle of less-eligibility, by making relief more meager and more onerous than the rewards of labor, kept the "pauper class" in its "proper position" below that of the "lowest class" of independent laborer. "It is only by keeping these things separated, and separated by as broad and as distinct a demarcation as possible, and by making relief in all cases less agreeable than wages, that any thing deserving the name of improvement can be hoped for."[40]

Derived from the principle of less-eligibility was the most famous—infamous, in some circles—feature of the report: the proposal that relief for the able-bodied and their families be given only within the confines of the workhouse (except for medical relief, which could be continued "outdoors"). In itself the institution of the workhouse was no novelty; it was as old as the poor law itself and had been a constant challenge to the imagination of reformers and the resourcefulness of legislators. It had been generally intended as a means of caring for those among the poor who could not care for themselves (in this sense it was identical with the almshouse or poorhouse—terms often used interchangeably), or as a way of making the pauper pay at least part of the cost of his upkeep (in the case of Bentham's industry-houses, considerably more than the cost of his upkeep). What was new about the present workhouse proposal was its function in distinguishing pauper and poor and in implementing the principle of less-eligibility. In the workhouse the pauper, whether able-bodied or infirm, was literally, physically separated from the independent laborer. And by controlling conditions within the workhouse—food, shelter, work, discipline—the less-eligible status of the pauper could be enforced; indeed, the very fact of confinement in a workhouse, the deprivation of liberty, was itself a primary condition of less-eligibility.

The workhouse, as the commission described it, had the paradoxical effect of carrying out the principle of less-eligibility and at the same time maintaining a humane standard of living for the inmates. There was no need to reduce the food or comforts of the pauper to the barest level of subsistence. On the contrary, physical amenities in the workhouse could actually be better than those outside—cleaner, more wholesome, more moral, the food more ample—and still satisfy the principle of less-eligibility, since it was the mere fact of confinement, the loss of liberty, that made the workhouse less desirable. It was also this fact that made it suitable for the able-bodied and the infirm alike: the able-bodied who would be disagreeably affected by the loss of liberty, the discipline, and the lack of such "luxuries" as liquor and tobacco; and the infirm who might voluntarily enter the workhouse because by their standards it would be more agreeable than life outside, a "place of comparative comfort."[41]

The suitability of the workhouse for all varieties of paupers required a further refinement in the principle of separation. Paupers would be separated from the independent poor by the simple existence of the workhouse, and within the house the different categories of paupers would be separated from each other: the impotent (aged and infirm), children, able-bodied men, and able-bodied women. Chadwick proposed separate buildings for each of these groups; later he bitterly complained that the New Poor Law, in establishing "general" workhouses, violated his principle of "classification."

The workhouse had yet another purpose; it would serve as a "self-acting test of the claim of the applicant." Instead of requiring magistrates to judge the neediness of each applicant, the offer of relief within the workhouse would in itself be the decisive test of need. "If the claimant does not comply with the terms on which relief is given to the destitute, he gets nothing; and if he does comply, the compliance proves the truth of the claim, namely, his destitution." Since the workhouse was, by definition, less eligible than any other mode of life, only the most severe destitution would induce a man to enter it. The "workhouse test" obviated the need for any "merit test" (what was later to be called a "means test") and did away with all the complicated, expensive, time-consuming procedures and appeals which made for so much ill-will and which were, in any case, inconclusive. Under the new system there would be no need for any inquiry into the condition or resources of the applicant. "When that principle [the workhouse] has been introduced, the able-bodied claimant should be entitled to immediate relief on the terms prescribed, wherever he might happen to be; and should be received without objection or inquiry; the fact of his compliance with the prescribed discipline constituting his title to a sufficient though simple diet." Thus the instrument of relief was itself the test for relief. It was also the infallible means of separating pauper and poor, since by this test "the line between those who do, and those who do not need relief is drawn, and drawn perfectly."[42]

If this self-acting test recalls the self-acting principle of laissez faire, other aspects of the report were notably at variance with that principle. The very establishment of the workhouses required a considerable degree of government involvement—a greater degree, opponents were quick to point out, than was entailed in outdoor relief. A more serious violation of laissez faire was the proposal to establish a "central board," with commissioners and assistant commissioners empowered to frame and enforce regulations for the management of the workhouses, the kind and amount of relief to be given in them, and the labor to be exacted from the inmates. Those regulations, moreover, were to be, as far as practicable, "uniform throughout the country."[43] More than any other feature of the report (and of the New Poor Law) it was this central board, charged with imposing a uniform policy and a uniform set of regulations upon the entire country, that was hotly contested. Even the most ardent advocates of reform were hard pressed to defend it except as a necessary evil to correct an intolerable situation. The anomaly was recognized at the time and has been much belabored by historians since: the New Poor Law, so solicitous of the natural laws of political economy, so determined to establish a free market in labor, so insistent upon the responsibility of the individual, was also the occasion for the most important extension of government power and of the administrative apparatus of the state in more than half a century.*

Another seeming anomaly in the report (and still more in the act) was the fact that it did not propose to abolish the law of settlement. The law had been amended in 1795 to permit the removal of a man from his parish only after he had actually applied for relief. But the Speenhamland policy introduced at the same time vastly increased the number of laborers who received parish relief during the course of the year and who were therefore subject to removal. The poor rates, swollen by the allowance system and the economic hardships of these years, were further burdened by the costly litigation encumbering the process of settlement. For these reasons among others, Senior and Chadwick were as opposed to the law of settlement as Smith and Malthus had been. The obvious solution, as the commission reported, would have been to abolish settlement requirements entirely by making relief a "national charge" instead of the responsibility of the parish.[46] After arguing the merits of such a policy, the report did not recommend it, on grounds which were not altogether persuasive (which would, in fact, have told against a central board as well): it would be too drastic a change; the absence of local control might invite abuse; it would create difficulties in regard to taxation. Instead the commission proposed to revise the law by establishing a single settlement qualification (that of birth) and creating

---

*It is no wonder that the celebrated jurist A. V. Dicey, writing at the turn of the century, had trouble assimilating the New Poor Law to his characterization of this period, 1825–1870, as "Benthamism or Individualism" (words which he thought synonymous). He admitted that it would be a "straining of terms" to make of the New Poor Law—"the most celebrated piece of legislation" of this period—an example of the triumph of individualism, when the popular view at the time saw it as an attempt to imprison the poor in Bastilles. A policy more consistent with individualism would have been the abolition of the poor laws. The long history of poor relief had unfortunately made that alternative impracticable, so that reformers were left with the only means available to them of protecting the freedom of property that was essential to individualism—the "property" in this case being that of the "hardworking men" who had to support the "laggards" among them.[44]

The issue Dicey did not deal with, because it conformed even less to his individualist interpretation, was the administrative aspect of the law: the authority it gave the state over economic and social affairs, and, as recent historians have pointed out, the model it provided for other administrative agencies to identify and define social problems in such a way as to make them amenable to governmental solutions.[45]

larger administrative districts. (This recommendation was whittled down as the bill went through both houses until the amended law of settlement was only a modest improvement over the old. One of the clauses was so complicated Senior professed not to understand it.) If, as is commonly said, the primary object of the New Poor Law was the institution of a free labor market, the failure to abolish the law of settlement, which even more than the poor law itself hindered that free market, is extraordinary.*

What all these supposed "anomalies"—the establishment of a central board, the retention of the law of settlement, even the decision to amend rather than abolish the poor law—suggest is that the doctrine of laissez faire, however important as part of the ideological background of the New Poor Law, was not the primary and compelling motive for reform. The more urgent issue was what contemporaries said it was: the "dispauperizing of the poor." There was an obvious connection between dispauperization and a free labor market. If the able-bodied poor could be dissuaded, by the workhouse test and the less-eligibility principle, from seeking relief, they would be obliged to find employment in the free market at the prevailing wages. And free employment made for independent, industrious laborers. The free market, however, was not the end but a means to the end, which was reducing the dependency of the poor. If it could be shown that that end could be achieved by compromising the principles of laissez faire—by expanding the role of government, perpetuating the system of settlements, and amending rather than abolishing the poor laws—the reformers were entirely amenable to those compromises.

Introducing the bill in the House of Commons, Lord Althorp, Chancellor of the Exchequer, admitted that it violated the economic law that required everyone to "provide his own subsistence by his own labour." But he went on to defend it as fulfilling a higher law, the religious and human duty to support those who were "really helpless, and really unable to provide for themselves."[49] While some of the reformers may have been less interested in helping those who really needed relief than in deterring and punishing those who did not, there is no doubt that the report (and the law) appealed to many who sincerely wanted to do both. The principle that permitted them to do both, to relieve not only the impotent but also the able-bodied pauper, while at the same time discouraging the independent

---

*It is sometimes assumed that the law of settlement was repealed in 1834.[47] In fact it remained in effect with some modifications until after the Second World War, when it was finally superseded, together with the poor law, by the welfare state. Reviewing the checkered history of the law of settlement, one historian has offered a number of reasons why it was not abolished or even seriously reformed: it did not immobilize labor as much as was thought because it was more flexible in practice than in theory; it was useful as a deterrent to excessive claims for relief; it was a stabilizing influence in a period of great change; and above all, it reflected a powerful commitment to local government and a fear of centralization.[48] But most of these reasons would have argued against the passage of the New Poor Law as well.

laborer from seeking relief, was the distinction between pauper and poor. It was this distinction that dominated the analytic part of the report and was the rationale for most of the remedial measures. It was the same distinction that led to the passage of the Poor Law Amendment Act, an "amendment" that transformed the poor law into a pauper law.

The act that was finally passed was more lenient than the recommendations of the report. Instead of having the power to "disallow" outdoor relief, the Poor Law Commissioners were merely authorized to "regulate" such relief, a concession taken advantage of by many parishes to continue a policy of outdoor relief. Where the original plan would have compelled localities to raise rates for the building of workhouses, the cabinet placed so low a ceiling on that compulsory levy that it deprived the law of the financial resources required for its most important provision. The powers of the central board (the Board of Commissioners, or Commission, as it was called) were reduced; instead of having the authority to commit for contempt, for example, it had to rely on the weaker device of a writ of mandamus. And the life of the board was limited to five years, after which it would have to be renewed by act of Parliament. (In 1847 the Commission was converted into a Poor Law Board whose president sat in Parliament and the Cabinet, thus giving him a constitutional responsibility the earlier commissioners did not have.) In these and other respects the New Poor Law diverged from the report. And the application of the law diverged still more, as innumerable studies in local history have demonstrated.[50] Yet the principles continued to engender heated controversy and remained a source of conflict and resentment for generations.

The *Poor Law Report* was obviously a response to the growing sentiment for reform. But it also helped channel that sentiment, directing it to a particular conception of the problem and a particular solution. After 1834 little was heard of the abolition of the poor law, apart from occasional mutterings which sounded more like mindless regressions than serious proposals. Lord Brougham, for example, moving the second reading of the act, delivered a tribute to Malthus in the course of which he endorsed Malthus's objections to a "permanent fund" for the poor; he then went on to defend the whole of the new act, including the provision for a central board to supervise just that permanent fund.[51] *The Times,* reporting the speech, thereupon attacked the act as Malthusian, much to Malthus's chagrin.

The movement from abolitionism to reform may be traced in the writings of Harriet Martineau, one of the most influential advocates of the New Poor Law and publicists for the new political economy. Convinced that the working classes were sorely in need of instruction in the natural laws governing their lives, she decided to edify them in the most agreeable fashion, by means of fiction. This was hardly a novel idea; indeed, it was so commonplace that she felt obliged to distinguish her own work from the more banal examples of that genre. "It is many years," she introduced her series, "since we grew sick of works that pretend to be stories, and turn out to be catechisms of some kind of knowledge which we had rather become acquainted with in its undisguised form."[52] Her own tales, she prided herself, were genuine works of fiction which happened to convey lessons in political economy.*

Martineau's first series of "novels" (novelettes really, each running to about 130 small-sized pages) appeared in 1832–33 under the general title *Illustrations of Political Economy*. Each "illustrated" a different principle, and each was accompanied by a "Summary of Principles" that was only slightly more didactic than the story itself. Or so, at least, a present-day reader might think. At the time, her great success was attributed to her skill as a storyteller. Charles Knight, her friend, adviser, and occasional publisher, who was also prominent in the affairs of the Society for the Diffusion of Useful Knowledge, which specialized in this kind of popularization, suspected that many people read her stories as fiction without being in the least affected by the principles. Yet the message was so intrusive, the moral assumptions so pervasive, it is difficult to see how even the most casual reader could have escaped them. And the sheer quantity of readers was impressive. Ten thousand copies of each book were sold at a shilling and sixpence, many of these to the libraries of Mechanics' Institutions, so that each tale was read, her publisher estimated, by as many as 144,000 people.

One of these, *Cousin Marshall,* published early in 1833, was a homily on the poor laws. An unabashedly Malthusian tract (although it avoided mentioning Malthus, his name being anathema among the working classes), it argued for the abolition of the poor laws on the ground that relief diverted the available "subsistence fund" from the productive part of the population to the unproductive, thus lowering the living standards of the working

---

*In dissociating herself from some of her predecessors, she did not mean to belittle the most notable of them, Jane Marcet, whose *Conversations on Political Economy* she acknowledged as the inspiration for her own work. The *Conversations,* published in 1816 and eventually going through sixteen editions, was in the form of a dialogue rather than a story and was a more straightforward primer than Martineau's. The dialogue was Mrs. Marcet's trademark. She had earlier written a *Conversation on Chemistry* which had also gone through many editions, and she followed the political economy book with a series of other "conversations" on a multitude of other subjects: Natural Philosophy, Evidences of Christianity, Vegetable Physiology, the History of England. Mrs. Marcet was no mean publicist. Although Joseph Schumpeter disparaged her political economy book as "economics for high-school girls," she received impressive tributes from her contemporaries. Macaulay said that any girl who had read her book "could teach Montagu or Walpole many lessons in finance"; Jean-Baptiste Say, France's leading economist, pronounced her "the only woman who has written on political economy and shown herself superior even to men"; and as late as 1845 J. R. McCulloch, himself a notable economist, wrote that her book was "on the whole perhaps the best introduction to the science that has yet appeared."[53]

classes as a whole. It even reproduced Malthus's timetable for the abolition of the laws, and in almost exactly his words. "The best plan, in my opinion, yet proposed, is this: to enact that no child born from any marriage taking place within a year from the date of the law, and no illegitimate child born within two years from the same date, shall ever be entitled to parish assistance."[54] Most of the story was more artful than this and some parts were even diverting—the descriptions of the "wily tricksters" who pretended to be paralyzed or disabled, or who claimed allowances for dead children, or who deliberately left home so that their families could apply for relief. But the fictional veneer was never permitted to obscure the moral of the work: the essential difference between pauper (the indigent) and poor.

> "We are too apt," she [the heroine] said, "to regard all the poor alike, and to speak of them as one class, whether or not they are dependent; that is, whether they are indigent or only poor. There must always be poor in every society; that is, persons who can live by their industry, but have nothing beforehand. But that there should be able-bodied indigent, that is, capable persons who cannot support themselves, is a disgrace to every society, and ought to be so regarded as such as to make us very careful how we confound the poor and the indigent."[55]

Predating the *Poor Law Report, Cousin Marshall* made no mention of the principle of less-eligibility or of the workhouse test. To the question, "How to prevent the poor becoming indigent," Martineau gave the classic Malthusian answer: increase the subsistence fund by making the poor more productive, and abolish the poor laws that "snatch the bread from the industrious and give it to the idle."[56]

A second series of tales, *Poor Laws and Paupers, Illustrated,* published in 1833–34, reflected the progress of opinion under the influence of the Royal Commission. Martineau had been given an advance copy of the *Extracts* and some of the reports of the assistant commissioners, including Chadwick's. As a result her new tales resembled the earlier ones in their characters and situations but were very different in their practical recommendations. Instead of calling for the abolition of the poor laws she now recommended their "amendment" along precisely the lines of the report: workhouse relief in place of outdoor relief, the principle of less-eligibility, and the establishment of a central board with paid officials. The ease of her transition from abolitionism to reformism, from no poor law to a new poor law, suggests that for her, as for so many others, the specific solutions to the problem were less important than the diagnosis of the problem and the determination to solve it one way or another. That problem was the familiar one: "Except the distinction between sovereign and subject, there is no social difference in England so wide as that between the independent labourer and the pauper; and it is equally ignorant, immoral, and impolitic to confound the two."[57]

While Harriet Martineau was issuing manifestos in the form of fiction, one of the most popular novelists of the time was turning his hand to social commentary. Edward Lytton Bulwer (later known as Bulwer-Lytton) was a Member of Parliament and the author of several "silver-fork novels," tales of romance and intrigue in high society. In *England and the English,* published in 1833, he ventured into another genre that was enjoying some vogue at the time, reflections on the "spirit of the age."* Associated with the small group of Philosophic Radicals in Parliament, Bulwer was even then something of a maverick, expressing publicly some of the reservations about Benthamism that John Stuart Mill was confessing to only in private. A good many of Mill's views found their way into *England and the English,* in the appendix on Bentham written by Mill although not attributed to him (he took pains to keep its authorship secret even from his friends), and in the body of the work, parts of which were obviously inspired by him. When Mill in his autobiography described *England and the English* as "greatly in advance of the public mind," it was because it anticipated the critique of Benthamism he himself was to develop several years later in his essays on Bentham and Coleridge.[60]

For Bulwer, as for Mill, Bentham's "half-truths" turned out to be considerably less than half the truth. At one point Bulwer praised Bentham for combining the "spirit of the Philanthropic with that of the Practical," the enlightenment principle of "Humanity" with the utilitarian principle of "Great Happiness."[61] More often he praised such notable enemies of Benthamism as Coleridge, Wordsworth, and Southey, and his caricatures of the Benthamites were worthy of a Carlyle or a Dickens. "Samuel Square," a man without "pith and succulence, dry as a bone," was the very model of Carlyle's "dry-as-dust," "logic-chopping machine": knowing nothing but "first principles," he "put the feet of his mind into boxes, in order that they may not grow larger"; caring only for humanity at large and for no person in particular, "he never relieveth any one: he never caresseth any one: he never feeleth for any one—he only reasoneth with every one."[62] "Mr. Bluff," the prototype of Dickens's Mr. Gradgrind, was a "sensible, *practical*

---

*William Hazlitt in 1825 and John Stuart Mill in 1831 published essays under that title. Mill explained that the expression was no more than fifty years old, and that while the idea of comparing one's age with former ages was hardly new, the idea of defining one's age in terms of a dominant "spirit" was new.[58] By 1834 the expression had become so common that Cobbett, protesting against the proposed changes in municipal government, accused the government of "pursuing this jack-o'-lantern, which you call the 'Spirit of the age.' "[59] On the Continent, the idea had long been familiar, in France in the works of Saint-Simon and Comte, and in Germany among the Romantics and, in its most sophisticated form, in Hegelianism.

man" who started every harangue with "Now, my friends, let us look *to the facts,*" and was so enamored of facts that "if you could speak to him out of the multiplication table, he would think you a great orator."[63]

Aristocrats fared even worse than the utilitarians. The heroes of Bulwer's novels appeared here as the villains of society. These were the lords and ladies who worshipped fashion and made money the "mightiest of all deities." Themselves corrupt, they succeeded by their example in corrupting the middle classes, for whom "virtue" came to mean "respectability," and respectability a "decent sufficiency of wealth." If only a man made a good appearance, paid his bills on time, subscribed to the proper charities, went to church regularly and to bed on time, he would be a member in good standing in good society, however immoral and mean-spirited he might be.[64]

It was these aristocrats and middle classes who conspired together to degrade the poor. Measuring respectability by wealth, they made poverty seem disreputable and even criminal. "In other countries poverty is a misfortune—with us it is a crime." And because it was thought a crime, they had no scruples in enacting laws injurious to the poor or in denouncing social meetings and amusements as evidence of idleness and disorder. Left with nothing by way of distraction save what they might find in the alehouse, the poor naturally became intemperate and improvident. Unlike French peasants who saved more because they enjoyed themselves more, who did not think it wicked to bring children into the world and took care, once they were in the world, to provide for them, English farm laborers squandered their pittance out of sheer misery. Theirs was the familiar chronicle: "Early marriages; many children; poor-rates, and the workhouse"; "they are born; they are wretched; they die."[65] Nor did factory workers fare better. Debilitated by the unwholesome conditions in which they lived and worked, by hereditary taints, overwork, and undernourishment, they were the ready victims of drink, dissipation, and despair.

For these evils, Bulwer saw only three remedies: legislation limiting the hours of work of women and children, education to promote "social as well as individual morals," and the reform of the poor laws. The poor laws were the heart of the matter. Intended to relieve distress, they had become the "arch-creators of distress."

> The operation of the Poor-laws is the History of the Poor. It is a singular curse in the records of our race, that the destruction of one evil is often the generation of a thousand others. The Poor-laws were intended to prevent mendicants; they have made mendicancy a legal profession; they were established in the spirit of a noble and sublime provision, which contained all the theory of Virtue; they have produced all the consequences of Vice.[66]

In creating pauperism, the poor laws also created crime. It was not poverty that was the "parent of crime," as was often said, but pauperism—and "pauperism is not poverty." The distinction, Bulwer emphasized, was "delicate and important." He quoted the treasurer of Spitalfields parish (the center of the silk-weaving industry in East London, which was in a state of severe depression), who testified before the Poor Law Commission that in all his twenty-five years as an official of that parish, he had come across only a single instance of a "poor but industrious man" charged with stealing —and that was a piece of bacon. There was crime, but it came less from the want of employment than from the idleness fostered by pauperism and the bad habits of those who found it so easy to obtain money and food without having to work.[67]

Bulwer's indictment of the poor laws echoed the *Poor Law Report:* the laws aided the sturdy and indolent young more than the aged and sick because the former were more violent and threatening; they helped dissolve the already fragile links between rich and poor because they made relief a right rather than an act of charity; they encouraged licentiousness and illegitimacy because bastards were supported by the parish; they deadened the social affections because children became "a matter of mercantile speculation." And Bulwer's recommendations were almost identical with those in the report: the abolition of outdoor relief for the able-bodied, workhouse relief under conditions of less-eligibility, the separation of different groups of paupers, the consolidation of parishes, the simplification of the laws of settlement, the creation of a central board responsible for the "sole management of the Poor."[68]

In one respect, Bulwer went far beyond the commission, enunciating a theory of government that was bold even by the standards of Bentham's "omnicompetent legislature."[69] "A good government is a *directive government,*" Bulwer wrote. "It should be in advance of the people—it should pass laws *for* them, not receive all laws *from* them."[70] It was this theory that legitimized not only a central poor law board and factory acts but also, Bulwer recommended, a Minister of Public Instruction on the Prussian model to supervise a system of public education, and in general a larger, more positive, more active government than the English normally tolerated.

> At present, my friends, you only perceive the Government when it knocks at your door for taxes; you couple with its name the idea not of protection, but of extortion; but I would wish that you should see the Government educating your children, and encouraging your science, and ameliorating the condition of your poor; I wish you to warm while you utter its very name, with a grateful and reverent sense of enlightenment and protection; I wish you to behold all your great Public Blessings repose beneath its shadow.[71]

This vision of government, as Bulwer well knew, was anathema to most of the poor law reformers. If he shared their position on the poor laws, he came to it from a very different ideological and emotional stance, his idea of a "directive government" being much closer to Carlyle or Coleridge (or, later, Matthew Arnold) than to Smith or Malthus, and his sympathy for the poor more reminiscent of a Tory Radical than of a Philosophic Radical. His poor were not so much the victims of circumstances over which they had no control as the victims of an aristocracy (and the middle classes aping the aristocracy) which venerated money and denigrated poverty. Yet in spite of these distinctive principles and attitudes, Bulwer ended up exactly where the other poor law reformers did, with a set of proposals that was identical with theirs (adopted, probably, from them), and with the distinction between poverty and pauperism that was essentially theirs—a distinction that could only be implemented by something like the New Poor Law.

Bulwer was not the only maverick among them. Considering the host of people who bore the label "poor law reformers," one might be more impressed by the variety among them than by their common allegiance to this reform. The Rev. Thomas Chalmers, for example, is generally identified as a Malthusian—the McCulloch of the Malthusians, Schumpeter dubbed him.[72] In many respects the designation is apt: he was a confirmed, almost zealous, believer in the principle of population; he was prominent in the movement first for the abolition of the poor laws, then for their reform; and he made a strenuous effort to reconcile Malthusianism and political economy with Evangelicalism and theology. But his Evangelicalism made all the difference, so that even his bitterest opponents did not deride "Parson Chalmers" as they did "Parson Malthus."

Chalmers did not merely assert that voluntary charity was in principle preferable to the poor laws. As minister of the largest and poorest parish in Glasgow, he devoted a good deal of time, energy, and imagination—and publicity—to establishing a comprehensive, church-based system of charity in that impoverished urban parish, a system that he claimed, and many believed, to be more effective than legal, compulsory, public relief. He did this in the name of a Malthusianism that was professedly Christian and a political economy that was something like a "moral economy." The author of a two-volume *On Political Economy* which earned him the respect of economists of his own time (as well as the grudging tribute of Schumpeter), he also delivered much publicized and widely circulated sermons appealing to "the pure, the patriarchal economy of the olden times," praising Malthus for being a political economist who was preeminently a Christian economist, paying tribute to a benevolent God who made the spiritual virtue of moral restraint an economic virtue as well, enjoining the poor to exercise the restraint that would ensure their material and spiritual redemption, and exhorting the rich to exercise the spiritual discipline that would enable them to curb their desire for excessive riches.[73]

The poor law reformers, it is evident, came in all shapes and sizes. They were utilitarians and Unitarians, Evangelicals and orthodox Anglicans, Dissenters and atheists, Whigs and Tories, manufacturers and landlords, countrymen and townsfolk, preachers and philosophers, philanthropists and politicians. They differed radically in their attitudes toward the poor, their theories of economics, their ideas about the proper role of government, their visions of a good society, their views of human nature and divine providence. But they agreed upon the urgency of the problem and the essential solution. The problem was the pauperization of the poor, the solution the removal of the poor from the fatal contamination of the pauper.

Malthusianism had brought that problem into focus and had provided the terms of discourse, the rhetoric and imagery, which dominated the debate over poverty and the poor laws in the first third of the nineteenth century. In its original form it had not provided for any separation between pauper and poor, either in theory or in practice; on the contrary, Malthus, like Smith, had assumed a continuum of pauper and poor. It was, to be sure, a very different continuum. Where Smith's poor, even the very poor, were expected to move gradually to the upper end of the spectrum as the economy expanded and progressed, Malthus's poor, confronted with the inexorable law of population and a restrictive economy, faced the dismal prospect of moving downward to the status of paupers. In this sense Malthus pauperized, potentially at least, the entire body of the poor, and it was to prevent this total pauperization that he insisted upon a total abolition of the poor laws. The poor law reformers hoped to achieve the same end by other means: by deliberately breaking the continuum of pauper and poor, rigorously separating the two so that the poor might be spared the fate of the pauper.

The New Poor Law, then, was not a Malthusian law, either programmatically or theoretically. Yet it was often referred to, especially by critics, as Malthusian, and it is still sometimes spoken of as such. The misconception is not altogether unwarranted. For even as the separation of pauper and poor was being insisted upon in theory, and as attempts were made (although less consistently so) to carry it out in practice, the Malthusian image of pauperization was so dramatic it unwittingly spilled over to the image of poverty itself. The "mischievous ambiguity in the word *poor*" survived the passage of the New Poor Law. Indeed it took on a new significance and a new lease on life. If the poor were no longer subject to the old poor law, if that law was superseded by a "pauper law," the poor nonetheless remained under the shadow of pauperism. The intention had been to remove the stigma of pauperism from the poor by confining it to the pauper class. The reality turned out to be quite the reverse. A stigma so visible and obtrusive could not be so neatly contained. In spite of all the efforts to distinguish, separate, and segregate pauper and poor, the stigma attached to the one inevitably tainted the other. This was perhaps unavoidable in times of great distress, when many of the laboring poor were so indigent they were obliged to seek relief. But the situation was exacerbated by the law itself, by the threat of the workhouse hanging over the heads of the poor, a workhouse that deliberately, publicly carried with it the stigma of pauperism.

It was this stigma, as much as the practical effects of the New Poor Law, that provoked a wave of opposition in the 1830s and 1840s. The opposition came not from the paupers, who were powerless and voiceless, but from the poor who felt degraded by the very idea of the workhouse (the "parish," as it was known), from local authorities who resented the usurpation of their traditional functions and were dismayed by a social ethos that was unfamiliar and uncongenial, from critics who looked back to a Golden Age of social harmony and hierarchy, and from radicals who looked forward to a political or economic egalitarianism that would eliminate pauperism by reforming the suffrage and redistributing property. As opposition to the old poor law provided the agenda for reformers in the first three decades of the century, so opposition to the New Poor Law provided the agenda for many conservatives and most radicals in the following two decades.

VII

THE TORY OPPOSITION:

PATERNALISM AND

HUMANITARIANISM

The New Poor Law, which seemed the very epitome of the "spirit of the age," the application to social problems of the laws of nature and political economy, of reason and utility, triggered a powerful movement of resistance, a movement which cannot be measured by the number of local authorities who covertly or openly sabotaged the law or by the number of laborers who rioted against it. Behind all the opposition was the assertion of something like a counter-spirit, a protest against the principles embodied in the law, and, more important, against the very idea of applying such rational, uniform, doctrinaire principles to social affairs.

The protest came from different groups in the name of different interests and ideas—from Tories (although not from the party itself, which officially endorsed the New Poor Law), Radicals (but not, of course, the Philosophic Radicals, who helped write the law), and even some Whigs (under whose auspices the act was introduced and carried); from the most respectable of all papers, *The Times,* and from the underground radical press; from country squires and provincial trade unionists; from orthodox Anglicans, Evangelicals, and Nonconformists; from agricultural laborers in the south and factory workers in the north; from Chartists, Christian Socialists, factory reformers, suffrage reformers, currency reformers, corn law reformers, education reformers, temperance reformers.[1]

A good deal of the opposition turned on the issue of centralization, the creation of a central board empowered to impose a uniform policy over the entire country. A later generation, accustomed to a much larger degree of centralization, may be inclined to see this issue as a camouflage for the "vested interests" threatened by the new system: the local magistrates, gentry, and clergy deprived of political and social power, and the farmers who profited from the old allowance system. Such interests did play a large part in the opposition, but they were by no means the whole of it. There were those who were exercised by the issue of centralization who had no personal stake in it (the arch-Tory Lord Eldon, for example, who was as violently opposed to the New Poor Law as he had been to the Reform Act of 1832), and those who did have a stake in it and opposed the law for quite other reasons. Even when the question was one of "social control"—who was to exercise what kind of control over whom and to what purpose—there were principles inherent in that question, principles that determined how that question was posed and how it was answered.[2]

On one level, the opposition of *The Times* can be explained in terms of professional interests and personal feuds. Harriet Martineau, who was taken aback by the venom of its editorials, first speculated that the editors were trying to humor the country justices who were "a most important class of customers," and then that it was the editor, Thomas Barnes, who was giving vent to his personal animus against the Lord Chancellor, Brougham.[3] (Barnes also heartily disliked three members of the Royal Commission: the economist Nassau Senior, the Benthamite Walter Coulson, and Blomfield, Bishop of London.) It was also well known that the proprietor of *The Times*, John Walter, had special reason to feel vindictive toward Chadwick. As a justice of the peace in Berkshire, Walter repeatedly decided appeals in favor of paupers, thus frustrating the attempts of another magistrate to restrict relief and keep the poor rates down. In his preliminary report, Chadwick quoted extensively from the testimony of the other magistrate and implied (without naming Walter but clearly referring to him) that by involving the parish in costly litigation, Walter had misused parish funds. Even in these instances, however, the personal issues reflected differences of principle. Barnes disliked Brougham, Senior, and the others because they represented political economy, utilitarianism, and everything else he despised in contemporary affairs. And Walter's feud was a dispute over the proper conception and scope of relief, Walter insisting that the parish had an obligation to provide its needy with work that would neither "degrade the party receiving it, nor change his domestic habits"—which meant work outside the workhouse.[4] This conception of relief was rooted in a conception of society that later made Walter the candidate of the Chartists when he stood for Parliament in 1841, and a friend of the Young Englanders, who met in his house and received a friendly hearing in his paper.

Whatever the motives of the editor or of the publisher, the fact that *The Times* took the position it did was of enormous importance, as Chadwick and Senior well knew. What they could not have known at the time was that the paper would keep up the campaign for over a decade, fanning the flames of the opposition, providing it with arguments and facts (or supposed facts), and giving credibility and respectability to the entire movement against the New Poor Law. Respectability, however, did not mean temperateness. From the beginning, *The Times* was as vitriolic as the radical press. It launched its campaign by thundering (it was for good reason that it was known as "The Thunderer") against "the plotting pericrania of Mr. Senior," "the handywork of some sucking Solon of the Benthamite breed, or . . . some retired and super-annuated sage of the same spawn."[5] That tone was sustained for the better part of a decade, in part provoked by its competition with the *Morning Chronicle,* which was no less vehement in support of the New Poor Law (having been purchased for precisely that purpose).

Initially *The Times* directed the brunt of its attack against the commissioners, the "Three Tyrants of Somerset House," who were nothing less, it claimed, than a dictatorship. With unlimited, irresponsible powers (they were not answerable to Parliament), they could make the law as well as administer it, and from their decisions there was no appeal. This combination of executive and legislative authority was so blatant a violation of the British Constitution that it only remained to repeal habeas corpus for the despotism to be complete. Should the bill carry, "no Englishman, who is not dead to shame, will again hear the words British liberty pronounced without a blush or a sigh."[6] For the poor that tyranny was nothing less than penal servitude. Shortly after the report was released *The Times* protested against the workhouse proposal: "Why not at once have the boldness to declare poverty 'penal'?" After the law was passed this became a major complaint. "Such a system amounts to a declaration that every pauper is a criminal, and that, under the name of workhouses, prisons shall be erected throughout the land for their safe custody and punishment." Every poor man would be at the mercy of the commissioners, who could "bully, tyrannize over, and trample upon him with perfect impunity." The erection of that expensive machinery and the myriads of functionaries required to operate it would "perpetuate the system of pauperism for ever." It was also an incitement to republicanism, since it would alienate the poor from the political system, keep them in a state of irritation, and set an example for a sweeping departure from the ancient constitution. It was, in short, as subversive a measure as any that the "most *farouche* republican could have desired or devised."[7] When it ran out of arguments such as these, *The Times* reprinted sections of Swift's *Modest Proposal* and the "Nature's feast" passage, which it resurrected from the second edition of Malthus's *Essay.* [8]

The Times had the great advantage of being able to harp daily on the iniquities of the New Poor Law. But the quarterlies had the space in which to do justice to the complexities of the argument and an audience capable of appreciating them. The Tory *Quarterly Review,* with a circulation of 10,000, published some of the most telling critiques. One major article (by G. Poulett Scrope, it is thought, a Member of Parliament and a political economist of some note) is less interesting for its criticism of the new law than for its defense of the old—not, to be sure, the old law as it was on the eve of the reform, but as it had been before Speenhamland. For centuries the poor law had permitted England to enjoy an "internal tranquility, security of property, and general prosperity unexampled in the history of nations." That happy situation could have been restored merely by abolishing allowances and returning to the status quo ante Speenhamland. Instead the bill proposed so fundamental an alteration of the law as to deprive England of its unique good fortune.[9]

Unlike *The Times,* the *Quarterly Review* did not quarrel with the centralizing provisions of the bill. On the contrary, it entirely approved of the establishment of a central board with paid officials empowered to regulate the workhouses, keep accounts, authorize the union of parishes, and otherwise supervise the system of relief; and it would have gone even further in giving the board the authority to review the assessment as well as the disbursement of the poor rates. Its objections were on a quite different level. Where the New Poor Law proposed to give relief only as a last resort, under conditions of less-eligibility and the stigma of pauperism, the *Quarterly* wanted to do exactly the opposite: to reassert relief as a matter of right, a right rooted in law as well as in humanity and expediency. The "poor man's rights and securities," it maintained, were as firmly grounded in statute and judicial precedent as were the rich man's right to property and title; to abrogate the former was to subvert the latter.[10] In a curious twist of the argument, the *Quarterly* interpreted the amendment which made the workhouse permissive rather than obligatory—an amendment intended as a concession to the opposition—as a retreat not from compulsory workhouse relief but from compulsory relief per se, and sharply criticized it on that account. Its disapproval of the workhouse provision, however, implied no disapproval of the principle of work. Unlike the new law, it would have made work a condition of outdoor as well as indoor relief, and it looked to parish employment (on the highways, for example) as a substitute for relief. This was its answer to the familiar argument that "to give the able-bodied poor a claim for support is to give the idle a claim to the produce of the labour of the industrious." The able-bodied poor who asked for parish employment were not asking to be maintained in idleness. They were asking to work, to share in "the curse inflicted on our first parents, namely, 'to gain his bread by the sweat of his brow.'" Only when they were deprived of this natural right were they tempted to take by fraud or violence what they could not obtain by work.[11]

[1] William Hogarth, from *Industry and Idleness* (1747).

The FRIEND of HUMANITY and the KNIFE-GRINDER, _ Scene. The Borough
in Imitation of M.ʳ Southey's Sapphics, _ Vide. Anti-Jacobin p.15.

London. Pub.ᵈ Dec.ᵗ 4.ᵗʰ 1797. by H. Humphrey 27. S.ᵗ James's Street

Friend of Hum.ᵗ _ "Needy Knife-grinder! whither are you going?
  Rough is the road, your Wheel is out of order.
  Bleak blows the blast; _ your Hat has got a hole in't,
          So have your Breeches!
  "Weary Knife-grinder! little think the proud ones,
  Who in their coaches roll along the turnpike-
  -road, what hard work 'tis crying all day 'Knives and
          "Scissars to grind O!"
  "Tell me, Knife-grinder, how came you to grind knives?
  Did some rich man tyrannically use you?
  Was it the Squire? or Parson of the Parish?
          Or the Attorney?
  "Was it the 'Squire for killing of his Game? or
  Covetous Parson for his Tythes distraining?
  Or roguish Lawyer made you lose your little
          All in a law-suit?
  "(Have you not read the Rights of Man, by Tom Paine?)
  Drops of compassion tremble on my eye-lids,
  Ready to fall, as soon as you have told your
          Pitiful story"

Knife-grinder._ "Story! God bless you! I have none to tell, Sir,
  Only last night a-drinking at the Chequers,
  This poor old Hat and Breeches, as you see, were
          Torn in a scuffle.
  "Constables came up for to take me into
  Custody; they took me before the Justice;
  Justice Oldmixon put me in the Parish _
         -Stocks for a Vagrant.
  "I should be glad to drink your Honour's health in
  A Pot of Beer, if you would give me Sixpence;
  But for my part, I never love to meddle
         With Politics, Sir."

Friend of Hum.ᵗ "I give thee Sixpence! I will see thee damn'd first,
  Wretch! whom no sense of wrongs can rouse to ven-
  Sordid, unfeeling, reprobate, degraded,   -geance.
         Spiritless outcast!
  (Kicks the Knife-grinder, overturns his Wheel, and exit in
  a transport of republican enthusiasm and universal-
         -philanthropy)

To the Independant Electors of the Borough of Southwark, this Print is most respectfully dedicated.

[2] Print by James Gillray (1797).

THE "MILK" OF POOR-LAW "KINDNESS."

ABOVE: [4] "Tremendous Sacrifice!" George Cruikshank, from *Our Own Times,* 1846.
BELOW: [5] From *Punch,* 1843.

REBECCA AND HER DAUGHTERS.

Tolltaker . . Sɪʀ R. P—ʟ.   *Irish Rebecca* . D—ʟ O'C—ʟ.   *Rebecca's Daughters* by Mᴇᴍʙᴇʀs of the Rᴇᴘᴇᴀʟ Ass——ɴ.

[6] "The Ragged School." George Cruikshank, from *Our Own Times,* 1846.

The Life of **WILLIAM-COBBETT**, — *written by himself* —
— *" Now you lying Varlets you shall see how a plain Tale will put you down !"*

1st Plate.

Father kept the sign of the Jolly-Farmer at Farnham. I was his Pot Boy and thought an Ornament to the profession, — at Seven Years Old my natural genius began to expand, and display'd itself in a taste for Plunder and oppresion ! — I robbed Orchards, set Father's Bull-Dog at the Cats — quarelled with all the Poor-Boys, and beat all the little Girls of the Town, — to the great admiration of the inhabitants; — who prophecied that my talents (unless the Devil was in it,) would one day elevate me to a Post in some publick situation.

[7] Print by James Gillray, for *Political Register* (1809).

The Life of WILLIAM-COBBETT. written by himself.

London. Publish'd Sept 29 1809. by H. Humphrey, 27 S! James's Street.

2ª Plate.

— as I shot up into a hobble-dehoy, I took to driving the Plow for the benefit of mankind, which was always my prime object ; — hearing that the Church-Wardens were after me, I determined to become a Hero, and secretly quitting my agricultural pursuits, and Sukey Stubbs, — Voluntered as a Private- -Soldier, into the 51st Regiment, commanded by that tried Patriot and Martyre Lord Edwd Fitzgerald, — and embarked for the Plantations.

[8] Print by James Gillray, for *Political Register* (1809).

[9] Illustrations from the Mine Commission Report.

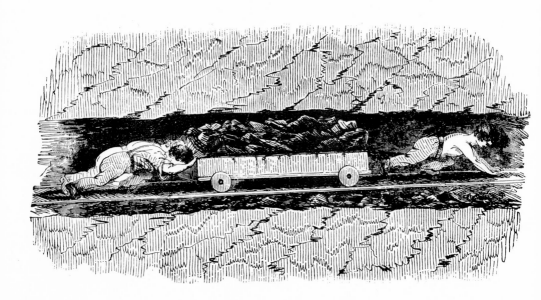

The *Quarterly* would also have reversed the principle of less-eligibility. The condition of the pauper, rather than being worse than that of the independent laborer, should be much the same, for the sake of the laborer as well as the pauper. Since the "parish rate of pay" determined the general level of wages in any district, employers had to meet that rate in order to attract workers. If the parish authorities were authorized to set relief at a "natural level" appropriate to poor and pauper alike, they would be sending a message to the local employers:

> Unless you will offer wages sufficient to maintain the families of your labourers, you will not get them. We will, as we are bound to do by law, maintain and employ them on the account of the public. And we will maintain them in such a manner as the necessity of their case and the humanity of the law require; not at any lower scale calculated from the insufficient pittance you offer them.[12]

That "natural level" of relief should be determined by the "natural wants" of the pauper, and this, in turn, by the "habitual standard of necessaries" among the population as a whole, a standard which "the people of this wealthy and civilized land . . . considered essential to the decent support of an Englishman." Any attempt to lower that standard by basing it on potatoes, barley, or any other inferior food would be an act of inhumanity toward the pauper and would inevitably lead to a deterioration of the condition of the entire laboring population, reducing them to the state of the "half-naked, and potato-fed, and wretched savages of Ireland."[13] (In Ireland itself, the *Quarterly* said, the absence of a poor law and thus the lack of any natural level of wages and subsistence, was responsible for the abject state of the poor.)

This argument was the mirror image of the Poor Law Report. It advocated exactly what the report decried: uniting pauper and poor in a common bond, making their interests identical, restoring them as a single class. Where the reformers had used the principle of less-eligibility to create a gap between the rate of relief and the rate of wages, the *Quarterly* wanted to eliminate that gap by making a single rate apply to both, a rate based upon a standard appropriate to the independent laborer. Where the reformers sharply differentiated between paupers and poor in terms of their qualities, needs, and rights, the *Quarterly* used "pauper" and "poor" interchangeably, attributing to them precisely the same qualities, needs, and rights. Where the reformers sought to convert the poor law into a pauper law, the *Quarterly* urged the restoration of the old law that had served "the whole labouring population of England." No radical put the case for the old law and against the new more persuasively than this high-Tory journal.

Not all Tories shared this view; a majority of the party actually favored the New Poor Law. Even the *Quarterly* wavered; in 1835 it published an article defending the law written by one of the assistant commissioners who were engaged in implementing it. Yet there were far more Tories than Whigs in the opposition and among them were some of the most passionate opponents of the law. They also had available to them another Tory journal, *Blackwood's Magazine,* whose circulation was less than the *Quarterly*'s but still a respectable 8,000. *Blackwood's* made little attempt to argue the economic merits of the case; instead it put it entirely on humanitarian grounds. Thus the Professor of Moral Philosophy at the University of Edinburgh denounced the "audacious doctrine" that the poor should be compelled to provide for themselves out of their savings for sickness, loss of employment, or old age, and failing that, that they should be "left to their fate." "It is indeed shocking to think how people, sitting in easy chairs at blazing firesides, and tables covered with wine and walnuts, will belch out opinions on the duties of the poor," or, the professor snidely added, to watch the members of the Political Economy Club spinning out their theories while devouring "venison pastry."[14]

With the same passion and his own inimitable rhetoric, Disraeli attacked the "flagitious statute" in his election address of 1837. Five years earlier, in his first bid for a seat in Parliament, he had urged a return to the "system of 1795."[15] He now reminded his audience of his opposition to the New Poor Law from the beginning, a law that contained "fearful tidings for the poor."

> One of our poets has beautifully said—'Sweet is the music of the Sabbath bells,' but of this music the Whigs have deprived the poor and the aged. For him the Sabbath bells sound no more. Immured in a prison, no spiritual consolation can he derive in the hallowed temple of his ancestors; but, at length, broken-hearted, he quits a world with which he is disgusted.

The new law was based on the false and immoral principle that relief was charity instead of a right. "I consider that this Act has disgraced the country more than any other upon record. Both a moral crime and a political blunder, it announces to the world that in England poverty is a crime."[16] Two years later, in the debate on the Chartist petition, he rejected the demand for political equality while agreeing that the New Poor Law was an "invasion of their civil rights," an attack on "the mainstay, the living source of the robustness of the Commonwealth."[17]

"Poverty is a crime." This was the gravamen of the indictment. To the traditional-minded Tory, poverty, so far from being a crime, was what it had always been, a natural condition to be alleviated by the charity of those who, by the grace of God and their own efforts, were happily able to afford it, and by a public system of relief which testified to the obligation of society to care for those who were so unfortunate as to be unable to care for themselves. This paternalistic creed survived long after political economy had pronounced it dead. It was a creed which spoke of "rights" and "obligations" as uninhibitedly as it spoke of "rich" and "poor." And it was able to persist in the old faith partly because it retained that old vocabulary.

If political economy had no room for rights and obligations, neither did it have room for rich and poor, except as emotive terms. In its lexicon the primary categories were capital, land, and labor, the share of each being determined by the prevailing conditions of supply and demand. Poor relief was not a right, because the marketplace recognized neither rights nor obligations but only, as the *Poor Law Report* said, "contracts"— contracts freely entered into by free men, by "independent laborers" and (it went without saying) independent employers. In that contractual world the pauper had no part. He might be taken care of, indeed the New Poor Law made elaborate arrangements to take care of him, but it did so outside the framework of the market. Since that framework defined the boundaries of society, the pauper was, by definition so to speak, an outcast —an outcast not so much by virtue of his character, actions, or misfortunes, but by the mere fact of his dependency, his reliance on relief rather than his own labor for his subsistence. From being an outcast it was only a short step to being regarded as a criminal. Hence the workhouse, the visible confirmation of his status as an outcast, was also, in popular parlance, a prison, a "Bastille."

The issue was then and is still often posed in terms of "humanitarianism." Was it on essentially humanitarian grounds that many Tories opposed the law? There is no doubt that humanitarianism played a large part in the opposition, but something more was meant by this than the harsh treatment meted out to the paupers, the onerous conditions to which they were subjected, the deprivations they suffered, the cruelties inflicted on them. The basic, radical inhumanity of the law was the ejection of the pauper from the society of his own kind, the poor, and from the larger society in which poor and rich were bound by human ties that could not be contracted away. In this sense humanitarianism merged with paternalism, and it was the amalgam of these sentiments that accounted for a large part of the Tory opposition.

The paternalistic ethic has been characterized by the historian David Roberts as "authoritarian, hierarchic, organic, and pluralistic," these features not always being present together or to the same degree, but in some combination and in one form or another.[18] In the large spectrum of belief comprised within that ethic, it was possible for some paternalists to approve of the New Poor Law and of political economy, although that approval was apt to be grudging and expediential. More often, they were ambivalent or hostile. As magistrates and poor-law guardians they frequently took it upon themselves to mitigate the effects of the law or to bypass it entirely, partly because they regarded it as inhumane, and partly because they saw it as inimical to a society in which they liked to think of themselves as "guardians" of the poor in more than the legal sense of that term.

"How cruel was the Victorian poor law?" That question exercised contemporaries as it has historians.[19] One memorable answer was provided by *Oliver Twist*. The opening chapter, published in *Bentley's Miscellany* in January 1837, described Oliver's birth in the workhouse, his first cry advertising to the inmates "the fact of a new burden having been imposed upon the parish." The second chapter had him farmed out to the branch-workhouse, where twenty or thirty other "juvenile offenders against the poor-laws" rolled about the floor all day "without the inconvenience of too much food or too much clothing," supervised by an elderly woman who received sevenpence-halfpenny a week for each of them, most of which she appropriated for her own use. In "eight and a half cases out of ten"—Dickens parodied the statistics bandied about by the reformers—the child perished from want, cold, and neglect, and was thus "summoned into another world, and there gathered to the fathers it had never known in this." Oliver, having defied the odds by surviving, was duly transferred at the ripe age of nine to the workhouse where the famous "More" scene took place, which gave Dickens the opportunity to explain the rule propounded by some deep philosophers that "all poor people should have the alternative (for they could compel nobody, not they), of being starved by a gradual process in the house, or by a quick one out of it."[20]

Parts of these opening scenes were reprinted in *The Times,* which followed them with a series of reports designed to give truth to the fiction. This was not the usual sensation-of-the-day exposé. For five years *The Times* kept up the campaign, demonstrating the cruelty of the workhouses by means of its own statistics (41 percent of the inmates were reported to have died in one house) and by harrowing accounts complete with names, dates, and places. Naked men were reported to have been sloshed with water in an open courtyard in the middle of winter; a woman was stripped to the waist and whipped; a mother whose two children had died in the workhouse was forbidden to leave until she had removed the bodies; a child was so hungry he ate a mouse; and so on, through instance after instance of starvation, deprivation, disease, exposure, flogging, to say nothing of the mundane cases of crowding, solitary confinement, and the breakup of families. This "compendium of poor law crimes" has been calculated as comprising some 290 episodes of abuse and cruelty recounted in something like

2,000,000 words in a five-year period.[21] The stories were widely reprinted, and they inspired countless similar ones. In Parliament alone, 65 cases of this sort (some from *The Times*) were cited during this period. The same stories (and a few new ones) reappeared in a compendium volume entitled *The Book of the Bastilles*. All of this gave the unmistakable impression of a policy not of random or occasional abuse, but of deliberate, systematic cruelty inspired by a conscious, ruthless ideology.

The indictment did not go unchallenged. The reformers conducted their own counter-campaign, citing in their defense the annual reports of the Poor Law Commission. If there were instances of cruelty, the rebuttal went, it was not because of but in spite of the new law, which explicitly forbade whipping, starving, freezing, overcrowding. Conceding these as unfortunate vestiges of the old law, the reformers insisted that conditions in and out of the workhouses had improved. The number of paupers had declined, laborers were receiving higher wages, the aged were being taken care of more humanely, and the workhouses were reasonably clean and decent. The commissioners also discovered, after instituting inquiries of their own, that the most flagrant and most frequently cited cases of cruelty—the woman stripped and beaten, the men sloshed with water in the icy court-yard, the boy who ate the mouse—were all false. *The Times,* it appeared, had made no attempt to substantiate them before publication, not even to the extent of determining whether the stories were consistent with the physical features of the workhouse in which they were presumed to have occurred. Although *The Times* dutifully reported the commissioners' findings, it neither retracted its charges nor ceased its campaign. The stories themselves, the false together with the true, continued to circulate, each repetition seeming to substantiate and reinforce the case against the New Poor Law.

Summing up the evidence, David Roberts has concluded that the reports of cruelty were often exaggerated and sometimes completely fab-ricated, and that some of the abuses which did exist were, as the commission-ers claimed, the heritage of the old workhouses which they tried vainly to correct. There was, to be sure, a "psychological discomfort" which was deliberate in the separation of families and other practices much resented by the inmates—early rising, prayers before meals, the lack of beer and tea. In general, however, the commissioners were less doctrinaire in practice than in theory, countenancing a good deal of outdoor relief and even, on occa-sion, allowances to supplement wages. And the theory itself, while commit-ted to the workhouse and the less-eligibility principle, did not sanction the kinds of cruelty which were so highly publicized, and which proved to be highly fictionalized as well.[22]

Yet the same evidence lends itself to a different interpretation. Conceding much of Roberts's case—that the reports of cruelty were exaggerated and even false, and that conditions in the workhouse, in spite of the principle of less-eligibility, were not necessarily worse than those outside—Ursula Henriques points to another kind of cruelty, reflected, for example, in the obtuseness of one of the Poor Law Commissioners, George Nicholls (later the author of a voluminous history of the poor laws), who, when told that the inmates of a workhouse were so hungry they ate the bones they were crushing as part of their work assignment, complained of the "depraved appetites" of the paupers. More pervasive and insidious forms of cruelty were the removal of old people from the communities in which they had lived their entire lives, the separation of families within the workhouse, and other regulations that were eminently reasonable to the reformers and profoundly offensive to the poor.[23]

Contemporaries were well aware of both sides of the argument: the fact that in some respects the new law was less cruel than the old and that in others it was more cruel. If the "myth" of cruelty was so widespread, if it persisted in spite of all the evidence to the contrary, it must have corresponded to some reality, although perhaps not the reality claimed for it.

By a kind of poetic justice, that myth may be laid at the door of the reformers themselves. The opponents of the law were responding precisely to the idea of pauperism that the reformers had deliberately and proudly written into the law. That idea prevailed even when the reality was other-wise. In spite of their complaints about the persistence of outdoor relief and the evasion of the workhouse test, the reformers had wrought better than they knew. Their much vaunted principle of less-eligibility had not been merely a means of ensuring that the rewards of labor would be greater than the rewards of idleness. That could have been done without the establish-ment of workhouses or the abolition of outdoor relief; all that would have been required was a statute fixing the rate of relief at some fixed figure or percentage below that of the prevailing wage. If the reformers did not avail themselves of this simple expedient, it was because they were seeking not a quantitative distinction between pauper and poor, a distinction that would simply make the pauper poorer than the poor, but a qualitative distinction, one that would make pauperism so odious that no respectable poor man would be tempted by it.

It was in this sense that the workhouse was meant to be cruel—not in terms of food, or physical conditions, or arduous labor, but conceptually, the very idea of it being shameful and disgraceful. And it was in this sense that it was perceived as cruel. The stigma of the workhouse constituted its cruelty. The tales of horror, often false in themselves, testified to a symbolic truth, so to speak. The commissioners might protest that the workhouses were tolerably clean, the food adequate, the conditions decent enough, at least by the standards of the very poor. But they themselves had said that it was not these conditions that made the workhouse less eligible; it was the fact of confinement and the stigma attached to the confinement.

After *The Times* started its series of exposés, the proprietor John Walter visited several workhouses and was reported to have been "much disappointed" to find a reasonable degree of "order, regularity, and *comfort.*" At the same time he was quoted as saying that "no facts" would persuade him to alter his opinion.[24] The statement (if indeed he made it—it comes from a prejudiced source) may be taken to mean that these particular houses may have been tolerable but others probably were not, or, more cynically, that he was not about to let the facts get in the way of a cause in which he had a large personal and professional stake. It may also suggest that "no facts" of that order were relevant to the real issue, that the significance of the workhouses did not lie in the apparent facts of their orderliness, regularity, or comfort but in what they represented. In this sense, *The Times* and other publications, in perpetuating the mythical cases of cruelty even after they had been exposed as myths, were doing what Dickens did in his fiction, attesting to an order of truth that could best be expressed mythically, fictionally. When Mrs. Higden, in *Our Mutual Friend,* vowed that she would sooner die than suffer the disgrace of the "accursed workhouse," and when she did in fact contrive to die on the road rather than in the house, she confirmed what Harriet Martineau, with far less grace and art, had said in her *Illustrations* and Chadwick in the *Poor Law Report:* to be poor was respectable but to be a pauper was disgraceful. It was the workhouse that established the identity of the pauper, that stigmatized him as a pauper and confirmed him in his disgrace.

This is not to say that the old workhouse had been much more respectable. In 1783 George Crabbe wrote of one "pauper palace" in Norfolk.

> Your plan I love not,—with a number you
> Have placed your poor, your pitiable few:
> There, in one house, throughout their lives to be,
> The pauper palace which they hate to see:
> That giant-building, that high-bounding wall,
> Those bare-worn walks, that lofty thund'ring hall!
> That large loud clock, which tolls each dreaded hour,
> Those gates and locks and all those signs of power;
> It is a prison with a milder name,
> Which few inhabit without dread or shame.[25]

During the following half-century, new and grander workhouses were built, so that the term "pauper palace" acquired an even more ironic tone. In 1810 Crabbe wrote of them more respectfully but still ruefully.

> Be it agreed—the Poor who hither come
> Partake of plenty, seldom found at home;
> That airy rooms and decent beds are meant
> To give the poor, by day, by night, content: . . .
> I own it grieves me to behold them sent
> From their old home; 'tis pain, 'tis punishment,
> To leave each scene familiar, every face,
> For a new people and a stranger race.[26]

Yet even in East Anglia, where workhouses had long been familiar and where they were known to be not excessively noxious—"palaces" indeed compared with some of the hovels of the poor—there were riots after the New Poor Law was passed. What was objected to was an official policy identifying relief with the workhouse. The persistence of the riots, there and elsewhere, even after local authorities had made it clear that they did not intend to impose that policy systematically, suggests that the meaning of the act as much as its execution was abhorrent. However authorities sought to mitigate its effects, the odium of pauperism remained.

The great offense of the new law was moral, not material or physical. This was also its great paradox. In trying to prevent the pauperization and demoralization of the poor, the reformers pauperized and demoralized the poor more profoundly than they knew. The New Poor Law did not invent the distinction between pauper and poor any more than it invented the workhouse. But where before pauper and poor had been temporary, contingent categories, a laborer being one or the other at one time or another (or even, as in the Speenhamland situation, at the same time), now these categories were hardened and sharpened, applying to whole classes rather than to individuals, and making it more difficult for individuals to move from one class to another. Contrary to the reformers' intentions, it was the poor, not the paupers, who felt most aggrieved by this classification. Knowing their own condition to be perilous, at the mercy of the economy, of nature, and of their own infirmities, they confronted the very real possibility that their poverty would one day degenerate into pauperism. The stigma of pauperism was more threatening to them than it was to the "idle vagabond" or "sturdy beggar" who was callous to that stigma, who indeed publicly displayed it, traded on it (literally), and thrived on it. When opponents of the New Poor Law raised the cry of cruelty, it was generally this idea of pauperism they had in mind. This is why they did not call for a reform of the workhouses—for improved administration and supervision, more plentiful food and medical care, better living and sanitary conditions. Instead they attacked the workhouse itself as the symbol of an idea they found degrading and immoral.

If we can sympathize with the poor who harbored memories (and illusions) of a more humane "moral economy," we should also be able to respect those among the upper classes who cherished the ideal—and, it may be, the illusion—of a humane, paternalistic, benevolent, organic, hierarchic society. Both as ideal and as reality, paternalism was no doubt, as is now often said, a form of "social control" peculiarly suited to the habits and interests of the aristocracy and gentry. But it also characterized a society that the paternalists (and not a few of the spokesmen of the poor) genuinely believed to be more moral and humane than the system that was displacing it.

The decline of paternalism is generally associated with the rise of laissez faire and the market economy, an ideology and an economy that broke the "cake of custom," the "chain of connexion," the "social fabric," and set individuals free to pursue their own interests, in their own ways, for their own purposes. A more immediate cause of that decline was the physical, and hence social, dislocation resulting from industrialism. The movements of population from country to town, agriculture to industry, domestic industry to factories, can be much exaggerated; England was not urbanized and industrialized as rapidly or as thoroughly as the image of the "industrial revolution" suggests. But the rate of urbanization and industrialization vastly increased within the lifetime of a single generation, and even those who remained in their old occupations and locations were aware of the movement going on all around them. That mobility, geographic and occupational, inevitably loosened the old paternalistic, deferential structure of society.

In these circumstances, the most visible remnant of paternalism was the poor law, a law that proudly traced its lineage to Elizabethan times and that confirmed the "ancient" responsibility of society for the infirm and the needy. And the most visible bearers of paternalism were the people charged with fulfilling that responsibility and executing that law: landlords, overseers of the poor, vestrymen, churchwardens, magistrates. If local farmers, who bore the heaviest burden of the poor rates, were inclined to lighten that burden by reducing relief, others in that social network, for whatever motives, tended to be more solicitous of the poor.* The magistrates, for

*On the other hand, the farmers had a stake in the old poor law, especially the allowance system, which permitted them to pay lower wages. There is, in fact, much confusion over the economic and social motives of the various parties, their claims to influence and power, and their roles in the administration of relief after the passage of the new law. Anthony Brundage, for example, maintains that the authority of the magistrates, and thus of the landed interests, increased under the New Poor Law, whereas Ursula Henriques sees the law as a transfer of power to the middle or "middling" classes.[27]

example, who were generally the larger landlords, decided cases in favor of the poor more often than the reformers would have liked. The *Poor Law Report* testified to this fact when it rebuked those magistrates who, for reasons of "misdirected benevolence, or desire of popularity, or timidity," were profligate in dispensing other people's money.[28] It was to eliminate such benevolence and profligacy that the central board of commissioners was empowered to prescribe and supervise the terms of relief.

Those who deplore the loss of the old moral economy cannot be entirely dismissive of the idea of paternalism that was an integral part of that moral economy. One may question the viability of the paternalistic ethic in an industrial age or be suspicious of the motives and interests of those who professed it. But one cannot dispute the fact that such an ethic existed, that large numbers of people spoke and acted in its name, that it played a considerable part in the opposition to the New Poor Law, and that it was conducive to a more generous, less punitive form of relief than the utilitarian ethic espoused by most of the reformers. So, at any rate, it appeared to a good many contemporaries, including those reformers who were hostile to that paternalistic ethic. So too, as will be seen, it appeared to a good many radicals at the time, some of whom shared that ethic and even grounded their own radicalism in it.

VIII

CARLYLE:

RADICAL TORYISM

When Thomas Carlyle attacked the "false, heretical and damnable" theory that lay behind the New Poor Law, he was called a Tory—"stranger Tory," he protested, than any in recent generations. Several weeks later, he found that he was being described as a Radical. "The people are beginning to discover that I am not a Tory. Ah, no! but one of the deepest, though perhaps the quietest, of all the Radicals now extant in the world."[1] But that label too was not quite right. Neither were those which one desperate reviewer tried on for size: "philosophic Ultra-Radical," "Tory-Radical," "half Radical," "Utopian Toryism," "heroic Toryism."[2]

The book that inspired these ill-fitting labels was *Chartism*. It was in 1838, when the Chartist movement was beginning to emerge into national prominence, that Carlyle first thought of writing an essay on the "claims, conditions, rights and mights" of the working classes. He proposed it to John Stuart Mill, his friend and editor of the *Westminster Review,* who turned it down, Carlyle later explained, because it would have been uncongenial to the Philosophic Radicals associated with that journal.[3] A year later, as Chartism gained momentum and prepared for its dramatic confrontation with Parliament, Carlyle returned to the theme, this time offering it to the Tory *Quarterly Review.* The long essay (70-odd pages) was completed several months later, by which time the Chartist petition had been rejected by the House of Commons, the Chartist convention had dissolved, and the movement itself appeared to be spent. Carlyle then gave the piece to the *Quarterly,* but without any expectation that it would be accepted. "Such an article equally astonishing to Girondins, Radicals, do-nothing Aristocrats, Conservatives, and unbelieving dilettante Whigs, can hope for no harbour in any Review."[4] And so it turned out, the editor apparently liking the essay but not daring to print it. Carlyle then showed it to Mill, who this time was enthusiastic. The *Westminster Review* was about to suspend publication, and Mill wanted to publish it in the final issue as the "last dying speech of a Radical Review."[5] It was now Carlyle's turn to reject the offer. That "whole beggarly unbelieving Radicalism" was a sinking ship, he decided, and it was best to let it go down in the hope that it would make way for a "believing Radicalism."[6] It was thus that the essay appeared as a separate book late in 1839.

If *Chartism* could find no place in the leading Tory and Radical journals, it was because it was sui generis, as Carlyle himself was. The book was not pro-Chartist; on the contrary, it attacked the kind of "reform-mongering" typified by the Charter, the puerile idea, as Carlyle thought it, that a sick society could be cured by votes, ballot boxes, and speeches in Parliament. Neither was the book anti-Chartist. Elevating Chartism above the paltry "Five Points" of the Chartist petition,[7] Carlyle made of it something like the English equivalent of the French Revolution, a revolution that could not be put down by rejecting the petition or arresting the leaders. The "living essence" of Chartism would live on, because that essence was the "bitter discontent" of the working classes.[8]

The opening chapter was entitled "Condition-of-England Question," an expression which Carlyle probably coined; certainly he was the first to give it such prominence. But he did not mean by it what it came to mean: the material condition of the working classes. His first sentence spoke of "the condition and disposition of the Working Classes." If "condition" was largely a matter of wages and prices, "disposition" involved the "thoughts, beliefs and feelings" of the people, their sense of what was right and wrong, just and unjust.

> Is the condition of the English working people wrong; so wrong that rational working men cannot, will not, and even should not rest quiet under it? . . . Or is the discontent itself mad, like the shape it took? Not the condition of the working people that is wrong; but their disposition, their own thoughts, beliefs and feelings that are wrong?[9]

These were not easy questions to answer, but they were the critical questions. And they were not being asked, still less answered, by the "national Palaver," the "Collective Folly of the Nation," which went by the name of Parliament. Nor were they being asked or answered by those busily collecting statistics and compiling tables. "Tables are like cobwebs, like the sieve of the Danaides; beautifully reticulated, orderly to look upon, but which will hold no conclusions." Tables were abstractions, whereas their subjects were concrete and complicated. "Conclusive facts are inseparable from inconclusive except by a head that already understands and knows." Statistics might prove that the average duration of life had increased; but they showed nothing of the kind of life that had been prolonged, of the outward suffering or inner discontent of those who were living longer. Statistics could say something about the wages a worker received and the amount of bread he could buy for those wages; but bread was only one small item in his well-being. Moreover, the quantity of his wages was less important than the quality. "Is it constant, calculable wages; or fluctuating, incalculable, more or less of the nature of gambling?" And the quality of wages was less important than the worker's prospects, his relationship to his employer, and his own sense of satisfaction or dissatisfaction. Could the worker hope to rise, by his own thrift and industry, to the position of master, or was that possibility denied him? Was he related to his employer by "bonds of friendliness and mutual help," or by "hostility, opposition, and chains of mutual necessity alone"? What was the real misery that afflicted him even when his real wages were sufficient? How could "figures of arithmetic" express "the labourer's feelings, his notion of being justly dealt with or unjustly; his wholesome composure, frugality, prosperity in the one case, his acrid unrest, recklessness, gin-drinking, and gradual ruin in the other"?[10]

If statistics did not address themselves to the real condition-of-England question, still less did the New Poor Law. England was lying in "sick discontent, writhing powerless on its fever-bed," when the Poor Law Commissioners came forward with the new dispensation: "Let there be workhouses, and bread of affliction and water of affliction there." The workhouse was a simple invention, as all great inventions were, and it was effective, up to a point. It operated on the principle of rat-catching.

> If paupers are made miserable, paupers will needs decline in multitude. It is a secret known to all rat-catchers: stop up the granary-crevices, afflict with continual mewing, alarm, and going-off of traps, your "chargeable labourers" disappear, and cease from the establishment. A still briefer method is that of arsenic; perhaps even a milder, where otherwise permissible.[11]

Paupers, like rats, could indeed be eliminated by this method, or at least driven out of sight. All that was required was the determination to treat them like rats, on the assumption that the "poor and luckless are here only as a nuisance to be abraded and abated." This assumption derived from the simple credo, "laissez faire, laissez passer," which supposed that whatever happened ought to happen, that the world required only to be "well let alone," that in this mad scramble of a world, everyone had only to "scramble along." If ever there was a "false, heretical and damnable principle," it was this.[12]

Yet no sooner had Carlyle delivered this damning indictment of the New Poor Law than he hastened to dissociate himself from those who called for its repeal. The law may have been "heretical and damnable as a whole truth," but it was "orthodox and laudable as a *half*-truth." It had been devised by men "filled with an idea of a theory," the theory that the "one thing needful" was the abolition of outdoor relief. That theory, half-truth though it was, may have been the only means of doing away with outdoor relief. And outdoor relief, Carlyle agreed, was an unmitigated evil. If the new law was lacking in any principle of justice, if it could think of nothing better to do with those poor unfortunates than sweeping them out of sight, the old law had been equally lacking in any principle of justice, for it too had fatally divorced reward from work, putting a bounty on "unthrift, idleness, bastardy and beer-drinking." The new law was thus an "indispensable element, harsh but salutary, in the progress of things."[13]

The new law was salutary in restoring the one thing Carlyle believed to be truly needful: not workhouses or outdoor relief but work itself. Work was the "mission of man in this Earth," the first law of nature, the first principle of justice. Neither Chadwick nor Malthus, neither the most obdurate poor law guardian nor the most ruthless employer, would have dared to speak as Carlyle did of the evil of idleness.

> In all ways it needs, especially in these times, to be proclaimed aloud that for the idle man there is no place in this England of ours. He that will not work, and save according to his means, let him go elsewhither; let him know that for *him* the law has made no soft provision, but a hard and stern one. . . . He that will not work according to his faculty, let him perish according to his necessity: there is no law juster than that.[14]

While the dictum "No work no recompense" was naturally imposed first on the largest class, the manual laborers, it was a universal principle binding on all persons and all classes. To the extent that the New Poor Law succeeded in protecting the honest workingman from the "thriftless and dissolute," the honest worker had reason to be grateful. This was, to be sure, a *"half-*result, detestable, if you will, when looked upon as the whole result"; but without that half the whole was unattainable. The poor law administrators, deluded by an imperfect theory, were instruments of a providence which used them for its own purpose, to achieve an "indispensable fractional" part of the truth.[15]

If this halfhearted defense of a "half-result" was calculated to offend both sides in this controversy, another part of Carlyle's argument was no less disagreeable to both. The New Poor Law, he said, tacitly acknowledged that the upper classes had some responsibility, some "general charge" for the lower classes. The centralization feature of the law, bitterly criticized by some and reluctantly defended by others, was to Carlyle one of its chief virtues. The supervision of the central government, in whatever spirit and by whatever means, had at least the merit of being supervision from a center. This the old law had never provided. For all its doles, allowances, and workhouses, it never gave the poor that "guidance and government" which the poor could not provide for themselves and which, in the modern complex world, they needed more than ever. The principle of guidance and governance was comprehended in the very idea of justice or just wages. The worker, an "ever-toiling inferior," wanted, even when he did not know it, "a superior that should lovingly and wisely govern: is not that too the 'just wages' of his service done?"[16]

The principle of authority was a corollary of the principle of work. This was why Carlyle could interpret "just wages" to include both the right to be properly recompensed and the right to be properly guided and governed. Together these rights assured the worker a "manlike place and relation" in the world. It cast no discredit on a worker that he needed the guidance of a superior; his work itself was a title of distinction. "He that can work is a born king of something; is in communion with Nature, is master of a thing or things, is a priest and king of Nature so far." It was only the man who worked at nothing who was a "usurper," the "born slave of all things."[17]

This was Carlyle's quarrel with the Chartists. They thought the "rights of men" were to be found in charters, reform bills, ballot boxes, and debates —the trappings of "self-government," a government "of the multitude by the multitude." Such a democracy, even if it were attainable, would be self-defeating, its victory signifying the victory of "nothing," of "emptiness." By its nature democracy was a "self-cancelling business" having a "net result of *zero.*" In America, where land was boundless and work plentiful, democracy was conceivable, but in Europe it was only a "regulated method of rebellion and abrogation," the "consummation of No-government and Laissez-faire." Democracy had nothing to do with the real rights or needs of people. What the people needed was neither self-government nor no-government but "veritable government." Behind the clatter of ballot boxes could be heard the desperate prayer for leadership: "Guide me, govern me! I am mad and miserable, and cannot guide myself!" This was the true right of men, the right enjoined by nature, the "right of the ignorant man to be guided by the wiser."[18]

It was this right that was being violated not only by the Chartists but by the traditional rulers of the people, the aristocracy. If democracy was the heresy of the Chartists, laissez faire was that of the aristocracy. Forfeiting their proper role as governors, the upper classes had fallen prey to the gospel of the marketplace, the belief that "Cash Payment" was the "universal sole nexus of man to man."[19] Money, mediating between supply and demand, had become the only medium of relationship, as it was the only medium of exchange. What it could not purchase, however, were those things the people were most in need of, work and leadership. In a "do-something world" the aristocracy had taken retreat in a "do-nothing" philosophy.[20]

In the final chapter of the book, Carlyle anticipated the obvious criticism: what did he suggest by way of positive reforms? His proposals, frankly introduced as sops to the "practical man," were universal education and emigration—both of which, as reviewers pointed out, were banal and anticlimactic. He himself put no great stock in them, and it was not for them that he was so widely read and praised. What was remarkable about the book was precisely what was not "practical": a definition of the condition-of-England question that was moral rather than material, a defense of the New Poor Law that was an attack on laissez faire and political economy, an affirmation of the principles of justice, work, and authority in terms that were not readily translated into programs and reforms.

It is interesting that so many practical people were attracted to Carlyle even as he denounced and vilified them. Their practical beliefs were his "false gospels": "Mammonism" (materialistic economics), "Dilettantism" (laissez faire), "Sansculottism" (democracy), "the pig philosophy" (utilitarianism), "Morrison's pill" (legislative reforms). In *Past and Present* these themes came to a focus. Carlyle described the book as a "red-hot indignant thing," its 300 pages having been written in seven weeks early in 1843. The previous summer, during a tour of Cromwell country, he had been appalled by the sight of fifty or more paupers sitting outside the poorhouse of St. Ives, men who were able and willing to work, and wretched for lack of it. That scene, together with newspaper reports of an "insurrection" in Manchester, convinced him that England was on the verge of revolution, and a secret voice whispered to him, "Thou, behold thou too art of it—thou must be of it!"[21] Putting aside the book on Cromwell which he had been planning to write, he started *Past and Present*.

This account of the genesis of *Past and Present,* it has been suggested, is somewhat mythical.[22] The book probably took a good six months in the writing, and Carlyle had been toying with the idea well before the visit to St. Ives or the Manchester riots. He had long had misgivings about devoting himself to the seventeenth century when the nineteenth was in such a parlous state. (Besides, the Cromwell book was not going well.) If *Past and Present* was not written in a red-hot fever of indignation, it read as if it had been. It opened with the familiar paradox of an England overflowing with wealth and dying of "inanition." Of 15,000,000 workers, "the strongest, the cunningest and the willingest our Earth ever had," 2,000,000 were rotting in workhouses or reduced to outdoor relief. Never had the working classes sunk so low, never had wealth been so unavailing to relieve want, never were so many perishing in the midst of plenty. England had become Dante's hell, the accursed world of Midas, "Jerusalem fallen under the wrath of God."[23]

In some respects *Past and Present* was a more radical book than *Chartism*. Instead of an equivocal defense of the New Poor Law, it presented an unequivocal indictment of an economic system that drove men to the workhouse or, at best, to the dubious rewards of the marketplace. Denouncing the principle of supply and demand, Carlyle proposed in its place the classical (by now radical) principle of "a fair day's-wages for a fair day's-work." He was also more conventionally radical in his practical recommendations, endorsing not only education and emigration but some of the standard "Morrison's pills": factory acts, sanitary regulations, mine inspection, the repeal of the corn laws, and anything else that might mitigate the "lawless anarchy of supply-and-demand."[24] In other respects, however, the book was even more distinctively Carlylean, and less conventionally radical, than the earlier one.

Between *Chartism* and *Past and Present* Carlyle had delivered his lectures, *On Heroes, Hero-Worship, and the Heroic in History,* and this idea of the heroic permeated *Past and Present.* Contrasting the "Unworking Aristocracy" to the "Working Aristocracy" and "Mill-ocracy" (the mill owners), he found among the latter the true heroes of the time. "Men do reverence men"—and these were the men worthy of reverence. Reverence, hero worship, was a fundamental fact of human nature, the manifestation of spirit in man, the "perpetual presence of Heaven in our poor Earth." In its absence "there is no worship, or worth-ship, or worth or blessedness in the Earth any more." "Worth-ship" was not a product of birth; it had to be earned, literally worked for. Any "master-Worker," even a "Plugson of Undershot," the most mundane and unimaginative of mill owners, was capable of it, if only he knew it. The Master-Workers, the Captains of Industry, were England's best hope at present; they were "virtually the Captains of the World; if there be no nobleness in them, there will never be an Aristocracy more."[25]

The ennobling of the industrialist, his elevation to the rank of the new aristocracy, is so striking it may distract attention from Carlyle's main protagonist: the worker. For the master-worker was only a species of worker; if he was the quintessential hero of modern times, it was because work was the quintessence of man. Hannah Arendt once wrote that Karl Marx, more than any other philosopher, presumed to define man totally in terms of work, making work the essential condition of his being, the cause of his alienation and the means of his salvation.[26] Carlyle had done that before Marx, and more thoroughly than Marx. Unlike Marx, Carlyle encompassed all men—capitalists as well as the proletariat—within the single category of "workers," making work the defining quality not of a class of men but of "species man" or "generic man," as the young Marx might have said.

Carlyle also endowed work with a religious quality, making it the condition of man's spiritual as well as material and social existence. Just as his idea of hero "worship" was infused with religiosity, so was his idea of work—and so too his idea of the worker. There was hardly a sentence about work or workers which was not permeated with the language and imagery of religion.

> For there is a perennial nobleness, and even sacredness, in Work.
> . . . Consider how, even in the meanest sort of Labour, the whole soul
> of a man is composed into a kind of real harmony, the instant he sets
> himself to work! . . . The blessed glow of Labour in him, is it not as
> purifying fire, wherein all poison is burnt up, and of sour smoke itself
> there is made bright blessed flame! . . . Blessed is he who has found
> his work; let him ask no other blessedness. . . . Labour is life; from the
> inmost heart of the Worker rises his god-given Force, the sacred
> celestial Life-essence breathed into him by Almighty God; from his
> inmost heart awakens him to all nobleness. . . . Work is of a religious
> nature:—work is of a *brave* nature; which it is the aim of all religion
> to be. . . . All true Work is Religion: and whatsoever Religion is not
> Work may go and dwell among the Brahmins, Antinomians, Spinning
> Dervishes, or where it will. . . . *Laborare est Orare,* Work is Worship.
> . . . All true Work is sacred; in all true Work, were it but true
> hand-labour, there is something of divineness. . . . No man has worked,
> or can work, except religiously; not even the poor day-labourer, the
> weaver of your coat, the sewer of your shoes.[27]

This idea of work may be dismissed as romantic, utopian, poetic, ethereal, as anything but work in the familiar, prosaic sense, certainly not that most prosaic kind of work, factory work. Yet it was exactly this last sense that Carlyle dwelt upon most insistently. His was no pastoral idyll. In spite of his penchant for medieval allegories, his archetypical worker was not, like Cobbett's, the peasant of Ye Olde England but the modern industrial worker. The captain of industry was the distinctive hero of modernity, and the industrial worker, the man who worked in Plugshot's factory, was the distinctive worker of modernity.

The sanctification of industrial work is all the more remarkable because it did not depend upon a providential, optimistic theory of political economy. Adam Smith could take a benign view of industrialism because he saw the "system of natural liberty" as the instrument of salvation, the means by which the poor would share in the wealth of the nation, self-interest would promote the general good, and economic prosperity would bring about moral progress. Carlyle rejected the whole of this teleology. For him political economy was not the work of a benevolent God but the invention of the devil; it was profoundly, irredeemably immoral. He insisted upon the spirituality of work in spite of the malignant influence of laissez faire, self-interest, and the "cash nexus." Like Hegel's spirit struggling to overcome its self-alienation, Carlyle's industrial laborer tried to escape from the bonds of Mammon.

> Industrial work, still under bondage to Mammon, the rational soul of it not awakened, is a tragic spectacle. Men in the rapidest motion and self-motion; restless, with convulsive energy, as if driven by Galvanism, as if possessed by a Devil: tearing asunder mountains,—to no purpose, for Mammonism is always Midas-earled! This is sad, on the face of it. Yet courage: the beneficent Destinies, kind in their sternness, are apprising us that this cannot continue. Labour is not a devil, even while encased in Mammonism; Labour is ever an imprisoned god, writhing unconsciously or consciously to escape out of Mammonism![28]

Had Carlyle deliberately set out to defy the reigning ideologies, he could not have done so more effectively. If he shared the Chartists' concern for the condition-of-England question, he thoroughly opposed the means by which they thought to remedy that condition; their cure, democracy, was for him a principal symptom of the disease. And if his antipathy to democracy seemed typically Tory, he mercilessly attacked the traditional Tory constituency (the "Idle Aristocracy"), the most cherished Tory causes (game laws and corn laws), and the Tory Party itself (the "do-nothing" party). There was something of the Tory Radical in his contempt for political economy, although not in his cult of hero worship or his reverence for the captain of industry. A political economist would have found much to praise in the "mill-ocrat," but not what Carlyle praised in him. Even on the subject of the poor law, which more than any other issue divided people into opposing camps, Carlyle belonged to neither camp. He denounced the workhouses as Bastilles while conceding the need for them. He derided the "rat-catching" principle behind the New Poor Law while defending the law itself as a half-truth and as wholly superior to the old law. He argued against the repeal of the new law, but in a rhetoric (that eye-catching "rat-catching" phrase) that has earned him a prominent place among the opponents of the law.[29]

His passionate denunciations of political economy, laissez faire, the cash nexus, and self-interest have endeared Carlyle to some Socialists, even prompting one biographer to make of him something of a Marxist (a "young Marxist").[30] But he was hardly a Socialist, still less a Marxist. Although he spoke of the need for some kind of "organization of labour," he did not at all mean by it what either Louis Blanc, the French Socialist who had recently published a book under that title, or the Saint-Simonians who had earlier used the expression, had in mind. Carlyle's "organization of labour" was to be under the firm direction of the captains of industry, who would respect the heroism, the "chivalry," of labor, and who would satisfy the workers' need for security by giving them "permanent contracts." "Despotism is essential in most enterprises"; to reconcile that despotism with freedom, all that was necessary was that the despotism be "just."[31] This was hardly the credo of the Owenite or Ricardian Socialist of his time, still less of a latter-day Marxist.

Permeating all of Carlyle's views was a profound if ill-defined, perhaps indefinable, religiosity. His protests against the false gospels of the age reflected a passionate hatred of materialism, skepticism, rationalism, secularism, and the kind of liberalism that fostered atheism in the guise of tolerance. Without God, he was convinced, man would be less than human and the society of men a jungle of lawless, soulless beasts. "A man's religion," he said, "is the chief fact with regard to him."[32] But he did not make it easy to elucidate the facts of his own religion. He belonged to no church, adhered to no established creed, did not believe in revelation, miracle, the literal truth of Scripture, or even a personal God in the form of Christ. What he did believe in, and what was implicit in everything he wrote (although he never formulated it explicitly), was a God who did not reveal Himself in Scripture or miracle because He revealed himself in His creation, a world that was itself divine and miraculous. His contemporaries, bewildered and disturbed by a credo that lacked the familiar ingredients of a credo, labeled it transcendentalist, pantheistic, heretical, infidel. His friend and biographer, James Froude, who understood him better, described his faith as "Calvinist without theology."[33]

Whatever difficulties contemporaries had in characterizing his faith, they had no doubt that Carlyle had one and that it was the basis of his social philosophy. Reviewers of *Chartism* and *Past and Present* devoted far more space to his religious beliefs (or, as some thought, lack thereof) than to his view of the condition-of-England question, the poor laws, Chartism, or political economy. Even Engels, praising *Past and Present* in a radical German journal as the only book published in England that year worth reading and Carlyle as the only educated Englishman concerned with the social conditions of England, dwelt at length on the misbegotten "pantheism" that distorted his social philosophy. Unlike "German philosophy" (by which Engels meant Young Hegelianism), which understood that "God is man," Carlyle made the mistake of seeking something beyond man and ended by making a cult of heroes and aristocrats. "If he had understood man as man in all his infinite complexity, he would not have conceived the idea of once more dividing mankind into two lots, sheep and goats, rulers and ruled, aristocrats and the rabble, lords and dolts."[34] The following year, having decided that England was in fact divided into two classes, Engels dropped his criticism both of Carlyle's religion and of his penchant for heroes, quoting instead, in his *Condition of the Working Class in England,* Carlyle's description of the wretched state of English workers and the famous "cash-payment cash-nexus" phrase.*

What made Carlyle's unconventional ideas about poverty and the poor laws, religion and work, heroes and leaders, more than the idiosyncratic creed of an eccentric was the fact that he was enormously popular in the most diverse circles, including those which were most committed to the false gospels he incessantly denounced. Later, especially after the publication in 1850 of the aggressively anti-liberal, anti-democratic *Latter-Day Pamphlets,* some of his admirers became disaffected, but in the thirties and forties (and in many cases well after that) he received accolades from a most varied and distinguished body of compatriots. Their names read like a roll call of the Victorian greats: Mill, Southey, Martineau, Dickens, Eliot, Gaskell, Morris, Ruskin, Swinburne, Thackeray, Hughes, Thomas Arnold, Kingsley, Maurice, Harrison, Morley. Abroad he was lavishly praised by Goethe, Thoreau, Emerson, and Whitman. Whatever reservations his admirers had about this or that of his ideas, they agreed that he was one of the most important thinkers of the age.

It was an extraordinary phenomenon. Carlyle attacked Chartism and was praised by the Chartist poets Thomas Cooper and Ebenezer Elliott. He attacked the Philosophic Radicals and received laudatory notices in their journal, the *Westminster Review.* He attacked political economy, and Harriet Martineau took it upon herself to arrange a lecture series for him. He attacked the Poor Law Commissioners and was treated respectfully by Chadwick. He attacked Peel (under the name of Sir Jabesh Windbag in *Past*

---

*The passage in the review of *Past and Present* rebuking Carlyle for not understanding "man as man in all his infinite complexity" was typical of the "young" Engels still under the influence of Feuerbach. Although the *Condition* had many such echoes, the dominant theme was the class struggle between the proletariat and bourgeoisie which would inevitably culminate in revolution. But even there Engels was much better disposed to Carlyle than he was later to be. The original German edition of the *Condition,* published in 1845, had a footnote comparing Carlyle to the Young Englanders, to the former's advantage:

> Wholly isolated is the half-German Englishman, Thomas Carlyle, who, originally a Tory, goes beyond all those hitherto mentioned. He has sounded the social disorder more deeply than any other English bourgeois, and demands the organisation of labour. I hope that Carlyle, who has found the right path, will be capable of following it. He has my best wishes and those of many other Germans.

The last two sentences were omitted in the English translation (published in America in 1887 and in England in 1892). The German edition of 1892 retained those last sentences and added: "But the February Revolution made him an out-and-out reactionary. His righteous wrath against the Philistines turned him into a sullen Philistine grumbling at the tide of history that cast him ashore."[35]

and Present), and Peel sought out his company. He attacked the Church and was acclaimed by the Bishop of St. David's. And so it went, one after another of the false gospelers paying tribute to the man who anathematized them. Emerson said of *Past and Present* that it was "as full of treason as an egg is full of meat."[36] If treason it was, it was so insidious it made converts of those it betrayed.

Agreeing with almost no one and unsparing in his contempt for almost everyone, Carlyle came as close as anyone to being the intellectual hero of the age. In 1840 the Anglican theologian Frederick Denison Maurice (later a leader of the Christian Socialists) explained to a friend that he would have to tone down his own praise of Carlyle because "his fame is most rampant, and men are beginning to talk and cant after him in all directions."[37] Another admirer recalled that his name was "running like wildflower" throughout the English-speaking world, young people especially reading him avidly, echoing his sentiments, and mouthing his phrases until his language permeated the "public speech."[38] Even after he had grievously offended liberal sensibilities by defending slavery and attacking democracy in his *Latter-Day Pamphlets,* George Eliot testified to his enduring influence over herself, her entire generation, and, she predicted, generations to come.

> It is an idle question to ask whether his books will be read a century hence: if they were all burnt as the grandest of suttees on his funeral pile, it would be only like cutting down an oak after its acorns have sown a forest. For there is hardly a superior or active mind of this generation that has not been modified by Carlyle's writings; there has hardly been an English book written for the last ten or twelve years that would not have been different if Carlyle had not lived.[39]

Carlyle's appeal was all the more remarkable because he seemed to go out of his way to outrage and provoke, by his mode of discourse as much as by his opinions. At a time when the essay form was being cultivated by such superb stylists as Hazlitt, Macaulay, and Mill, and when even the less famous contributors to the great journals were distinguished for their elegance and lucidity, Carlyle flaunted a style that was tortuous, convoluted, and turgid. It was also sometimes vulgar to the point of being scatological. (One of his favorite characters was Professor Teufelsdröckh—"Devil's Dung," in its politest translation. Perhaps it was this professor who emboldened Dickens to name the financier in *Little Dorrit* "Mr. Merdle.") Apart from the liberal use of German, Carlyle was given to unconventional syntax (solecisms, to put it harshly), labored metaphors, expletives and imperatives, capitalized nouns and italicized adjectives, all overlaid by an irony that made it difficult to know when he was being serious or sarcastic, and by a tone of moral urgency that did not always have a clear referent, so that the reader was sometimes left with a sense of a free-floating, self-generating passion. To complicate matters, one of his works, *Sartor Resartus,* was a parody of a German philosophical treatise, with all the ponderous abstractions (and ponderous wit) of that genre; and a good part of *Past and Present* was an account of a medieval chronicle which, as it happened, was real (it had recently been reprinted by the Camden Society), but which could as well have been fanciful.

It was in this fashion that Carlyle chose to communicate his exceedingly controversial views, and with extraordinary success. He had his critics, to be sure; his opinions were hotly contested and his style was ridiculed. John Sterling, an admirer and friend, complained of his barbarous language and neologisms, and Matthew Arnold called him a "moral desperado."[40] But his intellectual power and moral passion were such that even those who disagreed with him agreed that he was one of the most important and influential men of the time—the most important and the most influential, some maintained. His influence even extended to those who were themselves of a very different cast of mind. "Many of the men who have the least agreement with his opinions," George Eliot said, "are those to whom the reading of *Sartor Resartus* was an epoch in the history of their lives."[41]

Eliot could understand Carlyle's appeal to those whose philosophy was antithetical to his because she herself was in that position. "When he is saying the very opposite of what we think, he says it so finely, with so hearty conviction—he makes the object about which we differ stand out in such grand relief under the clear light of his strong and honest intellect—he appeals so constantly to our sense of the manly and the truthful—that we are obliged to say 'Hear! hear!' to the writer before we can give the decorous 'Oh! oh!' to his opinions."[42] Richard Hutton had a different explanation. Carlyle's attraction, he said, especially in the 1830s and '40s, was to the young who were adrift and without any sense of direction; to them his prophecies came with the "force of a revelation."[43] He also attracted those who were not adrift, who were riding the wave of the future, borne along by currents of opinion which they found irresistible and at the same time fearful.

Carlyle's "revelation," his admirers and critics agreed, was that of a "prophet"—this was the word used of him again and again. And it was the prophetic mode that made his style appropriate and acceptable. Henry James said that his style perfectly suited his thought. "It is not defensible but it is victorious."[44] So people felt about his ideas. He was a Jeremiah not a Moses, a moralist not a legislator, a social critic not a reformer. He was the great dissenter from the prevailing orthodoxies, an iconoclast come to destroy all the "foul and vile and soul-murdering Mud-Gods of my epoch."[45] Those "Mud-Gods"—rationalism, utilitarianism, secularism, individualism, liberalism—were too deeply embedded in the culture to be displaced by his alternatives—justice, passion, authority, heroism—especially since the latter were not readily translated into policies or programs. That it was his jeremiads rather than his feeble positive proposals that attracted his contemporaries explains the fact that he had many admirers and few disciples. When he spoke of the "chivalry of labour," or the "law of union" governing rich and poor, or the "blessedness" of work, they heard him not as advocating any particular policy but as exposing the superficiality of the liberal, democratic, rationalistic temper to which they themselves were irrevocably committed but about which they had deep misgivings. He gave voice to their inner doubts; he was their alter ego which could not be denied and yet could not be unequivocally affirmed. He did for morality, Harriet Martineau said, what Wordsworth did for poetry: he released the English from the bonds of conventionality, timidity, and immorality.[46] He was the very model of his own "prophet as hero."

> Such a man is what we call an *original* man: he comes to us at first-hand. A messenger he, sent from the Infinite Unknown with tidings to us. We may call him Poet, Prophet, God—in one way or another, we all feel that the words he utters are as no other man's words. Direct from the Inner Fact of things,—he lives, and has to live, in daily communion with that. Hearsays cannot hide it from him; he is blind, homeless, miserable, following hearsays; *it* glares-in upon him. Really his utterances, are they not a kind of 'revelation';—what we must call such for want of some other name? It is from the heart of the world that he comes; he is portion of the primal reality of things.[47]

Carlyle was an "original." His readers did not look to him for specific recommendations about the poor laws or for ways of implementing a "just wage." They looked to him for a moral critique of institutions, policies, and doctrines which they themselves subscribed to, for which they (and perhaps Carlyle himself) had no practical alternatives, but which they suspected were morally dubious and even dangerous. It is in this sense that Carlyle may be counted among the "opponents" of the New Poor Law. He was not, strictly speaking, an opponent of that law, although those who thought of him as such (his own contemporaries as well as later historians) may be forgiven for thinking so. What he was strenuously, unequivocally opposed to was the set of ideas, attitudes, and values which had given rise to the New Poor Law, the ethos which made that law appear to be a natural, rational way of coping with the problems of pauperism.

There was no more radical critique of the prevailing ethos than Carlyle's indictment of a society in which "cash payment" was the "sole nexus of man to man." It was more radical, one might argue, in the context of his thought than in that of Marx and Engels. In the *Communist Manifesto* Carlyle's phrase appeared in the famous passage:

> The bourgeoisie, wherever it has got the upper hand, has put an end to all feudal, patriarchal, idyllic relations. It has pitilessly torn asunder the motley feudal ties that bound man to his "natural superiors," and has left no other nexus between man and man than naked self-interest, than callous "cash payment."[48]

Marx and Engels did not propose to restore those old ties and relations. Nor was their own system, from Carlyle's point of view, more than a variation on bourgeois political economy. Their critique of capitalism was rooted in Ricardianism; their "historical materialism" was as "mammonist" as utilitarianism; their doctrine of class interests was as interest-centered as the doctrine of laissez faire; their class struggle was even more divisive and destructive than the struggle of individuals in the marketplace; only in the remote future, with the establishment of true communism, would man and society be truly transformed. For Carlyle that transformation lay neither in a transcendent future nor in an irrecoverable past, but in the present. All the ingredients of redemption—heroism, authority, nobility, spirituality—were at hand; they only needed to be liberated and legitimated.

Carlyle's formulation of the condition-of-England question was also more radical, more fundamental, than the question posed by most radicals. It was not only a matter of better wages, not even a "fair day's wages for a fair day's work," but a sense of justice that went beyond wages, material conditions, even life and death. "It is not what a man outwardly has or wants that constitutes the happiness or misery of him. Nakedness, hunger, distress of all kinds, death itself have been cheerfully suffered, when the heart was right. It is the feeling of *injustice* that is insupportable to all men."[49]

Perhaps the most radical part of Carlyle's enterprise was that which later radicals have been most suspicious of: his attitude to work and the worker. It was here that he altered the very terms of discourse. The condition-of-England question was for him less a question of poverty than of work. It is interesting that neither "pauper" nor "poor" figured prominently in his writings. His protagonist was the "worker." Where the poor law reformers were obsessed by the need to separate pauper and poor, and where most of the opponents of the law wanted to restore the pauper to the main body of the poor by reinstating the old poor law, Carlyle sought to elevate pauper and poor alike to the status of worker by endowing them with the dignity, meaning, and "chivalry" that came only from work. It was as if he suspected that "poor," like "pauper"—the words as well as the people to which they referred—had become hopelessly discredited, beyond redemption, so that the only hope for the poor was to think of them and treat them as workers. It had once been the poor who were blessed, who were of the Kingdom of God. Modernity had changed that. Work was the new salvation, the source of "blessedness."

If modernity transformed the poor into workers, it also created a distinctively new kind of worker. One of the many myths about Carlyle is that he despised industrialism just as he despised political economy.[50] In fact, like many of his contemporaries, he was careful not to implicate industrialism in his indictment of laissez faire. When he used "steam engine" and "machinery" as epithets, it was because he thought them symbolic of a temper of mind that sought mechanical solutions for human problems, reducing workers to engines and social relations to the machinery of politics and economics. One may wonder how Carlyle proposed to operate an industrial system without some cash-payment mechanism, but one cannot doubt his respect for industry itself or for the workers and master-workers who were the heroes of that system.

Carlyle eulogized not the poor but the worker. It was work that was the "grand sole miracle of Man," the means by which "man has risen from the low places of this Earth, very literally, into divine Heavens." In Carlyle's pantheon, the worker took his place beside the other heroes of history: "Ploughers, Spinners, Builders; Prophets, Poets, Kings; Brindleys and Goethes, Odins and Arkwrights; all martyrs, and noble men, and gods are of one grand Host; immeasurable; marching ever forward since the beginnings of the World."[51]

IX

COBBETT:

RADICAL POPULISM

William Cobbett was to the working classes what Carlyle was to the intellectuals, a man more often praised than heeded, a maverick without party (and, some thought, without principle), who was nevertheless presumed to have a large and devoted following and to wield considerable influence. They had other qualities in common: a passion that communicated itself in every line they wrote, an uninhibited eccentricity, a style designed to provoke and shock (and by means of the same rhetorical devices—neologisms, expletives, invectives, extravagant images and judgments), an overweening egotism, and an inordinate sense of moral righteousness. Prophets and moralists, they were more persuasive in criticism than in constructive guidance, in exposing evils than in proposing remedies. Their admirers did not necessarily agree with them, still less follow their precepts, but they credited them with having penetrated to some elemental truth, some "primal reality," which evaded more practical men. Like Carlyle's prophet-as-hero, they were "originals." It is a commentary on the age that two of its most influential men should have been so unique and intractable, so impervious to "enlightened" ideas, so indomitably opposed to the rationalism, utilitarianism, and laissez-faireism associated with their times.

One might continue in this vein, pitting the two men against each other, comparing Carlyle's "Mud-Gods" with Cobbett's "Thing," dwelling on their common animosities (Jews and Negroes, Benthamite "feelosofers" and "Scotch" economists), dramatizing their differences (Cobbett's commitment to the parliamentary reform that Carlyle ridiculed, and Carlyle's glorification of the captain of industry whom Cobbett execrated). To play them off against each other in this way would do an injustice to both, for they were not reacting against each other but against what each took to be that "jack-o'-lantern," as Cobbett called it, the "Spirit of the age."[1] They never met, Carlyle having moved to London only a year before Cobbett's death, and while some of Carlyle's writings had already attracted attention (his *Life of Schiller* and *Sartor Resartus*), they were not the kind of books Cobbett was inclined to read. On one of the few occasions when Carlyle mentioned Cobbett, it was to praise him as a healthy man in a sickly age, "the pattern John Bull of his century, strong as the rhinoceros, and with singular humanities and genialities shining through his thick skin."[2]

Others might wonder what century this "John Bull" was presumed to represent—not, it would seem, the nineteenth century against which Cobbett railed so incessantly. He himself boasted of his birth in "old England," in 1766 (or 1763, as most biographers now believe), in a small market town in Surrey, in a comfortable farming family, in the heart of what he fondly thought of as the most beautiful countryside in the world and the happiest country in the world.[3] He remembered the cottages of the laborers adorned with brass and pewter, furnished with curtains and feather-beds, filled with objects "worth possessing and worth preserving." A laborer would live out his whole life in the same cottage, just as he often worked for the same master (sometimes the same master his father had worked for) the whole of his life, without a contract but with the assurance of mutual good-will, "the liberality and kindness of the employer . . . repaid by the respect and fidelity of the servant." Master and worker would dine together, partake of the same homemade bread and beer (not those modern abominations, potatoes and tea), work side by side in their common interest, and share the same virtues: "early rising, industry, good hours, sobriety, decency of language, cleanliness of persons, due obedience." In that society, "all was in order" and "everyone was in his place." And from that society came the tradesmen and merchants of the city and the hardy men of the fleet and army, "fashioned to due subordination from their infancy."[4]

When foreigners heard of these idyllic conditions, Cobbett remarked, they thought they were "listening to romances."[5] And so they were. The image of a Golden Age in the past often serves as a literary device to cast into sharper light the evils of the present. In Cobbett's case, he seems to have meant it literally. When he said that he could wish for no more than to "see the poor men of England what the poor men of England were when I was born," he was making a statement about the kind of society he thought existed in his youth and had to be restored if people were to be happy again.[6] Today we may find his indictment of the nineteenth century more persuasive than his eulogy of the eighteenth; in his time they complemented each other. The invocation of that happy past provided an interlude of recollected tranquillity, a respite from his frenzied assault upon the present, as well as an invitation to regain that lost paradise.

Cobbett's main claim to fame, and the main vehicle for his views, was the *Political Register,* a weekly paper which he founded in 1802 and edited for more than thirty years, while he was in and out of jail and in and out of the country. He also published scores of books and pamphlets (many reprinted from the *Register*), lectured, became briefly involved with other radicals (and as quickly, and acrimoniously, disengaged from them), and was a member of the Reformed Parliament for three years until his death in 1835. In his early years (or not so early, this period lasting until he was about forty), he attacked Jacobins and republicans, peace lovers and rabble rousers, as ferociously as he was later to attack Tories and royalists, militarists and oppressors. His conversion took place around 1806, when his dissatisfaction with the particular policies of particular men became generalized into a wholesale condemnation of the "System." In London the System appeared in the guise of the "Great Wen" which "sucked up the vitals of the country";[7] in the country it was the "Old Corruption," or the "Thing," or "It"—an interlocking web of political, fiscal, and military establishments, of stock-jobbers, tax-farmers, fund-holders, borough-mongers, placemen, and pensioners, all of whom conspired to keep the country in a state of war, burdened by debt and taxes, demoralized and impoverished.

In a rare moment of modesty, Cobbett explained that he had first learned of the iniquities of the System from Thomas Paine's *Decline and Fall of the English System of Finance,* which was published in 1796 but which he read only in 1804.* That pamphlet determined him to "open the eyes of my countrymen to the truths which I myself had learnt from him."[9] Paine's thesis was that the national debt had been increasing at a rate that would ensure the collapse of the entire fiscal system of England sometime between 1805 and 1815. Expanding upon that idea, Cobbett associated the debt with all the other evils of the System: paper money, war, corruption, and above all taxes. Taxes were the linchpin of the System; in order to extract from the people as much money as possible to support the myriad of fund-holders, placemen, pensioners, and other parasites, the System was obliged to wage war, maintain a large debt, and issue worthless paper money.

It was to relieve the people of the burden of taxes and undermine the System that pressed so hard upon them that Cobbett became an ardent proponent of parliamentary reform. Like most of the radicals of the time, he advocated manhood (not universal) suffrage, an annually elected Parlia-

---

*In 1796, at the very time Paine wrote this pamphlet, Cobbett published his very critical and abusive *Life of Thomas Paine.* Perhaps it was to atone for this work that Cobbett later conceived the plan of disinterring Paine's bones and returning them to England to be enshrined in a mausoleum. Cobbett brought the bones back in 1819, but he was never able to raise the money to reinter them and the bones remained in his possession until his death, when they were bequeathed to his eldest son. The episode was widely reported and ridiculed in the British press at the time. When Cobbett acknowledged his debt to Paine in 1822, he explained that Paine's pamphlet had little effect when it first appeared because the government was then suppressing his work and because Paine "rendered himself unpopular amongst the very best of the people, by his gratuitous and rude assault on the Christian religion." Cobbett neglected to mention his own part in the discrediting of Paine.[8]

ment, and the secret ballot. The lack of access to parliamentary power, he argued, had caused the evils of the System and only parliamentary reform could remove them. What was required was a Parliament *"annually chosen by all the people,* seeing that they all pay taxes."[10]

The one tax the poor did not pay and which was to their benefit was that which the System was determined to abolish, the poor rates. After taxes and parliamentary reform, it was the poor law that most exercised Cobbett. His very last article, appearing in the *Register* in June 1835, a few weeks after his death, was a warning against the new "Rural War" that was being provoked by the New Poor Law, a war, he predicted, which would be far more devastating than the Swing riots five years earlier. He concluded by repeating the argument he had made so often before, that the old poor law was part of the fundamental principles of the English government as established at the time of the Reformation, and that to annul that law was to jeopardize the whole of that constitutional settlement.[11]

This genealogy of the poor law may have been of dubious historical merit but it had great polemical value. As both sides invoked nature in support of their positions—the reformers appealing to the natural laws of political economy, and the radicals to the natural right of subsistence—so both sides also invoked history. While Chadwick represented the New Poor Law as an "amendment" intended to restore the original Elizabethan laws by removing the excrescences of later centuries, the opposition insisted that the new law effectively abolished the old. But only Cobbett went so far as to claim that the poor laws were an essential part of the Reformation settlement and thus of the foundations of the English polity. Not content with that, he went further back into history, to the Conquest and beyond, to the very beginning of society, at each stage finding evidence of a public commitment to the relief of the poor.

The theory was worked out in great detail in *A History of the Protestant Reformation in England and Ireland* (1824–27) and in the tract, *A Legacy to Labourers,* published shortly before Cobbett's death. If the first was the more popular book (30,000–40,000 copies of each of the original parts were sold, a total of about 700,000 copies), the second was more lucid and coherent. Citing the Bible, Sir Edward Coke, Locke, Montesquieu, Paley, and Blackstone (Blackstone, curiously, more extensively than any other authority), Cobbett began by positing a state of nature in which everyone had an equal claim to the resources and products of nature. Private property, and thus inequality, arose when people applied their labor to the natural resources and then claimed a special right to the fruits of their labor. To protect them in the enjoyment of those fruits, civil society was instituted, with civil laws securing the property that had originated in labor. The Norman Conquest interrupted that natural process by making the King of England the sole proprietor of all the land. Those who came to be known as "landowners" were, in fact, "landholders," holding their land in tenure from the king. The king, in turn, held the land in trust for the nation, the terms of the social contract requiring that every person be secure in his right to life—and therefore in the right to relief.

Long before the Conquest the Bible had established a "legal provision" for the poor in the form of the tithe, a fixed charge upon the land for the relief of the destitute. With the Reformation the tithes, together with the property of the monasteries, were transferred to the king, who parceled them out to individuals. As a partial compensation to the poor, the poor laws were enacted, not to give the poor some new right or privilege but to restore to them, in some small measure, what had always been theirs by right and law. The poor rates became what the tithes had been, a legal charge upon property, and poor relief became a legal claim upon the rates. The poor law was thus a form of property, the property of the poor. If this form of property was denied, all of property was jeopardized, and with it the very foundation of society.

> If you maintain that the poor have no right, no legal right, to relief, you loosen all the ligaments of property; and begin that career, which must end in a contest for property, between the poor and the rich; you loosen all the bonds of allegiance; you get rid of all its duties; you proclaim that *might,* and not *right,* is to prevail; and, in short, you do all in your power to break up the social compact; to produce confusion, and to leave to chance a settlement anew.[12]

The New Poor Law was not a new form of that ancient right; it was an outright denial of it. By prescribing the kinds of conditions it did— imprisoning the poor in workhouses, compelling them to wear special garb, separating them from their families, cutting them off from communication with the poor outside, and, when they died, permitting their bodies to be disposed of for dissection—the law in effect condemned the indigent to slavery or death.* And that, as Locke had demonstrated, was a denial of the basic right to life which no civil law could abrogate, for to deny that right was to return to the state of nature. The New Poor Law did just that: it

---

*Cobbett was especially outraged by the practice of dissection, which he took to be the ultimate degradation and desecration caused by the New Poor Law. This was not, of course, part of the law, and it is not clear how common it was for workhouses to dispose of bodies for this purpose. But it was widely believed to be the case, partly because of Cobbett's repeated charges to this effect.

freed the poor of the bonds of civil society, of the duty to bear arms in defense of their country, obey its laws, and pay its taxes. When Malthus announced that the poor had no claim upon the community for even the smallest portion of food and were "thrown on their own resources," he was sending them back to the state of nature. In that state, Cobbett recalled, there was no property. Rather than spelling out the implications of this ominous situation, he quoted from Paley: "A man in a state of extreme necessity, has *a right to use another's property,* when it is necessary for his own preservation to do so; a *right to take, without or against the owner's leave,* the first food, clothes, or shelter, he meets with, when he is in danger of perishing in want of them."[13]

To throw men "on their own resources," then, was to throw them on other people's property. The reformers claimed that they wanted to make property secure by removing the heavy burden of the poor rates, but the effect of the new law was to jeopardize all property, ultimately to negate the very right of property.* It was more than a concealed threat that was contained in the quotation from Paley and in the epigraph on the title page by the seventeenth century jurist Sir Matthew Hale:

> A due care for the relief of the poor is an act of great civil prudence and political wisdom: for poverty in itself is apt to emasculate the minds of men, or, at least, it makes men tumultuous and unquiet. Where there are many very poor, the rich cannot long or safely continue such.[15]

This was obviously a highly tendentious and largely mythical reconstruction of the history of the poor law—and an extremely useful one, for it permitted Cobbett to anchor his utopia in what he took to be the historic institutions, traditions, and values of his country. If he cited Locke more than Paine, it was not because he wanted to cloak himself in the mantle of the more respectable philosopher (on the contrary, he denigrated Locke as a self-seeking placeman), but because he was, on this issue, genuinely closer to Locke than to Paine. Natural rights did not mean for him, as they did for Paine, that all men were equal, nor that every generation was a new "creation," nor that the past was a dead weight, an encumbrance and a hindrance to living men. To the extent to which he can be said to have had any philosophical theory, it was a Lockean one, which

---

*The argument that relief was a form of property and that to deny the right to relief was to deny the right to property as such was to be heard again and again in the course of the decade. The Tory Radical Richard Oastler made the same point shortly before the New Poor Law was passed. "If paupers have no right to parish pay, *no person in England has any right to any property whatever.*"[14]

legitimized inequality as it also legitimized private property, civil society, and the state.

Nor was it an accident that Cobbett preferred Blackstone to Bentham. His quotations from Blackstone (like those from Locke) were highly selective, designed to lend authority to the policies and laws he himself favored. But the fact that he quoted Blackstone so often and approvingly was itself provocative, Blackstone hardly being a name in good repute in radical circles. Jeremy Bentham had launched his own career, half a century earlier, by attacking Blackstone as an arch-conservative and the English constitution (or what passed as such, an unwritten constitution, in his view, being no constitution) as irrational, irreformable, and thoroughly mischievous.[16] As between Bentham and Blackstone, Cobbett's sympathies were all with the latter. He hated the Benthamite "feelosofers" as much for their irreverent attitude toward the institutions and constitution of England as for their opposition to the old poor law, and he accused Bentham personally of seeking to abolish the common law, erase twelve hundred years of history, and "rub out the recollections of the people of this country."[17] (Bentham, for his part, denounced Cobbett as an "odious compound of selfishness, malignity, insincerity, and mendacity.")[18]*

Cobbett's appeal to old England was a double-edged sword directed against new England—the England of the new industrial economy, the new political economy, and the New Poor Law—and against the kind of radicalism that wanted to destroy the old together with the new. The great enemies of reform, Cobbett said again and again, were those who thought there was nothing good in English laws and institutions, that everything had to be uprooted. He prided himself on being the real reformer—that is, the real conserver.

> I want to see no innovation in England. All I wish and all I strive for is *The Constitution of England,* undefiled by corruption.

> What do we wish for? *We wish to destroy no establishment.* We want nothing newfangled. We want no innovation. All we ask for is, such a reform as would effectually secure us against the effects of corruption.

---

*Their enmity seems to have dated from 1810, when Cobbett refused to publish in the *Register* Bentham's *Catechism of Parliamentary Reform,* a rebuff Bentham never forgave. Even without this episode, their ideas were divergent enough to account for their hostility. Yet in some respects they had more in common than either would have admitted. They were equally crotchety, intemperate, and egotistic; they shared the same demonology, the "System" or "Old Corruption" that governed and misgoverned England; and they personalized both the System and their own relationship to it, each regarding himself as the arch-foe of the King and his ministers.

We have great constitutional laws and principles, to which we are immovably attached. We want *great alteration,* but we want *nothing new.* Alteration, modification to suit the times and circumstances; but the great principles ought to be and must be, the same, or else confusion will follow.[19]

If Cobbett's idea of the constitution was not really that of Blackstone, still less was it that of Paine or Bentham. His "great alteration" did not require, as Paine's and Bentham's did, the abolition of the monarchy and the House of Lords; on the contrary, he wanted to preserve those institutions, purged of the "old corruption" that now disfigured them, because they were essential parts of the traditional, hierarchical, "mixed" government that was the genius of the English Constitution. While he hated the monarch and aristocrats of his time, he did not hate the institutions of monarchy and aristocracy; and except in moments of pique he hated republicanism almost as much. In 1829, when the Society for Radical Reform proposed to issue a republican declaration, Cobbett strenuously argued against it, and when that declaration was adopted, he resigned from the society.

In his own struggles against the government, he often protested against the infringement of his liberty, and, by extension, the liberty of all Englishmen. But he was also capable of the kind of pronouncement more often associated with Burke: "I have had too much opportunity of studying men and things to be led astray by any *wild theories about liberty.*"[20] He was even less well disposed toward any "wild theories" about equality. "As naturally as the sparks fly upwards, the mass of any people will prefer superiors to equals in all cases where trust is to be reposed and where their choice is free."[21] Insisting upon a natural right to subsistence and to participation in government, he also argued that equality of wealth was contrary to "the order of the world and the decrees of God," that it was "perfectly proper, that people in the lower walks of life should carry themselves respectfully towards those whose birth, or superior talent, or industry, have placed above themselves," and that the people themselves were perfectly content with this natural, hierarchical order. It was not the early Tory Cobbett but the later radical one who repeatedly used, and favorably, Hume's expression, "the natural magistracy."[22] The poor themselves, he was convinced, had no aspirations to equality, whether of wealth or of status, and no designs on the property of the rich. Only fools talked about revolutions *"made for the purpose of getting possession of people's property."* Revolutions might result in some redistribution of property, but they never sprang from that motive. Even after the Swing riots and during the agitation over the Reform Bill, Cobbett never wavered in this conviction. "In the whole body of the industrious and working people of England, there was scarcely a single man to be found, that had ever entertained the slightest thought of envying his richer neighbour, of wishing to share in his property, of wishing to see all men pulled down to a level."[23]

Like Carlyle, Cobbett was for an aristocracy in principle—a social aristocracy, however, not a political one. In the making of laws, especially those which so vitally concerned them such as taxes, the poor had the same rights as the rich and therefore the same claim to the suffrage. In other respects, in wealth and birth, talent and industry, there was no equality and could be none. The laborer himself would not have it otherwise; the difficulty was in finding a natural, legitimate aristocracy which could command his respect. A large part of the landed aristocracy had forfeited that respect by allying itself with the "monied interests" and pursuing policies—enclosures, game laws, corn laws, the New Poor Law—injurious both to farmers and to laborers. Unlike Carlyle, however, Cobbett had no alternative aristocracy, no captains of industry to take the place of the landed aristocracy. Where Carlyle's "millocracy" was a term of approbation, Cobbett's "Cotton Lords" was a term of opprobrium.*

In his biography of Cobbett, G. K. Chesterton argued that Carlyle was much the inferior of Cobbett because he never "contradicted the whole trend of the age as Cobbett did"; where Carlyle rejected the profit-and-loss philosophy but idealized capitalism itself, Cobbett rejected both the philosophy and the system of capitalism.[25] The comparison is intriguing but inaccurate. Both repudiated a free market economy, but both accepted other aspects of capitalism—the profit system and the private ownership and inheritance of land and goods. Where they differed, and where Cobbett did go against the "whole trend of the age," as Carlyle did not, was in his distrust of industrialism. The only kind of industry Cobbett entirely approved of was the cottage industry of the "dark ages," as it was mistakenly called, when the women and children sat at home spinning and weaving while the men worked in the fields.[26] That domestic system was socially desirable, he argued, because it made for a healthy, industrious, self-sufficient family, and it was economically necessary because it provided an indispensable income for the agricultural laborers and was an integral part of the rural economy.

The new industry undermined the old economy and society, and

*He sometimes included landlords—some landlords, at least—among those who were interested in preserving the best of the old society. One of his complaints against the New Poor Law was that it took the management of poor relief away from the gentry and local magistracy and put it in the hands of "three extraordinary gentlemen, perhaps from Scotland—perhaps, for what he knew, from Hanover."[24]

jeopardized as well the health and morals of those unfortunates doomed to toil in the hellish factories. Long before Cobbett had ever been inside a cotton mill, long before he had so much as visited Manchester, he described, on the basis of a newspaper account, a typical cotton mill in that "blood-stained town," where thousands of miserable creatures were locked up for fourteen hours a day in a temperature of eighty to eighty-four degrees, forbidden to open a window or to pause for so much as a drink of water, and were thrown together in "hotbeds of vice and corruption." Compared with these wretched factory workers, agricultural laborers were in "heaven" and the black slaves in the West Indies in a veritable "paradise."[27] Yet it was not primarily on humanitarian grounds (at least not in the usual sense) that Cobbett objected to factories. Just as the opponents of the New Poor Law were not really addressing themselves to the question, "How cruel was the law?" so Cobbett was not really concerned with the question, "How cruel were the factories?" The cruelty and inhumanity lay not in the heat or hours of work, not even in the promiscuity or temptations to vice, but in impersonal, non-familial institutions which violated his sense of what was natural and human. Like the publisher of *The Times* who, after discovering that the workhouses he visited were tolerably clean and comfortable, confessed that "no facts" would alter his low opinion of them,[28] so Cobbett, after finally visiting a few factories, admitted: "I have never been into any manufacturing place without reluctance, and I positively refused to go into any of them here [Scotland], alleging, that I had no understanding of the matter, that the wondrous things that are performed in these places, only serve, when I behold them, to withdraw my mind from things which I do understand."[29]

Cobbett did not "understand," or want to understand, a world of factories and factory towns. Yet he was not quite the primitive he sometimes appeared to be. At the height of a wave of machine-breaking episodes in 1816, he wrote one of his most important tracts, the "Letter to the Luddites," which opened by defending the Luddites against their "calumniators," and then proceeded to rebuke them, first for engaging in a form of violence that could only harm them, and then for the mistaken idea that machines were responsible for their distress. Machines, he assured them, were not an evil, not even a necessary evil, but a positive good. "Machines are the produce of the *mind* of man; and their existence distinguishes the civilized man from the savage." They permitted people to enjoy more goods and to use their time and energy more productively. The most primitive tool was a machine; there was no essential difference between a flail and a threshing machine, between a hand-loom and a power-loom. To destroy the machine, in the factory or in the field, was to retreat from civilization to barbarism.[30] Nor were the profits of middlemen excessive or unwarranted. After citing statistics of the cost of wheat to the miller and the price to the consumer, he was surprised to find how low the rate of profit was, and he could only wonder how the miller and baker managed on that modest return. The real problem lay elsewhere, not in the production of manufactured goods or in the profits derived from them, but in their consumption, the insufficient demand caused by the want of employment and low wages. And these were the results of taxes and paper money.

> Thus, then, my fellow-countrymen, it is not *machinery;* it is not the grinding disposition of your employers; it is not improvements in machinery, it is not extortions on the part of Bakers and Butchers and Millers and Farmers and Corn-Dealers and Cheese and Butter Sellers. It is not to any causes of this sort that you ought to attribute your present great and cruel sufferings; but wholly and solely to the great burden of taxes, co-operating with the bubble of paper-money.[31]

The "Letter to the Luddites" corrects and complicates the familiar image of Cobbett as a simple agrarian radical unable to come to terms with the realities of industrialism. In the mid-twenties, to be sure, when he was trying to recover his waning popularity, he lashed out against machines and factory owners. But he often resisted that temptation. Even when he confronted the classic, tragic case of technological unemployment, the Spital-fields silk weavers, he attributed their plight to high taxes rather than the introduction of machinery. Still, there remains a good deal of truth in the conventional image. Whatever degree of sophistication Cobbett could summon up in defense of mechanical progress, there was no question of his own preference for a "cottage economy." The book of that title, as well as the *Register,* were full of schemes for the development of such an economy; the most famous, for which he was much ridiculed, was his plan for the production of "Leghorn bonnets." In spite of his "Letter to the Luddites," he had a profound suspicion of machinery and an abiding distaste for the factory. He once went so far as to suggest that the government encouraged the growth of factories because large manufacturing "congregations" were more easily taxed than the dispersed units of domestic industry.[32] Yet even here the real villains of the System were not machines or manufacturers but the familiar demons: tax collectors, borough-mongerers, stock-brokers, placemen, Jews.

The heroes (or victims) in this morality play were the farmers and laborers. The latter were frankly modeled on the idealized agricultural laborers of old and were endowed with all the virtues the most high-minded Puritan could want of them. "They are industrious, they are virtuous, they are good and true in their very natures"; "they are content as to their station in life;

they are unpresuming; they are honest; they are sincere."[33] They were also manly and self-respecting without being disrespectful of their superiors; they were loyal to their country even though the leaders of the country were squandering its resources and betraying its interests; they were good family men in the face of every temptation and in the most trying circumstances; they even managed to remain sober while imbibing the ale of good old England. If they failed in any respect, succumbing to the insidious habits of tea-drinking or wife-beating, losing heart and becoming demoralized, it was all the fault of the System.

Cobbett had not always thought of them so. In his Tory period his image of the laboring classes had been markedly Malthusian; indeed, he had praised Malthus as a latter-day Newton. Like Malthus, he had attributed the degradation of the laborers to the allowance system and the old poor law. "*All,* all, the labourers, having families, are now paupers! . . . The labourers are humbled, debased, and enslaved."[34] That image was so powerful it persisted for a while even after he turned against Malthus in 1807, when the *Register* printed Hazlitt's bitter attack on Malthus. Yet an article by Cobbett the following year contained the classical Malthusian account of the evils of "giving wages in the shape of relief." The allowance system made paupers of honest laborers who "sink quietly and contentedly into that state, from which their grandfathers, and even their fathers, shrunk with horror." Any kind of relief that went beyond the acceptable limits of charity created dependence and thus pauperism.

> I cannot endure the idea of a labourer's receiving regularly, while he and his family are all in good health, a part of his subsistence in the character of a pauper. Nothing does good but that which is *earned.* There are particular cases when acts of charity (properly so called) are useful; but I like not the system of *presents* and *rewards.* . . . The "comforting" system necessarily implies *interference* on one side, and *dependence* on the other; and, if these exist, it matters not whether you *call* the "comforted" family paupers; for, they will feel themselves dependent, and will have no other than the mind and character which belong to the pauper state.[35]

Only later, when Cobbett became the great defender of the old poor law (allowance system and all), did he abandon this distinction between pauper and poor, and with it the idea that pauperism was a disgrace from which every honorable man shrank with horror. "What is a pauper; what is one of the men to whom this degrading appellation is applied? A very poor man; a man who is, from some cause or other, unable to supply himself with food and raiment without aid from the parish-rates." That aid did not demean or "pauperize" him because it was his by right. "He receives it not as an alms: he is no mendicant; he begs not; he comes to receive that which the laws of the country awards him in lieu of the larger portion assigned him by the law of nature."[36]

If there were no paupers, only poor men exercising their right to relief, the exercise of that right could hardly disqualify them for any of the other rights that properly belonged to all Englishmen—the right to the suffrage, most notably. This may have been the most radical part of Cobbett's argument: the idea that the recipient of relief was not only a member in good standing in the community of the poor but a citizen entitled to all the rights enjoyed by other citizens. It had always been the law (and was to remain so until 1918) that anyone who received parish relief within the year could not be an elector even if he otherwise qualified for the vote. When the reform of the franchise was being debated, Cobbett made a large issue of this provision. Why, he asked, should a poor man, who was more in need of the vote than any other man, be deprived of it merely because he was exercising his natural and legal right to relief? How could one legal right be the ground for the denial of another legal right? Was it "consistent with justice, with humanity, with reason, to deprive a man of the most precious of his political rights, because, and only because, he had been, in a pecuniary way, singularly unfortunate?"[37]

"Singularly unfortunate"—it was because Cobbett had this view of pauperism that he could so readily assimilate the pauper within the class of the poor, and pauper and poor within the larger body of the citizenry. There were some men, he granted, who were reduced to poverty by their vices. Far more common were those impoverished by misfortunes to which the most industrious and virtuous of men were exposed, without fault or folly on their part. And more common still were those who were victimized by the System, drained of their vitality and virtue by the machinations of the "monied interests." In this view of poverty, any distinction between pauper and poor was invidious and unjust.

"Pass this bill," Cobbett wrote while the New Poor Law was being debated, "and you destroy the constitution as far as relates to the necessitous. . . . You dissolve the social compact, as far as relates to the working people."[38] The "necessitous," the "working people"—Cobbett moved effortlessly from the one to the other because he saw no essential difference between them. If he hated the word "pauper" (hence the uncharacteristically graceless word "necessitous"), he was not much more comfortable with the word "poor." Like Burke, although for quite different reasons, he objected to "poor" applied indiscriminately to the laboring classes. "The *Poor* . . . ought always to mean the *helpless* only."[39] In one of his last books, *A Legacy to Labourers,* he cited approvingly a statement by Montesquieu: "that a man ought not to be called poor, merely because he has neither land, nor house, nor goods; that his labour is property; that it is better than an annuity; that the mechanic who gives his art to his children has left them a fortune."[40] He was not entirely consistent in this usage, sometimes lapsing into the more familiar, comprehensive sense of "poor" as in the title of his favorite book, *The Poor Man's Friend.*

Cobbett generally preferred to speak of the "labouring classes," "working classes," "working people," or, simply, "the people." When an appeal for funds for a Mechanics' Institution referred to the "lower orders," he protested against the "insolence" implied in that phrase, pointedly contributing his own five pounds to the "working classes of the community." On another occasion he objected to what he called the French word "peasantry," which originally meant simply "country folk," but had come to connote a *"distinct and degraded class of persons,* who have no pretensions whatever to look upon themselves, in any sense, as belonging to the same *society,* or *community,* as the Gentry; but who ought always be 'kept down in their proper place.' " The Malthusian word "population" was even more objectionable, suggestive of the word "stock" used of animals on a farm. "These the insolent wretches call you *the peasantry,* or the *population;* they never call you the *people.* The word people is quite out of use with them."[41] He also disliked the "new-fangled jargon of *Employer* and *Operative,"* which sounded to him as mechanical and impersonal as the new-fangled industry that gave rise to them, and which gave the impression of two distinct and unbridgeable classes. The older terms, "masters" and "men," evoked a time when "everyone was in his place" but everyone was also free to rise, when journeymen could "wriggle" themselves up and become masters, laborers become farmers, clerks become merchants, and privates in the army become (as Cobbett himself had done) sergeant-majors and even generals. The fixed gap implied in "employers" and "operatives" had the effect of "cutting off the chain of connection between the rich and the poor," "reducing the community to two classes: *Masters* and *Slaves."*[42]

Whatever confusions there were in Cobbett's own terminology, his intentions were clear. The older vocabulary gave the poor a more secure and dignified place in society, and at the same time greater opportunities to better themselves, to "wriggle" upward. In that society poverty, even "extreme poverty," so far from being shameful, was natural and inevitable. Indeed, poverty—or rather the "fear of poverty"—was actually desirable, for it was the source of all virtues and pleasures: "early-rising, sobriety, provident carefulness, attentive observation, a regard for reputation, reasoning on causes and effects, skill in the performance of labour, arts, sciences, even public-spirit and military valour and renown." Without the "salutary fear" of poverty, there would be no virtue, no industry, no civilization.

> Therefore, there must be extreme poverty in the world: it must exist; and, accordingly, the word of God tells us, that "the poor shall never

cease from out of the land"; that is to say, that there always must be, and shall be poor people; that is, people in extreme poverty.

God has said, for such is the order of the world, that the far greater part of mankind shall live by labour of one sort or another; and that the far greater part shall be subject to what may be called toil, or hard work. . . . Therefore, the order of the world; and, indeed, the happiness and harmony of mankind, render it necessary that the great body of the working people should not be owners of house or land; and thus it has been from the days of Moses to the present hour, in all nations of the world.[43]

It might have been Malthus preaching the gospel of poverty—except that Cobbett made of it a gospel of relief. If poverty was a necessary part of civilization, so was a legal provision for the relief of poverty.* If it was natural that some should be poor and others rich, some "men" and others "masters," it was also natural that there be a "chain of connection" between them, a chain of rights and duties and also a chain of opportunity and advancement.

Again and again one returns to a Cobbett who, in spite of occasional attempts to come to terms with the new world, had "no understanding" of that world and preferred, as he said, to "withdraw" his mind from it. He was for the Ten Hours Bill of 1833 because he had no objection to government regulation, but he did not believe that such measures went to the heart of the problem, which for him, in 1833 as in 1805, remained high taxes. He was for the repeal of the Combination Laws and the legalization of trade union activities, including the right to strike. But he counseled against strikes and belittled trade unionism, again on the ground that the conditions they hoped to remedy were not the fault of any one master but of the System —and not the industrial or capitalist system, but the fiscal system. And the reform of the System required not so much the raising of wages as the lowering of prices, which meant the elimination of taxes, sinecures, paper money, and the debt, all of which called for political action rather than trade union organization.

If Cobbett was tolerant (although only that) of factory legislation and trade unionism, he was positively hostile to all proposals for popular education. He opposed the bill of 1833 providing government subsidies for schools because it left the schools under the control of religious bodies. He disliked

*This is not inconsistent with his remark in *The Poor Man's Friend:* "Poverty is, after all, the great badge of slavery. Bare bones and rags are the true marks of the real slave." "Poverty," in this context, was "slavery" because it was not relieved, because it was permitted to remain in the condition of "bare bones and rags."[44]

Mechanics' Institutions because they were run by the same contemptible "feelosofers" who controlled the Society for the Diffusion of Useful Knowledge. And he distrusted schools in general, private or public, because the teachers were government agents, spies, and propagandists, because the only proper kind of education was that acquired in the bosom of the family, and because book-learning made children feel superior to their parents and dissatisfied with their stations in life.* A visit to Robert Owen's school in New Lanark confirmed him in all his prejudices. He was appalled by the sight of boys and girls in the same room, half-naked, he said (the boys wore kilts and the girls were bare-headed and bare-footed), reciting their lessons in unison. It was unnatural and tyrannical, a flagrant violation of the principles of "domestic life" and of the "order of nature." His only consolation was that this kind of schooling could never become common for the nation at large, since nine-tenths of the people would always have to be employed on the land and therefore be too scattered to attend schools. (This was in 1832, when one-fourth of the population already resided in cities with a population of 20,000 or more, and when 1,000,000 children were in day schools and another 1,500,000 in Sunday schools.) A year later he cited the nine-tenths figure again, this time as the number of children who had to "live by manual labor, or become thieves and strumpets"; surely it was undesirable for them to be "crammed up in schools, instead of being employed from their infancy in those little labours and cares which make them valuable when they grow up to be men and women."[47]

Along with school teachers and government agents, Jews occupied a prominent place in his demonology. Cobbett's admirers have been so embarrassed by this subject that they have tended to ignore or belittle it, as if it were an innocent crotchet on the order of his dislike for tea or potatoes, or as if it were too common a prejudice to be noteworthy.[48] In fact his anti-Semitism was far more virulent than the common garden variety, because it formed an integral part of his social and political views. The Jews were usurers, parasites, upstarts, loan-jobbers, stock-brokers, speculators; they bought up old estates, displaced old English families, and ruined old England.[49] And, of course, they were "Christ-killers." At the same time that he was agitating for parliamentary reform, Cobbett took the time to publish a pamphlet, *Good Friday; or the Murder of Jesus Christ by the Jews,* a classic specimen of anti-Semitism. He found the persecution of the Jews one of the

---

*It was one of his many inconsistencies to boast of his own "family of scholars." He hastened to point out that his children (like himself) were taught at home, that each sex had its "appropriate species of learning," that no one was forced to learn, and that none of that learning was attained at the expense of work.[45] He never confronted the larger paradox that his very calling, as writer, publicist, and publisher of a popular newspaper, depended on a literate public. In fact he deplored the "habit" of reading, for the middle classes as well as the working classes. The habitual reader of newspapers and books, he wrote in a book addressed to middle-class young men, had his head "stuffed with such a jumble that he knows not what to think about anything."[46]

endearing features of the Middle Ages, and he acquitted the Tsar of Russia of the charge of being a tyrant on the ground that no tyrant would have been so enlightened as to banish the Jews from his realm.[50] Needless to say, he opposed the bill introduced in 1833 which would have permitted Jews to sit in Parliament by exempting them from the standard oath "on the true faith of a Christian."

If Cobbett was less virulently anti-Negro, it was only because the Negroes were thousands of miles distant. For over twenty years he opposed the campaign waged by Wilberforce, Brougham, and others to abolish slavery in the West Indies. He sometimes claimed to have no objection to emancipation as such, only to the priority given to that issue. "Charity begins at home, and so ought *humanity.*" And humanity dictated that attention be paid to the condition of English laborers, which was far worse, he insisted, than that of the Black slaves. "It is notorious that great numbers of your *free* British labourers' have actually *died* from starvation; . . . [and] equally notorious that no black slave ever suffered from want of food"; nor was any slave so degraded as to be forced to eat potatoes. Contemplating the "fat and lazy and laughing and singing and dancing negroes," Cobbett found it hard to get exercised about slavery. When the issue came to a vote in 1833 and it became obvious that the abolitionists were going to prevail, Cobbett reluctantly voted with the majority, but only out of deference, he explained, to the wishes of his constituents.[51]

In one notable respect, he departed from the usual litany of populist prejudices. He was well disposed to the Catholics and generally (though not always) supported Catholic emancipation, in part as a means of undermining the establishment, in part because of his adulation of pre-Reformation England.[52] He compensated for this, however, by vilifying other religious groups whom he identified with the System: Quakers, Unitarians, Methodists, Evangelicals. The Quakers, for example, were a "sect of *non-labourers*"; "they are, as to the products of the earth, what the *Jews* are as to gold and silver." And the "nasty, canting, lousy Methodists," inveigling pennies from servant girls, were no better.[53]

It is impossible to know what Cobbett's readers made of him, what appealed to them in this melange of ideas, attitudes, prejudices, obsessions, and passions. There is no doubt that he commanded a large audience, both among the middle classes and the working classes—the latter especially after the appearance of the twopenny edition of the *Register* in November 1816, when sales rose from a thousand or two to 40,000 or 50,000. Earlier volumes were reissued (under the title *Cobbett's Annual Register*), and individual articles were reprinted, the most successful of them, "Address to the Journeymen and Labourers" (from the first twopenny issue), selling, by

Cobbett's count, 200,000 copies within a year. In 1819, when the Six Acts made it difficult to evade the tax on newspapers, the price of the *Register* went up to sixpence and sales fell drastically. The paper remained in a decline throughout the twenties, reviving only in the early thirties when Cobbett took up the issues of the suffrage and the poor law. Even at the price of sixpence, circulation far surpassed that of *The Times* or even the most popular of the cheaper, unstamped papers. Articles from the *Register* were also reprinted in a monthly journal Cobbett started for just that purpose, *Two Penny Trash* (the name originally applied derisively to the twopenny edition of the *Register*).[54]

An enterprising businessman as well as journalist, Cobbett exploited every commercial technique: serial publication, cheap editions, reprints of individual articles in pamphlet form and of collections of articles in bound volumes, and other means of recycling the same material. He also set up the most efficient system of distribution in the country, priding himself on the fact that his distributors had a stake in keeping up circulation because they profited so handsomely from it. (He once boasted that he himself had a clear profit of £200 a week, but his financial affairs were generally in disarray, partly because he invested in land and farms beyond his means.) Some of his most successful books were of the "how-to" genre. His *Grammar of the English Language* sold 13,000 copies when it was first published in 1818, 100,000 by the time of his death (this apart from numerous pirated editions), and continued to be reprinted well into the twentieth century. Its grammatical lessons were conveyed by such model sentences as: "The evil *is* the taxes," not "the evil *are* the taxes"; or "The borough-tyrants, generally *speaking,* are great fools as well as great rogues."[55] *Cottage Economy,* published in 1821–22, sold 50,000 copies in six years. A celebration of the good life as well as a practical manual, it contained instructions (as advertised in the subtitle) for the "brewing of Beer, making of Bread, keeping of Cows, Pigs, Bees, Ewes, Goats, Poultry, and Rabbits, . . . the selecting, the cutting and the bleaching of the Plants of English Grass and Grain, for the purpose of making Hats and Bonnets; and also instructions for erecting and using Bee-Houses after the Virginian manner." *Advice to Young Men and (incidentally) to Young Women,* in 1829, was another species of this genre, a manual of conduct for young men (the women were the beneficiaries of the advice, not the recipients of it), which laid down models of right-thinking and right-living for those of the "middle and higher ranks" at various stages of their lives, as youth, lover, husband, father, and citizen, all of which could have been heartily endorsed by Benjamin Franklin or Samuel Smiles.[56]

Cobbett's most enduringly popular book was *Rural Rides,* published in 1830, a collection of articles that had appeared in the *Register* during the twenties. Neither the sentimental journey nor the bucolic travelogue that some editors have made of it, it was thoroughly penetrated by his political and social views, the descriptions of country scenes interrupted by "Rustic Harangues" against the System, and punctuated by his usual fulminations against tax-collectors, borough-mongers, jobbers, and Jews, and his usual denunciations of tea and potatoes, canals and railroads. As he traveled about the country, noting the destroyed cottages and empty churches, he jeered at the official census returns which had the population increasing by 4,000,000 in twenty years. "A man that can suck that in will believe, literally believe, that the moon is made of green cheese."[57]

By obvious standards—the sheer bulk and variety of his work, circulation and sales figures, involvement in one after another episode which kept his name before the public—Cobbett was obviously a figure of some importance, although not as important as he thought. As he personalized the System, so he also personalized his own relations to it. Pitt, Malthus, Wilberforce, every fund-holder, tax-collector, and borough-monger, were his personal enemies, and he himself was the most formidable force opposing them. A "new era" in the political education of the people dated from 1804, when he began to "open the eyes" of his countrymen to the truths discovered by Paine. At another time the decisive eye-opening event was the first twopenny issue of the *Register,* which "occupied the conversation of three-fourths of all the acting men in the kingdom" and came as a revelation to the labouring classes. "The effect on their minds was like what might be expected to be produced on the eyes of one bred up in the dark, and brought out, all of a sudden, into broad daylight." Later still it was his lectures in 1830 which, more than "all other causes put together," brought about the Reform Bill.[58]

If Cobbett's own claims are excessive, so are those advanced on his behalf by the Lancashire Radical Samuel Bamford.

> At this time [late 1816] the writings of William Cobbett suddenly became of great authority: they were read on nearly every cottage hearth in the manufacturing districts of South Lancashire, in those of Leicester, Derby, and Nottingham; also in many of the Scottish manufacturing towns. Their influence was speedily visible; he directed his readers to the true cause of their sufferings—misgovernment; and to its proper corrective—parliamentary reform. Riots soon became scarce, and from that time they have never obtained their ancient vogue with the labourers of this country.[59]

This passage has been cited so often that by sheer force of repetition it has acquired a credibility it does not deserve. Apart from the fact that it was written almost thirty years after the event, it is on the face of it suspect. Soon after Cobbett's famous "Letter to the Luddites" in November 1816, urging the workers to remain calm and advising them not to blame their ills on the machines, a series of Luddite riots broke out, starting in Spa Fields in December and continuing throughout the following year; another outbreak in 1819 culminated in what came to be called the "Peterloo Massacre"—hardly evidence of his great influence in preventing riots. Nor was he widely seen as a force for peace in 1830 at the time of the Swing riots. Certainly the government did not see him as such, for it then brought charges against him for incitement to sedition. If this part of Bamford's testimony is untrustworthy, other parts of it may be as well—the claim, for example, that Cobbett was being read at all those "cottage hearths" in all those manufacturing towns.

This is not to belittle Cobbett's influence, only to suggest that it is not easy to determine its extent or exact nature. Although the charges against him were finally dropped, he was at least partly confirmed in his own sense of importance; clearly the government and the press thought him capable of inspiring and inciting the masses, even if it could not be proved that he had done so. However much one may discount the circulation figures he himself provided (figures too often cited by historians without indicating the source), there is no doubt that his work did sell in impressive quantities and that he did have a considerable working class audience. His peak periods of popularity corresponded, not by accident, with the periods of greatest economic distress and political turmoil, 1816–19 (when he himself was in America) and 1830–32. In the twenties, when the circulation of the *Register* dropped precipitously, his books had respectable sales.

Popularity, however, did not necessarily translate itself into influence. Cobbett could only have been dismayed by the upsurge of Methodism among the working classes or the popularity of the Sunday schools and Mechanics' Institutions, and he could not have been much more pleased with the growth of trade unionism. Nor could he take credit for some of the major reforms of the time: the revision of the penal code, the abolition of the income tax and lowering of tariffs, the establishment of the police force, the legalization of trade unions, the admission of Dissenters to public office, the abolition of slavery in the colonies. Although he supported the Reform Act of 1832 it was only after fifteen years of agitating for a very different kind of reform, which led to renewed accusations of inconsistency and inconstancy. Even his efforts on behalf of Catholic emancipation may have been irrelevant, the Catholics being loath to be associated with him and the working classes remaining largely impervious to his attempts to enlist them in the Catholic cause.

Like Carlyle, Cobbett had little to show by way of practical achievement. Yet somehow he struck a chord that resonated throughout society. William Hazlitt declared him "a kind of *fourth estate* in the politics of the country . . . unquestionably the most powerful political writer of the present day." Yet even Hazlitt, who agreed with him on such matters as Malthusianism and utilitarianism, parliamentary reform and the poor law, thought him unprincipled, capricious, inconstant, ineffectual—"like a young and lusty bridegroom that divorces a favourite speculation every morning, and marries a new one every night."[60] Lytton Bulwer was similarly bemused by him. Caricatured as "William Muscle," a radical of the "old school," Cobbett was said to be "the Incarnation of popular prejudices and natural sense . . . the living representation of the old John Bull."[61] In its obituary notice, *The Times* paid him the same ambiguous tribute. This "self-taught peasant," the most extraordinary Englishman of his time, belonged to no part of England and made no real impact upon the country.

> Though a vigilant observer of the age, and a strenuous actor in it, he lay upon the earth as a loose and isolated substance. He was incorporated with no portion of our political or social frame. He belonged neither to principles, to parties, nor to classes. . . . He was an English episode, and nothing more, as greater men have been; for what is Napoleon, while we write, but an *episode*?[62]

This was, of course, a commentary as much on *The Times* as on Cobbett. An "episode"—like Napoleon! One can hear Cobbett cursing the "bloody old *Times*" for its complacency and condescension. (One also recalls Cobbett's dislike of the word "peasant," signifying, as he thought, a "distinct and degraded class" unworthy of associating with the gentry.)

If the nature of the power exercised by that "most powerful political writer" was elusive, so was the nature of the constituency he appealed to and supposedly represented. To Marx, Cobbett was an "anticipated modern Chartist" and an "inveterate John Bull," "the purest incarnation of Old England and the most audacious initiator of Young England."[63] To the radical historians, the Hammonds, he was "the most powerful tribune that the English poor have ever known."[64] To his biographer, G. D. H. Cole, who was no less radical than the Hammonds but was more aware of Cobbett's complexities and ambiguities, he appeared "not as the apostle of the modern working-class movement, but as the tribune of the transition, the faithful representative of the feeling of the dispossessed of his time, not the preacher of strange new doctrines, but the John the Baptist, linking old and new together."[65]

E. P. Thompson's Cobbett had a still more ambiguous relationship to the working classes, his ideology being that of the "small producers" or "little bourgeoisie"—farmers, tradesmen, artisans—and his ideal society one in which landowners, tenants, and laborers were united in a system of mutual rights and obligations. Only in one respect was he a spokesman of the "working class"; in giving the poor a claim upon society as a matter of right rather than charity, he sowed the seeds of new claims that were potentially revolutionary. Apart from this, it was not what he said, still less what he did, that Thompson finds memorable or commendable, but how he said it, his habit of addressing his readers as though they were capable of reasoning and as though their problems could be settled by their "common understanding." While his ideas were often stupid and contradictory, his tone, style, and mode of argument were truly democratic. By his rhetoric he brought "the weaver, the schoolmaster, and the shipwright into a common discourse," and out of the diversity of their grievances and interests, he created a "Radical consensus," a "Radical intellectual culture." This was his contribution to the making of the English working class: "he nourished the culture of a class, whose wrongs he felt, but whose remedies he could not understand."[66]

By making Cobbett a culture hero rather than an ideologue, one avoids having to take seriously ideas which may be embarrassing or reprehensible. One also runs the risk of a certain condescension, not so much toward Cobbett himself as toward all those weavers, schoolmasters, shipwrights, farmers, tradesmen, and artisans, who read him and listened to him, yet presumably responded to his tone and style rather than his ideas. There is also something odd about the radical culture he is supposed to have created. If it represented so many schoolmasters as well as weavers, farmers as well as laborers, it could only have been a non-working class culture, a "consensus" culture; and if it exalted the values of a traditional, paternalistic, patriarchal, hierarchical society, it had also to be a non-radical culture. To the extent to which Cobbett exercised a powerful cultural influence upon workers as well as the "petty bourgeoisie," this would seem to belie Thompson's theory of a distinctive, radical (even revolutionary) working class culture and working class consciousness. In fact Cobbett's ideas and values have made of him a culture hero of the Right as well as of the Left. When G. K. Chesterton praised him for his sense of "human equality" and sympathy with the poor, he meant a human equality consistent with a large degree of economic and social inequality, and a sympathy for the poor consistent with a large sympathy for the aristocracy and gentry in contrast to the bankers, businessmen, and bureaucrats who (Chesterton, like Cobbett, believed) were destroying the old England.[67]

The "paradox" of Cobbett, if it can be called that, is symbolized in the fact that excerpts from his writings have found their way into both the "Radical" and the "Conservative" volumes of the *British Political Tradition* series.[68] (Not the "Liberal" volume—but then no one ever accused Cobbett of being a liberal.) This may be a paradox to historians, but not to Cobbett or his contemporaries. For his was the kind of populist ideology that lent itself to conservative and even reactionary causes—and in the service of those causes had a radicalizing effect. He made no secret, for example, of his hostility to any kind of schooling for the working classes; yet his own writings, by encouraging the habit of reading which he deplored and helped foster, created a demand for schools on the part of parents who, for obvious reasons, were unable to follow his advice and teach their children at home. So with trade unionism, for which he had no great liking but which he may have promoted unwittingly because of his own militant stance and the adversary posture he assumed for himself and for the working classes. Insisting that he sought no "innovation," no great "alteration," "nothing new," he proposed such radical innovations in the constitution as manhood suffrage, annual parliaments, and the secret ballot. Professing to defend King, Church, and Country, he bitterly denounced the monarch, the prelates, the aristocracy, the bureaucracy, the army. He preached class cooperation and harmony while fomenting class antagonism and discord. He was, as the government charged, profoundly seditious, even if he had nothing to do with the riots he was supposed to have inspired.

Cobbett was, in short, a familiar type of populist who appealed to several classes in the name of "the people," who tapped a reservoir of popular discontent in which the sense of grievance was more powerful than any specific grievance, who expressed an outrage that seemed plausible even if the objects of his wrath were not, who combined compassion with bigotry, passion with crankiness, equality with hierarchy, defiance with deference. Cobbett reminds us how untidy, unstructured, unfocused his world was, in spite of the attempts of political economists and reformers in his own day, and historians since, to reshape and reform it, to make it coherent and intelligible.

This may be the most salutary lesson to be learned from "the Poor Man's Friend." It is almost as if Cobbett had deliberately set out to confound all the tidy definitions and distinctions which others were trying to impose on the poor. In his world there were no paupers, only the "very poor" who were an integral part of the "people." In that world the poor were jealous of their rights and property (their property in the poor law, for example) and had no designs on the rights and property of the rich. They knew their place, but they also knew how to "wriggle" up to a better place. They wanted no part in Owen's "community of paupers," preferring to remain in a community, a "chain of connections," with their betters.[69] They were not engaged in a class struggle with their masters, but they were engaged, together with their masters, in an implacable struggle against the System that was thought to be oppressing them both. They were not even engaged in a struggle against poverty—only against a poverty that was unnatural and unrelieved, a new kind of poverty that threatened to make of them paupers rather than the worthy poor of old.

X

THE POOR MAN'S GUARDIAN:

THE "NEW RADICALISM"

In 1830 Colonel T. Perronet Thompson was pleased to inform the readers of the *Westminster Review* that "the term Radical, once employed as a name of low reproach, has found its way into high places, and is gone forth as the title of a class, who glory in their designation."[1] The radicalism Thompson was glorying in was Philosophic Radicalism, he himself being so enthusiastic a Benthamite he was sometimes an embarrassment even to Bentham, who was not normally discomposed by excessive praise. But there were other kinds of radicals abroad, some who had been prominent in the Peterloo period and a younger generation emerging at this time.* There were populist radicals (Cobbett), Tory radicals (Richard Oastler), "cooperative" socialists (Robert Owen), agrarian socialists (Allen Davenport), Ricardian socialists (Thomas Hodgskin), republicans (Richard Carlile), trade union militants (John Doherty), atheists (G. J. Holyoake), "demagogues" (Henry Hunt), "agitators" (against the New Poor Law or for the Ten Hours Bill), "radical reformers" (for universal suffrage), currency reformers (for or against paper money)—"a motley, confused, jarring miscellany of irreconcilable theorists," Lytton Bulwer (himself a somewhat unorthodox Philosophic Radical) called them.[3] What was remarkable about this motley crew was not only the variety but the extent to which they overlapped and interlocked with each other, so that even the most discordant of them had enough in common to warrant that common label.

Contemporaries tried to bring order out of this chaos by distinguishing between radicals and "ultra radicals," or moderates and extremists. The difficulty with these categories is that on any one issue there was a range of alternatives, so that one person's extremism was another's moderation, and

---

*According to Harriet Martineau, "radical" as a noun first appeared in 1819 after the Peterloo affair, when "reformers" proudly assumed that title.[2]

a moderate on one issue (the suffrage) might be an impassioned partisan on another (factory laws). Another distinction, more common among historians than contemporaries, is between working class and middle class radicals. But this too is difficult to sustain, since there was no clear correspondence between social status and ideological persuasion, some of the most militant radicals being of middle class background, and some notable moderates coming from the working classes. Nor does it help to use these terms in a purely ideological sense, "working class radicals" referring to those who were most solicitous of working class rights, interests, and desires, since it was precisely the nature of those rights, interests, and desires that was in dispute. Even the issue of the working class suffrage provides no clear guide. Was Oastler a "middle class radical" because he was opposed to the suffrage, and Cobbett a "working class radical" because he favored it?

Another distinction focuses on the differences between the "old" radical ideology and the "new," the former typified by Cobbett's "Old Corruption"—tax-collectors, fund-holders, war-mongers, job-seekers—and the latter emphasizing theories of property, class, labor, and exploitation. This distinction emerges most sharply in Patricia Hollis's study of the "unstamped" press, the illegal, semi-underground papers which flourished in the early 1830s. "Old" and "new" obviously carry the connotation of regressive and progressive, and Hollis herself does not conceal her judgment that the old ideology was "irrelevant" to the real problems of the working classes, and that the new was both more "sophisticated" and more "appropriate," a "stricter working-class theory." But she also makes it clear that the new never displaced the old, that both were represented in the unstamped press (not only in different papers but in the same paper, often in the same article), that both persisted in the Chartist period and beyond, that in spite of superficial similarities the new ideology was not Marxist, and that the "socialist patina was always very thin."[4]

If the "new ideology" was only one element, and not the dominant one, in the radicalism of the time, radicalism itself was only one element in the unstamped press, much of which was not political, still less radical. There were good commercial, as well as political, reasons to defy the stamp tax, and many papers devoted to fiction, crime, comedy, religion, "useful knowledge," and other respectable and not so respectable subjects availed themselves of that opportunity.* The original purpose of the stamp tax had been entirely political; one of the Six Acts passed after Peterloo, it had been intended to put an end to penny and twopenny papers such as Cobbett's *Political Register* and the even more provocative *Black Dwarf.* It had served

---

*The titles were often deceptive, perhaps deliberately so. The *People's Police Gazette,* for example, specialized in sensational crime stories, but *Cleave's Weekly Police Gazette* was highly political. The frequent change of titles, the irregular appearance of some and the very brief duration of others, made it as difficult for the authorities as for the historian to keep track of them.

its purpose well during the twenties, the circulation of the *Register,* for example, falling precipitously when the price went up to sixpence. (*Black Dwarf* ceased publication in 1824 when Cartwright, who may have subsidized it, died.) The unrest of the early thirties led to a widespread defiance of the tax. Although the *Register* continued as a stamped paper, dozens of newer radical papers joined the ranks of the unstamped.

The illegal nature of the enterprise was itself an invitation to radicalism. With publishers, printers, editors, writers, distributors, and vendors subject to arrest and imprisonment, the struggle against the authorities became a powerful stimulus to the development of a radical ideology. A primary tenet of that ideology, and the common denominator of all the papers, was the commitment to a free press—free not only in the editorial sense of an uncensored press but also in the sense of a cheap press available to the poor. That issue generated others, so that the unstamped papers came to reflect the entire spectrum of radical thought.

In the process of developing a remarkably efficient system of distribution, the unstamped press created something like a radical movement, a network of people and organizations associated with one or another of the papers devoted to one or another radical cause. The papers assumed an organizational as well as ideological character, *The Poor Man's Guardian,* for example, being the unofficial house organ of the National Union of the Working Classes, reporting on its meetings, activities, debates, and resolutions. There was a good deal of dissension among the papers on matters of policy, tactics, and, of course, personalities. But there was also a good deal of agreement and cooperation. And even in taking issue with each other they served as a medium for the dissemination of each other's ideas. The many articles on Owenism in *The Poor Man's Guardian* brought that doctrine to the attention of a larger, somewhat different audience from that reached by the Owenite journals, *Crisis* and *New Moral World.*

Apart from ideology, the simple fact of the cheapness of the papers had an unwitting political effect. Intended for those who could not afford the "respectable" papers, they acquired a readership that was largely (although not exclusively) working class. It might be claimed that this was the most important fact about them—not their ideology but their readers. Whatever the contents of the papers, whatever issues they focused on and whatever positions they took, they had the effect, even when they were entirely unpolitical, of contributing in some sense to the development of a working class culture and "consciousness."

The most successful and influential of the radical unstamped papers was *The Poor Man's Guardian,* the title an ironic play on the "guardians" who administered the poor law.* The first issue appeared in July 1831 with the provocative subtitle: "A Weekly Newspaper for the People, Established Contrary to 'Law' to Try the Powers of 'Might' against 'Right.' "[5] Its circulation was a modest 2,000 or 3,000 until its owner, Henry Hetherington, was arrested, when it rose to about 10,000, reaching 12,000 to 15,000 during most of 1832 and 1833—this compared with *The Times,* which averaged 10,000 readers. The *Guardian* declined in its last year to 3,000 or 4,000 and suspended publication in December 1835, just before the reduction of the tax signaling the death of all the unstamped papers. Like the other papers, it was read (and sometimes read aloud) in workshops, public houses, coffee houses, and reading rooms, so that its readership was considerably larger than its sales; at its peak Hetherington estimated it at around 50,000.[6] Although Hetherington was nominally the editor as well as printer, publisher, and owner, the actual editor and author of most of the leading articles, especially those of the "new ideology" type, was James Bronterre (as he was known) O'Brien.[7] (Hetherington and O'Brien also collaborated on other papers of a similar political disposition: *The 'Destructive' and Poor Man's Conservative* and *Hetherington's Twopenny Dispatch.*)

One of the themes of the *Guardian,* especially in the early years, was the stamp duty itself, the "taxes on knowledge." While this was obviously of great concern to the editors of the *Guardian* and the other unstamped papers, it was not what gave them their distinctive political tone or impact. The Philosophic Radicals and even many Whigs and Tories also favored the repeal or reduction of the tax, on the ground that the lower classes would then be able to afford the "respectable papers" rather than these "foul," "pernicious," "obscene" pennypapers (as Lord Brougham, one of the great advocates of repeal of the tax, described them).[8] Where Brougham and his colleagues saw "cheap knowledge" as the means of inculcating the lower classes in the true principles of political economy, Hetherington and O'Brien saw it as the instrument for "radical reform."

"Radical reform" was universal suffrage, or what the *Guardian* and most radicals of the time meant by that—manhood suffrage. "It is only necessary that we have a legislature freely chosen by the whole people, *alias,* by all the adult males, not disqualified by insanity, crime, or other sufficient bar to the exercise of political rights."[9] This definition was so widely accepted that the *Guardian* rarely spelled it out. What was at issue, and was the subject of countless editorials, was a reform that would enfranchise not only the £10 householders, as provided in the Reform Bill of 1832, but those

*More ironic is the fact that a dozen years after the demise of this *Poor Man's Guardian* another journal of the same title, but with no ironic overtone, started publication as the organ of the Poor Man's Guardian Society. The earnest, middle class reformers involved in that society obviously had no knowledge of their radical predecessor.

whom the *Guardian* professed to represent: "the working, productive, and useful but *poor* classes, who constitute a very great majority of the population of Great Britain."[10] To the argument that the majority of these classes favored the Reform Bill, the *Guardian* replied that if that were so it was only because they were too oppressed to know their own rights; those who did know them opposed the bill. The latter, the *Guardian* was confident, were "a very large portion, and that portion decidedly the most enlightened and educated" of the working classes, including the "hundreds of thousands" of *Guardian* readers. The rest were "politically speaking, sick to death," too sick to know the nature of their ailment, let alone the cure for it. Fortunately, they had a "guardian and Physician" elected by the "most intelligent and convalescent of them" who could diagnose their disease and prescribe the remedy—the disease, "Abject Poverty and Slavish Degradation," the remedy, "Universal Suffrage and Vote by Ballot."[11] It was without irony that the *Guardian* pronounced universal suffrage to be the "grand panacea for all our evils."[12] A right in itself, the suffrage was also the remedy for all the other ills afflicting the poor. "The rich have no sympathy or fellow-feeling with the poor. They never had any, and never can have any." So long as they made the laws, the laws would be such as to maintain their own power and wealth.

> By the law they can make wrong right, and right wrong—they can make bad money good money and *vice versa,* they can make blasphemy religion, and religion blasphemy. They can even draught off one section of the people to slaughter the other.[13]

So far the *Guardian*'s argument for universal suffrage was not very different from Cobbett's. Where it differed was in the diagnosis of the disease to be remedied by the suffrage. What to Cobbett were the primary causes of the disease—taxes, paper money, sinecures—were to the *Guardian* symptoms or effects. The primary cause was the "vile system of property exclusiveness." As universal suffrage was the "grand panacea" for all evils, so property was the "one great Cause of all these evils"—poverty and degradation, crime and immorality, disease and death, armies and prisons, unjust laws and corrupt judges, dissension and misery.[14]

Sometimes the *Guardian* implied that property itself, the right of "exclusive possession," was the problem. In its most extensive analysis of the subject, it modified that view, acknowledging the legitimacy of one kind of property, the right of every industrious person to the produce of his own labor, even if that produce was in excess of his needs. It also granted to everyone the right to dispose of the excess as he liked, or to transmit it to his heirs. In this sense the *Guardian* recognized the "inviolability of property." But the property claimed by landlords was different; this was the right to "appropriate the fruits of other men's services." This kind of property, acquired by "brigandism" and transmitted by the aid of "priestcraft and exclusive law-making," was "downright robbery." And it was this kind of property that divided society into two warring camps: "the disguised cannibal, and the emaciated helot—the men of prey, and the men preyed upon."[15]

Although this analysis was often put in terms of landed property, it was meant to apply to capitalist property as well, indeed to the latter even more than the former. Like the landlord, the capitalist lived off the labor of others by manipulating the laws and institutions so as to transfer the wealth of the producer to himself. Capitalists constituted a *"monied monopoly, which is (if possible) a thousand times more baneful than the monopoly in land."* Together with the landlords, that other "useless class," they conspired to plunder the "useful classes" of their rightful property.[16]

These views were anathema to most reformers and many radicals. Francis Place denounced the "absurd and mischievous" belief, widespread, he suspected, among the working classes, that the whole produce of their labor should remain in their hands.[17] Nor was Cobbett better disposed to that idea. To Cobbett property as such, whether of land or capital and whether acquired by one's own labor or not, was entirely legitimate. What was illegitimate was the denial of the poor man's "property" in the poor law, and the expropriation, by means of taxes, paper money, and the like, of the property of both the laborer and his employer. When Cobbett extended this defense of property to include a justification of poverty, on the ground that men would not labor unless they were propertyless and poor, the *Guardian* was provoked beyond endurance. For three months it devoted itself to the "Exposure of Cobbett's Damnable Doctrine that the Poor are Predestined to be the Slaves of the Rich." In declaring property to be part of the divine order, was Cobbett blasphemously suggesting that God approved of all the crimes and miseries of mankind? Or was he trying to make his doctrine palatable by giving it the specious authority of religion? The people, the *Guardian* was confident, were not so easily gulled. They knew that any religion that would sanction the robbery of the many for the benefit of the few was a religion not of God but of cheats and robbers, "invented by villains to reconcile the multitude to their crimes and depredations." Nor would the people be content to be drudges and slaves if only they had enough bacon and beer, as Cobbett thought. God ordained that men should live by their labor. But how could they be expected to labor when they saw the fruits of their labor stolen from them by "brute force and fraud"?[18]

The attack on property, and, more important, on "capitalists" (not "capitalism," that term being of later vintage), may suggest that the "new ideology" of the *Guardian* was socialism. This may also be inferred from the frequent references to Thomas Hodgskin, the "Ricardian socialist," as he is generally known. Hetherington probably knew Hodgskin in the twenties, when they were both active in the London Mechanics' Institution. And he almost certainly read the pamphlet published in 1825, *Labour Defended Against the Claims of Capital*, which made Hodgskin's reputation in London radical circles, and his *Popular Political Economy*, originally delivered as lectures to the Mechanics' Institution and published in 1827.

If Hodgskin's theory of value seemed to anticipate Marx's, it was because both derived from Ricardo. But other aspects of his thought, deriving from Godwin, were notably un-Marxist and un-Ricardian.[19] Like Ricardo, Hodgskin believed labor to be the source of all value; but he also believed, like Godwin and unlike Ricardo, that all property not derived from labor, notably rent and capital, was artificial and unjust, the creation of arbitrary laws and institutions. What made Hodgskin's argument seem more modern than Godwin's was his insistence that capital rather than land was the greater of the two evils, and that "the reproaches so long cast on the feudal aristocracy should be heaped on capital and capitalists." To the extent to which the capitalist was genuinely productive, Hodgskin conceded, his profit was a proper return for his managerial labor, a form of wages. For the rest, profit was nothing more than a brute act of usurpation made possible by laws and institutions that were no more legitimate than property itself. And as property was artificial, so was poverty. The great fallacy of the political economists was to attribute to natural laws the poverty that was the result of social institutions, institutions which either did not permit the laborer to use his productive powers to their full capacity or which robbed him of the fruits of his labor.[20]

Hodgskin's theories constituted a radical critique of capitalism, although not a socialistic one. He himself repudiated the varieties of socialism available in his own time—Owenism, St. Simonianism, agrarian radicalism —and in terms that would also preclude anything like Marxism. The only kind of property he recognized as natural and legitimate was that which was "individual, not common; selfish, not general," the "right of every individual to own for his separate and selfish use whatever he can make."[21] Any communal or nationalized property was as much a violation of natural rights, as much a usurpation by government, as feudal or capitalist forms of property. This hostility to law, government, and social institutions carried over to parliamentary reform and social legislation. Nothing good, not even reform, could come from the state or organized society, which were by nature instruments of oppression and injustice. (Even voluntary cooperative schemes were suspect, although Hodgskin made an exception for the Mechanics' Institutions, which he approved of because they taught men to help and better themselves and encouraged them to be sober.) Halévy may have overstated the case when he characterized Hodgskin's philosophy as a form of "anarchism";[22] "radical individualism" may describe it more accurately. Later that philosophy was to make of him an ardent free-trader and a disciple of Herbert Spencer. But in the twenties and thirties, even during his Chartist days, his critique of capitalism had a large Godwinite element in it. To the extent to which it also drew upon Ricardian economics, that too gave it an individualistic character, so that the familiar label, "Ricardian socialist," is singularly inapt.

The *Guardian* drew upon both Hodgskin and Godwin, but upon both selectively, and in espousing universal suffrage it departed radically from both. Godwin was in fact cited more often than Hodgskin, but there was so large an affinity between them that a typical quotation from Godwin could as well have come from Hodgskin.

> It is a gross imposition that men are accustomed to put upon themselves, when they talk of the property bequeathed to them by their ancestors. The property is produced by the daily labour of men, who are now in existence. All that their ancestors bequeathed to them was a mouldy patent, which they show as a title to extort from their neighbours what the labour of those neighbours has produced.[23]

The *Guardian* (and other radicals influenced by Hodgskin) were not so much propounding a "new ideology" as harking back to an old one, the highly individualistic, almost anarchic radicalism of Godwin. What was new was the linking of the radical critique of property with the radical reform of the suffrage.

Although Hodgskin and Godwin did not provide the *Guardian* with any system that could properly be described as socialistic, such an alternative was available in the doctrine of Owen. Marx's later critique of "utopian social-ism," which made any kind of socialism other than Marxism seem unworthy of the name, has done much to discredit Owenism as a serious form of socialism. Yet the word "socialist" was coined in 1827 to apply specifically to Owenism.[24] By 1848 it had become so closely identified with Owen that when Marx and Engels wrote the *Manifesto,* they were obliged, as Engels later explained, to call it a "communist," rather than "socialist," manifesto.[25] Whatever latter-day socialists might think of the merits of Owenism, there is no question of its historic right to that title.

Nor is there any question of the importance of Owenism in the radical movements of the thirties. Hetherington himself was a disciple of Owen as early as 1820 and a charter member of the British Association for Promoting Cooperative Knowledge, an Owenite organization which included others who later figured prominently in the unstamped press (William Carpenter, John Cleave, James Watson) and in the Chartist movement (William Lovett, most notably). But Owen, like Godwin and Hodgskin, provided no basis for a radical reform of the suffrage. When the Reform Bill became an urgent issue for Hetherington and other radicals, in contrast to the orthodox Owenites who looked upon it (and upon politics in general) as a distraction from the true tasks of cooperation, education, and moral reform, the dissidents formed the National Union of the Working Classes. Under that banner they declared their allegiance to both cooperative socialism and political radicalism. The *Guardian* became the unofficial organ of the National Union, while the *Crisis,* another unstamped paper edited for a time by Owen himself, represented orthodox Owenism.

In spite of its deviation, the *Guardian* maintained cordial relations with the Owenites, partly because the latter were then cultivating a working class and trade union constituency. In the early 1820s Owenism had been a largely middle class movement devoted to the education and moral reformation of the working classes, but by the end of the decade, having witnessed the failure of some of its communities and the growth of working class militancy, it began to direct its efforts to the working classes en masse. It penetrated the existing trade unions and founded new trade union associations, established a much publicized National Equitable Labour Exchange, and set up hundreds of cooperative stores in working class neighborhoods. Between 1829 and 1834, according to the historian J. F. C. Harrison, "the British working class movement was saturated with Owenism."[26] By the same token, Owenism was saturated with a new kind of radicalism, the radicalism reflected in the unstamped press.

Yet this new radicalism did not sit easily with Owenism. In its headlines the *Guardian* boldly called for a united front of Radicals and Owenites, "a real 'Holy Alliance,'" to put down Despots and Spoliators of all Creeds and Classes." But its editorials were uncompromising on the issue of parliamentary reform and thus in conflict with one of the basic tenets of Owenism. There was no redress for the working classes, the *Guardian* insisted, except that which came from the power of the law, and that power required a radical reform of the suffrage. It was not from the "justice or benevolence" of the aristocracy that the working classes could look for an improvement in their conditions but only from their own political power.[27] Interwoven with this political argument was an economic one that also went well beyond the principles of Owenism. When the *Guardian* claimed that their differences were only in respect to means, that they shared the same end— "to establish for the workman dominion over the fruits of his own industry" —it did not mean by "dominion" the kind of voluntary cooperative communities the Owenites had in mind. The suffrage was to permit the workers to recover what was rightfully theirs, the full fruits of their labor, and that meant abolishing the rents, profits, tithes, annuities, and taxes which had deprived the workers of those fruits. Political power would permit the laborers to say to the landlord, "You shall have no more rent, because you were 'hard of heart,'" and to the capitalist, "Henceforward you have no capital, because we will it."[28] This was a far cry from the class cooperation, social harmony, communality, rationality, and morality which were at the heart of the Owenite enterprise.

After 1834, when the Owenites reverted to type, dissociating themselves from working class movements and committing themselves, more boldly than ever, to radical moral reform, the *Guardian* became even more critical. The new Owenite gospel, repudiating marriage as the worst kind of social tyranny, the family as the bastion of private property and selfishness, and religion as the primary obstacle to the creation of a "New Moral World" (the title of the Owenite journal), was denounced as unnecessarily provocative and utterly irrelevant. Whatever evils there were in marriage, the family, religion, or "anything else," the *Guardian* argued, were the results of the system of property. "Property, property is the great denaturalizer—the grand demoralizer, the universal destroyer." But it was not property per se that was evil, the kind of property implied in the idea of the family, for example. What was evil was the property that derived from "bad institutions," the institutions of rent and profit, and it was these institutions that had to be abolished.[29]

In the course of this critique of Owenism, the *Guardian* proposed an elaborate program for the reform of society. The fundamental principle was simple: "that there shall be henceforward no idlers, or uselessly-employed persons in society, and that each individual shall receive the full equivalent of his services, and no more." The first step would be the "appropriation of the whole soil of the country to the whole people of the country." The landlords would be compensated over a twenty-year period, after which the income from the land would accrue to the nation and be used for national purposes. Since the nation would then be the "sole landlord," there would be no question of the private accumulation of property or of inheritance. Nor would there be any problem of resistance on the part of the landlords, since they would be conscious of their "weakness and unworthiness" and would not dare challenge so generous a settlement.[30]

Capitalist enterprises would also be "appropriated," the owners compensated for their machinery and "fictitious capital," and the income from the establishment then accruing to the "whole concern, each member receiving a share of it proportional to his services." The *Guardian* did not explain the apparent discrepancy between the respective proposals regarding capital and land—the ownership of the capitalist enterprise to be vested in the single firm and its earnings distributed to its employees, whereas the land was to be nationalized and the income used for national purposes.* It did, however, make the point that the scheme would prevent the "unjust" accumulation of property, whether in capital or in land. While every individual would be permitted to accumulate the fruits of his own labor, the prohibition of interest and inheritance would make it impossible to accumulate large amounts of property. The national debt and all other "vested interests" (church property, for example) were to be similarly disposed of, and the fund-holders similarly compensated. Thus, after twenty years "every man might start fair, in the field of competition or co-operation as they thought fit, and be in full condition to receive the full equivalent for their services to society."[31]

In that last sentence, as much as in the scheme itself, the *Guardian* revealed how far it had come from Owenism, not only in the solution of the social problem—the "appropriation" (expropriation, some might say) of all property, in contrast to the voluntary, cooperative communities favored by the Owenites—but, perhaps more significantly, in the very conception of the problem. For Owen, the basic problem was the irrationality and immorality of present society as exhibited in self-interest, acquisitiveness, competitiveness, disharmony, conflict. The solution to that problem lay in the kind of education and social environment that would reshape the character of individuals so as to make them perfectly rational and moral—although not necessarily equal. Owen himself was not averse to equality, but his system could tolerate a fair amount of inequality, political, economic, and social. Indeed equality itself would be undesirable if it proved to be conducive to irrationality. This was one of his arguments against universal suffrage. "Were you to have a Parliament chosen next year, by Universal Suffrage and Vote by Ballot, it would be most probably the least efficient, most turbulent, and worst public assembly that has yet ruled this country."[32]

For the *Guardian* the problem was not the irrationality and immorality of a competitive society, but the immorality and injustice of a society that did not recognize the "moral necessary of perfect Equality," the principle of "Equal Rights and Equal Obligations."[33] This is why in its prospectus for the future society (after the twenty-year period of compensation) it left to individuals the choice of entering into the "field of competition or co-operation as they saw fit." It did not try to eliminate the spirit of competitiveness; it only sought to prevent that competitiveness from resulting in inequality. While Owen rebuked the *Guardian* for thinking that the suffrage and ballot would promote rationality and cooperation, the *Guardian*

---

*O'Brien remained faithful to this land program. After he had abandoned "Physical Force" Chartism in the 1840s, he continued to advocate the nationalization of the land, in opposition to Feargus O'Connor, who favored a peasant-proprietorship scheme.

rebuked Owen for thinking that the small Owenite communities could survive in the face of large inequalities of wealth. "Benevolent designs," it argued, were no substitute for equality. "There can be no community of feeling between rich and poor. Extreme wealth and extreme poverty can never enter into community."[34]

When Owen complained of the *Guardian*'s habit of applying "epithets" not only to individuals but to "classes of individuals," he was exercising remarkable restraint. The worst epithets were reserved for capitalists and the middle classes—the "shopocrats" and "middlocrats," "robbers," "tyrants," "plunderers," "usurpers," "oppressors," and "villains."[35] Occasionally the *Guardian* permitted itself to contemplate a future when universal suffrage would have so united the country that "the term *classes* will merge into some comprehensive appellation."[36] Until then, it saw society as divided into classes of rich and poor, masters and slaves, who had no common interests or feelings. And the middle classes, even those who were not rich, exacerbated the conflict by throwing their weight onto the side of the rich. They were even more oppressive than the aristocracy, because they were in the closest relationship to the poor and because they were so numerous—more than 6,000,000 people, the *Guardian* calculated (almost half the entire population of England). They were the "shopkeepers and master manufacturers" (very small shopkeepers and masters, it must have been, to amount to that number) whose business it was to "buy labour *cheap* from the poor, and sell it *dear* to the aristocracy."

> Taken as a body, they are the basest of society. Occupying an intermediate position between the workman and the aristocrat—employing the one and being employed by the other, they insensibly contract the vices of both tyrant and slave. Tyrants to those below them—sycophants to those above them—and usurers from necessity and habit—they prey on the *weakness* of the workman, while they extort all they can from the *vanity* of the aristocrat. Indeed the middle classes are the destroyers of liberty and happiness in all countries.[37]

In a passage that seems to anticipate Marx's theory of the proletarianization and pauperization of the petty bourgeoisie (an idea that was, in fact, something of a cliché at the time), the *Guardian* explained that the only hope for the working classes lay in the impoverishment of the middle classes. And this was already coming about: as a result of competition and Peel's currency reforms, large numbers of the middle classes were already being reduced to the "ranks of pauperism." But those who remained in the middle classes continued to be the worst enemies of the people. "Don't believe those who tell you that the middle and working classes have one and the same interest. It is a damnable delusion. Hell is not more remote from heaven, nor fire more averse to water than are the interests of the middle to those of the productive classes."[38]

The *Guardian*'s views of poverty and the poor were a corollary of its views of property and class. At first sight, it may seem remarkable that a journal called *The Poor Man's Guardian* should have paid so little attention to the poor law at a time when most radicals, and a good many non-radicals, were passionately exercised about it. For two years, while the Royal Commission conducted its hearings, while its preliminary and then its final report were published and widely reviewed, while something like a pamphlet war raged and the *Political Register* and *The Times* made common cause against political economists and poor law reformers—during all this time the *Guardian* had almost nothing to say on the issue of the poor law.

The first important (but not leading) article on the poor law appeared in May 1834, when the bill was being debated in Parliament. The article did not attack the bill as a whole but only the bastardy clause, and on grounds similar to those given by *The Times*. By making the mother of an illegitimate child responsible for its support, the *Guardian* complained, the bill was reversing the natural order of things: "Women are the weaker vessels, and the laws ought to be made for their preservation."[39] On August 16, two days after the bill was officially signed into law (and after four months of extensive public debate), the *Guardian* repeated its objections, again to the bastardy clause alone. Not until October did it begin to express the kind of outrage against the New Poor Law that one might have expected—and it then did so in the middle of an article on the "Profit-Hunting System." Pronouncing the law "one of the most inhuman and widely-devastating acts of robbery ever heard of in the world," it agreed with one of its correspondents that it might more fittingly be called "The Poor Man's Destruction Bill." If that title recalls Cobbett's "Poor Man's Robbery Bill," the echoes of Cobbett can also be heard in the argument that the right of relief derived from the Reformation when it was given to the poor in exchange for "their share of the church property" and thus became their "vested interest."[40]

Only to this point, however, did the *Guardian* follow Cobbett. Beyond that its argument took a distinctive turn, the New Poor Law becoming yet another occasion for an attack on the capitalists. The landed aristocracy, it pointed out, had never proposed such a bill. Not until the creation of the "usurer's ten-pound Parliament" had the middle classes become bold enough to commit such infamous robbery. "Of this most sacred of all sacred properties have the poor been despoiled by the capitalists. 'The Poor Man's Destruction Bill' is purely and solely the work of the middle or profit-hunting classes." Disclaiming any intention of seeking to incite class conflict, to "excite the poor and the work-people against the middle classes," the *Guardian* protested that it wanted only to give each "equal liberty and protection against the other." Without the equal protection of the suffrage the workers would never be more than the serfs of the middle classes. If the latter, having the power to provide that equality, chose not to do so, they could hardly be surprised at the hatred—and worse, the *Guardian* intimated—of the working classes. "Injustice always begets revenge, and though revenge is a hateful passion, it is not those who feel it, but those who give just cause for it, that are to blame."[41] Shortly afterward, commenting on a wave of arson in the countryside, the *Guardian* reminded its readers of its prediction that arson would be one of the legacies of the law. Although it did not remind them of its repeated assertions that the capitalists, not the landlords, were the true enemies of the working classes, it did explain that the particular targets of the incendiaries were not necessarily the worst employers but the most vulnerable ones. Only toward the end of this article did it come out unambiguously for the repeal of the New Poor Law and a return to the Elizabethan law —"till other measures are adopted for their relief, which might thenceforward render all poor laws unnecessary."[42]

That last phrase was crucial, for it explains the curious reticence of the *Guardian* for so long, and the tone of its comments when it finally spoke out. If it was less exercised over the New Poor Law than either *The Times* or *Political Register*, it was because it thought less well of the old poor law —or, indeed, of any poor law. For Tories and radicals of the "old school," the Elizabethan poor law was a necessary part of the structure of society because the poor themselves were a necessary part of society; and the New Poor Law was both a betrayal of humanity and a break in the social contract that bound the poor to society. For the *Guardian,* the poor law itself was a symptom of the disease afflicting the poor, and the New Poor Law was only an aggravation of that symptom. The disease, as it never ceased reminding its readers, was "property," the "only one cause" of all social evils. What the New Poor Law demonstrated was how much worse things had become since the middle classes took power, for they, even more than the landed aristocracy, represented property in its most naked, brutal form.

The *Guardian* took no part in the agitation against the proposed reform before the actual passage of the act, in part because it was not averse to seeing the system exposed in its most brutal form—the familiar radical tactic of "worse is better"—and in part because it did not want to put itself in the position of sanctioning the old poor law and thus the old system of property and political inequality. After the enactment of the New Poor Law it was free to join the opposition, denouncing the new law as evidence of the ruthlessness of the propertied classes and of the misery of the poor, as "frightful, inhuman, unprecedented, detestable, and damnable."[43] It then called for a restoration of the old law, with the proviso that this would be an interim measure until such time as other steps would be taken to "render all poor laws unnecessary."

An anonymous correspondent to the *Guardian* (possibly O'Brien himself—it was not unknown for editors to use the letter columns as a vehicle for their own opinions) said boldly what the editorials only intimated: that Cobbett's defense of the old poor law was part of his idealization of the "old system," in which the bulk of the working classes were presumed to be content with bacon and beer while the rest enjoyed the "right of being kept in pauperism." The real issue was not the "advocacy of poor laws" but the advocacy of universal suffrage; indeed the franchise was required in order to "supersede poor laws and pauperism." The "intelligent part of the industrious classes," the writer felt assured, had already gone beyond Cobbett in the perception of their rights; only the "unreflecting portion of the nation" could be won over by an appeal to the old system of "indiscriminately relieving able-bodied paupers."[44]

For the *Guardian,* as for the writer of this letter, the poor law was a distraction because pauperism itself was not the essential problem—not the problem, at any rate, for the working classes, who were more interested in wages than in relief, and who might even resent the relief given "indiscriminately" to able-bodied paupers at their own expense. In one of its last issues, the *Guardian* repeated the familiar objection to the New Poor Law: the less-eligibility clause made the pauper's condition worse than that of the convicted criminal, reducing the pauper to something like starvation, since the independent laborer was already at the barest level of existence. But the crux of its argument was the plight of the independent laborer himself: by making relief worse than any alternative, the law compelled the laborer to take whatever wages were offered him and thus put him at the "utter mercy of the capitalist."[45] This was the heart of the issue. Where others were concerned primarily with the effect of the law on the pauper, the *Guardian* was more concerned with its effect upon the independent laborer. The problem was poverty rather than pauperism, and no poor law, new or old, could address that problem.

One might suppose that the *Guardian* was less than enthusiastic about the old poor law because it was less concerned with the agricultural laborers who were then more dependent upon poor relief. There is some truth in this. Although the *Guardian,* like all self-designated spokesmen for the poor, professed to be representing the largest constituency—"the working, productive, and useful but *poor* classes, who constitute a very great majority of the population of Great Britain"[46]—it took as the model of those "poor classes" the industrial worker, which is why its main enemy was the capitalist rather than the landlord.

It was a difficult assignment the *Guardian* took upon itself: to defend industrialism while attacking capitalism. This agenda sharply distinguished it from some of the competing forms of radicalism: from Cobbett's nostalgia for an agrarian society and domestic economy, from the incipient Luddism of some of the other unstamped papers (the *Poor Man's Advocate,* for example), even from the ambivalence toward industry displayed by that socialist manufacturer, Robert Owen.[47] (It is not sufficiently appreciated how suspicious Owen was of the industry to which he owed his wealth, how much he associated the competitive, acquisitive, hedonistic spirit with the industrial system, and how hostile he was to the division of labor, the source of "poverty, ignorance, waste . . . crime, misery, and great bodily and mental imbecility.")[48]

Only rarely did the *Guardian* lapse into the familiar rhetoric about the good old times before the "accursed Manufacturing System," when tradesmen required not capital but industry and skill, when goods were made to last and to serve the real needs of the people, when everyone (except the "naturally vicious") was well fed and happy, when seven-year-olds were not doomed to a "worse than Egyptian bondage." Even then it pointed out that the "accursed" system was not manufacturing as such but the laws and institutions that gave the benefits of machinery to idle employers rather than to the workers.[49] More often it went out of its way to defend manufacturing and machinery against those among its own readers who cherished illusions about a halcyon, preindustrial age. "Before steam power was known," it reminded them, "there was more general poverty in the world than there is now." Machinery and factories were not the causes of poverty but the means of alleviating it. Under a just system of property, where everyone received the full value of his labor, it would be to everyone's interest to make that labor as productive as possible by using more machinery, so that everyone would have a larger share of the increased produce. Machinery would then become the "greatest blessing ever vouchsafed to man," the means of delivering mankind from the primeval curse of work and transforming "grovelling beasts of burden into intelligent and happy beings."[50] And as with machinery, so with capital. If the increase of capital was now a curse rather than a blessing, it was only because it had been monopolized by the capitalist. "Capital is like muck or manure, there is no good in it unless it is spread; when properly diffused, it enriches and fertilizes; but if suffered to lie in idle heaps, it breeds nothing but stink and vermin."[51]

This bias in favor of industrialism makes it all the more interesting that the *Guardian* did not assume the leadership in those movements that were specially pertinent to the factory workers: the Ten Hours Bill and trade unionism. It did, to be sure, support these causes, but in the same spirit in which it supported the old poor law—belatedly and guardedly. Like the Marxists of a later generation, it looked upon them as "immediate demands," melioratory measures worthy in themselves but harmful if allowed to distract attention from the only issues that were, finally, decisive: a radical reform of the suffrage and a radical change in property rights.

The *Guardian* was as slow in entering the lists for factory legislation as it was in taking up the issue of the poor law. Well after Richard Oastler, Michael Sadler, John Fielden, and others had made the Ten Hours Bill a major public issue, after Short-Time Committees had been set up throughout the country, and after the *Poor Man's Advocate* had devoted itself almost entirely to this one subject, the *Guardian* finally came out in favor of the measure. Even then it used it as the occasion to point up the evils of a system of property that made child labor profitable, and of a Parliament impervious to those evils because it did not represent the classes most sorely affected by them. When Althorp's Act was finally passed in 1833, providing a twelve-hour limit for older children and eight hours for younger, the *Guardian* welcomed it as "half-a-loaf" which was better than none, and praised it as the achievement not of the Reformed Parliament but of the working classes —this in spite of the fact that it was passed by a Parliament that did not represent or include the working classes. Yet even on that memorable occasion the *Guardian* did not devote its leading article to the act; that was reserved for yet another sermon on "The Best Mode of Obtaining Universal Suffrage."[52] (There were, in fact, no leading articles on factory reform, most of the discussion appearing in the form of extracts from Sadler's Select Committee report, resolutions passed by the National Union of Working Classes, and letters to the editor.)

Trade unionism received more prominent treatment, although here too with qualifications. The important thing, the *Guardian* emphasized, was for the workers to secure the "largest possible share of their produce from the hands of the common plunderer."[53] For this purpose, they had to combine in whatever fashion they could, and trade unions and cooperative associations were among the means available to them—necessary but not sufficient means. The "Great Error of Trade Unions," as the title of one leading article put it, was in separating the issue of unionism from politics. Without a radical reform of the political system and a consequent radical change in the economic system, trade unionism was doomed to defeat. Combinations of workers would inevitably lead to counter-combinations of employers, and the latter, with all the resources of the state at their disposal, were bound to prevail. Unions might also make demands which, under the present system, the employers could accede to only by raising prices or laying off workers, which would make the situation worse than it was at present.[54]

The *Guardian* made this case so strenuously, and in terms so suspiciously reminiscent of political economy, that it had repeatedly to defend itself against the charge of being the "enemy of trade unions." But even as it assured its readers that it was a "zealous and staunch" advocate of unions, supporting, for example, a demonstration in Manchester demanding a full day's wages for an eight-hour day, it accompanied these assurances with its usual warnings against the futility of relying upon unions alone. To demand an increase of wages and a decrease of hours was a "two-fold attack on 'property,'" and that attack could succeed only if the workers had the political power that would give them control over the laws of the country and thus over property. What was needed was a united front against the common enemy. "Let the Universal-Suffrage men co-operate with the Trades, and the Trades' Unions with the Universal-Suffrage men. . . . The emancipation of Industry is our common aim; unity of action can alone accomplish it; let unity of action be therefore our motto."[55]

In the same spirit, the *Guardian* cautioned against the other "nostrums" favored by some radicals: Irish independence, the abolition of slavery, currency reforms, economy measures, emigration schemes, repeal of the corn laws, proposals to abolish the army, monarchy, or church. Some of these were innocuous, even salutary, but the best of them could not significantly affect the fundamental relations of "labour and capital." If the army were drastically reduced, the savings would only find their way into the "coffers of the capitalist and landowner." If the monarchy, church, and House of Lords were abolished, they would be replaced by even more oppressive institutions, like the "usurer's parliament." In any case all the talk about kings, aristocrats, priests, and armies was "humbug that ought to be discarded with our nursery tales."[56] Even taxes were less than a "mole-hill to Mont Blanc" compared with the burdens of rents and profits. If all taxes were repealed, the poor would be as poor as ever, and the rich (except for the "tax-eaters") as rich; in fact, the "pauperization" of the tax-eaters would only make the rest of the rich even richer. "Talk of tithes and taxes, indeed! Pshaw!—what signifies the parson's plundering, or the tax-eater's, compared with that of the remorseless capitalist?"[57]

Occasionally, especially in its early issues, the *Guardian* lapsed into the rhetoric of the Old Corruption, protesting that the "poor" were ground down by taxes to keep a "parcel of lazy, big-bellied sinecurists in idleness and luxury," or that workers were reduced to rags and potatoes while the "overflowing community of guzzlers and consumers," "retired profit-hunters, or the sons of profit-hunters," gorged themselves on the most sumptuous luxuries.[58] But even when it denounced the villains of the Old Corruption, it treated them as pseudo-villains, surrogates for the real culprits. "The priest, the soldier, the hangman, the banker, the lawyer, the exciseman—in short, all who live by the crimes and ignorance of society, are, under divers pretences, hired to prop it up"—by the landlords and capitalists who were the real beneficiaries of the system. And some of those lesser villains should not even be blamed for their actions. "The crime is in supporting the system, not in filling any particular function which the system renders necessary."[59]

Even the *Guardian*'s anti-Semitism had a different character from that of the *Register*. Not always, to be sure; sometimes it was the familiar, automatic kind that made of Joseph Hume a "jew-pedlar politician," or gave the Jews priority on the enemies list—"the Jews, and the parsons, and the statesmen, and the hangman, and the slave-drivers"—all of whom, in the "paradise of earth" to be ushered in by universal suffrage, would become honest men, "not from any love of honesty, but because they will have nobody to cheat."[60] When a Mr. Salomons was elected sheriff for Aldgate and was denied the position because he refused to take the required oath "on the faith of a Christian," the *Guardian* had little patience with the sentimental talk about his religious scruples. "Salomons will buy cheap and sell dear; he will lie, and cheat, and speculate all day: he will take advantage of the necessities of his fellow-creatures, and get their goods out of them at half their value: he will lend money at exorbitant interest, and exact his pound of flesh, like Shylock." But he did all this, the *Guardian* said (an admission Cobbett would never have made), "in the teeth of his own religion, which condemns such practices." And he did it not for religious but for economic reasons, for the same reasons that prompted all rich men, Jews and Christians alike, to rob, cheat, and plunder the poor.[61]

The Salomons episode is instructive because it suggests how even the most primitive prejudice was put to ideological use. Where Cobbett's venom was directed against the Jew *qua* Jew (the "Christ-killer"), the *Guardian* (like Marx) vilified the Jew *qua* capitalist. Its anti-Semitism was no less anti-Semitic for being anti-capitalist as well; in one sense it was even more so, since it gave anti-Semitism a new rationale and thus a new plausibility and legitimacy. It was also more virulent in denying any appeal to religious conscience or religious liberty which might serve as an antidote to persecution. The whole issue of religion, the *Guardian* argued, was spurious. Religion was nothing more than a "conspiracy" of the rich against the poor, part of the ceremonies and codes, manners and morals by which the rich "agreed to know one another," their "passport" to a society from which the poor were excluded. If the rich, Christian or Jew, really believed in their religion, they would not rob and oppress the poor. The fact that they behaved as they did meant that they believed in religion only as a "political engine to keep the useful classes in subjection to the rich." Those who prated about religious liberty or persecution were distracting attention from real grievances and fixing it upon imaginary or remote ones, exactly as those who shed tears for Negro slaves were deliberately belittling the plight of English laborers. Such people "will bawl about everything, or any thing, but the thing we want." The thing that was wanted was a change in property, which in turn required a change in the suffrage.

Property, property—this is the subject of subjects. You may always ascertain the true friend of his species by hearing what he has to say on property. . . . *Property, Universal Suffrage, a Free Press*—these are the questions to try a man's pluck. Any vagabond may cant on negro slavery; any rogue may shed tears for Poland; any imposter may declaim on 'religious' liberty. These are nothing now-a-days. We have got beyond them; we want something solid—we want self-protection —we want the privilege of governing ourselves—we want a voice in the laws, a share in those institutions by which our minds are formed, and by which the produce of our toil is distributed. We want no demagogues, or canters, or smooth-tongued hypocrites among us, to pester us about what does not concern us. Equal rights and equal laws for all—this is what we want. No man is the people's friend who does not labour for this paramount end.[62]

. . .

"Property, property—this is the subject of subjects." The *Guardian* had come a long way from the old "subject of subjects," poverty. In an early issue it had diagnosed the disease afflicting the poor as "abject poverty and slavish degradation," and the remedies as universal suffrage and the redistribution of property.[63] As it pursued that theme, poverty and degradation became the symptoms of the disease and the disease itself was revealed to be the unequal distribution of property. In this sense the "new ideology" was not only different from the old, it was more ideological, more removed from the existential nature of poverty itself.

For all his obsession with the Old Corruption and idealization of the old society, Cobbett communicated a vivid (if perhaps fanciful) image of the poor. If he personalized the agents of the Old Corruption, he also personalized their victims—the old men huddled in front of the workhouse, laborers enervated by a diet of tea and potatoes, women and children shut up in stifling factories, choking on cotton fuzz, half naked and more than half savage. His readers may have suspected him of romanticizing the conditions of the old poor, but they were likely to credit his harrowing accounts of the new poor. The *Guardian* had far fewer portraits of this sort, its occasional descriptions of handloom weavers or lace makers being rare interludes in its unremitting ideological campaign. In terms of that ideology, the actual state of the poor, the degree and quality of their poverty, the conditions in which they lived and worked, were basically irrelevant. The real grievance was injustice rather than inhumanity, the injustice that came from an inequitable system of property and an unequal suffrage. It was for this reason that the *Guardian* could not get passionately concerned with such melioratory measures as an increase of wages and decrease of hours, or with such mediating institutions as cooperatives and trade unions. The decisive fact, the subject of subjects, was "property, property." And that fact would yield only to a radical change in the suffrage.

As the rhetoric of poverty gave way to the rhetoric of property and political equality, the protagonists in the drama were recast. In place of the tax collectors, pensioners, and parasites of the Old Corruption, the new villains were the capitalists and middle classes. Against these class adversaries, "the poor" too acquired a class character, appearing increasingly in the guise of "working classes," "labouring classes," "industrious classes," even "poor classes." The implications of this "language of class" will be dealt later; at the moment it may be enough to point to the presence of this language and to suggest its role in the new ideology.

What was new about the "new ideology" was not the demand for universal suffrage; that had been the staple of radicalism for half a century. Nor was the scheme for the redistribution of property and nationalization of land; the followers of Thomas Spence were only the best known of the agrarian socialists calling for some kind of "agrarian law." The conjunction of the two was somewhat more novel. But the real novelty came from the simultaneous redefinition of poverty and the redefinition of the radical enterprise, the first making poverty a function of property and political equality, the second making radicalism a function of class and class struggle.

If this ideology was largely, even exclusively, a reflection of the ideas of the editor, Bronterre O'Brien, rather than of a movement or party, it became the editorial voice of the *Guardian* (and of the other papers edited by him) as surely as if it had the endorsement of a party. It was not a sophisticated, systematic, or entirely consistent ideology, but it was sufficiently coherent and sustained to communicate itself to readers, and its effect may even have been the greater because it was not sophisticated. (Hodgskin never commanded anything like the following of the *Guardian*.) It was also less parochial and sectarian than might have been expected. Whatever differences the *Guardian* had with other radicals, the paper remained on reasonably good terms with them, reporting on their meetings and activities, welcoming letters from them, in effect making of them unwitting accomplices. When the Owenites, for example, assembled a "Congress of Co-operative and Trades' Union Delegates," the *Guardian* projected upon that body its own revolutionary agenda: "Their report shows that an entire change in society—a change amounting to a complete subversion of the existing 'order of the world'—is contemplated by the working classes. They aspire to be at the top instead of at the bottom of society—or rather that there should be no bottom or top at all."[64] This was not, in fact, what the Owenite Congress was about; but it was what the *Guardian* chose to make of it.

It is tempting to see in this ideology and rhetoric something like a premature or incipient Marxism. But this is to distort the distinctive quality both of Marxism and of the *Guardian*.[65] The "working classes" on whose

behalf the *Guardian* spoke were not Marx's "proletariat" or "working class";
nor were its "middle classes" Marx's "bourgeoisie." Nor was its emphasis
upon universal suffrage consistent with the Marxist schema in which the
suffrage was part of the "epiphenomena" of politics, merely the "first step
in the revolution," as the *Communist Manifesto* said. To an ear attuned to
Marxism, numerous passages in the *Guardian* strike a sensitive note—its
definition of government, for example.

> Fools imagine that it is the government that makes itself what it is,
> when the real fact is that the government is only the creature of the
> usurious classes to protect them in their exorbitant profits, rents, and
> impositions on the labouring classes. . . . Government is but a tool in
> their hands to execute their nefarious purposes.[66]

In fact, the idea of government as the "tool" or "creature" of the ruling
classes was a commonplace in radical thought, long predating both Marx
and the *Guardian*. And so too was the labor theory of value, which reflected
a long and honorable tradition going back at least to Locke, and which, by
the early nineteenth century, was a staple of political economy as well as
radicalism.[67]

The more impressed one is with the boldness of the new ideology, the
more important it is to be wary of exaggerating its practical effects, to be
mindful of the fact that the new never succeeded in displacing the old or
becoming the dominant radical ideology, still less the dominant working
class ideology. The circulation of the four papers representing the new
ideology has been estimated at 25,000, but the old ideology appeared in a
larger number of papers with a much larger circulation.[68] The sales of the
Guardian, the largest of the radical unstamped papers, were 16,000 at its
peak, while those of the twopenny *Register* had been more than twice that.
There was, moreover, enough overlap between the new and the old to blur
the picture. The *Register,* like the *Guardian,* vigorously supported universal
suffrage; and the *Guardian* had enough vestiges and rhetoric of the Old
Corruption to make it congenial to the readers of the *Register.* The other
papers confounded the confusion by pursuing their favorite causes: the poor
law, taxes, currency reform, factory legislation, trade unionism, religion (or
antireligion), temperance, education, self-help. At one point or another most
of these issues crisscrossed, the leaders of one appearing in the forefront of
another, with much duplication among the rank and file. (The Short Time
Committees agitating for the Ten Hours Bill became the vehicle for the
anti–poor law movement in the north, and both then merged with Chartism.) While all these causes added up to something like a general working
class radical movement, they did not add up to a coherent ideology, new
or old.

If in this larger perspective the *Guardian* seems diminished in importance, it also assumes a greater significance. For it demonstrates that there was available in the early 1830s the kind of self-conscious, class-conscious, potentially revolutionary ideology that E. P. Thompson has described (but which he attributed to an earlier period). It also demonstrates that, in spite of the availability of such an ideology, it did not prevail, either then or later. It did not capture the unstamped press, although the illegal status of the press made conditions ripe for a revolutionary ideology. Nor did it capture the Chartist movement later in the decade. In this sense "old" and "new," if they are presumed to connote past and future, are misleading. For the old continued to exist, and not vestigially or peripherally among an older generation, but at the very heart of radicalism well into the forties and beyond.

So too the older idea of poverty persisted, not only among Tories and radicals of the old school but among the Chartists. Even as the condition-of-England question became more acute and social antagonisms sharpened, the conflict continued to be waged under the banners of "rich and poor" rather than "Capital and Labour." And even as the "language of class" became more familiar, the older language of "poverty and poor" continued to prevail and to dominate social discourse.

XI

CHARTISM:

THE POLITICIZATION

OF THE POOR

Chartism, the climax of a decade of radicalism, was in one sense anticlimactic. It was a reprise of all the issues that had been exercising radicals throughout the 1830s: the suffrage, the poor law, factory laws, trade unionism, Owenism, Methodism, education, temperance. It even inherited the leaders of the earlier radical movements, the unstamped press alone bequeathing to it Henry Hetherington, Bronterre O'Brien, John Cleave, James Watson, William Carpenter, Richard Lee, James Lorymer, Joshua Hobson, Robert Hartwell. Even such newer recruits as George Julian Harney and Robert Lowery had served their radical apprenticeship as shop-boys or street-sellers for the unstamped papers. William Lovett, the principal author of the Charter and one of the founders of the London Working Men's Association which sponsored it, had been involved earlier in Owenite organizations and in the National Union of the Working Classes (whose activities were regularly reported in *The Poor Man's Guardian* in the early thirties). Others made their way to Chartism from the Short Time Committees agitating for the Ten Hours Bill, the anti–poor law campaign which had revived with the introduction of the New Poor Law into the industrial towns of the north, trade unions which were feeling the brunt of the industrial depression, Mechanics' Institutions, Methodist chapels, and temperance groups.

What was new about Chartism was its sheer magnitude. Originally an amalgam of two separate organizations, the London Working Men's Association and the Birmingham Political Union, it soon became a loose association of similar groups throughout the country. Their rallying point was

"The People's Charter" drafted by the London Working Men's Association in May 1838. The contents of the Charter were hardly new. The "Six Points" had been the agenda of "radical reformers" for half a century: universal manhood suffrage, annual elections, secret ballot, equal electoral districts, no property qualification for members of the House of Commons, and payment for members.* But never before had a manifesto of this sort acquired such symbolic import or generated such widespread interest and activity among the working classes. Meetings were held throughout the country to endorse the Charter and to elect delegates to a national convention that would submit it in the form of a petition to Parliament. The convention met in February 1839; the national petition was presented to the House of Commons in July and was rejected by a large majority; the convention dissolved in September. The history of Chartism, however, as Carlyle predicted, continued. The Newport "uprising" in November (the "Welsh rebellion," it was sometimes called) was followed by sporadic demonstrations, riots, and threats and fears of riots; within several months as many as five hundred Chartists were arrested or deported. A second petition was presented to Parliament in 1842 and was again rejected. After a period of relative quiet and decline, punctuated by disputes over land nationalization and redistribution schemes, the bad winter of 1847–48 precipitated another spurt of activity, another convention, demonstration, petition, and rejection—and the virtual end of Chartism.

In an obvious sense the "Age of the Chartists," as it has been called, is a misnomer. The Chartists hardly dominated the decade between the drafting of the charter and the rejection of the last petition, still less the larger period (1832 to 1854) to which their name has lent itself.[2] But if some historians have inflated their influence, so did many contemporaries, and not only the Chartists themselves. To some people, like Carlyle and Disraeli, Chartism symbolized the "social problem": the "condition and disposition" of the working classes, the gulf between the "two nations." To others it signified nothing less than a revolutionary challenge to the entire social order. The very fact that it was so large and amorphous, bringing together within a single "movement" so many groups and factions, causes and grievances, meant that every event, every speech, demonstration, or meeting, was magnified, as if part of an organized, countrywide conspiracy. The Charter itself read like a declaration of rights that was tantamount to a declaration of revolution. The convention assumed the guise of a Parliament

---

*There were variants of the Charter that had only five points. O'Brien left an account of a meeting in February 1837 which omitted the provision for payment for the Members of Parliament. The petition of 1839 left out equal electoral districts (because, it is presumed, the Birmingham Chartists did not look kindly upon the possibility of doubling the representation of the Irish), and the 1842 petition restored it. Although Chartism was generally symbolized by the "Six Points," Carlyle and others often spoke of the "Five Points."[1]

(some of the members of the convention took to appending the initials "M.C." after their names, on the model of "M.P.," Member of Parliament). The 1,250,000 signers of the petition of 1839, and more than double that number of the 1842 petition, looked to many like a horde of potential revolutionaries. And the movement appeared to have at its command a national network of associations and underground cells, a well-developed propaganda machine consisting of a host of newspapers, a trained corps of speakers, a professional cadre of leaders, a hard core of activists, and a large body of supporters who could be called into action at moments of crisis. The impression was of a vast organization, dedicated to a specific program, and prepared to take "ulterior measures" (the Chartist euphemism for violence) if that program was not met.

This, at any rate, was how Chartism looked from the outside. And this perception of it was an important part of the reality. The other part of the reality was a highly disorganized, differentiated, factionalized movement consisting of groups so diverse in character—geographically, occupationally, socially, ideologically—that it might better be described as a conglomerate or confederation, a "popular front" held together by the most tenuous connections. Even before the publication of the Charter, a militant group under the leadership of George Julian Harney seceded from the London Working Men's Association and formed the rival East London Democratic Association.[3] The union between the London Working Men's Association and the largely middle class Birmingham Political Union was short-lived; although Thomas Attwood, the leader of the Birmingham group, dutifully presented the petition to Parliament, he and his followers had withdrawn from the convention months before. The convention itself was riven with dissension and factionalism. And the Chartist press was almost as diverse as the unstamped press earlier in the decade.

The most publicized dispute was between the advocates of "Physical Force" and those of "Moral Force," the dominance of the former symbolized by the removal of the convention to Birmingham. Recalling the distinction between the "old" and "new" radicals, one might suppose that this corresponded to the distinction between the Physical Force and Moral Force factions. In fact there was no such correlation. Hetherington and O'Brien, who were in ideological agreement on the need for radical economic as well as political reform, were on opposite sides of the great divide on the subject of force (at least in the early period of Chartism—later O'Brien abandoned the idea of violence); while the Physical Force faction included the Tory Radicals Richard Oastler and Joseph Rayner Stephens, who made strange ideological bedfellows with such "new" radicals as Bronterre O'Brien and Feargus O'Connor.

Even in respect of tactics, there were large differences within the Physical Force faction. For some, force was a threat to be used against the government, much as the threat of force had been manipulated by the reformers of 1832 to secure the passage of the Reform Act; the rhetoric of violence, they hoped, would do what the rhetoric of justice had not succeeded in doing. For others, force served an important function within the movement itself, the brandishing of pikes and torches uniting and inspiring the ranks, keeping up morale when petitions failed. Still others took the rhetoric of violence literally, believing that the time had come to use physical force against the enemies of reform. There were speeches urging the people to arm themselves and reports of training sessions in the use of arms; there were instructions for the making of bombs out of ginger beer bottles (an early version of the Molotov cocktail) and for techniques of street fighting. A former radical, alarmed by the possibility of a revolution fought out on the streets of London and Birmingham, wrote a series of pamphlets under the title, "Dissuasive Warnings to the People on Street Warfare," which may have had the effect of publicizing the idea of street warfare as much as warning against it.[4]

In hindsight the fears of violence and revolution seem grossly exaggerated. The only episode that could qualify as an "uprising" was the Newport affair in November 1839 when a few thousand Welsh colliers were dispersed by thirty soldiers stationed in the local hotel. But this "rebellion," led by John Frost, a prosperous, respectable draper known as a moderate Chartist, started with the relatively innocent intention of protesting the arrest of the popular Chartist leader Henry Vincent. The much celebrated "Rebecca riots" in the summer of 1839, as well as those in the winter of 1842–43, involved little more than the destruction of some tollgates at the turnpikes—and never on Sunday, the "Daughters of Rebecca" being Sabbath observers. The last demonstration in April 1848, the "fiasco of Kennington Common," as the press referred to it, was dissipated as much by the rain as by the request of the police, promptly acceded to by O'Connor, that the marchers give up their plan to carry the petition from South London to Westminster; Punch dubbed it the Chartist "rain of terror."[5]

Yet in the beginning even sympathetic observers, and still more, of course, hostile ones, thought that Chartism might well unleash a genuine "reign of terror," or at the very least provoke the kind of violence (as Dickens intimated in Barnaby Rudge) reminiscent of the Gordon riots of 1780—anti-Catholic in that case, anti-property in this. At the close of 1839, reflecting upon the tumultuous events of that year, the Annual Register ascribed to the Chartists the aim of seeking a "violent alteration in the form of the government," not simply for the purpose of acquiring more power and privileges for the lower classes but in order to bring about "some hitherto unexperienced state of society."[6] For years thereafter, the word

"Chartism" evoked for many people an image of disaffected, seething masses organized and manipulated by unscrupulous demagogues seeking to overthrow the established political order.

The conflict over physical and moral force was only one source of tension within the movement. There were also conflicts between Christian Chartists and rationalist or atheist (often Owenite) Chartists, between temperance and anti-temperance Chartists, between education reformers and land reformers, between land nationalizers and land redistributors, between corn law repealers and those who regarded the corn laws as a distraction from the real issue, between parliamentary reformers and "knife and fork," "bread and cheese" radicals. Over and above all of these were the differing interests and traditions of miners and weavers, factory workers and agricultural laborers, Londoners and north countrymen, Welshmen and Scotsmen, and all the other highly differentiated regions, trades, classes, and, not least, personalities that went into this curiously anomalous, heterogeneous "movement" known as Chartism.

Richard Oastler was one of the most prominent and perhaps the most anomalous of Chartists. Generally identified with the most militant faction, he opposed every point of the Charter—and not, like the other Tory Radical Chartist, J. R. Stephens, because he thought political reform irrelevant, but because he thought political democracy undesirable and dangerous. When he made his rousing speeches calling on the masses to arm themselves, he did so in the name of "the Altar, the Throne, and the Cottage." While he was as aggressively anti-capitalist as O'Brien, he was so in the spirit of Cobbett, denouncing the middle classes as the "money-and-steam interest," "slaughter-house men," " 'Money Dealers' who hover about trade like locusts."[7] One can sympathize with the historian G. D. H. Cole, who first denied Oastler the title of Chartist and then proceeded to include him among the dozen leading figures in his *Chartist Portraits.*[8]

The greatest anomaly of Chartism was also its greatest strength: the fact that it could embrace such disparate interests, ideologies, and personalities, and still constitute a distinctive movement. Asa Briggs, who has done more than any other historian to focus attention on the diversity of groups, regions, interests, and ideas subsumed under the name of Chartism, has also testified to the importance of that diversity in giving the movement its character and its influence.

> The more eclectic Chartism had been, the more it retained its vigour as a mass movement. The more it had drawn on material discontents and local grievances as well as on ideological inspirations, the more it prospered. The more it had attracted those people who looked back to

the past as well as those who looked forward to the future, the more
it spread.[9]

Perhaps the single most important factor which brought unity out of
diversity, and which helped sustain the movement during the quiescent
periods when there were no dramatic events to mobilize its members, was
the *Northern Star.* Although privately owned by Feargus O'Connor, it was
generally recognized as the national organ of the Chartists, and although
O'Connor himself was identified with the Physical Force wing, for commercial as well as organizational reasons he was thoroughly latitudinarian
in his editorial policies. The *Northern Star* helped integrate the movement
precisely because it did not try to integrate it ideologically. All the themes
of the Old Corruption were there—taxes, war, paper money, monopoly,
lords, pensioners, bankers, priests—interlarded with the no longer "new"
ideology of property and equality. The paper provided a forum for the
debate over force and all the other issues which agitated different groups at
different times in different places: the poor law and corn law, factory
legislation and trade unionism, religion and rationalism, education and
teetotalism.

Because it was so hospitable to so many different ideas and interests,
the *Northern Star* enjoyed a loyalty that made it more a social institution
than a newspaper, part of the "larger Chartist cultural experience," as one
historian put it.[10] Chartist meetings often opened with a reading of the
leading article and a vote of confidence and expressions of thanks; anniver-
sary dinners celebrated the founding of the paper and toasts were drunk to
it; banners praising it were displayed at mass rallies and reprints of its
"Portrait Gallery of People's Friends" were hung in homes and clubrooms.
At its peak it reportedly sold 50,000 or 60,000 copies, not a mean achievement at fourpence-halfpenny.[11] Because it was so expensive, it was widely
read in working men's clubs, coffeehouses, public houses, and Mechanics'
Institutions. When Disraeli, in *Sybil,* wanted to portray a group of politically alert workers, he had them boasting of their local institution's three
subscriptions to the *Northern Star* and two to the Owenite *New Moral World.*

That Chartism was as much a "cultural experience" as a political
movement is evident from the other activities that gave it its distinctive
character: lectures, sermons, classes, plays, poetry readings, concerts, dances,
celebrations commemorating the birth of its heroes (Paine, Cartwright,
Cobbett, Hampden), and meeting halls decorated with their portraits. All
of these provided a sense of "fellowship," as Asa Briggs has described it, for
large numbers of Chartists who were not political activists but who had a
more sustained commitment than the signing of a petition or participation
in a rally.[12] One militant Chartist, raising money for O'Brien when he was
in jail, found himself at a benefit party near Brighton. "I observed several

hundreds of Chartists enjoying themselves with all kinds of games, and the various groups of cricket players, dancers, etc., formed a picturesque sight on the green grass. After tea the drums and fiddles beat and played for the gathering." When he interrupted this pastoral scene to make his usual speech, his audience fidgeted and looked uncomfortable. Only later that day, when he met with the "unadulterated democrats—the real grain and no chaff," did he find the kind of "energy, enthusiasm and principle" he was accustomed to.[13] There were those, however, who recognized the connection between the innocent fun and games on the village green and the political demonstrations and torchlight parades that took place on that same green on other occasions.

This cultural or social aspect of Chartism is so reminiscent of Methodism that it comes as no surprise to find that Chartist meetings were often held in Methodist chapels, that many Chartist hymns were adaptations of Methodist hymns, and that the organization of the National Charter Association was modeled on Methodist "classes."* It was also well known that some of the most prominent Chartists had been (in some cases continued to be) active Methodists: Lovett, Oastler, Stephens, Thomas Cooper, John Skevington, Joseph Capper, George Russell. Although Chartism also embraced a vocal antireligious, even atheistic, element, the Methodist influence was more pervasive and influential. If, as has been claimed, the larger Methodist sects had become increasingly quiescent and conservative, it may be significant that Chartism emerged at just this time to give expression to a radical temper that could not find satisfaction in religion. On the other hand, the existence of some smaller radical Methodist groups, and the fact that they sometimes flourished in the same places at the same time as Chartism, suggests that the two reinforced each other.[15] In either case, whether Chartism served to compensate for a conservative religion or to complement a radical one, the more interesting point is the way each transcended its ostensible purpose. Just as Methodism fostered a sense of fraternity that had only a peripheral relationship to its theology, so Chartism provided a sense of fellowship that went well beyond its official program.

The sense of fellowship evident in the mundane activities of the local groups was also reflected in a class consciousness that transcended regional, occupational, and ideological differences. The common bond that united Chartists was the recognition of a common cause, a cause defined not ideologically, not programmatically, not even organizationally, but in terms of its constituency—the "people" or "working classes."

*The National Union of the Working Classes, founded in 1831, also consisted of "classes" of thirty or forty members meeting weekly under the direction of "class leaders." Lovett explained that it had been "organized somewhat on the plan of the Methodist Connexion."[14]

The creation of such a constituency was deliberate. From the beginning the London Working Men's Association, the parent body of Chartism, defined itself as a working class organization. While it was not averse to joining with other groups—the largely middle class Birmingham Political Union, for example—to promote the Charter, its primary objective, as the first clause of its founding document stated, was "to draw into one bond of *unity* the *intelligent* and *influential* portion of the working classes in town and country."[16] According to Francis Place, the idea for an exclusively working class organization originated with a Dr. J. R. Black who persuaded Place that nothing could be done for the working classes "till they did something for themselves."[17] Lovett had long since come to that conviction on his own. It had prompted him to join the National Union of the Working Classes five years earlier, and it inspired him to help found the London Working Men's Association. The working classes, he explained in his autobiography, had too often been "swayed to and fro in opinion and action by the *idol* of their choice" and were left divided and bereft when that idol was destroyed. Instead of placing their faith in "great men," they were better advised to rely on "great principles" and to propagate those principles on their own behalf. While the cooperation of other classes was welcome, they had learned that the division of interests among those classes was too often destructive of that "union of sentiment" required for any great project. For that reason the association was determined to "confine their members as far as practicable to the working classes."[18]

Having agreed to restrict membership to the working classes, the association confronted the problem of deciding who the working classes were and "where the line should be drawn which separates the working classes from the other portions of society."[19] Lovett proposed to resolve that problem by leaving it to the members themselves to make that decision. The difficulty of drawing such a line is suggested by Place's account of the founding meeting of the association held at the Crown and Anchor Tavern in the Strand on a Tuesday evening, February 28, 1836.* The chairman was Robert Hartwell, a journeyman printer, and the speakers included two other printers (Vincent and Hetherington), a cabinetmaker (Lovett), a shoemaker, a carpenter, a pamphlet seller, a tailor, and two unspecified "working men." "Besides these," he added, "there were two speakers who were not of the working class—namely Feargus O'Connor and John Bell both of whom were considered intruders."[21]

In the Chartist movement there were many such "intruders," men who were not of the working classes or who were in that gray area where

---

*In his memoir Lovett made a great point of the decision to acquire a regular meeting place so that they would not have to assemble in a tavern. "No healthful tone of political morality could be formed . . . so long as our fellow-workmen continued to croak over their grievances with maudlin brains, and to form and strengthen their appetites for drink amid the fumes of the tap-room."[20]

class identity was by no means clear. O'Connor, formerly a Member of Parliament, proudly (and falsely) claimed descent from the "ancient kings of Ireland"; O'Brien, the son of an Irish merchant and manufacturer, was a university graduate who had trained for the law; Oastler had been a merchant and then a steward on a large estate; Joseph Sturge came from a comfortable farming family; John Frost was a prosperous draper; Hetherington was the publisher and owner of several successful papers; and Place, the "radical tailor of Charing Cross," had been the owner of a thriving establishment employing, at one point, as many as thirty workers. Yet in spite of these and a host of other such cases in both the leadership and the rank and file of the movement (which included a large contingent of schoolmasters, doctors, and other professionals), Chartism conceived of itself as a working class movement and was accepted as such by most contemporaries.

It was this image of itself as a working class movement that accounts for the great paradox of Chartism: the fact that in an important sense it succeeded even as it patently failed. In spite of the rejection of the petitions and the inability to realize a single one of the Six Points, in spite of the dissipation of the movement and the dispersal of its leaders, it achieved what may have been its most important goal. It generated a self-consciousness among a large part of the working classes, a sense of a common cause which went beyond specific grievances, demands, or interests, and which sustained itself even after the failure of the program and the disappearance of the movement.

In the conventional reading of Chartism, its failure signified a lack of militancy, a predilection for moral causes and values, a willingness to cooperate with the middle classes and to join forces with liberalism. That view, Brian Harrison and Patricia Hollis have shown, derives from the perspective of labor or socialist history rather than from the contemporary reality. In the career of Robert Lowery, they find the example of a Chartist who was militant in the 1830s, moderate in the '40s, and liberal in the '50s, while remaining faithful to his basic principles. Even in his most militant phase he exhibited all the religious, moral, and liberal concerns which were later to come to the forefront, so that his subsequent career, so far from being a betrayal of his earlier ideas, can be understood as a fulfillment of them. If during the '40s he, like many other Chartists (including O'Brien), came to see the interests of the working classes and of the middle classes as convergent, or at least reconcilable, this may well have been not a "wrong turning," as some historians think, but a right one, a realistic assessment of the situation confronting them, and a more practical policy than the alternative of intransigent class struggle. From this point of view, the evolution of Chartism into a radicalized liberalism was as consistent with Chartism itself as was any of the variants existing at the time—"Teetotal Chartism," "Christian Chartism," or "Knowledge Chartism."[22]

This "revisionist interpretation" may be carried further, suggesting that the significance of Chartism lay not so much in its ideology as in the promotion of a class consciousness that transcended ideology, that did not necessarily imply a commitment to class conflict, still less to revolution, but found its deeper meaning in a "cultural experience," a sense of fellowship among Chartists most immediately and, beyond that, among the working classes as a whole. If the Chartists did not speak with one voice on any particular issue, principle, or policy, they did speak, or claim to speak, on behalf of all of the unrepresented. In this sense Chartism subordinated ideology to constituency. The Chartist could be a "new" ideologue or an old, a socialist or a Tory, a Physical Force or Moral Force man, an advocate of class cooperation or class struggle. But whatever his ideology or strategy, his allegiance and commitment were unquestioned, not so much to the movement as to the working classes. This was the common denominator that united militants and moderates, parliamentary reformers and bread-and-cheese radicals, teetotalers and educators, land nationalizers and redistributors. The Chartists never pretended, as did the Tory, Whig, and Radical members of Parliament, to represent the nation as a whole; on the contrary, they boasted of representing only the unrepresented part of the nation. But neither were they a class party defined, as the later socialist parties were, primarily by an ideology; in this respect Chartism was distinctively a movement rather than an organized party.

Because Chartism was a movement rather than a party the question of the size of the membership is less important than might be thought (fortunately so, since reliable numbers are not available). A Chartist activist, recalling the events of 1848, complained that even after the revolutions on the Continent had shamed the English working classes to that last abortive effort, there were only three or four hundred who regularly paid the weekly dues of a penny. "I cannot count the thousands, or say millions, who made noises at monster meetings. Indeed they were never counted. Why should they have been? They were no part of our party."[23] Even a party requires its sympathizers ("fellow-travelers," as they later became known), and a movement like Chartism was still more dependent upon that large, amorphous, peripheral body of followers. "They gave it," Asa Briggs has said, "its colour, its force, its power of threat to the established order."[24] The whole of the movement, even in its most extended sense, probably did not comprise even a majority of the working classes, possibly not even a majority of that *"intelligent* and *influential* portion of the working classes" whom Lovett had hoped to attract.* Yet it gave the illusion of a mass movement representing the working classes. And that was formidable enough.

If Chartism succeeded in "raising the consciousness," as we now say, of the working classes, it did the same as well for the middle classes. It stimulated both their specifically "middle class consciousness"—their greater awareness of their own interests in opposition to those of the working classes —and at the same time their consciousness of the legitimate interests of the working classes.[26] This "social consciousness," or "social conscience," gave the decade of the forties its distinctive character. It was then that the middle and upper classes in and outside of Parliament (the "Reformed Parliament" as it was generally called, the "Unreformed Parliament," as the Chartists knew it), publicized the condition-of-England question, wrote essays, tracts, parliamentary reports, and novels dramatizing that condition, and passed the Ten Hours Act and other social legislation that helped mitigate it. Chartism may have been a failed revolution, judged by the Charter itself. But it was eminently successful in bringing the working classes to the center of the stage. If they did not become the principal actors in history, the makers of their own history, as the Chartists would have liked, they did emerge as prominent subjects in the drama of history.

To some historians the purely political nature of the Charter, the Six Points devoted entirely to parliamentary representation, was the strangest of all the anomalies of Chartism. One historian has commented on the "paradox" of a working class movement totally unable to agree on any program of economic and social change but managing to produce an utterly precise program of political reform.[27] Others have suggested that this political program was retrograde, harking back to the individualistic, natural rights, pre-industrial tradition of Price and Cartwright. The founders of the London Working Men's Association were described by G. D. H. Cole as skilled, well paid craftsmen with "bellies full enough and minds well-stored enough" to await patiently the fulfillment of their political gospel, in contrast to the handloom weavers, factory workers, miners, and unemployed laborers who could not afford that luxury and who had more urgent material needs. It was the Londoners, Cole said, who wanted the Charter; the main body of the Chartists wanted bread. The latter prevailed, and the movement that started as a political gospel turned into a "vast revolt of the hungry and the intolerably oppressed."[28]

---

*At its height the membership of the London Working Men's Association was all of 279. But this does not include the other associations formed throughout England by "missionaries" of the London group.[25]

This view of Chartism seems to be borne out by the famous speech by J. R. Stephens.

> Chartism is no political movement, where the main question is getting the ballot. . . . This question of universal suffrage is a knife and fork question, after all, . . . a bread and cheese question, notwithstanding all that has been said against it; and if any man asks me what I mean by universal suffrage, I would answer: that every working man in the land has the right to have a good coat to his back, a comfortable abode in which to shelter himself and his family, a good dinner upon his table, and no more work than is necessary for keeping him in good health and as much wages for that work as would keep him in plenty and afford him the enjoyment of all the blessings of life which a reasonable man could desire.[29]

This may be the most frequently cited quotation in the whole of Chartist literature. But it hardly proves what it is taken to prove: that Chartism was primarily a bread and cheese, knife and fork movement rather than a political movement centered upon the suffrage. For the purpose of that speech was to dispute the prevalent view of Chartism, which was precisely the political view. Like Oastler, Stephens was a Tory Radical who made common cause with the Chartists on some issues (the poor law and factory bill) but notably not on the suffrage. When he was arrested in August 1839, less than a year after he delivered that speech, he disavowed Chartism, chiefly because he disagreed with it on the subject of universal suffrage.

If Chartism had been essentially a bread and cheese question, it could have found a more suitable sponsor than the London Working Men's Association and a more appropriate founding document than the People's Charter. Other organizations would have been happy to supply an alternative manifesto: the East London Democratic Association founded by G. J. Harney, the Central National Association organized by O'Brien and O'Connor, or one of the other associations that sprang up throughout the country. In fact it was the Charter that brought into being the first truly national, radical, working class movement, that continued to be the rallying point for the movement, supplied the program for each of the petitions presented to Parliament, and integrated the movement in spite of all the centrifugal forces threatening to tear it apart. Cole quoted the Chartist addressing a meeting in Leicester in 1840: " 'Cheap Bread!' they cry. But they mean 'Low Wages!' Do not listen to their cant and humbug. Stick to your Charter! You are veritable slaves without your votes."[30] That Chartist was arguing against the Anti-Corn Law League, not so much because he was against the repeal of the corn laws—he may even have been for their repeal —but because he did not believe that issue to be fundamental. Nor were the other issues raised by this or that group of Chartists. The one overriding principle for the movement as a whole, the one idea that defined it and united it, was political equality—not social democracy but political democracy.

So far from being regressive, the Charter represented Chartism at its most progressive, its most radical. It is true that Paine, Cartwright, Cobbett, Hunt, Bentham, and scores of others had been there before—but in a historical and ideological context so different as to give the suffrage a quite different meaning. It was precisely now, in the context of a frankly class-oriented politics, that the suffrage acquired a new significance. Where before it had been an expression of Enlightenment universalism, or populist agrarianism, or individualistic utilitarianism, it was now the reflection of a thoroughly class-conscious radicalism. The language sometimes sounded universalistic, as in the statement of the Crown and Anchor meeting which based the suffrage on a "universal," "sacred" right.[31] But it was the working classes who claimed that right for themselves at a time when the middle classes had already obtained it.

Of all the issues exercising the Chartists, the suffrage was if not *primum mobile,* at least *primus inter pares.* The disfranchisement of the poor was doubly resented, the ignominy of exclusion from the polity compounding the ignominy of poverty. And the one condition was believed to exacerbate the other. Even O'Brien, committed to a radical program of economic change and the use of violence if necessary, insisted that the poor were poor because they did not have the vote: "Your poverty is the *result,* not the *cause* of your being unrepresented."[32] The "only difference," it was often said, between the English freeman and a Russian serf or American slave was the vote.[33] Again and again the same figures were cited: of 6,000,000 adult men only 840,000, one-seventh, had the franchise.

For most Chartists, as for most Englishmen, it was axiomatic that universal suffrage was manhood suffrage. When O'Brien complained that only one-seventh of the "population" had the vote, he meant by "population" the adult male population.[34] Some Chartists, however, and not the most militant of them, took so exalted a view of the suffrage that they wanted to make it genuinely universal by extending it to women as well. Lovett, a Moral Force man and a great believer in education and self-improvement, included female suffrage in the original draft of the Charter and was persuaded to remove it only when the rest of the committee insisted it would be unacceptable even to the working classes. He always regretted that decision, and in 1840 he restored female suffrage in the plank of the National Association for the Improvement of the People, overruling other members who warned that it would put the organization "out of the pale of practical politics."[35] The suffrage, he argued, was necessary to protect women against tyrannical husbands and oppressive laws, and for women as much as for men, it was a "natural right," a "civil right," a "political right."[36]

With the conspicuous exception of the occasional Tory Radical like Oastler or Stephens—and they were very much the exception—the suffrage was the primary principle of Chartism and the single cohesive principle, unifying both the movement itself and those the movement professed to represent. Unlike the other issues that appealed to particular groups—the poor law or factory bill, temperance or education—the suffrage appealed to the whole of the Chartist constituency: the "working classes," the "people," the "poor." John Stuart Mill saw this as the essence of the movement. Chartism, he said, represented "the whole effective political strength of the working classes: classes deeply and increasingly discontented, and whose discontent now speaks out in a voice which will not be unheard; all whose movements are now made with an organization and concert of which those classes were never, at any former period, capable." There were as many different opinions and objectives among the Chartists as among the moderate radicals of his own party, but their strength lay in leaving aside these disputed questions and concentrating upon the one issue that bound together all the "disqualified classes," the one issue that made them all "natural Radicals."[37] Mill himself would have preferred to enfranchise only the best educated of them, but that was because he was, after all, a moderate radical rather than a Chartist. The distinctive radicalism of Chartism consisted in not making those distinctions, in insisting upon the enfranchisement of all the disfranchised. The suffrage was not only a means to another end, the answer to the knife and fork question; it was also an end in itself, a claim to political equality as an assertion of human equality.

The political gospel of Chartism had momentous, if unwitting, implications for the idea of poverty, precisely because it did not make poverty the center of attention. If disfranchisement was the common bond uniting the "disqualified classes," the one circumstance that made of them all "natural Radicals," it meant that degrees of poverty were essentially irrelevant. It was not poverty as such, not even extreme poverty, not even pauperism, that defined a particular person or class; the crucial fact was the political disability shared by the vast majority of the population. Lovett thought of his own constituency, the "intelligent and influential portions of the working classes," as the vanguard of those "natural Radicals." But in claiming the franchise for everyone, for the least intelligent and influential as well as the most, for the poorest laborer and pauper (even for the poorest woman), he "qualified," so to speak, the most disqualified. The objective was to enfranchise all the disfranchised, and in this Chartism failed. The more immediate effect, however, was to unite all the disfranchised under the same banner, to elevate the poorest to the status of the least poor, to give them all the same definition—a political and civic rather than an economic and social definition.

The truly radical, even revolutionary nature of this achievement can best be appreciated by recalling something of the historical background. Forty years earlier Malthus had observed that the law of population had gone unnoticed so long because the "histories of mankind" had been exclusively the histories of the upper classes rather than of the lower classes where the pressures of food and population had taken their worst toll.[38] Malthus's *Essay* provided that missing history, a natural history, as it were, of the poor. In that Malthusian version, the poor were not only pauperized; they were also "naturalized," portrayed as creatures of nature subject to the most primitive biological passions (hunger and sex) and to the vicissitudes of the natural order (famine and death). The next generation of political economists and reformers, recoiling from that dismal image, tried to rewrite the history of the poor by reforming the poor law. The laboring poor, separated from the paupers, would be "socialized" and "moralized," made free men in a free economy and society; while the paupers, removed from the Malthusian state of nature, would be assured a minimal subsistence, although under conditions of dependency that reduced them to the status of minors—literally, "dependents."

Cobbett's response to this revisionist history was to restore the poor to their old status by reinstating the old poor law and reviving the old society. Paupers and poor would be reunited in a single community and reintegrated into a society that was hierarchical, paternalistic, and traditional. The only modification he proposed in that old society was the enfranchisement of the poor—not to make them the equal of their betters but to assure them their historic rights. *The Poor Man's Guardian,* in turn, had the double task of rebutting the new reformism of the political economists as well as the old radicalism of Cobbett. Universal suffrage served both purposes: it asserted the political equality of the working classes, and it proposed to use their political power to effect a radical change in the economy and society.

Chartism added another momentous chapter to the history of the poor. Hostile to the new political economy and refusing to commit itself to the new radical ideology, it transcended, in effect, the old problem of poverty. The heroes of its "history of mankind" were the "people" or "working classes" whose principal grievance was neither pauperism nor poverty, neither the exploitation of their labor nor the expropriation of their rightful property, but the simple, single fact of their exclusion from full membership in the polity.[39] They experienced, to be sure, other serious deprivations, and different groups of Chartists concerned themselves with one or another of these: the onerous conditions of poor relief, the grueling hours of factory work especially for women and children, the lack of education, the debilitating effects of drink. The essential deprivation, however, the one crucial disability shared by all the poor, was their disfranchisement. Under the terms of the Charter, this became the defining characteristic of the poor. And this was the historic achievement of Chartism. The social problem was redefined so as to make of it a political problem, the solution to which was neither the restoration of the old society nor the creation of a new one but the integration of the poor into the polity. It was membership in that polity, which for so long had been the proud preserve of the rich and which had only recently deigned to admit the middle classes, that was now the coveted goal of the working classes and the poor.

The political agenda of Chartism—the politicization of the poor—was a response to the peculiar situation brought about by the conjunction of the Reform Act and the New Poor Law. It is commonly said that both acts were of a piece, the first reflecting the political interests and ideology of the middle classes, the second their economic interests and ideology. But in an important sense the two acts worked at cross purposes. Where the New Poor Law tried to separate paupers and poor, the Reform Act, by excluding them both, brought them together into a single community. The Charter was thus a response to both measures, to the New Poor Law by asserting the communality of pauper and poor, their equal status in society, and to the Reform Act by asserting their common claim to the suffrage, their equal status in the polity.

In his classic essay, "Citizenship and Social Class," T. H. Marshall described the evolution of the three phases of citizenship: civil rights (liberty of the person, freedom of speech) emerging primarily in the eighteenth century, political rights (participation in political power) in the nineteenth, and social rights (economic welfare and security) in the twentieth.[40] From the perspective of a twentieth century social democrat or socialist, this is an altogether plausible sequence. And it is this sequence that gives rise to the familiar idea that political rights are less advanced, less progressive than social rights, that they are "merely formal," insubstantial, illusory, until fleshed out with a full complement of social rights.

A nineteenth century radical might have had a different sense of chronology and a different set of priorities. An Old Corruption Radical or a Tory Radical would have located social as well as civil rights in the eighteenth century, with its "moral economy" and paternalistic "old society," and political rights in the nineteenth, as a later stage in the advance of civilization. Even a "new" radical, whose conception of social rights derived from labor and property rather than tradition and prescription, gave the highest priority to political equality. If he sometimes spoke of political equality as a means to political power and thus to a more equitable distribution of property, it was so exalted a means—the "grand panacea for all our evils"—that it was practically an end in itself. O'Brien, the most consistent and systematic of the new radicals, never belittled the suffrage, never suggested that political rights were merely formal, instrumental, or anything less than fundamental.

For the Chartist, political rights were the highest rights because they represented the true equality of mankind. If, as Malthus had said, the "histories of mankind" thus far had excluded the lower classes, it was because those lower classes had been excluded from the making of history, from the conscious, deliberate, political decisions that had hitherto been reserved for the privileged. The Charter proposed to bring the poor into history by making them active participants in history, the authors of their own history. This was as far as they could get from the lowly "natural" status to which Malthus had relegated them. The poor law reformers had "socialized" the poor in one sense, by bringing the laboring poor (but not the dependent poor) into the free society of free men. The "old" radicals had "socialized" them in another sense, by restoring laborers and paupers alike to a single society of the poor. The "new" radicals "socialized" them in yet another sense, by claiming for them a new social right, the right to the full produce of their labor. It remained for the Chartists to "politicize" the poor, not so much by radicalizing and activating them, making them a political force to be reckoned with, as by endowing them with the highest qualities of human beings, qualities that made them truly, fully human in the classical sense: "political animals," people "born for citizenship."[41]

XII

ENGELS:

THE PROLETARIANIZATION

OF THE POOR

To Friedrich Engels, writing in 1845, Chartism was only one manifestation of the "social war" that was being waged in England, a war that was bound to issue in a full-scale revolution. And this not in the remote future but within a few years, following the economic crisis he predicted for 1846–47, or the one after that in 1852–53.

> The proletarians, driven to despair, will seize the torch which Stephens [the Chartist] has preached to them; the vengeance of the people will come down with a wrath of which the rage of 1793 gives no true idea. The war of the poor against the rich will be the bloodiest ever waged. Even the union of a part of the bourgeoisie with the proletariat, even a general reform of the bourgeoisie, would not help matters. . . . The revolution must come; it is already too late to bring about a peaceful solution.

Nothing could now prevent that revolution. All that could be hoped for was some mitigation of the violence, and that would depend on the "development" of the proletariat. "In proportion, as the proletariat absorbs socialistic and communistic elements, will the revolution diminish in bloodshed, revenge, and savagery."[1]

In most commentaries on *The Condition of the Working Class in England,* this scenario of revolution has been dismissed as a *folie de jeunesse,* a youthful excess of zeal which was surely mistaken, at least in its timing, but which did not seriously affect the substance of the book or the subject denoted by the title.* Questions have been raised about the accuracy of Engels's citation of documents and the accuracy of the documents themselves, about the bias in his selection of sources and the bias in the sources themselves, about the representativeness of his examples and the validity of his generalizations.[2] But there is another question that is no less pertinent: To what extent was his account of the condition of the English working class shaped by his prognosis of social war and revolution? He himself claimed that the class struggle and revolution were the logical, necessary consequences of the total impoverishment of the proletariat—"immiseration," in the language of later Marxism. One may well be wary of an ostensibly descriptive or empirical account of the condition of the English working class which so neatly confirmed his ideological predispositions. This does not necessarily invalidate his account; it may be that his ideology was firmly rooted in the actuality. It does, however, mean that the whole of the historical record has to be examined: the reports, articles, and books cited by Engels, his personal observations and reflections, and another set of sources he did not cite or make explicit—the ideas he brought with him to his study of the English working class. To raise this issue is not to subject Engels to any special or invidious kind of examination. It is only to take seriously ideas he himself took seriously. In the preface to the English edition written many years later, he observed that the book revealed the "stamp of his youth," "traces of the descent of modern Socialism from one of its ancestors, German philosophy"[3]—by which he meant that he had not yet emancipated himself from the philosophy and politics of Young Hegelianism.

Die Lage der arbeitenden Klasse in England was published in Leipzig in 1845; the first English language edition appeared in 1887 in America, and in 1892 in England, under the title *The Condition of the Working Class in England in 1844.* The date in the English title reminds us that almost half a century intervened between the original publication and its first appearance in England, a period during which the book was known only in Germany (and mainly in the German radical movement) and not at all in the country that was the object of its concern (except perhaps among the small group of German émigrés in London).[4] Whatever else may be said about it—as social reportage, ideological polemic, literary text, psychobiographical revelation, or "semiotic" exercise[5]—it was not, in the context of early Victorian England, a contemporary document in the way that Carlyle's or Cobbett's writings were. It was contemporary in the sense of being contemporaneous with the period it was describing. But it had no public resonance, no echoes

---

*Engels himself was so little discomfited by the patent failure of this prediction that in supervising the English edition almost half a century later, he let stand the whole of this passage (and others to the same effect), noting only that he had been right in predicting the repeal of the corn laws.

in public opinion, no part in the shaping of the public consciousness. Later, to be sure, it did enter the public domain, at a time, not by accident, when English socialism finally emerged as an important force. It has since become so much a part of the historical record, of the consciousness of historians if not of contemporaries, that it has been accused of unduly dominating that record.[6] For this reason as well as its intrinsic interest—as a picture of the English working classes seen through the eyes of a German radical newly resident in England—the book is a fascinating historical document.

Engels was twenty-two when he arrived in Manchester in November 1842 to join a textile firm in which his father was a partner. He remained in England for twenty-one months and started his book after his return to Germany in September 1844; it was completed by March and published in May. These bare facts are suggestive enough, although they hardly begin to tell the story. By the time the young man came to England, he had been initiated into the various factions of German radicalism known collectively as Young (or Left) Hegelianism, had met the leading figures in that movement (Wilhelm Weitling, Moses Hess, Bruno and Heinrich Bauer, Arnold Ruge, and Karl Marx), had published articles on various subjects (including an attack on the mill owners of his own town, of which his father was one), and had become a regular contributor to the radical journal, the *Rheinische Zeitung*. Before leaving for England he paid two visits to Cologne to meet with the staff of the *Zeitung*. On one occasion he was coolly received by the newly appointed editor, Karl Marx, who disapproved of his association with the "Freien" sect in Berlin, the extremist faction led by the Bauers and Ruge. Another editor, Moses Hess, befriended him and engaged him in long discussions. "We spoke about current questions," Hess wrote to a friend several months later, "and he, an Anno I revolutionary, departed from me an enthusiastic communist."[7] Those "current questions" must have included England, for Hess had just published his book, *Die europäische Triarchie*, describing the three stages in the history of human emancipation: the German Reformation which he identified with religious freedom, the French Revolution with political freedom, and a future English Revolution which would establish social freedom.

When Engels arrived in England, it was as a confirmed communist and an avowed revolutionary. His first weeks were spent in London, and either then or on a subsequent visit he met the German colony of exiled revolutionaries, members of the League of the Just who had been implicated in the Blanquist uprising in Paris in 1839; they were, he later explained, the first "proletarian revolutionaries" he had met.[8] During his first week in London he wrote three articles for the *Rheinische Zeitung,* one of which assured his German readers that the inherent "contradictions" in the English economy could be resolved only by revolution.[9] No sooner had he installed himself in Manchester than he sent off an article entitled "The Condition of the Working Class in England," which opened by asserting that that condition was becoming "daily more precarious," in spite of the fact that unemployment had recently decreased and the English worker was generally in a far better state than the German or French worker.

> The worker there [in Germany and France] earns just enough to allow him to live on bread and potatoes; he is lucky if he can buy meat once a week. Here he eats beef every day and gets a more nourishing joint for his money than the richest man in Germany. He drinks tea twice a day and still has enough money left over to be able to drink a glass of porter at midday and brandy and water in the evening. This is how most of the Manchester workers live who work a twelve-hour day.[10]

But this affluence, he warned, was only temporary, for the smallest fluctuation of trade would throw thousands out of work and a major depression was in the offing.

In the following months, in the spare time left him from business, Engels managed to write a series of articles for a German émigré magazine in Zurich (the *Rheinische Zeitung* having ceased publication), other articles for the Owenite *New Moral World* and the Chartist *Northern Star,* and a long essay, "Outlines of a Critique of Political Economy," for the *Deutsch-Französische Jahrbücher* edited by Marx and Ruge in Paris.* When the Soviet translator of the "Critique" later commented on the lingering traces of "ethical 'philosophical' communism" and "abstract principles of universal morals and humaneness," he had in mind such passages as that on the private ownership of land: "To make land an object of huckstering . . . was the last step towards making oneself an object of huckstering. It was and is to this very day an immorality surpassed only by the immorality of self-alienation."[11] For the most part, however, the "Critique" was an impassioned but not notably "philosophical" or moralistic analysis, using the language and concepts of political economy—wealth, value, price, capital, rent, wages—to criticize the system of private property that the political economists took for granted. That system, Engels argued, was destined to collapse as a result of its inherent contradictions. Competition would lead to monopoly and the centralization of property; economic crises would become more acute and widespread; the world would be divided into capitalists and workers, and eventually, with the impoverishment of the small capitalists, into millionaires and paupers; wages would decline to the point where the worker

*The February 1844 issue of the *Deutsch-Französische Jahrbücher,* the only issue to appear, contained, in addition to Engels's "Critique," his long review of Carlyle's *Past and Present* and two essays by Marx, "The Jewish Question" and "Introduction to the Critique of Hegel's *Philosophy of Right.*"

received "only the very barest necessities, the mere means of subsistence"; and the final crisis would result in the abolition of private property and the "total transformation of social conditions."[12] (Fifteen years later Marx, in his own *Critique of Political Economy*, paid tribute to Engels's "brilliant outline" which anticipated his own in so many respects.)[13]

The final words of Engels's essay read like an advertisement for *The Condition of the Working Class in England*. Having raised the question of machinery and the factory system, Engels explained that that subject was beyond the scope of the present essay. "Besides," he added, "I hope to have an early opportunity to expound in detail the despicable immorality of this system, and to expose mercilessly the economist's hypocrisy which here appears in all its brazenness."[14] The allusion was to the book he was planning on the political and economic state of England, with a chapter or two on the working class. Two articles on that subject were written early in 1844 and published in the summer (in yet another German émigré magazine). That same summer, returning from England, Engels stopped off in Paris to meet the exiled revolutionaries assembled there, including Marx. That visit marked the beginning of their lifelong friendship and collaboration. It may also have been then, perhaps on the advice of Marx, that he decided to devote the whole of his forthcoming book to the English working class.

Returning to his home in Barmen in the Rhineland, Engels immersed himself in the books and newspapers he had brought with him from England —not, however, to the exclusion of political activities. He joined Hess in founding a new radical periodical, helped organize a working class society, addressed two public meetings in which he explained why the continued expansion and impoverishment of the proletariat would lead to a social revolution "in a very short time,"[15] continued to write for the *New Moral World* and various German radical publications, and contributed his small part to *The Holy Family* (Marx's polemic against the Bauers and Stirner) —all this during the six or seven months in which he also wrote the 300-odd-page *Condition of the Working Class in England*. It was a prodigious accomplishment, testifying to his extraordinary intellectual vitality and his total political commitment.

Even if one were unaware of the ideological background of *The Condition of the Working Class in England*, one could not fail to see in it a good deal more than a descriptive account of that "condition." At the very least it included an analysis of the system responsible for that condition, a moral critique of both the condition and the system, and a prognosis of the development of the system and its eventual destruction by those who suffered so grievously under it. In a letter to Marx written soon after he started work on the book, Engels explained that he was drawing up a "bill of indictment" against the English bourgeoisie, and, by the same token, against the German bourgeoisie.

> I shall present the English with a fine bill of indictment. I accuse the English bourgeoisie before the entire world of murder, robbery and all sorts of other crimes on a mass scale, and am writing an English preface which I shall have printed separately and shall send to the English party leaders, literary men and Members of Parliament. Those fellows will have to remember me. Moreover, it is a matter of course that while I hit the bay I also mean to strike the donkey, namely, the German bourgeoisie, of whom I say clearly enough that it is just as bad as the English, only not so courageous, consistent and adept in sweat-shop methods.[16]

In the book itself Engels was entirely candid about his purpose, at least in respect to the English. In the preface addressed to "the Working Classes of Great Britain" he identified himself with the workers in the struggle against their "oppressors," and throughout the book he spoke of the middle classes as "murderers," the social order as a systematic form of "social murder," and the class struggle as a form of "social war."[17]

The bill of indictment consisted of descriptions, episodes, and statistics culled from parliamentary reports, newspapers, books, and pamphlets, supplemented by Engels's own observations and judgments. The effect was a picture of desperate, hopeless misery: workers dying of starvation or so malnourished and enfeebled as to be on the verge of death, fifty thousand homeless people wandering the streets of London and millions more crowded into the meanest, foulest slums, all of them clothed in rags, exposed to the damp and cold, their bodies sickly, crippled, stunted, deformed. Their moral state was no less appalling, as they drowned their sorrows in drink, vented their rage in crime and violence, and lost themselves in the only indulgence left to them, sexual licentiousness. As misery and vice was the refrain of Malthus's work, so degradation and demoralization was the refrain of this.

Occasionally Engels raised the issue that has exercised his critics: Was the condition he described the extreme or the average condition of the working class? What part of the working class was in that state of destitution, degradation, and demoralization? In the course of one chapter, caustically entitled "The Great Towns," he estimated that one-tenth of the workers were utterly degraded, that 12 percent lived in the foulest cellars, and that "the average is much nearer the worst cases than the best"—the "worst" having just been described as "bitter want, reaching even homelessness and death by starvation." Potentially every worker was in that worst condition.

"Every proletarian, everyone, without exception, is exposed to a similar fate without any fault of his own and in spite of every possible effort."[18]

It could be said that Engels's portrait was so stark because the reality itself was stark. He had arrived in Manchester, the worst of all industrial towns—"the shock city of the age," as Asa Briggs has aptly called it[19]— at the worst of all times, in the midst of the most severe economic depression in half a century. Even then, however, as he himself reported in the first of his newspaper articles from Manchester, less than 10 percent of the workers were unemployed, and those who were employed could afford a quantity and quality of meat and drink that would have been the envy of the German or French worker.[20] Engels did not reproduce that passage, or anything like it, in his book, but he could have done so without any logical inconsistency (although it would have detracted from the prevailing impression of gloom). For the point was not so much the actual, existential condition of the worker as his essential and potential condition, the condition that was his simply by virtue of his being a "proletarian," a member of the propertyless class. It was this state of propertylessness that doomed the worker to the "worst" condition even if, for the moment, he seemed to be in a "better" or "best" condition. In this sense the question of percentages and averages was irrelevant since it was the extreme, not the average, that was the essential condition of the whole of the working class.

In the same sense, every aspect of the worker's being, his moral and intellectual as much as his economic and physical condition, was in that extreme state. One might have expected a Chadwick to speak of the working class as a "race" so thoroughly degraded and demoralized that it "must really have reached the lowest stage of humanity," or to describe dwellings in which "only a physically degenerate race, robbed of all humanity, degraded, reduced morally and intellectually to bestiality, could feel comfortable and at home."[21] And it was in fact from Chadwick and his kind—J. P. Kay (later Kay-Shuttleworth), Peter Gaskell, Nassau Senior, and other "bourgeois" reformers, critics, and investigators—that Engels took his material. He went further than they did, however, because his purpose was different. They wanted to arouse the consciousness and conscience (and perhaps the fears as well) of the middle classes in order to promote specific reforms. Engels wanted to portray the workers in that condition of destitution and degradation which was a prelude not to reform but to revolution, a revolution to restore the humanity that the present system denied to them.

There was no hidden agenda here, no secret strategy. Engels was quite explicit about the revolutionary implications of his account. Again and again he interrupted his description of the vile state of the workers to hold out the promise of redemption, the redemption that would come not as the result of rebellion but in the very act of rebellion. The impulse to rebel was the saving grace, the one glimmer of humanity in an otherwise dehumanized race.

> There is, therefore, no cause for surprise if the workers, treated as brutes, actually become such; or if they can maintain their consciousness of manhood only by cherishing the most glowing hatred, the most unbroken inward rebellion against the bourgeoisie in power. They are men so long only as they burn with wrath against the reigning class. They become brutes the moment they bend in patience under the yoke, and merely strive to make life endurable while abandoning the effort to break the yoke.

> ... How can such a sentence [to the division of labor] help degrading a human being to the level of a brute? Once more the worker must choose, must either surrender himself to his fate, become a "good" workman, heed "faithfully" the interest of the bourgeoisie, in which case he most certainly becomes a brute, or else he must rebel, fight for his manhood to the last, and this he can only do in the fight against the bourgeoisie.[22]

At every point the same message came through: the condition of brutality was the precondition for change, the only kind of change that was of any consequence—revolution. "The Great Towns" opened with a memorable description of hordes of people crowded together, streaming past each other, yet brutally indifferent to each other and entirely separated from each other. It was an altogether repulsive sight, repugnant to human nature itself. "This isolation of the individual, this narrow self-seeking, is the fundamental principle of our society elsewhere, [and] it is nowhere so shamelessly barefaced, so self-conscious as just there in the crowding of the great city." The "dissolution of mankind into nomads" reminded Engels of the recent book by Max Stirner, the most anarchistic of the Young Hegelians, who described all of society, and capitalist society preeminently, as a "war of each against all." In this atomistic, ferociously competitive world, everyone looked upon everyone else as an object to be used and exploited, and the capitalists, being the strongest, were able to seize everything for themselves, leaving the mass of the poor with the barest means of existence.[23] But these same cities, the breeding places of misery and vice, were also—and here Engels parted from Stirner—the "birthplaces of the labor movements." Were it not for the cities, the workers, isolated and exploited as individuals, would have been slower in coming to a consciousness of their oppression, of their class interests and class identity. Thus the cities aggravated the social problem and, by aggravating it, helped solve it; they were the disease and the remedy. "The great cities have transformed the disease of the social body, which appears in chronic form in the country, into an acute one, and so made manifest its real nature and the means of curing it."[24]

Industrialism had the same dual aspect. It stupefied the worker by limiting him to a single process in the division of labor, enslaved him by the tyrannical discipline of the factory, dehumanized him by reducing him to a machine, a "chattel" to be used and discarded as his employer saw fit. But it was also the means of his salvation. The most highly industrialized part of the economy produced the most intelligent and energetic workers who were in the forefront of the labor movement and of the class struggle. Even those workers who were not so intelligent, whose "mental state" was as enfeebled as their physical condition, who were more ignorant than the working classes of Spain and Italy—even they, by sheer force of "necessity," came to know their own interests and to know them to be implacably opposed to the bourgeoisie. Similarly the immigration from Ireland, which had the immediate effect of degrading and barbarizing the English workers, also "deepened the chasm between workers and bourgeoisie, and hastened the approaching crisis."[25]

In each case the disease contained within itself its own antidote. Since the antidote matured only as the disease did, the disease had to run its course before the antidote became effective. As in a grave sickness where the fate of the patient was determined by the final, violent crisis, so the social disease had to await its crisis. The only difference was that the English nation, unlike an individual patient, could not die. "And as the English nation cannot succumb under the final crisis, but must go forth from it, born again, rejuvenated, we can but rejoice over everything which accelerates the course of the disease."[26]*

When Engels authorized the translation and publication of the book in 1887, in the midst of another economic crisis, he believed it to be as relevant and urgent as ever. The timing of the revolution may have been inexplicably delayed, but the revolution itself was still on the agenda of history. From the perspective of "mature Marxism," *The Condition of the Working Class in England* was a case study of capitalism *in extremis,* the existential confirmation of the scenario outlined in the *Communist Manifesto* and elaborated in *Capital.*

To be sure, there were some deviations, some traces of "German philosophy" which gave it the "stamp of his youth." Engels's own example of that vestigial idealistic philosophy was the passage: "Communism is a question of humanity and not of the workers alone. . . . Communism stands

---

*This is another example of the "worse is better" principle—the principle that makes reactionaries preferable to reformers ("reformists," as later Marxists called them) and, in one famous instance, Nazis preferable to Social Democrats.

above the strife between bourgeoisie and proletariat."[27] He might also have cited the image of the city as the "dissolution of mankind"; or the portrait of the worker deprived of his "humanity" and "manhood," forced to rebel in order to assert himself as a "human being"[28]; or the Feuerbachian "generic" or "species" man in the preface addressed to the "Working Classes of Great Britain":

> I found you to be more than mere *Englishmen,* members of a single, isolated nation, I found you to be *Men,* members of the great and universal family of Mankind, who know their interest and that of all the human race to be the same. And as such, as members of this Family of "One and Indivisible" Mankind, as Human Beings in the most emphatical meaning of the word, as such I, and many others on the Continent, hail your progress in every direction and wish you speedy success.[29]

Apart from these occasional idealistic effusions, as he later thought them, and some unfortunate predictions, Engels had good reason to be pleased with the *Condition,* for it gave every appearance of corroborating the *Manifesto* both in its general thesis and in its details. The pauperization of the English working class appeared here, as in the *Manifesto,* as the necessary precondition for the historical process that would inevitably lead to revolution. And in the *Condition,* again as in the *Manifesto,* material impoverishment was accompanied by a moral degradation that ensured the total alienation of the working class. Although the word "alienation" did not appear in the *Condition* (or for that matter in the *Manifesto,* except to deride the "True Socialists" who still talked of the "alienation of humanity"), it was a thoroughly alienated working class Engels described, a class alienated from "generic" humanity as well as from bourgeois society and culture.

Like the proletariat in the *Manifesto,* which was utterly divorced from bourgeois family relations, national character, law, morality, and religion, the English working class in the *Condition* was a "race wholly apart" in just these respects. "The workers speak other dialects, have other thoughts and ideals, other customs and moral principles, a different religion and other politics than those of the bourgeoisie."[30] In some ways the workers were more humane than the bourgeoisie, friendlier, more generous, less greedy, less bigoted. But it was their less agreeable traits Engels dwelt on at much greater length and in starker detail: drunkenness, brutality, licentiousness, and criminality. To be sure, there was an explanation for each of these. They drank themselves into a state of bestiality and engaged in hideous sexual practices because these were the only pleasures they had. They stole and committed crimes because they were starving and desperate. They were irreligious for the same reason that they were illiterate, because the bourgeoisie totally ignored their education save for the futile attempt to inculcate the incomprehensible dogmas of conventional religion. Their families were destroyed by the factories and by filthy, crowded homes devoid of any domestic comfort. Where the family was not "wholly dissolved," it was "turned upside down," with the wife working and the unemployed husband at home, a situation which "unsexes the man and takes from the woman all womanliness." In addition to the sexual promiscuity among the workers themselves, the women were at the mercy of their employers, who enjoyed the traditional privilege of the master over the slave, the *jus primae noctis* —except that the employer could choose to exercise that right at any time.[31]

The working class and the bourgeoisie were thus "two radically dissimilar nations, as unlike as difference of race could make them."[32] They were different as much by will as by circumstance. The rejection by the working class of bourgeois morality and culture was an expression of defiance, a conscious or unconscious act of rebellion. Crime was a form of "social war," a war which the bourgeoisie had been waging against the proletariat and which the proletariat was now turning against their exploiters. Stealing was more than a means of staving off hunger; it was a "primitive form of protest," a denial of the "sacredness of property," an assertion by the worker of "contempt for the existing social order" and of opposition to the "whole conditions of his life."[33] The "surplus population" which roamed the streets, begging, stealing, and murdering, was engaged in the same social war: "He among the 'surplus' who has courage and passion enough openly to resist society, to reply with declared war upon the bourgeoisie to the disguised war which the bourgeoisie wages against him, goes forth to rob, plunder, murder, and burn!"[34] These violations of the law were the evidence of a society "already in a state of visible dissolution," the prelude to that "universal outburst" whose symptoms were ordinary crimes.[35] Atheism was another form of that social war. Echoing Marx's essay "On the Jewish Question" published the previous year, Engels equated religion with the worship of money. "Money is the god of this world; the bourgeois takes the proletarian's money from him and so makes a practical atheist of him." That atheism announced to the world that the proletariat no longer respected the "sacredness and power of the earthly God" and was prepared to "disregard all social order."[36]

If the working class and bourgeoisie were "radically dissimilar," so were the modern working class and the preindustrial workers. Engels's account of the latter recalls the ambiguous passage in the *Manifesto* about the "feudal, patriarchal, idyllic relations" which had been "pitilessly torn asunder,"

leaving nothing but "naked self-interest" and "callous 'cash-payment.' "[37]
The *Condition* enlarged upon that idyllic preindustrial state.

> So the workers vegetated throughout a passably comfortable existence,
> leading a righteous and peaceful life in all piety and probity; and their
> material position was far better than that of their successors. They did
> not need to overwork; they did no more than they chose to do, and
> yet earned what they needed. They had leisure for healthful work in
> garden or field, work which, in itself, was recreation for them, and they
> could take part besides in the recreations and games of their neighbours,
> and all these games—bowling, cricket, football, etc., contributed to
> their physical health and vigour. They were, for the most part, strong,
> well-built people, in whose physique little or no difference from that
> of their peasant neighbours was discoverable. Their children grew up
> in the fresh country air, and, if they could help their parents at work,
> it was only occasionally; while of eight or twelve hours of work for
> them there was no question.[38]

Engels continued in this vein, rhapsodizing about those "respectable" workers who had a "stake in the country," who were good husbands and fathers,
drank no more than was good for them, mingled happily with the yeomanry, and had a comfortable "patriarchal relation" with their "natural
superior," the squire. Their children enjoyed the same natural relationship
with their fathers; working at home, and raised in "obedience and the fear
of God," they grew up in "idyllic simplicity and intimacy with their
playmates." (This moral regimen did not preclude the practice of premarital
intercourse, but since it was invariably followed by marriage, that "made
everything good.")[39]

The idyll went on for several hundred words before the fatal flaw
emerged. Just as in the *Manifesto*, where the "feudal, patriarchal, idyllic
relations" were shortly exposed as the "idiocy of rural life,"[40] so in the
Condition that comfortable, respectable, patriarchal existence suddenly appeared, in mid-paragraph, to be a life "not worthy of human beings." Spared
the violent fluctuations of the industrial cycle, the workers were also spared
all mental and political activity. "Comfortable in their silent vegetation,"
they were intellectually dead, aware only of their petty, private concerns,
and ignorant of the "mighty movement which, beyond their horizons, was
sweeping through mankind." "In truth, they were not human beings; they
were merely toiling machines in the service of the few aristocrats who had
guided history down to that time." It was only when the industrial revolution roused them out of that happy life, making them "machines pure and
simple," that they were forced to "think and demand a position worthy of
men," and thus were drawn into the "whirl of history."[41]

This portrait of the happy, healthy, moral, if mentally torpid preindustrial worker has been criticized by some historians as the familiar myth of the Golden Age, and defended by others on the ground that that age was indeed golden compared with that which followed.[42] The controversy, however important in its own terms, is largely irrelevant to Engels. For here, even more than in the rest of his book, he was concerned not so much with the actual condition of the preindustrial workers as with their role in his historical schema; and in that schema these workers had no role. If Engels's account of them seems mythical and unhistorical, it is because they themselves were unhistorical, which is to say, prehistorical—prehistorical from the perspective of the revolution that would bring them on the stage of history and make them the leading actors in history, the agents of the "dissolution" of society and the "transformation" of mankind.

It is no accident that the *Condition* was one of the first occasions when the phrase "industrial revolution" was used, not once but repeatedly, and with the full force of a revolutionary event.[43] The industrial revolution was for Engels the decisive "historical moment," the beginning of the expansion and concentration of the means of production which led to contradictions and crises. It was also then that the working class started its descent into pauperism and degradation which left it no choice but to rebel. The preindustrial workers, by contrast, were not "ripe for revolution" because the economy was not ripe for revolution. Spared the misery that was a precondition of revolution, they were healthy, happy, and comfortable; spared the self-consciousness that would have made them rebellious, they were apathetic and torpid. They had precisely the qualities required of them in a drama in which their only role was to exist and survive. Like a nation without a history, they were happy—and boring.

In the preface to the German edition, Engels explained that a "knowledge of proletarian conditions" was necessary to provide a "solid ground for socialist theories," and that only in England did these conditions exist "in their classical form and in their perfection."[44] *The Condition of the Working Class in England* was meant to give that solid, empirical "ground" for Marxist theory. All the essential ingredients were there: the preindustrial workers in a comfortable, unconscious, unrevolutionary state; the modern proletariat pauperized and degraded, reduced to a "slavery" worse than the serfdom of old, totally alienated from bourgeois morality and culture; the "lower middle class" impoverished and forced down into the ranks of the proletariat; society divided into two irreconcilable classes; the bourgeoisie, the "ruling class," exercising the "power of the State"; the increasing concentration of industry, wealth, property, and population; the increasing intensity of economic crises, misery, and "social war"; and finally the "violent revolution, which cannot fail to take place."[45] Although no one of these propositions was novel in England at the time, the totality was. And it was the totality that added up to an ideology significantly different from the prevalent modes of English radicalism and significantly similar to that of the *Communist Manifesto.* *

A distinctive and crucial part of this ideology was its vocabulary—"proletariat," most notably. The word was not invented by Marx or Engels. Derived from *proles,* offspring, it originally referred to the lowest class of Roman citizen who served the state only by producing children. In one variation or another (as an adjective, or in the French form of *proletaires*), it was used in England from at least the seventeenth century to describe either the ancient populace or the contemporary "rabble." In its modern meaning, applied to the working classes as a whole, it began to appear in Germany in the mid-thirties and was popularized in 1840 by Pierre Joseph Proudhon's *Qu'est-ce que la propriété?* and in 1842 by Lorenz von Stein's *Der Sozialismus und Communismus des heutigen Frankreichs.* (Unlike Proudhon, Stein was a conservative who was as wary of the proletariat as of socialism or communism.) By the time Engels wrote the *Condition,* "proletariat" was part of the vocabulary of French and German Socialists—but not of English radicals.[47]

Engels himself was fully aware of the alien connotation of "proletariat." The original preface to the *Condition,* written in English and intended for distribution to Members of Parliament and English literary men, was couched in the familiar English vocabulary. It was entitled, "To the Working Classes of Great Britain," its salutation read, "Working Men!" and the text itself referred to "working men." The German preface, however, which followed the English one, started by speaking of the condition of the "working class," went on in the next sentence to "proletarian conditions," and in the following paragraph to the "English proletariat"—all on the first page—and concluded with some comments on terminology.

> I have used the word *Mittelklasse* all along in the sense of the English word *middle-class* (or *middle-classes,* as is said almost always). . . .
> Similarly, I have continually used the expressions working men *(Arbeiter)* and proletarians, working class, propertyless class and proletariat as equivalents.[48]

The opening words of the book established the significance of the term. "The history of the proletariat in England," Engels explained, dated from

---

*There were innumerable other anticipations in the *Condition* of the *Manifesto*—Engels's criticism, for example, of the Owenites on the ground that they "acknowledge no historic development, and wish to place the nation in a state of Communism at once, overnight, not by the unavoidable march of its political development up to the point at which this transition becomes both possible and necessary."[46]

the second half of the eighteenth century with the invention of the steam-engine and textile machinery.[49] These inventions gave rise to an "industrial revolution, a revolution which altered the whole civil society." England was the "classic soil" of this revolution and, therefore, "the classic land of its chief product also, the proletariat." The preindustrial worker, the hand-weaver working at home, had been "no proletarian." With the appearance of the spinning jenny the class of farm weavers merged with the new class of weavers who lived entirely upon wages, had no property, and so became "working men, proletarians."[50] At the same time the propertyless, wage-earning agricultural laborers became an "agricultural proletariat." The proletariat was fully developed only in England because only there were both industry and agriculture transformed by the industrial revolution. "The industrial revolution is of the same importance for England as the political revolution for France, and the philosophical revolution for Germany." It was decisive for the development of the economy and even more for the development of the proletariat. "The mightiest result of this industrial transformation is the English proletariat."[51]

Engels prided himself on the fact that his was the first book to deal with "*all* the workers." And so it did, all workers being subsumed under the category of the proletariat. The "industrial proletariat," the "mining proletariat," and the "agricultural proletariat" shared the crucial characteristic of being propertyless. By the same token, the propertied classes—the middle class and landed aristocracy—belonged to the single class of the "bourgeoisie": "In speaking of the bourgeoisie I include the so-called aristocracy."[52]*

The condition of propertylessness proletarianized the workers and then, by the logic of capitalist development, pauperized them. Contemporaries (and historians) might object that not all workers were impoverished, that the navvy or artisan was in a far better state than the agricultural laborer, and the factory worker than the handloom weaver. Engels recognized these differences but regarded them as ultimately inconsequential. If some workers were not actually, currently impoverished, they were so essentially and potentially. They were a single class characterized by a single condition; the propertylessness that defined them as the proletariat pauperized them and revolutionized them. That single "class" and "condition" were reflected in the singular title. It was probably out of deference to English usage that

---

*In his *Economic and Philosophic Manuscripts* of 1844, Marx similarly assimilated the landed aristocracy into the class of "capitalists."

> The final consequence is thus the abolition of the distinction between capitalist and landowner, so that there remain altogether only two classes of the population—the working class and the class of capitalists. This huckstering with landed property, the transformation of landed property into a commodity, constitutes the final overthrow of the old and the final establishment of the money aristocracy.[53]

Engels chose to call his book *The Condition of the Working Class* rather than *The Condition of the Proletariat*. But he could not have adopted the more familiar "working classes," "poor," or "people" without doing violence to his thesis.

The idea of poverty that emerged from his book was implicit in the word "proletariat." It was total, unrelieved poverty, a poverty that extended itself to every realm of life—cultural, moral, and intellectual as much as material—a poverty that created a class so different as to constitute a different "race." The poverty of the proletariat was quantitatively different from the poverty of the old poor—the preindustrial poor were less impoverished, less hardworking, less miserable. And it was qualitatively different, creating a new consciousness, a new identity, and a new historical role. This is what impressed Lenin when he read the *Condition:* "Engels was the *first* to say that the proletariat is *not only* a suffering class; that it is, in fact, the disgraceful economic condition of the proletariat that drives it irresistibly forward and compels it to fight for its ultimate emancipation. And the fighting proletariat *will help itself.*"[54]

Engels was not, in fact, the first to say that. Stein had made it the crucial difference between the "proletariat" and the "poor." There had always been poor, he said. What was new, and dangerous, was the proletariat: "dangerous in respect of its numbers and its often tested courage; dangerous in respect of its consciousness of unity; dangerous in respect of its feeling that only through revolution can its aims be reached, its plans accomplished."[55] This dangerousness, which made the proletariat so perilous to Stein, was a source of pride and hope to the Young Hegelians. When they distinguished between the proletariat and the poor, it was precisely the size and courage of the new class, its unity, self-consciousness, and above all revolutionary character that made it superior to the old poor, that made it a historical class endowed with the highest historical mission.

In his "Introduction to the Critique of Hegel's *Philosophy of Right,*" published early in 1844, Marx described the proletariat (in a passage now regarded as the classic expression of Feuerbachian "humanism") as "a class of civil society which is not a class of civil society, an estate which is the dissolution of all estates, a sphere which has a universal character by its universal suffering." Less well known but equally notable was the next paragraph in which the "artificially *impoverished*" proletariat was contrasted to the *"naturally arising* poor"; the latter, impoverished by nature and natural circumstances, would be gradually absorbed into the larger class that was impoverished by the artificial institution of private property.[56] In *The Holy Family,* the following year, the proletariat retained some of that generic, humanistic character—"the abstraction of all humanity"—while acquiring a more historical, deterministic character, for it was driven to revolt against the inhuman conditions of its life by "absolutely imperative *need*—the practical expression of necessity," the necessity to abolish private property in order to "abolish" itself. "It is not a question of what this or that proletarian, or even the whole proletariat, at the moment *regards* as its aim. It is a question of what the *proletariat* is, and what, in accordance with this *being,* it will historically be compelled to do."[57] By 1847 Marx was attacking Proudhon, who had been one of the first to popularize the idea of the proletariat as well as the idea of property as "theft," for not appreciating the revolutionary nature of poverty, for seeing "in poverty nothing but poverty, without seeing in it the revolutionary, subversive side, which will overthrow the old society."[58] At the same time Engels, in the credo he drew up for the Communist League (parts of which were incorporated in the *Communist Manifesto*), explained the difference between the old poor and the new proletariat.

> Poor folk and working classes have always existed. The working classes have also for the most part been poor. But such poor, such workers as are living under conditions indicated above, hence proletarians, have not always existed, any more than free and unbridled competition has always existed.[59]

It was this new idea of poverty that pervaded the *Condition:* a poverty qualitatively different from the old, just as the proletariat was qualitatively different from the poor.* What was unique about the book, distinguishing it from everything else Marx and Engels wrote at this time or later, was the fact that here the proletariat was something more than a historical abstraction, a logical category subsumed under a larger historical schema, a "world-historical" class furthering the "world-historical" movement of communism.[61] Instead of the familiar, abstract, universal proletariat, Engels described a specifically English proletariat, located in real towns and villages,

---

*In his commentary on Engels's book, Steven Marcus has suggested a psychoanalytic distinction between "poor" on the one hand and "working class" or "proletariat" on the other. Inspired by Erik Erikson's observation that young Gandhi's interest in "the poor" rather than in "labor" was a symptom of what Gandhi himself had called his "mother complex," Marcus applied this distinction to Engels.

> As a boy, he [Engels] had often given his little savings to "the poor." As a young man, he has now decided in more ways than one actively to throw his lot in with labor, with the working class or proletariat. The difference between an identification with "the poor" and an identification with the "working class" represents, among many other things, the measure in which an idealistic and rebellious young man could appreciate for himself a traditional historical masculine identity and maintain that identity even in the role of insurrection against the world in which it was grounded.[60]

Whatever credibility one assigns to this feminine-masculine dichotomy, it is interesting that "poor" should be taken to connote an attitude of passivity or acquiescence and "working class" or "proletariat" an attitude of rebelliousness. This much, at least, is consistent with the Marxist interpretation.

living in real cottages and cellars, working at real jobs, participating in real events, suffering real hardships, and indulging in real vices. All this was attested to by real newspapers, books, parliamentary reports, and personal observations. Contemporaries may not have known Engels's proletariat under that name and might have disputed his descriptions, generalizations, and predictions. But they would have recognized the names of the towns and villages, the views of back streets and houses, the scenes of riots and demonstrations, the titles of newspapers and royal commissions, the identities of politicians and writers. And they would have responded (as readers still respond) to the emotive force of the book, the dramatic evocation of misery and the powerful sense of outrage. Almost twenty years later, rereading the *Condition* in preparation for the writing of *Capital*, Marx confessed to Engels that it made him feel his advancing years.

> How freshly and passionately, with what bold anticipations and no learned and scientific doubts, the thing is still dealt with here! And the very illusion that the result itself will leap into the daylight of history tomorrow or the day after gives the whole thing a warmth and jovial humour—compared to which the later "gray in gray" makes a damned unpleasant contrast.[62]

That passion and boldness, the illusion that his predictions would "leap into the daylight of history tomorrow or the day after," came in no small part from the powerful ideology Engels imposed on the actuality of history. His English proletariat was the "world-historical" proletariat writ small, a miniature version of the universal phenomenon. If the English working classes never carried out Engels's prediction of revolution, it was for the same reason that they resisted the label "proletariat"—resisted in fact the whole of the historical schema that would have made them what Lenin was pleased to call a "fighting proletariat."

XIII

THE LANGUAGE OF CLASS

"Language is called the Garment of Thought: however, it should rather be, Language is the Flesh-Garment, the Body, of thought."[1] That dictum comes with special authority from Carlyle, for whom language was indeed the body of thought. And it is especially appropriate to the early nineteenth century, when momentous social changes, dramatic public events, new ideas, attitudes, philosophies, and policies were intruding themselves upon every level of public consciousness, when debate became intensely passionate, and when some of England's finest writers and rhetoricians were on hand to publicize these great issues.

It was also a time when there were abundant opportunities for the expression of the most diverse opinions. The age of the illegal, unstamped press was also the age of a flourishing legal press. In 1830 London alone had seven daily morning papers and six evening ones—this for a population of less than 1,500,000. The combined sales of these papers was about 40,000, but this figure does not take into account the multiple readers. (A single copy of *The Times* might be lent out by the local newsman to dozens of readers at a penny an hour, and used copies were sent to subscribers in the country.) There were also provincial and Sunday papers, religious and secular journals of every description, weeklies *(Examiner, Athenaeum, Spectator)*, monthlies *(Blackwood's, Fraser's, Tait's Edinburgh)*, and, of course, the great quarterly reviews *(Edinburgh, Westminster, Quarterly)* with their distinctive constituencies and political dispositions. The play of mind, the passion of polemic, gave an enormous stimulus to the language, producing new expressions and giving old ones new connotations and emotive effects.

For the social historian the most striking linguistic feature of this period was the development of what Asa Briggs has called the "language of class."[2] Underlying all the other changes that were taking place in the idea of poverty and the image of the poor was the increasing use of the language of class to define poverty and describe the poor—the increasing, although not, as will be seen, the exclusive use of that language. If old and new ideologies, liberal and conservative as well as radical, persisted throughout this period, so did the old and the new language.

The old language—the language of "orders," "ranks," "sorts," "degrees," "estates"—was evocative of the old society. "Orders" suggested the idea of an orderly, stable, organic society; "ranks" and "estates" a stratified, hierarchical one; "sorts" and "degrees" a varied and finely graduated one. That vocabulary carried with it other connotations as well, of social relations defined largely in terms of birth but not rigidly or exclusively so, of distinctions and differences small enough to permit some measure of social mobility, and of a system of mutual dependency implied in such expressions as "chain of connection" and "bond of attachment."

The language of "class" was more mechanistic, less organic, connoting not a system of interrelations and interdependence but of separation and independence, not a "vertical" society (as Harold Perkin calls the old society) linked together by bonds of interest and allegiance, but a sharply demarcated "horizontal" society where each stratum was, potentially at least, in an adversary relationship to every other.[3] (The language of class could, however, adapt itself to the vertical structure as well, as in the expressions "landed classes" and "manufacturing classes.") The new vocabulary was used most commonly by two groups who were hostile to each other and, in quite different ways, subversive of the old society: the political economists and the "new" radicals. It was congenial to the political economists because it derived from the fundamental economic categories of rent, capital, and labor, and because it implied that class relations, in society as in the economy, were based on interest and contract rather than tradition and status. And it served the purposes of the new radicals because it was an invitation to radical social change. If class relations were contractual rather than conventional, if the legitimizing principle of social behavior was interest rather than obligation, the constraints of the old order were no longer binding, and the most radical ideas about power and authority, property and equality, could be advanced with impunity. This is not to say that the old society was lacking in a vocabulary suitable to its own radicals. Long before the language of class became prevalent, the language of the Enlightenment— "nature," "right," "reason," "equality"—was available to justify universal suffrage, the nationalization of the land, republicanism, secularism, or any other radical doctrine. But the new language of class was conducive to a new and bolder radicalism. It was easier to think in terms of radical change when there was no frame of reference to inhibit such change, no "chain of connection" to bind the "orders" to each other and to the established "order."

The language of class (class in the specifically social and economic sense as distinct from "classes" in botany or in school) emerged in the last quarter of the eighteenth century, began to be familiar in the first decades of the nineteenth, and became common only in the thirties—although even then it was not the exclusive or even dominant mode of discourse. The first of the classes to gain recognition were the "lower classes," as in Jonas Hanway's pamphlet of 1772, "Observations on the Causes of the Dissoluteness which Reigns among the Lower Classes of the People." Twenty years later "middling" and "middle classes" made their appearance in, for example, Thomas Gisborne's *Enquiry into the Duties of Men in the Higher Rank and Middle Classes of Society in Great Britain.* [4] "Higher classes," and somewhat later "upper classes," completed the trinity, but these terms never acquired the currency of the others, perhaps because the older language of "rank" was more appropriate to those more firmly rooted in the old society (hence Gisborne's "higher rank and middle classes").

"Working classes" (or "labouring classes") was a significant departure not only from the language of rank and order but also from the earlier language of class. "Lower classes" had an unambiguous place in the hierarchical structure, paralleling "middle" (or "middling") and "higher" (or "upper") classes. But "working classes" had a functional rather than a hierarchical connotation, just as Adam Smith's category of "labor" did. (By placing labor in the middle of the "rent-labor-profit" triad, Smith violated the ladder image which always had labor at the bottom rung.) One of the early appearances of "working classes" was in Owen's *Essays on the Principle of the Formation of the Human Character,* published in 1813 (and reprinted, with two additional essays, as *A New View of Society*). In the following years Owen used the term several times, most conspicuously in the titles of his "Two Memorials on Behalf of the Working Classes" and "An Address to the Working Classes."

To the modern ear "working classes" has a quite different tone from "lower classes," the former sounding objective and dignified, the latter pejorative and demeaning.* This was not, however, the contemporary im-

---

*Lower classes" has other connotations for the psychoanalytically minded historian. According to Bruce Mazlish, John Stuart Mill's use of "lower classes" revealed both his aversion to sex and his "elitist notions" about the working class. Since "lower" is "equated" with the body, especially the "baser" parts of the body, it implies that sexuality is low, dirty, animalistic. It also evokes the image of the savage who is "low in the scale of human evolution," thereby equating "lower-class sexuality" with "savagery." Mill's use of the term thus shows that, although ostensibly committed to social equality, he shared the low opinion of the "lower class" which was "typical of his time, society, and class."[5]

The difficulty with this theory is obvious. Are we to assume that everyone who used the expression "lower classes" for the better part of a century—and almost everyone did, including the most militant radicals—had a "disdain" for workers as well as an aversion to sex? In the case of Mill, there is a more decisive objection. Mazlish posits the theory in the course of discussing the chapter "On the Probable Futurity of the Labouring Classes" in Mill's *Principles of Political Economy,* and he finds a significant discrepancy between the manifest content of that chapter (an attack on those who wanted to keep the labouring classes in a position of dependency and inferiority) and its latent content, the "unconscious disparagement" revealed in the term "lower class." But throughout that chapter, as in

plication of those terms for much of this period. In a society, even a "new" society, that was unabashedly hierarchical, where inequality was as natural a fact of life as poverty, "lower classes" was an objective, descriptive term properly applied to people who occupied a lower place in society, in the polity, and in the economy. Even "inferior" was not at first invidious, "inferior ranks" or "inferior sorts" being synonymous with "lower orders" or "lower classes" through much of the eighteenth century. In 1773 John Wilkes proudly declared himself the defender of the liberties of "all the middling and inferior set of people"; three years later he argued that "the meanest mechanic, the poorest peasant and day labourer"—"this inferior but most useful set of men"—deserved a share in the making of the laws.[7] By the beginning of the nineteenth century, "inferior" had begun to acquire a pejorative connotation, but "lower" continued to be acceptable, especially in the form of "lower classes." Until at least the forties "lower classes" continued to be used as commonly as "working classes," and by radicals as often as not.

It is revealing that "working classes" was introduced (or popularized) by Owen, the least egalitarian of all radicals, and that it was used freely by others—Cobbett, most notably—who were not much more egalitarian. Owen himself, in the very sentence preceding his reference to "working classes," spoke of the "lower classes" in exactly the same sense; some pages later he referred to them as "lower orders," again without any invidious intent.[8] In 1823 Cobbett professed to take umbrage at a reference to "lower orders" by a Mechanics' Institution, but it was probably the institution rather than the expression that provoked him.[9] He certainly had no objection to "lower classes," which appeared frequently in the *Political Register*. By the late forties some stigma began to attach to that term in radical circles. Harriet Martineau, a sensitive recorder of social vocabulary (it was she who noted the origin of "radical"), wrote: "The term 'lower class,' or 'lower classes,' is gone out of use. The term is thought not complimentary to the democracy, and so we say 'the working-class,' which is less precise, and conveys false notions." She herself, in the course of the same book, went so far to conciliate the democratic spirit as to speak of "working classes."[10]

From a later perspective the language of class seems peculiarly the language of the working class (perhaps, as has been suggested, because social history has generally been written by labor historians and socialists). Asa Briggs has demonstrated that the language of class was at least as much the language

---

the title, Mill referred to "labouring classes," "working classes," "labouring people," "working men," and "the poor"—never to "lower classes," "lower class," or "lower orders." ("Inferior classes" appears once in these 45 pages.)[6]

of the middle classes as of the working classes—in the early decades of the century, probably more so—and that "middle classes" itself antedated "working classes" (although not "lower classes"). Moreover, the middle classes proudly took that designation for themselves. If the language of class is suggestive of the growth of "class consciousness" (a term of later Marxist origin), the middle classes may be presumed to have arrived at a consciousness of themselves—of their identity, interests, and aspirations—before the working classes did. Moreover, this middle class consciousness, Briggs suggests, may well have inspired a heightened working class consciousness, the working classes responding not only to their own problems, grievances, and demands, but to the success of the middle classes in asserting themselves.[11]

Neither the language of class nor the class consciousness reflected in that language necessarily implied a theory or policy of class struggle. The demands raised by the middle classes in the 1820s (free trade, fiscal reforms, legal reforms) did not present a threat to the working classes. Nor, at first, did the demand for parliamentary reform. Even the radicals committed to universal suffrage thought it possible to attain that end by cooperating with middle class reformers. In 1829 Thomas Attwood, busily promoting his paper currency scheme as well as parliamentary reform, formed an organization called the "Political Union of the Lower and Middle Classes of the People." A few months later Cobbett reported that everywhere he went he found the "middle class uniting with the working classes" for a reform bill that would enfranchise both.[12] The following year, with the reform crisis well under way, Lovett organized the "National Union of the Working Classes and Others." The "others" in the title provoked some debate at the time and was later tacitly dropped; but if the objections to it were significant, so was the fact that the word was initially inserted in the title in spite of those objections.

In the course of the 1830s, with the passage of one after another measure that radicals took to be in the interests of the middle classes and against the interests of the working classes—a Reform Act that enfranchised the former and not the latter, a New Poor Law that was popularly regarded as an "anti-poor" law, a Factory Act that fell short of the Ten Hours Bill —there was a rapid growth of both class consciousness and class antagonism.* Even those who were adamantly opposed to "physical force" were insistent upon class independence and class unity. When Lovett organized the successor to the National Union of the Working Classes (and the

---

*In a provocative study of the Reform Act and its effects, D. C. Moore refutes the conventional view that the middle classes came to "power" as a result of the act and that the reformed Parliament was a "middle class" Parliament. Instead, he sees the reform as designed to restore the traditional principles of representation and the primacy of the landed classes.[13] This thesis does not, however, dispute the fact that a good part of the middle classes felt excluded from the unreformed Parliament, that they agitated for the Reform Act, and that they were enfranchised (if not "empowered") by it.

forerunner, as it turned out, of Chartism), there was no question of adding "others" either to the title of the new organization or to the membership; the London Working Men's Association made it its avowed aim to confine itself "as far as practicable to the working classes."[14]

Historians have been so preoccupied with the problem of the "labor aristocracy," the relationship of the "superior artisan" to the rest of the working classes, that they have paid too little attention to the problem Lovett faced when he organized the London Working Men's Association: "where the line should be drawn which separates the working classes from the other portions of society"—from the middle classes, in short.[15] This difficulty was reflected in an ambiguity of language. During much of the first half of the century, "working classes" was used interchangeably with "labouring classes," "productive classes," "industrious classes," "useful classes." But for a good part of this time the latter three terms were also commonly applied to those of the middle classes who were engaged in industry—factory owners, for example. The terms were used in this sense not by aristocrats lumping together all the classes inferior to themselves, but by the middle classes themselves who were pleased to think of themselves as productive, industrious, and useful, and who proudly distinguished themselves from the landed aristocracy in these respects. There was the suggestion of Old Corruption radicalism in their flaunting of these terms, the implication that the aristocracy was unproductive, idle, and useless.

This connotation of "productive," "industrious," and "useful" classes had its rationale in Puritanism, mercantilism, and political economy, all of which put a premium on work and productivity and made capital and labor partners in the economic enterprise. It was also reflected in Adam Smith's famous statement: "I have classed artificers, manufacturers, and merchants among the productive labourers."[16] By the 1820s these "productive labourers" had become the "productive classes." It was in their name that the case for parliamentary reform was argued, by moderate reformers seeking to enfranchise the middle classes, and by radical reformers who wanted to enfranchise all the "productive" classes, including the working classes.

It remained for the "new" radicals of the thirties, whose animus was directed more against the middle classes than against the aristocracy, to try to dissociate the middle classes from such honorific terms as "productive," "industrious," and "useful," and reserve them exclusively for the working classes. *The Poor Man's Guardian* consistently used them as synonymous with the working classes, a usage that was itself an ideological statement, an assertion that the middle classes were not economically productive or socially useful, that the profits they claimed (except for a small part representing the wages of management) were an appropriation of the labor of the workers, and that they were as parasitic as Cobbett's Old Corruption types. By the end of the decade this restrictive usage, among radicals at any rate, was sufficiently common to permit the Chartists to name their convention "The General Convention of the Industrious Classes" and to submit their petitions on behalf of "the industrious classes of this country."[17] But even then the old usage persisted, so that it was not entirely eccentric of Carlyle to speak of the entrepreneur, the "captain of industry," as "productive" and "industrious" and to apply to him the term "master-worker" in contrast to the "non-working" aristocracy.[18]

If the language of class reflected the class consciousness of both the working and middle classes, and thus, potentially at least, a sense of class antagonism, the ambiguity of the language muted that effect. To the extent to which the middle classes were seen as "productive," "industrious," "useful," they were the natural allies of the working classes against the aristocracy. This was, in fact, how they appeared in 1842 to the "middle-class Chartists" in the Complete Suffrage Unions and to those working class Chartists (including such militants as O'Brien) who were prepared to join them in the movement for a new reform act.* So long as the language of class remained fluid, as it did until almost the last quarter of the century, that language implied a heightening of class consciousness but not necessarily an exacerbation of class conflict. Indeed the language lent itself, for those who wanted to avail themselves of it in this sense, to a mitigation of conflict, a collaboration between the working and middle classes, classes which were equally productive in the economy and useful in society, hence equally entitled to representation in the polity.

The adversary tone of the language of class was also mitigated by the plurality of classes. Even in its harshest form, in the rhetoric of *The Poor Man's Guardian* and of the Physical Force Chartists, it was generally the pluralized "working classes" who were pitted against the pluralized "middle classes." The consciousness of class, even when it involved a consciousness of class conflict, did not imply the kind of unity, the singleness of interest, purpose, and will, signified by a singular "working class" (still less by a singular "proletariat").

In the 1830s and 1840s, indeed well into the century, "working class" in the singular was relatively rare, much rarer than "middle class" in the singular.[19] As "middle classes" antedated "working classes," so "middle class" antedated "working class." When "working class" was singularized, it was sometimes because it was used in contraposition to "middle class." In 1830

---

*The power of words is suggested by the fate of this movement. The Complete Suffrage movement foundered on the single demand of the middle class members that the name "Charter," which for them was evocative of violence, be abandoned. But that name, even for so conciliatory and pacific a man as Lovett, was too precious to be given up, and he led his group out of the meeting, thus aborting what might have been a serious reform movement.

Cobbett reported that "the *middle class,* who always, heretofore, were arrayed, generally speaking, against the *working class,* are now with them." But in the very next sentence, having dropped that contraposition, he reverted to the more familiar "labourers." Earlier that year even a reference to "middle class" was not enough to produce the parallel "working class": "We see, at last, then, the middle class uniting with the working classes"; a few sentences later the "middle class" was said to be seeking the support of the "lower class."[20] Ten years later Place spoke of Hetherington's appeal to the Chartists to cooperate with the "middle class," since the "working people" by themselves would not be able to obtain the charter.[21] That conjunction of terms—a singular "middle class" and a plural "working classes" or "working people" —was typical even among the most radical groups.

If it is ironic that "working classes" should have been given currency by Owen, that notorious "class collaborationist" as the Marxist sees him, it is also ironic that the *Guardian,* which was as resolutely dedicated to the class struggle as any paper at the time, rarely if ever used the singular "working class" (although it did occasionally speak of the "middle class").[22] One leading article seemed to be preparing to make a large point of the singular form. "I have often," the editorial opened, "addressed you in the plural number. Allow me for once to address you in the singular." But the "singular" that was being addressed was the Grand National Consolidated Trades Union, and in the course of that editorial, it was the "working classes" who were said to be represented in that union.[23]

Engels, who gave "working class" the largest prominence it had until that time, was notably inconsistent in his usage. It may have been the title of his book, *The Condition of the Working Class in England in 1844,* that unwittingly imposed itself on later historians, inducing them to use the singular form more often than the contemporary evidence warranted. But in spite of his own conscious ideological bias in favor of a singular "working class," Engels himself could not entirely resist the weight of contemporary usage. The preface, originally written and published in English and intended for distribution in England, had "working classes" in the title and "working men" in the salutation. In the German preface he commented on the fact that the English habitually spoke of "middle classes" in the plural; that they even more commonly spoke of "working classes" in the plural could not have escaped him.[24] So far from validating a singular "working class," his book confirms the fact that that form was still, in the mid-forties, not at all common. And since the book was published in England only late in the century, the title could not have had any effect on contemporary usage. Indeed, after it was published (in the American although not yet the English edition), Sidney Webb cited it, in *Fabian Essays in Socialism,* as *Condition of the English Working Classes.* Such was the power of the conventional form even at that late date.[25]

To the Marxist who regards the "failure" to make the transition from "working classes" to "working class" as a failure of class consciousness, the frequent "lapses" from the language of class, the persistence of the old non-class vocabulary, are even more egregious. "Middle rank" and "middle ranks," or, vaguer still, "middling ranks," continued to be used by radicals as well as conservatives. James Mill, in his much discussed and criticized *Essay on Government*, argued that the majority of the people would always be guided by the "middle rank," the "most wise and the most virtuous part of the community."[26] The *Guardian* alternated between "middle classes" and "middlemen" or the "middling portion of the community"; and references to "working classes," "labouring classes," or "productive classes" were far fewer than to "working men," "working people," "labourers," "labouring men," "labouring people," "the people," "the poor." The latter terms, moreover, appeared even in those contexts where "working classes" might have been more appropriate and euphonious—in juxtaposition, for example, to "middle classes." A typical headline read, "No Confidence to be Placed in the Middle Classes as a Body—Necessity of Vigilance and Determination on the Part of the People."[27] Nor was it only in casual discourse, a hastily composed editorial or an improvised speech, that one finds a "regression" to traditional non-class terms. The titles of the radical organizations are revealing. One might have thought that the National Union of the Working Classes would have set a precedent for the later organizations. Instead its successor was the London Working Men's Association, which spawned the more militant East London Democratic Association and the Central National Association.

More striking were the names of the radical newspapers, *The Poor Man's Guardian* most notably. If "Guardian" in that title was intended ironically as a play upon the "Guardians of the Poor" who were charged with administering the poor law, "Poor Man" had no such ironic intent; nor did Cobbett's *Poor Man's Friend;* nor such unstamped papers as Hetherington's *'Destructive,' and Poor Man's Conservative, Poor Man's Advocate,* or *Poor Man's Paper.* Some variant of "worker" appeared in *Working Man's Advocate, Working Man's Friend,* and *Workman's Expositor.* But the most common term favored by the unstamped press (and some of the stamped) was "people": *People's Hue and Cry, People's Police Gazette, People's Weekly Dispatch, People's Weekly Police Gazette, Penny Papers for the People, Pamphlets for the People, Voice of the People, People's Conservative, People's Parliamentary Reporter, People's Press, People of England.* (When "people" did not appear in the title, it sometimes did in the subtitle, as in *The Poor Man's Guardian: A Weekly Paper for the People.*) It is also interesting that the middle class papers (and there were many unstamped among them) used the same terms to address their working class readers: the *Whig People's Friend,* the *Tory People's True Friend, Chambers's Information for the People, Poor Richard's*

Journal for Poor People.[28] None of the unstamped papers had "working classes," or any "classes," in the title.

If the increased use of the vocabulary of class signified the growth of class consciousness, the prevalent use of "people" signified the development of political consciousness. At first sight "people" might seem to be the least significant of terms, amorphous, banal, meaning anything or nothing. But even at its vaguest, it contained within it a radical potential that was at least as momentous as that implied by "class." Long before the appearance of "working classes," it was in the name of the "people" that universal suffrage had been demanded. And even when "people" was used in a more restrictive sense—when the Friends of the People, in its founding manifesto in 1792, called for a "more equal representation of the people," clearly intending something far more limited than the mass of the people[29]—the word itself, with all its ambiguities, pointed the way to a more comprehensive idea of "people" and a more egalitarian idea of representation.

"People" had always been a thoroughly ambiguous word. It ranged in meaning from the universal sense of mankind (Locke's "people" whose "lives, liberties, and estates" were secured by civil society);* to the "common people" in the sense of the "commonalty" as distinguished from the nobility (it was in this sense that the elder Pitt was the "Great Commoner"); to the electorate who constituted the "political nation"; and down to the lower orders of society, the "labouring people," "poor people," "mean people," "mere people."[31]

The most precise—or at least the most quantifiable—sense of "people" was the electorate, which was perhaps why Bentham used that definition in his *Constitutional Code:* "By the term *the people* is meant the whole number of persons, existing in any part of the territory of the State—such as are, at the moment of the time in question, admitted to act in the capacity of *electors.*"[32] It was also a concept that came naturally to politicians. When the younger Pitt dissolved Parliament in 1800 he explained, somewhat apologetically, "There may be occasions, but they will ever be few, when an appeal to the people is the just mode of proceeding on important subjects."[33] But even that idea of "the people" was far from precise, neither contemporaries nor historians knowing exactly the size of the electorate at any given time (or, for that matter, the size of the population). What was

---

*Locke's usage has been the subject of much controversy. C. B. Macpherson attributes to him so restrictive an idea of "people," and so property-minded an idea of "lives, liberties, and estates," that even in the state of nature (and still more in civil society) the propertyless are said to lack not only rights but full rationality and morality. Other commentators, attributing to Locke a more universal, generic sense of "people," and interpreting "property" as property in their lives and liberties as well as estates, find in his doctrine the basis for a democratic theory of politics, with everyone having the same claim to representation in the polity as in the society.[30]

known was that the electorate was a small part of the population. The "people" Pitt appealed to were perhaps six percent of the adult male population, and by the time Bentham wrote his *Code* in the twenties that proportion had declined. Even after the Reform Act, as radicals were fond of pointing out, only one-seventh of the adult male population qualified as electors.

More sensitive than Bentham to the nuances of language, and more respectful of them, Burke reflected in his writings the whole range of meanings commonly attributed to "people." In its most comprehensive usage, the people were members not of the polity but of "civil society," and were governed not by Parliament but by natural laws and a "natural aristocracy." "When multitudes act together, under that discipline of nature, I recognize the PEOPLE."[34] To the extent to which they had any political existence, it was by means of their "virtual" rather than "actual" representation in Parliament. Even when Burke interpreted "people" in a political sense, he did not mechanically equate them with the electorate. They were those "of adult age, not declining in life, of tolerable leisure for such discussions, and of some means of information, more or less, and who are above menial dependence (or what virtually is such)";[35] there were 400,000, he estimated, who fitted that description—a considerably larger number than the actual electorate at the time. Here, as in all his references to the "political nation," it was the moral and intellectual attributes of the people that gave them that political qualification. Even when he characterized them in economic or class terms, as "the great peers, the leading landed gentlemen, the opulent merchants and manufacturers, the substantial yeomanry," he went on to say that these were people who were "sensible of their own value," whose "opinion" was important, and who constituted the "natural strength of the kingdom."[36]*

Mediating between the people as "political nation" and the people as "civil society" were the "people out of doors." In 1779, at the height of the parliamentary reform movement, Charles James Fox announced to the House of Commons that "the people out of doors . . . possessed a right to declare their opinion of men and things, in order to do which they might meet and consult together, provided they did it in a peaceable, orderly manner."[38] On this issue, Burke agreed with Fox, defending the right of assembly as an essential part of the political process. No measure of reform, he insisted, should be considered until the "real sense of the people" was made known, for which purpose "open committees" should be formed in

---

*The narrowest definition of "people" emerged, not surprisingly, in the course of his polemic against the French revolutionists, who had driven into exile or opposition, he claimed, all the landed proprietors of France, some 70,000 in number. "I am sure, that if half that number of the same description were taken out of this country, it would leave hardly anything that I should call the people of England."[37]

which "no class or description of men is to be excluded."[39] That this was not a newfound principle designed to delay reform is suggested by his remarks a decade earlier when he had warned the king's faction not to "over-leap the fences of the law," lest that arbitrary act invite *the interposition of the body of the people itself*[40]—provocative language so soon after the Wilkes affair.

By the nineteenth century the "people out of doors" had become a recognized, quasi-official part of the political system. Unrepresented in Parliament, they "constituted" themselves, as it were, in extraparliamentary societies, committees, associations, conventions. Denied the franchise, they "voted" by means of petitions and demonstrations. The debate between the radical reformers and the moderates was in effect over the status of the people out of doors: the radicals sought to bring them indoors, into the formal political process; the moderates wanted to preserve the distinction between those who were full members of the political nation and those who had only a partial membership, whose voice was properly heard out of doors.

In the passion of that debate the people out of doors were often identified as the "populace," "mob," or "rabble." One of the most widely reported speeches was by Henry Brougham, the Lord Chancellor, who assured the House of Lords that the government had the entire support of "the people of this country"—"the people" as distinct from "the populace —the mob."

> But, if there is the mob, there is the people also, I speak now of the middle classes—of those hundreds of thousands of respectable persons —the most numerous, and by far the most wealthy order in the community; ... who are also the genuine depositaries of sober, rational, intelligent, and honest English feeling.[41]

The speech caused a furor among radicals, and Brougham became a byword for class privilege and arrogance.* The *Guardian* wrote a scathing article in which quotations from the speech were interspersed with sardonic commentaries on Brougham's "people," the wise and virtuous middle classes who wantonly plundered the hardworking "populace" that created all the wealth of the country. During the following year it repeatedly returned to this

---

*The speech created a sensation as much for its delivery as its content. Brougham's peroration was in his usual grandiloquent manner: "I warn you—I implore you—yea, on my bended knees, I supplicate you—reject not this Bill!" *The Times* reported that at this point Brougham "slightly bent his knee on the Woolsack." John Campbell, in his *Lives of the Lord Chancellors,* had him actually kneeling as if in prayer, and continuing in that unseemly position until his friends, "alarmed for him lest he should be suffering from the effects of the mulled port, picked him up and placed him safely on the woolsack." Although this version has since been discredited, it was only a slight exaggeration of reports widely circulated at the time.[42]

theme, citing Brougham's "contradistinction between people and populace" as if it encapsulated all the grievances of the working classes, of the "people" properly understood.[43]

The distinction between "people" and "populace" (the latter equated with "mob" or "rabble") had always been a sore point. Yet it was a distinction recognized by everyone, including radicals. Forty years earlier Paine accused Burke of charging a "whole people" with the "outrages" of the French Revolution. Those who committed these outrages—the assassinations and the parades through Paris with heads on pikes—were no more the people of France, Paine protested, than the Gordon rioters were the people of London or the Irish rioters the people of Ireland. They were the "populace," or "mob," the "lowest class of mankind" present in all countries of Europe because everywhere the people had been "debased" by their governments.[44] In fact Burke did not make the "whole people" of France responsible for these events; on the contrary, he attributed them precisely to the "mob," a band of ruffians whose passions were unleashed by the "metaphysicians" of the revolution.[45] In accusing Burke of identifying the people with the mob, Paine was really objecting to Burke's sense of "people," a people who neither sought nor required the "rights" Paine wanted to bestow upon them. The quarrel between Brougham and the *Guardian* was a reprise of that earlier debate, the *Guardian* accusing Brougham of debasing the "people," making of them a "populace" or "mob" by denying them the suffrage.*

From a Marxist point of view, "people" is a regressive term, suggesting an insufficiently developed class consciousness, a blurring of class distinctions and hence of class conflict. For the radicals of the 1830s, it was a highly charged word signifying a radical claim to power. It was in this sense that it was used in the titles of the unstamped papers, in editorials and manifestos calling for a popular suffrage, and in the "People's Charter." In one sense "people" was more radical than "working classes" or even "the working class." Evoking the idea of the "political nation," it would be satisfied with

---

*"Mass" and "masses" were less common at the time. They did not have the political implication of "people," nor quite the invidious intent of "mob," although they did sometimes carry a suggestion of mistrust or fear. For John Stuart Mill, "masses" had a largely cultural connotation, signifying the opinions, attitudes, tastes, and values of society as a whole, in contrast to the small group of people of superior wisdom and cultivation. In this sense the "masses" included the middle as well as the working classes—indeed, the former more than the latter because it was the middle classes who dominated public opinion. "With respect to knowledge and intelligence, it is the truism of the age, that the masses, both of the middle and even of the working classes, are treading upon the heels of their superiors."[46] Here, as in *On Liberty*—or Tocqueville's *Democracy in America,* or Matthew Arnold's *Culture and Anarchy*—the "masses" represented philistinism, mindless conformity, and a threat to individuality. Even when the Chartist William Lovett used "masses" in a more political context, it was their cultural and intellectual condition, their state of tutelage, that concerned him. Urging the creation of a working class organization, he deplored the fact that the "masses" had been taught to look up to "great men" instead of "great principles."[47]

nothing less than full membership in that nation. This was the implication of Place's comments a few days before the reform bill became law: "By the word 'people' when, as in this letter I use the word in a political sense, I mean those among them who take part in public affairs, by whom the rest *must* be governed."[48] Two years later *Pioneer*, the organ of the Grand National Consolidated Trades Union, gave "people" the same political meaning.

> Those who call themselves the liberal statesmen of the present day, must go progressively with the people; but in the word PEOPLE (a word very much misunderstood) they must, brethren, include *us*, the productive labourers, for what are the people without us? . . . The people have a political position, but we have none that we can make any use of with benefit to ourselves.[49]

If "people" had the rhetorical effect of politicizing the issue for the radicals of the thirties, it also served to enlarge the scope of the "social problem," to make it more comprehensive than it would have been had it been formulated exclusively in terms of the "working classes." For included in the "people" were all the "poor," not only the "productive labourers" who qualified as "working classes," but also those who did not work or were not notably productive: the young and the old, the unemployed and the irregularly employed, the "dependent" as much as the "independent" poor. For these groups the language of class was not especially appropriate. Yet they occupied a large place in the social reality and in the social consciousness of contemporaries. At a time when the poor law was a major social issue, the poor-*cum*-pauper had to be accommodated in the social vocabulary. The *Guardian*, dedicated to a "new ideology" that defined the social problem in terms of property and political equality, could regard the poor law as a peripheral issue, a minor incident in the class struggle. But those not committed to that ideology (and most radicals were not) had to address the problem of pauperism more directly.

Here again the comprehensive nature of Chartism revealed itself. Drawing upon the anti-poor law movement as much as upon the trade union and political reform movements, Chartism reflected in its vocabulary that larger constituency. If it was appropriate that the Charter be called "The People's Charter," it was also fitting that the first point of the Charter should read: "A vote for every man twenty-one years of age, of sound mind, and not undergoing punishment for crime."[50] Modern historians, commenting on this point, may be more sensitive than contemporaries were to those excluded by that provision—women. But at least as notable were those included by it—the paupers.[51]

The proposal to enfranchise the paupers was all the more striking precisely because of those who were not to be enfranchised—women, minors, criminals, and the insane—all of whom were presumed to be naturally, legitimately disqualified, unlike the paupers who were not. It was also a reproach to the Reform Act which had made a point of disfranchising the paupers. The thirty-sixth clause of the act, disqualifying anyone who had received parish relief during the year, was in one sense gratuitous, since such a person would in any case have been disqualified by the £10 clause. Yet it was an important statement of principle, for it gave notice to future reformers that whatever the franchise might be—and there were those who suspected that the Reform Act would not be the "final" measure that Russell declared it to be—the dependent poor should be excluded by virtue of their dependency alone, even if they should happen to meet the franchise qualification. (The pauper disqualification clause was finally eliminated in 1918, at the same time that women were enfranchised.) By the same token, the radicals made it a point of principle to include paupers within the community of the poor, to identify all the poor as the people, and to bestow upon them all the political rights that properly belonged to the political nation. It is here that the opposition to the Reform Act and to the New Poor Law coalesced. The Reform Act, as the radicals saw it, denied to the poor the right of citizenship, of membership in the polity; the New Poor Law denied to the poor the right of subsistence, of membership in society. Against that double disfranchisement, the radicals put forward the claims of the "people" —a comprehensive body which included workers of every description and the poor in every condition of poverty.

In this sense the old language, the language of "people" and "poor," was more radical than the new language of class. A "Working Class Charter" would not necessarily have enfranchised the very poor, still less the non-working poor. There might well, in fact, have been a presumption against their enfranchisement, just as the Marxist category of "proletariat" was to create a presumption against their inferiors, the "lumpenproletariat."[52] It was in the name of the "poor" that a greater measure of social welfare was demanded, and in the name of the "people" that a greater measure, indeed a complete measure, of political equality was demanded.

In urging the significance of the language of class, Asa Briggs has reminded us that this subject is not an "academic exercise in semantics," that the new language "reflected a basic change not only in men's ways of viewing society but in society itself."[53] If this is so, the persistence of the old language, long after the new had become available, must also be significant. Nor can it be dismissed merely as a "cultural lag," the residue of old habits of speech which die hard. There is always some dissonance between language and reality, even between language and the perception of reality. But there is also a good measure of correspondence, especially on the part of contemporaries who were consciously intent upon changing reality and deliberately casting about for theories and policies designed to effect that change. If the language of class did not take hold more firmly, if "workmen," "people," and "poor" continued to dominate even the radical literature, if plural classes prevailed over singular ones, this must tell us something about the way people thought about society and about society itself.

To a Marxist, the coexistence of the old and the new language suggests a defective sense of reality on the part of contemporaries, a "false consciousness."[54] To others it may suggest that both the reality and the contemporary perception of the reality were well served by that amalgam of languages. The ideological eclecticism of Chartism, Briggs has said, was one of its great sources of strength.[55] So, one may argue, the linguistic eclecticism of the age was a source of strength for radicals and non-radicals alike. If contemporaries did not define their terms precisely or use them consistently, if they did not insist upon the language of class or make the transition from plural classes to singular ones, it was not because they were thoughtless or unimaginative but because they were undoctrinaire and realistic. The age of Bentham and Mill, Cobbett and Carlyle, was hardly an age of intellectual or rhetorical timidity. It was, in fact, a time of great linguistic innovation, when neologisms were freely coined and circulated, when polemic was notably uninhibited, and when social discourse, at every level and in every form, was richer and more expressive than ever before (and, perhaps, ever since). Essayists, journalists, polemicists, publicists, politicians, were adept at making language do what they wanted it to do. One can only suppose that what they chose to do with it was adequate to their needs, faithful to their ideas and sensibilities, consonant with the reality as they understood it.

"For the purposes of the historian," E. J. Hobsbawm has said, "class and the problem of class consciousness are inseparable. Class in the full sense only comes into existence at the historical moment when classes begin to acquire consciousness of themselves as such."[56] That comes to us with the authority of an eminent Marxist historian. If it can also be assumed that consciousness expresses itself in language and ideas as well as behavior, it would follow that early nineteenth century England was not a fully developed class society. It was not the two-class society of Engels—proletariat and bourgeoisie; nor the three-class society of the political economists—landlords, capitalists, and laborers; nor the four- or five-class society proposed by recent historians (the four-class model featuring a professional as well as an entrepreneurial middle class, the five-class model two working classes and two middle classes).[57] On some occasions and for some purposes it seemed to approximate one or another of these class schemata. But it took other forms as well. It was a society of rich and poor, of the respectable and unrespectable, of town and country, of the provinces and the metropolis.

It was also a society that was becoming increasingly individualistic at the very time that it was becoming increasingly class conscious, an individualism that expressed itself in the language of "artisans," "labourers," "operatives," "mechanics," "workers," "workingmen."

Language is obviously not a sufficient guide to social reality, not even to the reality of social consciousness. But taken in conjunction with other facts, it is an important social indicator. In this case the eclectic, pluralist nature of the language points to a changing, mobile society with broadly conceived, heterogeneous classes, in which class consciousness did not necessarily imply an unremitting class struggle, still less a revolutionary class consciousness and struggle.*

*The old "classical" Marxism, having little regard for "consciousness" (except as a "reflection" of material reality or part of the "superstructure" of society), leaves the Marxist historian free to impose his categories upon the past without reference to the ideas or attitudes of contemporaries, whose consciousness can be dismissed as a form of "false consciousness." The new Marxism, supposedly deriving from the "young Marx," puts a greater burden both on the idea of consciousness and on the historian, who has to validate his theories of class by evidence of the class consciousness of contemporaries. This presents a problem for those historians who, following the example of Engels, posit the existence of a single English working class during this period. E. J. Hobsbawm, who holds class and class consciousness to be "inseparable," claims that "the very words 'working class' (as distinct from the less specific 'the working classes') occurs in English labour writings shortly after Waterloo, and perhaps even earlier."[58] But the essay by Asa Briggs that he cites does not bear out this contention, and he himself has not tried to demonstrate it; nor does he confront the fact that the relatively few singular forms in that period were vastly outweighed by the plural forms, even among the most militant radicals.

E. P. Thompson, whose main thesis is the emergence by 1832 of a single, united, self-conscious, potentially revolutionary working class, also comments on the unsatisfactoriness of the plural form. " 'Working classes' is a descriptive term, which evades as much as it defines. It ties loosely together a bundle of discrete phenomena." It evades, that is, the essential point of his thesis, which is that there were not "discrete phenomena" (workers) but a single "*historical* phenomenon" (a working class), and that this phenomenon was displayed in the "raw material of experience and in consciousness." Yet in spite of his own superb literary facility and his sensitivity to the rhetoric of contemporaries (as when he locates Cobbett's significance in his tone and style rather than his actual beliefs), he rarely presents the "raw material" of linguistic evidence which goes against his thesis. On one of the few occasions when he can cite the singular form he calls the reader's attention to it: "Note the early use of 'working class'." But there are few such instances in the thousands of quotations in his book, and the many examples of the plural pass without mention.[59]

PART THREE

"THE UNDISCOVERED
COUNTRY OF THE POOR"

XIV

THE "CULTURE OF POVERTY"

1. London: A Special Case

"Hell is a city much like London—a populous and a smoky city." Thus Shelley in 1819, voicing the familiar pastoral lament.[1] By the middle of the century Shelley would have had more reason to complain, for the population of London continued to grow at twice the national rate. During the first half of the century, while the population of the country as a whole doubled, that of London tripled; of the 18,000,000 people in England and Wales in 1851, London had over 2,350,000, more than one-eighth of the whole. (Paris, the next largest city in the world, doubled in the same period, bringing its population up to 1,000,000 by mid-century—but that was only one-thirty-fifth of the total population of France.) This unprecedented increase in population coincided with the building of the railroads and the laying out of new streets, which put even greater strains on the most densely populated and poorest areas—the slums, or "rookeries," as they were commonly known.*

"A populous and a smoky city." The most populous but not the smokiest, the mining and mill towns of the midlands and north competing for that distinction. Smoky enough, however, partly because of its populousness. Millions of open fires spewed out their fumes (and much of their heat) through as many chimney pots, producing that yellow fog which seems romantic in retrospect but was in fact a noxious form of pollution.

* "Rookery" was the more common word through much of the century. It derived from the "rookery," or rook's nest, that was the breeding place for that unattractive, harsh-voiced bird. The unsavory connotation of the word was reinforced by the verb "to rook," meaning to cheat or swindle, and by the noun "rook," a thief or swindler, or the crowbar used in housebreaking. ("Rook" in this sense went back to Elizabethan times.) More recent was "slum," which first appeared in Vaux's *Flash Dictionary* in 1812 ("flash" also meaning "thief"). "Slum" had at first a somewhat more innocuous meaning than "rookery"; supposedly derived from "slumber," it designated a "sleepy, unknown back alley." In 1850, Cardinal Wiseman complained of the "congealed labyrinths of lanes and courts, and alleys and slums" near Westminster Abbey.[2]

A good measure of that smoke was also contributed by the railroads, gasworks, and manufacturing establishments of the city. The industrial character of Victorian London tends to be overshadowed by the other qualities of the metropolis and by the more striking industrial development in other parts of the country. But even in this respect London retained its primacy. In the middle of the century it was still the major manufacturing center of England, more diversified than Manchester or Birmingham and in this sense less dramatic, but that very diversity provided its own drama.[3]

London was an invitation to superlatives. It was the largest center of industry, the largest port, the largest provider of services, the largest concentration of consumers, the largest source of all those needs, demands, and fancies that kept busy the "dark satanic mills" of the midlands and the "sweated workshops" of the East End.* It was also the political, cultural, and social center of the country, creating and disseminating the ideas and values that were reflected in the literature, legislation, and institutions of the age. The "provinces" had their distinctive cultures, but they were distinctively, consciously, sometimes aggressively provincial. London had a "moral density" (in Emile Durkheim's expressive phrase) commensurate with its "material density," a critical mass of intellectual and social consciousness that gave it a unique position and power.[4]

London was unique, for good and ill. If Shelley saw it as an unmitigated "hell" and Cobbett as a "great wen," a malignant excrescence on the body politic, there were those for whom it was an unfailing source of pride and delight, even its offenses being so outsized as to evoke perverse admiration. It was common to speak of London as a microcosm of England, of the world, indeed of civilization, exhibiting in heightened form all the virtues and vices of modernity. One writer managed to find cause for celebration even in its smoke, "the sublime canopy that shrouds the City of the World."[5] Others adduced the familiar metaphor of the heart and the body. "It is the centre, to which and from which the lines are radiating, which connect it with every point in the circumference: it is the heart to which and from which the life-blood circulates through every artery and vein of the entire body."[6]†

---

*Blake's "dark Satanic Mills" is generally taken to be a condemnation of the cotton factories. In the preface to *Milton,* where the phrase appears, it refers to the universities and intellectual establishments which worshipped the false gods of Homer and Ovid, Plato and Cicero, instead of the Bible, Shakespeare, and Milton. The image of the mill, here and in his other poems, derives not from the cotton mill but from the iron and steel mills producing the weapons of war. It was militarism more than industrialism that exercised Blake.

†In one sense, London was less a center of England than Paris was of France. The English had proudly and successfully resisted the kind of centralization that France had always been prone to and that had been much intensified under Napoleon. The difference between the two countries might be symbolized by the location of their major universities—Oxford and Cambridge, the Sorbonne and the Ecole Polytechnique. Yet it was, paradoxically, the Englishman's much vaunted attachment to land and locality, his resistance to centralization and suspicion of the metropolis, that made the

In the 1830s and 1840s, when both the material and the moral "dynamic" (again, Durkheim's term) were at their height, London seemed more than ever to be at the heart of things. This was true even of those matters that were not peculiar to London. The impact of Chartism, for example, was far greater in the provinces than in London. Yet it was London that gave birth to the movement and was the scene of its demise. Similarly the condition-of-England question was more urgent for the industrial north than for London. But it was London that brought that problem to the attention of the rest of the country, dramatized and publicized it, and proposed to alleviate it. The seat of Parliament, the location of the major newspapers and journals, the home of social critics, social reformers, and social commentators, London was the center of the newest "growth industry," one that was not listed in the official census returns but that was well known to contemporaries—the reform industry.

As London was the political, the financial, the commercial, the social, and the cultural capital of England, so it was also the "capital of poverty." It was the poorest city, if only because it was the richest. "Real poverty," André Gide once said, "is that of cities, because it is there such a close neighbor to the excesses." This too was London's distinction: it was the city of excesses par excellence. An American visitor in 1849, eulogizing London as the "heart of the great world," was overwhelmed by both its grandeur and its poverty. "In the midst of the most extraordinary abundance, here are men, women, and children dying of starvation; and running alongside of the splendid chariot, with its gilded equipages, its silken linings, and its liveried footmen, are poor, forlorn, friendless, almost naked wretches, looking like the mere fragments of humanity."[7] In London the "two nations" lived in the closest proximity—and were separated by the most impassable gulf.

The coexistence of poverty and riches was the least of the paradoxes for which London was famous. Another was the anomaly familiar to the ancients: *Magna civitas, magna solitudo*. The vision of a city so crowded that its very atmosphere was fetid—Rousseau meant it literally when he said that in the city "man's breath is deadly to his kind"[8]—was superimposed upon another image which had each man totally isolated from the neighbor who pressed so hard upon him, completely immersed in his own interests, absorbed by an *amour propre* that left no room for human compassion or social affections. Here, where each had most need of all, the "war of each against all" was being waged most ruthlessly.

---

physical growth of London and its magnetic attraction all the more striking. The University of London was never a threat to the intellectual hegemony of Oxford and Cambridge, but its founding in 1828 had a symbolic significance that far outweighed its institutional importance. Blake, Carlyle, and Cobbett all ranted about the "infernal wen" while comfortably ensconced there (just as Rousseau praised Geneva while yearning for Paris).

The rookery was the symbol of that war, of a state of anarchy in which the only law was the law of the jungle. The metaphors were familiar: the rookeries were "breeding grounds" for vice and disease, "schools" of crime and immorality. Inculcating no moral or religious habits, imposing no check on natural passions and inclinations, they gave the residents, as one contemporary critic put it, "a licence to do evil." Yet that critic also pointed out that there were in fact far fewer criminals in London than was commonly thought, less than one percent of the population. "It is the exception," he noted, "rather than the mass, which is thus putrid."[9] But the exception was enough to putrefy the whole, to create the impression of a massive rookery in which crime and disease were as rampant as poverty. For Robert Southey the image conjured up by London was of a wilderness swarming with every kind of physical and moral pestilence, of misery and vice.

> London is the heart of your commercial system but it is also the hot-bed of corruption. It is at once the centre of wealth and the sink of misery; the seat of intellect and empire, . . . and yet a wilderness wherein they, who live like wild beasts upon their fellow creatures, find prey and cover. . . . Ignorance and misery and vice are allowed to grow, and blossom and seed, not on the waste alone, but in the very garden and pleasure ground of society and civilisation.[10]

There were counter-images, to be sure. In contrast to the spectacle of a swarming mass of people without community, there was the vision of a city composed of many small communities, the poorest of which, precisely because they were so crowded, were the most neighborly; even the rookery evoked the fantasy of a fraternity happily united in crime. Where some saw the coexistence of wealth and poverty as the dramatic evidence of social injustice, a standing invitation to envy, discontent, and dissension, others saw it as a means of social amelioration, the luxuries of the rich providing employment and sustenance for the poor and thus the opportunity to "better themselves." The *amour propre* which Rousseau took to be the great vice of mankind, a vice that flourished especially in the modern city, was transmuted by Smith into the benign "self-interest" which, properly understood, became the most reliable (if unexalted) of social virtues and the most effective (if invisible) of social bonds. In "socializing" political economy, Smith also "socialized" the city.

One of Smith's disciples, Frederick Eden, defended the city against Rousseau. "Why is it," he quoted Rousseau, "that in a thriving city, the Poor are so miserable, while such extreme distress is hardly ever experienced in those countries where there are no instances of immense wealth?"[11] To which Eden gave the un-Rousseauean answer that the poor were poorer in the city because they were freer there. Unlike the agricultural laborer who was assured against want but only at the cost of his liberty (his freedom to move to another parish) and of his independence (his self-sufficiency), the town worker was free and independent—and, by the same token, more vulnerable and less secure in times of want. The poor themselves, Eden was convinced, preferred freedom even at the price of security. "A prisoner under the custody of his keeper, may perhaps be confident of receiving his bread and his water daily; yet, I believe, there are few who would not, even with the contingent possibility of starving, prefer a precarious chance of subsistence, from their own industry, to the certainty of regular meals in a gaol."[12] This defense of the city—the freedom to starve rather than the servitude of being fed—was not, to be sure, much of a recommendation; and it was hardly what Smith had in mind when he extolled freedom.

At a time when the condition of man was a subject of much agonizing, the condition of urban man, and of the Londoner particularly, began to be seen as the condition of modern man *in extremis:* spiritually and morally impoverished, anonymous, isolated, "alienated." So, too, the London poor seemed to be afflicted with a kind of poverty *in extremis,* a poverty that made them not so much a class apart, or even a "nation" apart (as in the "two nations" image), as a "race" apart. In fact the London poor were no poorer than the poor elsewhere and may even have been, on the average, less poor (although the poorest of them, the Spitalfields silk weavers, were in as depressed a state as any laborers in the country). Nor was the "anomie" of London life as severe or pervasive as has been made out; neighborhoods, streets, workshops, even public houses, generated distinctive loyalties, sentiments, and associations. Still, there was unquestionably an acute sense of uprootedness experienced by large numbers of immigrants from the countryside and Ireland, by workers displaced from their old crafts and having to seek new occupations (silk weavers, for example, driven to the docks), and by families disoriented in unfamiliar surroundings.

Thus London, the least typical of places with the least typical kinds of poverty, somehow became archetypical. Not that any kind of poverty was "typical." Contemporaries were well aware that the kinds of poverty were as various as the degrees, that rural poverty was significantly different from urban, the poverty in a textile mill from that of a mining village, the poverty of a declining trade from that of a stable one, the poverty of old age from that of youth. Yet by the middle of the century the problem of poverty was more and more identified with the city, and, paradoxically, with that most uncommon city, the city beyond compare, the metropolis.

London became the "capital of poverty" in part by default, at a time when poverty ceased to be an urgent problem in the rest of the country. By the middle of the century, the general improvement in the economy and a series of melioratory measures had removed the condition-of-England question from the center of public attention. If the 1840s were never quite the "Bleak Age," nor the 1850s the "Golden Age," some historians have made them out to be, there was nevertheless a conspicuous improvement in the condition and morale of the poor.[13] Yet just at this time, when social tensions were abating, when there were no sensational Royal Commission reports and no dramatic demonstrations of popular discontent, attention turned to London, where an attentive observer might find, in the midst of unparalleled riches and unmistakable progress, new social problems and new forms of poverty. If Manchester was the "shock city" of the forties, London was the "shock city" of the fifties, a new challenge to the social imagination and conscience.

In part London attained that dubious distinction because of the assiduous efforts of one of the most remarkable chroniclers of the time, Henry Mayhew. Mayhew was a one-man Royal Commission. His methods of inquiry were somewhat unorthodox (but so were those of some of the Royal Commissioners), and his work was profoundly ambiguous in its intentions and implications. Yet he succeeded in popularizing a new idea and image of poverty, a poverty that was not so much an economic phenomenon as a cultural one—a "culture of poverty," as we have since learned to call it.

2. Henry Mayhew: Discoverer of the "Poor"

It was in the autumn of 1849 that Henry Mayhew launched the series of articles that did more to focus attention upon poverty in London than any other single work. Until December 1850 the articles appeared in the *Morning Chronicle,* and then until February 1852 as weekly pamphlets (some of which were bound and issued as two volumes in 1851–52); a pamphlet series was briefly resumed in 1856; and the four-volume *London Labour and the London Poor* was published in 1861–62 and reprinted in 1864–65.[14]

Mayhew was a journalist, novelist, playwright, editor, humorist, satirist, moralist, commentator, advertiser, children's writer, travel writer, amateur scientist, and entrepreneur of sorts—of a rather unconventional sort, specializing in such schemes as the production of artificial diamonds. His father was a prosperous London solicitor who thoroughly disapproved of him (to the point, eventually, of disinheriting him) and who was heartily disliked in turn. But some of his brothers (there were seventeen children in all) were more congenial: the oldest, Thomas, was the editor of Hetherington's *Penny Papers* and *The Poor Man's Guardian* until he committed suicide in 1834; Horace was with Henry on the staff of *Punch;* and Augustus was a frequent collaborator.[15]

To some of his associates Mayhew appeared as the classic type of *Luftmensch,* a great schemer who never carried his schemes to completion.

One remembered him as "a genius, a fascinating companion, and a man of inexhaustible resource and humor," but felt obliged to add that "indolence was his besetting sin, and his will was untutored."[16] Yet, while many of his projects were left unfinished, "indolence" hardly seems the right word for someone who produced as much as he did, and sometimes at breathtaking speed. If much of his work was incomplete and ephemeral, that was the nature of his trade; he was primarily a journalist, not, as we have come to think of him, a sociologist or historian. What is remarkable, and what distinguished him from his colleagues, was the ambitiousness of some of his projects.

Mayhew's first important job, in the 1830s, was as editor of the satirical journal *Figaro in London*. That experience brought him into the small group that founded *Punch* in July 1841.[17] After serving as co-editor for a few months, he became an occasional contributor when Mark Lemon assumed the sole editorship late that year. (Another *Punch* writer, Douglas Jerrold, was his father-in-law.) In the early forties when Mayhew wrote for it, *Punch* was at its most radical, satirizing and commenting on political and social issues as well as featuring the comic trivia that later became its stock-in-trade. It has been suggested that Mayhew was largely responsible for the radical tone of the magazine during these years, a supposition that derives largely from Mayhew's subsequent career.[18] But it could as easily be argued that he was influenced by *Punch* rather than the reverse. One of *Punch*'s early coups was the publication of Thomas Hood's "Song of the Shirt," the famous poem of social protest which is said to have trebled the circulation of the magazine. According to one account, Lemon published it over the protests of the other contributors, including Mayhew.[19] The lesson of that episode could not have been lost on someone like Mayhew, who was so responsive to popular culture and whose livelihood was so dependent on it. This is not to say that he and others on the magazine were not genuinely interested in social issues and moved by social distress. It only suggests that they were primarily professional writers rather than publicists for a cause, and that the condition-of-England question was the liveliest journalistic subject at the time. The most serious political thinker on the staff (Mayhew himself was not a staff member, and had little to do with policy decisions) was Jerrold; it was he who had written the article in *Punch* on the meager earnings of a seamstress which had inspired Hood's "Song of the Shirt." Thus apart from the familial relationship, it was fitting that Mayhew should have dedicated to Jerrold the first volume of *London Labour and the London Poor*.

If Mayhew was not responsible for the social criticism of *Punch*, neither was he for that of the *Morning Chronicle*, with which he later became associated. When he started to write for the *Chronicle* in the summer of 1849, the paper had long since acquired a reputation for vigorous social and political commentary; among its more distinguished contributors were

Dickens and Hazlitt in the thirties and John Stuart Mill reporting on Ireland in the forties. It is difficult to know whether Mayhew was attracted to the paper because of the opportunity to write on such subjects, or whether he took whatever job came to hand and applied his versatile talents to it. He himself later claimed that he originated the idea for the series on the laboring poor, a contention disputed by the editor of the *Chronicle* and by one of the other correspondents. What is beyond dispute is the fact that while the genre itself—"investigative reporting," as it is now called—was well established by the time Mayhew came to it, his was the most ambitious private effort of its kind.

Mayhew's series in the *Chronicle* was inspired by an earlier article by him on the cholera epidemic. The disease, which had appeared sporadically throughout England (and more seriously on the Continent) in 1848, returned with a vengeance the following year, taking 20,000 lives in the rest of the country and another 15,000 in London (almost 4,000 in the City alone). It reached the metropolis in the summer of 1849, peaking in mid-September. Readers of the daily death count were beginning to take comfort in the declining figures when the *Chronicle* on September 24 published an unsigned article, "A Visit to the Cholera Districts of Bermondsey." Most of the article (3,500 words, two and a half long columns in small type) was devoted to the infamous slum known as Jacob's Island. It was there, in the "Capital of Cholera" as Mayhew called it, that the epidemic had first struck in 1832, and there that Dickens had located the grisly scene of Bill Sikes's death in *Oliver Twist*. If Dickens had been inspired by newspaper accounts of that earlier epidemic, it is probable that Mayhew was now inspired by Dickens to visit that notorious site. The result was an account that almost rivaled Dickens's in its grotesqueness.

Jacob's Island was dominated by the ditch that ran through it, an open sewer covered with scum and grease, filled with the refuse from the privies lining its bank, with an occasional swollen, putrefied carcass of an animal floating on the surface, all of which emitted the noxious vapors and "mephitic gases" that were presumed to be the cause of the epidemic. In grisly detail Mayhew described the inhabitants of the area (some of whose houses actually spanned the ditch), who breathed those deadly fumes, drank and washed in that foul water, and died in their hovels, their bodies left unattended for days. The editor of *Fraser's Magazine* was not being unduly squeamish when he said that he could not quote the article because it was "too loathsome to trust to the chance of its being read aloud."[20] Other journals and newspapers were less fastidious and did reprint some of the more shocking passages.

The article attracted a good deal of attention and gave rise to the ambitious idea of a series on "Labour and the Poor." The idea may have

been prompted by Mayhew's suggestion that there was a correlation between the incidence of disease and the geography of poverty.

> Indeed, so well known are the localities of fever and disease, that
> London would almost admit of being mapped out pathologically, and
> divided into its morbid districts and deadly cantons. We might lay our
> fingers on the Ordnance map, and say here is the typhoid parish, and
> there the ward of cholera; for truly as the West-end rejoices in the title
> of Belgravia, might the southern shores of the Thames be christened
> Pestilentia. As season follows season, so does disease follow disease in
> the quarters that may be more literally than metaphorically styled the
> plague-spots of London.[21]

· · ·

"Labour and the Poor" was inaugurated in the *Chronicle* on October 18,
1849, prefaced by an editorial note explaining that the series would give "a
full and detailed description of the moral, intellectual, material, and physical
condition of the industrial poor throughout England." There were to be
three sets of "letters" running on successive days: one on the rural communities, another on the manufacturing and mining areas, and a third on London.
Together, the editor hoped, they would equal or even surpass the parliamentary reports in "impartiality, authenticity, and comprehensiveness," and
would provide the facts with which an "energetic Government and an
enlightened Legislature" could improve the condition of the poor.

The initial article, by the "special correspondent" in Manchester
(Angus Reach, as we know from other sources), makes for an interesting
comparison with Mayhew's on London the following day. Promising to put
aside political and economic issues in order to concentrate on the "immediate
influences" affecting the workers, the reporter proposed to accompany them
to their looms, mines, and forges, their rooms, cellars, and cottages, to
observe the conditions under which they lived and worked, the effect on
their bodies and minds, their religious beliefs, reading habits, amusements,
family ties, sexual relationships, and political views. The latter prompted a
long defense of the Ten Hours Act and an even longer attack on the political
economists for exacerbating the relations between rich and poor. But if the
economists were wrong to set class against class, Reach thought their opponents equally misguided in their nostalgia for an idyllic rural England free
of the abominations of factory and city. The poet who longed for the "dewy
call of incense breathing morn" rather than the "dismal clank of the factory
bell" had not considered the man with a family to feed who preferred to
earn twelve shillings in noisy, smoky Manchester rather than six shillings
in the dewy fields of Wiltshire. To purify the air of Manchester was to

quench its furnaces and deprive its inhabitants of their dinners. Moreover, those sunlit hills and vales concealed a poverty more grinding and hopeless than was to be found in the cellars and garrets of Manchester. Whatever the faults of political economy, Reach concluded, it had helped create the industry that was the source of the prosperity and happiness of the entire country and even of the entire world. "Now it is for Social Economy to play its part—to investigate diligently into the condition, the comforts, the mode of work and of life, of our factory population, and to devise and to urge every possible means for the amelioration of their lot."[22]

Mayhew's article on London the following day was in one sense more ambitious. Where Reach proposed to treat the subject existentially, so to speak, describing the effects of the manufacturing system upon "the workman and the workwoman" in terms of their environment and relationships, their habits and opinions, Mayhew undertook to give an analytic account of "the poor of London" in terms of the different classes of poor and the different causes of poverty.

> Under the term poor I shall include all those persons whose incomings are insufficient for the satisfaction of their wants—a want being, according to my idea, contra-distinguished from a mere desire by a positive physical pain, instead of a mental uneasiness, accompanying it. The large and comparatively unknown body of people included in this definition I shall contemplate in two distinct classes, viz., the *honest* and *dishonest* poor; and the first of these I purpose subdividing into the striving and the disabled—or, in other words, I shall consider the whole of the metropolitan poor under three separate phases, according as they *will* work, they *can't* work, and they *won't* work.[23]

Those who *"will* work" were further subdivided into those who received relief and those who did not, and the latter into the "improvident" and the "poorly-paid." As Mayhew warmed to his subject, especially the case of the poorly-paid, he became more impassioned, promising to inquire into the causes of their inadequate income and miserable conditions, the exorbitant rent they paid for their "waterless, drainless, floorless, and almost roofless tenements," and the usurious interest exacted by the "petty capitalist" (the pawnbroker). At this point, however, he hastened to reassert his objectivity. However sensitive he was to the wrongs done to the poor, he would not be misled by a "morbid sympathy" into seeing them only as the victims of other people's selfishness. "Their want of prudence, want of temperance, want of energy, want of cleanliness, want of knowledge, and want of morality, will each be honestly set forth."

Having laid out the plan of the series, Mayhew went on to the subject of the introductory article: the extremes of wealth and poverty, power and weakness, knowledge and ignorance, which existed side by side in London, and, more startling still, the extremes of charity and poverty. The main distinction of the present age, he found, was not the steam-engine, the railroad, or the telegraph, but the "fuller and more general development of the human sympathies," especially toward the poor. Anyone nostalgic for the "good old times" should contemplate the reign of "bluff King Hal," when 72,000 thieves and rogues were hanged, twice as many as had been felled by the recent plague; or the act in the reign of Henry VIII which stipulated the penalties for the "sturdy beggar": whipping for the first offense, cropping of the right ear for the second, and jail for subsequent offenses; or more recent times when people found their pleasure in bull-baiting and badger-baiting, dog fights and cock fights. Instead of those sports, there were now laws and societies for the prevention of cruelty to animals, and in place of bear-gardens and cock-pits there were a "thousand palaces" to cater to every variety of want, ill, or benevolent impulse: societies for the visitation of the sick, the cure of the maimed, the alleviation of the pains of childbirth, the reformation of juvenile offenders and prostitutes, the suppression of vice, and so on and on.[24] As the list unrolled, the tone became unmistakably sarcastic, almost as if Mayhew were writing a squib for *Figaro* or *Punch.* Yet his original point about the growth of the spirit of benevolence had been serious enough. Perhaps it was the vision of all those "palatial institutions," of nobles and lords giving up their sponsorship of prizefights to assume the presidency of philanthropic societies, that brought to the surface his ingrained suspicion of reformers and philanthropists. The £15,000,000 expended each year on charity suggested to him not only the "liberal extent of our sympathy" but the enormous want and suffering requiring such large expenditures of charity and the still more enormous wealth that could afford them.

Much of the article had the character of a "set piece," the discourse on the contrasts of wealth and want being the staple of this genre. But an occasional vignette was pure Mayhew.

At night it is that the strange anomalies of London are best seen. Then, as the hum of life ceases and the shops darken and the gaudy gin palaces thrust out their ragged and squalid crowds, to pace the streets, London puts on its most solemn look of all. On the benches of the parks, in the niches of the bridges, and in the litter of the markets, are huddled together the homeless and the destitute. The only living thing that haunts the streets are the poor wretches who stand shivering in their finery, waiting to catch the drunkard as he goes shouting homewards. Here on a doorstep crouches some shoeless child, whose day's begging has not brought it enough to purchase it even the twopenny bed that its young companions in beggary have gone to. There, where the stones

are taken up and piled high in the centre of the street in a flag of flame
—there, round the red glowing coke fire, are grouped a ragged crowd
smoking or dozing through the night beside it. Then, as the streets
grow blue with the coming light, and the church spires and chimney
tops stand out against the sky with a sharpness of outline that is seen
only in London before its million fires cover the town with their pall
of smoke—then come sauntering forth the unwashed poor, some with
greasy wallets on their back, to haunt over each dirt heap, and eke out
life by seeking refuse bones or stray rags and pieces of old iron. Others,
on their way to their work, gathered at the corner of the street round
the breakfast stall, and blowing saucers of steaming coffee drawn from
tall tin cans, with the fire shining crimson through the holes beneath;
whilst already the little slattern girl, with her basket slung before her,
screams watercresses through the sleeping streets.[25]

The theme of incongruity and contrast was well served by the style,
passages such as this alternating with a barrage of statistics intended to point
up the "anomalies." The nighttime scene of poor wretches huddled in
doorways gave way to a daytime scene of twenty-nine bankers clearing an
annual total of nine hundred and fifty-four million pounds, an average of
over three million pounds a day. In a city where a poor man might lack
a roof over his head, property was insured to the value of five hundred
million pounds. Where some poor soul was in want of dinner, two hundred
and seventy million eight hundred and eighty thousand pounds of meat was
consumed annually. (These and a series of similar figures were spelled out
and sometimes italicized, as if to give them added weight.) A final set of
statistics on crime established London's preeminence in yet another respect:
the number of people taken into custody annually by the metropolitan
police was equal to the population of some of England's largest towns.

This introductory article set the agenda for the rest of the series in ways
Mayhew may not have intended. Instead of a systematic analysis of the types
and causes of poverty, there was more often a melange of facts, figures,
images, and impressions jostling each other in bewildering confusion, with
the author's voice alternately that of the dispassionate inquirer and the
passionate partisan, the satiric commentator and the social accountant. The
scientific impulse, the urge to define, categorize, quantify, and analyze, was
always there. But so was the impulse of the dramatist, satirist, novelist, and
activist. It was this combination of qualities that gave the *Morning Chronicle*
articles, and, later, the four volumes of *London Labour and the London Poor,*
their distinctive tone and dramatic force.

The original plan called for two articles a week by each of the correspondents, but after several months Mayhew settled into the routine of a weekly

article of three to four thousand words. He chose to open with the Spitalfields silk weavers, he explained, because they typified the poverty caused by low wages and because they were "notorious for their privations." Anticipating the charge of exaggeration, he promised to tell the truth in its "stark nakedness," to express views that were "wholly and solely of the weavers themselves," and to select his informants objectively. His procedure was to interview half a dozen workers chosen at random from the first houses on the nearest street, and then, upon the advice of two knowledgeable local residents, the doctor and a worker, to seek out examples of specific "classes" of workers: those with "violent political opinions" (Chartists), those of superior learning, and those in the lower ranks of the trade.[26] (In fact, he admitted, most of his informants came from the first and third classes, the most militant and the most destitute.)

Most of the articles followed the same pattern: a brief account of the history and nature of the trade (in the case of the weavers his main sources were the 1840 report of the Royal Commission on the Handloom Weavers, and Hector Gavin's *Sanitary Ramblings,* published in 1848); interviews generally presented in the first person, often reproducing the dialect and idiom of the worker; and Mayhew's own descriptions, observations, and judgments. In spite of his initial typology of poverty (or an alternative he introduced in the midst of the second article, this consisting of "artizans, labourers, and petty traders"),[27] his subjects succeeded each other in no logical order: weavers, dockworkers, various branches of the clothing trade ("slop-workers," army clothing workers, needlewomen), costermongers, papersellers, tailors, coal porters, ballast men, vagrants, shoemakers, toymakers, seamen, performers, carpenters, builders, transit workers. Nor was there any attempt to be systematic or consistent in the treatment of these trades. He used whatever facts happened to be readily available, many of them having less to do with the workers themselves than with the industry—the number of ships accommodated in the London docks, the area occupied by the docks, the cost of constructing them, the tons of goods transported annually. Nor were all the articles focused on the trades. The account of the dockworkers was followed by an article on the "low" lodging houses where many laborers lived (the inhabitants of the particular house described in that article were mainly thieves and beggars), and three articles on the "ragged schools" followed three others on merchant seamen.

Mayhew repeatedly apologized for the erratic nature of the series. It was impossible, he explained, to generalize or systematize his findings because he, like everyone else, was too ignorant of the poor. As each day brought him into contact with "a means of living utterly unknown among the well-fed portion of society," he thought it best to write about that subject while it was still fresh in his mind.[28] And he wrote about it, he insisted, without dramatizing it. Confessing that he himself would not have believed there could be such scenes of misery had he not personally witnessed them, he assured his readers that he portrayed them "in all their stark literality," that he wrote up his interviews "on the spot" and "in the self-same words in which they were told to me," and that he avoided "extreme cases." The last was especially important because if anything were to come of his work, it would only be by "laying bare the sufferings of the *class,* and not of any particular individuals belonging thereto"—the sufferings, that is, caused by "insufficient remuneration" rather than by "improvident expenditure."[29]

Other sources give a different impression of the conduct of the inquiry. One of Mayhew's friends recalled:

> He was in his glory at that time. He was largely paid and, greatest joy of all, had an army of assistant writers, stenographers, and hansom cabmen constantly at his call. London labourers of special interest, with picturesque specimens of the London poor, were brought to the *Chronicle* office, where they told their tales to Mayhew, who redictated them, with an added colour of his own, to the shorthand writer in waiting. His younger brother, Augustus, helped him in his vivid descriptions, and an authority on political economy controlled his gay statistics.[30]

Mayhew himself acknowledged the help of two assistants, one of whom, he said, contributed so much he might fairly be considered a co-author.[31] He made no mention of his brother Augustus, although other sources spoke of him as actively involved both in the research and in the writing of the articles. While there is, of course, nothing reprehensible in the use of assistants or collaborators—indeed, it is difficult to see how a project such as this could have been carried out without them—it does suggest that Mayhew was not as much in control of his material as he professed to be.

Even without such evidence, one would have good reason to doubt the "stark literality" of Mayhew's accounts. If his use of statistics was notably cavalier, it is probable that he was no more precise in his transcriptions of interviews and descriptions of scenes. Nor is it likely that a journalist writing in a daily newspaper could have resisted the temptation to dwell on "extreme cases" and "picturesque specimens," nor that, writing against a deadline, he could have been as accurate and systematic as he might have liked. Nor is it surprising that he failed to carry out his intention of taking testimony from all "classes" in each trade, or of distinguishing what was perhaps indistinguishable in reality (the suffering caused by low wages from that caused by improvident habits), or even of distinguishing the trades themselves at a time when unemployed weavers worked on the docks, seamstresses turned to prostitution, and Irish immigrants and country laborers took whatever jobs came their way. This would not need saying were it not for the excessive claims made on Mayhew's behalf by some recent historians, who credit him with being a more "systematic empirical investigator" than the social inquirers of the late nineteenth and early twentieth centuries (Charles Booth, Seebohm Rowntree, and Beatrice Webb), attribute to him the idea of the "poverty line" (this because he defined the "poor" as those whose "incomings are insufficient for the satisfaction of their wants"), and make much of his "life-histories" (an age-old technique used most successfully at just this time by G. W. M. Reynolds in his best-selling *Mysteries of London*).[32]

What is remarkable is the sheer quantity and variety of material, of whatever degree of "literality," that Mayhew managed to amass in the time available to him. Only three weeks after his Jacob's Island piece, he published the first of the articles on the London poor. During the next five months he wrote two articles a week on a dozen major subjects ranging from weaving and tailoring to docklabor, street-selling, vagrancy, and seamanship —about 150,000 words in all, the equivalent of a good-sized volume. Later, cutting back to one article a week, he produced what amounted to another volume on yet another group of diverse trades—street performers, carpenters, boat builders, transit workers. It was an extraordinary virtuoso performance, an impressive achievement in spite of its obvious deficiencies and inadequacies.

Even if Mayhew could have suppressed his natural inclinations and professional habits, if he could have resisted the temptations of the medium and overcome the limitations of time and sources, if he had become the very model of the objective investigator, the effect of his work would have been something less than objective. Just as his more moving and dramatic interviews necessarily overshadowed the pallid, commonplace ones, so his descriptions of the depressed, unskilled, underpaid branches of each trade (the "slop," "sweated," "dishonourable," "foul," "garret" work) necessarily overshadowed his accounts of the skilled and better-paid branches ("honourable," "society," "aristocratic"), and to a greater degree than was warranted by the actual proportion of workers in each.[33] However careful he might have been to present his material in proper balance, his readers would have remembered what was most memorable—which happened to be what was most miserable.

The series had been running only a few months when friction developed between Mayhew and the editor of the *Chronicle*. The quarrel came over the issue of free trade. Although the *Chronicle* was hardly a devotee of laissez faire—it had been attacked only recently by the *Economist* for encouraging a spirit of philanthropy that was subversive of political economy—it believed free trade to be in the best interests of the working classes, in proof of which it cited the salutary effects of the repeal of the corn laws. Mayhew's conviction, that the repeal of the corn laws and the accompanying reduction in the import duties on manufactured goods had resulted in unemployment and low wages, was reflected in his interview with a shoemaker, a "fine sample of the English artisan," who made out a persuasive case for higher duties. While that interview was permitted to stand, another, more provocative one on the same subject was deleted by the editor.[34] Mayhew objected to this censorship and was assured it would not happen again. But several months later it did, this time in an article on the timber trade, where he attacked not only the duty on timber but the repeal of the corn laws.

By October 1850, the disagreements on this and other issues had become so heated that Mayhew resigned. No sooner had he done so than another grievance arose. The *Chronicle* had published an article praising one of the tailoring establishments in the West End (an advertiser in the *Chronicle*, Mayhew later pointed out) for precisely the practices Mayhew had objected to: farming out the work to workers in their own homes and paying them by the piece instead of by the hour. When the paper refused to print a statement making it clear that he had not written that article, Mayhew made a public issue of it at a meeting of 1,500 tailors. Denouncing the editor who had tampered with his text and the firm that engaged in such reprehensible practices, he launched into a bitter attack on a system that depended on advertising, the production of cheap goods, the importation of foreign wares, and the immigration of foreign workers. He also took the occasion to attack another tailoring firm owned by the "Messrs. Moses," rousing the audience to cheers when he said that the magistrates were "too ready to listen to any paltry Jew who might come from Judas Iscariot, or any other Hebrew, to swear, by Barabbas, or Iscariot, or any of the brutal race that were thus festering upon us."[35]*

With his resignation from the *Chronicle,* Mayhew started preparations for the publication of his articles as pamphlets, or weekly parts, to be sold for twopence. The first of these appeared on December 14, 1850, the last on February 21, 1852—sixty-three in all. Some of the parts were issued as two volumes in 1851–52.[36] The four-volume edition of 1861–62 (reprinted in 1864–65) included these parts as well as others which had not previously appeared in volume form, extracts from the original *Chronicle* articles, and material prepared especially for this edition.[37] The title, both of the original series of pamphlets and of the four-volume edition, was *London Labour and the London Poor; A Cyclopaedia of the Condition and Earnings of Those That Will Work, Those That Cannot Work, and Those That Will Not Work.* The first three volumes bore the subtitle: "The London Street-Folk; comprising

---

*At the same time that *Punch* was celebrating the "Song of the Shirt," it was also making the firm of Moses and Son a symbol of sweated labor and a butt of anti-Semitic gibes. The slop-tailor in Charles Kingsley's *Alton Locke* was also named Moses.

Street Sellers, Street Buyers, Street Finders, Street Performers, Street Artisans, Street Labourers"; and the fourth: "Those That Will Not Work, comprising Prostitutes, Thieves, Swindlers and Beggars."

3. The "Moral Physiognomy" of the Street-Folk

It is this work, *London Labour and the London Poor,* that made the reputation of Mayhew in his time and that has become a major source for historians and sociologists since. (Several volumes of selections appeared in recent decades and a reprint of the entire work in 1968.)[38] The introduction to the latest edition praises Mayhew for having "uncovered and codified data on the modern proletariat that whole municipal and federal agencies are only now beginning to assemble."[39] And E. P. Thompson has described it as "the fullest and most vivid documentation of the economic and social problems, the customs, habits, grievances, and individual life experiences of the labouring people of the world's greatest city of the mid-nineteenth century."[40] In view of these and a host of similar commendations going back to Mayhew's own time, it is instructive to examine the work itself to see how that misapprehension came about, how a work dealing with the "London Street-Folk" and "Those That Will Not Work" could have been taken, by contemporaries and historians alike, as applying either to the "modern proletariat" or to the "labouring people" of the largest city of the mid-nineteenth century—or, indeed, to the *London Labour and the London Poor* of the title.

The misnomer of the title is readily explained. The original series in the *Morning Chronicle* entitled "Labour and the Poor" did in fact deal with "the poor" in the conventional meaning of that term. That Mayhew intended eventually to bring those poor into *London Labour* as well is suggested by the opening sentence of the preface to the first volume (a sentence quoted in some of the reviews): "The present volume is the first of an intended series, which it is hoped will form, when complete, a cyclopaedia of the industry, the want, and the vice of the great Metropolis."[41] When he briefly resumed publication of the pamphlets in 1856 under the title *The Great World of London,* he repeated that assurance, promising to do for "all classes" what he had already done for a "comparatively small and obscure portion of the community—viz., the London Street Folk."[42] He then proceeded, however, to deal with the prison population of London. Neither then nor later did he carry out his original intention, not even to the extent of reprinting the *Morning Chronicle* articles on the tailors, shoemakers, and other conventional trades. Instead, *London Labour* dealt almost entirely with the subjects of the subtitles: the "street-folk" and "those that will not work."[43]

The street-folk made a dramatic appearance in the introduction under the title "Wandering Tribes."

> Of the thousand millions of human beings that are said to constitute the population of the entire globe, there are—socially, morally, and perhaps even physically considered—but two distinct and broadly marked races, viz., the wanderers and the settlers—the vagabond and the citizen—the nomadic and the civilized tribes.[44]

"Race" and "tribe"—the words appeared repeatedly (and interchangeably) throughout the work, sometimes in the typical, loose Victorian sense of "race," in which the word might be used of any ethnic, national, religious, or cultural group, and sometimes in a biological sense. Thus the wandering race was distinguished by a "greater relative development of the jaws and cheekbones" and "broad lozenge-shaped faces," indicating an enlargement of "the organs subservient to sensation and the animal faculties," and by "distinctive moral and intellectual features."

> The nomad then is distinguished from the civilized man by his repugnance to regular and continuous labour—by his want of providence in laying up a store for the future—by his inability to perceive consequences ever so slightly removed from immediate apprehension—by his passion for stupefying herbs and roots, and, when possible, for intoxicating fermented liquors—by his extraordinary powers of enduring privation—by his comparative insensibility to pain—by an immoderate love of gaming, frequently risking his own personal liberty upon a single cast—by his love of libidinous dances—by the pleasure he experiences in witnessing the suffering of sentient creatures—by his delight in warfare and all perilous sports—by his desire for vengeance —by the looseness of his notions as to property—by the absence of chastity among his women, and his disregard of female honour—and lastly, by his vague sense of religion—his rude idea of a Creator, and utter absence of all appreciation of the mercy of the Divine Spirit.[45]

The phenomenon was universal, every civilized tribe harboring a wandering horde that preyed upon it. The Hottentots had their Bushmen and Sonquas (the latter defined by Mayhew as "paupers"), the Kafirs their Fingoes ("wanderers, beggars, or outcasts"), the Finns their Lapps, the Arabs their Bedouins. These wandering tribes persisted and perpetuated themselves in the midst of the civilizations around them, despite the privations and dangers of their life and the efforts of missionaries to civilize them.

"It is curious," Mayhew observed, "that no one has as yet applied the above facts to the explanation of certain anomalies in the present state of society among ourselves." He proposed to repair this omission by describing the English equivalents of the Sonquas and Fingoes: "paupers, beggars, and outcasts, possessing nothing but what they acquire by depredation from the industrious, provident, and civilized portion of the community." In the countryside the tribe consisted of vagrants, beggars, thieves, peddlers, showmen, harvestmen; in the cities pickpockets, beggars, prostitutes, street-traders, street-performers, carmen, coachmen, watermen, sailors. Each of these groups had its peculiar features, but all shared the same basic qualities: "a greater development of the animal than of the intellectual or moral nature," "high cheek-bones and protruding jaws," a "slang language," "lax ideas of property," "general improvidence," "repugnance to continuous labour," "disregard of female honour," "love of cruelty," "pugnacity," an "utter want of religion."[46]

Having described the generic characteristics of the race, Mayhew proceeded to distinguish the species native to London: street-sellers, street-buyers, street-finders, street-performers, street-artisans, and street-laborers. Each of these was divided into its various subspecies, the street-sellers, for example, into the sellers of fish, vegetables, fruit, greenery, "eatables and drinkables," stationery and literature, manufactured articles, and so on; and each of these, in turn, into its sub-subspecies—the sellers of "eatables and drinkables," including vendors of fried fish, hot eels, pickled whelks, sheep trotters, ham sandwiches, pea soup, and so on through twenty or so categories. In each case Mayhew described the specific nature of the occupation and those engaged in it, always in the context of their common racial characteristics. Thus the street-performers had an "indisposition to pursue any settled occupation," the street-patterers (who hawked their wares to the accompaniment of a "spiel" or "patter") a "natural," "innate" love of the "roving life," the street-children "vagabond propensities."[47]

The costermongers had these traits in so exaggerated a form as to be almost a "distinct race" in themselves (possibly, Mayhew speculated, because of their Irish extraction). In their constant warfare with the police they "resemble many savage nations, from the cunning and treachery they use"; their love of revenge was such that they were prepared to wait for months to wreak vengeance upon a policeman who had offended them; their love of play made of them incorrigible gamblers willing to lose every penny of their hard-gained earnings and the very clothes off their backs. Few of them married (less than one-tenth, Mayhew estimated, of the couples living together), and fewer still had ever seen the inside of a church or had the vaguest notion of Christianity. They prided themselves on their elaborate and obscure slang, which had no humor in it but only the single purpose of making them thoroughly incomprehensible to everyone else. The most honest of them were rarely known by their proper names, preferring, "like many rude, and almost all wandering communities," nicknames and pseudonyms.[48] These qualities displayed themselves in their earliest years, the children being distinguished by "a desire to obtain money without working for it; a craving for the excitement of gambling; an inordinate love of amusement; and an irrepressible repugnance to any settled in-door industry." Driven to the road by their "vagabond propensities," the children sold trifles or more commonly begged and stole. If they were not more brazenly dishonest, it was only because they associated jail with hard work, to which, "with the peculiar idiosyncrasy of a roving race, they have an insuperable objection." Their most remarkable trait was their "extraordinary licentiousness," an "extreme animal fondness for the opposite sex," a "precocity" so marked as to suggest that the age of puberty generally assigned to the human species might well have to be revised.[49]

The distinctive moral character of the street-folk was a conspicuous theme of *London Labour*. But it had appeared earlier in the *Chronicle* articles where Mayhew attributed to them the same "moral physiognomy." The street-performers, for example, were described as notoriously improvident ("let them make what they will in the summer, it is all squandered as soon as got, and they starve in the winter"), eager to "rebel at authority," impatient with the "irksomeness of labour," indisposed to any "settled occupation," inordinately fond of "novelty and amusement," and having a passion for a "roving life."[50] That Mayhew had this view of the street-folk from the beginning, long before he took them as his exclusive subject, suggests that it was not an afterthought contrived to augment the sale of the pamphlets or give them a specious unity. If this theme emerged so much more dramatically in *London Labour*, it was only because it was undiluted by the presence of any conventional workers.

From this account of the "moral physiognomy" of the street-folk, one might assume that Mayhew himself was less than sympathetic, or even hostile, to them. And so it must often have appeared to his readers. Yet this was far from his intention. In fact, some of his most shocking and seemingly harsh revelations of immorality and brutality were accompanied by explanations that were meant to excuse by way of explaining. If they did not quite succeed in this purpose, it was because the descriptions were so much more vivid than the explanations that the latter could never undo the effect of the former. The counterpoint of description and explanation appeared early in the work. Between the introduction on the "Wandering Tribes" and the account of the costermongers who exhibited those tribal characteristics in the most extreme form, Mayhew offered the first of several reasons for their "religious, moral, and intellectual degradation." Their degradation, he explained, was the inevitable result of privation and insecurity. To suppose that a precarious occupation would beget provident habits was "against the nature of things." What was natural was that the most precarious calling should engender the greatest degree of improvidence and intemperance. "It is not the well-fed man but the starving one that is in danger of surfeiting himself."[51]

Society bore a large share of blame for this condition, if only because it did nothing to alter it. It was a "national disgrace" that 30,000 people were permitted to remain in a "brutish" state. "If the London costers belong especially to the 'dangerous classes,' the danger of such a body is assuredly an evil of our own creation." Contrary to his earlier assertions, Mayhew now declared them pathetically grateful to anyone willing to give them the least bit of knowledge; unfortunately, no one was prepared to do that. He also now found them possessed of "the same faculties and susceptibilities as ourselves—the same power to perceive and admire the forms of truth, beauty, and goodness, as even the very highest in the state, . . . [the same] elements of manhood and beasthood." If the beast in them was more highly developed, it was because society allowed that to happen.[52] And if their children also had the "most imperfect idea of the sanctity of marriage," if their notions of morality were those of "many savage tribes," that too was to be expected; "indeed, it would be curious if it were otherwise." "I am anxious," Mayhew confessed, "to make others feel, as I do myself, that *we* are the culpable parties in these matters."[53] Concluding his first volume with an account of the immoral "propensities" of the street-children, their licentiousness, promiscuity, profligacy, gambling, and thieving, he hastened to explain the source of these vices. What little instruction they received came from the very worst class; their few amusements were poisonous; their homes were vile and base; their existence depended upon chicanery; their lives were spent in constant suffering. All the normal means of improvement —parental guidance, domestic comforts, social values, the influence of example and education— were denied them or were so tainted as to aggravate the evils they should have prevented.[54]

The effect of Mayhew's intercessions on behalf of the street-folk was, paradoxically, to make them seem even more "brutish," a "race" apart. The more passionate he was in their defense, the more indignant at the society that tolerated such vice and degradation, the more vicious and degraded they appeared. A long and moving passage, the most sustained effort at exculpation and the most bitter indictment of society, leaves a most ambiguous impression upon the reader.

The consciences of the London costermongers, generally speaking, are as little developed as their intellects; indeed, the moral and religious state of these men is a foul disgrace to us, laughing to scorn our zeal for the "propagation of the gospel in *foreign* parts," and making our many societies for the civilization of savages on the other side of the globe appear like a "delusion, a mockery, and a snare," when we have

so many people sunk in the lowest depths of barbarism round about
our very homes. It is well to have Bishops of New Zealand when we
have Christianized all *our own* heathen; but with 30,000 individuals, in
merely *one* of our cities, utterly creedless, mindless, and principleless,
surely it would look more like earnestness on our parts if we created
Bishops of the New-Cut and sent "right reverend fathers" to watch
over the "cure of souls" in the Broadway and the Brill. If our sense
of duty will not rouse us to do this, at least our regard for our own
interests should teach us, that it is not safe to allow this vast dungheap
of ignorance and vice to seethe and fester, breeding a social pestilence
in the very heart of our land. That the costermongers belong essentially
to the dangerous classes none can doubt; and those who know a coster's
hatred of a "crusher," will not hesitate to believe that they are, as they
themselves confess, one and all ready, upon the least disturbance, to
seize and disable their policemen.

It would be a marvel indeed if it were otherwise. Denied the right
of getting a living by the street authorities, after having perhaps, been
supplied with the means of so doing by the parish authorities—the
stock which the one had provided seized and confiscated by the other
—law seems to them a mere farce, or at best, but the exercise of an
arbitrary and despotic power, against which they consider themselves
justified, whenever an opportunity presents itself, of using the same
physical force as it brings to bear against them. That they are ignorant
and vicious as they are, surely is not their fault. If we were all born
with learning and virtue then might we, with some show of justice,
blame the costermongers for their want of both; but seeing that even
the most moral and intelligent of us owe the greater part, if not the
whole, of our wisdom and goodness to the tuition of others, we must
not in the arrogance of our self-conceit condemn these men because
they are not like ourselves, when it is evident that we should have been
as they are, had not some one done for us what we refuse to do for
them. We leave them destitute of all perception of beauty, and therefore without any means of pleasure but through their appetites, and
then we are surprized to find their evenings are passed either in brutalizing themselves with beer, or in gloating over the mimic sensuality of
the "penny gaff." Without the least intellectual culture is it likely,
moreover, that they should have that perception of antecedents and
consequents which enables us to see in the shadows of the past the types
of the future—or that power of projecting the mind into the space, as
it were, of time, which we in Saxon-English call fore-sight, and in
Anglo-Latin providence—a power so godlike that the latter term is
often used by us to express the Godhead itself? Is it possible, then that
men who are as much creatures of the present as the beasts of the field
—instinctless animals—should have the least faculty of prevision? or
rather is it not natural that, following the most variable climate of any
—they should fail to make the affluence of the fine days mitigate the

starvation of the rainy ones? or that their appetites made doubly eager by the privations suffered in their adversity, should be indulged in all kinds of excess in their prosperity—their lives being thus, as it were, a series of alternations between starvation and surfeit?[55]

Here, as on other occasions, every expression of compassion toward the street-folk was accompanied, however unwittingly, by yet another aspersion on their characters, every attempt at extenuation by additional evidence of their degradation. The "foul disgrace to us" was a reflection of the foul disgrace of the costermongers themselves. Their "utterly creedless, mindless, and principleless" state was a rebuke to the Christians who sent missionaries abroad while neglecting to look after the heathen at home—and at the same time a devastating picture of those native heathen. The "vast dungheap of ignorance and vice," the "social pestilence" threatening to infect the entire land, the "dangerous classes" lying in wait to attack the police, these were surely as much cause for alarm as for sympathy and good will. And it was hardly reassuring to be told that it was our fault rather than theirs that they were ignorant and vicious, lacking all foresight and prudence, indulging in every kind of excess, sunk in the "lowest depths of barbarism," behaving like "beasts of the field," "instinctless animals." The very metaphors—heathen, beasts, animals, barbarians, dungheap, pestilence—carried a more powerful, and very different, message than his plea for understanding and help.

If the plea was weak in comparison with the rhetoric, the one practical proposal Mayhew offered in the wake of this apologia was weaker still. It is hard to take seriously his suggestion that the "chief evils" of street-life would be mitigated by the establishment of a Friendly Association of London Costermongers which would provide insurance against sickness and old age, interest on savings, loans for the purchase of stock, the inspection of scales and weights, free education for the young, and "harmless, if not rational" amusements.[56] However commendable, such an association hardly seems commensurate with the evils that had just been depicted.

That feeble proposal points to a weakness in the argument itself. If that was all society could do by way of reform, it was perhaps because the moral condition of the street-folk was, as Mayhew elsewhere suggested, too deeply rooted within them to be amenable to reform. "Race," even in its loose Victorian usage, signified a distinctive physical, mental, and moral constitution, a "disposition," "propensity," or "physiognomy" which was "natural" and "innate." The love of the roving life, the repugnance to civilization, the incapacity for steady work—these were the marks of a "moral nature" as congenital as protruding jaws and cheekbones or lozenge-shaped faces. By this definition the street-folk were not a fortuitous, ephemeral, local phenomenon but a universal race which no amount of missionary endeavors or enlightened policies could eradicate.

Although Mayhew never explicitly confronted this difficulty, he came close to it when he invoked something like the nature-nurture distinction to account for the differences among various species of street-folk. The "patterers," for example, while less "brutified" than the costermongers, had the typical characteristics of the race: "an indomitable 'self-will' or hatred of the least restraint or control—an innate aversion to every species of law or government, whether political, moral, or domestic—a stubborn, contradictory nature—an incapability of continuous labor . . . —an unusual predilection for amusements, . . . utter absence of all religious feeling." They were, however, street-folk with a difference. Where the costermongers were "mostly hereditary wanderers" born and bred to the street (with a few "aliens" among them driven to the street by the lack of employment in their regular trades), the patterers "have rather *taken* to it from a natural love of what they call 'roving.' " Among them were men of "respectable connections, and even classical attainments"—the son of a military officer, a clergyman, a doctor, the natural sons of gentlemen and noblemen. In fact, in their more disagreeable traits, they resembled the "gent": "If an absence of heartiness and good fellowship be characteristic of an aristocracy—as some political philosophers contend—then the patterers may indeed be said to be the aristocrats of the streets."[57]

At one point Mayhew proposed a schema differentiating the street-folk in terms of their origins: those who were born to the street, those who took to it, and those who were driven to it. The first and largest group, of whom the costermongers were typical, were the "natives," the "indigenous" tribe "imbibing the habits and morals of the gutters almost with their mothers' milk." "Nursed in the lap of the kennel," the children naturally took on the character of their parents. "Surely there is a moral acclimatisation as well as a physical one, and the heart may become inured to a particular atmosphere in the same manner as the body; and even as the seed of the apple returns, unless grafted, to its original crab, so does the child, without training, go back to its parent stock—the vagabond Savage." The finest gentleman in Europe would have been the worst blackguard in Billingsgate had he been reared with a fish-basket on his head instead of a crown; conversely, the crudest "rough" on the streets would have had diamonds instead of fish-scales glistening on his shoulders had he been born "by the Grace of God, King, Defender of the Faith."[58] This was not to say, Mayhew hastened to add, that men were entirely the creatures of circumstance. On the contrary, to the extent to which they were men rather than beasts they were "self-agents," moving rather than being moved by events, stemming and directing the current rather than being swept along by it. Indeed, the proportion of the active and passive nature in any individual was the measure of the relative development of the human and the animal in him. The hero, the exceptional man, had the most active nature and was therefore able to overcome the material and external forces acting upon him. Because ordinary people lacked that "energy—principle—will (call it what you please)," they had to be helped to become better, and if they were not helped, if the brute in them dominated, it was our fault, not theirs. "Those who are bred to the streets must bear about them the moral impress of the kennel and gutter—unless *we* seek to develop the inward and controlling part of their constitution." The "indigenous" street-folk, then, were "improvable." But not by the feeble kind of education available to them. It was not enough to teach them to read, write, and "chatter a creed"; that was to make of them "human parrots," not human beings. What was needed was to arouse in them intellect, conscience, and taste. Without that they remained "the same brute creatures of circumstances—the same passive instruments—human waifs and strays—left to be blown about as the storm of life may whirl them."[59]

Toward the second group, those who took to the streets by choice, Mayhew was notably less sympathetic. These were the people for whom the "roving life" was a "passion," the "aversion to continuous labour" part of their "nature." Full of health and mischief, stubborn and willful, rebellious and libidinous, dishonest and predatory, they were beyond reform. "We might as well preach to Messrs. Moses, Nicol, and Co., in the hope of Christianising them."[60] Fortunately this group, the unimprovable one, was also the least numerous. The third group, almost as large as the first and at least as worthy of pity, were those driven to the streets: the maimed, aged, and young, victims of misfortunes beyond their control or of their own "imprudence and sluggishness," and workers who could not get employment in their own trades.[61] For some in this group street-selling was little more than an excuse for begging, but more often it was resorted to out of a horror of the workhouse and a desperate attempt to retain some sense of pride and independence.

This tripartite division did not inform the rest of the work and was not entirely consistent with it. Elsewhere the costermongers hardly seemed as "grateful for instruction" or "deeply moved by any kindness and sympathy" as they were made out to be here. And it is not clear how their protruding jaws and cheekbones could be reconciled with the "there but for the grace of God" argument which made them interchangeable with kings and noblemen. What is clear, however, is Mayhew's purpose in devising these categories, his desire to redeem most of the street-folk from the qualities he himself attributed to them. Having earlier consigned them all to the same race by virtue of their innate nature, he now attributed that nature to only one group of them, and that the smallest, making the rest reformable if only society would assume its proper responsibility. But even here, where he was most intent upon humanizing and socializing the street-folk, restoring them to the civilized world, he was also brutalizing and degrading them—and this with the best intentions: to dramatize the need for society's help and to condemn the society that withheld that help. Unfortunately the reader whose sympathies were being appealed to was also apt to be repelled by those brutish creatures of the "kennel and gutter."

4. Varieties of Street-Folk

In the preface to the first volume, Mayhew described himself, in a phrase that was much quoted, as a "traveller in the undiscovered country of the poor." Because he was bringing back reports from a people about whom less was known than "the most distant tribes of the earth," because the facts he adduced were so novel and extraordinary, he might be suspected of telling the kinds of tales travellers were supposed to delight in.[62] It was a theme reviewers were quick to pick up.

> He has travelled through the unknown regions of our metropolis, and returned with full reports concerning the strange tribes of men which he may be said to have discovered. For, until his researches had taken place, who knew of the nomad race which daily carries on its predatory operations in our streets, and nightly disappears in quarters wholly unvisited by the portly citizens of the East as by perfumed whiske-randoes of the West End? An important and valuable addition has thus been made to our knowledge. In a volume replete with curious facts, authenticated by absolute proof, as well as by the high character of the author, we have a description of a class of the population perfectly marvellous to contemplate.[63]

It was indeed a "marvellous" scene the reader was invited to contemplate: a population consisting exclusively of street-folk, more various, numerous, and curious than anyone might have suspected, full of dramatic, tragic, and, occasionally, comic stories—"romances," "tales stranger than fiction," as reviewers repeatedly remarked. Even if Mayhew had not made a point of introducing these street-folk as a separate race, the reader might have deduced as much from his accounts of them.

The costermongers were the most familiar variety of street-folk; few Londoners could have lived so sheltered a life as not to have encountered them. But by the time Mayhew finished with them, after 150 pages, they seemed odd indeed, with their peculiar occupations, dispositions, habits, and morals. Even the most straightforward expository details of their life and work made them seem strange and exotic. The very language was bizarre: the names of the different kinds of barrows and baskets, the "slang" (counterfeit) weights and measures, the youngsters paid for their labor by "bunts" (the profits over the set price), the "king's man" (silk neckerchief) which was their most prized article of dress, the "cries" and "calls" with which they hawked their wares. And the interviews, colloquial, ungrammatical, often in dialect, transformed the most mundane facts into quaint and dramatic oddities.

As if this were not enough to create the impression of a distinctive race, Mayhew devoted separate chapters to those costermongers who were (as these matters were then viewed) literally distinctive "races"—the Irish and the Jews. "The Irish street-sellers," he announced at the outset, "are both a numerous and peculiar class of people," peculiar in appearance ("low fore-heads and long bulging upper lips"), in dialect, and in religion. They were the lowest class of costermonger (although not the lowest class of Irish, the Irish laborers having that distinction), most having turned to costermonger-ing because they were ill fitted for any other trade, the women inept even at such tasks as sewing and housework. But they were also singularly ill fitted for costermongering, with no understanding of the elementary princi-ples of trade and no knowledge of any but the most common measures and calculations. Thus they were confined to the simplest transactions, selling, as one of them reported to Mayhew, "for a ha'pinny the three apples which cost a farruthing." They lived apart from the other costermongers, had a more austere diet, were more chaste and somewhat more provident. They were also notorious liars, but this, Mayhew explained, was because they were more imaginative, readier of wit and of speech than their English counter-parts; if the latter had those gifts, they too might take more liberties with the truth.[64]

Toward the street-Jews Mayhew's attitude was more equivocal. Com-pared with his earlier vitriolic comments about the tribe of Messrs. Moses which was "festering upon us," his remarks in *London Labour* were relatively temperate. Like the Irish, the Jews were a "distinct and peculiar part of street-life." Reviewing their checkered history in England, Mayhew at-tributed some of the prejudice against them to the vestiges of old feelings and some of it to their own greed and "unlawful and debasing pursuits." With a fine show of evenhandedness, he deplored the "rabid prejudice" that saw them only as "misers, usurers, extortioners, receivers of stolen goods, cheats, brothel-keepers, sheriff's-officers, clippers and sweaters of the coin of the realm, gaming-house keepers"—while conceding that there was "some foundation for many of these accusations."* If Jews were prominent in the

---

*Of some popular manifestations of anti-Semitism Mayhew was frankly contemptuous. In the 1790s, when attacks on Jews were frequent and the most harmless old-clothes man could not safely ply his trade, a common street cry was "No Jews! No wooden shoes!" That cry, Mayhew explained, was an amalgam of the hatred of Jews and the fear of a French invasion (the French being symbolized by wooden shoes, *sabots*), and was "certainly among the most preposterously stupid of any which ever tickled the ear and satisfied the mind of the ignorant."[66]

speculative branches of foreign trade (jewelry, fruit, cigars, delicacies), it was
because there were no fixed prices and therefore more opportunities for
profit; quoting Walter Scott's comment that this kind of trade had "all the
fascination of gambling, without the moral guilt," Mayhew accepted the
first part of that statement, but not the second—he would not absolve the
Jewish traders from moral guilt. In the buying of old clothes and the selling
of oranges the Jewish monopoly was being challenged by Irish boys who
were prepared to "live harder" (on a stolen turnip a day), "lodge harder"
(outdoors if necessary), do without shoes and stockings, proper meals and
recreation, whereas the city-bred Jewish boys were accustomed to more
comforts and even luxuries (concerts and plays, checkers and dominoes).
Gambling was their greatest vice, as the "extreme love of money" was their
principal characteristic. In other respects they compared favorably with
other street-folk: they were quick learners, relatively clean, sober, honest,
and chaste, faithful husbands and doting fathers. They were also known for
their communal spirit, helping each other in time of need and contributing
generously to Jewish charities so that no Jew ever had to die in a parish
workhouse—which was all the more remarkable "when we recollect their
indisputable greed of money."[65]

"Peculiar," "odd," "strange," "distinct"—the refrain appears in one after
another account of the street-folk. The reader of the work, in either its
weekly installments or the bound volumes, could not but be struck by the
strangeness of it all. The very multiplicity of trades contributed to this effect,
some of them totally unknown to the reader (the middle class reader, at any
rate), each sharply delineated by Mayhew's extraordinary eye and ear for
detail, his genius for the arresting fact and phrase.

The first volume, after describing the infinitely varied kinds of costermongers, devoted another hundred pages to yet another "wholly distinct"
group, the street-sellers of "stationery, literature, and the fine arts." Again
the varieties were dazzling: sellers of "long-songs" (songs printed on yard-
long paper), love letters, begging letters (written by "screevers"), murder
tales, comic tales, accounts of fires, "catechisms and litanies" (religious and
political satires), "cocks" (literary forgeries and disguised fiction), "straws"
(quack remedies), "sham indecent" literature (sealed packets purporting to
contain a lewd or scandalous publication), shorthand-cards (lessons in ste-
nography), race-cards, playing-cards, writing paper, memorandum books,
almanacks, diaries, ballads, "gallows" literature (about hangings), conun-
drums, squibs, magical illusions, play-bills, used books, newspapers and
periodicals (back-numbers and new), waste-paper, engravings, pictures.
"We are the haristocracy of the streets," one patterer assured Mayhew.

"People don't pay us for what we gives 'em, but only to hear us talk. We live like yourself, sir, by the hexercise of our hintellects—we by talking, and you by writing."[67]

The second volume featured an even more curious and motley crew: secondhand street dealers specializing in metals, linen, glass and crockery, apparel, or anything, as one dealer said, "from a needle to an anchor";[68] street-sellers of live animals, each with his own specialty (stolen dogs, birds painted to resemble exotic species, squirrels, rabbits, goldfish, tortoises, snails, worms, frogs, snakes, hedgehogs); street-buyers (old clothes, rags, waste paper, bits of metal, umbrellas, bottles, glass, keys, bones, kitchen grease, hogs' wash, tea leaves); and street-finders (bone-grubbers, rag-gatherers, pure-finders, dredgermen, mud-larks, sewer-hunters, dustmen, sweeps, scavengers). If some of these occupations were more familiar to Mayhew's readers than they are today, others were obscure and peculiar even then. Not many middle class or even working class Victorians knew of the considerable trade in bones (which were ground for manure) or "pure" (dog's dung used in the tanning, or "purifying," of leather). And few could have appreciated the social distinctions within these groups—the great wealth, for example, of a few rubbish contractors. (The "golden dustman" in Dickens's *Our Mutual Friend* revealed the potentialities of that trade; but that book was not published until 1865.)

Most of the finders belonged to the "very lowest class" of street people, lacking even that small degree of intelligence that would have permitted them to trade in some trifle, and unable to summon up the ingenuity required for begging. Yet even here there were distinctions. The bone-grubbers and rag-pickers were so benighted as to be "unconscious of their degradation, and with little anxiety to be relieved from it." The pure-finders, on the other hand, were clever enough to adulterate their product and pass it off as a superior grade of dung, prompting Mayhew to observe that "there is no business or trade, however insignificant or contemptible, without its own peculiar and appropriate tricks." The river-finders, the dredgermen of the Thames, were a hereditary class, the trade passing from father to son; in spite of their disagreeable occupation (their prize haul was a corpse, which brought a standing reward of five shillings in addition to whatever money or jewelry might be found on the body), they were hardworking and persevering, not given to drink, gambling, or brawling.[69]

Oddly enough, the sewer-men, exposed to unspeakable stench and filth, ferocious rats, and dangerous torrents of water—all for the sake of a few coins, scraps of metal, bits of jewelry, ropes, or bones—took "precedence" over all the other finders in earnings (often higher than those of the best paid artisans), skill, courage, and even health. Strong, robust, florid in complexion, they attributed their good health to the sewage odors, which they believed to have therapeutic qualities.* They were also more improvi-dent and intemperate than the others, repairing to the public house after each haul and venturing out again only to get money for a "fresh debauch."[70] The most pathetic of the finders were the "mud-larks," children and old women whose job it was to dredge the mud left by the receding tide. Wading and groping in the mud for pieces of coal, chips of wood, scraps of metal, and bones, they passed and repassed each other without speaking, their eyes fixed upon the ground, their bodies bent over, clad in tattered, befouled rags, "stiffened up like boards with dirt of every possible descrip-tion."[71] No less peculiar were the various types of street-cleaners—the "sifters," for example, half-buried in mounds of cinders and ashes, sieving through them to separate the fine dust from the coarse and both from other varieties of refuse. Garbed in heavy leather aprons, they wielded their sieves so violently that the noise of the sieves striking the aprons was like the sound of tenor drums.[72]

As one after another of the street-folk passed under review, the reader was overwhelmed by this multitude of highly specialized and exceedingly peculiar trades, some repulsive and grotesque (dead-body scavengers, rat-catchers, dung-collectors), others entertaining and exotic. The street-per-formers, for example, included a Punch-and-Judy puppeteer, juggler, strong man, acrobat, conjurer, clown, actor, dancer, stilt-walker, musician, singer, artist, animal trainer, sword-swallower, snake-swallower, knife-swallower, blind profile-cutter, and a "writer without hands." The impression of oddity sometimes came more from the descriptions of the trades than from the workers themselves. Thus the section on the destroyers of vermin said little about the men engaged in that occupation, but a good deal about the appearance, habits, and life-histories of the various species of vermin. At one point Mayhew paused to reflect upon the process of adaptation and differen-tiation which took place in these interstices of the economy. The passage might stand as the epigraph for the work as a whole.

It would be in itself a curious inquiry to trace the origin of the manifold occupations in which men are found to be engaged in the present day, and to note how promptly every circumstance and occur-rence was laid hold of, as it happened to arise, which appeared to have any tendency to open up a new occupation, and to mark the gradual process, till it became a regularly established employment, followed by a separate class of people, fenced round by rules and customs of their

---

*This conflicted with the "miasma" theory of epidemics held by most public officials. One of the difficulties encountered by the authorities during the cholera epidemic of 1848–49 was the habit of many working class families of heaping manure outside their houses and under the windows in the belief that the odor would protect them from the epidemic.

own, and who at length grew to be both in their habits and peculiarities plainly distinct from the other classes among whom they chanced to be located.[73]

. . .

Even such pedestrian street-folk as the coal laborers emerged from Mayhew's work as rather exotic types, if only by virtue of their specializations —"whippers," "backers," "pull-backs," "trimmers." To be among them was to be "in a new land, and among another race," a violent and lawless race.[74] They had nine times as many convictions for larceny and pugnacity, and five times as many for drunkenness, as the working classes in general. Even these statistics, the laborers told Mayhew, underestimated the extent of drunkenness, since only the most extreme cases came to the attention of the police and most of the other offenses were caused by drink. Mayhew himself rejected the familiar argument that drink was as necessary as food to hardworking laborers, some teetotalers having assured him that they actually worked better without drink. He also denied that drunkenness was simply a function of poverty; laborers, he pointed out, did not figure prominently in the pauper rolls. The main reason for their drunkenness was the "system" that "positively forced" them to get drunk. The system Mayhew had in mind was not capitalism but the "truck" or "tommy" system—payment in goods rather than wages. When wages were distributed in the public house and the coal-contractors were also the publicans, it was obviously in their interest to encourage the men to drink, even compelling them, in some cases, to spend a portion of their earnings on drink. Thus drunkenness was "the fault of the employer, rather than the man," indeed "something like a positive conspiracy on the part of the master."[75] That system, Mayhew admitted, had been abolished some years earlier when an act of Parliament required that the whippers be hired and paid at a special office set up for that purpose. Moreover, butchers and grocers were beginning to replace publicans as coal contractors, and while they too obliged their workers to make their purchases from them, at least that was an incentive to buy food rather than drink, thus benefiting the laborer's family. Yet drink, Mayhew found, remained a major evil, a cause of degradation and misery that could not begin to be measured by the statistics on crime.

The most degraded of all laborers were the casual dock workers, both because they were the lowest paid and because their employment was most insecure and irregular. They were the extreme type of unskilled workers, for whom mechanical and natural metaphors were more appropriate than human ones. The dock laborer was a "human steam-engine, supplied with so much fuel in the shape of food . . . a striking instance of mere brute force with brute appetites . . . as unskilled as the power of a hurricane." Muscle was all that was needed on the docks; "hence every human locomotive is capable of working there."[76] The climax of this section was the description of the tragic "struggle for life" that took place every day on the docks.

> In the scenes I have lately witnessed the want has been positively tragic, and the struggle for life partaking of the sublime. . . . The scenes witnessed at the London Dock were of so painful a description, the struggle for one day's work—the scramble for twenty four hours' extra-subsistence and extra-life were of so tragic a character, that I was anxious to ascertain if possible the exact number of individuals in and around the metropolis who live by dock labour. . . . That the sustenance of thousands of families should be as fickle as the very breeze itself; that the weathercock should be the index of daily want or daily ease to such a vast number of men, women and children, was a climax of misery and wretchedness that I could not have imagined to exist; and since that I have witnessed such scenes of squalor, and crime, and suffering, as oppress the mind even to a feeling of awe.[77]

Earlier Mayhew had explained that it was because these laborers were "shut out from the usual means of life by the want of character" that there were so many thieves among them. But now, as he described the scenes at the docks, every man pitted against the elements as well as against his neighbors, working like a "human locomotive" and getting drunk as soon as he was released from work, Mayhew decided that it was not any "malformation of his moral constitution" that made the dock worker what he was but the "precarious character of his calling." His vices were those of "ordinary human nature"; anyone else would have done the same under similar circumstances. "It is consoling to moralise in our easy chairs, after a good dinner, and to assure ourselves that we should do differently. Self-denial is not very difficult when our stomachs are full and our backs are warm, but let us live a month of hunger and cold, and assuredly we should be as self-indulgent as they."[78]

Mayhew was eloquent in defending the casual dock laborers, but he was equally eloquent in describing them. If the laborers' vices were those of "ordinary human nature" aggravated only by the special circumstances of their lives, the result was such as to make it difficult for the ordinary reader to see his nature in theirs, to sympathize, let alone empathize, with them. This was also the effect of Mayhew's description of one of the "low lodging houses" catering to the casual laborer. The conditions in the house were so foul and the inhabitants so repulsive that Mayhew tried to find out what brought people to that low state. Of 55 residents, he discovered, 34 had been in prison at least once and most several times, more often for theft than vagrancy. As many as 40 could read and write and another 4 could at least read, leaving only 11 illiterates. Most of their fathers had been respectable workers, and they themselves had been brought up to be laborers or skilled workers. Most drank occasionally, although not to excess; two were actually teetotalers. They started to steal when they ran away from home, or to keep up with "flash company," or to indulge small pleasures, or because the life of a thief, even in prison, was easier than that of a vagrant. Only one man said that he had stolen because he could not get work, another because he had no tools to work with, and a third because he was "hard up." Their delinquencies, Mayhew concluded, could not be attributed to want, ignorance, drink, or unfortunate associations, but rather to an "erratic and self-willed temperament," an inability or unwillingness to accept the restraints of home or of any continuous occupation. "Does the uncertainty of dock labour generate thieves and vagabonds, or do the thieves and vagabonds crowd round the docks so as to be able to gain a day's work when unable to thieve?"[79] Mayhew did not answer that question, but his readers might have been inclined to the second alternative. In any case they would have come away with the impression that for whatever reasons, most dock laborers were thieves, just as most coal laborers were drunkards.

The same ambiguity appears in Mayhew's discussion of vagrants: "those vagabond or erratic spirits who find continuity or application to any task specially irksome to them, . . . creatures who are vagrants in disposition and principle." This judgment was somewhat muted by the observation that all mankind was "innately erratic," all labor "naturally irksome," and only the cultivation of good character and habits could overcome the natural disinclination to work. Unfortunately, vagrants lacked the kind of "education, example, and deliberation" that would have made them willing to work. If they had been taught to read, it was without any "moral perception," so that reading itself became an instrument for their degradation, their favorite reading matter being tales romanticizing crime and violence. And their upbringing was either too lax to inspire them with any moral purpose or so severe that they were moved to rebel and run away. Thus it was the fault of others that these youths never developed the habits of industry that would have counteracted their natural sloth.[80]

On other occasions Mayhew was harsher toward vagrants, especially when he compared them with the laboring poor. "I am anxious that the public should no longer confound the honest, independent working men, with the vagrant beggars and pilferers of the country; and that they should see that the one class is as respectable and worthy, as the other is degraded and vicious." Laborers, with all their vices, now appeared to be the epitome of virtue, patient under the keenest privations, charitable beyond their means, intelligent in spite of a lack of education. "In a word, their virtues are the spontaneous expressions of their simple natures; and their vices are the comparatively pardonable excesses, consequent upon the intensity of their toil."[81] Vagrants, by contrast, were degraded, vicious, and dangerous.

The recurrent image was of a "pestilence," and not only as metaphor but as literal fact. The vagrants swarmed across the country carrying with them "tramp-fever" (a disease resembling typhoid and cholera), and with that a "moral pestilence . . . as terrible and as devastating as the physical pest which accompanies it." They were a "stream of vice and disease—a tide of iniquity and fever, continually flowing from town to town, from one end of the land to the other." When they settled down momentarily in town, as in an asylum for the homeless described by Mayhew, they were "a vast heap of social refuse—the mere human street-sweepings—the great living mixen— that is destined, as soon as the spring returns, to be strewn far and near over the land, and serve as manure to the future crime-crop of the country."[82]

Once again Mayhew was provoked to his usual "there but for the grace of God" reflections.

> Then get down from your moral stilts, and confess it honestly to yourself, that you are what you are by that inscrutable grace which decreed your birthplace to be a mansion or a cottage rather than a "padding-ken," or which granted you brains and strength, instead of sending you into the world, like many of these, a cripple or an idiot.
>
> It is hard for smug-faced respectability to acknowledge these dirt-caked, erring wretches as brothers, and yet, if from those to whom little is given, little is expected, surely, after the atonement of their long suffering, they will make as good angels as the best of us.[83]

It was a moving finale to a memorable vignette. But it did not erase the earlier images, which were not of cripples, idiots, or "erring wretches," but of "the lowest, the filthiest, and most demoralised classes," "the most restless, discontented, vicious, and dangerous elements of society," "habitual de-predators, house-breakers, horse-stealers, and common thieves," a "vast heap of social refuse."[84] After this long account of misery and vice, after being told that only five percent of the vagrants were "really destitute and deserv-ing" while the rest were "degraded and vicious," Mayhew's readers could have been forgiven if they did not take his belated advice "to acknowledge these dirt-caked, erring wretches as brothers."

The vagrants provided a natural transition to the final volume, "Those That Will Not Work, comprising Prostitutes, Thieves, Swindlers and Beggars." Most of this volume was written by others, Mayhew contributing a brief introduction and an elaborate "Classification of the Workers and Non-Workers of Great Britain."[85] The "Classification," he prided himself, was the first attempt to create "the natural history, as it were, of the industry

From *London Labour and the London Poor*.

TOP LEFT [1] Vagrant from the Refuge in Playhouse Yard, Cripplegate.
TOP RIGHT [2] The Crippled Bird-Seller.
BOTTOM LEFT [3] The Street-Seller of Nutmeg-Graters.
BOTTOM RIGHT [4] The Lucifer Match Girl.

From *London Labour and the London Poor.*

RIGHT [5] The London Costermonger.
"Here Pertaters! Karots and Turnups!
fine Brockello-o-o!"
BELOW [6] View of a Dust Yard.

From *London Labour and the London Poor.*

ABOVE [7] A Dinner at a Cheap
Lodging House.
RIGHT [8] The Sweeps' Home

George Cruikshank illustrations, from Dickens's *Sketches by Boz*.

LEFT [9] Seven Dials.
BELOW [10] The Streets—Morning.

George Cruikshank illustrations,
from Dickens's *Sketches by Boz*.

RIGHT [11] A Pickpocket in Custody.
BELOW [12] Monmouth Street.

George Cruikshank illustrations, from Dickens's *Oliver Twist*.

LEFT [13] Oliver Asking for More.
BELOW [14] Oliver Introduced to the Respectable Old Gentleman.

George Cruikshank illustrations,
from Dickens's *Oliver Twist*.

ABOVE [15] Oliver Amazed at
the Dodger's Mode of
Going to Work.
RIGHT [16] Oliver Claimed by
His Affectionate Friends.

USEFUL SUNDAY LITERATURE FOR THE MASSES;

OR, MURDER MADE FAMILIAR.

Father of a Family (reads). "The wretched Murderer is supposed to have cut the throats of his three eldest Children, and then to have killed the Baby by beating it repeatedly with a Poker. * * * * * In person he is of a rather bloated appearance, with a bull neck, small eyes, broad large nose, and coarse vulgar mouth. His dress was a light blue coat, with brass buttons, elegant yellow summer vest, and pepper-and-salt trowsers. When at the Station House he expressed himself as being rather 'peckish,' and said he should like a Black Pudding, which, with a Cup of Coffee, was immediately procured for him."

[17] From *Punch*, 1849.

and idleness of Great Britain in the nineteenth century." Defining "workers" as "all those who do *anything* for their living, who perform any act whatsoever that is considered worthy of being paid for by others, without regard to the question of whether such labourers tend to add to or decrease the aggregate wealth of the community," he extended that term to include soldiers, sailors, officials, capitalists, clergymen, lawyers, and wives.[86] "Nonworkers" included "those who cannot work," "those who need not work," and "those who will not work." The latter, the subject of this volume, were the "outcast class." By elucidating the "physics and economy of vice and crime," he hoped to make society "look with more pity and less anger" on these wretched outcasts and try to alleviate the social evils responsible for much of that vice and crime.[87]

The mere enumeration, let alone the elaborate descriptions, of the myriad varieties of outcasts made it difficult to sustain the posture of "more pity and less anger." Confronted with an extraordinary array of vice and crime—the "multifarious tribe of 'sturdy rogues' " who roamed the countryside in the summer and London in the winter, the professional beggars posing as "pretended starved-out manufacturers," "pretended unemployed agriculturalists," "pretended frozen-out gardners," and a dozen other kinds of "pretended" unfortunates, the 15 categories of cheats, 48 of thieves, and 26 of prostitutes—even the most compassionate reader might find himself more impressed by the ingenuity of these outcasts than by their miseries. A more cynical reader would surely be confirmed in his suspicion that there were people who would do anything, subject themselves and their families to any degradation, rather than put in an honest day's work. Mayhew himself often fell into this kind of moral outrage. His comments on prostitution were worthy of the most bourgeois *paterfamilias*. "Prostitution is the putting of anything to a vile use . . . the base perversion of a woman's charms —the surrendering of her virtue to criminal indulgence." Even if it were legal it would be immoral, since unchastity itself was an offense to the moral sense.[88]

The classification points to another ambiguity in Mayhew's work. In all of this elaborate schema, there was no category of street-folk. Some of the groups dealt with in the earlier volumes—dock workers, coal laborers, dustmen—did appear, but under such different names and widely separated rubrics that one could never deduce from them anything like the common denominator of "street-folk." And some of the most prominent street-folk never figured in the classification at all. There were no costermongers, except those who might appear in "markets, or weekly gatherings of buyers and sellers"; and performers, known here as "exhibitors or showmen," were included among "servitors," a category they shared with such other "temporary servitors" as the Queen and Members of Parliament.[89] The omission of the very concept of street-folk is a curious commentary on the three volumes which had made that their exclusive subject.

Early in his work Mayhew announced his intention to eschew all "opinions" so that his inquiry might be strictly factual and objective.[90] He did not, of course, hold to that resolve. In the course of his account of street cleaners, for example, he commented on the use by some parishes of pauper labor. He objected to that practice on the ground that the pauper laborer displaced the independent laborer and made them both compete for the same "wage fund." "It is impossible to make labourers of the paupers of an over-populated country without making paupers of the labourers." The laborers were twice injured: by having their jobs taken away from them and by making them bear the burden of maintaining the paupers. In effect, the poor rate was paid out of the wages of the workers instead of the profits of the traders, and the poor were saddled with responsibility for their "poorer brethren."[91] Mayhew also objected to putting paupers to work breaking up paving stones, a practice justified as a "labor test" (a variant of the "less-eligibility" principle). It was an "unequal" test, he pointed out, for what came easily to an agricultural laborer or quarryman was a great hardship for the starving tailor. Moreover, it had exactly the opposite of the effect intended: instead of cultivating a respect for work and encouraging the will to work, it made work repulsive and idleness attractive, in this respect resembling the onerous and unproductive work provided in the workhouse. For the same reason he disapproved of all the other devices used to distinguish pauper employment from regular employment—the practice, for example, recently discontinued, of "badging" the pauper laborer (printing the name of the parish on his clothes), or requiring him to wear distinctive attire, both of which were especially unjust at a time when even criminals were no longer degraded in this manner. To expose the pauper to public scorn was to make the occasional recipient of relief into a "hardened and habitual pauper."[92]

It was not the employment of paupers as such that Mayhew objected to, but only their employment under conditions that would injure other workers. Thus he was enthusiastic about the street orderly system instituted by the recently founded Philanthropic Association. Since it was a new technique and therefore a new trade, it did not take employment away from the independent laborers. Moreover, the new employer, being a private agency rather than the parish, was not bound by the principle of less-eligibility. The paupers did not have to wear distinctive attire, were not subject to a humiliating labor test, and, most important, were not paid at a rate lower than that of the independent laborer. The single rate of wages had the effect of raising the pauper to the level of the independent laborer instead of forcing the laborer's wages down to the rate paid the pauper. "Elevate the condition of the labourer, and there will be no necessity to depress the pauper. Make work more attractive by increasing the reward for it, and laziness will necessarily become more repulsive."[93]

Even while praising the Philanthropic Association, Mayhew could not refrain from criticizing the philanthropic enterprise itself. When it started the street orderly scheme, the association had imposed conditions which were humiliating, not because they were less eligible but because they were a misguided attempt to be more eligible. The men were lodged in special houses with superior living and sanitary accommodations, given abundant and nutritious food, provided with a library and writing materials, and invited to attend religious services. Although these lodging houses and amenities had recently been discontinued, Mayhew used the experiment to discourse upon the evils of paternalistic philanthropy.

> This is all very benevolent, but still very wrong. There is but one way of benefiting the poor, viz., by developing their powers of self-reliance, and certainly not in treating them like children. Philanthropists always seek to do too much, and in this is to be found the main cause of their repeated failures. The poor are expected to become angels in an instant, and the consequence is, they are merely made hypocrites. . . . This overweening disposition to play the part of *ped-agogues* (I use the word in its literal sense) to the poor, proceeds rather from a love of power than from a sincere regard for the people. . . . The curfew-bell, whether instituted by benevolence or tyranny, has the same degrading effect on the people—destroying their principle of self-action, without which we are all but the beasts of the field.[94]

If Mayhew was critical of philanthropists who wanted to "do too much" for the poor, his real animus was reserved for the political economists who wanted to do too little for them. His views on this subject appeared not in *London Labour* itself but on the covers of the weekly parts under the heading "Answers to Correspondents."[95] It was on these "waste pages," as he called them, that he explained his objection to free trade: to the extent to which free trade succeeded in lowering the price of food, it also lowered the wages of labor, which were determined, under the system of supply and demand, by the cost of subsistence.[96] It was here too that he made out a case against machines, the millions of "steam men" who made of real men a "surplus population."[97] "Study Ricardo," he sternly admonished one correspondent who ventured to suggest that machinery enhanced productivity and thus the living standards of the workers.[98] To another he cited Ricardo's admission that he had once thought that the workers, like everyone else, would profit from the cheaper commodities produced by machinery, but had since discovered that the interests of all the classes were not identical, that the fund from which landlords and capitalists derived their revenue might get larger while that of the laborers diminished, and that machinery inevitably led to lower wages.[99] Ricardo's discovery, Mayhew wrote, made a mockery of Adam Smith's dream of an expanding industrial economy that would benefit all classes alike, a dream that could only have come to a man who spent the better years of his life in an obscure village in Scotland spinning out his "cobweb philosophy," his "arm-chair science."[100]

From Ricardo, as he understood him, Mayhew drew the un-Ricardian conclusion that the only remedy for the working classes was the abandonment of political economy and especially of that "invidious" law of supply and demand which presumed to fix the rate of wages. That law, so far from being natural, violated natural justice, right, equity, and "moral equality." Supply and demand was nothing more than a struggle between two parties to determine how much one could extort from the other; it had as much to do with equity as a standing army had with the rights of nations. What equity required was not a struggle between capital and labor but a "partnership" based upon a contract assuring each a "fair share of the produce" as determined by the "equitable wage-principle." (Not, it should be noted, the full share of the produce, as might be implied in a labor theory of value.) Such a partnership would put an end to the class enmity reflected in the "new-fangled" schemes of socialism, communism, and Chartism, and would finally "wed the two great clans of this country—the savers and the workers —into one united family."[101]

Mayhew did not specify the terms of that partnership except to propose, on one occasion, that the trade unions, in addition to seeking higher wages, should provide a "uniform rate of income" for workers in slack seasons and a basic subsistence for the aged and disabled.[102] Disparaging those "new-fangled" ideas, he assured his readers that he himself was "neither Chartist, Protectionist, Socialist, Communist, nor Co-operationist."[103] Yet he was as impassioned as the most extreme radical in denouncing the "infamies" of the capitalists, their "brutalizing love of gain," and the injustice of a system that freed the laborer from the "tyranny of the noble" only to subject him to the "greed of the trader."[104] As his attacks on the capitalists became shriller, they fell into the familiar anti-Semitic mode, the "perfection" of political economy appearing in the guise of "Ikey Solomons, the Jew fence," "Ikey, the economist": "He buys in the cheapest market and sells in the dearest, and he is regulated in all his dealings *solely* by the principle of supply and demand."[105]

The anti-Semitism was predictable enough; it was a staple of radical thought throughout the period. Other of Mayhew's views, however, were less predictable, as some of his readers discovered when they sent him money to distribute to the "distressed persons" he had reported on in his columns.

One reader, contributing half a sovereign (and apologizing for that small sum) to a young flower girl so that she could continue in her honest trade instead of lapsing into the all too common life of sin, was lectured about the "evils of promiscuous charity," the danger of encouraging people to think that "there are other means of obtaining money than by working for it." "To bestow alms upon a struggling, striving man, is to destroy his independence, and to make a beggar of one who *would* work for his living."[106] Another correspondent, offering goods instead of money, was sternly reminded that the same objection held against gifts of all kinds. The only remedy for the able-bodied was to put them to work. "To do other than this is to destroy a man's self-reliance; and this is perhaps the greatest injury that can be inflicted on the poor, being often the main cause of their poverty." Mayhew relented only to the extent of permitting goods advanced as loans of stock, a plan that had succeeded admirably, he said, among the Jews.[107] But when another reader sent a pound to be loaned for the purchase of stock—without interest, he specified—he too was admonished. "To allow the poor the use of money at less than the fair market value is to bestow alms upon them to precisely the extent of the deficient interest." It was one thing to protest against the usurious interest exacted from the poor, another thing to suggest to the poor that interest itself was wrong. Interest was a legitimate return for the use of money and as much a share of the product as labor. "Let us not, in our wish to have justice done to the workman, forget what is due to the capitalist, who supplied the materials, tools, and subsistence, without which the cleverest operative would not only have no work to do, but no strength to do it even if he had the work."[108]

As firmly as Chadwick or Martineau, Mayhew drew the line between the "deserving" and the "undeserving" poor, between those worthy of assistance and those not.

> All that the better part of the working-classes desire is, to live by their industry; and those who desire to live by the industry of others, form no portion of the honest independent race of workmen in this country whom Mr. Mayhew wishes to befriend. The deserving poor are really those who *cannot* live by their labour, whether from under-payment, want of employment, or physical or mental incapacity; and these Mr. Mayhew wishes, and will most cheerfully do all he can, at any time and in any way to assist.[109]

That Mayhew accepted this distinction and was prepared to base social policy on it is all the more significant in view of his own unconcealed fascination and sympathy with those whom he himself labeled the "undeserving." In his book on the prisons of London, published at the same time as the four-volume edition of *London Labour,* he tried to reconcile the proper claims of the deserving poor with the compassion that should be extended to the least deserving. "Are we all so immaculate that we have no sympathy but for the *deserving* poor. Is our pity limited merely to those only who suffer the least, because they suffer with an unaccusing conscience; and must we entirely shut out from our commiseration the wretch who is tormented not only with hunger, but with the self-reproaches of his own bosom."[110] On the face of it, there was nothing inconsistent in such a plea for compassion, in trying to bring the undeserving within the compass of "pity" and "tenderness" while insisting upon the superior moral claims of the deserving. But in Mayhew's case it betrayed a tension that pervaded all his work. Having represented the undeserving in the starkest, most dramatic terms, as incapable of normal civilized life or deliberately, perversely resistant to such a life—in either case preying upon the civilized members of the community, including the honest workmen—he went on to ask for a sympathy and understanding that his own account rendered all the more difficult. Not, perhaps, for someone of Mayhew's temperament—a bohemian instinctively attracted to the outcast who flouted society's laws and the trickster who made fools of conventional men. But his readers were more apt to identify themselves with the victims of those outcasts and tricksters, to be impressed less by the supposed "tormented" conscience and "self-reproaches" of the transgressors than by their willful, persistent, ingenious transgressions.

5. A Confusion of Identity

If Mayhew's attitude toward the street-folk was ambiguous, it was partly because their identity was ambiguous. He had gone to great pains to describe that "wandering tribe" in all its peculiarity, and had even made an effort to determine its size. Yet the effect of his work was to blur the distinction between the street-folk and the "London Labour and the London Poor" of the title.

London Labour was full of numbers, in the text, in charts and tables, even in interviews. The numbers were not always reliable, consistent, logical, or relevant; but they were there, in great profusion. Among these numbers were estimates of the population of the street-folk. Early in the first volume Mayhew spoke of "upwards of fifty thousand individuals, or about a fortieth-part of the entire population of the metropolis getting their living in the streets."[111] This figure, which included workers and their dependents, comprised street buyers, sellers, finders, cleaners, and performers, but not the coal laborers, dock workers, transit workers, and vagrants of the third volume, or the prostitutes, thieves, and beggars of the fourth. The individual figures for each of these other groups were so imprecise and overlapping that no total figure can be ventured, but it must have fallen far short of even ten percent of the population of London.

Mayhew was well aware of the importance of relative figures, the proportion of street-folk to the population at large. Repeating the one-fortieth figure in the introduction to the second volume, he stressed the need to determine "the precise extent of the proportion which the Street-Traders bear to the rest of the Metropolitan Population . . . the want, the ignorance and the vice of a street-life being in a direct ratio to the numbers."[112] Only rarely, however, did he act on this advice, as when he compared the proportion of laborers convicted of petty larceny (one in 28) with that of Londoners as a whole (one in 266).[113] Some of the most revealing figures were tucked away in the middle of the third volume in the chapter on the coal heavers, where Mayhew suddenly introduced the census figures on occupations in London. Domestic servants were the largest single group (168,000), followed by laborers (50,000, including indoor laborers), boot-makers and shoemakers (28,000), tailors (23,500), milliners and dressmakers (20,000).[114] (These figures represented individual workers, not their fami-lies.) Mayhew commented on the fact that the number of laborers was less than one-third that of servants, but not on the much greater disparity between the street-folk and the servants. Indeed, apart from this passing reference and their appearance in the Classification, servants did not figure at all in *London Labour*. (This is all the more remarkable because Mayhew and his brother had recently co-authored a comic novel, *The Greatest Plague of Life: or the Adventures of a Lady in Search of a Good Servant*.) Nor did the shoemakers, tailors, milliners, dressmakers, and a good many other workers and their families. Mayhew complained that most of his street-folk were missing from the census.[115] But if the census had its nonpersons, so did *London Labour,* and in far larger numbers.

Mayhew, one of his editors has it, was "obsessed with statistics."[116] But the obsession had the effect, as often as not, of distorting the reader's perspective. Many of his charts and tables, like his long descriptions of technical processes, seemed to have no other purpose than to fill space. Whatever their purpose, they left the impression of a vast domain of street-folk. The plethora of figures on all manner of subjects—the number of rats inhabiting the sewers and the projected number after several genera-tions if permitted to multiply naturally; the number of oysters consumed each year and the amount of oyster shells in the refuse heaps; the miles of streets and roads, the cost of constructing, repairing, and cleaning them, and the quantity of mud, dung, and dust removed from them; the number of fish, fruits, vegetables, rabbits, matches, and flowers sold on the streets; the tons of goods loaded and unloaded at the docks, the value of those goods, and the cost of constructing the docks; the number of omnibuses, the riders served by them, the miles of road traversed, and the fare collected—all of these had the effect of magnifying the image of the street-folk themselves. It was as if the human population had to be commensurate with the material phenomena: 650,000,000 oyster shells, 1,932,480 feet of sewers, 1,350 miles of macadamized streets. The magnitude and profusion of these numbers gave the impression of a profusion of street-folk. And as if to magnify them even more, the figures were sometimes written out and italicized—the 1,397,760 pounds of wastepaper traded every year being sufficient for *"forty-four millions, seven hundred and twenty-eight thousand, four hundred and thirty"* half-ounce letters.[117]

Among the other illusions fostered by this plenitude of statistics were those of precision and certitude. That so many different kinds of facts could be reduced to hard, precise numbers seemed to be a warrant of accuracy. In fact the statistics were often as faulty as they were irrelevant. Appended to the 1851 edition of the first volume was an errata list of some 80 items, most of which were mistakes in numbers. (These may have been called to his attention by readers of the weekly pamphlets.) Later editions, rather than correcting the errors in the text, simply reproduced the errata list. The other volumes contained no similar list, although the mistakes were at least as numerous. The most obvious errors ranged from simple arithmetical miscalculations to gross logical fallacies. One of Mayhew's most dramatic findings —that 14 percent of the population of England "continue their existence either by pauperism, mendicancy, or crime"[118]—contained several typical errors: a simple arithmetical mistake resulting in an overestimate of almost 300,000 people; the comparison of noncomparables (using data from different periods and different kinds of sources); equating the incidence of pauperism, vagrancy, and criminality with the number of paupers, vagrants, and criminals, as if there were no recidivists among them, no criminal committing several crimes each year, or vagrants lodged in different casual wards at different times; and adding up each of these categories as if they were mutually exclusive, as if paupers were not also, on occasion, vagrants, or vagrants criminals. Each of these errors was an overstatement, and compounded they egregiously exaggerated the situation.*

---

*This is not to apply to Mayhew standards of accuracy and sophistication appropriate to a later time. The "science" of statistics may be said to have come formally of age in 1833 with the formation of the Statistical Section of the British Association for the Advancement of Science, and the founding, later that year and the following year, of the statistical societies of Manchester and London. From the beginning the London society took as its main purpose the compilation and elucidation of "facts calculated to illustrate the condition and prospects of society," which included statistics about industry and commerce, births and deaths, as well as "moral and social statistics": housing, sanitation, education, child labor, crime, illiteracy, pauperism.[119] And from the beginning there was a determined attempt to exclude personal judgments and to present a balanced view of social conditions. The year before Mayhew started his series for the *Chronicle,* the *Journal of the Statistical Society* published an article on housing conditions in St.-George's-in-the-East, explaining that it had chosen that parish as an example of the *"average* condition of the poorer classes of the metropolis" rather than the "condition of any one of those lowest sinks of barbarism and vice."[120]

Rather than labor the point, one need only endorse the judgment of one of Mayhew's admirers, E. P. Thompson: "Every single table and set of statistical data in Mayhew must be scrutinized, not for dishonesty or manipulation, but for sheer slipshod technique and haste in getting to press"; indeed, several tables were "sheer gibberish." Thompson made almost a virtue of this statistical sloppiness. "His method is in fact anti-statistical and constructively so: by counterposing statistical generalities with actual life-histories and individual witness, he is both offering a running commentary—and criticism—of the generalities, and offering a different framework within which they may be read."[121] A more mundane explanation is that the statistics were meant to confirm the life-histories, to give precision, objectivity, and scientific authority to what might otherwise appear impressionistic, exaggerated, or fanciful. For someone venturing into the "undiscovered country of the poor," bringing back stories that "lie under the imputation of telling such tales as travellers are generally supposed to delight in," it was important to have the credibility that came with cold, hard numbers.[122]*

Neither the "flesh and blood" of the life-histories nor the "bare bones" of the statistics succeeded in removing the confusion surrounding the identity of the street-folk. The expectations aroused by the title, the massive, cyclopedia-like appearance of the work, the multitude of species and subspecies which seemed to enhance the size of the street population, the profusion of statistics which had the same inflationary effect, and, perhaps most important, Mayhew's own attitude toward his subjects, his insistence that, for all their peculiarities and faults, they were worthy of the considerable attention and sympathy he gave them—all had the effect of equating the street-folk of the subtitle with the "labour" and "poor" of the title.

*That this imputation was not entirely undeserved is suggested by the research of one historian who inquired into the details of one of Mayhew's "life-histories," the experiences of a convict transported to Australia. Claiming to have "confirmations" of the convict's story, Mayhew declared it "altogether truthful." In fact, F. B. Smith discovered, the account was contradicted by readily available sources and was patently self-serving and untrue. "Like many journalists landing a good story, Mayhew seems to have willingly suspended disbelief to the point of becoming an accomplice in falsehood."[123]

Mayhew's biographer, Anne Humpherys, found·two misquotations on the cover pages of the pamphlets "so wantonly wrong that one's faith in Mayhew's accuracy is almost shaken." The first was a quotation attributed to Carlyle about workers displaced by machinery. "Soot them," Mayhew quoted Carlyle, "and sweep them into the dustbin." What Carlyle had in fact said—not about workers but about criminals, in a pamphlet entitled "Model Prisons"—was that the "besom" (broom) should be used to sweep those criminals into the dustbin. A week later Mayhew again cited Carlyle, this time as recommending, "in grim earnest," the "painless extinction" of every poor man's child. This was an apparent allusion to a passage in *Chartism* commenting sardonically on the well known and much derided infanticide scheme of "Marcus," the Malthusian fanatic. Carlyle, who was as critical of Malthusianism as Mayhew himself, cited Marcus's proposal as the pronouncement made in "grim earnest" of a "Benthamee-Malthusian."[124]

This confusion of identity was abetted by the much-cited image of the "traveller in the undiscovered country of the poor." Commentators on both the *Chronicle* articles and the weekly parts of *London Labour* had remarked upon the "unknown," "undiscovered," "foreign," "strange" country unearthed by Mayhew. That image served as a blank check on credibility, an invitation to the suspension of disbelief. Since it was an unknown country that was being explored for the first time, anything might be true, nothing was inconceivable. However strange "the poor" might seem, the strangeness was to be attributed to the simple fact of ignorance. The *Spectator* was the first to advise its readers to see for themselves the parts of the metropolis described by Mayhew—an area "stranger to you than Brussels, Lyons, or Genoa."[125] The strangeness, the foreignness, of that country of the poor was all the more striking because it existed, as one reviewer after another said, unbeknownst to everyone else living there. The *British Quarterly Review* commended the "wonderful series of revelations suddenly disclosed in our own country, existing as it were, under our very feet; a mass of social woe and putridity that France itself could not parallel."[126] Douglas Jerrold, Mayhew's father-in-law and former colleague on *Punch,* wrote to a friend praising "those marvellous revelations of the inferno of misery, of wretchedness, that is smouldering under our feet," adding, with typical self-reproach, "We know nothing of the terrible life that is about us,—us, in our smug respectability."[127] William Thackeray, another friend of Mayhew's, struck the same posture of astonishment and remorse.

> What a confession it is that we have almost all of us been obliged to make! A clever and earnest-minded writer gets a commission from the *Morning Chronicle* newspaper, and reports upon the state of our poor in London; he goes amongst labouring people and poor of all kinds—and brings back what? A picture of human life so wonderful, so awful, so piteous and pathetic, so exciting and terrible, that readers of romances own they never read anything like to it; and that the griefs, struggles, strange adventures here depicted exceed anything that any of us could imagine. Yes; and these wonders and terrors have been lying by your door and mine ever since we had a door of our own. We had but to go a hundred yards off and see for ourselves, but we never did. . . . Of such wonderous and complicated misery as this you confess you had no idea? No. How should you?—you and I—we are of the upper classes; we have had hitherto no community with the poor. We never speak a word to the servant who waits on us for twenty years. . . . Some clear-sighted, energetic man like the writer of the *Chronicle* travels into the poor man's country for us, and comes back with his tale of terror and wonder.[128]

"Romances," "adventures," "tales," "fiction"—the words appear again and again, and with no invidious intent. The *Chronicle* was pleased to quote the tribute paid it by its rival, the *Sun:* "At this auspicious moment the *Morning Chronicle* has published a series of revelations of London life—revelations so marvellous, so horrible, and so heartrending, that few histories can equal, and no fiction surpass them."[129] Those "revelations" resembling nothing so much as "fiction" recall the cliché about truth being stranger than fiction; indeed, the stranger the tales, the more truthful they seemed. When Thackeray and others marveled at the "strange adventures," the "wonders and terrors" taking place all about them, they took their own ignorance to be part of that strange and terrible reality. They did not question the facts of which they were so abysmally ignorant; they only deplored the complacency, the "smug respectability," that had kept them in ignorance. Their ignorance became, in a sense, a confirmation of the reality; the reality was what it was precisely because they suffered it to be so, because they had deliberately closed their eyes to it, had chosen not to see what was under their very feet, outside their very doors.

It is curious that so many reviewers of *London Labour* responded to these volumes with the same expressions of wonder and guilt that had earlier been elicited by the *Chronicle* articles. Yet the two series were quite different. However strange the tales brought back from Mayhew's first excursions into "the poor man's country," some of them, at any rate, were tales about the familiar, recognizable poor—weavers, dockers, shoemakers, tailors. The critical reader might have wondered whether those tales were representative or the facts accurate; he might have been suspicious of Thackeray's statement about the upper classes who "never speak a word to the servant who waits on us for twenty years"; it might even have occurred to him that if the rich ignored their servants, so, evidently, had Mayhew. But whatever his reservations, he would have had reason to think that it was "the poor man's country," the country of "labouring people and poor of all kinds," that was being explored in the *Chronicle,* and reason to feel guilty about his ignorance of that country.

London Labour, however, was another matter. Here Mayhew, by his own admission, was traversing only a small and remote corner of that poor man's country, a region totally devoid of domestic servants, tailors, dressmakers, shoemakers, carpenters, and the like. And many of those portrayed by Mayhew were, by his account, so exceedingly strange, deliberately cultivating their isolation and peculiarity, that the reader need have felt neither surprise nor shame at his ignorance. What is surprising is how many reviewers did nevertheless react so guiltily, and, more important, how many unwittingly identified the most distinctive street-folk with the generality of "London Labour and the London Poor."

The *Eclectic Review* was typical. Under the familiar title "Mayhew's Revelations of London," it praised the work that would give a new cast to contemporary history, and paid tribute to the intrepid explorer responsible for these revelations. "Henry Mayhew has dug up the foundations of society, and exposed them to light. He has travelled through the unknown regions of our metropolis, and returned with full reports concerning the strange tribes of men which he may be said to have discovered." For ten pages the review quoted and paraphrased Mayhew's most extravagant descriptions of these tribes—"more degraded than the savages of New Zealand, than the blacks of the Great Karoo . . . greater development of the animal than of the intellectual or moral nature . . . intellectually, morally, and religiously degraded . . . overwhelmed by ignorance, vice, and poverty." This was no "petty tribe," the reviewer pointed out, but rather a "large class," a "nation numbering thousands," "fifty thousand individuals," "one-fortieth" of the population of London. But as the review progressed, the subject expanded until it became "the poor" who were excluded from the advantages of civilization. By the end, Mayhew's "noble" work had become "a history of the poor in the nineteenth century."[130]

The equation of the street-folk with "the poor" was a common feature of most of the reviews, and this while quoting Mayhew's most lurid passages and citing his estimate of "one-fortieth" of the population. Even a critical notice like that in the *Athenaeum* fell into the same trap. It intimated that Mayhew, a writer of comic stories and an editor of the *Comic Almanac,* might have carried over to the present work some of the literary habits appropriate to that other genre. Recalling his controversy with Lord Ashley over the ragged schools, the *Athenaeum* suggested that the "proved exaggeration" in that case made questionable some of the present "revelations" (this last word in quotation marks), and suspected that Mayhew's sketches may have been as effective as they were because they had been drawn "for the mere sake of effect." But it expressed no such suspicions about the identity of Mayhew's subject; on the contrary, the review itself could well have misled the unwary reader. It opened by explaining that such an inquiry into "the actual condition of the London poor" had long been desired by statisticians and philanthropists, for in spite of all the parliamentary committees, commissioners, and special correspondents, there had been no general study of "the actual state of the million poor of London." Only now, it was pleased to report, was a private inquirer doing what the state had so long neglected. At the very end of the review, following two long pages of extracts, it observed that the monthly installments of the second volume were "still occupied with the Street-Folk." But that casual and belated observation could hardly erase the impression left by the opening paragraph, that this important work was indeed the long-awaited inquiry into "the actual state of the million poor of London."[131]

Sometimes the distinctive character of Mayhew's street-folk was noted, but so casually that it hardly registered. The *Quarterly Review* described those who derived their living from the streets as "a class decidedly lower in the social scale than the labourer and numerically very large, though the population returns do not number them among the inhabitants of the kingdom." This single sentence came in the middle of a long omnibus review of seventeen books and articles under the title "The Charities and the Poor of London," the subject of which was "the London poor," the "metropolitan poor," the "laboring classes." Making a large point of the connection between poverty and crime—"Guilt and poverty are closely connected. Misconduct leads to poverty, poverty tempts to crime"—the *Review* insisted that it was poverty as such, the poverty of all the poor, not just that of the "lower" class of street-folk, that had that unfortunate association with crime.[132]

The *Edinburgh Review* also remarked upon "the existence in our great towns of a class of being *below* the working classes, permanently and almost hopelessly degraded." The reference, however, was not to the street-folk but to the subjects of the *Morning Chronicle* articles, the impoverished tailors, needlewomen, and agricultural laborers. The reviewer conceded that the "individual pictures" of suffering and misery were basically true, if exaggerated. He only questioned the representativeness of those pictures. "They are true as scenes; are they true as general delineations? Are they *specimens,* or *exceptions?* How deep do these miseries go? Are they characteristic of a class, or only of individuals of that class?" His own suspicion was that the miseries, though real enough, were those of a relatively small group, of a few thousand out of the 31,000 needlewomen, certainly not of the working classes as a whole. The conditions of most workers, the reviewer was convinced, had actually improved. If it seemed otherwise, it was because the social sensibilities of the public had progressed even more rapidly. "How much more sensitive to suffering, how much more quick to detect and prompt to pity misery, the public mind has of late years become; and how many phases of wretchedness formerly hidden in secrecy and silence are now made known through a thousand channels."[133]

The Christian Socialist J. M. Ludlow drew exactly the opposite conclusions from the same data. Writing in *Fraser's Magazine* a few months after the *Chronicle* series started, he anticipated the objection of the *Edinburgh Review*. "Still, it may be said, your accounts apply only to the emphatically underpaid and suffering classes. Starvation wages and unwholesome diets are not the characteristics of the bulk of London workmen." To which he replied that if these characteristics were not yet typical of the working classes as a whole, they were already typical of a daily increasing class, and that the wretched Spitalfields weaver was the "full-developed type of what is everywhere taking place." The poor were getting poorer while the comparatively well-off were sinking into poverty or becoming the "parasites of labour," thus swelling the ranks of the helpless and enslaved.[134]*

Mayhew's first articles appeared just at the time when the Christian Socialists were girding for action. Charles Kingsley, F. D. Maurice, Ludlow, and other "gentlemen of known philanthropic zeal," as the *British Quarterly Review* described them, had called a series of meetings to inquire into the means of ameliorating the condition of the workers in accord with the principles of Christian Socialism. "Precisely at this moment," the *Review* said, "came the stimulus of Mr. Mayhew's revelations, urging into immediate execution what might else have been delayed."[135] The result was the founding of the Working Tailors' Association and the Needlewomen's Association. Although Mayhew himself was not a Christian Socialist and had not been present at the meetings, it was assumed that his articles had provided the impetus for these associations.†

The articles may also have provided the inspiration for some of the scenes in Kingsley's *Alton Locke,* published the same year. While Kingsley himself, in a letter written shortly afterward, denied "picking and stealing" bits from Mayhew—the philanthropic activities of his mother, he explained, and the experiences of his father as rector of a large metropolitan parish had long familiarized him with the conditions of the London poor—he commended the articles as a "clear view of the real state of the working classes."[136] In his pamphlet *Cheap Clothes and Nasty,* published several months before *Alton Locke,* he quoted at length from the articles on the tailors, from which, he said, "we learnt too much to leave us altogether masters of ourselves."[137] A footnote in *Alton Locke* entreated all Christians to read the "noble letters" on labor and the poor in the *Chronicle.*[138] And some of the scenes in that novel (whose hero was a tailor) may have owed something to Mayhew: the Irishman enticed into the sweatshop and kept there by the employer who took away his clothing, the profiteering in the purchase of army uniforms, the needlewomen forced into prostitution, the slum that was suspiciously reminiscent of Jacob's Island.[139]

At just this time, when Kingsley was enlisting Carlyle's help to find

---

*Today this reads like the Marxist theory of immiseration: the pauperization of the proletariat and the proletarianization of the petty bourgeoisie. But Ludlow was writing without benefit of Engels's *Condition of the Working Class in England* or the *Communist Manifesto.* (The latter was published in England for the first time in *The Red Republican,* ten months after this issue of *Fraser's.*) The theory of immiseration (although not under that name) had in fact long been a staple of English radicalism.

†The idea of such associations antedated Mayhew's articles. Lord Ashley had previously organized a Milliners' and Dressmakers' Association which *Fraser's Magazine* spoke of approvingly in the November 1849 issue. It may have been Ashley rather than Mayhew who galvanized the Christian Socialists.

a publisher for *Alton Locke,* Carlyle himself was issuing the first of his *Latter-Day Pamphlets.* In that pamphlet Carlyle praised the *Chronicle* for bringing home to its readers the "unspeakable" thought of "thirty thousand outcast Needlewomen working themselves swiftly to death . . ., thirty thousand wretched women, sunk in that putrefying well of abominations." This unspeakable thought prompted another: that in spite of all these wretched creatures, a housewife looking for the services of a seamstress would find none worthy of hire. "Imaginary needlewomen, who demand considerable wages, and have a deepish appetite for beer and viands," were abundantly available, but not a competent seamstress satisfied with fair wages.[140] The *Economist* seized upon this passage to discredit Mayhew. Having made some inquiries of its own, it assured its readers that Carlyle was not indulging in his usual "grotesque and perverse paradoxes" but was telling the literal truth; none of these needlewomen was so distressed as to be willing to work at the regular wage of a shilling a week.[141]

Dickens is also said to have been influenced by Mayhew, although the evidence here is still more tenuous. In this case it is not the articles on tailors or needlewomen which are cited, but those on the more bizarre types of street-folk. Since the typically Mayhewian characters were also typically Dickensian, it is difficult to know who was indebted to whom. Long before *London Labour* Dickens had given ample evidence of his fondness for the picturesque and grotesque, for social outcasts and eccentrics, for street-folk and street-scenes. In any event, there was surely enough in London to fire the imagination of both men without recourse to claims of "borrowing" or "indebtedness."[142]

It was less, however, among the eminent Victorians than among the not so eminent ones that Mayhew's influence was felt.[143] The weekly parts of *London Labour* sold 13,000 copies, a respectable number for a work of that sort—and respectable, too, by comparison with the circulation of the *Chronicle* series, which was perhaps a third of that.[144] A more important measure of influence was the number of imitators he spawned and the genre of literature he brought into vogue. While isolated specimens of the genre had always existed, it was not until the fifties that his "unknown country" became almost too well known in works whose very titles are often evocative of Mayhew: Thomas Beames, *The Rookeries of London* (1850); C. M. Smith, *Curiosities of London Life* (1853); John Garwood, *The Million Peopled City: Or, One-Half of the People of London Made Known to the Other Half* (1853); George Godwin, *London's Shadows* (1854); Watts Phillips, *The Wild Tribes of London* (1855); M. A. S. Barber, *The Sorrows of the Streets* (1855); J. E. Ritchie, *Night Side of London* (1857); John Hollingshead, *Ragged London* (1861). Adaptations from Mayhew also appeared on the popular stage. J. B. Johnstone's *How We Live in the World of London* and J. Elphinstone's *London Labour and the London Poor; or, Want and Vice* made their debuts within a week or so of each other in 1854 and both were later revived.

The popularity of these books and plays may have inspired Mayhew to issue the four-volume edition of 1861–62. His earlier articles on the conventional trades, on the other hand, evoked so little interest that Mayhew himself, who was always alert to the commercial potentialities of his work, did not reprint them. Nor did anyone else for over a century. When the first selection from his *Chronicle* articles appeared in 1971, it was under the fitting title *The Unknown Mayhew*. [145] The "historic" Mayhew, the Mayhew best known in his own time and for generations to come, was not this "unknown" Mayhew reporting on the conventional laboring poor, but the chronicler of the street-folk—the "Mayhewian poor," as they may be called, in tribute to their "discoverer."

6. The "Residuum"

Mayhew did not, in fact, discover the Mayhewian poor. One of the reasons his "revelations" had the effect they did was because they were not entirely unfamiliar; the shock of discovery was actually a shock of recognition. His revelations had been anticipated by the Royal Commission and Select Committee reports of the early forties, which had also been received with dismay and horror. Even the metaphors were the same: the travelers' tales brought back from foreign parts, the fictional tales that were all too true. The reports of 1842 on the mines were described by the *Quarterly Review* as disclosing "modes of existence . . . as strange and as new as the wildest dreams of fiction," and by the *Spectator* as revealing "scenes of suffering and infamy which will come upon many well-informed people like the fictions or tales of distant lands."[146]

That same year saw the publication of another document, perhaps the most influential since the Poor Law Report: the *Report on the Sanitary Condition of the Labouring Population of Great Britain*. The *Sanitary Report*, as it is generally known, elicited the usual protestations of disbelief; indeed, it foresaw just that reaction. In almost exactly the words with which Thackeray was to greet Mayhew's work, Edwin Chadwick, the principal author of the report, commented on its revelations.

> The statements of the condition of considerable proportions of the labouring population of the towns into which the present inquiries have been carried have been received with surprise by persons of the wealthier classes living in the immediate vicinity, to whom the facts were as strange as if they related to foreigners or the natives of an unknown country. . . . We have found that the inhabitants of the front

houses in many of the main streets of those towns and of the metropolis, have never entered the adjoining courts, or seen the interiors of any of the tenements, situate at the backs of their own houses, in which their own workpeople reside.[147]

Chadwick invoked the image of the "unknown country" for much the same reason Mayhew later did, to account for the public's ignorance of the abysmal conditions in which so large a part of the laboring population lived —the foul odors of open cesspools, the garbage, excrement, and dead rats rotting in the streets, the filth and scum floating in the river, the sewage that passed as drinking water. Chadwick's principal concern (his obsession, critics complained) was the "miasma" emanating from all that decaying matter, the "fetid effluvia," "poisonous exhalations," and "reeking atmosphere" which were the source of the physical, moral, and mental deterioration of the poor.[148] It was this miasma theory that caused him, at the height of the cholera epidemic, to have the sewers flushed in order to dissipate the deadly vapors, thus further contaminating the water supply and aggravating the epidemic—this against the advice of those who maintained that the disease was caused by germs and infection rather than by the miasma.*

Like the *Poor Law Report* which it resembled in so many respects (not surprisingly, since Chadwick had so large a part in both), the *Sanitary Report* included a distinctive theory of the cause of the problem, a body of evidence to support that theory, and a set of practical recommendations by way of remedy. The evidence itself, again like the earlier report, was selective and biased. Although the report was full of figures, they were not always pertinent or accurate, and the analysis was conspicuously nonquantitative at precisely those points where it should have been quantitative. If there was so little hard statistical evidence, it was partly because the miasma, by its nature, defied measurement. The miasma theory was also inconsistent with the "unknown country" metaphor. Surely that pungent stench could not entirely have escaped the notice of the rich who lived in such disagreeable proximity to it; surely the occupants of those "front houses" must have had some whiff of the odoriferous world at their very backs.

A more serious difficulty was the failure of the report to address the crucial question: How large a part of the "labouring population" did in fact live in the midst of those noisome sights and smells? After 400 pages the report concluded that what had been described at such length was the "condition of considerable proportions of the labouring population of the towns."[149] (Earlier it had said that conditions in rural areas, contrary to

*Chadwick had a powerful ally in Florence Nightingale, who shared his disbelief in the germ theory of disease. Long after the work of Jacob Henle, Louis Pasteur, and Joseph Lister, she mocked the idea that syphilis, any more than smallpox or cholera, was carried by infection; in each case the fault was the lack of sanitation, clean water, and fresh air.

popular belief, were no better than those in the towns.) In the absence of
any more precise estimate of those "considerable proportions," the "labouring population" of the title (the "poorer classes of the population," as the
first sentence put it) were implicitly identified with that odious "sanitary
condition." And because that condition was so much worse than anything
the reader could be presumed to have witnessed—hence the unknown
country metaphor—the report had the effect of reducing the "natives" of
that unknown country to the status of "foreigners" or, worse, "savages" and
"animals." One London magistrate was quoted as saying that there were no
living quarters so wretched as to have no occupants, that if empty casks were
placed in the streets they would soon be tenanted by a "race lower than any
yet known." "If you will have marshes and stagnant waters, you will there
have suitable animals, and the only way of getting rid of them is by draining
the marshes."150

There is a striking correspondence between the *Sanitary Report* and
London Labour, not only because the Mayhewian poor lived and worked
under the worst sanitary conditions, but because they themselves were, in
a sense, that "sanitary condition." It is significant that the same words—
"residuum," "refuse," "offal"—were used to denote the sewage waste that
constituted the sanitary problem and the human waste that constituted the
social problem. And it is no accident that some of the characters in the
Sanitary Report reappeared in *London Labour.* One "eye-witness" description
of the "class of bone-pickers, mud-rakers, people living on the produce of
dung-heaps," was worthy of Mayhew himself.

> The bone-pickers are the dirtiest of all the inmates of our workhouse;
> I have seen them take a bone from a dung-heap, and gnaw it while
> reeking hot with the fermentation of decay. Bones, from which the
> meat had been cut raw, and which had still thin strips of flesh adhering
> to them, they scraped carefully with their knives, and put the bits, no
> matter how befouled with dirt, into a wallet or pocket appropriated
> to the purpose. They have told me, that whether in broth or grilled,
> they were the most savoury dish that could be imagined. I have not
> observed that these creatures were savage, but they were thoroughly
> debased. Often hardly human in appearance, they had neither human
> tastes nor sympathies, nor even human sensations, for they revelled in
> the filth which is grateful to dogs, and other lower animals, and which
> to our apprehensions is redolent only of nausea and abomination.151

Mayhew improved upon this account. His bone-pickers not only ate (and
relished) this revolting fare but made a livelihood out of it; after gnawing
at the bones, they sold them. And so with the other scavengers, who lived
in the midst of that filth and lived off it, made a living and a way of life
out of it. One of the most memorable impressions of *London Labour* is of

a "refuse" class whose sole occupation was the finding, collecting, sorting, treating, and selling of every conceivable kind of refuse: dung, dust, bones, offal, rags, rats, dead bodies.

Like the scavengers themselves, Chadwick too wanted to put that refuse to use, although in a manner that would have deprived some of that class of their livelihood. He was offended by the dung on the streets as much because it was uneconomic as because it was unhealthy. Convinced that untreated human sewage was the best and cheapest kind of fertilizer, he was outraged at the thought of all that manure being wasted on the city streets —and laying waste to the people there—while the fields were starved of fertilizer. He encouraged the efforts of a Metropolitan Sewage Manure Company to sell that sewage, and he himself engaged in experiments to convey it to the countryside by means of pipes and canal boats. In Chadwick the sanitary reformer and the political economist were perfectly complemented. "All smell is disease," pronounced the former; and the latter: "All smell of decomposing matter may be said to indicate loss of money."[152]*

The *Sanitary Report,* Chadwick's biographer has said, "burst on a startled middle-class public."[155] Its sales exceeded those of any other blue book; thousands of copies were distributed free; and it was widely reviewed, excerpted, analyzed, and agonized over. Yet that "startled" public had been recently startled by no fewer than three similar revelations in as many years: one inquiry by Southwood Smith, another by Neil Arnott and James Kay, and the report of the Select Committee on the Health of Towns in 1840. After the publication of the *Sanitary Report,* the subject was kept alive by a series of other government reports—on Intramural Interments (1842–43), the Health of Towns (1844–45), the Metropolitan Sanitary Commission (1847–48). In 1844 alone, no fewer than three associations were formed to propagate the "sanitary gospel": the Association for Promoting Cleanliness among the Poor, the Society for the Improvement of the Conditions of the Labouring Classes, and the Health of Towns Association, all of which held meetings, sponsored lectures, and issued reports which were duly publicized in the press.

The climax of all this missionary activity came in 1848 with the passage of the Public Health Act and a supplementary health bill for London. These

---

*It is tempting to think of such schemes as typically Benthamite—maximizing utility by converting evils into goods. In fact the utilization of human waste, especially from the cities which produced such huge quantities of it, occupied reformers and radicals of every description. William Lovett (then prominent in the National Union of the Working Classes and later a founder of Chartism) deplored the fact that the Thames was carrying away daily "seven thousand loads of poisonous filth that might have been converted into the most valuable manure."[153] It might have been a character in a Dickens novel, but it was in fact Dickens's brother-in-law, Henry Austin, who explained to the Board of Health in 1857 that because of the greater quantity of animal food in the diet of the rich, their feces were richer in nitrogen than the feces of the poor; hence "the value of the refuse of Belgravia would, no doubt, exceed that of Bethnal Green."[154]

measures, hotly debated in and out of Parliament, were as much exercises in propaganda and public instruction as in legislation and administration. And the agencies created by these acts, the General Board of Health and the Metropolitan Commission, continued to focus attention on the issue by the constant release of reports, statements, and dire warnings. When John Simon, the first Medical Officer for London, gave a preview of his first annual report in October 1849, *The Times* commented (not in criticism but in praise) that it promised "to equal, in the fearful interest of its unvarnished disclosures, the vivid horrors of those fictitious chronicles, the *Mysteries of Paris*, and the *Revelations of London.*"[156]

What made Simon's report so "fearful" was the same event that precipitated Mayhew's work, the cholera epidemic. (The Public Health Act of 1848 had been passed in the shadow of the cholera epidemic then raging on the Continent.) The sanitary issue, so long the subject of reports and debates, had become a tragic reality. Whatever quarrels there might be about the cause of the disease, there was no quarreling with the fact of the epidemic itself, whose daily reality was brought home to the public (if they needed reminding of it) in the daily death toll featured on the front pages of the newspapers. These mortality figures gave immediacy and urgency to the *Chronicle* series, to Simon's "Medical Report" (the complete text of which was also published in the *Chronicle*), and to a host of similar "revelations."

Although the epidemic revived the familiar theory that cholera was the "disease of the poor," the statistics did not always bear that out. "The epidemic was no respecter of classes," wrote one of the medical inspectors of the Board of Health. "Rich and poor suffered alike or escaped alike, according as they lived in the observance or violation of the laws of their physical well-being."[157] The latter qualification, of course, meant that the poor and rich did not suffer or escape "alike." But it did mean that the rich were not quite as immune nor the poor as fatally vulnerable as had been thought at the time of the previous epidemic in 1832. The comparison with that earlier epidemic was frequently made, and it was noted that while the victims in 1832 had been drawn largely from the "destitute and reckless class," they now included many of the "respectable class" of workmen, shopkeepers, even gentlemen.[158] Reviewing the mortality statistics after the epidemic had subsided, *Fraser's Magazine* tried to correct the popular misimpression. While at first sight, it reported, the figures suggested a vast disproportion of deaths among the poor—3,489 working men compared with 558 tradesmen and 135 gentlemen—in proportion to the population the figures were far less discrepant: 1 in 120 working men, one in 150 tradesmen, and one in 200 gentlemen.[159]

Yet the identification of cholera with the poor persisted, in part because there was in fact some correlation, in part because the epidemic drew attention once again to the slums of London. Thus *Fraser's,* after warning against too facile an equation of poverty with cholera, concluded by recommending to its readers the *Chronicle* article on Jacob's Island. Even the *Economist,* normally more given to preaching the gospel of political economy than the gospel of sanitary or social reform, reported that the epidemic raised anew the question of the "actual condition of the lower classes."

> It has opened up to the view of all the world the innermost parts of our great metropolis. It has shown the people lying eight or ten in a room, men and their wives dying unnoticed and unattended in dark and filthy dens, the living and the dead huddled together; it has shown to the whole world what a festering mass of destitution and demoralization spreads through a large part of our splendid city.[160]

The *Economist* was not so moved as to forget its basic principles. If the welfare of the lower classes commanded the immediate attention of the authorities, that was no warrant for a further centralization of power in the form of an expanded Board of Health, a measure that could only play into the hands of "chartists, red republicans, and socialists." But by equating the condition of the lowest classes in the worst of all times and places with the "actual condition of the lower classes," the *Economist* itself may have played into the hands of social reformers as well as socialists.

Written in the aftermath of the epidemic, *London Labour* had the smell of the miasma in it. Not all the street-folk resembled the "festering mass of destitution and demoralization" the *Economist* associated with the disease, but enough of them did to warrant the constant imagery of disease: the sickly, filthy, vermin-ridden, barely human men taking refuge in the "low" lodging houses; the scavengers plying their trades in the sewers, gutters, and garbage heaps of the city; the vagrants carrying with them a "stream of vice and disease," a "tide of iniquity and fever," a "moral pestilence . . . as terrible and as devastating as the physical pest which accompanies it."[161] Those of the street-folk who were not in that condition of moral and physical decay exhibited more subtle symptoms of the epidemic. Existing in a state of anxiety and crisis, of feverish, frenetic activity, they were prone to every variety of psychic and physical disorder, every kind of abnormality, excess, and perversion. And their poverty was equally unnatural. It was not the natural poverty of a pre-industrial world, the poverty that came with the inadequate resources of nature or the frailties of the human condition. Nor was it the poverty associated with industrialism and urbanism, the poverty that political economists regarded as the natural by-product of the laws of population, wages, and supply and demand. The poverty of the street-folk was not so much an economic condition as a pathological one, less a social problem than a social disease, a peculiar malignancy that could neither be explained nor cured.

7. Progress and Poverty

What made this poverty even more disturbing was the sense that it was regressive. The historian, especially the radical historian, may feel this most acutely and may therefore feel ambivalent toward *London Labour* itself. That the "Age of Chartism," when the working classes supposedly came to maturity, achieving a new level of consciousness, assertiveness, and unity, should have been succeeded by a period in which the major social document was a chronicle not of the working classes but of a small, heterogeneous group of street-folk, an urban "wandering tribe," seems an affront to the historical imagination, a violation of the orderly progress of history. It is all the more vexing because Mayhew himself originally gave promise of becoming the chronicler of the working classes and abandoned that mission, so it has been suggested, either because he reverted to his old romantic bohemianism or because he sought to promote sales by pandering to the taste for the sensational and the grotesque.[162]

Whatever the reason for the change of subject, the fact is that *London Labour* did pass over the conventional working classes, the bulk of the laboring poor, in favor of marginal types who resembled a lumpen-proletariat more than a proper proletariat. The street-folk were literally regressive, a throwback to a pre-industrial, even pre-civilized state, a primitive "tribe" surviving in the very heart of civilization. This was Mayhew's "revelation." And this was what was shocking about it: it gave evidence of the persistence, in the midst of the greatest metropolis of the world, of an archaic, anarchic, barbaric people.

This kind of poverty seemed all the more regressive at just this time. The *Chronicle* articles appeared at the turn of the mid-century, the pamphlet parts and first two volumes of *London Labour* in the early fifties, and the complete edition in the early sixties—a period recognized by contemporaries (and confirmed by historians) as one of relative well-being for the poor. Some contemporaries had been saying for some time that the condition-of-the-people question had been exaggerated, that the state of the majority of the working classes, so far from having deteriorated with the advance of industrialism, had considerably improved. In 1836 G. R. Porter opened the first volume of his *Progress of the Nation* by announcing that the present generation had witnessed the "greatest advances in civilization that can be found recorded in the annals of mankind," and subsequent volumes demonstrated that those advances were shared by most of the working classes (with such notable exceptions as the handloom weavers). There remained, Porter conceded, considerable inequality in the distribution of the products of industry, more than was consistent with the "degree of perfection to which human institutions may at some time be brought"; but there was less inequality than there had been earlier in the century, and there would be still less, he predicted, as production continued to rise and the rate of increase of the population declined. In later editions of his work, published in 1847 and 1851, he found even more reason for optimism, although again with reservations—the moral progress of the nation unfortunately lagged behind its material and social progress, the crime rate, for example, outstripping the increase both of population and of wealth.[163]

Macaulay, taking a longer historical view, found an even greater degree of progress. The condition of the poor in the present, he wrote in 1848, was infinitely better than that of the poor on the eve of the "Glorious Revolution," and compared favorably with the condition even of the rich in that "golden age."

> It is now the fashion to place the golden age of England in times when noblemen were destitute of the comforts the want of which would be intolerable to a modern footman, when farmers and shopkeepers breakfasted on loaves the very sight of which would raise a riot in a modern workhouse, when to have a clean shirt once a week was a privilege reserved for the higher class of gentry, when men died faster in the purest country air than now die in the most pestilential lanes of our towns, and when men died faster in the lanes of our towns than they now die on the coast of Guiana.[164]

This message appeared in the first volume of the *History of England* in the memorable chapter on the "State of England in 1685," a chapter which said almost as much about early Victorian England as about post-Restoration England. Indeed, the *History* itself was as much a social and cultural document of its time as a work of history, not only for the ideas it reflected—the famous "Whig interpretation" of the Revolution—but for the fact that those ideas were conveyed to so large an audience, and so formidable a work (five weighty tomes dealing with a period of seventeen years) with so austere a title *(The History of England from the Accession of James II)* could attain the popularity it did. The first two volumes, of 600-odd pages each, sold 22,000 copies within a year, subsequent volumes were even more successful, and by 1875 the first volume alone had sold over 133,000 copies.*

*Not all of those copies were destined for the library shelves of learned gentlemen. Mudie's lending libraries took 2,400 copies of the third and fourth volumes, and had to set aside a special room to handle them. One gentleman, living on the outskirts of Manchester, invited his poorer neighbors to his house every evening and read the entire *History* aloud to them. At the end of the last reading one of the audience rose and moved a vote of thanks to the author "for having written a history which working men can understand."[165]

The testimony of a Porter or a Macaulay might be discounted as that of an unimaginative civil servant (Porter had been chief statistician in the Board of Trade) or of a complacent Whig. But by the late 1840s some radicals were beginning to voice the same sentiments. Charles Kingsley was at the height of his radical period in the autumn of 1848 when he published *Yeast.* In that novel the hero, countering the spiritual blandishments of Rome, cited the evidence of social and material progress as proof of the existence of a God. "So give me the political economist, the sanitary reformer, the engineer; and take your saints and virgins, relics and miracles. The spinning-jenny and the railroad, Cunard's liners and the electric telegraph, are to me, if not to you, signs that we are, on some points at least, in harmony with the universe."[166] Mayhew's articles on the tailors in the *Chronicle* gave Kingsley pause, but a year and a half later the opening of the Great Exhibition moved him to tears and inspired him to preach a sermon in which the Exhibition appeared as a visible demonstration of Divine Providence. Had our forefathers been alive today, he assured his audience, they would have seen in the hospitals, railroads, and other scientific achievements of the day "confirmation of that old superstition of theirs, proofs of the kingdom of God, realizations of the gifts which Christ received for men, vaster than any of which they had dreamed."[167]

By the time the Exhibition opened in May 1851, Chartism with all its symbolic overtones—"the bitter discontent grown fierce and mad," as Carlyle put it—was a lingering memory to all but the most intransigent radical. The Crystal Palace, a million feet of glass in the shape of a huge dome containing thousands of exhibits (and some of the most magnificent elms in Hyde Park), was heralded as the beginning of a new era, the advent of modernity. Many years later Thomas Hardy recalled the impression the reports of the Exhibition made upon young people in a remote village in Wessex.

> For South Wessex the year [1851] formed in many ways an extraordinary chronological frontier or transit line, at which there occurred what one might call a precipice in Time. As in a geological "fault," we had presented to us a sudden bringing of ancient and modern into absolute contact, such as probably in no other single year since the Conquest was ever witnessed in this part of the country.[168]

Dedicated to the "working bees of the world's hives," the Great Exhibition was taken as a tribute to the great nation that had produced it, a nation made great, the exhibition suggested, by the gospel of work to which all classes were committed. "The Bees are more considered than the Butterflies of society," the *Economist* was pleased to report. "If the poor do not yet work less, the rich certainly work more."[169] The Crystal Palace was an extraordinary feat of industrial engineering and an equally extraordinary manifestation of the work ethic, of will, energy, and resourcefulness. Today more than ever we can appreciate the prodigious effort required to convert the initial idea into the completed structure in ten and a half months. The Exhibition's mottoes might have been devised by Carlyle: "The workers, of all types, stand forth as the really great men"; *"Pulcher et ille labor palma decorare laborem."*[170] These were not the slogans of "two nations," but of a single nation sharing a single ethos and exulting in the monumental product of that ethos.

It is against this background, the background of Hyde Park as well as the East End, that *London Labour* must be viewed. While England was congratulating itself on the "moral and material progress" that was so dramatically exhibited in that "fairy palace," as the cliché had it (and while Mayhew himself found time to write a novel on the Exhibition and a series of articles for the *Edinburgh News,* both of which overlapped with *London Labour*), *London Labour* was giving evidence of quite another England. Mayhew's street-folk were not part of the nation celebrated in the Great Exhibition, not even part of that "other" of Disraeli's "two nations," but rather a primitive "tribe," "folk," or "race." At just this time, when Adam Smith seemed finally to be vindicated, when the "natural progress of opulence" seemed to be benefiting the poor as well as the rest of the nation, Mayhew revived the Malthusian image of the poor—depressed, degraded, averse to labor except under the direst necessity, unaffected by the progress of industry and civilization.

What made the situation more paradoxical was the fact that at just this time the street-folk were actually decreasing in numbers. Mayhew himself reported that the number of costermongers had diminished in recent years as a result of legislation regulating street-trading.[171] More important in reducing their numbers was the laying of the railway lines which led to the creation of new streets, the destruction of many of the old rookeries, and the dispersion of their inhabitants. (This was often done as a conscious social policy, the new streets being deliberately designed to cut through the rookeries.) To be sure, the influx of Irish immigrants compensated for some of that decrease and dispersion, so that the improvement of some slums was accompanied by the deterioration of others. But the "hereditary" class of street-folk that Mayhew described was clearly declining, and with it the vitality of street life.

Less visible and less numerous, the street-folk nevertheless continued to be conspicuous, especially by contrast to the rest of the poor who gave every indication of sharing in the "moral and material progress" that was as much a refrain of the 1850s as "misery and vice" had been of the thirties and forties. This was the true paradox of *London Labour.* If the street-folk were an aberration, an atavism, they were nonetheless an important part of the social reality, important not so much in themselves, not even in relation to the rest of society, as in revealing the limits of progress, the precariousness of civilization. There evidently existed, not in "darkest Africa" but in the most advanced city of the most advanced country in the world, at the very apex of civilization, the equivalent of Bushmen and Fingoes, tribes which resisted amelioration and acculturation, refused to be drawn into the mainstream of the culture, perversely persisted in a way of life and work that was an affront to civilized society. It was as if some primitive spirit, some vestige of primeval nature, were mocking the proud presumptions of modernity.

Mayhew had not originally intended to make this his theme. He had started the *Chronicle* series with the classic two-nation problem, the contrast between the rich and the poor. But no sooner had he entered the world of the street-folk than that contrast gave way to the contrast between the civilized and the uncivilized. Some of the subjects of *London Labour* were not, in fact, notably poor; some earned enough to lead "respectable" lives were it not for drink, dissipation, and improvidence. In any event, it was not poverty as such that defined them, not even the poorest of them, so much as a mode of life and work that condemned them to a "culture of poverty." This "culture of poverty" was not the culture of "the poor," the other of the two "nations," but of a small and distinctive "tribe" which was a permanent feature of society, a testament to that part of society that resisted civilization. It was for this reason that Mayhew made no serious attempt to propose remedies or reforms to integrate them into society. Nor did he look to the expansion of industrialism and the growth of opulence for their melioration and assimilation. That might have been the prognosis of Smith. But Mayhew had too little faith in industrialism, and too much faith in the enduring resolve of this defiant tribe of nonconformists, to anticipate its disappearance. Nor, perhaps, would he have been pleased with that prospect. To more conventional souls, the street-folk were a standing reproach to civilization; to Mayhew, one suspects, they were a rebuke to the bourgeois spirit, a saving remnant of dissent, an adversary culture worthy of respect.

In making poverty a form of social pathology, a cultural rather than an economic condition, Mayhew and his flock of imitators gave yet another turn to the ideological history of poverty. In only half a century the social problem had gone through a series of redefinitions: from the population problem of Malthus to the pauperization problem of the poor law reformers, from Carlyle's condition-of-England question to the political inequality of the Chartists and the economic inequality of the "new" radicals. Now, at mid-century, when these issues seemed to be in abeyance, when the specter of overpopulation had receded and pauperism had declined, when economic improvements and social reforms had dissipated the demands for equality, the problem of poverty emerged in yet another guise, as a cultural and moral phenomenon. With the redefinition of the problem came a reidentification of the poor. It was neither the paupers nor the laboring poor, still less the "working classes," who were now deemed to be problematic, but a small, distinctive group that had the character not so much of a class as of a "tribe" or "race."

Mayhew's term for this group, "street-folk," never became part of the social vocabulary, perhaps because it was too restrictive.* There were clearly Mayhewian types indoors as well as out, underground as well as on the streets. Yet "street-folk" was more apt than some of the alternatives that have since been proposed—"underworld," for example, the label used for a selection of excerpts from the fourth volume of *London Labour.*[172] Most of the subjects of that volume (prostitutes, swindlers, beggars) plied their trades openly, on the streets, in defiance of law and convention. This, indeed, was the main feature of the street culture as Mayhew saw it. The street was a place where conventional distinctions of what was legal and illegal, moral and immoral, proper and improper, permissible and impermissible, did not prevail. This was its great attraction to a race of "wanderers" who could not bear the physical and psychic confinements of "civilized" life, who could not live indoors, within the closed walls of home and workshop, bound by the constraints of time, place, and convention.

"Street" has always had a connotation of freedom, even license. It had it all the more for the proper Victorian who made a fetish of domesticity and privacy, whose house was a castle in ways never intended by his forefathers, who fortified himself behind closed doors as if to ward off the temptations and provocations lurking outside, who shrouded himself, even in the fastness of his house, in veils of shame and guilt. That much of this obsession with privacy and secrecy had to do with sexuality is obvious: the trousers that went by the name of "unmentionables," and bodily organs too unmentionable even to have euphemisms, the "five and twenty breadths of petticoat" that sheathed the "nether parts" of a proper young lady, the blushing that was rampant and that testified to an impropriety of thought as shameful as any impropriety of action. In this milieu the street symbolized a sexual license the Victorians publicly deplored and, perhaps, privately envied. The "street-walker" was the most blatant example of the flaunting in public of a sexuality some Victorians thought illicit even in the privacy of their bedrooms. Other street-folk were almost as notorious: the street

---

* "Street-musicians," "street-beggars," "street-sweepers," "street-walkers," "street-wanderers," and the like had long been part of ordinary speech, but the collective term "street-folk" was not.

urchins whose "licentiousness" and "unnatural precocity" fascinated Mayhew, the costermongers who were so free and easy in their relationships, the men and women who lived in overcrowded quarters, besotted with drink and all too prone to promiscuity (even to that dreaded Victorian vice, incest). A French visitor to London in the 1850s commented on the anomaly: "However rigid English prudery may be in the home circle, it is shocked by nothing in the street, where licentiousness runs riot."[173]

Sexuality was only one respect in which Mayhew's "other Victorians" flouted the conventional ethos. No less flagrant was their defiance of the "work ethic." That too was perfectly symbolized by the street. An entire volume of London Labour was devoted to the hundreds of ingenious ways by which "Those That Will Not Work" managed to earn a living, and the other three volumes were full of people who, out of choice or necessity, worked in highly irregular occupations, with no fixed hours, no established place of work, no routine or rules, no production quota, and no regular income.

Some historians have made much of the "work and time discipline" imposed by industrialism.[174] As late as 1851, while the Crystal Palace was celebrating the glories of the new technology and the new civilization—three-quarters of a century after the supposed start of the industrial revolution—a good part of the economy had not been industrialized or revolutionized. Agriculture was still the principal occupation for men, and domestic service by far the largest for women. Next in the table of occupations was construction, which, according to one historian, was still in a "medieval" state.[175] The textile factories did impose a discipline of work and time. But even within the industrial sector the factory was atypical, more people working in their own homes or small workshops than in large, mechanized establishments. This was especially the case in London itself.

Yet there was a "work ethic," even if it was not rationalized, routinized, and mechanized. It was an ethic that derived more from Puritanism than from industrialism or capitalism and that manifested itself as much on the farm and at the handloom as in the factory or banking house. Those virtues which now seem quintessentially "bourgeois" and "capitalist" were far older, more deeply rooted in the culture, and more widespread among the population than those terms suggest. Industriousness, diligence, prudence, temperance, thrift, honesty, independence, the desire for self-betterment, the capacity for deferred gratification—"middle-class values," as they are now called—were shared, as values, by most of the working classes even if they were not always observed in practice. It was the Chartist, socialist, and militant atheist G. J. Holyoake who included, in his working class primer published in 1846, a poem by Frances Gage entitled "The Sounds of Industry."

> I love the banging of the hammer
> The whirring of the plane.
> The crushing of the busy saw
> The creaking of the crane . . .
> The puffing of the engine,
> And the fans' continuous boom . . .
> The sounds of busy labour,
> —I love, I love them all.[176]

However ambivalent Mayhew himself was toward this work ethic, he testified to its importance when he made it the basis of his distinction between the "civilized" and "nomadic" tribes. Whether it was the lack of a work ethic that made his street-folk take to the street or the lack of employment that drove them to it, the result was the same. They worked, but only reluctantly and on the street where they could maintain some freedom or illusion of freedom. They worked intermittently, by preference or necessity, and the harder they worked the more dissipated they were in their periods of idleness. Some were well paid for their work, but this too was irregular, the unpredictability of their earnings and the improvidence of their natures making them as needy, on occasion, as the least well paid. Even those street laborers who worked desperately hard did so in a spirit that violated the work ethic—erratically, peculiarly, intemperately.

More than any other feature of their lives, it was this that set apart the Mayhewian poor: the implicit or explicit affirmation of an alternative ethos that was more profoundly radical than anything proposed by the radicals of the time. If most of the street-folk had little interest in radical politics, or politics of any kind, they embodied in their lives a principle of radicalism far more revolutionary than the political equality of the Chartists or the economic equality of the socialists. Theirs was a moral radicalism as subversive of working class radicalism as it was of bourgeois society, subversive, indeed, of the culture that sustained both. It was this spectacle of an alien ethos and culture that magnified a small, pathetic tribe into something so threatening as to be mistaken for the "country of the poor."

The effect of Mayhew's revelations, the images and fears evoked by them, and the distortions and exaggerations induced by them, might seem improbable were it not for the fact that much the same thing has happened in our own time. When Oscar Lewis (exactly a century, as it happened, after the publication of the complete edition of *London Labour*) gave the "culture of poverty" that label, he carefully defined and delimited it, locating it not in some "unknown country" but in a real and identifiable foreign country.[177] The "children of Sanchez," one might think, would not easily be confused with the children of Smith. Yet the term, "culture of poverty," was picked up by journalists, commentators, and even some sociologists as if it pertained not to *a* culture of poverty but to *the* culture of poverty, the culture of the poor as a whole. It took a second round of discussion and reevaluation to clarify the concept and to understand how that misapprehension came about.

We can now see how we were beguiled by the romantic appeal of dissidence and deviance, how we were shocked by the vulnerability of the dominant culture and by the weakness of those processes of acculturation and "bourgeoisification" which we had once relied upon to assimilate marginal and immigrant groups, how we were disillusioned by a "Great Society" that had boldly undertaken to wage a "war against poverty" only to find itself confronted with a moral, psychological, and cultural (spiritual, one might once have said) poverty more debilitating and refractory than material poverty. Yet even now the dramatic image of the "culture of poverty" tends to overwhelm the prosaic image of the ordinary, conventional poverty of the "working poor." And even now that dramatic image is often seen as the extreme condition of all poverty instead of as the special condition of a very distinctive kind of poverty.

So it was in mid-nineteenth century England. If Victorian England had no illusions about being a "great society" in our sense—if it was not affluent enough to aspire to "abolish" poverty, nor institutionally capable of doing so, nor, for that matter, ideologically disposed to do so—it had its own sense of greatness, the conviction that it was the most advanced society in the history of mankind. If it did not presume to "solve" the problem of poverty, it did take pride in having ameliorated it. Yet at this very time it was confronted with the revelation of a kind of poverty that seemed intractable, a class of the poor that seemed irredeemable. That revelation was a shock not only to the social conscience of the Victorians but to their social cosmology, as it were—the expectation that the steady, ineluctable progress of civilization would inevitably raise the cultural, moral, and intellectual level of the entire society, including the poor. And that shock was sufficiently disorienting to create the confusion between the Mayhewian poor and the laboring poor.

It is one of the many ironies of this period that just at the time when the poor were finally relieved of the stigma of pauperism, when they seemed to be following the model laid down by Adam Smith rather than that of Malthus, Mayhew came along and, with the most laudable of intentions and the most generous of sympathies, inflicted upon the poor a new stigma and saddled society with a new social problem, the "culture of poverty."

XV

"RAGGED CLASSES" AND "DANGEROUS CLASSES"

For centuries the poor—all the poor—had been referred to, for obvious reasons, as "the ragged." By the early nineteenth century that label was being applied more selectively to the very poor or to those Mayhewian types who, willfully or out of necessity, were conspicuously ragged. In *Chartism*, Carlyle derided the Irish immigrants whose "rags and laughing savagery" revealed a state of "degradation and disorder" worse than anything experienced by the poorest Englishman. In a typical hyperbole he described the Irishman's "suit of tatters, the getting off and on of which is said to be a difficult operation, transacted only in festivals and the hightides of the calendar."[1] Engels was so taken with this passage that he quoted it twice, cautioning against Carlyle's exaggerated and biased view of the Irish national character while insisting that the description was "perfectly right," and adding details of his own about the dirty, rough, brutal, improvident, intemperate Irishmen who degraded still further the already degraded English proletariat.[2]

The condition of clothing was so important an indicator of poverty that G. R. Porter took it as evidence of the progress of the working classes. The reduction in the price of manufactured goods, he wrote in 1838, enabled most of the poor to dress better than ever before, so that now one rarely saw anyone in the street who was not decently attired "except it be a mendicant, whose garb is assumed an auxiliary to his profession." Those who were still ragged unwittingly testified to the higher standards prevailing among the poor, for if they happened, by reason of improvidence or misfortune, to lack the kind of clothes appropriate to the "improving customs of the people," they were so ashamed that they remained, for the most part, in their homes.[3]

As raggedness became associated with the very poor or the very peculiar, it acquired a metaphoric meaning. The ragged lived in "ragged homes," squalid, slovenly, untended; and they lived "ragged lives," disorderly, unsettled, unconventional.[4] By extension the word also took on a political connotation. The radicals of 1819 were referred to, first derisively by their opponents and then satirically by themselves, as "ragged Radicals," to differentiate them from the Philosophic Radicals and other respectable middle class radicals.* The term might have died out had it not been for the fame of the "ragged schools" which kept it alive through the whole of the century. The first of the ragged schools is said to have been founded in the 1830s by John Pounds, a poor shoemaker in Portsmouth. By 1844 there were enough such schools to warrant the establishment of the Ragged School Union under the presidency of the indefatigable Lord Ashley.[6]

This was hardly the first attempt to educate the "ragged classes." The charity schools of the early eighteenth century had been created for much the same purpose, to provide some kind of education not merely for the poor but for the very poor.[7] Unlike the older grammar schools which permitted a small number of the children of the most able and ambitious poor (artisans, for the most part) to have the same kind of classical education enjoyed by the rich, the charity schools were intended for those who did not aspire to such an education, or, indeed, to any education at all—the children of laborers, domestic servants, even paupers. Sponsored by the Society for Promoting Christian Knowledge, and subsidized by small contributions (rather than, like the grammar schools, large endowments), the schools provided free instruction as well as meals, clothing, and apprenticeship fees. Although their purpose was avowedly religious and moral (the primary, sometimes the only, textbook being the Bible), they provided a basic if primitive level of literacy, at the very least the ability to read and often to write and perform sums. These were the schools criticized by Bernard Mandeville for catering to "slovenly sorry Fellows that are used to be seen always Ragged and Dirty," initiating them into a life of crime, sloth, and discontent, and permanently incapacitating them for hard, honest labor.[8] In fact the schools turned out to have quite the opposite effect. As

---

*Even then the literal meaning of the word hovered over the political. In his *Autobiography of a Working Man*, Alexander Somerville recalled his schooldays in 1819, when the term "ragged Radicals" was much in the press. His schoolmates, hearing it at home, brought it to school as a "name of reproach," and devised a game in which "soldiers" were pitted against "radicals," the soldiers the sons of farmers and tradesmen and the "radicals" the poorer children, the two sides being distinguished by "the quality of the clothes worn." By that criterion the young Somerville was readily identified as a radical. In the course of the first day's battle his ragged (but clean and carefully mended) clothes were badly torn and he retreated home in a thoroughly unrespectable state. His mother spent the night cleaning and repairing his clothes and he went forth the next morning, only to be set upon with the same unfortunate results, this time giving as many blows (and inflicting as much damage to his opponent's attire) as he received. This was his initiation into "ragged radicalship"—a radicalism that in his case turned out to be notably moderate. (He was, for example, strenuously opposed to Chartism.)[5]

day schools they appealed to families sufficiently comfortable and farsighted to be able and willing to forgo the labor of their children for several years. And because so few grammar schools were established in the course of the century, the charity schools were attended by the children of artisans who might otherwise have gone to the grammar schools, as well as by those of the "respectable" laboring poor who sought a more elementary kind of education.

The social vacuum left by the charity schools was filled toward the end of the eighteenth century by industrial schools, which were not unlike the "schools of industry" favored by the philanthropic-minded mercantilists of the late seventeenth century, and by Sunday schools, which also had existed earlier in the century, though in far fewer numbers. In the 1780s, under the impetus of the movement for the "reformation of manners and morals," Sunday schools proliferated and became a major instrument in the education of the poor. Today "Sunday school" conjures up the image of an hour or two of religious instruction; in the early nineteenth century the school occupied the better part of the Sabbath, four to six hours, and included reading from the Bible and other texts (one of the important by-products of the Sunday school movement was the children's literature it spawned), as well as writing and some arithmetic.* The average length of attendance was four years, sometimes supplemented by intermittent spells at a day school; more often the Sunday school was the only education available to a considerable number of children. Between 1801 and 1851, the number of schools and attendance multiplied tenfold, from 2,300 to 23,000 schools and from 200,000 to 2,000,000 children.[9]

The redoubtable Sarah Trimmer, a great enthusiast for Sunday schools and a leading figure in the moral reformation movement (her *Oeconomy of Charity* contains some of the choicest specimens of the rhetoric of that genre), saw the schools as instruments for social differentiation as well as moral edification. "There are degrees of poverty as well as of opulence," she observed, and just as the children of the higher orders should not be educated "promiscuously," so the children of the poor should be taught with a due regard for the different circumstances of their parents and of their own capacities. In the Sunday schools the children had an opportunity to prove themselves and sort themselves out, the "dull and bad children" going on to industrial schools or to the more menial kinds of domestic employment, while those of the "first degree among the Lower Orders" were encouraged to attend the day schools.[10]

If the Sunday schools did not have quite that tidy effect, separating the superior from the inferior children and sending them on their respective

---

*While some Wesleyans opposed the teaching of writing, most did not, the Arminian and New Connection sects actually favoring it. By the second quarter of the nineteenth century, writing was as much a part of the curriculum in almost all Sunday schools as reading.

ways, neither were they the simple instruments of "social control" some historians have made of them. The most recent study refutes the familiar theory that the schools were insidious devices used by the middle classes to wean the poor away from their indigenous culture and from the natural rhythms of pre-industrial life in order to subject them to the "new universe of disciplined time."[11] In the early part of the nineteenth century, Thomas Laqueur demonstrates, the schools increasingly came under the control of the working classes themselves, who taught in them and often organized and financed them. So far from imposing an alien, dehumanizing discipline upon the hapless children, the schools were a vital part of the working class culture and community—of the "respectable" working classes, to be sure, committed to a "Puritan ethic" that was by no means the exclusive preserve of the middle classes. The Sunday schools were obviously below the educational level of the day schools, in some instances failing entirely of their purpose and leaving the children ignorant of the most elementary religious principles. As was often the case, the most egregious conditions were publicized by the middle class reformers themselves, in this instance in the reports of the Children's Employment Commission of 1842.* For a considerable body of the poor, however, especially outside of London, the Sunday schools provided a level of literacy that, however minimal, was clearly distinguishable from illiteracy. If, as is now generally thought, between two-thirds and three-quarters of the English working classes could read in the early nineteenth century, and a larger proportion by the middle of the century, that achievement must be credited in large part to the Sunday schools.[13]

To the degree that they were successful, the Sunday schools, like the charity schools before them, departed from their original mission. By enlarging the body of literate, respectable poor, they made all the more conspicuous the state of the illiterate and unrespectable, those who were too ragged, literally and metaphorically, to send their children to school. It was for these children (and sometimes adults as well) that the ragged schools were intended: for the children of the very poor or the very demoralized who could not or would not attend charity schools, Sunday schools, or the day schools operated by the National Society (for Anglicans) and the British and Foreign School Society (for Nonconformists). By 1855 there were more than 300 ragged schools with 18,000 students.

The supporters of the ragged schools had no doubts about their pur-

---

*Engels, who had contempt for the very idea of religious education, was delighted to quote from these reports examples of the abysmal ignorance of the children on the subject of religion: the child who had attended Sunday school regularly for five years and recognized the name of Jesus Christ but did not know who he was, or others who identified Christ as Adam, or an apostle, or a "king of London a long time ago."[12]

pose, but they did have some compunctions about the name. "We entertain no fanatical passion for the name," Ashley once confessed, but upon reflection he decided that it did have the great merit of reassuring those for whom the schools were intended and who might be put off by a more conventional, respectable-sounding name. His explanation was as candid as the name itself: "Some of the most degraded of the race have been invited by the belief that the place and the service were not too grand for their misery."[14] But the discomfort persisted, even among admirers of the schools. The *Quarterly Review* once regretted that the schools had not been called "Free Schools";[15] and T. H. Huxley, defending their existence even after the passage of the Education Act of 1870, suggested that the name be changed to "Substrata Schools."[16] (That the latter too might be thought invidious did not occur to Huxley, perhaps because "substrata" had a nice, objective, scientific ring, rather like geological strata.)

"Ragged classes," "substrata," "residuum," "outcasts"—these, the lowest of the poor, were the clients of the ragged schools. The metaphors were brutally revealing. "The eels which are in the mud the Government have been trying to catch with nets, and they have caught nothing but the fish that swim. The conductors of the Ragged Schools have gone down into the mud, and have caught the eels."[17] Three years before Mayhew discovered them, Ashley described the "curious race," the "tribe," that desperately needed some civilizing influence.

It is a curious race of human beings that these philanthropists have taken in hand. Every one who walks the streets of the metropolis must daily observe several members of the tribe—bold, and perty, and dirty as London sparrows, but pale, feeble, and sadly inferior to them in plumpness of outline. Their business, or pretended business, seems to vary with the locality. At the West-end they deal in lucifer matches, audaciously beg, or tell a touching tale of woe. Pass on to the central parts of the town . . . many are spanning the gutters with their legs, and dabbling with earnestness in the latest accumulations of nastiness; while others, in squalid and half-naked groups, squat at the entrances of the narrow, fetid courts and alleys that lie concealed behind the deceptive frontages of our larger thoroughfares. Whitechapel and Spitalfields teem with them like an ant's nest, but it is in Lambeth and in Westminster that we find the most flagrant traces of their swarming activity. There the foul and dismal passages are thronged with children of both sexes, and of every age from three to thirteen. Though wan and haggard, they are singularly vivacious, and engaged in every sort of occupation but that which would be beneficial to themselves and creditable to the neighbourhood. Their appearance is wild; the matted hair, the disgusting filth that renders necessary a closer inspection before the flesh can be discerned between the rags which hang about it, and the barbarian freedom from all superintendence and restraint, fill the mind of a novice in these things with perplexity and dismay. . . . At an age when the children of the wealthy would still be in leading strings, they are off, singly or in parties, to beg, borrow, steal, and exercise all the cunning that want and a love of evil can stir up in a reckless race.

Ashley's conclusion, like Mayhew's, was that the children of that "reckless race," living "within a walk of our own dwellings," were "beings like ourselves," whose condition was all the more unfortunate because they were regressing, physically and morally, even as the metropolis advanced toward the "pinnacle of magnificence and refinement."[18]

Mayhew could hardly have quarreled with that account. Indeed, he quoted it at length in the *Chronicle,* and had it not been explicitly identified as Ashley's, the reader might well have taken it as his own.* But he quoted it in the course of his attack on Ashley and the ragged schools in a series of articles in March and April 1850. Unlike Dickens—who supported the principle of the schools and approved of their general effect while objecting to what he saw as their excessive religious orientation, mean facilities, and pretentious teachers—Mayhew was utterly opposed to the schools in principle as well as practice.[21] It is curious that he should have been so hostile to the one institution designed specifically for the classes he himself had singled out for attention, and even more curious that he should have opposed it on the grounds he did. He did not complain about the emphasis on religion, the inadequacy of the schooling (most of the schools met on Sundays and one or two evenings a week), or the invidious separation, as we might think today, of the ragged from the respectable children. Nor did he take exception to Ashley's description of that "wild and lawless race" capable of every kind of vice, crime, and degradation.[22] On the contrary, he professed to have an even lower opinion of that race. Neither ragged schools nor any other kind, he argued, could reform children who were unreformable; they could only corrupt them still more, and corrupt everyone who came into contact with them. He cited statistics showing a correlation between the growth of juvenile crime and the increase of schools, teachers, and students. Juvenile illiteracy, to be sure, had decreased, but this meant that the young criminal had moved from the class of the "utterly ignorant" to that of the "imperfectly educated." Since crime was not caused by illiteracy, it could not be

---

*A speech by Ashley in 1845 suggests how prevalent were the sentiments and phrases Mayhew was later to make his own. "Thousands may be found in our highways and hedges, in our streets and alleys, in our courts and lanes, who are living in a state of practical heathenism—a heathenism as complete as if they were found in California or Timbuctoo."[19] In other respects too, Ashley anticipated Mayhew. Some years before Mayhew thought to assemble a group of 50 "ticket-of-leave men" (parolees) to inquire into their circumstances, Ashley presided at a meeting of some 400 thieves. Unlike Mayhew, Ashley opened the meeting with a prayer, after which the thieves were invited to talk about their lives and careers.[20]

cured by education; in fact, the process of education was itself an education in crime, the only certain effect being the emergence of a more skillful and sophisticated race of criminals.* A knowledge of arithmetic enabled the children to steal articles marked at a higher price, and the ability to read made them avid readers of crime stories.[24]

If illiteracy was not the cause of crime, Mayhew argued, neither was poverty. He quoted the report of the Royal Commission on the Constabulary which found that crimes against property were rarely the result of "blameless poverty or destitution" but were generally motivated by the simple desire to "obtain property with a less degree of labour than by regular industry."[25] The ragged schools were as ineffectual in coping with such utilitarian calculations as they were with the vicious characters of the young criminals. Even if education itself did not have the perverse effect of increasing crime, the ragged schools did, because there innocent children were thrown together with youngsters who had the most "vicious propensities and depraved habits." He was not opposed, Mayhew assured his readers toward the close of his final article, to schools for the "honest poor." His objection was to the "instruction of the honest poor *in connection* with the dishonest, believing that any attempt to educate *the two together* must necessarily, from the force of association, be productive of more harm than good to the community."[26]

The problem of "promiscuity"—the lumping together of different species of poor, male and female, young and old, honest and dishonest, deserving and undeserving—exercised reformers of all kinds. In Mayhew's case, however, it was a somewhat specious argument. *London Labour* dramatically testified to the infinite capacity of his subjects to defy conventional catego-

---

*In Thomas Peacock's novel *Crotchet Castle* (1831), the Reverend Dr. Folliott is engaged in a long polemic with the utilitarian and political economist Mr. Mac Quedy (the "son of a Q.E.D.") on the subject of the "march of mind," which Mr. Mac Quedy regards as the salvation of mankind. The Reverend has just had a demonstration of that "march of mind."

> The Rev. Dr. Folliott.—Sir, I have seen it, much to my discomfiture. It has marched into my rick-yard, and set my stacks on fire, with chemical materials, most scientifically compounded. It has marched up to the door of my vicarage, a hundred and fifty strong; ordered me to surrender half my tithes; consumed all the provisions I had provided for my audit feast, and drunk up my old October. It has marched in through my back-parlour shutters, and out again with my silver spoons, in the dead of the night. The policeman, who was sent down to examine, says my house has been broken open on the most scientific principles. All this comes of education.
>
> Mr. Mac Quedy.—I rather think it comes of poverty.
>
> The Rev. Dr. Folliott.—No, sir. Robbery perhaps comes of poverty, but scientific principles of robbery come of education. I suppose the learned friend has written a sixpenny treatise on mechanics, and the rascals who robbed me have been reading it.[23]

ries and labels, their ingenuity in accommodating themselves to the interstices of the economy and society, their obduracy in resisting the attempts
of reformers to understand, let alone reform them. It was almost with pride
that Mayhew described the children who used their education for their own
perverse and nefarious purposes, converting the schools into schools of
crime, and mocking the earnest, naïve reformers who tried to categorize and
civilize them. The reformers, on the other hand, believed in the necessity
and feasibility of reform precisely because they thought it possible to
differentiate and separate the various classes of the poor and create institutions designed specifically for each. For poor-law reformers, the crucial
distinction was between paupers and independent laborers; for educators,
between the working classes and the ragged classes; for prison reformers,
between the ragged and the dangerous classes.*

When Mary Carpenter, the founder of a ragged school and the leading
proponent of reformatory schools, was called before the Select Committee
on Juveniles in 1852, she assured them that she had much experience with
the "lower classes of our population, especially the respectable labouring
classes," and that she was much impressed by "the very strong line of
demarcation which exists between the labouring and the 'ragged' class, a line
of demarcation not drawn by actual poverty."[28] She had made the same
point the previous year in her book on reformatory schools. "There is, and
will long be, a very strongly defined line of separation between them, which
must and ought to separate them, and which requires perfectly distinct
machinery and modes of operation in dealing with them." She also sought
to draw another line separating the "perishing classes" from the "dangerous
classes."

> That part of the community which we are to consider, consists of those
> who have not yet fallen into actual crime, but who are almost certain
> from their ignorance, destitution, and the circumstances in which they
> are growing up, to do so, if a helping hand be not extended to raise
> them—these form the *perishing classes;*—and of those who have already
> received the prison brand, or, if the mark has not been yet visibly set
> upon them, are notoriously living by plunder, who unblushingly ac-
> knowledge that they gain more for the support of themselves and their

*Differentiation, specialization, separation, segregation—Donald Olsen has pointed out that this
was one of the principal characteristics of the architecture and geography of Victorian London, as
well as of other aspects of material life. Each course had its distinctive cutlery and china; each meal
its distinctive food (cold toast and marmalade at breakfast, warm toast and jam at tea, and never the
reverse); each time of day its distinctive attire; each class its own compartment in the train, to say
nothing of its own dress, speech, meals, drink, manners. "Subdivision, classification, and elaboration,"
George Augustus Sala wrote in 1859, "are certainly distinguishing characteristics of the present era
of civilization."[27]

parents by stealing than by working, whose hand is against every man, for they know not that any man is their brother—these form the *dangerous classes.* [29]

That second line was far less distinct than the first, and the terminology was inconsistent. Sometimes the "perishing classes" seemed to occupy a terrain somewhere between the "ragged classes" and the "dangerous classes"; sometimes they were identified with the one or the other or with both, in which case "ragged," "perishing," and "dangerous" were more or less synonymous. There was good reason for this semantical confusion, since individuals as much as groups resisted these tidy classifications. If Carpenter tried so strenuously to maintain them in spite of all the difficulties, it was because she needed these distinctions, both for analytic clarity and for the practical purposes of reform, to create the "perfectly distinct machinery and modes of operation" essential for education, rehabilitation, and reform.

The "machinery" itself, in Carpenters's schema, defined those classes. For the working classes there were the day schools run by the National and British societies. For the ragged classes whose "want of character or necessary clothing" made those schools impractical, there were the ragged schools (which Carpenter wanted to convert into free day schools). For the perishing classes who had not yet fallen into crime but were likely to do so, there were industrial schools. And for "juvenile offenders" or "delinquents" (both terms were current at the time) who had already committed crimes which brought them within the "iron grasp of the law" and who were, in effect, "children of the state," there were reformatory schools.[30] (Carpenter did not mention the pauper schools attached to some workhouses or the factory schools mandated by the Factory Acts, perhaps because she thought them unsatisfactory and would have liked them abolished.)

The schema was not always so neat, the lines dividing the schools sometimes getting blurred, just as the lines dividing the classes did. What was unambiguous, however, was the principle: "That, as a general rule, all children, however apparently vicious and degraded, are capable of being made useful members of society, and beings acting on a religious principle, if placed under right influences, and subjected to judicious control and training."[31] This principle of rehabilitation and redemption was universal, even if the "machinery and modes of operation" were highly differentiated. What was also universal was the regimen of religion and love: religion, assuring the children of their absolute worth in the eyes of God (the "equal value in His sight of each one of these poor perishing young creatures with the most exalted of our race"), and love, a natural sentiment in the rearing of all children and all the more essential for these children who had never known the love of their own parents.[32] (It was the principle of love Carpenter invoked to prohibit corporal punishment in the reformatory schools—a radical idea at a time when caning was common in the most prestigious schools.)

Carpenter was a familiar type of philanthropist, religious and at the same time thoroughly utilitarian, pursuing moral reform by way of social reforms, and relying on the machinery of institutions and the mechanism of the state. Bentham might have jeered at her appeal to God and love, but he would have been delighted with her idea of distinctive schools for distinctive classes and purposes, and even more, with her proposal to bring all the schools into a single, comprehensive, compulsory, state-organized, state-subsidized system of education. From a later (much later) perspective, the idea of segregating these classes in separate schools seems invidious or punitive, yet another attempt to stigmatize them and isolate them from the community of the poor. At the time it had the opposite significance. The children of the ragged, perishing, and dangerous classes were not being removed from the schools attended by the children of the working classes; they had never attended those schools, or, for that matter, any schools. Carpenter's proposal was meant to provide schooling where there had been none. And the labels she attached to those classes were meant to identify problems for which she was seeking solutions. If her characterizations seem harsh, they were those in common use at the time; the only difference was her conviction that even the lowest of these classes, the most "vicious and degraded" of them, could be redeemed, if only their specific problems were addressed in an appropriate and rational manner. The "judicious control and training" to be provided in each of these schools was designed not only to control and train these classes so that they would do least harm to society, not only to rehabilitate them so that they would become "useful members of society," but also to make them "beings acting on a religious principle" —to save their souls. To the historian who does not recognize that principle, the enterprise may seem an elaborate exercise in "social control." To Carpenter and her associates, the "control" was that which enabled human beings, even the lowliest of them, to behave like the highest, controlled by their best natures rather than their worst impulses.

"The people perisheth," Ashley bemoaned.[33] All his efforts—to limit the hours of work of women and children, provide better care for the insane, improve the housing of the poor, maintain schools for the ragged—were designed to prevent that dire fate, to redeem the poor spiritually and morally while ministering to their physical and material needs. So too Mary Carpenter, coming from a Unitarian rather than Evangelical tradition, sought the same end. Writing to an American friend who was involved in the Abolitionist movement, she compared her ragged flock with the slaves her friend was trying to liberate.

My mind is now almost as much engrossed by our Ragged School as yours is by the Abolition question. Indeed they are very kindred subjects; you are trying to free the god-like spirit which has been enthralled by the wickedness of man, by external force; we are trying to free that divine nature from the still more than heathenish darkness in which it is growing to become a fiend, a worse than American slave.[34]

As "ragged classes" sounds more invidious today than it did in the early nineteenth century, so "dangerous classes" sounds more ominous, as if the working classes themselves were "dangerous," discontented, and potentially revolutionary. In contemporary usage the expression was far less alarming. "Dangerous classes" referred to that small part of the population which was thought especially prone to crime—the "criminal" or "predatory classes," as they were also known. While "ragged and dangerous classes" were often linked together, "working classes" and "dangerous classes" were not; on the contrary, the line between them was sharper than that which Carpenter found between the ragged classes and the working classes. Mayhew put it succinctly: "The predatory class are the non-working class."[35]

Another "line of demarcation," unambiguous in theory but difficult to sustain in practice, separated the dangerous classes from the pauper classes. A major objective of reformers was to discourage paupers from crossing the line into criminality, just as the New Poor Law was designed to prevent the laboring poor from crossing the line into pauperism. Ironically, it was the New Poor Law itself which exacerbated the problem. To the degree to which it succeeded in separating pauper and poor by making the condition of the pauper less eligible than that of the poor, it inadvertently made the condition of the pauper less eligible than that of the criminal. Thus the dangerous classes emerged as a social problem in the wake of the law that was intended to solve the problem of pauperism.

Just before the passage of the New Poor Law, Lytton Bulwer, in his *England and the English,* published a table of the weekly food allowance for the agricultural laborer (122 oz.), the soldier (168 oz.), the able-bodied pauper (151 oz.), the suspected thief (181–203 oz.), the convicted thief (239 oz.), and the transported thief (330 oz.), from which he concluded that "the industrious labourer has less than the pauper, the pauper less than the suspected thief, the suspected thief less than the convicted, the convicted less than the transported, and by the time you reach the end of the gradation, you find that the transported thief has nearly three times the allowance of the honest labourer."[36] Similar tables appeared elsewhere, citing different figures but making the same point. The report of the Royal Commission on the Constabulary of 1839 conceded the difficulty: "In point of sensual gratification, the condition of the habitual depredator is, during his career, much higher than that of the honest labourer."[37] The report did not add (perhaps because it would have reflected badly upon the New Poor Law) that the condition of the criminal was *a fortiori* higher than that of the pauper. But others were quick to make that connection, and the inequity of the pauper vis-à-vis the criminal became something of a public scandal.

The scandal was fed by statistical evidence, by the testimony of paupers, criminals, and officials, by squibs in *Punch* and indignant editorials in *The Times.* Carpenter reported that young vagabonds in the workhouse were being deliberately insubordinate so as to be removed to some "favourite gaol, where it is known that every attention will be paid them."[38] Old men and women, faced with the prospect of the workhouse, were reputed to be committing crimes for the express purpose of being caught and imprisoned. One old woman, urged by her minister to enter the "House" rather than suffer the ignominy of jail, retorted: "Excuse me, sir, have you tried both places? No? Well, I have, and I know where I am best off."[39] A magistrate explained the wave of window-smashing that had recently taken place: "The fact was that the convict prisons were made so comfortable by the humane excesses of some people, that the lazy and vile availed themselves of the facilities which shop windows presented to aid them in getting into prisons where they could maintain comfortable quarters for the year."[40] The public was regaled with tales of criminals, young and old, luxuriating in the delights of prison.

> A poor ragged sweep, about 16 years of age, without shoes or stockings, and his red legs cracked with the cold, was brought to prison for some trifling offence. The warm bath into which he was put much delighted him, but nothing could exceed his astonishment on being told to put on shoes and stockings. "And am I to *wear* them? and this? and this too?" he said, as each article of dress was given to him. His joy was complete when they took him to his cell; he turned down the bedclothes with great delight, and, half-doubting his good fortune, hesitatingly asked if he was really to sleep in the bed! On the following morning, the governor, who had observed the lad's surprise, asked him what he thought of the situation? "Think of it, master! why I'm damn'd if ever I do another stroke of work!" The boy kept his word, and was ultimately transported.[41]

The superior status of the prisoner was reflected in the superior status of the prison-keeper, who was often a gentleman, unlike the workhouse-keeper, who was more often of a lower class. (Bentham, one remembers, did not find it at all unseemly to aspire to the position of master jailer in his Panopticon.)[42] The architecture and internal structure of the new prisons also had the effect of making them seem respectable, even palatial—"prison palaces," as they were called, echoing the familiar complaints about "pauper palaces." Some of the improvements were fortuitous, the by-products of the single cell system: private washing and toilet facilities, central heating, meals served on trolleys, and books provided to the inmates (reading being one of the few activities that lent itself to separate confinement). These amenities made the new prisons superior not only to the workhouses and houses of the poor (and not so poor), but even to most hotels at the time, in appearance as well as amenities. The new prisons, a source of pride to the local community and to the architect, were often elaborately embellished, in contrast to the ordinary commercial hotel, which was typically bare and mean-looking.[43]

Prison reformers, distressed by the unwonted effect of reforms which made the condition of the prisoners "more eligible" than that of worthier elements of the population, tried to compensate for this by making crime "less eligible" in other respects. Criminals, they were convinced, engaged in crime, or "depredation," because it was more agreeable than honest labor: like the pauper calculating the advantages of relief as against work, the criminal calculated the pleasures of a free and easy life of crime compared with the pains of regular, honest labor. The reformer could only respond with a kind of counter-calculus, a system of apprehension and confinement which would make it difficult to pursue a life of crime, and painful if caught. Thus the *Constabulary Report* recommended the establishment of a strong, centralized, much expanded police force which would deter a criminal bent on a career of crime and punish him if deterrence failed. The same kind of calculations lay behind Carpenter's insistence upon a compulsory system of industrial and reformatory schools. Juvenile delinquents, she reasoned, found their mode of life too lucrative and agreeable to be given up voluntarily; filth and rags did not disturb them, for these were the "implements of their trade," nor cold and hunger so long as they had an occasional luxurious meal, nor the "noisome dens" they lived in so long as they could freely ply their trade. Since they could not be enticed by better conditions or the prospect of a better life, they could only be forcibly consigned to school much as prisoners were consigned to jail.[44]

This utilitarian conception of crime had important implications for the idea of poverty. If crime was the result of a rational calculus on the part of the criminal, it could not be said to be the result of poverty or even destitution. The Commission on the Constabulary professed to have discovered by empirical investigation that most crimes against property were ascribable to one cause: "the temptations of the profit of a career of depredation, as compared with the profits of honest and even well paid industry." These temptations and illicit profits could be reduced only by an effective police force. The question of poverty was irrelevant. "The notion that any considerable proportion of the crimes against property are caused by blameless poverty or destitution we find disproved at every step."[45] The parallels between the *Constabulary Report* and the *Poor Law Report* five years earlier, both written largely by Chadwick, were obvious. The recommendation for a centralized police force was equivalent to the central Poor Law Board (and aroused the hostility of critics for the same reason); the principle of less-eligibility had a prominent part in both; and in both there was a conscious attempt to dissociate poverty from the "social problem" under consideration —from criminality in the one case, from pauperism in the other. Just as the *Poor Law Report* insisted upon the sharpest distinction between pauperism and poverty, so the *Constabulary Report* distinguished between crime and poverty. And as the first proposed a solution to the problem of pauperism which was addressed exclusively to that problem, which was intended to deter pauperism while leaving poverty alone (indeed, poverty was explicitly said to be not a social problem), so the problem of crime was defined in its own terms, and the solution found in a policy of deterrence that would make crime less "eligible" and more painful.

A dozen years later another writer, not a disciple of Bentham, came to similar conclusions about the nature of crime and the character of the criminal. In 1851, the Leeds reformer Thomas Plint reported that the total amount of crime in England had decreased in the preceding half-century, the only category showing an increase being nonviolent offenses against property.* More significant than this overall decrease, he argued, was the increasing concentration of crime within a small, well-defined part of the population, the "criminal or dangerous classes," which included "not only the professional thief or burglar, but the whole rabble of the vagrant and dissolute classes, who labour by fits, and eke out subsistence by pilfering, and who are ever on the verge of a more serious breach of the laws." Although these dangerous classes lived among the working classes, they were not part of them. The incidence of crime was greater in urban centers, the "seats of industry," not because industrial workers committed more crimes but only because the cities provided ideal conditions for the criminal classes, opportunities for plunder and concealment. "It is not manufacturing Manchester," the superintendent of police had said, "but multitudinous Manches-

---

*It may have been this exception that led G. R. Porter to the opposite conclusion. Otherwise optimistic about the "progress of the nation," Porter was dismayed to find that crime had increased in recent years out of proportion to the increase of population. But as he himself was quick to observe, "There is a constant tendency in the human mind to magnify the importance of all that belongs to the present moment; and this tendency is peculiarly active as regards the evils by which we may be assailed or surrounded."[46] Others pointed out that the statistics were deceptive: improved recording of crime tended to magnify the figures, and juvenile crime assumed a disproportionate importance at a time when an unprecedentedly large percentage of the population was below the age of twenty-five.

ter, which engenders crime." Plint himself found that during the worst of the trade depression in Manchester, the conduct of the working classes had been exemplary. There, as in the rest of England, in spite of great suffering there had been no violence and, except for petty thefts, no increase in crime. Crimes, he concluded, did not arise out of the manufacturing system, nor criminals from the ranks of the factory workers. Nor were the criminal classes driven to crime by bad sanitary or housing conditions, by poverty or the lack of employment; these were "concomitants, not causes, of the moral debasement of that class."[47]

The argument that poverty was not a cause of crime was all the more remarkable because of the widespread belief that drunkenness was intimately related to both poverty and crime. There was hardly a working class, radical, or Chartist memoir which did not attest to the "evil" of drink—the perennial temptation that the ambitious young apprentice managed to resist only by great force of will and character, or that the feckless worker succumbed to, thereby degrading himself and his family until he saw the light and "took the pledge."[48] And there was hardly a social critic who did not associate drink, whether as cause or as effect, with poverty and pauperism, immorality and crime. The historian confronting this contemporary evidence is apt to be embarrassed and apologetic. "One is bound to look suspiciously," J. J. Tobias has said, "on ideas so redolent of Victorian morality as these." Having said that, however, he was obliged to admit that there was "more than an element of truth" in these Victorian ideas and "little doubt that crime and drink were often associated."[49]*

What is interesting is that in spite of the fact that drink was commonly linked to both poverty and crime, the line separating the criminal classes from the laboring classes remained sharp. The habitual drunkard might cross that line, might take to a life of crime and become a habitual criminal. But the kinds of crime committed by the poor laborer in a state of intoxication (most commonly petty theft and brawling) were regarded as qualitatively different from the crimes committed by the criminal classes, the professional "depredators." That difference did not emerge clearly from the statistics,

---

*Another historian, Brian Harrison, points to the fallacies in the statistical evidence purporting to show a correlation between gin and crime. But he also makes it clear that such a correlation was generally assumed at the time and that it was partly responsible for the passage of the Beer Act of 1830, which reduced the tax on beer and thus its price, beer being presumed to be a "moral species of beverage," as Brougham put it, in contrast to the "demon gin." Without minimizing the gravity of the problem of drink, Harrison removes it somewhat from its usual moral context—the laborer drinking to drown his miseries, avoid his responsibilities, or willfully indulge himself—by suggesting a variety of other reasons for the high consumption of alcohol: the impurity of the water supply, the public house as a social center, the truck system (paying wages in the public house), and the real or reputed functions of liquor as anesthetic, antiseptic, aphrodisiac, tonic, and insulation against cold in the winter and heat in the summer.[50]

which usually failed to distinguish between habitual offenders and occasional ones. Contemporaries, however, were well aware of the difference, a difference of such large moral consequence that they made of it a class difference.

The association between drink and crime, however distressing in one respect, was reassuring in another. For if drink, rather than poverty, was a major cause of crime, that cause was more easily addressed than poverty. The Temperance Chartists, for example, were convinced that even the poorest menial laborer could be weaned from the addiction to drink and thus from crime and violence. The solution to this problem did not have to await the solution to the more difficult and recalcitrant problem of poverty; in fact, temperance or teetotalism could actually alleviate the problem of poverty by preventing the laborer from dissipating his meager earnings and encouraging those habits of sobriety and diligence which would enable him to augment his income and better his condition. Even when this modest solution failed, when laborers resisted the ministrations of teetotalers and temperance preachers and persisted in their besotted ways, the problem of drink was regarded as of a different order from the problem of crime. Drunkenness separated the "rough" from the "respectable" poor, a distinction that was as important to the working classes as to the middle classes. It was a less important distinction, however, than that which separated the criminal classes from the working classes, respectable or unrespectable. The characteristic feature of the criminal classes, even temperance reformers agreed, was not drunkenness—those criminals whose craft required skill and discretion had a reputation for sobriety to the point almost of teetotalism —but a peculiar disposition or proclivity to crime.

This peculiarity of temperament, it was thought, a product of nature and environment, made some people take to a life of crime as others took to a life on the streets. Plint's criminal class was reminiscent of Mayhew's street-folk. It was a class determined by "descent," isolated from other classes "in blood, in sympathies, in its domestic and social organizations, . . . in the whole 'ways and means' of its temporal existence." It was a "pariah and exotic tribe," a "foreign," "non-indigenous body" preying upon the "indigenous and really working population," a "moral cesspool, into which all the offscourings and dregs of the community settle down and corrupt," a "moral poison," a "pestiferous canker."[51] No one could mistake that criminal class for the working classes. And, unlike Mayhew, Plint allowed for no ambiguity. As Carpenter insisted upon the strong line of demarcation between the laboring and ragged classes, "a line of demarcation not drawn by actual poverty," so Plint insisted upon the absolute moral separation between the working classes and the criminal or dangerous class. Unfortunately, the separation was not a geographical one as well. The dangerous class was "in the community, but neither of it, nor from it."[52] This was the great problem.

It was dangerous not only to the rich upon whom it preyed but to the poor among whom it lived.

> The criminal class live amongst, and are dove-tailed in, so to speak, with the operative classes, whereby they constitute so many points of vicious contact with those classes—so many ducts by which the virus of a moral poison circulates through and around them. They constitute a pestiferous canker in the heart of every locality where they congregate, offending the sight, revolting the sensibilities, and lowering, more or less, the moral status of all who come into contact with them. Their very presence, and the daily commission of offences by them, is an evil; because it so habituates society to the loathsome spectacle of the one, and the constant *recurrence* of the other, that the sensibilities become blunted, and the judgment benumbed and stupefied.[53]

. . .

This dangerous class inevitably recalls Marx's "dangerous class," the "lumpenproletariat." Yet the differences are at least as striking as the similarities. To see the Victorian classes as the Victorians saw them, it is necessary to dispel the shadow of the Marxist image, to understand the ideological background in which the Marxist concept took shape and the historical purposes it served.

The lumpenproletariat received its classic definition in the *Communist Manifesto*.

> The "dangerous class," the social scum, that passively rotting mass thrown off by the lowest layers of the old society, may here and there be swept into the movement by a proletarian revolution; its conditions of life, however, prepare it far more for the part of a bribed tool of reactionary intrigue.[54]

"Dangerous class" (in quotation marks in the authorized English translation of 1888) was a translation of *Lumpenproletariat* (not in quotation marks) in the original German edition. The earlier, little known English translation of 1850 had rendered it "the mob."[55] A more literal translation would have been the "ragged proletariat," or, more loosely, the "ragged class," *lumpen* meaning "ragged." In choosing "dangerous class," Engels (who personally supervised the 1888 translation) amalgamated "ragged and dangerous classes" into a single class under the more pejorative label, a label that accurately reflected the idea of the lumpenproletariat as it had developed in the Marxist tradition. For the lumpenproletariat was more dangerous than ragged—far more dangerous, and dangerous in a different sense, than the English dangerous class.

The "proletariat" itself was dangerous, in the sense that it was a potentially revolutionary class. This was the meaning Engels gave that term in *The Condition of the Working Class in England,* and Lorenz von Stein before him when he distinguished the "proletariat" from the "poor," the latter being merely destitute while the former was "dangerous" in its courage, unity, and revolutionary intentions.[56]* The Marxist lumpenproletariat was dangerous in quite another sense—conscious neither of its unity nor of its aims, and counter-revolutionary rather than revolutionary. But before it acquired that meaning, it evolved from the Young Hegelian idea of the *Lumpen,* a ragged class that was dangerous precisely because it was revolutionary.

There had always been a "ragged" class in Germany, just as there had been in England. Max Stirner transformed that relatively innocent class into a dangerous one in his *Ego and His Own* published in 1844. The book created a great stir among German radicals because it carried the Feuerbachian critique of Hegel to what seemed to be its ultimate limit, making the "ego" the final, ineluctable, "unique" reality compared with which all else remained in the realm of theology. The book was properly recognized by the Young Hegelians as a critique of socialism as well as bourgeois society, the socialist ideas of social order and social justice being as much a fetter on the individual as the "bourgeois" ideas of law, morality, society, or the state. In the course of developing this radical nihilism Stirner introduced the class of *die Lumpen,* who were superior to the proletariat in being free of all possessions, thus in a totally impoverished, "have-nothing" state that was the precondition of true "ownness," pure "egoism." This state of *Lumperei,* raggedness, would characterize the proletariat under communism, where instead of being a term of derision it would become an honorable form of address, like "citizen" in the French Revolution. "To be a ragged one is an ideal, ragged ones we shall all become." Beyond communism Stirner foresaw the ultimate ideal, in which raggedness itself would be stripped off and

*Robert Tucker relates Stein's "proletariat" to Hegel's *"Pöbel,"* a "rabble of paupers," as it has been translated. In fact the *Pöbel,* as Hegel described it in *Philosophy of Right,* was closer to Marx's "lumpenproletariat" than to Stein's "proletariat." Marx, who had written a critique of the *Philosophy of Right* in 1844, may well have received the first glimmerings of the idea of the lumpenproletariat from Hegel (although the term was probably inspired by Stirner's *Lumpen*). In the *Philosophy of Right* Hegel commented on the unfortunate tendency of modern civil society to create a disproportionately wealthy class on the one hand and a *Pöbel* on the other, the latter accompanied by a "loss of the sense of right and wrong, of honesty and the self-respect which makes a man insist on maintaining himself by his own work and effort." Poverty itself, Hegel explained in a note, did not produce a rabble. "A rabble is created only when there is joined to poverty a disposition of mind, an inner indignation against the rich, against society, against the government, etc." Like the Neapolitan *lazzaroni,* the rabble claimed subsistence from society "as a right." In England, Hegel observed, the problem was most acute, because there the poor rates, combined with generous private charity, had persuaded "even the very poorest [to] believe that they have rights." To prevent the creation of a rabble, a class without "shame and self-respect," the English would have to harden themselves to the most drastic measure: "to leave the poor to their fate and instruct them to beg in the streets."[57]

man would be exposed in his "real nakedness, denuded of everything alien."[58]

For Stirner, the ragged class was dangerous in both the revolutionary and the criminal senses. In that "have-nothing," ragged state, the individual was as devoid of principle as of property, recognizing no value, no commitment save to himself, his own ego—thus a criminal. "The self-willed egoist is necessarily a criminal, and his life is necessarily crime."[59] This was the familiar form of antinomianism in which the totally liberated individual was liberated from law and morality as much as from material possessions and political domination, from everything conventionally deemed sacred. The *Lumpen* were not merely paupers; they were criminals and potential criminals, existing outside the law and in defiance of the law. If they rebelled, it was not as revolutionaries seeking another social order or political system but as "primitive rebels," rebelling for the sake of rebellion.[60]

Stirner's book provoked rebuttals by the leading Young Hegelians—Feuerbach, Hess, Bruno Bauer, and, most extensively, Marx and Engels. In more than 400 pages of the *German Ideology* (Stirner's book was only half as long), they mercilessly dissected every phrase and turn of his argument. Deriding his "spirituality," his idealistic "spectres" and "phantoms," they baptized him "the blessed Max," "Saint Max," "Saint Sancho." They ridiculed the idea of a "dangerous proletariat" made up of "rogues, prostitutes, thieves, robbers and murderers, gamblers, propertyless people with no occupation and frivolous individuals." And they scorned the idea of "crime" as a means by which the "unique" man, the egoist, would transcend convention and defy the sacred.[61]

In the course of the attack on Stirner, Marx and Engels described the *Lumpen* as an "unsuccessful travesty" of Weitling's "thieving Proletariat."[62] Although they did not pursue the point, and even crossed out that sentence in the manuscript, the introduction of Wilhelm Weitling suggests another source of their lumpenproletariat. It also points to the inadequacy ("travesty," one might say, echoing Marx) of most English accounts of Weitling, in which he appears as a "social reformer," "utopian communist," or apostle of a "New Christianity."[63] Weitling, like Stirner, assigned a progressive role to the "thieving proletariat," in fact a more active role than Stirner gave it. Where Stirner simply had the *Lumpen* emerge as the dominant class under communism, Weitling gave it the task of bringing about the communist revolution. The outlaws and outcasts of society, criminals, vagabonds, and hoodlums, were the truly revolutionary class because they were totally dispossessed, totally alienated from society. They had nothing to lose, not even their chains, because they were completely outside the system. And since they alone were uninhibited by bourgeois morality, they alone were capable of the kind of violence necessary for a successful revolution. (At one point Weitling called upon socialists to open up the jails and impress the convicts into the service of the revolution.)

If Marx and Engels were at first reluctant to denounce Weitling, it was because, unlike Stirner, he was an active revolutionary, one of the guiding spirits of the League of the Just (a sect composed not of *Lumpen* or criminals but of respectable artisans, mainly tailors like Weitling himself).* It was not long, however, before his religious and apocalyptic views, his invocation of a "new messiah" and a "second coming," became an embarrassment, and his concept of the revolution as a spontaneous act of violence requiring no organized party, no coherent or conscious ideology, no historical stages, conditions, or preconditions, went exactly counter to the historical and material determinism Marx and Engels had begun to insist on as the only "scientific" form of socialism. Although Weitling himself emigrated to America shortly after a stormy meeting with Marx and Engels in Brussels in 1846, his ideas remained anathema to them, all the more because Bakunin seemed to be espousing some of them, so that by the time of the *Manifesto* he was as much an enemy as the other "reactionary," "petty bourgeois," and "utopian" socialists denounced in the final section of the *Manifesto*. 66

It is in the light of this ideological background that the description of the lumpenproletariat in the *Manifesto* must be read. The *Manifesto* was not only a prospectus for revolution but also an "internal" document, a polemic against rival revolutionary creeds. In that polemic the idea of the lumpenproletariat assumed a special significance. Where Stirner and Weitling looked to the "dangerous class" as the bearer of revolution, Marx and Engels thought it dangerous because it could as easily be suborned by the bourgeoisie and made the "bribed tool of reactionary intrigue"—of counter-revolution. This warning was delivered on the eve of the revolutions of 1848. After the failure of these revolutions they saw their worst fears confirmed. In Vienna they found "the lazzaroni, the armed and bought lumpenproletariat, fighting against the working and thinking proletariat," in Naples allied with the monarchy against the bourgeoisie, in Paris with

---

*When Engels was in England in 1843 he tried to arrange for a translation of Weitling's *Garantien der Harmonie und Freiheit,* a book whose innocent title belied its contents. It was there that Weitling called for a "new Messiah" to lead the revolution and usher in that new state of harmony and freedom. "There must be no searching around for a leader, and no fussing about the election of a leader. Whoever rises first, whoever takes the lead, whoever shows the bravest perseverance and places his life in the balance with all the others, is leader."64 In November, in an article in the Owenite journal, *The New Moral World,* Engels spoke sympathetically of Weitling and of this book, without, however, commenting on either his religious or his undemocratic predilections. Two months later in the same journal, he singled out for praise Weitling's proposal for the "abolition of all government by force and by majority" and its replacement by a "mere administration" whose officials would be nominated not by a majority of the community but by those who alone had knowledge of the work of each official; the final selection of officials was to be made on the basis of anonymous "prize essays," thus guaranteeing the choice of the "fittest person." This method of selection rather than election, Engels assured the readers of the journal, was entirely in keeping with the principles of Owenism.65

the bourgeoisie against the proletariat.[67] *The Class Struggles in France,* written in 1850, was even harsher than the *Manifesto.* Here the lumpenproletariat was "a mass sharply differentiated from the industrial proletariat, a recruiting ground for thieves and criminals of all kinds, living on the crumbs of society, people without a definite trade, vagabonds, *gens sans feu et sans aveu";* if it was sometimes capable of "the most heroic deeds and the most exalted sacrifices," it was equally capable of "the basest banditry and the foulest corruption."[68] Twenty years later, the defeat of the Paris Commune evoked the same sentiments. "The *lumpenproletariat,* this scum of the demoralized elements of all classes, which establishes its headquarters in all the big cities, is the worst of all possible allies. This rabble is absolutely venal and absolutely brazen."[69]

Apart from the experiences of 1848 and 1871, Marx and Engels had ample ideological reasons to distrust the lumpenproletariat. That class was not only a danger to the revolution; it was a danger to socialism itself. If Mayhew had cause to think that his street-folk were not reformable, not amenable to the well intentioned designs of philanthropists, Marx had still better reason to suspect that the lumpenproletariat would resist his far more ambitious plans for the reconstruction of society and the transformation of man. Like the street-folk, the lumpenproletariat consisted of social deviants and dissidents. Bourgeois society could tolerate such types even if it could not domesticate and assimilate them. But a socialist society, requiring a high degree of planning, regulation, and organization, would find them (as Stirner recognized) irredeemably anti-social and anti-socialist. Nor could a socialist society accommodate the street-folk among the lumpenproletariat —all those street-buyers and street-sellers who were neither bourgeois, petty-bourgeois, nor proletariat, and who displayed a peculiar, not always licit, passion for private enterprise. Adam Smith's famous description of the instinct underlying modern industry and trade—"the propensity to truck, barter, and exchange"—could stand as the epigraph of the street-folk. In this respect they were parodies of bourgeois man, tributes to the infinite ingenuity of the commercial spirit. If the bourgeoisie was made uncomfortable by this exuberant zeal for free enterprise, a socialist could hardly look benignly upon this primitive and totally unrestrained form of capitalism.*

---

*Before his position on the lumpenproletariat had hardened, Engels had been better disposed to the criminal elements in the English working class, who were engaged, as he saw it, in a form of "social war." He also singled out for praise a German poem that sympathetically portrayed the street-folk, characterizing it as a fine picture of the "lumpenproletariat."

> Who day by day unwearyingly
> Hunts garbage in the fetid gutters;
> Who flits like sparrows after food,
> Mending pans and grinding knives,
> Starching linen with stiff fingers,
> Pushing breathless at the heavy cart,

In other respects, notably the total absence of a "work ethic," the lumpenproletariat, like the street-folk, were hardly paragons of the bourgeois spirit. Marxist historians have accused capitalism of imposing on its labor force a regimen of time, a discipline of work, and a rhythm of life geared to the mechanical, "dehumanizing" processes of industrial production. But this work ethic is as essential for the functioning of a socialist society, which is no less dependent on industry and productivity. It was Stirner who first pointed out that "only the Sunday side of communism" took man to be man; the "workday side" of communism saw man only as "human laborer or laboring man." The communist, he predicted, looking at a "lazybones," would try to cleanse him of his laziness and convert him to the *"faith* that labor is man's 'destiny and calling.' "[71] Hannah Arendt made a similar point when she found Marx unique among philosophers in giving absolute primacy to the idea of work, defining classes in terms of their relationship to the means of production and individuals in terms of classes, allowing people no significant identity apart from their class identity, making their very "consciousness" a product of their "social nature," their relationship to the means of production.[72]

Even more than the counter-revolutionary tendency of the lumpenproletariat, it was the lack of any "social" character, any productive function (apart from the production of progeny, *prolis* in the original sense) that aroused Marx's contempt. He despised the lumpenproletariat as he did not despise the bourgeoisie. The bourgeoisie was the class enemy; it played a historically necessary and respectable role in the class struggle. The lumpenproletariat, having no relationship to the means of production, was, in effect, a non-class. Thus it had no historical function, no role in the class struggle, no legitimate place in society, no redemptive role in history. Even when it was reactionary, it was so by accident, so to speak, "bribed" to be the tool of reaction. And the members of that non-class, having no "social nature," were not real human beings but gross matter—"scum," "dregs," a "rotting mass."

It was not London that provided Marx and Engels with their examples of the lumpenproletariat at its worst; Paris had that dubious distinction. Even those who did not share Marx's view of that class agreed that Paris was its capital. A popular French book by Flora Tristan, published in 1840 under the title *Promenades dans Londres* and later reissued as *La ville monstre,* made London the heartland of immorality and crime.* But this may be an instance

---

Laden with but scarcely ripened fruits,
Crying piteously: Who'll buy, who'll buy?[270]

*Flora Tristan is better known today (where she is known at all) as Gauguin's grandmother. Her only English biography makes that her major claim to fame: *Gauguin's Astonishing Grandmother: A Biography of Flora Tristan,* by Charles N. Gattey (London, 1970).

of the literary convention whereby one's own country is criticized under the guise of another (as in Montesquieu's *Persian Letters*); or perhaps it is simply a device by which a familiar phenomenon is made more dramatic and exotic by locating it abroad—the "foreign country" tactic used so effectively by Mayhew. Two other books published that same year gave Paris a better claim to the title of "la ville monstre," and unlike Tristan's frankly sensationalistic book, these were serious inquiries by reputable social critics.

Honoré Frégier's *Des classes dangereuses de la population dans les grandes villes* and Eugène Buret's *De la misère des classes laborieuses en Angleterre et en France* drew upon official documents and statistics as well as personal observations. Frégier came to the subject from his experiences in the Paris police department and was inspired to write about it by an essay posed by the Academy of Moral and Political Science in 1838: "To discover what are the elements, in Paris or any other great city, which made up that part of the population which forms a dangerous class by virtue of its vices, its ignorance and its pauperism." Buret was responding to a later question set by the Academy: "What does pauperism consist of, by what symptoms does it show itself in different countries; what are its causes?"[73] Both books implied a closer connection between pauperism and the dangerous classes, even between the laboring classes and the dangerous classes, than was common in England. And although both professed to be speaking of England as well as France, it was the example of France that was dominant, and a French audience that was being persuaded of the dangerousness of their lower classes.

Buret blamed society for pauperizing the laboring classes and thus for making of them barbarians, outlaws, and criminals.

> The lower classes are gradually expelled from the usage and laws of civilized life and are reduced to the state of barbarism through the sufferings and privations of destitution. Pauperism is tantamount to exclusion from society. The destitute resemble the bands of Anglo-Saxons who took to a nomadic life in the forests to escape the Norman yoke. They are outside society, outside the law, outlaws, and almost all criminals come from their ranks. Once distress has brought its weight to bear on a man, it gradually presses him down, degrades his character, strips him of all the benefits of civilized life one after another and imposes upon him the vices of the slave and the barbarian.[74]

Frégier more often held the dangerous classes responsible for their own degradation.

> The poor and the vicious classes have always been and will always be the most productive breeding ground of evildoers of all sorts, it is they

whom we shall designate as the dangerous classes. For even when vice
is not accompanied by perversity, by the very fact that it allies itself
with poverty in the same person, he is a proper object of fear to society,
he is dangerous. . . . These unfortunates, who were still seemingly
attached to the mass of honest and industrious workers by the practice
of their trade, gradually shed their remaining habits of industry under
the malign influence of their companions in disorder and ended by
embracing their idle and criminal life.[75]

The historian Louis Chevalier, drawing heavily upon these books, tele-
scoped their titles in the double-barreled title of his own influential work,
*Classes laborieuses et classes dangereuses à Paris pendant la première moitié du XIXe
siècle,* thereby telescoping the classes themselves. His Paris was one in which
Buret's "nomadic wanderers" and Frégier's "poor and vicious classes" mingled with Hugo's *"les misérables,"* Balzac's beggars "situated between crime
and charity," and Eugène Sue's "barbaric tribes" and "savage hordes."
It is not clear whether the social critics were influenced by the novelists
or vice versa, or whether both were responding to a phenomenon so striking
as to call forth the same kinds of observations and judgments. In any event,
fiction and reality (or what was presumed to be reality) were so closely intertwined they could hardly be dissociated. Balzac's novels were studded with
presumed facts, such as that Paris had a "ratio of one villain to ten honest folk"
—which was not far removed from Frégier's finding that one-eighth of the
working classes were criminals (one-eighth of the working classes being
roughly equivalent to one-tenth of the population).[76] Sue borrowed from
Frégier and others not only statistical data but entire scenes of the denizens and
haunts of the Parisian underworld. And the French and English, novelists and
critics alike, shamelessly imitated and exploited each other. Tristan's *Promenades dans Londres* (1840) inspired Sue's *Mystères de Paris* (1842–43), and the
latter, in turn, G. W. M. Reynolds's *Mysteries of London* (1845–48). Tristan's
book was not translated into English, perhaps because Londoners would not
have recognized their city in it, or perhaps because they would not have taken
kindly to a foreigner's "revelations" of their vices. But the works of Sue,
Hugo, and Balzac were translated. John Stuart Mill and Sue exchanged books
and letters and found that while they disagreed about economics, they were
allies in the cause of sexual equality.[77] Marx cited Buret in his *Economic and
Philosophic Manuscripts of 1844* and in another article that year; Engels recommended Sue's book to the readers of the *New Moral World;* and *The Holy
Family* contained lengthy quotations from both Sue's book and Tristan's.[78]
Even the government reports and statistical surveys of each country
found an audience in the other. In his commission reports, Chadwick
frequently had occasion to cite data collected in other countries; in the
Sanitary Report, he quoted from the French report on the sewers of Paris

which had inspired some of the most memorable passages in Hugo's *Les Misérables*. It was the English, however, who were the acknowledged masters of this genre. Buret, who was himself much indebted to the "Blue Books," paid tribute to England as "the prime country for social studies, the country from which we had more to learn than from the whole of the rest of the world." He was especially impressed by the *Poor Law Report,* which helped men understand "the social mystery we are trying to solve."[79]

The "social mystery" England was presumed to be solving was pauperism; the mystery that still eluded solution was criminality. If the first was the English malady, the second was the French vice. "Criminal," Chevalier wrote, "is the key word for the Paris of the first half of the nineteenth century"; "the theme of crime was in fact the principal theme in the history of Paris in the nineteenth century."[80] Chevalier may have overstated the situation in Paris, but no historian, however inclined to exaggeration, could make a similar statement about London. Nor did any serious contemporary critic. Even the "Newgate" novelists, chronicling the exploits of fictional (or fictionalized) villains, adhered to a literary convention according to which the criminal classes existed within clearly defined social and geographical boundaries; they lived in a particular area of London, sometimes in a single rookery, and were instantly identified by their peculiar surroundings, language, dress, and comportment. Theirs was an "unknown country" that was rapidly becoming all too well known. But the persistence of the metaphor suggests that they were still a curiosity, more exotic than menacing.

The English dangerous classes, however illicit their activities and unconventional their manners and morals, were engaged in crimes of the most prosaic kind, crimes against property and persons of varying degrees of seriousness (most were relatively trivial)—but not crimes against the state or social order. Whatever transgressions they were guilty of, political subversion was not one of them. They were not thought capable of revolution or, like Marx's lumpenproletariat, of counter-revolution. In 1850 the French minister Adolphe Thiers, defending a bill to control and if necessary expel the "multitude of vagabonds," charged that this "vile mob" had brought "every Republic down in ruin."[81] No English statesman could have made such an accusation against the English dangerous classes. But some did believe the Parisian mobs to be capable of just that. When Palmerston heard of the establishment of the French Republic, he dismissed it as the rule of 40,000 or 50,000 "scum of the faubourgs of Paris."[82]

This, of course, was the crucial difference. England had no 1789, 1830, or 1848, no mobs marching on Versailles and the Bastille, ripping up paving stones for barricades or raiding gunsmith shops for arms, no massive bloody battles in the streets and no *Grande Peur* in the countryside. The Wilkes and Gordon affairs, which had earned the London mobs a reputation for violence in the eighteenth century, paled into insignificance beside the violence unleashed across the Channel by the French Revolution. And whatever the turbulence in England in the early nineteenth century, it was nothing like that on the Continent. The conspiracy of Despard in 1802 and that of Thistlewood in 1820, the Luddite riots in 1811–13 and the Swing riots in 1830, the Peterloo massacre of 1819, the Newport uprising of 1839, the Plug riots of 1842—singly or collectively, they were no match for the massive eruptions abroad. One historian has commented on the incidence of violence in modern England.

> A nation which commemorates 10th May, 1768, when about half a dozen rioters were killed, as the 'massacre' of St. George's Fields, 15th August, 1819, when eleven people were killed, as the 'massacre' of Peterloo, and 13th November, 1887, when no one was killed, as 'Bloody Sunday,' measures its public violence by high standards.[83]

It was not only by the standards of the great French Revolution that these "massacres" pale into insignificance. The casualties in Paris in the "June days" of 1848, according to the police estimate, were 2,000 killed or wounded, with thousands more killed subsequently. And these casualty figures are only tokens of the momentous political changes they signified —of revolutions, in short.

If the English working classes were so much less dangerous than the French, less violent and certainly less revolutionary, the English dangerous classes were far less political. Very occasionally, usually in the aftermath of a revolution in France, some hysterical Englishman might be heard sounding the alarm of an impending insurrection. During the height of the Reform Bill crisis, one pamphlet entitled "Householders in Danger from the Populace" described the radicals as "desperadoes" who were prepared to unleash the "helots of society"—"costermongers, drovers, slaughterers of cattle, knackers, dealers in dead bodies and dog's meat, cads, brickmakers, chimney-sweepers, nightmen, scavengers, etc."—to further their nefarious ends. "If an insurrection of the London populace should take place, they will be found at the most dangerous posts, leading the thieves and rabble, pointing out the most effectual measures, and dying, if the lot fall on them, with cries of defiance."[84] Mayhew was not above playing on the same fears. At one point he described the costermongers as "nearly all Chartists"—or rather, he corrected himself, not themselves Chartists (they knew nothing of such abstruse matters as "Six Points") but under the influence of one or two artisans in the neighborhood who were Chartists. Hating the police who harassed them, the costermongers could not understand why the Chartists tried to dissuade them from battling the police. "I am assured," Mayhew commented, "that in case of a political riot every 'coster' would seize his policeman." Elsewhere he said that "there are thousands in this great metropolis ready to rush forth, on the least evidence of a rising of the people, to commit the most savage and revolting excesses"; these were men who regarded all law as "organized tyranny," who had no religious or moral principles to restrain them, and who were "necessarily and essentially the dangerous classes."[85]

What is remarkable is not the few comments of this kind, but the fact that there were so few. Even during the Chartist period, when there was much talk of "agitators" and "demagogues," there was little attempt to link the criminal classes with the Chartists, to identify them both as "dangerous classes" involved in the same dangerous enterprise. The *Constabulary Report* appeared in 1839 at the height of the Chartist crisis. It would have been a telling argument in favor of a strong police force had Chadwick suggested that the Physical Force Chartists might enlist the help of criminals or might themselves be criminals. Yet there is no intimation of this in the report. Nor were the opponents of a strong constabulary reconciled to it by the fear of a political uprising abetted by the criminal elements. Nor were the Chartists themselves, even the most militant of them, tempted to use that threat; if some justified violence, they did not glorify or romanticize it. Indeed, the first point of the Charter stipulated that the vote not be given to anyone of unsound mind or convicted of a crime, the latter condition being as self-evident as the former.

The English dangerous classes, then, were dangerous without being subversive. Unlike Stirner's *Lumpen* or Weitling's "thieving proletariat," they violated the laws of the state but did not defy the law or the state as such. They usurped other people's property but did not challenge the system of private property itself. Their "depredations" did not even seriously injure the economy. They themselves were unproductive, destructive, and a burden on the taxpayers, but the "pecuniary evil," as Plint said, was "light and insignificant compared with the moral."[86] This was the real danger: they were the "virus of a moral poison" that threatened to contaminate those around them. Unfortunately, those most exposed to that virus and most vulnerable to it were those who had the most to lose—the working classes, the laboring poor. And what they had to lose was their most important asset in the present and their most important investment in the future—their respectability.

There had always been marginal types among the poor—paupers, beggars, vagrants, street-folk, drunkards, brawlers, thieves, prostitutes. And they had always been distinguished, to some degree, from the laboring poor; they

were the lowliest of the poor, the lowest of the lower classes, the most
inferior of the "inferior orders." But they had previously existed in a
continuum with the poor. Depending on age and health, character and
family, location and occupation, the state of the harvest and the conditions
of trade, any laborer might find himself, at one time or another, more or
less destitute, more or less dependent on charity or relief, more or less idle
or dissolute. And among his family and neighbors might be found some who
existed more or less permanently on the fringes of society, in and out of
the workhouse or jail, often enough drunk and violent to be classed among
the "roughs."

The breakup of the continuum, the sharpening of "lines of demarcation," was partly a result of industrialism and urbanism, partly of ideology
and social policy. So long as all the poor were ragged, there were no "ragged
classes." The latter emerged as a distinctive group when the development
of the textile industry and a general rise in the standard of living made
clothes cheaper and more available. It was then, when most of the poor
ceased to be ragged, literally and metaphorically, when the laboring poor
started to become known as the "working classes," that the "ragged classes"
also assumed something of a class character. Under that distinctive appellation they became a distinctive social problem—a problem to the poor who
were not themselves in that condition and were fearful of lapsing into it,
and a problem to social reformers who sought to prevent that lapse, to
redeem at least the ragged children, and to forestall the degeneration of the
ragged classes into the dangerous classes.

There had also always been identifiably criminal, dangerous elements
in society; there was an Elizabethan underworld, a Restoration underworld,
a Hogarthian underworld. But with the growth of cities, and of London
especially, these elements acquired the status of "classes." In the densely
populated slums the criminals and semi-criminals became a "critical mass,"
and thus a social problem. Again, they were a problem to the laboring poor
who were in the closest proximity to them and in the greatest danger from
them, not so much as the victims of their "depredations"—the criminals
more often found their prey outside the slums—but as the victims of their
contamination. And they were a problem to social reformers who tried to
prevent that contamination and to rehabilitate the children so that they did
not perpetuate that taint.

A generation later, after the passage of the second Reform Act enfran-
chising most of the working classes, Walter Bagehot proposed as the slogan
of the time: "Educate! Educate! Educate!"[87] So, one might say, the motto
of the earlier reformers was "Separate! Separate! Separate!" In a sense they
were charged with this mission by Malthus, who confronted them with the
prospect of a massive pauperization of the poor. The New Poor Law was
the most dramatic effort to prevent that pauperization by separating the

independent laboring poor from the paupers, re-moralizing the poor at the expense, if need be, of the de-moralized pauper class. The factory acts had a similar strategy: concerned not with factory workers in general but only with women and children, they were intended to protect those who were most vulnerable, most likely to be injured and to injure the working classes as a whole. Similarly, the public health measures were designed to correct the worst sanitary conditions, conditions that threatened to reduce all the poor to the state of the "residuum," infecting them all with the miasma of Jacob's Island. And so too the ragged schools and reformatory schools were meant to educate and rehabilitate the children of the most destitute and depraved, and to do so in separate institutions where they would not contaminate each other or, worse, the laboring poor.

At every point the distinctions, the lines of demarcation, were primarily moral. Paupers were not distinguished from the poor in terms of income or even standard of living; the crucial distinction was dependency and the degradation that was presumed to accompany dependency. Nor were the street-folk necessarily poorer than the laboring poor, indeed many were richer; but the quality of their lives was distinctively, morally different, so distinctive as to make them a species apart, an uncivilized, barbarous race. Both the ragged and the dangerous classes were even more sharply distinguished from the respectable poor, the former displaying, sometimes flaunting, their unrespectability in their very appearance, the latter making a career of it, carrying immorality to the ultimate end of criminality.

In the initial reaction against "middle class history," "history from above," some historians recoiled from such words as "respectable" and "unrespectable," "deserving" and "undeserving," as if they were the inventions of "culture-bound" middle class historians reflecting the prejudices of narrow-minded middle class Victorians. More recently, it has been recognized that such moral concepts were an important part of the social reality for people of all classes and persuasions. "Respectability," for example—the public analogue of private morality—was not confined to the middle classes or the "labor aristocracy" but was just as much a fact of life for the poor.[88] And the distinction between the "respectable" and the "rough" was even more critical at the lower rungs of society, where any misstep, any misfortune or imprudence, could be catastrophic. This is the significance of all those revelations about the street-folk and residuum, the ragged classes and dangerous classes. To a historian today, such concerns may seem like a diversion from the real problem, the problem of the working classes, and especially of the new industrial working classes—the problem of poverty in the sense of low wages, long hours, unemployment and irregular employment, unsavory working and living conditions. To contemporaries, however, they were very much a part of that problem, indeed the most crucial part. The "line of demarcation" between the laboring classes and the "ragged, perishing, and dangerous" classes was never as clear and firm as reformers would have liked. But it was clearly impressed upon the contemporary consciousness—of the poor as much as the rich, of Chartists, radicals, and socialists as much as conservatives, liberals, and reformers.

PART FOUR

THE FICTIONAL POOR

XVI

FICTION AS HISTORY

It should not be necessary, in a study of this kind, to defend the use of fiction as a historical source. A medium which, then far more than now, was full of the "hum and buzz" (in Lionel Trilling's memorable phrase) of cultural and social implication must surely be valuable in elucidating contemporary ideas of poverty.[1] Yet the source has been so much abused that some caveats are in order.

Historians have always used fiction to illustrate the "spirit of the times," generally in a final chapter of miscellanea containing all those odds and ends of intellectual, cultural, and social history which could not be accommodated in the text proper. The historian for whom these subjects are the heart of the matter may be inclined to give fiction a greater centrality and prominence, all the more so in a study of early Victorian England, when an entire genre of fiction, the "social novel" as it is now called, was devoted to the "social question." Yet it is in this period, when the novel most insistently intrudes itself upon history, that it is most problematic. W. O. Aydelotte expressed the concerns of many historians (and not only those of the "quantitative" school with which he is identified) when he complained that the information provided by these novels was "spotty, impressionistic, and inaccurate," and that any reliance upon them for purposes of social history was "a kind of dilettantism which the historian would do well to avoid." At best, they would reveal not the "facts of the age" but the "mind of the novelist," not "social conditions" but "attitudes towards social conditions."[2]

This criticism may be carried further. If the novels seem to support the "pessimistic" position of some historians, Michael Jefferson has suggested, it is because the novelists themselves shared the attitudes of these historians, attitudes which disposed them to typical inaccuracies and distortions: the failure to make crucial chronological distinctions (attributing to a later period abuses which had been removed by earlier reforms),

generalizations based on a single incident or on spurious or unrepresentative incidents, the contrast between industrialism and a mythical pre-
industrial Golden Age, and in general an overly dismal view of social
conditions and an overly polarized view of social relations.[3] Historians
have since compounded these errors by the selective, tendentious use of
such novels, citing as evidence of contemporary attitudes and facts those
passages which conform to their own views and ignoring or dismissing as
fictitious those which do not.

Another objection derives from the supposed gap of sensibility, sympathy, and knowledge between the middle class novelists and the lower classes
they purported to describe, so that the novelists would inevitably see their
characters through the distorting lens of their own values.* In a sense, the
novelists brought this charge upon themselves by making so large a point
(in some cases, their main point) of the unbridgeable chasm supposedly
separating the "two nations," and locating that other "nation" in a "foreign"
or "unknown" country. By their own testimony, the novelists would seem
to disqualify themselves as authorities on that other nation in that unknown
country. Since many of the novels were written for as well as by the middle
classes, the authors could take even greater license with their subjects, their
readers presumably knowing no more about the lower classes than they did.
They could feel free to create characters sharing their own values and
feelings, on the assumption that all human beings were essentially the same;
or they could create characters with exactly the opposite values and feelings,
on the assumption that these were, after all, alien creatures belonging to
another nation or race. Caught up in the illusory power of the fiction, their
readers would forget the disclaimer implicit in the "two nations" and
"foreign country" metaphors, and would take these imaginative creations
at face value, thus further confounding fancy and reality.

This difficulty may be exaggerated—as exaggerated as the metaphor
of the foreign country. That country was not, in fact, as foreign as it was
made out to be; if it were, the metaphor would not have appeared as
frequently as it did. With predictable and monotonous regularity every
parliamentary report, social novel, and journalistic exposé announced itself,
and was hailed by reviewers, as an excursion into "distant lands," "dark and
unknown regions," populated by "aborigines" and "unknown tribes" as
peculiar as the "people of Lapland or California," their tales as "strange and
new as the wildest dreams of fiction."[5] At some point, those unknown tribes

---

*Those literary critics who make the most of this problem are often confident that they themselves
(however middle class) do not suffer from this distortion, and so can discern the distortion in others
and distinguish it from the reality. Their conception of that reality, however, often derives not from
an independent study of the historical sources but from their own assumptions about what constitutes
"authentic" working class experience and consciousness—immiseration, alienation, and rebelliousness.[4]

must have become familiar, the tales less exotic, the mysteries less mysterious, even banal, as they were exposed in one "revelation" after another, by one intrepid and all too voluble explorer after another. Even if these explorers were of the middle classes, they could not have continued to be as hopelessly ignorant of that other country as they pretended to be. Nor were the readers of these revelations exclusively of the middle classes and therefore ignorant and gullible. The greatest novelist, Charles Dickens, had a considerable working class following, especially for the novels in the serial form in which they originally appeared. And the more sensationalistic writers—G. W. M. Reynolds, William Ainsworth, and a host of others who are less well known today—attracted a still lower and larger class of readers. It is interesting that the novels containing the most villainous types of poor were read most widely and eagerly by the poor themselves.

If the novels had only a tangential, fantasized relationship to the reality, the fantasy itself permeated the reality, shaping the ideas, opinions, attitudes, and behavior of the readers, no less, perhaps, than the commission reports, newspaper accounts, tracts, and broadsheets, which were also, to one degree or another, removed from the reality. If the novel cannot be taken as historical evidence *tout court,* neither can these other sources; it might even be salutary if all sources were seen as, in some sense and in some measure, fictional, to be used warily, skeptically, critically, but also appreciatively. Whatever else may be said about the novels, they were undoubtedly one of the most important means by which the "anonymous masses," in however fictionalized or fantasized a form, were brought to the attention of the public, assimilated into the social consciousness, and made the concern of an increasingly sensitive and vigilant social conscience.

Of all forms of fiction, the "social novel"—or "industrial novel" or "social-problem novel," as others prefer to call it—would seem preeminently suited to the social historian.[6] That novel was concerned primarily with the state of the lower or working classes under the new conditions of industrialism. The archetypes of this genre are Benjamin Disraeli's *Sybil* (1845), Elizabeth Gaskell's *Mary Barton* (1848) and *North and South* (1855), and Charles Dickens's *Hard Times* (1854), with such lesser exemplars as Harriet Martineau's *A Manchester Strike* (1832), Frances Trollope's *Michael Armstrong: The Factory Boy* (1839–40), and Charles Kingsley's *Alton Locke* (1850).[7] One can understand why these novels have been singled out for attention, and why some have been given preeminence over others. For purposes of social history, however, great books—even great books which happened to be popular as well—have to be put in the context of other popular books which are not so great. More important, the "social novel" has to be put in the context of other novels not explicitly or primarily addressed to the "social problem." An idea of poverty or image of the poor may emerge as clearly from a book which does not intentionally deal with that problem as from one which does. It might be argued that if the object is to elicit the prevailing ideas and images of an age, they might better be sought precisely where they are not the subject of conscious attention and reflection, where they reveal themselves inadvertently and unconsciously.

The social novel, then, as it is usually defined, is itself problematic if it focuses attention unduly on a particular social problem and a particular class. To the degree to which it encourages us to speak of "working classes" rather than "the poor," it points to a significant change in the social and intellectual climate. Yet even the most "industrial" of these novels were not confined to the industrial working classes—which suggests not, as some critics have complained, that the authors were insufficiently attentive to the nature and problems of industrialism, but that they were acutely aware of a larger social reality of which industrialism was only one element. For the most part, the new condition-of-England question merged with the old question of poverty, and the industrial working classes with the more amorphous body of the poor. In *Sybil,* Disraeli made a deliberate effort to address the "condition-of-the-people question," but his most memorable pronouncement about the "two nations" identified them, in bold capitals, as "THE RICH AND THE POOR."

In the largest sense of the term, almost every novel is a social novel.* The historian interested in ideas of poverty may find significance in the absence of any visible poverty in Thackeray's best novels, which were located, as was said at the time, in the "debatable land between the middle classes and the aristocracy."[9] Thackeray's "poor" were the *déclassés,* characters like Becky Sharp, whose "dismal precocity of poverty" obliged her to teach French for a living, which she managed to do in a pure Parisian accent. Yet he too thought of his novels as having a social purpose—the exposure of the moral and spiritual poverty of the upper classes, the "undeserving rich," one might say. It was in this sense that one contemporary critic claimed that the world of his novels was more "real" than that of Dickens.[10]

If social historians tend to ignore novels that are not on obvious social themes, they also tend to make too much of those passages that are most conspicuously on those themes—passages signaled by such code words as "rich" and "poor," "Capital" and "Labour." In the case of the famous

---

*This is not, however, to say, as does the opening sentence of a recent book, that "any novel written between roughly 1780 and the 1850s is necessarily an expression of and a response to the events we have come to call, somewhat narrowly, the Industrial Revolution"[8]—if only because in the early part of that period in many parts of the country, the industrial revolution had neither industrialized nor revolutionized the economy, still less social relations, social sensibilities, or the social consciousness. Even for the later part of that period (or any period) the relationship between a novel and the economic and social environment of the author is never as mechanical, reductivistic, and deterministic as this statement implies.

Disraeli quotation, its importance is attested to in the novel itself and in the fact that it immediately entered the social vocabulary. In other instances, the passages may be of little significance in the context of the novel and of still less import in the consciousness of the ordinary reader. However wary the historian may be of reading the novel as a social tract, the temptation will be to focus on those parts of it which allude more or less explicitly to social issues or problems. Yet the "social message" of the novel may lie elsewhere, in ideas and attitudes communicated less overtly, in language, style, plot, characters, and scenes which were not intentionally didactic or programmatic, in meanings and emotions which may not be readily accessible to the modern reader. In this sense, the novel is both a work of art and a contemporary artifact, transcending and at the same time firmly rooted in its time and place. If one cannot now weep at the death of Little Nell, as readers all over England wept when that installment appeared, one can at least try to understand that response and give proper weight to it.

By the same token, the historian must take seriously novels which may be mediocre and meretricious, which are no part of the "great tradition" or even of any lesser "selective tradition," the literary canon as it has come down to us.[11] This does not require any suspension of literary judgment, any assumption that the distinction between good and bad literature is "class bound" or a matter of personal taste.* It merely testifies to the fact that a novel with no redeemable literary value may have considerable historical value.

At this time especially, there were so many crosscurrents between the traditional and the popular culture, between "high" literature and "low," that neither can be entirely understood without the other. *Nicholas Nickleby* and *Vanity Fair* were both conceived, at least in part, as parodies of one of the favorite genres of the time, the "silver fork" novel, which appealed to readers of all classes but drew most of its characters and scenes from high society.[13] An occasional ostensibly lower class character might wander into these novels: a poor maiden speaking faultless English (as Becky Sharp spoke faultless French), seduced by an aristocrat, and eventually revealed to be a foundling or changeling of good family, or a poor but dashing young man

---

*Populist history, "history from below," lends itself to such a relativistic view of literature:

> The overwhelming condescension of scholars toward the literature written by working people arises out of a long tradition of judging art from a position of educational superiority. What we call literature, and what we teach, is what the middle class—and not the working class—produced. Our definition of literature and our canons of taste are class bound; we currently exclude street literature, songs, hymns, dialect and oral story telling, but they were the most popular forms used by the working class.[12]

One might argue that the greater "condescension" is to adopt different literary standards—or no standards—in discussing working class literature.

defrauded of his rightful title and inheritance who recovers them after many installments of travail and adventure. The social message in these tales was ambiguous. If the hero or heroine was upper class, so was the villain. Indeed, the villain was quintessentially aristocratic, since it was the convention of the genre that in this rarefied social sphere good and evil were transcended. The true aristocrat was a Nietzschean character, willful, imperious, amoral, even, when it pleased him, vicious and sadistic; the reader was not expected to approve of him, only to be thrilled and titillated by him.

A chaster kind of romance was provided by the "domestic" novel. Here the characters were not so much middle class as classless, their heroes and heroines professedly "ordinary" people. But some of these ordinary people led quite extraordinary lives, rarely seeming to work, devoting themselves to the most improbable love affairs, and often becoming more upper class as the plot unfolded until they ended where the silver fork novels began. The illusion of classlessness was sometimes achieved by the pastoral setting, a mythical version of the simple country life. In one of these novels, the "village maid" inhabited a cottage that was a miniature version of a country estate, complete with china figurines, tastefully arranged vases of flowers, and a loving collection of books presumably typical of the cultivated woman of leisure: "Byron, Shelley, Chateaubriand's Génie de Christianisme, Volney's Ruins, the Corinna of Madame de Stael, Holstein, and Paul and Virginia of St. Pierre."[14]

The hortatory novel was more austerely domestic, resisting any impulse to romance, except, as the author might say, the romance of hard work, clean living, and self-improvement. Frankly addressed to the poor and featuring them as the main characters, it had all the characteristics of a morality play, in which the virtuous, deserving poor battled with the demon drink. The message of these novels was so blatant and the litany so familiar —the misery and degradation caused by drink, the rewards of temperance in the form of a comfortable subsistence, domestic serenity, and social advancement—that the modern reader finds it difficult to understand how people could be entertained or moved by them. But this is to underestimate the power of the didactic mode in an age which, unlike our own, had a high tolerance for sermons, lectures, moralistic biographies, tales of political economy, and self-help tracts.* Charles Knight, Harriet Martineau's publisher, was dubious about the pedagogic effect of her *Illustrations of Political Economy;* most of her readers, he suspected, came away from the monthly installment without the least idea of the principle it was meant to inculcate. He did, however, credit her with influencing the development of the social novel and encouraging other writers to take as their subject "the characteris-

---

*The archetype of the didactic tale, Hannah More's *Cheap Repository Tracts* (1795), sold 2,000,000 copies within a year of their publication. This, to be sure, was the total figure for some fifty tracts, each priced at a halfpenny, penny, or penny-halfpenny. But it is still a remarkable number.

tic relations of rich and poor, of educated and uneducated, of virtuous and vicious, in our complicated state of society."[15]

The most popular novels were anything but morality plays. To some contemporaries they were, rather, invitations to immorality. The typical Newgate novel was a tale of crime, imprisonment, escape, recapture, and hanging, while the Gothic novel specialized in the exotic, the grotesque, and the macabre. These themes were so popular that they became staples of the other genres as well, the social novel, for example, often containing a Newgate or Gothic subplot, a scene of murder or terror. (Lytton Bulwer's *Paul Clifford,* published in 1830, which is sometimes given the distinction of being the first social novel, was also one of the most successful Newgate novels.) When Thackeray complained that the Newgate novelists were sentimentalizing and romanticizing crime, he did not mean that they were representing crime as innocent (the pauper driven to steal to feed his starving children), or virtuous (Robin Hood taking from the rich to give to the poor), or innocuous (the debtor punished out of all proportion to his offense). These were not, in fact, the usual themes of these novels. What he objected to was that they habituated the reader to gratuitous violence, made crime seem romantic and heroic, and condoned the vices of drunkenness, dissipation, and dissoluteness which accompanied a life of crime. "We have our penny libraries for debauchery as for other useful knowledge; and colleges like palaces for study—gin-palaces, where each starving Sardanapalus may revel until he dies."[16]*

To be aware of these varieties of fiction flourishing in the thirties and forties is to see in better perspective the handful of "social novels" that are usually dignified with that title. It is also useful to remember that all these varieties, including the silver fork novels, had large numbers of working class readers. Any illusions one may have of a working class or "folk" culture of a kind that would have met with the approval of Ruskin or Morris cannot survive the least familiarity with the popular literature of the time. This is all the more true if one considers other forms of literature besides the novel, the street literature described by Mayhew—broadsheets, for example, publicizing a murder, fire, or hanging—or the abundant supply of "penny dreadfuls." Dickens remembered reading one of these serials as a schoolboy, "making myself unspeakably miserable, and frightening my very wits out of my head," very good value, he thought, "considering that there was an illustration to every number in which there was always a pool of blood, and at least one body."[17]

*Thackeray's casual reference to Sardanapalus, his confidence that the reader of *Fraser's Magazine* would understand the allusion to the king of Nineveh who was the symbol of luxurious effeteness, is itself a "social message" of considerable significance.

Dickens himself was enormously popular, although not as popular as William Ainsworth, G. W. M. Reynolds, Frederick Marryat, J. F. Smith, and other writers who are now almost forgotten except by the social historian. Charles Kingsley, visiting a Chartist bookstore in London, was appalled to find that in addition to radical papers and the works of Voltaire and Paine, most of the stock consisted of " 'Flash Songsters,' and the 'Swell's Guide,' and 'Tales of Horror,' and dirty, milksop French novels."[18] If Chartists—the sort who frequented bookstores, moreover—were attracted to that kind of literature, one need not be surprised to learn that Mayhew's costermongers, having had their fill of "tales of robbery and bloodshed, of heroic, eloquent, and gentlemanly highwaymen, or of gipsies turning out to be nobles," had gone on to stories about "Courts, potentates, or 'harristo-crats.' "[19]

Even the fiction written by Chartists conformed to the familiar models. Their hortatory tales, unlike those of the Society for the Diffusion of Useful Knowledge, made much of the grievances of the poor, but they too extolled the virtues of temperance, diligence, prudence, and self-help. And their romantic tales, again laced with sentiments of sympathy for the poor, contained the obligatory scenes of seduction and plots about changelings and long-lost heirs. Sometimes the melodrama was so overwhelming as to leave little room for the theme of social protest. Ernest Jones introduced his serial *Woman's Wrongs* by declaring his intention "to paint life *as it is*—no poet's fancy, no romancer's dream."[20] That "romance of truth," however, was hardly a romance of working class heroism, oppression, or tragedy. The real villain of the piece was the worker, who was far more cruel to his long-suffering wife than his employer was to him. Drunk, violent, and bestial, he beat his wife, watched impassively as his daughter almost burnt to death, became a robber and murderer, and was finally hanged at Newgate. A subplot had the daughter become a prostitute after being seduced by her employer; but if she was a victim of society, she was a thoroughly disagreeable one, almost as callous and depraved as her father. The only sympathetic character was the much abused wife. If, as the title suggests, the serial belongs more to the genre of women's literature than to that of working class literature, it is an unorthodox specimen of this genre as well, since the daughter hardly typifies the virtuous woman wronged.* Assuring his readers that this was "life *as it is*," Jones also promised them that the book was so

---

*It has recently been criticized on both counts, as insensitive to the woman's issue and irrelevant to the working class problem. Because Jones did not portray women from the same class as his readers (radicals and Chartists), Martha Vicinus argues, he never posed the question of "how politically aware men treat their women"; as a result, his readers could be repelled by the mistreatment of women of other classes without having to confront their own failings. Similarly, the working class problem was obscured by the melodramatic episodes (the murder of the employer, the mutilation of the body, the gory burial) and by a plot that put the worker in the wrong. "Social criticism remains oblique; the husband is fired because he is drunk and inefficient, and not for political reasons."[21]

pure and inoffensive it could be read by anyone. "This novel will portray the working of our social system in *the domestic sphere,* and while replete with incident, with passion and excitement, will be kept so pure of all objectionable matter, and inculcate so true and just a moral, that the father and husband may freely give it to the wife and child."[22]

All of this is a far cry from Engels's account of working class literature, which had the proletariat (and chiefly the proletariat) reading "the epoch-making products of modern philosophical, political, and poetical literature": Helvétius, Holbach, Diderot, Strauss, Proudhon, Bentham, Godwin, Shelley, Byron. He was especially pleased to report that Shelley and Byron found most of their readers among the proletariat, the bourgeoisie having "only castrated editions, family editions, cut down in accordance with the hypocritical morality of today." Ignoring the less edifying and far more plentiful kinds of literature available to the working classes, Engels concluded that proletarian literature was "far in advance of the whole bourgeois literature in intrinsic worth."[23]*

It is notoriously difficult to determine which books were read by which classes, but some clues are provided by the economics of the publishing industry. The familiar three-volume novels selling for a guinea and a half were bought only by the affluent (a guinea and a half being a good weekly income for a working class family), or by the lending libraries which were to be found by the middle of the century in every town of any size and which served rural customers through the post. Mudie's was the best known of the libraries, but there were many others which, for a membership fee of a guinea or a guinea and a half a year, permitted a family to borrow as many novels as it liked; the three-volume novel was well suited to this purpose since it could be read by different members of the family at the same time. While this fee (and sometimes an initiation fee as well) limited the use of these libraries to the upper and middle classes and to the more prosperous and intellectually ambitious artisans, others catered to the poorer classes: the libraries of the Mechanics' Institutions (about seven hundred of

---

*Other writers also credited the artisans with extraordinary literary interests. Charles Kingsley claimed that Isaac Watts's *Logic* and Locke's *Essay on Human Understanding* were well known to artisans. Mrs. Gaskell described the handloom weavers in Lancashire who worked with an open copy of Newton's *Principia* beside them "to be snatched at in work hours, but revelled over in meal-times or at night."[24] One is reminded of the lectures and courses provided by the settlement houses later in the century, which (if the titles are to be believed) would be formidable by the standards of a modern university, and which, one suspects, testified more to the enthusiasm of the lecturers than to that of the audience. So with Locke and Newton; the aspiring artisan may have felt that these were the symbols of literacy and intellectual respectability, but it is hard to believe that he "revelled" in them. At least one of those artisans, John Passmore Edwards, the son of a carpenter who later became a millionaire newspaper proprietor, confessed that in his youth he had bought used copies of Locke and Newton, but found them utterly baffling.[25]

these, some of which refused to stock novels but made exceptions for favorite authors), libraries attached to Sunday schools and ragged schools, cheap commercial libraries in tobacconist and stationery shops, libraries at railway stations where a book could be read for a penny while waiting for the train or for slightly more during the trip, and public houses and coffee shops which stocked the installments of a novel or magazines to be read on the premises for the price of a mug of beer or a cup of coffee.

Mudie's was reputed to have used its influence to maintain the high price of the three-volume novel and to keep it in that three-volume format, but it could not prevent cheaper modes of publication which brought the novel within the means of the poor. Many novels were reissued after two or three years in a one-volume edition for a shilling, and others appeared in reprint series such as the Parlour and Railway Libraries. A still wider circulation was made possible by the serial form in which most novels originally appeared, serialization having the double advantage of prolonging the suspense of the plot and reducing the cost of the book. The more respectable novels usually appeared in monthly journals such as *Fraser's Magazine* and *Blackwood's;* at half-a-crown an issue these periodicals were bought mainly by the middle classes. For the working classes there were countless weeklies of the sensationalist type *(London Journal, Lloyd's Penny Weekly Miscellany, Reynolds's Miscellany),* as well as more respectable ones *(Penny Magazine, Family Herald, Family Journal, Household Words)* which also cost only a penny or two and published Dickens, Thackeray, Mrs. Gaskell, and the like. Since these journals included much other reading matter in addition to the serial, they were good value for the money. (Mayhew remarked upon the "commercial spirit" of the costermongers who bought these magazines with an eye to their resale, for when "they've got the reading out of it," they sold them for a halfpenny to a secondhand dealer.)[26] The novels—the best as well as the trashiest of them—were also sold in separate monthly parts for a shilling or in weekly parts for a penny or two, some of the serials going on in this form for years.* Sometimes friends or neighbors shared the cost of a particular novel, the parts of which would be passed from one member to another or read aloud to the group.

The literary effect of serialization on the structure, style, and content of novels has often been noted: the pressure on the author to produce his

---

*The appearance of the shilling monthlies in 1859–60 *(Macmillan's Magazine* and the *Cornhill)* doomed the publication of the novels in monthly parts at a shilling apiece, since for that price the reader could obtain an entire journal. It should not, incidentally, be thought that serialization was an invention of the Victorians; the practice went back at least to the late seventeenth century. Nor was it confined to fiction. In the nineteenth century, nonfiction was often "recycled" in the same way, appearing first in parts or journals, then in volumes and cheap reprints. Bagehot's *The English Constitution* first appeared in the *Fortnightly Review* and Newman's *Apologia Pro Vita Sua* in eight weekly parts.

weekly or monthly allotment encouraging repetition, verbosity, and such stylistic peculiarities as single-sentence or even single-word paragraphs; the predetermined length of each installment requiring suitably spaced climaxes; the plot adapted to readers' reactions, a new character or dramatic episode introduced when sales began to fall. The social implications were no less striking. The fact that novels were available in different forms and prices suggests that there was a large popular demand for fiction among all classes. But if the demand generated supply, the reverse was also true: the accessibility of novels created a still larger body of consumers. In this sense, the penny dreadfuls played a significant part in the development of a literate working class and of a popular literary culture. It was not, to be sure, the highly political and sophisticated culture described by Engels, nor the kind of culture later romanticized under the label of "folk culture." It was, however, a reading culture, one in which even the poorest had some relation to the written word—even if only to be read to by a more literate neighbor, and even if the reading matter was a penny installment of a second-hand copy of a third-rate novel.

In fact more people than one might suppose could and did read, and this well before the compulsory education provided by Forster's Act of 1871. The manager of one of Edward Lloyd's publishing enterprises, which catered to the very lowest classes, explained: "Our publications circulate among a class so different in education and social position from the readers of three-volume novels, that we sometimes distrust our judgment and place the manuscript in the hands of an illiterate person—a servant, or machine boy, for instance. If they pronounce favourably upon it, we think it will do."[27] What is most remarkable about this statement is the assumption that that "illiterate person" was literate enough to read the manuscript and to express an opinion on it.

    Literacy figures are notoriously difficult to come by, not only because the sources are inadequate but because the definition and measurement of literacy are debatable. Is schooling an appropriate index of literacy, or reading and writing, or reading alone, or signing the marriage register? By any of these standards, conditions varied so much among different groups in different parts of the country (even among different parishes in one area) that aggregate national figures are most unsatisfactory. The best overall estimate is that in the early Victorian period two-thirds to three-quarters of the working classes had some reading ability.[28]* If there were no other

*A quite different impression is given if these figures are reversed, if, as is sometimes said, "nearly one-fourth of the population" could neither read nor write.[29] Most contemporaries were more impressed with the literacy of the great majority than with the illiteracy of the minority, and even

evidence for this relatively high degree of literacy, something like it is suggested by the sheer quantity and variety of publications intended primarily for the working classes. In 1840 there were 80 cheap journals in London alone; by 1860 there were 100, more than half of which were devoted entirely to fiction. In the course of these decades, the *London Journal,* whose normal circulation was 100,000 copies a week, reached a sale of 500,000 when an especially popular novel (the now totally unknown *Minnigrey* by the equally unknown J. F. Smith) was being serialized. One of its rivals, *Reynolds's Miscellany,* at times sold as many as 200,000 copies a week. The more respectable *Family Herald,* appealing to both the working classes and the lower middle classes, had a weekly circulation of 125,000. The *Penny Magazine,* founded in 1832 by the Society for the Diffusion of Useful Knowledge, had a regular circulation of 200,000 almost from the start. These figures do not take into account the number of readers of any single copy within a family or among friends or their resale to dealers who then resold them in turn. Nor do they include the even more ephemeral literature such as broadsheets and chapbooks, songs and ballads. In 1848–49, while *The Times* was reporting on revolutions abroad and Chartist demonstrations at home, outbreaks of cholera and public health reforms, two broadsheets recounting the gory details of murders sold 2,500,000 copies apiece—this, it must be remembered, at a time when the population of England and Wales was 18,000,000.[31]

The readers of *The Times* did not buy broadsheets and the purchasers of penny dreadfuls did not usually buy three-volume novels. But between these extremes there was a large area where both the readers and the genres overlapped. Dickens had a considerable working class audience, and Reynolds a not insignificant middle class one. The most popular authors in the Parlour and Railway Libraries, catering primarily to the middle classes, were G. P. R. James (47 titles), Bulwer Lytton (19), Mrs. Marsh (16), Frederick Marryat (15), William Ainsworth (14), and others still less familiar today. Most of these were what contemporary critics called "sensation novelists," which prompted *The Times* to observe that "persons of the better classes who constitute the larger portion of railway readers lose their accustomed taste the moment they enter the station."[32] (Had *The Times* considered some of the books circulating in Mudie's, it might have had a less exalted notion of the "accustomed taste" of these classes.) While historians scour the "social

more so with the growing rate of literacy. Arguing for state-supported education, the Chartist and popular writer G. W. M. Reynolds addressed the largely working class readers of his own journal: "You are intelligent and enlightened by *self*-education (no thanks to the State!); whereas, fifty years ago, not one of your class was able to read, now a hundred can not only read and write fluently, but are also possessed of much useful information and miscellaneous knowledge."[30] That contrast was undoubtedly exaggerated, but it testifies to the common impression of a vast improvement in literacy during the first half of the century.

novels" for evidence of the influence of the Blue Books (the Royal Commission reports bound in blue-paper covers), it may be useful to recall that other kind of "blue book" which was at least as influential: the stories and short novels (frequently Gothic tales) published in the twenties which were bound in blue and cost sixpence or a shilling. By the 1850s these blue books had given way to the "yellow-backs," full-length novels (and some nonfiction), usually with yellow covers and colored illustrations on the cover, and selling for two shillings or so at the railway bookstalls.[33] The fact that perfectly respectable novels as well as "sensation novels" were published in the same format, sold for the same price at the same place, and bought by the same kinds of readers, says a good deal about the culture and the society in which they flourished.

The mixed readership of these novels may account for one quality that comes as a surprise to the modern reader: the fact that even the most sensationalistic and meretricious of them had an occasional flair, a flamboyance and exuberance, which did not make them better works of art but did make them more artful than comparable works today. Mayhew quoted a passage from a story read to a group of costermongers which "took their fancy wonderfully."

> With glowing cheeks, flashing eyes, and palpitating bosom, Venetia Trelawney rushed back into the refreshment-room, where she threw herself into one of the arm-chairs already noticed. But scarcely had she thus sunk down upon the flocculent cushion, when a sharp click, as of some mechanism giving way, met her ears, and at the same instant her wrists were caught in manacles which sprang out of the arms of the treacherous chair, while two steel bands started from the richly-carved back and grasped her shoulders. A shriek burst from her lips—she struggled violently, but all to no purpose: for she was a captive—and powerless!

What caught Mayhew's interest was the costermongers' fascination with those elegant manacles. "Aye! that's the way the harristocrats hooks it. There's nothing o' that sort among us; the rich has all that barrikin to themselves."[34] The passage may also impress the modern reader with a certain sophistication of language. One does not know what the costermongers made of that "flocculent cushion," but it is obvious that the author made no attempt to talk down to his audience. On the contrary, he seems deliberately to have cultivated a haughty tone, perhaps because that was appropriate to his aristocratic subject—or perhaps because it appealed to readers who, however lower class, had a fancy for high-flown language, as they had a fancy for high society. That lofty tone also made the novel acceptable to middle class or would-be middle class readers who could feel flattered that they were reading the work of an educated man writing for educated people, even while they were being diverted by the same vulgarity and sensationalism that appealed to the costermongers. If the growth of literacy had a democratizing influence upon the culture, so did the romantic sensibility, which pervaded the language of the novel as much as the plot and which seduced readers of all classes.

There were "two cultures," as there were "two nations." But in some respects they were less far apart than might be thought. The silver fork and Newgate novels, the domestic romances and edifying tales, the three-volume novels sold in monthly parts and the weekly parts that were later bound as volumes, the libraries and reading clubs, the habit of reading aloud and being read to, all had the effect of mediating between the two cultures. The novels themselves had the same effect, the respectable and the unrespectable sharing, to some extent, common themes and rhetoric, as they also shared, to some extent, a common audience. If *Hard Times* qualified for the "Great Tradition" by virtue of sheer literary genius, it also revealed its affinity with the "low tradition" in its sentimentality and melodrama, qualities which later critics, knowing more about the high culture than the low one, find embarrassing and inexplicable.

The two cultures had one other common characteristic: both appealed powerfully to the visual sense. Those who could not read could listen—and they could also pore over the illustration highlighting the current episode of their penny serial or Dickens novel. Today, when novels (serious adult novels, at any rate) are rarely illustrated (perhaps because they are no longer serialized and there is no need to sustain interest from one part to the next), it may be difficult to appreciate the effect of those illustrations.* Unaccustomed to them, many of us tend to pass over unseeingly the plates in our edition of Dickens, much as we ignore the advertisements in our newspapers. But in the nineteenth century, when there was a well established tradition of illustrations (going back to the late seventeenth century), readers paid at least as much attention to them as to the text—more attention, obviously, in the case of those readers who did not have the habit of reading or who read with difficulty. For the latter, the illustrations were not the frosting on the cake but the cake itself. Or perhaps bread and butter would be a more appropriate metaphor, for it was not only fiction that was illustrated but the Bible and *Pilgrim's Progress,* self-help and temperance tracts, broadsheets and ballads, histories and homilies, the *Penny Magazine* dedicated to the

---

*One of the few exceptions today is the novels of John Gardner. In an age as visual as ours—witness the importance of television not only in reporting the news but in making it—it is interesting that serious fiction should have forfeited the use of pictures, leaving them to the domain of children's books and "true romance" magazines.

diffusion of useful knowledge and the *Penny Sunday Times* specializing in murders and kidnappings, *London Labour and the London Poor* and the *Report to Her Majesty of the Commissioners for Inquiring into the Employment and Condition of Children in Mines and Manufactories.* [35]

After 1840, with advances in the techniques of photography, daguerreotypes began to replace woodcuts (as in *London Labour*); these enhanced the authenticity of the illustrations but also deprived them of some dramatic effect. On the other hand, the illustrations to the report on the employment of children were sketches supposedly done on the spot by the assistant commissioners. Enormously effective and widely reproduced (the most famous was of a naked child on all fours hitched by leather straps to a wagonful of coal), they helped bring about the passage of the Mines Act.* Because they were woodcuts rather than photographs, opponents of the act were able to claim that they were inaccurate or exaggerated. The more pertinent objection—that they focused attention on the worst cases, and possibly atypical ones—would have applied to photographs as well.

Some high-minded literary critics objected to "low" illustrations on the same grounds that they objected to "low" literature, as encouraging the lower classes in their basest instincts, making familiar and attractive a life of debauchery and crime. Others were impressed by the potentialities of illustrations for instruction and edification. Charles Knight, the enterprising publisher of the Society for the Diffusion of Useful Knowledge, used woodcuts liberally in the tracts issued by the society, and George Cruikshank, the most successful of the illustrators, applied the techniques he used so effectively in *Oliver Twist* to his later series of temperance cartoons, "The Bottle" and "The Drunkard's Children." Perhaps more important than the moral—or immoral—effect of the illustrations was the impetus they gave to literacy. Just as the penny dreadfuls, by encouraging the habit of reading, also promoted the reading of newspapers (often Chartist papers), so illustrations whetted the appetite for the text and provided an incentive to learn to read.

It was not only the lower classes who were moved by the illustrations. The literary and social critic Frederic Harrison was grateful to his enlightened parents for sparing him the ordeal suffered by other children of his class who were subjected to a "literature of devildom and of everlasting fire," copiously illustrated by pictures guaranteed to induce nightmares.[36] Thackeray, who never missed an opportunity to belittle Ainsworth, said of *Jack Sheppard* that "Mr. Cruikshank really created the tale, and that Mr. Ainsworth, as it were, only put words to it"; all a reader would remember of the novel some months after he had read it were the pictures. Although Thackeray was better disposed to Dickens, grudgingly acknowledging his

---

*See illustration #9 in the insert following page 180.

genius, he found even his characters made memorable by Cruikshank. "Once seen, these figures remain impressed on the memory, which otherwise would have had no hold upon them"—a tribute Dickens would hardly have appreciated.[37] Even Henry James, so preternaturally sensitive to words, found the illustrations in *Oliver Twist* more compelling than the text: "It was a thing of such vividly terrible images, and all marked with that peculiarity of Cruikshank, that the offered flowers of goodnesses, the scenes and figures intended to comfort and cheer, present themselves under his hand as but more subtly sinister, or more suggestively queer, than the frank badnesses and horrors."[38]

The intimate connection between illustration and text made it possible for Cruikshank later to claim that he had helped create two of Ainsworth's novels as well as *Oliver Twist*. Dickens, he said, had chanced to see some of his earlier drawings and had been inspired by them to revise the plot and give greater prominence to the figures Cruikshank had drawn.[39] Most historians give little credence to these claims, but there is a sense in which the novels were undoubtedly shaped by the illustrations.* The knowledge that there had to be an illustration for each installment made it necessary to devise some scene or character that lent itself to illustration; and the fact that Cruikshank was the illustrator may well have inspired the kinds of scenes and characters that made the most of his genius. Fagin, for example, was irrevocably cast in the shape given him by Cruikshank, and this image powerfully affected the reading of the novel. Cruikshank, recent critics have pointed out, is said to have modeled that portrait at least partly upon himself, or some fanciful sense of himself.[41] But it also reflected an old stereotype of the Jew evident in the prints of Hogarth and Rowlandson and in cartoons whenever the subject became a matter of public concern—in 1753, for example, during the debate over the naturalization of Jews, and eighty years later, when the question of their admission to Parliament was raised.[42] This stereotype was as familiar to Dickens as to Cruikshank, so that it shaped the literary description of Fagin as much as the illustration.

If illustrators and authors were responding to a common pictorial convention, they also helped create a common literary culture. This may be the most important social effect of the illustrations. Were it not for them, one might assume that the upper and lower classes, the sophisticated and the untutored, read Dickens's novels in the light of such different experiences and sensibilities that they might almost have been reading different books.

*Pickwick Papers was originally intended to be merely the text accompanying Robert Seymour's drawings of Cockney sportsmen, but the publisher was apparently persuaded by Dickens's argument that "it would be infinitely better for the plates to arise naturally out of the text." In his preface Dickens went to great pains to refute the claim, current at the time, that Seymour had an important part in the "invention" of his book.[40] (Seymour committed suicide before the second number appeared, and the rest of the illustrations were by Hablot K. Browne, better known as "Phiz.")

While the illustrations themselves were open to differences of interpretation, they did fix the images of some of the most memorable characters and scenes, gave them a definition and a finality that were as compelling for the cultivated as for the unlettered. Apart from making Dickens accessible to all classes of the population, arousing the interest and stimulating the imagination of people at every stage of literacy (and illiteracy), they also ensured that everyone carried away from the novels at least some of the same impressions and feelings. The schoolboy at Eton and the barrow-boy in the East End had at least this world in common.

The illustrations democratized the culture in yet another sense, by creating a common denominator not only between upper and lower classes but between high and low literature. Today one might take, as a measure of the seriousness and respectability of a work of fiction (or of nonfiction), the amount and kind of illustrations accompanying it, ranging from the pristinely unadorned text of the "high-brow" novel or article, to the occasional illustrations in the popular journals, to the comic book where the text is an appendage to the picture. In early Victorian England almost every kind of literature was illustrated, ranging from the Bible (and not a comic-book version of the Bible) to the cheapest broadside. And almost every illustrator applied his art to a variety of subjects. Cruikshank illustrated political satires, radical pamphlets, fairy tales, histories, newspaper articles, books on phrenology and demonology, a "Comic Alphabet," temperance cartoons, and a host of novels ranging from the eighteenth century classics (Smollett, Fielding, Sterne, Cervantes) to Scott, Ainsworth, Mayhew *(1851)*, and, of course, Dickens.

A recent writer who happens to be a namesake of Cruikshank, noting his "gallery of fat ladies and human skeletons, of villains looking like earwigs and eccentric creatures looking like fungus, of children terrible as withered goblins," was moved to reflect upon the changes that had taken place in England since those memorable figures had been produced. "A century of healthier living has improved the physical appearance of the ordinary people out of all Cruikshankian recognition, and for this shall we not praise the parks and playing fields as well as the hospitals and sanitary engineers?"[43] It is an extraordinary tribute to this remarkable artist that a century later a writer should be so forgetful, at least momentarily, of the fact that the illustrations were caricatures as to identify them with the reality, and then summon up parks and playing fields, hospitals and sanitary engineers, to account for the differences between the cartoon figures of the nineteenth century and the "ordinary people" of the twentieth.

Those "Cruikshankian"—or, as is more commonly said, "Dickensian" —images imposed themselves upon the imagination of contemporaries as well as historians. With text and illustration conspiring together to give the illusion of reality, it is no wonder that readers and critics often responded to the novels as if they were social documents. Even when the novels were most highly fictionalized, most blatantly melodramatic and sensationalistic, they had enough of a semblance of reality to make critics worry that impressionable readers, especially the lower class readers of the lower forms of literature, would be seduced by them, would be tempted to carry out in their own lives the "message" of the novels. It is in this double sense that the novels, high and low alike, were "social novels": they conveyed an image of the poor—or rather, images of varieties of the poor—which bore some recognizable relationship to the reality, however mediated by the literary imagination; and they affected the reality itself by assimilating the products of the literary imagination into the moral imagination of readers of all classes and dispositions.

XVII

THE NEWGATE POOR

A reader of *Bentley's Miscellany* early in 1839 would have had the good fortune to read simultaneously the final four chapters of *Oliver Twist* and the first four chapters of *Jack Sheppard*. Today those novels stand as the exemplars of high and low literature. At the time the distinction was not so clear. Although Dickens's literary superiority was obvious, it was also obvious that the books had a good deal in common and that there was nothing unseemly in their appearance in the same journal at the same time.

Nor was it an accident that they did appear there, Dickens being the editor of *Bentley's* and William Harrison Ainsworth one of his best friends. They had met five years earlier, when Dickens was twenty-two and Ainsworth, twenty-seven, had just had his first great success with his novel *Rookwood*. Ainsworth introduced Dickens to John Forster, who became his good friend (and after his death his official biographer), to Cruikshank, who illustrated both *Oliver Twist* and *Jack Sheppard,* to John Macrone, who published *Sketches by Boz,* and to others in the literary circles frequented by both of them. In 1837, when *Pickwick Papers* turned out to be such a success, Dickens presented three "extra-super" bound copies to his wife, Forster, and Ainsworth. They traveled together, partied together, entertained each other, and cooperated in various literary ventures. Ainsworth published in *Bentley's* when Dickens edited it, and took over the editorship when Dickens resigned. They gave each other ideas for plots, characters, and episodes. Abraham Mendez, in *Jack Sheppard,* owed some of his features and characteristics to Fagin, while *Oliver Twist*'s Bill Sikes took his name from James Sikes, a friend of the real Jack Sheppard. Ainsworth's *Rookwood* inspired Sam Weller in the *Pickwick Papers* to sing about "Bold Turpin," and Ainsworth's Manchester friends were the prototypes of the Cheeryble Brothers in *Nicholas Nickleby*. At one time Ainsworth and Dickens considered collaborating on a Pickwickian book to be called *The Lions of London* which would counterpose the London of the past with that of the present,

Ainsworth doing the ancient, tragic part, and Dickens the modern, humorous part. If their novels looked more alike than they were, it was partly because they had the same illustrators, first Cruikshank and then "Phiz."

Today, when Ainsworth is a footnote in the literary history of the period, it is useful to recall the qualities which, according to Forster, endeared him to Dickens: his "sympathy in tastes and pursuits, accomplishments in literature, open-hearted generous ways, and cordial hospitality."[1] Although Dickens's superiority was undisputed, the gap between them was that which separated the first-rate novelist from an enormously popular second-rate one, a large enough gap but not an unbridgeable one. When their joint publisher advertised *Jack Sheppard* as "uniform in style and price with *Oliver Twist,*" he may have been seeking to elevate Ainsworth's novel by associating it with Dickens's.[2] But the association was commonly made (and, occasionally, objected to, by Forster especially). Esthetically worlds apart, as we may properly judge them today, at the time they were neighbors and friendly competitors.

Whatever differences there were in their social backgrounds would have been of little consequence in the circles in which they traveled, had Dickens himself not been so exceedingly sensitive about his lowly origins. Ainsworth came from a comfortable middle class family long established in the countryside around Manchester. His father was a successful lawyer, and for a time Ainsworth contemplated following the same career, but even while he was ostensibly reading for the law, he was publishing poems, stories, and sketches, and soon settled into the life of a professional writer. A prominent figure in London literary life, he continued to regard Manchester as his native city and was sometimes described as a "Lancashire novelist"—in the literal, geographical, rather than "social novel" sense of that phrase.

The novel that made Ainsworth famous was hardly a social novel. *Rookwood,* a retelling of the famous tale of Dick Turpin the highwayman, was published in 1834 and was an instant and phenomenal success. When Dickens dwells, compulsively as it may seem, on the melodrama of crime, the critic is tempted to give it some personal significance, to interpret it as an anxiety-ridden fantasy induced by the bitter experience of poverty, an experience that left him with the stigma of the social outcast or criminal. In Ainsworth's case, there seems to have been nothing personal in his preoccupation with crime, certainly no poverty to contend with, no psychological identification with the outcast, nothing but a literary tradition to inspire him. He had not even the curiosity to acquaint himself with real outcasts and criminals. When it was once suggested to him that he must have interviewed many thieves and gypsies to have become so familiar with their language and ways, he scoffed at the idea.

Not at all. Never had anything to do with the scoundrels in my life. I got my slang in a much easier way. I picked up the *Memoires* of James Hardy Vaux—a returned transport. The book was full of adventures, and had at the end a kind of slang dictionary. Out of this I got all my "patter." Having read it thoroughly and mastered it, I could use it with perfect facility.[3]

The famous account of Dick Turpin's ride from London to York— an entirely fictional event as we now know, but then so much part of the established folklore that it was often taken to be true—was written in a fevered transport of imagination, a hundred pages in a single sitting. Only when it was in proof did Ainsworth make the ride himself to check the localities and distances, and he was pleased to find that his account had been accurate. He would also have been gratified to know that Jack Sheppard's fictional grave in Willesden churchyard was later visited by hordes of sightseers, the sexton making a tidy sum, as he told Ainsworth's daughter, selling pieces of wood from the supposed monument marking the site. If *Rookwood,* and the still more successful *Jack Sheppard* five years later, seemed so authentic, it was partly because they were based on real historical charac- ters whose exploits had been recounted in scores of broadsides, ballads, and stories, and whose trials and executions had been recorded in volumes bearing such official-sounding titles as the *Newgate Calendar* and the *Annals of Newgate.* (The real Dick Turpin was hanged in 1739, the real Jack Sheppard in 1724.)

The basic plot of *Jack Sheppard* is simple and familiar: a series of robberies, murders, imprisonments, and escapes, culminating in the hanging of the "hero" at Tyburn. Interwoven with these exploits are subplots centering on the other characters: "Thames" Darrell, fished out of the river as an infant, raised by the carpenter Mr. Wood (to whom Jack Sheppard was also apprenticed), and eventually discovered to be an English aristocrat and a scion of the "blood royal" of France; Darrell's uncle, Sir Rowland Trench- ard, who tries to prevent him from assuming his rightful name, title, and fortune; Jack's mother, who turns out to be Sir Rowland's long-lost sister; Jonathan Wild, "the Napoleon of knavery," who had been responsible for the hanging of Jack's father and is determined to see the son share the same fate; and the company of thieves, including the memorable Master, Blueskin, and the Fagin-like Abraham Mendez. These characters and subplots keep the novel going for the mandatory three volumes, the plots ingeniously inter- woven and the banalities of missing heirs, betrayed women, abandoned children, incorrigible criminals, and sluttish "molls" infused with some complexity of character and situation. Apart from the conventional rhetoric of melodrama—"Betrayed! . . . These cries will avail you nothing. . . . Execrable villain!"[4]—the style is competent if undistinguished, and some of the scenes are genuinely dramatic. At one point the narrative is interrupted by a brief historical exposition that is considerably better than the usual bits of potted history inserted in such novels—an account of the Jacobites which makes it credible that a woolen draper would passionately ally himself, at great personal risk, with one royal faction against another.

The more interesting complications of the novel are those of class. If Ainsworth had deliberately set out to distribute virtue and vice evenly among the various social classes, he could not have done so more scrupulously. The villainous Sir Rowland has his counterpart in the equally villainous Jonathan Wild; the good-hearted carpenter, Mr. Wood, has a mean shrew of a wife; Jack's mother, alcoholic and thoroughly demoralized in the opening episode, is rehabilitated by the good offices of Mr. Wood and by her own heroic efforts; and Jack himself is not without redeeming virtues, deliberately risking capture in order to visit his mother on her deathbed and to attend her funeral. This evenhanded distribution of virtue and vice does not obscure the essential distinctions of class—above all, the crucial distinction between the respectable and the dangerous classes. By heredity and by character Jack is a full-fledged member of the dangerous class. Born the day his father was hanged, brought up in the shadow of that grisly event (literally in its shadow, the most prominent decoration in his room being the poster advertising "The Last Dying Speech and Confession of TOM SHEPPARD"), haunted by the prophecy that pursues him from infancy ("Little Jack will never die in his bed"), he can no more escape his heritage than change his name. ("Thames" Darrell becomes Lord Trafford, but Jack Sheppard remains a Sheppard.) Jack is hanged (in fact, as in the novel) shortly after coming of age—coming into his estate, so to speak. Neither the rehabilitation of his mother nor the revelation of her gentle birth can avail against that tainted heritage, as if destiny, like title or estate, is transmitted in the paternal line.

Like the street-folk born and bred to the streets, Jack Sheppard is born and bred to a life of crime. And as the street-folk display their calling in their features, so Jack's villainy is revealed in his physical appearance. He and young Darrell, ostensibly of the same class, living in the same house, apprenticed to the same master, preparing for the same career, "contrasted strikingly with each other." Tall and robust, Darrell shows in his bearing and in his every feature the "promise of a glorious manhood," while Jack's "physiognomy" betrays his incorrigible "cunning and knavery." The differences of complexion, hair, nose, lips, eyes—a veritable catalogue of racial characteristics—represent class differences as unalterable and unmistakable as race itself.

Jack's complexion was that of a gipsy; Darrell's as fresh and bright as a rose. Jack's mouth was coarse and large; Darrell's small and exquisitely carved, with the short, proud upper lip, which belongs to the highest order of beauty. Jack's nose was broad and flat; Darrell's straight and fine as that of Antinous. The expression pervading the countenance of the one was vulgarity; of the other, that which is rarely found, except in persons of high birth. Darrell's eyes were of that clear grey which it is difficult to distinguish from blue by day and black at night; and his rich brown hair, which he could not consent to part with, even on the promise of a new and modish peruke from his adoptive father, fell in thick glossy ringlets upon his shoulders; whereas Jack's close black crop imparted the peculiar bullet shape, already noticed, to his head.[5]

Jack retains those dark, coarse, vulgar features throughout his short, ill-fated life. His mother, on the other hand, undergoes a remarkable "transformation" of appearance and character, testifying to her social elevation (she turns out to be Sir Rowland's sister) and her moral redemption. In her worst days, oppressed by poverty and shame, she had sought relief in "the stupefying draught—that worst medicine of a mind diseased"—a combination of alcohol and opium.[6] In an eloquent apologia (too articulate and literate for so ill-educated a person, but this implausibility is common to all these novels), she explains why she had fallen so low. "Oh! madam, there are moments—moments of darkness, which overshadow a whole existence —in the lives of the poor houseless wretches who traverse the streets, when reason is well-nigh benighted; when the horrible prompting of despair can alone be listened to; and when vice itself assumes the aspect of virtue." But even the most debased creature, she hastens to add, is not "irreclaimable," not beyond the "hope of reformation."[7] Her own reformation is sorely tested, her son's exploits driving her literally mad and into that notorious insane asylum, Bedlam. Eventually she commits suicide rather than suffer a "fate worse than death," but even in madness and death she retains her gentility of birth and newfound respectability.

If physique and physiognomy are tokens of class, so is geography. The London of the Newgate novel is even further removed from the London of the respectable poor than Mayhew's London. A major factor in Mrs. Sheppard's rehabilitation is her removal from the neighborhood which had witnessed her original degradation and which remained the haunt of her son. The "Old Mint" (deriving its name from the time of Henry VIII, when it had housed the royal mint) had been, until just before the time of the real Jack Sheppard, a legal sanctuary for debtors. Although its immunities had since been abolished, its denizens remained: the "dregs of society," the "lowest order of insolvent traders, thieves, mendicants, and other worthless and nefarious characters," the "grand receptacle of the superfluous villainy of the metropolis."[8] The "Master" of the Mint, the local publican, prides himself on being an absolute sovereign in his domain, more absolute than the English monarch, which is perhaps why, in addition to his grievance against King William for having abolished the immunities of the district, he is so ardent a Jacobite. He enjoys all the trappings of monarchy: bodyguards, weapons, ceremonies, court dress, a hierarchy of lieutenants and sublieutenants, and a loyal if disorderly populace. He also has imperial ambitions, aspiring to rule over all of London by making it one vast underworld. "I hope to see the day, when not Southwark alone, but London itself, shall become one Mint—when all men shall be debtors, and none creditors—when imprisonment for debt shall be utterly abolished—when highway-robbery shall be accounted a pleasant pastime, and forgery an accomplishment—when Tyburn and its gibbets shall be overthrown."[9] It is the classic antinomian fantasy in which crime would be legitimized and vice made virtuous. In the meantime, while awaiting that messianic day, the Master is content to lord it over the Mint, directing its criminal activities and presiding over its orgies.

In spite of the charges made at the time that Ainsworth was romanticizing crime, the novel itself concludes on a properly moral note, with virtue rewarded and vice punished. Moreover, that retribution is not merely the act of an external authority; the robbers bring about their own downfall through dissension in their ranks. And while Jack's cronies are clearly more sympathetic than Jonathan Wild's, they too can be gratuitously brutal, as in the murder of the "dwarfish Jew." Nor is Jack himself blameless. Only reluctantly does he agree to burglarize the house of the worthy Mr. Wood, his kindly master and his mother's great benefactor, and having participated in that burglary, he feels morally responsible for its outcome, the gory murder of Mrs. Wood by his best friend, Blueskin. More shocking is the death of Jack's mother, at her own hand, to be sure, but in a manner that makes Jack morally culpable. She has been kidnapped by Jonathan Wild, who plans to marry her in order to mortify her son. When Jack comes to her rescue, breaking down the door to free her, she mistakes him for Wild and stabs herself.

> "I have killed you," cried Jack endeavoring to stanch the effusion of blood from her breast. "Forgive—forgive me."
> "I have nothing to forgive," replied Mrs. Sheppard. "I alone am to blame."[10]

The reader is left in no doubt that it is Jack who is to blame. Had the author intended it otherwise, he would have had Wild kill Mrs. Sheppard, thus permitting Jack to avenge his mother's death and emerge as the hero. Instead the author went out of his way to justify, morally as well as legally, the hanging of Jack Sheppard.

The real Jack Sheppard was hanged for housebreaking, a capital offense at the time. In the novel the moral offense is matricide, the ultimate, unforgivable crime, and no more forgivable because it is unwitting. On the contrary, the fact that here, as on other occasions in the novel, Jack's good intentions go awry suggests a flaw in his nature so deep, a character so tainted, as to be beyond redemption. Whatever the other ambiguities in the novel, this is unambiguous: from the beginning, Jack is fated to be hanged. In spite of his mother's pleas that the most wretched creature is not "irreclaimable," there is never any doubt of Jack's irreclaimable nature. By character, heritage, environment, and will, he is a member of the "dangerous classes." The final scene at the gallows is not merely the pious tribute that vice pays to virtue, not the conventional affirmation of law and order, not even the familiar climax to the familiar tale. It is as necessary and compelling as any act of poetic justice or divine retribution.

This was not, however, the way some important contemporary critics read the novel. They were deeply troubled by what they took to be its essential immorality, in spite of Ainsworth's efforts to forestall just this objection. In his original draft he had prefaced each section of the novel with a biblical text, and had deleted them only after a friend convinced him that the mixture of "sacred texts with a work of fancy" would offend the ordinary reader without placating the critics.[11]* In fact most of the critics seemed to be reacting less to this particular novel than to the genre as a whole. There had been grumblings about earlier Newgate novels, and *Jack Sheppard*, coming on the heels of *Oliver Twist*, brought the issue to a head.

Jack Sheppard was even more successful than *Oliver Twist*. Before the serialization had been completed in *Bentley's*, it had spawned a host of imitations, plays, ballads, satires, spurious memoirs, and histories. At one point in the autumn of 1839, no fewer than eight plays about Jack Sheppard were running simultaneously in London, and this did not include countless "penny gaffs," performances in cheap theaters or on the streets. (The custom of hissing the stage villain is said to have started with the Jack Sheppard plays.) The competition from imitators, adapters, and plagiarizers induced Ainsworth's publishers to produce the three-volume edition even before the serialization had come to an end; 3,000 copies of this edition were sold the first week while the book was still appearing in *Bentley's*. The following year it was reissued in fifteen monthly parts. A veritable Jack Sheppard industry sprang up, and with it something like a Jack Sheppard cult, in the course of which whatever moral lessons Ainsworth may have tried to impose

*The idea for such texts came to him from Hogarth, who had appended a scriptural motto to each of the plates of his *Industry and Idleness* series. Ainsworth was a great admirer of Hogarth, and fancied *Jack Sheppard* to be a "Hogarthian novel."[12]

on the story disappeared. (Twenty years later the final volume of *London Labour* reported an interview with a thief—a "poor wretched creature, degraded in condition, of feeble intellect, and worthless character"—who said that the only books read in the low lodging house where he and his friends lived were *Jack Sheppard, Dick Turpin* [presumably *Rookwood*], and the *Newgate Calendar.*)[13]

Thackeray, leading the campaign against the Newgate novels, wrote his mother that in the lobbies of theaters people were said to be selling "Shepherd-bags" [*sic*] containing pick-locks. "One or two young gentlemen have already confessed how much they were indebted to Jack Sheppard who gave them ideas of pocket-picking and thieving which they never would have had but for the play."[14] Some months later it was widely reported that a valet named Courvoisier who had murdered his master confessed that he had been inspired to do so by reading *Jack Sheppard.* Ainsworth wrote letters to the newspapers saying that he had inquired into the affair and that the man denied having made any such statement. After the execution, however, the sheriff affirmed the truth of the original report, adding that the book had been lent to Courvoisier by a valet of the Duke of Bedford.[15]

If the Victorians had great confidence in the edifying effects of good books—hence the voluminous tracts of the Society for Promoting Christian Knowledge, the Society for the Diffusion of Useful Knowledge, and all the other benevolent societies—they were also impressed by the corrupting effects of bad books, especially the "low" books intended for the lower classes who were presumed to be most impressionable and most susceptible to corruption. *Jack Sheppard,* the *Athenaeum* protested, was "a bad book, and what is worse, it is of a class of bad books, got up for a bad public." It was bad because it had all the "inherent coarseness and vulgarity of the subject," portraying people in a state of "corrupted, stunted, and deformed degradation"; and it was worse because of the special "relation of the author to his public." When Henry Fielding (in *Jonathan Wild*) and John Gay (in *The Beggar's Opera*) had dealt with similar themes, they had done so from a level above that of the public; thus their effect was to "raise the public in the moral and intellectual scale." *Jack Sheppard,* however, was on the same level as its readers, and this at a time when the public itself was in a perilous condition, beset by all the difficulties of industrialism: "the struggle for existence, the aggregation of the population into large towns, the universal preoccupation of mind on the routine habits of a sordid industry."[16]

The reviewer in the *Examiner* shared these fears. "Public morality and public decency have rarely been more endangered than by the trumpeted exploits of Jack Sheppard. . . . Crime—bare, rascally, unmitigated, ferocious crime—becomes the idea constantly thrust before us." Bad as the morals of the book were, the "puffs" were even worse—the adaptations and imitations which found their way into the low smoking rooms, common barbershops, cheap reading places, and theaters. It was there that the book was served up in the most attractive form to "all the candidates for hulks or rope—*and especially the youthful ones*—that infest this vast city."[17] After the Courvoisier affair, an editorial in the *Examiner* declared the novel to be nothing less than "the cut-throat's manual, or the midnight assassin's *vade mecum*"; if ever there was a book that deserved to be burned, it was this.[18]

The review in the *Examiner* (but not the editorial) is especially interesting because it was written by John Forster, Dickens's good friend and, until then, Ainsworth's. Forster (and Dickens) may have been upset because *Jack Sheppard* was outselling *Oliver Twist,* or perhaps because the resemblances between the two threatened to bring discredit upon *Oliver Twist* as well. For whatever reason, the whole of the review was an elaborate attempt to dissociate the two novels, and this without mentioning *Oliver Twist* lest the association be unwittingly reinforced.

If Forster had to frame his criticisms in such a way as to absolve Dickens from the same charges, Thackeray had no such problem. He attacked them both with the same venom that for years he had been directing against Lytton Bulwer. Thackeray's motives were not above suspicion. The popularity of these novelists was all the more galling because he himself never enjoyed anything like their success although he tried his hand at the same themes. "I always find myself competing with him," he confided to his diary about the same time that he was preparing to launch yet another attack on Bulwer.[19] The personal motive is significant, not because it discredits Thackeray's arguments but because it elucidates an important aspect of the social reality. Today Dickens and Thackeray seem worlds removed from Ainsworth and Bulwer; at the time, however, they were very much in the same world, competing for the same readers, seeking the acclaim of the same critics, and exploiting the same plots and techniques.

Three months after *Jack Sheppard* started to appear in *Bentley's* (and while *Oliver Twist* was still running), *Fraser's Magazine* began a new serial by Thackeray, *Catherine,* published under the pseudonym "Ikey Solomons, Esq. Junior." Intended as a parody of *Jack Sheppard,* it was far more violent and sadistic than the original, including a gruesome scene in which the corpse was dismembered for easy disposal. In *Jack Sheppard,* the murder was an unintended consequence of the burglary; in *Catherine,* the murder was as willful as the hacking away at the corpse. This was consistent with Thackeray's criticism. Ainsworth, he said, made crime attractive by deliberately placing in the background the horrors and brutalities of crime. By bringing them to the foreground, Thackeray was presumably restoring them to their rightful place. Yet one cannot resist the suspicion that here too he was competing with Ainsworth, trying to outdo him in violence in the hope of matching him in popularity. Disappointed in the reception of the novel, he confessed to his mother that he had not made it "disgusting enough" lest his readers throw it up in horror, and that he himself had developed a "sneaking kindness for his heroine, and did not like to make her utterly worthless."[20]

Lest the point of his novel be lost on his readers, Thackeray devoted the final chapter (some of which was deleted from later editions) to a polemic against the genre as a whole, starting with *Oliver Twist*. Dickens, he said, made his villains so interesting, amusing, even attractive, that the reader breathlessly watched the crimes of Fagin, tenderly deplored the errors of Nancy, pitied and admired Bill Sikes, and positively loved the Artful Dodger. When a dramatization of the novel was staged, the London public, "from peers to chimney sweeps," was regaled with the adventures of a gang of thieves, murderers, and prostitutes—"a most agreeable set of rascals, indeed, who have their virtues, too, but not good company for any man." Craving still more extravagant fare, the public was then presented with Jack Sheppard, his two wives, his faithful followers, and his "gin-drinking mother, that sweet Magdalen," and asked to admire the gallantry and loyalty of those "prodigies of evil."[21]

While Thackeray's moral indignation may have been fed by envy and resentment (the failure of *Catherine* did not help matters), his attitude was shared by those who had no personal interest or animus. Mary Mitford, the poet, novelist, and self-described Radical, confessed that on reading *Jack Sheppard* she was struck by the "great danger, in these times, of representing authorities so constantly and fearfully in the wrong." Ainsworth, she knew, had no such intention; her friend Thomas Hughes (author of *Tom Brown's Schooldays*) had spoken well of him. But the low plays based on the book were most unfortunate. "All the Chartists in the land are less dangerous than this nightmare of a book, and I, Radical as I am, lament any additional temptations to outbreak, with all its train of horrors."[22] The reviewer in the *Spectator* was more sanguine, finding the book powerful but improbable and in any case not immoral. "Though some of the scenes are necessarily low, there is nothing offensive to propriety, or with the slightest tendency to corrupt."[23] Even here, however, the defensive tone suggests how widespread the criticism was. Five years earlier, following the publication of *Rookwood*, Ainsworth had been welcomed into high society, invited to parties at Holland House and soirées at Lady Blessington's. After *Jack Sheppard*, perhaps because of the atmosphere created by the Chartist demonstrations, he was blackballed from one club (the letter informing him of that decision was written, with many professions of regret, by John Forster), and withdrew his nomination from the much-coveted Athenaeum rather than risk a similar embarrassment there. And after the Courvoisier episode the Lord Chamberlain refused to license any new theatrical productions of *Jack Sheppard*. Although the prohibition did not apply to performances already on the stage and was easily evaded by changing the name of the proposed play, the intent was clear. The plays, even more than the novel, were a public danger because they reached a large and impressionable public—the "millions" who, as Miss Mitford said, were exposed to them in the "low" theaters and might become "dangerous" as a result.

Whatever fears Thackeray, Mitford, and others might have had about the corruption of the lower classes, there was little in the novel itself to warrant those fears. Here, even more than in Mayhew's work, the dangerous classes were a species apart, in every way distinct from the respectable working classes; they looked, dressed, spoke, and behaved differently. Their criminality was not an incidental, part-time affair; it was their profession and way of life. (Jack Sheppard ceased being a carpenter's apprentice when he joined the company of thieves.) Moreover, it was a profession they took up voluntarily because it conformed to their nature and disposition, not because they were driven to it by intolerable poverty. They were poor, to be sure, but poor with a difference—basely poor, tainted by character rather than circumstances. When the *Athenaeum* reviewer wanted to distinguish Dickens from Ainsworth, he ascribed to Dickens a "high moral object," his scenes of vice displaying the "peculiar phasis of degradation which poverty impresses on the human character under the combinations of a defective civilization."[24] No one suggested that Ainsworth's characters were degraded because of poverty or society. On the contrary, the criticism was that young boys would be enticed into a life of crime by the example of Jack Sheppard and the promise of an adventurous, romantic, carefree life, not because it was the only livelihood available to them. Certainly these youths were not so poor as to lack the penny or sixpence for the serial or play.

Nor did Ainsworth himself, however much he may have romanticized crime, exonerate it by making it the result of extenuating circumstances. He did not attribute it to hunger, destitution, parental neglect (whatever her other faults in the beginning of the novel, Mrs. Sheppard was a devoted, even doting mother, and Mr. Wood a model surrogate father), bad environment (the Wood house and neighborhood were thoroughly respectable), or the lack of any alternative (Jack had a perfectly good trade had he chosen to pursue it). The closest Ainsworth came to any hint of excuse was when Mrs. Sheppard, speaking of her own unfortunate past, explained to Mrs. Wood "how much misery has to do with crime"—prefacing that remark by saying that she did not mean it to "extenuate my guilt, far less to defend it."[25] In any case, the kind of crime she was referring to was her own vices, the vices of the undeserving poor, drunkenness and improvidence, not those of her son and the dangerous classes, thievery, violence, and murder.

One of the few occasions when the book resembled anything like the conventional social novel was a passage contrasting the old and the new Newgate. Those modern writers who complained of the demoralizing effect of prison society were quite right in respect to the old Newgate; it was indeed the "grand nursery of vice." But that was the Newgate of Sheppard's time. Since then, Ainsworth observed, as a result of the philanthropic exertions of John Howard, a new prison had been erected on the same site, inspiring the "cheering reflection, that in the present prison, with its clean, well-whitewashed, and well-ventilated wards, its airy courts, its infirmary, its improved regulations, and its humane and intelligent officers, many of the miseries of the old gaol are removed."[26] If this sounds sarcastic to the modern reader, there is no suggestion that Ainsworth intended it so. Nor was there any intimation that the evils of the old Newgate excused or even explained the vices of the inmates. The prison was a nursery of vice because everyone in it was vicious; "the gaolers robbed the prisoners; the prisoners robbed one another."[27]

It is curious that the novel did not have more of the character of the conventional social novel, that Ainsworth did not take the opportunity of reflecting on the causes of crime, the current state of the law, or proposals for reform. This was, after all, a period of great activity in the reform of criminal laws and penal institutions: the death penalty had been abolished for a multitude of crimes, public executions had become a rarity, and new prisons were built and old ones remodeled. In *Paul Clifford,* Bulwer consciously provided the rationale for these reforms by creating a hero who was drawn into crime by bad associations in the slum and in the prison itself. Convicted of a crime he did not commit, he became a professional criminal only after being exposed to the hardened inmates of Bridewell. Even as a highwayman, however, he was charming, elegant, and scrupulously careful not to shed blood unless absolutely necessary. The real villains of the novel were the lawyers, the politicians, and the king himself, who were no better than a gang of thieves and who drove Clifford to crime by not providing for him in his time of need. Clifford's summation in his own defense at his trial is the classic indictment of society and exoneration of the criminal.

> Your legislator made me what I am! and it now *destroys me, as it has destroyed thousands, for being what it made me!* . . . Let those whom the law protects consider it a protector: when did it ever protect *me?* When did it ever protect the poor man? The government of a state, the institutions of law, profess to provide for all those who "obey." Mark! a man hungers—do you feed him? He is naked—do you clothe him? If not, you break your covenant, you drive him back to the first law of nature, and you hang him, not because he is guilty, but because you have *left* him naked and starving.[28]

Dedicating the novel to the legal and penal reformer Albany Fonblanque, Bulwer explained that his book had two objectives: to expose "a vicious

Prison-discipline and a sanguinary Criminal Code ... and to show that there is nothing essentially different between vulgar and fashionable vice—and that the slang of the one circle is but an easy paraphrase of the cant of the other."[29]

There was none of this in Ainsworth's work, no exposure of social evils or demand for social reforms. It is also interesting that those who criticized the Newgate novels for making crime attractive did not criticize the reforms which had liberalized the criminal law, made the prisons more habitable, and thus made crime more "eligible." On these issues most of the critics were as liberal—"radical," in Mitford's sense—as any reformer. The reviewer in *Fraser's Magazine,* who castigated Ainsworth for transforming a "vulgar ruffian into a melodramatic hero," concluded with an account of the real Jack Sheppard which was far more sympathetic, if less melodramatic, than the character in the novel. Attributing Sheppard's downfall to the "brutality and inefficiency of the criminal jurisprudence of England," the reviewer launched into an attack on the criminal system of the eighteenth century which came perilously close to exculpating Sheppard, explaining that after his unfortunate experiences he naturally "looked upon society as an enemy against which he had to wage battle with whatever arms he could find." But even this reviewer, who went much further in extenuation of the real Jack Sheppard than Ainsworth had of the fictional one, found the novel "dangerous," an incitement to moral laxity and a temptation to the lower classes to lapse from their hard-earned respectability.[30]

It is here that the "social significance" of the novel may be found. On one level, of course, it was pure romance, a classic tale of adventure and danger, of exotic characters in menacing situations, of heroes tempting fate, pursuing fantasies, and coming to spectacularly good or bad ends. In another sense, it was very much of its time and place. If it was not a social novel in the conventional sense, if it did not deal with the usual social issues and problems, still less provide answers for them, it did convey an image of a class that, however romanticized, fantasized, and fictionalized, gripped the imagination of readers, in part because it had a visible relation to the social reality, to the dangerous class that did in fact exist in the metropolis. That sense of reality was enhanced by the historicity of the novel, and enhanced still more by the fact that its readers had long been familiar with that historical reality (or what they took to be such).

Like other Newgate novelists, Ainsworth borrowed his chief characters and the main line of his plot from the *Newgate Calendar* and the *Annals of Newgate.* He embroidered upon the reality but did not invent it. There had been a Dick Turpin, a Jack Sheppard, a Jonathan Wild.* There had even

*The ambiguous relationship between fact and fiction is nicely illustrated in the *Columbia Encyclopedia,* which has an entry for Richard Turpin but not for Ainsworth. The brief account of "Turpin,

been a real Ikey (Isaac) Solomons, the prototype of Dickens's Fagin and Ainsworth's Mendez (and the nominal author of *Catherine*). Solomons, whose case was widely reported in the press, had worked his way up from pickpocket and counterfeiter to a successful career as a dealer in stolen goods before he was finally transported to Australia in 1831. (In "flash" language, "Ikey" was the generic term for a "fence," a receiver of stolen goods.) It was surely a highly fictionalized and grossly debased Solomons who made his appearance in the guise of Fagin and Mendez (the anti-Semitic distortions giving him an exotic fillip lacking to his English confrères), but the awareness of even the semblance of fact behind the fiction gave credibility to this most melodramatic of characters. (Edward Lloyd gave an additional twist to this fact-fiction turnabout in his plagiarism of *Oliver Twist,* entitled *Oliver Twiss,* when he restored Fagin's patronym by renaming him Ikey Solomons.)[31]

When critics complained of the "dangers" of *Jack Sheppard,* it was partly because of this confusion of fact and fiction, a confusion which made the novel more "real" and therefore more insidious. A worse danger, however, was another kind of confusion, the potential confusion between the readers of the novel and the characters in the novel, the possibility that the working classes would find the dangerous classes so glamorous and exciting as to tempt them to forfeit their coveted respectability. If the conventional poor did not figure prominently in the novel, they did in the consciousness of the critics. They were the invisible protagonists of the novel, the real victims of the villainous heroes.

It is hardly surprising that the "lower classes"—the conventional, respectable, hard-working poor—were not the subjects of the "low" novelists. At no time has it been easy to dramatize ordinary poverty. At this time, when even social reformers deemed ordinary poverty to be unproblematic, it is little wonder that most novelists found it unromantic as well, so that even the social novelists were easily diverted from the respectable poor to the less respectable, from the laboring poor to the street-folk, from the working classes to the dangerous classes, from the drama of poverty to the melodrama of crime.

Richard (Dick Turpin, 1706–39, English robber)" testily complains of the unwarranted notoriety achieved by this commonplace robber, mainly through Ainsworth's *Rookwood.*

XVIII

THE GOTHIC POOR

"Jack Sheppard is immoral," Thackeray said, "actually because it is decorous."[1] No one could accuse *The Mysteries of London* of that failing. It was, in fact, brutally candid in its depiction of vice, violence, and depravity. Yet it is doubtful that Thackeray would have found it any the less immoral.

The Mysteries of London by G. W. M. Reynolds was a "low" version of the Gothic tale, savage in its portraits of low life and cynical in its depiction of high life. Appearing weekly from 1845 to 1848, it was followed by a sequel, *The Mysteries of the Court of London,* which went on to 1856; together they were probably the longest, best selling fiction of the time. The 1840s are more often remembered for the novels that make it one of the great decades in English fiction: *Barnaby Rudge, Martin Chuzzlewit, Dombey and Son, Coningsby, Sybil, Vanity Fair, Pendennis, Jane Eyre, Wuthering Heights, Mary Barton.* But these books should not suggest any fanciful ideas about the beneficent effects of literacy upon the literary culture, for side by side with them there flourished a considerable trade in the lowest kind of fiction. *The Mysteries of London* was a much lower form of literature than *Jack Sheppard* and far more popular—and not the lowest of this genre, that distinction being reserved for literature so ephemeral it never had the privilege of being bound in hard covers and preserved for posterity.

What makes this genre all the more interesting is that Reynolds, its most successful practitioner, was a Chartist, and a militant one.[2] Although he did not take a prominent part in the movement until the demonstrations of 1848, he made no secret of his political views in his earlier writings, either in fiction or nonfiction, and he was one of the few who continued to preach and act on behalf of Chartism long after most of its leaders had abandoned it. Like Ainsworth, Reynolds came from a solid, middle class family. His father was a naval captain of some means, and he himself was sent to Sandhurst to prepare for a military career. Finding the school and the profession uncongenial, he left Sandhurst for the Continent, where he acquired a taste for literature and the bohemian life. The death of his father provided him with a substantial inheritance which he invested and soon lost in an Anglo-French journal. Returning to England in the late thirties, he embarked upon a literary career that made him one of the most versatile and prolific writers in a literary generation famous for its versatility and productivity. He turned out fiction in huge quantities and of every description. And his nonfiction ranged from a two-volume study of the modern literature of France, to articles of the self-help type ("Etiquette for the Millions," which initiated the masses into the proper use of knives, forks, and other such niceties), columns on the political situation abroad (applauding the revolutionary movements on the Continent), and Chartist tracts addressed to the working classes. He also found time to edit two of the most popular mass journals of the time, *The London Journal,* which had a circulation of 500,000 at its peak, and *Reynolds's Miscellany,* with less than half that. *Reynolds's Weekly Newspaper* (edited for a while by the Chartist Bronterre O'Brien) was more political and less popular, although even it sold almost 50,000 in the mid-fifties at a time when political passions had notably cooled.[3] A uniform edition of his collected (but not complete) works published after his death came to forty-two volumes.

Although Reynolds was writing and editing in London at the same time as Ainsworth and Dickens, he was not part of their circle. In the public mind, however, his name was linked with theirs.

To them as makes the Cracksman's life, the subject of their story,
To Ainsworth, and to Bullvig [Bulwer], and to Reynolds be the glory.[4]

Quoting that verse, Ainsworth's biographer identified Reynolds condescendingly as a "voluminous romance writer of the period, whose books, though picturesque and prolific in incident, are almost forgotten now"— a description that would apply equally well to Ainsworth and that hardly conveys the quality of Reynolds. "Grotesque" might be more fitting than "picturesque," and "prolific in incident" is a feeble intimation of the wild episodes and hectic pace of his stories.

The Mysteries of London, published in weekly parts for a penny and in monthly parts for sixpence, had an average circulation of 40,000 apart from the sale of back numbers and the annual volumes.[5] This would have been a substantial number for any series but was still more impressive for one that went on as long as this did. Several dramatic versions appeared; at one time in 1846 three productions were being staged in London alone. Translated editions were published abroad (in Russian as well as the more customary languages), and at home there were the usual pirated editions, imitations, adaptations, and plain plagiarisms.

This large circulation, especially in the form of penny parts, suggests a large lower class audience; according to Mayhew, Reynolds was the most popular writer among the costermongers.[6] It was not exclusively lower class, however, the bound volumes selling for 6s.6d. obviously intended for readers of some means and book-buying habits. (The volumes read by the present writer are in the half-Moroccan binding suitable for a Victorian gentleman's library.) Even the penny parts found their way among the middle classes, if sometimes surreptitiously. A Manchester bookseller, testifying before a parliamentary committee on newspapers in 1851, explained that while Reynolds drew "scenes of profligacy as strongly as it is possible for any writer to do, and the feelings are excited to a very high pitch by it," his work was not really "indecent" because no "vulgar" words appeared in it. "A great many females buy the 'Court of London,' and young men; a sort of spreeing young men; young men who go to taverns, and put cigars in their mouths in a flourishing way."[7]

Reynolds was as popular as he was, in part because he worked in a thoroughly familiar and popular genre. Even the title was derivative, an unabashed imitation of Eugène Sue's *The Mysteries of Paris,* which had appeared in France in 1842–43 and in translation in England in 1844. Circulating throughout the world, Sue's book gave rise to a host of local adaptations: *The Mysteries and Miseries of New York, The Mysteries of Berlin,* and at least two *Mysteries of London.* (The other book of that title, published soon after Reynolds's, was by a well-known French writer, Paul Féval, who started it before he had so much as set foot in London; when he did arrive, he was pleased to announce that the city was exactly as he had represented it.) Reynolds's work, in turn, inspired others. Ainsworth, who had once tried to get Dickens to collaborate with him on a book on London, started such a serial himself in 1846, changing its original title, *The Lions of London,* to the more fashionable *Revelations of London.*[8] The common theme of these *Mysteries* was the counterpoint of high life and low life, with aristocrats conspiring to defraud their kin and criminals plotting to break into the aristocrats' houses, beggar boys turning out to be long-lost heirs and well-born maidens turning into prostitutes, masquerades and machinations in high society and drunken, brutal, mindless violence among the dregs of society. The locale was always the metropolis, a city containing only two classes, an opulent, often decadent aristocracy, and a "lowest class" of outcasts and criminals.

"It was on a cold and rainy night, towards the end of October 1838," *The Mysteries of Paris* opened, and after a brief glimpse at the tapis-franc, the drinking house "frequented by the refuse of the Parisian population," the scene returned to the "night in question": the wind howling fiercely in the dark, the swaying lamps revealing the murky houses and dark, noisome alleys.[9] *The Mysteries of London* opened on the same stormy scene and in the same menacing style.

Our narrative opens at the commencement of July, 1831.

The night was dark and stormy. The sun had set behind huge piles of dingy purple clouds, which, after losing the golden hue with which they were for awhile tinged, became sombre and menacing. The blue portions of the sky that here and there had appeared before the sunset, were now rapidly covered over with those murky clouds which are the hiding-places of the storm, and which seemed to roll themselves together in dense and compact masses, ere they commenced the elemental war.

In the same manner do the earthly squadrons of cavalry and mighty columns of infantry form themselves into one collected armament, that the power of their onslaught may be the more terrific and irresistible.[10]*

Where *The Mysteries of London* differed from the others in this genre was the occasional injection, sometimes suggested by the turn of the plot, sometimes entirely gratuitous, of social and political commentaries which gave it something of the character of a social novel. More effective by way of social commentary than these homilies delivered by the author were the "histories" supposedly originating with the characters themselves, autobiographical accounts of their lives, often in dialect and always studded with the "flash" language appropriate to their particular criminal callings. Unlike Mayhew (who may have borrowed the device from him), Reynolds did not insist upon the literal truth of these "histories." But he did leave that impression, if only by labeling them "histories," setting them off from the rest of the work, and inserting an occasional reference to some well known event or situation. In the midst of the most outlandish episodes and improbable coincidences, the "histories" served as interludes of "social realism," firsthand documents attesting to truths stranger than fiction.

The prologue to *The Mysteries of London* is the familiar discourse on the excesses of "WEALTH AND POVERTY" which are the distinctive feature of London. "The most unbounded wealth is the neighbor of the most hideous poverty; the most gorgeous pomp is placed in strong relief by the most

---

*Gothic tales have an obvious penchant for dark and stormy scenes, but the conspicuous dating of both books is more surprising. Perhaps it is an attempt to give historicity and authenticity to the bizarre tale, to give the fantasy an illusion of reality, or even to heighten the fantasy by juxtaposing it with this misplaced bit of reality. In Reynolds's case the dates have an additional function. The first volume opens in July 1831 and concludes on New Year's Day, 1840, thus placing the action in the very recent past, so recent as to verge on the present and have all the urgency of contemporaneity, and yet sufficiently in the past to predate the reforms of the 1840s so that social evils could be seen at their worst. One "history," for example, makes much of the payment of wages in public houses, a practice made illegal in 1842–43, and of very young children working in mines, which was outlawed by the Mines Act of 1842.

deplorable squalor; the most seducing luxury is only separated by a narrow wall from the most appalling misery." The announcement that wealth and poverty are generally equated with virtue and vice prepares us for something like the morality play that is then described: two youths are to make their way through this "city of fearful contrasts," one taking a road through the "noisome dens of crime, chicanery, dissipation, and voluptuousness," the other following a path that has its difficult spots but also its "resting places of rectitude and virtue."[11] Those separate roads, needless to say, do not remain separate long. The paths of the protagonists constantly cross and merge, with far more occasions for vice than virtue along the way. The life of luxury turns out to be as voluptuous and vicious as the "noisome dens of crime," and the latter prove far more noisome than the reader might have expected.

A chapter fittingly titled "A Den of Horrors" contains one horrific scene after another, each worse than anything depicted in *Jack Sheppard*. What makes them worse still is the presumption that, unlike *Jack Sheppard*, which takes place a century earlier, these scenes are located in the recent past. (At one point Reynolds reminds his readers that however bad conditions are in 1845, they were worse a decade earlier, a comment that does little to mitigate the horrors.) The chapter opens in Smithfield, the meat market of London, where the usual filth and squalor of the slum are compounded by the sights and smells of decaying carcasses. This graphic and malodorous scene is followed by a description of the wretched hovels with pigs rooting about in the backyards, which in turn recalls the supposedly true story of a mother who left her house to arrange for the burial of her dead infant and returned to find that a pig had wandered in and "feasted upon the dead child's face!" In these houses, we are told, an entire family may live and sleep in a single room, so that if one of them dies, the rest have to remain in the same room with the corpse until they can raise the money for its burial; days, even weeks, may thus pass, the body decomposing until "myriads of loathsome animalculae are seen crawling about." Among the other loathsome results of this forced intimacy is that "odious crime . . . the crime of incest!" For once Reynolds shrinks from further description, contenting himself with the reflection that "the wealthy classes of society are far too ready to reproach the miserable poor for things which are really misfortunes and not faults."[12]

The scene that follows is so gratuitously sadistic that even the most sympathetic reader would have difficulty attributing it to any "misfortunes" of poverty. Two beggar children, a boy of seven and a girl of five, ragged and bare-footed, are returning home one night, the boy trying to comfort his tearful sister by assuring her that he will take the blame for their paltry earnings so that their mother will beat him rather than her. Entering their house in trepidation, they are delighted to find that their father has just returned from jail. He rebuffs them, and their mother, enraged because their day's begging has netted only eightpence-halfpenny—"not more than enough to pay for the beer"—falls upon them, beating and kicking them until forced to stop by sheer exhaustion. It is their own fault, she complains to her husband, that they earn so little, "for people grows more charitable every day." The children are given a crust of moldy bread and sent to their mattress in the corner, where they clutch each other in fear and misery, "repulsed by a father whose neck they had longed to encircle with their little arms, . . . trembling even at the looks of a mother they loved in spite of all her harshness towards them."[13]

The story is interrupted by the author's assurance that this is no "over-drawn picture," that there are indeed such "monsters in a human form." There then ensues a conversation between these monsters, who have by now finished their "plentiful" meal of meat and bread. The boy, they agree, can be useful in helping the father break into houses, but the girl is a problem because she seems loath to beg. The mother has a plan to make her beg, "aye, and be glad to beg—and beg too in spite of herself," a plan that will "put her entirely at our mercy and at the same time render her an object of such interest that the people *must* give her money." Slowly, after tantalizing hints, the plan emerges: the mother will "put her eyes out." The father, although "a robber—yes, and a murderer," is startled by this proposal, which the mother then lays out in detail.

"There's nothin' like a blind child to excite compassion," added the woman coolly. "I know it for a fact," she continued, after a pause, seeing that her husband did not answer her. "There's old Kate Betts, who got all her money by travelling about the country with two blind girls; and she made 'em blind herself too—she's often told me how she did it; and that has put the idea into my head."

"And how did she do it?" asked the man, lighting his pipe, but not glancing towards his wife; for although her words had made a deep impression upon him, he was yet struggling with the remnant of a parental feeling, which remained in his heart in spite of himself.

"She covered the eyes with cockle shells, the eye-lids, recollect, being wide open; and in each shell there was a large black beetle. A bandage tied tight around the head, kept the shells in their place; and the shells kept the eyelids open. In a few days the eyes got quite blind, and the pupils had a dull white appearance."

"And you're serious, are you?" demanded the man.

"Quite," returned the woman, boldly: "why not?"

"Why not indeed?" echoed Bill, who approved of the horrible scheme, but shuddered at the cruelty of it, villain as he was.

"Ah! why not?" pursued the female: "one must make one's children useful somehow or another. So, if you don't mind, I'll send Harry

out alone tomorrow morning and keep Fanny at home. The moment
the boy's out of the way, I'll try my hand at Kate Betts's plan."[14]

This conversation is interrupted by the arrival of an old friend and
fellow house-breaker who takes the husband off to a "boozing ken," a low
public house catering to "sweeps, costermongers, Jews, Irish bricklayers, and
women of the town," where they plot their next burglary. Returning home
after a night of revelry and drink (the liquor is laced with drugs), the
husband, rebuked by his wife, proceeds to hit and kick her until she is almost
senseless, while the children cry bitterly. When the mother recovers, she
turns her rage upon the weeping children and beats them with "demoniac
cruelty," whereupon the father, not out of sympathy for the children but
to annoy his wife, tells her to stop beating them. She continues and he hits
her again, causing her to fall forward and strike her face on the corner of
the table. "Her left eye came in contact with the angle of the board, and
was literally crushed in its socket—an awful retribution upon her who only
a few hours before was planning how to plunge her innocent and helpless
daughter into the eternal night of blindness." She recovers long enough to
fix upon her husband, with her one good eye, a look so malignant that no
words, the author protests, could describe it. She then dies, her features
distorted by a "horrible expression of vindictive spite." The father, realizing
that he has murdered her, flees, leaving the terrified children alone with the
corpse of their mother.[15]

This is one of the more repulsive scenes of the novel, but not the only
one of its kind. A pornography of violence—deliberate, brutal, gratuitous
violence—characterizes the scenes of low life, just as a pornography of
sexuality pervades those of high life. The alternation of the two makes for
a powerful counterpoint, an ironic comment on the wealth-and-poverty
dichotomy that is presumed to be equivalent to virtue-and-vice. The sexuality, to be sure, unlike the violence, is not quite so explicit, the climax being
indicated (but clearly indicated—there is nothing ambiguous about that) by
a series of asterisks.

The chapter immediately following the murder opens cheerfully in the
drawing room of a villa in Upper Clapton, where a young woman (dressed,
for complicated reasons which had been explained earlier, in the garb of a
man and bearing a man's name) is being courted by a handsome and
seemingly proper young man. The courtship is interrupted by two burglars
(one of whom is the father of the children) who are chased off by the young
man. Flushed by excitement and aroused by the disheveled state of the
woman, he tries to rape her. She saves herself by producing a dagger from
under her pillow. "Villain, that you are—approach this bed, and, without
a moment's hesitation, I will plunge this dagger into your heart!"[16] The
ludicrous situation (the dagger conveniently hidden under the pillow) and

the banal prose—his "hot and burning kisses," his hand "invading the treasures of her bosom," his imagination envisioning "scenes and enjoyments of the most voluptuous kind"[17]—make it difficult for the modern reader to appreciate how prurient this scene is, as prurient as the preceding one is sadistic. And it is all the more titillating because of the pervasive overtones of sexual perversion. Throughout the whole of this seduction scene, the woman is dressed—and addressed—as a man.

What distinguishes this work from others of its kind is neither its sexuality nor its violence but its politics. Echoing the wealth-poverty theme of the prologue, the epilogue to the first volume proclaims the author as "the scourge of the oppressor and the champion of the oppressed," determined to expose tyranny and vice wherever he finds them and to "dwell as emphatically upon the failings of the educated and the rich, as on the immorality of the ignorant and poor." The "grand moral" of the work is simple: "Crime, oppression, and injustice prosper for a time; but, with nations as with individuals, the day of retribution must come."[18]

In the course of the volume, the plot is periodically interrupted to impart this moral. One discourse on "Wealth and Poverty" features a series of single-sentence paragraphs (a device copied from Sue's *Mysteries of Paris*).

> In England men and women die of starvation in the streets.
> In England women murder their children to save them from a lingering death by famine.
> In England the poor commit crimes to obtain an asylum in a gaol.
> In England aged females die by their own hands, in order to avoid the workhouse.

A diagram of the "social scale of these realms," with the sovereign at the top of the ladder, followed by the aristocracy and clergy, the middle classes, and, at the bottom, the "industrious classes," is accompanied by a chart of statistics on the average annual incomes of the individuals in each of these classes (ranging from £500,000 for the sovereign to £20 for the industrious classes), and a typical menu of the rich man's New Year feast compared with the pauper's workhouse meal. Finally the familiar words, "But to proceed," signal the return to the plot.[19]

This is one of Reynolds's more elaborate digressions. Generally he is content with brief asides, such as that delivered by the heroine who earlier so resourcefully defended her honor and was then unjustly jailed. Bidding farewell to a friend leaving for America, she confesses that she finds nothing in England to endear it to a "sensitive mind." She has read much since her release from jail and has discovered that England is the only civilized country where death from starvation, "literally starvation," is common. She cannot help feeling that "there must be something radically wrong in that system of society where all the wealth is in the hands of a few, and all the misery is shared by millions." Her supposed friend (who is taking the occasion of this sermon to slip a sleeping potion into her drink) asks whether this is not true of the other great cities of Europe. Not at all, she assures him. Were a person to die of starvation in Paris, the whole population would "rise in dismay," whereas in England, in spite of the immense machinery of the poor laws, there is more wretchedness than anywhere in the world, not excepting "the myriads who dwell upon the rivers in China."[20]

One of the frequent themes of these homilies is the inequity of English law and justice. When a grave-stealer befouls the air by digging up rotten corpses, someone suggests that the poor people in the neighborhood bring an indictment against him, which inspires some satiric reflections on poverty and the law.

> The poor, indeed! who ever thought of legislating for the poor? Legislate *against* them, and it is all well and good: heap statute upon statute—pile act upon act—. . . convert the whole legal scheme into a cunning web, so that the poor man cannot walk three steps without entangling his foot in one of those meshes of whose very existence he was previously unaware, and whose nature he cannot comprehend even when involved therein;—do all this, and you are a wise and sound statesman; for this is legislating *against* the poor—and who, we repeat, would ever think of legislating *for* them?[21]

The law is an instrument for the rich, not for justice. It is what a judge and jury decide it is, and they are more inclined to favor the testimony of a well dressed, well spoken man than of a ragged and ignorant one. Indeed the law is so arbitrary and omnipotent, one lawyer informs his client, it even "makes religion," defines the attributes of the deity, and obliges everyone to accept that definition. It also makes morality. "If I murder you," the lawyer continues, "I commit a crime; but the executioner who puts me to death for the action, does *not* commit a crime. . . . Thus, murder is only a crime when it is not legalised by human statutes,—or, in plain terms, when it is not according to the law."[22] The same argument is echoed by the "Resurrection Man" who, when not engaged in his regular trade of grave-stealing, does the odd job of blackmail. At one point his victim, a weak but virtuous middle class young man, remonstrates with him: "Tell me—by what right, by what law, do you now endeavour to extort—vilely, infamously extort —this money from me?" "My law," the Resurrection Man replies, "is that practised by all the world—*the oppression of the weak by the strong;* and my right is also that of universal practice—*the right of him who takes what will not dare to be refused.*"[23]

The gang of thieves to which the murderer in the earlier episode belongs is obviously intended as a microcosm of society. If conventional law is the law of the rich and powerful, the law of the underworld is the law of the violent and powerful. And it is conventional law that makes the lawless what they are. The Resurrection Man, looking about the Dark House (the public house frequented by the gang), observes that of the twenty thieves and prostitutes in the room "the laws and the state of society made eighteen of them what they are."[24] Elsewhere, speaking in his own voice, Reynolds accuses the law of being "vindictive, cowardly, mean and ignorant": vindictive, for inflicting punishments more severe than the offences and for going to any length to get a conviction; cowardly, for putting to death men whose dispositions it could not curb; mean, because it proceeds most harshly against the poor who cannot defend themselves; and ignorant, because "it erects the gibbet where it should rear the cross." The novel part of this argument is the idea that instead of greater leniency being given in the case of a crime of passion—as was the conventional practice —consideration might better be given to the "cool and calculating" criminal, since it is he who is the more reformable, the more apt to be "led by reflection to virtue."[25]

It is here that Reynolds distinguishes himself from his reform-minded contemporaries, including the more radical of them. They too tried to understand and even, on occasion, sympathize with the dangerous classes, but they did not give them the same moral status as the rest of society. Certainly they did not seek to legitimize the outlaw by illegitimizing the law. Reynolds does just this, and without in any way sentimentalizing the criminal or mitigating the heinousness of his crime. On the contrary, it is the basest criminal who inspires his vehement attack upon the law. The "cool and calculating individual" on whose behalf special "consideration" is claimed is the man who plots to blind his daughter, murders his wife, and is engaged in other crimes when the law finally catches up with him. On the eve of his execution he has nightmares of "hideous monsters, immense serpents, formidable bats, and all kinds of slimy reptiles . . . all the phantasmagorical displays of demons, spectres, and posthumous horrors ever conceived by human mind." These nightmares, however, come from the simple, primitive fear of death; Reynolds makes it clear that he feels no remorse or guilt and gives no thought to his children. There is one feeble suggestion that if the murderer were permitted to live he might "see the horrors of his ways, and learn to admire virtue."[26] But this unlikely possibility does not account for the author's protest against his execution. Reynolds himself expresses neither compassion for the condemned man nor a principled objection to the taking of life—only a contempt for law and society so powerful that the most monstrous murderer is more defensible, in a perverse sense more moral, than law and society.

The "histories" of these victims of society, the anti-heroes of the novel, have the same morally ambiguous quality, most of the victims being as brutal as society itself. The "Buffer" is shown committing his first crime at the age of twelve (stealing from his overindulgent parents to pay his gambling debts), and going on to a career of knavery, duplicity, burglary, and premeditated murder. Finally caught and tried on one of the lesser charges, he is imprisoned for two years in Newgate, where he reflects on his evil ways and is tempted to reform. But the system does not allow him to reform; knowing only how to punish, it fails to provide him with work when he is released. Thus he goes from prison to the workhouse, where he discovers that paupers are treated worse than convicts, a fact he proves by citing tables giving the exact quantities of bread, gruel, meat, and other foods allotted to each pauper for each day of the week.*

These criticisms of the prison and workhouse are put in the mouth of "one of the most unmitigated villains that ever disgraced the name of man," whose wife, a fitting helpmate, exhibits "every evil passion that can possibly disgrace womanhood."[28] By the Buffer's own account, they are leniently treated by the law. An unsympathetic reader might come away from the tale deploring not the rigors of the penal system but its laxity, the failure to apprehend the criminal earlier or punish him for any of his more serious crimes (including murder), and the commutation of his sentence of seven years' transportation to two years at Newgate. The reader might also wonder whether even the most enlightened system could ever reform a character like the Buffer.

Whatever the faults of the prisons, it is not poverty that puts the Buffer and most of his friends there. The Buffer's parents were fairly prosperous street-folk, sellers of coal and potatoes on a large scale, with some illicit trading on the side; and the Buffer and his wife are hardly destitute. Nor are the abominable husband and wife who discuss the blinding of their daughter after a "plentiful" dinner of meat, bread, and drink, and who use the proceeds of their children's begging, as they repeatedly say, to keep them in beer and gin. Even the tales featured under the title, "The Wrongs and the Crimes of the Poor," convey an ambiguous message, the "wrongs" done to the poor being done to them, as often as not, by their own parents.

*The Buffer also recites the seven stanzas of a "Song of the Workhouse" composed by one of the inmates. As if to give plausibility and authenticity to this history (including the dietary details itemized down to the last half-ounce), Reynolds explains that he has taken the liberty of "altering and improving" the Buffer's language, correcting his "grammatical solecisms," and putting his "random observations into a tangible shape."[27]

These tales have as their setting the Dark House, a "notorious resort for thieves and persons of the worst character." Among the habitués of the house are the "paramours" of the thieves, "viragoes" whose language is as foul as that of the men and their behavior not much better, who would as soon, we are told, dash out the brains of the landlord as quaff a tumbler of raw gin. It is they who prompt the observation, "There is no barbarism in the whole world so truly horrible and ferocious—so obscene and shameless —as that which is found in the poor districts of London!" This leads Reynolds to the familiar criticism of the missionaries who seek converts in the farthest corners of the world while London swarms with far more dangerous "infidels." "How detestable it is for philanthropy to be exercised in clothing negroes or Red Men thousands of miles distant, while our own poor are cold and naked at our very door"[29]—a peculiarly inappropriate comment since these women are neither cold nor naked but well warmed by gin and gaudily attired.

It is in the unsavory atmosphere of the Dark House that the thief and the prostitute relate their histories. The thief was a coal-whipper who became a drunkard and then a "prig" (thief) when he was obliged to take part of his earnings in drink. His wife and children are forced into the workhouse, and he himself, drowning his sorrows in the Dark House, reflects upon his life.

> "It's only the poor that's treated so. And now I think I have said enough to show why I turned prig, like many more whippers from the port of London. There isn't a more degraded, oppressed, and brutalised set of men in the world than the whippers. They are born with examples of drunken fathers afore their eyes; and drunken fathers makes drunken mothers; and drunken parents makes sons turn out thieves, and daughters prostitutes;—and that's the existence of the coal-whippers of Wapping. It ain't their fault: they haven't edication and self-command to refuse the drink that's forced upon them, and that they must pay for; —and their sons and daughters shouldn't be blamed for turning out bad. How can they help it? And yet one reads in the papers that the upper classes is always a-crying out about the dreadful immorality of the poor!"[30]

The prostitute also attributes her career to drink, although in her case it was not an employer who was responsible for her downfall but her own father, whose trade was the sale of "jiggered gin," a combination of molasses, beer, and vitriol guaranteed to make "the strongest man mad drunk." Her mother, besotted by drink, had fallen into the fire and burnt to death. At the age of eleven the daughter was sent out by her father "upon the town" and thrashed if she returned with too little money. Since his death she has been plying her trade under various auspices ("dress-houses," for example, which were also whorehouses) and with varying fortunes; she was once imprisoned, often beaten, and in her present position has "capital fun." In the course of the tale she explains the pleasures of "jiggered gin" and provides such bits of information as that there are 80,000 "unfortunate gals" in London. (A long footnote enumerates the various causes of prostitution and the proportions assignable to each cause.)[31]

The "Rattlesnake's" history opens as a conventional horror story of child labor in the coal mines, a footnote at the beginning assuring the reader that its accuracy is vouched by the report of the Children's Employment Commission of 1842. The Rattlesnake tells of children sent down to the pits at the age of seven, maimed by accidents or crippled by the distorting positions in which they have to work, and of the evils of the "truck" or "tommy" system requiring the laborer to spend a portion of his wages on goods purchased from the employer's store.[32] But the tale dwells more on the moral degradation of the miners than on their physical conditions or economic grievances. It is the Rattlesnake himself, not some bourgeois moralist like Chadwick, who says: "The habits of the colliers are hereditarily depraved: they are perpetuated from father to son, from mother to daughter; none is better nor worse than his parents were before him." The Rattlesnake is illegitimate, which is no disgrace, he explains, "morality being on so low a scale amongst the mining population generally, as almost to amount to promiscuous intercourse."[33] His career in crime starts when he flees from the mines after overhearing his mother and father plot the murder of his father's crippled wife (herself the mother of five children), and has reason to suspect that they are planning to do away with him too. (The murder of the wife is duly recounted in all its gruesome details.)

This is not the usual exposé of child labor, not the kind calculated to arouse the compassion of the reader and the zeal of the reformer. Nor are the other histories the familiar morality tales in which the virtuous poor succumb to the temptations and misfortunes visited upon them by an immoral, inequitable system. The nearest approximation in the whole of the first volume to the conventional tale of unjust, undeserved poverty is the story of Ellen Monroe, prefaced by the author's assurance that here is to be found "perhaps less romance and more truth" than in any previous tale.[34]

Ellen makes her first appearance on a cold December evening in a bare and fireless room, the wind whistling through the broken pane of the paper-covered window, and the flickering light of a single candle revealing the scantily clad figure of a seamstress hunched over her work. The description of the young woman ("the cast of her countenance was purely Grecian —the shape of her head eminently classical—and her form was of a perfect and symmetrical mould") makes it clear that this is no ordinary seamstress but a well-born lady fallen on hard times.[35] For much of the novel Ellen's fate works itself out in predictable ways, although even here there are distinctive touches and an unconventional ending. When sewing fails to provide the barest living for herself and her father, she becomes a model, first for a sculptor, then for an artist, and finally for a photographer, each job more degrading—and financially more remunerative—than the preceding one (the degree of degradation and remuneration being proportionate to the degree of nudity). These jobs last only long enough to compromise the heroine and make her ripe for the ultimate degradation: becoming mistress to the "heartless voluptuary" who earlier had designs on the other heroine of the novel. At this point the story takes a decidedly un-Victorian turn, for instead of taking to the streets after the birth of her illegitimate child, she manages to get one interesting job after another, none quite respectable by conventional standards but in her own eyes (and obviously those of the author) satisfying and not at all demeaning; she becomes an assistant to a mesmerist (a "Professor of Animal Magnetism"), then a dancer, and finally an actress.* Eventually she regains her child (who has been cared for by a kindly doctor while she has been otherwise engaged) and her self-respect. The hero, who gives her refuge in his comfortable home, assures her that her sin is "not criminal," only "unfortunate," and that her soul is "pure and spotless."[36]

Like the other stories, this is no more the conventional morality tale than it is the conventional tale of the oppressed working classes. If one did not know better, if Reynolds's political opinions were not a matter of public record, one might even suspect him of parodying the radical cause. "In England," he interrupts his story to protest, "men and women die of starvation in the streets. In England women murder their children to save them from a lingering death by famine."[37] But his characters do not die of starvation in the streets; they live comfortably off the proceeds of their crimes, dying of alcoholism and debauchery, of violence at each other's hands, or on the gallows. And the women do not murder their children to save them from starvation; they murder or plot to murder them for their own selfish and wicked reasons.

If the book is not a parody of radicalism, it is an assertion of a radicalism so absolute as to make all other forms seem sentimental and banal. In his prologue, Reynolds promised to confront the reader with the extremes of poverty and wealth. The extremes of poverty, however, appear to be not starvation and misery but crime and vice. This might be attributed to the demands of the genre, the vicious crimes of the dangerous classes being obviously more interesting than the virtuous miseries of the industrious

---

*"Animal magnetism," or "mesmerism" as it was otherwise known, enjoyed a great vogue at the time. The original of this Professor of Animal Magnetism was probably Dr. John Elliotson, who published a book in 1843 on mesmerism as an anesthetic device. In the *Athenaeum* in 1845 Harriet Martineau described her cure by mesmerism from her addiction to opiates. She then proceeded to mesmerize Charlotte Brontë and to convert other friends to the cause.

classes. But he pursued this theme so relentlessly that one has to credit him with something like a conscious strategy and ideology.

Part of this ideology emerges in the story of the Republican and the Resurrection Man. These characters make their first appearance together in the jail where the hero is confined, each offering to counsel and befriend him. The Republican has been jailed for arousing "the grovelling spirit of the industrious millions to a sense of the wrongs under which they labour," the Resurrection Man for "body-snatching" and, he intimates, worse. The hero shudders when the Resurrection Man announces his name (and thus his occupation), but it is the Republican who is regarded as a "moral pestilence," a "social plague," "loathed and shunned by all virtuous and honest men."[38] Both hold out the promise of freedom, the one through republicanism, the other through some more covert and unspecified means. Four volumes later, largely through the efforts of our hero (now turned general), republicanism is established, poverty "extirpated," and the people made "contented, free, and prosperous"—this in the Republic of Castelcicala, the "Model-State" of Europe, at a time when, as the press of Castelcicala reports, people are still starving in the streets of England.[39] Although Castelcicala is frankly a utopia (*cicalata* implies the empty, idle chattering of the cicada), Reynolds does not conceal his hope that ultimately republicanism will be established even in his own benighted homeland, "sweeping away the remnants of feudal barbarism, leveling all oppressive institutions, compelling tyrants to bend to the will of the masses"—and this to be accomplished not "by degrees but at once and in a moment."[40] That, however, is in the future. In present-day England it is the devious methods of the Resurrection Man which prevail. "We shall both be tried together," the Resurrection Man predicts. "Fifteen years for him—freedom for me! That's the way to do it!"[41] What "freedom" there is now is the freedom of the outcast, the criminal. The Republic of Castelcicala is a utopia; the Dark House in London is the reality.

The few commentators who have taken Reynolds seriously find in his work a fundamental ambivalence, contradiction, or betrayal of principle. Margaret Dalziel makes much of the fact that this republican, Chartist, and champion of the poor created heroes and heroines who were generally rich and of noble birth. (The hero of *Mysteries of London,* who eventually helps found the Republic of Castelcicala, has earlier reinstated his father-in-law as grand-duke of Italy, has been himself ennobled, and enjoys, with no apparent guilt, all the prerogatives and luxuries of his class.) To Dalziel this suggests that Reynolds wanted to appeal to his readers with his democratic views and at the same time allow them "the pleasure of imaginative participation in the life of a wholly undemocratic society."[42] Another critic, Louis

James, portrays him as an intelligent, thoughtful man with a genuine social conscience who fell prey to the "lure of sensation and easy popularity," so that his radicalism succumbed to the conventions of romance.

> The pauper classes are caricatured, and are either idealized royalty in disguise, or soul-less monsters. The middle classes are hardly represented at all. The lower classes are made up of thugs, resurrection men, fences, prostitutes, or starving paupers. The best of the working classes as they really existed—the courageous artisan overcoming his difficulties by hard work and determination, is never shown.[43]

Like those who fault Mayhew for abandoning his proper subject, the working class, these critics see Reynolds as having been distracted from his true radical mission. Dalziel complains that he failed to carry out in his fiction the role of the "genuine radical," James that his popularity interfered with his convictions and prevented him from making "a real contribution to the popular culture of his time."[44]*

These critics have imposed upon Reynolds their own ideas of what a "genuine radical" would have done and what a "real contribution" to popular culture would have been. They are also asking of him the kind of "social novel" that no radical of the time, not even Ernest Jones, ever wrote. The fact is that Reynolds was a social novelist of a most unusual kind, as he was also a Gothic novelist, with a difference. Neither the conventions of the genre nor the desire for popularity required him to express the views he did, or would have precluded him from expressing others had he so chosen; within the constraints of that form and market, there was a large latitude for differences of ideas and attitudes. Sensationalism and romance, violence and terror, the extravagant depravity of high life and the villainy of low life—these were obligatory in the Gothic novel. But it was not obligatory to ascribe such unadulterated villainy to characters ostensibly representing the poor. The monstrous wife and husband could have been driven to their foul deeds by misery and desperation instead of sheer selfish-

---

*Q. D. Leavis, on the other hand, attributes to Reynolds her own notions of a decent, idealistic, radical politics and culture. From an apparently cursory examination of *Reynolds's Miscellany*, she makes him out to be the "Northcliffe of his age," albeit a benign version of that species.

> There is an impressive decorum about the *Miscellany* which the age of Northcliffe and the Beaverbrook Press can hardly understand. Its most striking feature is a complete absence of any emotional appeals. . . . The constant insistence on open-mindedness in politics and non-material standards in living without any appeals to religious sentiment or anything cheap in the radicalism for which Reynolds stood, is a considerable achievement. It is a heritage from the eighteenth-century revolutionary idealists and the vogue of Godwin and Tom Paine.[45]

This is a much idealized reading of the *Miscellany*, and it entirely ignores the *Mysteries of London*, which was at least as influential and anything but decorous, unemotional, open-minded, or idealistic.

ness and callousness; the prostitute might have been corrupted by an unscrupulous employer rather than her own father; the Rattlesnake might have had a mother tragically starving to death instead of coolly planning to murder her lover's wife and her own child; the Resurrection Man might have been a little embarrassed by his calling and less arrogant about his success. And they all might have been somewhat more remorseful, more inclined to mend their ways and atone for their sins.

This is not to expect from the Gothic novelist a swarm of deserving, respectable poor; that would have been out of keeping with the genre. Within the limits of the genre, however, even the lowest classes of the poor could have produced, in addition to their quota of unregenerate villains, an occasional heroic character, not the humble, deserving sort but romantic, flamboyant, bohemian, someone who rose above his poverty not by discovering his noble birth but by turning his low birth to good account, defying authority for the sake of others rather than his own gratification—a Robin Hood type, perhaps. If Reynolds created no such heroes among the poor, it was not necessarily, as his critics suppose, because he was insufficiently resolute and radical to withstand the temptations of sensationalism. It may have been because his radicalism was of an entirely different order and because his idea of poverty was nihilistic rather than compassionate or heroic.

By temperament and instinct rather than conscious ideology, Reynolds was more in the tradition of a Stirner or Weitling than of a Dickens or an Ainsworth. If there was any social message to be drawn from *The Mysteries of London,* it was that violence and depravity, licentiousness and criminality, were the only forms of existence, and potentially the only means of redemption, available to the poor. (The Resurrection Man may have implied another kind of "resurrection" than grave-stealing.) In a world where, as Reynolds repeatedly said, poverty was regarded as a vice, the poor had no recourse but to be vicious. In that world there were no "deserving poor." To appear deserving was to be false to oneself, to deny one's poverty and the degradation of poverty. Like the *Lumpen* who had to realize, in consciousness and in actuality, the utter "raggedness" of their condition before they could transcend it, so Reynolds seemed to require his poor to experience the full effect of their degradation in order to be "resurrected."

It may well be that Reynolds was not entirely aware of what he was doing, and his readers were certainly less aware of it. Yet to some extent and in some fashion, part of that message must have been intended by him and must have communicated itself to his readers. And if not the message, then the image of poverty which carried the burden of that message. His readers were surely less interested in his commentaries on "Wealth and Poverty" than in his pictures of the voluptuous pleasures of high life and the horrors of low life. And while the scenes of high life were represented as pure fantasy, the scenes of low life—interspersed with those commentaries, "histories," facts and figures, footnotes citing parliamentary reports, and the author's personal testimony—seemed intended to convey something like reality. Whatever Reynolds himself understood by poverty, whatever he said in his asides, his stories depicted a poverty that was not that of the hardworking, oppressed, deserving poor, not even of the indolent, improvident, undeserving poor, but of the dangerous, degraded, brutalized poor.

If the domestic novel had the effect of domesticating poverty, taming it, making it seem natural and tolerable, Reynolds's work as surely had the effect of "gothicizing" poverty, making it seem barbarous, grotesque, macabre. In this respect he went far beyond Ainsworth. Reynolds could not be charged, as Ainsworth was, with romanticizing or sentimentalizing the "dangerous classes," making them appear attractive, adventurous, heroic. No reader would be tempted to identify himself with the Rattlesnake or Resurrection Man as he might with Jack Sheppard or even Jonathan Wild. (Nor were there any murderous mothers in Ainsworth's novel; on the contrary, Sheppard's mother was self-sacrificing to the point of being, literally, suicidal.)

It was a peculiar genre Reynolds created: the social novel-*cum*-Gothic romance. If the Gothic tale in general gives us a new perspective on early Victorian culture, a culture far less inhibited, conformist, and bourgeois than that commonly associated with Victorianism, Reynolds's work shows us a new dimension of the social novel, a novel shaped as much by the Gothic imagination as by a radical ideology, and presenting a peculiarly "Gothicized" image of poverty.* His dangerous class was far more dangerous than the conventional one (which consisted, for the most part, of petty criminals), more dangerous even than the lumpenproletariat (which was dangerous chiefly to the Marxist revolution). It was dangerous as only the *Lumpen* were in the febrile imagination of the "ultra" revolutionaries, a class utterly impoverished, de-moralized, and alienated, whose "immiseration" was so total that it went to the very heart of their moral being. It was, of course, for Reynolds as for Stirner or Weitling, a nihilistic fantasy—but what better place for such a fantasy than the Gothic novel.

---

*Reynolds's work also provides an interesting commentary on Mill's *On Liberty*. The central thesis of that book—the need for the largest degree of liberty and individuality consistent with the injunction not to harm others—was meant to counteract the intolerable "social tyranny" exercised by the majority, the yoke of "conformity" and "uniformity" imposed on every individual, the single "pinched and hidebound type of human character" which was the model for everyone. "In our times, from the highest class of society down to the lowest, everyone lives as under the eye of a hostile and dreaded censorship."[46] If there was such a tyranny or censorship, Reynolds and the other "sensation novelists," writing for the "highest class of society down to the lowest," clearly knew nothing of it. By the same token, Mill evidently knew nothing of the kinds of popular literature available or of the varieties of character and behavior displayed in that literature. One suspects that had he known of it, he might willingly have retreated to the "pinched and hidebound" Calvinist types he so deplored in *On Liberty*.

XIX

THE DICKENSIAN POOR

To the social historian or the socially minded literary critic, Dickens offers a cornucopia of treasures, a plethora of social problems, conditions, classes, attitudes, and ideologies. Paupers, workhouses, infant "farms," prisons, crime, poor relief, child labor, old age, factories, trade unions, education, housing, sanitation, the law, civil service, Parliament, philanthropy, political economy, Malthusianism, utilitarianism, industrialism, urbanism—there was hardly a social issue that did not make its appearance in one novel or another.

Contemporaries were as aware as we are of the need to approach these subjects with great caution, not to take Dickens's fictional account of the workhouse, school, or factory as literal truth. The *Westminster Review,* reviewing *Our Mutual Friend* in 1866, suggested that if Dickens were serious about the poor laws he should write a pamphlet or go into Parliament; to use the novel as an instrument of reform was as "absurd as it would be to call out the militia to stop the cattle disease." The very idea of the social novel was an anomaly; "like an egg with two yolks, neither is ever hatched."[1] Historians have good reason to endorse these sentiments, reminding us of the perils not only of fictionalized history but also of fictionalized biography, the fallacy of assuming that Dickens's own position on any particular issue could readily be deduced from his novels. One of the best social commentators on Dickens, Philip Collins, has pointed out that he was a prominent advocate of two educational institutions which he mercilessly satirized in his novels: training colleges (in *Hard Times*) and ragged schools (in *Our Mutual Friend*).[2]

More recently, literary critics have gone so far in the other direction as to warrant a different kind of cautionary note. In the effort to reconstruct the "imaginary universe" of the novels, they have virtually constructed that universe *de novo,* with little regard for the universe Dickens himself inhabited or for his own creative intentions. In this new mode of literary criticism, the novels are said to be "autonomous works of art"—autonomous, that is, in relation to history and society, not to other works of literature with which they are presumed to have the closest relationship.[3] Divorced from the world of Victorian England, Dickens's novels are located in an imaginative universe cohabited by Dante, Dostoyevsky, Kafka, D. H. Lawrence, and T. S. Eliot, a universe dominated by language, structure, rhetoric, myth, symbol, metaphor, allegory. Lionel Trilling, gently chiding his students who vied with each other in finding symbolic parallels between *Our Mutual Friend* and *The Waste Land,* recalled his own discovery of the historical reality of what he himself had thought of as pure symbols.

> Since writing this, I have had to revise my idea of the actuality of the symbols of *Our Mutual Friend.* Professor Johnson's biography of Dickens has taught me much about the nature of dust heaps, including their monetary value, which was very large, quite large enough to represent a considerable fortune: I had never quite believed that Dickens was telling the literal truth about this. From Professor Dodds's *The Age of Paradox* I have learned to what an extent the Thames was visibly the sewer of London, of how pressing was the problem of the sewage in the city as Dickens knew it, of how present to the mind was the sensible and even the tangible evidence that the problem was not being solved. The moral *disgust* of the book is thus seen to be quite adequately comprehended by the symbols which are used to represent it.[4]

The actuality, and the reader's awareness of the actuality, so far from vulgarizing or demeaning the imaginative universe of the novel, enhances it, all the more in the case of someone like Dickens who was himself so engaged in the actuality, as reporter, social critic, and social reformer. He was also, of course, the social novelist par excellence, expressing in his fiction the widest range of social concerns and appealing to the widest audience. The world of his novels was part of the world, imaginative and real, of generations of men, women, and children. He did for the nineteenth century what Bunyan had done for the seventeenth, providing a common cultural denominator, a common stock of characters, situations, expressions, and witticisms for people of all classes, occupations, regions, ages, and persuasions. For countless Englishmen Mrs. Gamp was more real than Mr. Gladstone, Scrooge as familiar as Father Christmas.

An obvious measure of Dickens's appeal is the sale of his books. One is not surprised to find that *Pickwick Papers* sold 40,000 copies a week, *The Old Curiosity Shop* 100,000, or the Christmas tales as many as 250,000. The figures for his more sober books are no less impressive: 33,000 copies of *Dombey and Son* (which sold out on the first night of its issue), 35,000 of *Bleak House* and *Little Dorrit,* 50,000 of the first part of *The Mystery of Edwin Drood.* These figures represent only the original serialized parts (the weekly parts selling for a penny-halfpenny, and the monthly parts for a shilling). The sale of the innumerable editions of volumes is incalculable, but some measure of its magnitude may be suggested by the fact that in the dozen years following his death well over 4,000,000 copies of his books were sold in England alone.[5] These are sales, not circulation or readership, figures; they do not take into account the copies passed on among friends, or sold and resold by secondhand dealers, or borrowed from the circulating libraries. (Mudie's complained that no set of books wore out as quickly as Dickens's.)

In his obituary of Dickens, Anthony Trollope said that his books would become staples, like "legs of mutton or loaves of bread," a sentiment echoed by *The Times* when it memorialized him as "the intimate of every household."[6] It did not take Dickens's death to make people aware of his universal appeal; from the beginning that had been his great distinction. In 1837 G. H. Lewes reported that he often saw the butcher-boy with his tray on his shoulder avidly reading the latest number of *Pickwick,* and that the maidservant, footman, and chimney sweep were following the tales of "Boz" with the same fascination.[7] One of Mayhew's informants told him that Dickens had been a great favorite of the "patterers" (the street-sellers of songs, broadsheets, and ballads) until *Household Words* offended them by publishing a piece attacking the professional begging-letter writers.[8] Reviewing *Great Expectations* in 1861, *The Times* was pleased to find that although it was addressed to a "much higher class of readers," a "better" class than that catered to by Reynolds's penny journals, it was sensational enough to compete successfully with those journals.[9] Walter Bagehot explained that the phrase "household book" was peculiarly apt for Dickens, there being no other writer "whose works are read so generally through the whole house, who can give pleasure to the servants as well as to the mistress, to the children as well as to the master."[10]

The memoirs of the time are full of such accounts, of reports of the poorest people reading Dickens, and those who could not read listening to the latest installment read aloud in the servants' hall, lodging house, public house, or tea shop. Dickens's son recalled that a walk with his father in the streets of London was a "royal progress, people of all degrees and classes taking off their hats and greeting him as he passed." After his death, the son was recognized by a taxi driver. "Ah! Mr. Dickens, your father's death was a great loss to all of us—and we cabbies were in hopes that he would soon be doing something to help us." A costermonger girl was reported as saying, "Dickens dead? Then will Father Christmas die too?" Most critics, whatever their other reservations, took it as a tribute to him that he was able to appeal to the literate and illiterate alike. An early review praised him for performing the function of "moral teacher" to the "millions who are just emerging from ignorance into what may be called reading classes."[11] Only occasionally was this fact recorded with the snide overtone of Leslie Stephen's later comment: "If literary fame could safely be measured by popularity with the half-educated, Dickens must claim the highest position among English novelists."[12]

One of the ways in which Dickens reached the poor was through the numerous dramatizations of his novels, most of them unauthorized, and performed in the cheap theaters frequented by the poor. The fictional imitations catered to the same audience. In an age when plagiarism and literary piracy were rife, *Pickwick Papers* had the distinction of being the most plagiarized and pirated book of the time. Reynolds made his debut as a popular writer with *Pickwick Abroad,* and Edward Lloyd, the most enterprising and unscrupulous of the penny publishers, entered the lists with the periodical *Penny Pickwick.* Refusing to restrain the publication of *Penny Pickwick,* the judge argued that no one could possibly confuse it with the original—a dubious consolation to Dickens, who had to witness the appearance of one after another plagiarism of his later books: *Oliver Twiss* published by Lloyd under the pseudonym of "Bos," which inspired yet another *Oliver Twiss,* this under the name of "Poz"; *Nickelas Nicklebery* and *Nicholas Nicklebury, Mr. Humfries Clock, Martin Guzzlewit, Dombey and Daughter.* [13] (Dickens was not alone in suffering these transmutations. W. H. Ainsworth's *The Tower of London* was issued by Lloyd as *The Legend of the Tower of London* by W. H. Hainsforth.)

The judge who said that no one could mistake the copy for the original was quite right; the style was flatter, the humor broader, the plot more melodramatic, the social message either omitted or grossly exaggerated. In one version of *Oliver Twist,* Oliver's father starved to death in prison, his mother was driven to suicide, and Oliver himself was more grossly maltreated than his prototype. In another version, the Fagin character (renamed Solomons) was made to deliver a speech more appropriate to a high-minded Chartist than to a low criminal.

> If the wealthy of our land choose to lay claim to those things that are intended as much for the use of the poor man as for the rich one, we cannot be much surprised that men are to be found who will resist the laws that have been made for the purpose of depriving them of their share in the gifts of heaven. The poor man feels his wrongs, and boldly asserts his rights.[14]

It would be interesting to know whether these sentiments reflected the political views of the hack writer or whether they were the unwitting result of vulgarization, the politics becoming exaggerated along with the characters and situations. Whatever the case, plagiarization often had the effect of magnifying both the melodrama and the social criticism, the commentaries on poverty becoming more radical as the murder scenes became more gruesome.

Dickens was a "low writer," it was said at the time; he wrote about low subjects, for a low audience.[15]* Some thought him as low as Reynolds. A reviewer of *Bleak House* complained that it was "meagre and melodramatic, and disagreeably reminiscent of that vilest of modern books, Reynolds's *Mysteries of London*."[17] John Ruskin later defended Dickens against this charge by distinguishing him not from Reynolds but from Sue. Unlike *The Mysteries of Paris,* that loathsome specimen of "prison-house literature," *Oliver Twist* was an "earnest and uncaricatured record of the state of criminal life, written with a didactic purpose, full of the gravest instruction."[18] Dickens himself was sensitive to this criticism, and sensitive especially to the comparison with Reynolds, who was "low" both in his writing and in his politics. When he started *Household Words,* which might be thought to be competing with Reynolds's *Miscellany* (which was in fact competitive in terms of circulation, the first number of *Household Words* selling 100,000 copies), his introductory editorial denounced the periodicals that were "Bastards of the Mountain, draggled fringe on the Red Cap, Panders to the basest passions of the lowest natures."[19]

When contemporaries accused Dickens of being a low writer, it was generally because of his Newgate characters and scenes, reminiscent more of Ainsworth than of Reynolds. But there was little objection to those characters and scenes which were socially rather than morally low, depicting the lower classes rather than the dangerous classes. Lord Melbourne, to be sure, disliked both kinds of lowness. Persuaded to read *Oliver Twist* by Queen Victoria, he confessed he could not get beyond the opening chapters.

---

*Almost a century later, this charge was echoed by Q. D. Leavis, who associated Dickens with the other sensation-seeking novelists catering to the new reading public, an "uncultivated and inherently 'low' " class of readers brought into being by the cheap serials. Dickens was so successful, Mrs. Leavis argued, because he shared the childish sensibility of his readers. The fact that he laughed and cried aloud as he wrote proved that he was "not only uneducated but also immature." When he had to create upper class characters, they were "the painful guesses of the uninformed and half-educated writing for the uninformed and half-educated." All this in contrast to the eighteenth century novelist, who wrote for "the best, because it was the only public," and whose fiction revealed a "mature, discreet, well-balanced personality," an "adult and critical sensibility." Only in *David Copperfield* and *Great Expectations* did Dickens rise above his public and produce novels that could genuinely be called "literature." This was written in 1932. Later the Leavises reread Dickens and admitted him to their literary canon, the "Great Tradition." But even then there remained some discomfort with the "low" scenes, the picaresque and melodramatic—"exposure" scenes, as Q. D. Leavis called them.[16]

It's all among Workhouses, and Coffin Makers, and Pickpockets. I
don't like *The Beggar's Opera;* I shouldn't think it would tend to raise
morals; I don't like that low debasing view of mankind. . . . I don't
like those things; I wish to avoid them; I don't like them in *reality,* and
therefore I don't wish them represented.[20]

Queen Victoria, on the other hand, reading the book over the objections of
her mother (who disapproved not only of low books but of all "light
books"), found *Oliver Twist* "excessively interesting."[21] Even Thackeray,
who suspected that the Fagin scenes pandered to the sensational tastes of the
age, did not object to Dickens's other low themes and characters. "The pathos
of the workhouse scenes in *Oliver Twist,* or the Fleet prison descriptions in
Pickwick, is genuine and pure—as much of this as you please; as tender a hand
to the poor, as kindly a word to the unhappy as you will; but in the name of
common sense, let us not expend our sympathies on cut-throats, and other
such prodigies of evil."[22] *Blackwood's Edinburgh Magazine* complimented
Dickens on his ability to find a "counter-picturesqueness" in the poor which
made his "washerwomen as interesting as duchesses."[23] Richard Horne, a
friend of Dickens (and, later, an editor of *Household Words*), defended him
against the charge of romanticizing criminals by suggesting that he only
romanticized the poor. Dickens, he said, left no doubt of the villainy of his
criminals, reserving his compassion for those worthy of it—the poor woman
in *Oliver Twist,* for example, who died gasping the names of her children.
"O, ye scions of a refined age," he rebuked those who pronounced Dickens
"a low writer, and a lover of low scenes": "Look at this passage—find out
how low it is—and rise up from the contemplation chastened, purified—
wiser, because sorrow-softened and better men through the enlargement of
sympathies."[24]

　　Oliver Twist, the most Hogarthian of Dickens's novels, alternated
between low characters of both kinds, and it is hard to say which fascinated
readers the more. (Or, for that matter, Dickens himself; the murder of
Nancy was his favorite reading piece.) Some critics see an intimate relationship between the two species of lowness. To Steven Marcus, Fagin and
Oliver are "alike if not identical" in their "alienation" from respectable
society, a society in which "poverty was tantamount to crime."[25] The
strongest support for this view comes from an autobiographical memoir in
which Dickens recalled that unhappy period of his childhood in the blacking
warehouse when he was obliged to associate with "common men and boys."
"I know that I lounged about the streets, insufficiently and unsatisfactorily
fed. I know that, but for the mercy of God, I might easily have been, for
any care that was taken of me, a little robber or a little vagabond." This
passage appears almost verbatim—not, however, in *Oliver Twist* but in
David Copperfield.[26] And David (like Dickens himself) never ran the least

risk of becoming "a little robber or a little vagabond." The streets of London he wandered through were perfectly respectable, and he never so much as encountered anyone like the Artful Dodger, let alone a Fagin or a Bill Sikes.

In his maudlin recollections of his childhood, Dickens may have fancied himself a robber or vagabond, much as another child might fancy himself dead, to avenge himself on his parents. But even the novel ostensibly based on his own life belies that fantasy. Little Oliver, thrown into the company of criminals, is never really in danger of becoming one of them. Throughout the novel he is sharply distinguished from the others, in character, in appearance, and in that crucial class indicator, clothing. When Oliver runs away from the undertaker to whom he has been apprenticed, he is shabbily and meagerly dressed, but he manages to include in his little bundle a spare shirt and two pairs of stockings. Ragged, hungry, and footsore after a week of wandering, he is still not peculiar or strange-looking. The Artful Dodger, on the other hand, even in the eyes of Oliver, accustomed to the ragged children in the poorhouse, is "one of the queerest looking boys" he has ever seen.[27]

The gulf between pauperism and criminality, in the novel as in reality, is large although not unbridgeable. If some pauper children, like Noah Claypole, join the community of thieves, others, like Oliver, do not. So far from Fagin and Oliver being "alike if not identical" in their alienation from respectable society, Dickens made them utterly unlike. Oliver is not in the least alienated from respectable society; he is entirely at home in the company of the proper Mr. Brownlow and Mrs. Maylie. What he is alienated from, indeed repelled and terrified by, is the dark, dirty, dangerous underworld of the criminals. This is not a world of "outcasts" in anything like the sense in which that word might be used of paupers. Fagin is not an outcast from respectable society; he is an outcast from humanity. He has no redeeming qualities because he is not human. A "loathsome reptile, engendered in the slime and darkness through which he moved," he is, like that primordial creature, evil incarnate, a "villainy perfectly demoniacal."[28] He is as quintessentially vicious as the dying pauper child, who bids farewell to Oliver when he flees the workhouse, is quintessentially virtuous.*

Fagin and the saintly pauper child are extremes of type; they are what makes *Oliver Twist*, as Steven Marcus has said, a morality play more than a social novel.[29] It is because Dickens was more concerned with moral types than with social classes, because he defined social problems as essentially

---

*If Fagin was to some extent inspired by the real Ikey Solomons, the notorious fence, his name derived from a real Bob Fagin, the boy who befriended the young Charles Dickens in the blacking warehouse. That Dickens should have attached the name of that good-natured child to that evil old man has been a source of much speculation. The moralist might take it as a classic instance of that well-known maxim, "No good deed goes unpunished." The biographer and the social historian are reminded once again of the treacherous gap between fiction and reality.

moral problems, that the social implications of this novel (as of his others) are not as unequivocal, and the class distinctions not as decisive, as some critics might like. While some pauper children are too good to be true (indeed, too good to live), others (like Noah Claypole) are clearly "bad 'uns." Even the poor-law officials are not all of a kind; the magistrate who prevents Oliver from being apprenticed to the odious chimney sweep is kindly and humane—if also somewhat senile, but it is this that saves him from the cruel rationality of the other authorities. And it is another inmate of the workhouse, not the matron, who robs Oliver's mother on her deathbed. Oliver's half-brother, Monks, better born and bred than Oliver, is an evil man, bearing the brand of the social outcast and eventually suffering the fate of the outcast, while Oliver, an illegitimate child born and raised in the workhouse, is the true, natural gentleman. Character is evidently more important than class in distinguishing heroes from villains.

If there is no simple social message to be drawn from the class status of the characters, neither is there from the theme of the novel. Published in 1837–38, *Oliver Twist* was a powerful indictment of the New Poor Law, a law that gave the poor, as Dickens said in that much-quoted passage, the alternative "of being starved by a gradual process in the house, or by a quick one out of it."[30] In more subtle ways, however, the book affirmed and validated one of the principles that inspired the law. The law was meant to separate the pauper from the independent poor so as to prevent the pauperization of the poor; by the same token, the pauper had to be separated from the criminal to prevent the dependent class from becoming a dangerous class. The workhouse may have seemed to Dickens and others like a prison, in some respects worse than a prison. But it was meant to keep the pauper out of prison, to give him an alternative to a life of crime. For all of Dickens's hatred of the workhouse and the new poor law, he was as insistent as any reformer, as insistent as Chadwick himself, on the need to distinguish the pauper from the criminal, to separate, physically and conceptually, the unfortunate victim of circumstances from the willful villain, Oliver from Fagin.

In his provocative, oddly querulous essay on Dickens, George Orwell mocked G. K. Chesterton's characterization of Dickens as "the spokesman of the poor." Chesterton had called Sam Weller "the great symbol in English literature of the populace peculiar to England"—Sam Weller, Orwell protested, who was "a valet!" Orwell suspected that Dickens knew as little about the poor as Chesterton did. "He is vaguely on the side of the working class—has a sort of generalised sympathy with them because they are oppressed—but he does not in reality know much about them; they came into his books chiefly as servants, and comic servants at that." And not even "modern" servants. Sam Weller is so much the "feudal" type of servant that he offered to work without wages, deliberately got arrested in order to serve his master in jail, and was so lacking in a proper sense of class as to sit down in his master's presence. This "idealised" view of the servant, Orwell suggested, was perhaps all Dickens could envisage in a world where domestic service took the place of labor-saving devices. "Without a high level of mechanical development, human equality is not practically possible; Dickens goes to show that it is not imaginable either."[31]

If equality was "not imaginable" to Dickens, it was for reasons other than technology. The idea that "human equality" was dependent on "mechanical development" was precisely the kind of mechanistic, utilitarian thinking he despised. He had no difficulty imagining the idea of equality; he simply refused to make equality the measure of human worth and dignity. Though the servants in his novels are not the social equals of their masters, this in no way degrades or dehumanizes them. Sam Weller has a powerful sense of dignity and a lively, indeed peculiarly modern sense of his rights. When Pickwick proposes to engage him, Weller insists on spelling out carefully the terms of employment, a parody of a businessman negotiating a contract. It is he who takes the initiative by putting the questions to his prospective employer:

> "Wages?" inquired Sam.
> "Twelve pounds a year," replied Mr. Pickwick.
> "Clothes?"
> "Two suits."
> "Work?"
> "To attend upon me; and travel about with me and these gentlemen here."
> "Take the bill down," said Sam emphatically. "I'm let to a single gentleman, and the terms is agreed upon."[32]

Only later, when he has come to appreciate Pickwick as a human being as well as a generous employer, does he offer to work without wages in jail. He does this in a spirit of friendship rather than servitude; there is little or no service required of him in jail, except to initiate Pickwick into the strange mores of prison life. (There was nothing peculiar about having a servant in jail; Dickens's own family took a servant girl with them when they were committed to Marshalsea prison.)

So far from being a caricature of the feudal servant who knows his place, Sam Weller is a caricature of the independent, irreverent servant who does not know his place, who can even fancy himself a gentleman. Shortly after their acquaintance, Sam has occasion to tell Pickwick something of his background. Before being a bootboy, he had been a waggoner's boy and before that a carrier's boy. "Now I'm a gen'l'm'n's servant. I shall be a gen'l'm'n myself one of these days, perhaps, with a pipe in my mouth, and a summer-house in the back garden. Who knows? I shouldn't be surprised, for one."[33] (Nor would "jolly" Mark Tapley, in *Martin Chuzzlewit,* have been surprised. First a hostler at The Blue Dragon Inn, then Martin Chuzzlewit's servant, he returns from America to marry the innkeeper and become the proprietor of the inn, renamed The Jolly Tapley.) If Sam is a caricature, it is of a type rather than a class, and a more human type than some of Dickens's upper class caricatures—Lord Decimus Tite Barnacle, for example, the high official in the Circumlocution Office in *Little Dorrit,* who is entirely defined by his calling, satirized solely in terms of his occupation.

If there is hardly a novel by Dickens that does not have its quota of servants, this itself was a reflection of the social reality. By the middle of the century no fewer than 1,000,000 people, of a total population of 18,000,000, were domestic servants. They were the largest single group of employed people after the agricultural laborers, thus a considerable portion of the poor. When *Punch* seemed obsessed with the "servant problem," it was because its middle class readers were. But that problem was more urgent for the lower classes, many of whom were servants for at least part of their lives, or had parents, children, or other relatives in service. There were even working class families, themselves barely above the servant class, who managed to keep a much overworked and underpaid maid-of-all-work. At a time when, as Orwell said, the slavey drudging in the basement kitchen was "too normal to be noticed,"[34] it was surely to Dickens's credit that he did notice her and made so much of her. His servants, instead of being a distraction and irrelevancy, are a reminder of how important a part of the poor they were—and how varied. Apart from such major characters as Sam Weller, Mrs. Peggotty, and Mark Tapley, there are a host of minor but memorable ones: Sloppy, the "love-child," brought up in the poorhouse, given a home by Betty Higden, the washerwoman, and then sent into service with the Boffins; the "orfling" girl who works for the Micawbers and is distinguished chiefly by her habit of snorting; Susan Nipper, Florence Dombey's maid, who boldly stands up to the master of the house and then marries the rich, amiable, dotty Mr. Toots; and dozens of others occupying every kind of position, in every kind of household, in all sorts of conditions and circumstances.

The conventional image of the model Victorian servant is like that of the model Victorian child, silent, invisible, and dutiful. He entered rooms without knocking as if his presence were unnoticeable, conversation went on in his hearing as if he were deaf, he was privy to all the family's secrets because he could be counted on to be loyal and discreet. Dickens's servants are of another species. They are visible, vocal, and frequently "uppity." They are conscious of themselves and others are conscious of them. They live lives of their own and often impinge dramatically on the lives of others. By creating such outsized characters, Dickens helped rescue from oblivion those among the poor who, as Orwell rightly said, were too often out of sight and out of mind.

Orwell complained that there was no proletariat in Dickens's novels, that if a reader were asked which "proletarian characters" he remembered, he would almost certainly mention Bill Sikes, Sam Weller, and Mrs. Gamp— a burglar, a valet, and a drunken midwife.[35] The complaint was an old one, going back at least to George Gissing in the late nineteenth century, who found many "poor people" but not a single "representative wage-earner" outside of *Hard Times,* and this he judged the least successful of Dickens's novels. "The working class," he concluded, "is not Dickens's field, even in London."[36] A few years later Louis Cazamian, in what is still one of the best books on the English social novel, addressed the same question. "If Dickens could make his poor characters alive, and give them a striking realism even while he romanticized them, precisely who were these representatives of the poor?" Cazamian's answer was that the poor whom Dickens found most attractive, whom he celebrated as the glory of England, came from the "lower middle class." It was they who practiced the "philosophy of Christmas"—love, charity, generosity, warmth, good humor.[37]

Typical of that lower middle class, according to Cazamian, are the Cratchits. They are "poor and needy," the family of eight subsisting on the father's salary of 15 shillings a week, supplemented by a few shillings earned by his daughter as a milliner's apprentice. They live "in a very small way" in a four-room house in Camden Town, suffer their privations cheerfully, make the best of their world, and are altogether admirable specimens of their class and of mankind. If Bob Cratchit's occupation as Scrooge's clerk qualifies him as a member of the lower middle class, his daughter, a milliner's apprentice, should surely be counted in the working class (unless, as a secondary contributor to the family income, her work is discounted). But whatever class a clerk might be said to belong to (an occupation that is a problem for sociologists even today), in terms of income the Cratchit family, with eight mouths to feed on little more than a pound a week, was below the level of most working class families of the time.*

The other examples of this type fit even more awkwardly into the lower middle class—the Nubbles family, for example, in *The Old Curiosity Shop.* Mrs. Nubbles is a widow who takes in laundry to support herself

---

*The average unskilled industrial worker at the time earned 18 shillings or more, the average skilled worker in the cotton industry 20 to 25 shillings, and the London artisan between 25 and 40 shillings.[38] These are rough averages for individual workers. A family having more than one worker would have a higher family income, often considerably higher than that of the Cratchits.

and her three children, the oldest child, Kit, contributing the few shillings he earns as an errand boy. The reader is introduced to her at midnight when she is still hard at work, having been at it, we are told, since morning; Kit, having just returned from work, is having his supper. Later in the novel, after Kit loses his job (through no fault of his own), he earns some pennies minding horses, in the course of which he meets the Garlands, who offer to take him in as a servant and give him board, lodging, and the munificent sum, it seems to him, of £6 a year. Delighted with his new home, a little thatched cottage in Finchley, he is still prouder of his own family's modest home. "Was there ever such comfort in poverty," the author comments, "as in the poverty of Kit's family, if any correct judgment might be arrived at, from his own glowing account?"[39] Eventually, after many misfortunes (including the memorable death of Little Nell) and some simple pleasures (an outing to the circus), Kit marries the Garlands' other servant and leaves their service for a "good post," presumably another domestic position.

The Nubbleses are a perfect example of the kind of family Dickens most admired—warm, spontaneous, cheerful, good-natured, devoted to each other, eminently deserving of each other's love and of everyone's respect. But surely by no stretch of the imagination can they be regarded as lower middle class. The hardworking widow washing and ironing from morning until midnight, her son earning what he can at odd jobs or domestic employment and overjoyed with an annual wage of £6—surely these are of the lower ranks of the working classes.

The Peggottys are another such family. Clara Peggotty is Mrs. Copperfield's servant, not a pampered lady's maid but a maid-of-all-work. While she is on the most intimate relations with her mistress and spends her evenings in her company, quite like one of the family, she occupies her time even then sewing. (One of David Copperfield's strongest memories is of the touch of her pin-pricked fingers, "like a pocket nutmeg-grater.")[40] Her marriage to Mr. Barkis, the carrier, she explains to David, means that she will be "independent," able to work in her own house instead of as a "servant to a stranger."[41] Although Barkis manages to put away a considerable sum of money (he leaves £3,000 at his death), Peggotty ends the novel as she began, as a servant still working away at her needlework. The other Peggottys are in more modest circumstances. Daniel, Clara's brother, is a simple, hardworking fisherman, rough but ready, as he describes himself. The fact that he owns his own boat does not make him less poor, any more than it did his partner, Mr. Gummidge, who "died very poor."[42] To Orwell the Peggottys "hardly belong to the working class."[43] But Emily, their niece, has a different sense of it. "Your father," she tells David on their first meeting, "was a gentleman, and your mother is a lady; and my father was a fisherman, and my mother was a fisherman's daughter, and my uncle Dan is a fisherman."[44]*

And so too some of the other supposedly lower middle class characters: Polly Toodle, Paul Dombey's nurse, and her husband, a stoker on steam engines who can neither read nor write and is pleased to be offered the job of engine-fireman on the railroad; or Charley, the thirteen-year-old girl in *Bleak House* who does washing to earn a few "sixpences and shillings" to support her younger brother and sister, before she has the good fortune to be taken on as a maid and taught to write (which she does with the greatest difficulty). There is nothing lower middle class about them, not their occupations, or conditions of life, or pretensions, or aspirations.

Although Cazamian distinguished between the "proletarian" and the "non-industrial working class," it is interesting that he did not avail himself of this last category to describe the Peggottys, Nubbleses, Toodles, and the others.[45] Perhaps this is because he assumed that the "working classes" constituted the "social problem" and therefore must have been miserable and discontented. The families so lovingly portrayed by Dickens do not think of themselves and are not thought of by others as a social problem. They are happy, warm, cheerful, respectful and self-respecting, devoted to their families and satisfied with their jobs, making their way, in their own way, in the society in which they find themselves (hence Dickens's famous happy endings)—all this while being "poor and needy." Because these poor families defy the conventional image of a pauperized, alienated working class, Cazamian assigned them to a class with a more benign image, a "lower middle class," which is not so much a class as an amorphous category to accommodate those who are not problematic, not wretched or alienated.

Contemporaries had their own terms for these people, not "lower middle class" or "non-industrial working class," but "lower classes," "lower orders," the "poor," or, more specifically, the "deserving poor."† If one does not think of Dickens as celebrating the deserving poor, it is because "deserving" has been given a bad name, as if to be deserving is to be calculatingly, grudgingly, joylessly virtuous. So perhaps it was for some of Dickens's contemporaries. Chadwick may not have approved of the Nubbleses' outing

---

*David Copperfield's mother—a "lady," as Emily calls her—was an orphan who had worked as a nursery governess before her first marriage. The governess had an anomalous position in Victorian society, a servant in one sense, but a very special kind of servant since this was one of the few occupations open to the well-bred lady fallen upon bad times. Even after her marriage, Mrs. Copperfield was a rather impoverished lady, employing only one servant when she was widowed and living on an annuity of £105 a year.

†"Lower orders" had become less common by the 1840s, but it was by no means unusual. The reviewer of *The Chimes* who used that phrase in 1844 meant nothing demeaning by it when he said that Dickens "first drew those admirable portraits of the poor—called lower orders—which have rendered his name so truly dear to every lover of his country."[46]

to the circus or the Cratchits' Christmas "feasting"; certainly Gradgrind and Bounderby would not have approved. But even Chadwick could not have asked more of them by way of hard work, a spirit of independence, and—the epitome of these virtues—cleanliness. It is with the eye of a superior housewife that Dickens observes that Cratchit's threadbare garments are "darned up and brushed" in readiness for the Christmas dinner, and that after the feast, "the cloth was cleared, the hearth swept."[47] The old barge in which Daniel Peggotty and his assorted dependents live is "beautifully clean inside and as tidy as possible."[48] When Susan Nipper finally locates Polly Toodle in her new home, she is ushered into a "clean parlour full of children."[49] Little Charley, who has the compulsive habit of "folding up everything she could lay her hands on," is complimented on the exemplary state of the sickroom, "so fresh and airy, so spotless and neat."[50] The Nubbleses, the poorest of them all, live in a house that is "an extremely poor and homely place, but with that air of comfort about it, nevertheless, which—or the spot must be a wretched one indeed—cleanliness and order can always impart to some degree."[51]

The repeated refrain, "cleanliness and order," comes oddly from Dickens—not quite in keeping, one might think, with the joyousness and spontaneity he valued so highly. Yet if Dickens could make so much of these virtues, one should perhaps be more tolerant of those reformers and philanthropists who tirelessly harped on them. In the Victorian version of the Puritan ethic, cleanliness was next to industriousness and temperance, a not unreasonable set of priorities in the circumstances. In their mean and cramped quarters, it was only by the greatest effort of cleanliness and orderliness that the poor could make their homes livable. The symbol of the hearth in Dickens's work has often been commented on; it is the symbol of the family, of warmth and brightness, intimacy and devotion. Poverty might sometimes extinguish the fire in the hearth, but the hearth remains as the center of the family. And a clean hearth means that it is being tended, that someone cares enough to make that effort, so that whatever other misfortunes strike, the family is united and sustained (so unlike Dickens's unhappy memories of his own family).

Dickens himself may not have used the expression "deserving poor." It was redolent of the kinds of reformers he despised: the utilitarians who thought the poor deserving only when they led lives that were as crabbed and joyless as their own, or the "telescopic philanthropists" who found the natives of Borrioboola-Gha more deserving of attention and assistance than the poor in their own backyards (or than their own families, for that matter).[52] Dickens's deserving poor are hardworking, sober (but not teetotalers—theirs is the time-honored drink of the poor, beer or ale, not gin), independent, honest, chaste, clean, orderly—and at the same time lively, spirited, good-humored, and good-natured. In Dickens's moral economy, these virtues were domesticated and socialized, serving the welfare of family and friends rather than of the individual, and exercised naturally, spontaneously, not dutifully and self-righteously. The reformers might have objected to Dickens's representation of themselves, but not to his representation of the class that was his constituency as much as theirs—the independent, respectable, moral poor.

"It is Dickens's delight in grotesque and rich exaggeration which has made him, I think, nearly useless in the present day." This was John Ruskin writing to his friend Charles Eliot Norton just after Dickens's death.[53] Much of the exaggeration Ruskin complained of had to do with Dickens's portraits of another group of poor, neither the admirable Cratchits and Nubbleses nor the despicable Sikes and Fagin, but an assortment of bizarre characters, strange-looking, strange-speaking, and above all engaged in strange occupations—sometimes grotesque in their strangeness, sometimes picturesque or quaintly amusing.

Almost all his novels have such types, but none in such profusion as *Our Mutual Friend*. The powerful opening scene tantalizingly introduces one of the more memorable characters, a boatman, we are told, who is neither fisherman, nor waterman, nor lighterman, nor river-carrier, a man who is not rowing the boat (a girl is doing that) but only holding the rudder, staring intently at the river, trying to penetrate below the "slime and ooze" on its surface. The man is "half savage," bare-chested, his hair matted, his dress seemingly made out of the same mud that begrimes the boat. A sudden flash of light dimly illuminates, in the bottom of the boat, a "rotten stain" resembling a human form. The boatman is finally identified as Gaffer Hexam, a dredgerman, and the object in the boat as a dead man fished out of the Thames. The horror of the scene is highlighted by the matter-of-fact argument between Gaffer and another dredgerman about the morality of robbing a dead man compared with robbing a live one, and by Gaffer's rebuke to his daughter Lizzie, who is terrified by the body and by the river that yielded it. The river, he reminds her, is her best friend; the fire that warmed her when she was a baby, the basket she slept in, the rockers of her cradle, were all flotsam picked out of the water.

It has been said that the main character in *Our Mutual Friend* is the Thames, and much has been made of the symbol of the river coursing through the city, carrying with it the filth and refuse of London, the remains of all the dirty secrets and criminal acts which tainted the lives of everyone coming in contact with it. When Lionel Trilling spoke of the "actuality of the symbols" in Dickens's work, he mentioned the sewage in the Thames which was so sensibly, compellingly present in the consciousness of contemporaries.* What they were also conscious of were the men who made their living out of that "ooze and scum," hauling out the flotsam of wood which might be used for firewood or a baby's cradle, or the occasional corpse which could be turned in for a reward after the pockets had been picked. Whatever symbolic value might be attached to that occupation, there is no doubt that the symbol was solidly rooted in reality, and that it was better able to bear that symbolic burden because of that reality. Gaffer had a worthy confrere in the dredger interviewed by Mayhew, who insisted that there was nothing bizarre or repulsive in his job. He even defended himself, as Gaffer did, against the charge that it was dishonest to rifle the pockets of a dead man. Where Mayhew's dredger merely argued that he had a better right to the money than the police who would otherwise appropriate it, Gaffer's little speech has the echo of Shylock:

> "What world does a dead man belong to? T'other world. What world does money belong to? This world. How can money be a corpse's? Can a corpse own it, want it, spend it, claim it, miss it?"[55]

The recent revival of interest in Mayhew has drawn attention to the Mayhewian types in Dickens's novels, suggesting to some scholars that Dickens may have borrowed these characters from Mayhew.[56] There is no hard evidence of this, no reference to Mayhew in Dickens's writings, and no copy of *London Labour and the London Poor* in his library (which did contain other books on London). Yet Dickens evidently knew Mayhew personally. He was a friend of Horace Mayhew, Henry's brother, and of others in the *Punch* circle; they wrote for the same journals (although not at the same time—Dickens had been a reporter for the *Morning Chronicle* in the mid-thirties and wrote occasionally for it later); they even once appeared in the same amateur theatrical production. An avid reader of newspapers, Dickens must have come across Mayhew's work at one time or another. Yet even when the parallels between them are most striking, it is by no means clear that Mayhew was the source; on some occasions the reverse is at least as probable. Mayhew's initial article in the *Morning Chronicle* was a report on the cholera epidemic in that notorious slum,

---

*In June 1858 the stench from the river was such as to cause a rapid evacuation of the Houses of Parliament. *The Times,* whose offices must have been afflicted by the same stench, described the men rushing out of a committee room, "foremost among them being the Chancellor of the Exchequer [Disraeli], who, with a mass of papers in one hand and with his pocket handkerchief clutched in the other, and applied closely to his nose, with body half bent, hastened in dismay from the pestilential odour, followed closely by Sir James Graham, who seemed to be attacked by a sudden fit of expectoration." A fortnight later Disraeli introduced a bill for the financing of new sewage drains —eleven years after the establishment of the Metropolitan Commission of Sewers for that purpose.[54]

Jacob's Island, which owed its notoriety in large part to Dickens, for it was there, in "the filthiest, the strangest, the most extraordinary of the many localities that are hidden in London," that Bill Sikes met his gruesome death.[57] It may well have been the memory of that powerful scene in *Oliver Twist* (next to *Pickwick Papers,* Dickens's most popular novel) that caused Mayhew to select Jacob's Island as the locale for his *Morning Chronicle* piece.

On the basis of chronology alone, one might suppose that *Our Mutual Friend* was heavily indebted to Mayhew, this novel (Dickens's last completed one) coinciding with the reprint of Mayhew's volumes in 1864–65. But this is to consider the two works in isolation, divorced from the social reality as well as from the whole of contemporary literature reflecting that reality—the newspapers, journals, and Mayhewian exposés of London life which proliferated in the fifties. Dickens did not have to go to Mayhew for the unsavory details of Gaffer's occupation; the recovery of dead bodies from the Thames was regularly reported in the papers, together with the amount of the reward and details about the clothing and state of the body. Nor did he need Mayhew for the model of Noddy Boffin, the dustman who inherited three dustheaps worth £100,000; it was common knowledge that several London dust-contractors were exceedingly wealthy. Nor did he need him for all the other "Mayhewian" characters in *Our Mutual Friend:* Mr. Venus, the seller of stuffed animals and birds; Betty Higden, the laundress whose fear of dying in the workhouse makes her take to the road and become an itinerant seller; the professional begging-letter writers who besiege Boffin with their importunities; Jenny Wren, the doll's dressmaker. Henry James criticized Dickens for making so outlandish a character of Jenny Wren;[58] but he could have made her even more outlandish by giving her the occupation of two of Mayhew's real-life characters who specialized in making doll's eyes. One critic, locating the prototype of Betty Higden in the "pure-finder" (dung-collector) in *London Labour* who had an obsessive fear of the workhouse, regards it as significant that Dickens, in order to create a paragon of the "deserving poor," felt obliged to transform a dung-collector into a washerwoman, thus purifying, so to speak, the pure-finder.[59] Since the only point of resemblance between this pure-finder and the laundress is their dread of the workhouse, it seems improbable that Dickens, who had done as much as any single person to discredit the workhouse, had to draw upon Mayhew for an example of a poor old woman fearful of "the House."*

---

*Another of Mayhew's characters cited as the "source" and "inspiration" of Dickens is the marine-store (used-goods) dealer in *London Labour* who is said to resemble Krook, another marine-store dealer, in *Bleak House.* [60] But Mayhew himself, earlier in that volume, had quoted a long passage from Dickens which included a description of a marine-store dealer and his shop. That passage (not identified by Mayhew) was the better part of one of the *Sketches by Boz* published more than a dozen

If there are dozens of Mayhewian characters in Dickens's novels—or Dickensian ones in Mayhew's work—it is because such characters were a conspicuous part of the London scene, conspicuous quite out of proportion to their actual numbers. Long before *London Labour and the London Poor,* even before *The London Charivari* (better known as *Punch*), Dickens had established himself as the chronicler and celebrant of the streets of London. Most of the *Sketches by Boz* deal with some aspect of London street life, featuring costermongers, cab drivers, old-clothes dealers, street vendors, street performers, street laborers and street walkers (in both senses). And Cruikshank's illustrations include a breakfast cart in the street in the early morning, a quarrelsome crowd at Seven Dials, clothes strung along the shop fronts on Monmouth Street, a First-of-May street festival. The most prominent street character is Boz himself, the indefatigable wanderer, observer, and commentator, who refers to himself in the first-person-plural but who puts his singular stamp upon this vista of London street life. If one were looking for the inspiration of Mayhew's work, one might be tempted to find it here, in Boz's description of his "amateur vagrancy" in that "unknown region" of London.

> We have a most extraordinary partiality for lounging about the streets. Whenever we have an hour or two to spare, there is nothing we enjoy more than a little amateur vagrancy—walking up one street and down another, and staring into shop windows, and gazing about as if, instead of being on intimate terms with every shop and house in Holborn, the Strand, Fleet-street and Cheapside, the whole were an unknown region to our wandering mind.[63]

There are echoes of Boz in all of Dickens's work, even in a novel like *Dombey and Son* which takes place in the dark and gloom of the counting-house. The house fronts on a street which every morning witnesses a procession of street-folk: "the water-carts and the old-clothes men, and the people with geraniums, and the umbrella-mender, and the man who trilled the little bell of the Dutch clock as he went along."[64] One of the more dramatic episodes involves the odious "Good Mrs. Brown," the ugly, old, ragged woman carrying rabbit skins over her arm, who accosts little Florence, takes her to her home (a hovel crammed with rags, old clothes, bones, dust, and cinders), robs her of her clothes, and refrains from cutting off her hair only because of the memory of her own long-lost daughter.[65] That

---

years earlier. If there is any suspicion of "inspiration," it could well be Mayhew who was inspired by "Boz."[61] Another bit of "conclusive external evidence" that Dickens was familiar with Mayhew's work is the supposedly "uncanny echo" of Mayhew in *Little Dorrit,* where Dickens described the extremes of luxury and poverty that coexisted in London—a theme that was one of the set pieces of every commentary on London.[62]

cameo sketch is the archetype of the Mayhewian street-finder, for whom every conceivable object, including human hair, was a source of trade. The fourth volume of *London Labour* (published fourteen years after *Dombey and Son*) had an entire category corresponding to Mrs. Brown: "child stripping," an occupation of "old debauched drunken hags who watch their opportunity to accost children passing in the street, tidily dressed with good boots and clothes." In 1860 ninety-seven such cases were reported.[66]

Much has been written about Dickens's image of himself as a poor, undernourished, neglected child roaming the streets of London at night, making his way, like the thieves in *Oliver Twist,* through the "cold wet shelterless midnight streets," or, like David Copperfield, wearing down the cobblestones in his daily walk from the warehouse in Blackfriars to Micawber's prison in Southwark.[67] At its worst the city appears, in this image, as a black, mysterious, dangerous place, a maze where every turning conceals some impending horror; at its best as foggy, gray, melancholy, anonymous, callous, materialistic. This is the city of the ragged and dangerous classes, the "unknown country" exposed to view again and again only to remain obstinately, frighteningly unknown, a London where, in the words of one of Dickens's reviewers, "one half of mankind lives without knowing how the other half dies," where the inhabitants are "as human, at least to all appearances, as are the Esquimaux or the Russians, and probably (though the Zoological Society will not vouch for it) endowed with souls."[68]

But there is another London celebrated by Dickens, a familiar and friendly country where men embark on adventures knowing they will turn out well and where even misadventures are more often comic than tragic. *Pickwick Papers* is not usually regarded as a "social novel" because it is not usually identified with the "social problem," the problem of the working classes. In one sense, it is the most middle class of Dickens's novels. Samuel Pickwick, Esq., Augustus Snodgrass, Esq., Nathaniel Winkle, Esq., and the other members of the club are not rich, certainly not "upper class," but their means are sufficient to support them in retirement and permit them to indulge their hobby of travel. The casual description of Pickwick, offered well into the book, as a retired businessman and a "gentleman of considerable independent property," is probably an exaggeration (it is provided by his defense counsel to establish his respectability).[69] He lives modestly in a small apartment in Mrs. Bardell's house in Goswell Street, not a fashionable part of London, and is attended to by her and, later, by Sam Weller. Yet those contemporary reviewers who made a point of class associated the book with the lower classes, and specifically with the lower classes of London, although much of the action takes place on the open road and in country inns and houses. The *Quarterly Review* attributed its success to Dickens's felicity in conveying "the genuine mother-wit and unadulterated vernacular idiom of the lower classes of London." And Lytton Bulwer praised him for depicting the "humors of the lower orders of London" with the precision and comic effect of a Teniers, the seventeenth century Flemish painter famous for his scenes of peasant life.[70]

It is, of course, Sam Weller who dominates the book and gives it the appearance of being about the "lower orders of London." Until his arrival in the fourth number, the serial, in spite of an extensive publicity campaign, had sold poorly and reviews had been less than enthusiastic. After his appearance sales dramatically improved, and by the end of the serial in 1837, 40,000 of each number were sold. Where Orwell saw Weller as a parody of a feudal servant, contemporaries saw him as the epitome of the Cockney, the lower class Londoner who was the true urban aborigine. Accompanying the Pickwickians on their travels, he puts the impress of London on all of England, making the entire country a provincial outpost of the metropolis. It is his voice and spirit, the primitive, untutored, caustic wit of the Londoner born and bred within the sound of Bow Bells, that give the novel its distinctive tone and vitality. The relationship of Pickwick and Weller is not that of benevolent master and obsequious servant—Weller is, in fact, independent to the point of impertinence—but that of the naïve, bumbling, genial master and the shrewd, articulate, world-wise (street-wise, we would now say) servant.

Mary Mitford expressed a common view of *Pickwick Papers:* "It is fun —London Life—but without anything unpleasant: a lady might read it all *aloud;* and it is so graphic, so individual, and so true, that you could curtsey to all the people as you met them in the streets."[71] Yet even here there are intimations of the "dark side" of Dickens, in the tragic stories of the dying clown and his destitute family, the convict who broke his mother's heart and then killed his father, the man ruined by a long legal suit, the debtor in prison watching his child and wife die in poverty and later cruelly exacting his vengeance. These bitter tales presage an unhappy turn in the plot when Pickwick is imprisoned and discovers what Weller and his kind have always known: that even in prison there are vast differences between the classes, some enjoying prison as a "regular holiday . . . all porter and skittles," while others pine away in misery and despair. Weller, as usual, delivers the final word: " 'It's unekal,' as my father used to say wen his grog warn't made half-and-half; 'It's unekal, and that's the fault on it.' "[72]

If this is not the message most readers took from the book, if *Pickwick Papers* was not read as a social novel in this sense, as an exposé of the unequal conditions in prison or the inequities of the legal system, it is because this and other episodes function as tragic relief in an otherwise comic tale. Looking at *Pickwick Papers* from the perspective of Dickens's later novels, one may be inclined to reverse the ratio of comedy and tragedy, to read the comic as sardonic, to find the good humor forced, fraught with despair. Such a reading may appeal to the modern literary sensibility, but it violates the contemporary sensibility. To contemporaries, *Pickwick Papers* took place in a familiar society, "unekal," often unjust, sometimes tragic, but basically decent, hopeful, and humane. What makes the Pickwickian world a place of good cheer, for the Wellers of that world as well as the Pickwicks, is the promise of freedom rather than equality. As the Thames casts its malignant spell over the London of *Our Mutual Friend,* so the road is the dominant and benign symbol of *Pickwick Papers.* And not, as one might think, because it permits men to escape from the evil city. When the coach makes its way through the streets of London, they are not the dark, treacherous alleys that terrify Oliver Twist, nor the gloomy back streets that oppress David Copperfield; they are well-lit, cheerful thoroughfares where a Miss Mitford might well curtsey to everyone she meets. For Pickwick and his friends, the open road is a release not from the prison of the city but from the bonds of a prosaic, routinized, if comfortable and decent, existence.

Today Pickwickians of both classes—Pickwick and his friends, Sam Weller and his—are regarded as picaresque characters, romantic fantasies, "quasi-mythical" creatures who, as Steven Marcus put it, represent a form of "transcendence," a vision of the "ideal possibilities of human relations."[73] At the time they appeared in a very different guise, as perfectly ordinary people of middle and low rank, of no special distinction except their great good will and good humor. Reviewers spoke of them as "droll," "comic," "original," "curious," "whimsical"; and at the same time as "realistic," "true," "natural," "veritable," "actual." "All of it," John Forster said, "is real life and human nature. It is not a collection of humorous or pathetic dialogues about people who have no tangible existence in mind; but it is a succession of actual scenes, the actors of which take up a place in the memory."[74] Even Thackeray, who was not always generous to his rivals, praised it for portraying "true characters under false names," and for giving a "better idea of the state and ways of the people than one could gather from any more pompous or authentic histories."[75]

One does not know what the butcher-boy, the footman, the maidservant, and the chimney sweep—those whom George Lewes saw reading the latest issue of *Pickwick Papers*[76]—made of it, whether they too thought Sam's wit and dialect true to life, to their own life. If they did not, if they enjoyed it as fantasy, it was evidently a fantasy much to their liking, which is itself a social fact of some importance. At least as important is the fact that other readers thought that Dickens captured the idiom and image of the lower classes, perhaps, one reviewer conceded, in a slightly "heightened" but still realistic and "veritable" form.[77] It is interesting that throughout the period when the Newgate and Gothic novels were popular, indeed when Dickens himself was exploiting those themes, *Pickwick Papers* continued to be reissued and reread, as if to provide an antidote to that other, more forbidding and dangerous image of the poor.

All the earlier novels have "dark" overtones, but none is as unrelievedly dark as *Hard Times.* This reflects both the subject of that novel and a sensibility that was becoming increasingly pessimistic, even tragic, about man's nature and fate. The working classes in *Hard Times* exemplify humanity *in extremis.* Coketown is "representative" of England, not in the sense that industrialism is typical of England (later, in *Our Mutual Friend,* that same dark sensibility pervades the pre-industrial world of the Thames bargeman), but in the sense that all problems, individual and social, become more acute under the conditions of industrialism. Industrialism is a microcosm of modernity; it magnifies those aspects of the modern world which Dickens found most disagreeable— its cold, calculating rationality, its impersonality and lack of community.

It is a familiar criticism of Dickens (in his own time and still more today) that in this novel, when he finally confronted the industrial problem, he was distracted by such extraneous issues as utilitarianism, education, marriage, and divorce.[78] To Dickens, however, these were not extraneous. For him the problem of industrialism was not that of an oppressed or exploited class, of inadequate wages or intolerable working and living conditions. What was at issue was the way people felt and thought about themselves and each other, their ability to understand, sympathize, suffer, enjoy, love, work. If the factory was oppressive, it was because it was destructive of these natural human emotions and experiences. And the factory was only the reflection of more grievous faults, of the crabbed spirit generated by a system of education designed to transform children into reasoning machines, by marriages held together by unjust laws and calculations of interest, and by a philosophy that decreed pleasure to be sinful and love illicit.

While he was working on the novel, Dickens presented Forster with a choice of titles.

1. According to Cocker.	2. Prove it.
3. Stubborn Things.	4. Mr. Gradgrind's Facts.
5. The Grindstone.	6. Hard Times.
7. Two and Two are Four.	8. Something Tangible.
9. Our Hard-headed Friend.	10. Rust and Dust.
11. Simple Arithmetic.	12. A Matter of Calculation.
13. A Mere Question of Figures.	14. The Gradgrind Philosophy.[79]

Forster chose 2, 6, and 11, whereupon Dickens admitted that he preferred 6, 13, and 14. Because 6 was the only one on which they both agreed, the novel became *Hard Times*. Were it not for that, the title might well be *A Mere Question of Figures* or *The Gradgrind Philosophy*, either of which would make utilitarianism rather than industrialism the main theme.

The dedication is also ambiguous. Asking Carlyle for permission to inscribe the novel to him, Dickens assured him that "it contained nothing in which you do not think with me."[80] The obvious assumption is that Dickens had in mind the condition-of-England question which Carlyle had done so much to popularize. Even in 1839, however, when Carlyle first raised that question, he gave it the largest connotation, making it a question of the moral and social as well as the material condition of the working classes, of a society that was increasingly materialistic and atomistic, and of a philosophy that reduced all human relations to calculations of interest and the "cash nexus." By 1854, when *Hard Times* was published, Carlyle had gone so far in his critique of that "pig philosophy" that he had alienated many of his earlier admirers (John Stuart Mill, most notably). To dedicate the book to him at this time was to dedicate it not only to the author of *Chartism* and *Past and Present* but to the author of "The Nigger Question" (published in 1849 and reprinted in 1853) and *Latter-Day Pamphlets* (1850), both of which were an uncompromising repudiation of every tenet of conventional liberalism.*

The opening words of *Hard Times* go to the very heart of the utilitarian temper, the spurious rationalism that Carlyle saw as the *fons et origo* of the modern disease.

> "Now, what I want is, Facts. Teach these boys and girls nothing but Facts. Facts alone are wanted in life. Plant nothing else, and root out everything else. You can only form the minds of reasoning animals upon Facts; nothing else will ever be of any service to them. This is the principle on which I bring up my own children, and this is the principle on which I bring up these children. Stick to Facts, sir!"[82]

It is Mr. Gradgrind, the schoolmaster, who delivers this memorable speech to his pupils and who dominates the opening chapters. The industrialist, Josiah Bounderby, is introduced only later, when he is identified not as the local mill owner but as a "rich man: banker, merchant, manufacturer, and what not"; and he makes his first appearance not in his factory in Coketown but in Gradgrind's house a mile or so out of town.[83]

Coketown comes into view somewhat later, as Gradgrind and Bounderby make their way into town.

*In the notorious Eyre case in 1865, in which Governor Eyre was charged with the brutal suppression of an uprising of Jamaican Negroes, Dickens, much to the consternation of the liberals, sided with Carlyle in defense of Eyre. Well before this, Dickens was more in agreement with Carlyle —the "late" Carlyle—than is generally thought. At the very time "The Nigger Question" was republished and while he himself was about to start *Hard Times,* he published an article in *Household Words* entitled "The Noble Savage" which savagely exposed that myth.[81]

It was a town of red brick, or of brick that would have been red if the smoke and ashes had allowed it; but as matters stood it was a town of unnatural red and black like the painted face of a savage. It was a town of machinery and tall chimneys, out of which interminable serpents of smoke trailed themselves for ever and ever, and never got uncoiled. It had a black canal in it, and a river that ran purple with ill-smelling dye, and vast piles of buildings full of windows where there was a rattling and a trembling all day long, and where the piston of the steam-engine worked monotonously up and down like the head of an elephant in a state of melancholy madness.[84]

This is the familiar description of the textile town—dark, dirty, noisy, smoky, smelly—and the familiar prelude to an attack on the factory system. The emphasis soon shifts, however, and the great evil, of the town as of the factory (which is described only once, and then briefly), becomes not the pollution of the atmosphere but the pall of utilitarianism that hangs over Coketown. Everything is "severely workfull." The chapel resembles the warehouse, the jail looks like the infirmary, the town hall and the school are indistinguishable from the rest. The factory itself as it appears here is more a monument to fact than to industry, less a means of production than a mode of behavior and attitude of mind, a routinized, rationalized, fact-ualized institution, the incarnation of the spirit of the town. "Fact, fact, fact, everywhere in the material aspect of the town; fact, fact, fact, everywhere in the immaterial."[85]

When Gradgrind and Bounderby walk to town, their destination is the public house where Sissy, one of Gradgrind's pupils, lives with her father. There they meet some of the members of the circus troupe to which Sissy's father belongs. Thus the reader is introduced to the circus people before meeting a single factory worker. The circus folk are yet another variety of street-folk—"vagabonds," "strollers," "comers and goers," "queer," "rakish and knowing," "not at all orderly in their domestic arrangements," peculiarly dressed, and speaking a language so strange as to be almost incomprehensible to Gradgrind and Bounderby.[86] What is most disturbing to the worthies of Coketown is the troupers' attitude to work. It is not that they are idlers; like the other street-folk, the circus people work as hard as ordinary folk. (When Bounderby and Gradgrind meet Sissy in the street, she is bringing a bottle of "nine oils" to her father to soothe the bruises he has acquired in the ring.) But they are workers of another species, working outdoors, at their own pace, at activities of their own choice, in keeping with their own instincts and skills. Bounderby explains the difference between them: "We are the kind of people who know the value of time, and you are the kind of people who don't know the value of time." One of the circus men amends this: "If you mean that you can make more money of your time than I can of mine, I should judge from your appearance, that you are about right."[87] The trouper's point is well taken. It is not that the circus people have no regard for time; on the contrary, time for them is of the essence. (Sissy's father has to leave the circus because he is "missing his tip," his timing is off.) It is only that they do not "value" their time, as Bounderby and his kind do, in terms of money.

In one sense the circus is obviously a counterpoint to the factory, the natural, graceful, spontaneous rhythm of the performers contrasting with the artificial, rationalized, mechanized rhythm of industry. The circus, however, is a supplement, not an alternative, to the factory. Had Dickens wanted to present such an alternative, he might have put Sissy's father on a farm, or in domestic industry, or in a traditional craft, or even in a model factory. By putting him in the circus he gave him a peripheral role in society, much like that of the street-folk. In other respects the circus people were quite unlike the street-folk. Where the latter were cunning and conniving and even the children precociously mature, the circus folk are above all "childish." The owner of the circus speaks with a pronounced childish lisp, and all of them display a "remarkable gentleness and childishness" which would have made them incapable of surviving on the streets of London. They are also utterly, unambiguously deserving—"deserving often of as much respect, and always of as much generous construction, as the everyday virtues of any class of people in the world."[88] Not more deserving; there is no intention of demeaning the "everyday virtues" of ordinary people. Nor are the circus folk meant to be a model for everyone else. Sissy's father, who loves her and wants the best for her, deliberately removes her from the circus and places her in Gradgrind's school, not knowing the exact nature of that school but knowing that some schooling, some education and maturation, will be good for her. The circus owner, also out of love for her, counsels her to return to the Gradgrinds, and Sissy acquiesces, remaining with them until she is old enough to go to work—in the factory, not in the circus.

The real counterpoint to the circus is not Bounderby's factory but Gradgrind's school, which tries to turn children into fact-grinding machines ("logic-chopping engines," as Carlyle described the youthful Mill).[89] The disaster is compounded when the adult world, the industrial, commercial world, adopting the same utilitarian philosophy, commits itself to a regimen of "facts, facts, facts," and adamantly opposes anything that smacks of the childish: pleasure, fantasy, imagination, playfulness, spontaneity, sentiment, love. The factory itself, Dickens implies, would be tolerable were not everything else in the town exactly like the factory. What is intolerable is the relentless sameness of everything—church, jail, hospital, town hall, school—everything "severely workfull." The circus helps relieve this utilitarian sameness, the deadly monotony of workaday life. It is a transient, marginal affair, a traveling circus set up temporarily on the outskirts of town, and not meant to have any more central or permanent status than that. That, however, is enough to make it an essential, if peripheral, part of society, recalling adults to the pleasures of childhood and keeping alive in them the spark of innocence without which adulthood would be unendurable.[90]

It is interesting that this idea of pleasure should appear in the context of an attack on utilitarianism. For "pleasure" was one of the key words in the Benthamite vocabulary, the maximization of pleasure and minimization of pain being the basis of the "felicific calculus." This was a special kind of pleasure, however, the equivalent of interest or utility, the antithesis of the playfulness and fancifulness that Dickens, and common usage, associated with the word.* In Freudian terms, one might say that Bentham's "pleasure" corresponded to the "reality principle" and Dickens's to the "pleasure principle." Dickens himself associated utilitarianism with a rigorous commitment to reality. When Mr. Gradgrind is first introduced, it is as a "man of realities."[92] And repeatedly "reality," like "fact," is invoked to describe the material, mechanical, utilitarian world of Gradgrind and Bounderby, a world without sensual pleasure or mental fancy, without romance or love, without any of the childish delights which make the adult world, the world of "everyday virtues," livable. Even to the rich (Miss Gradgrind, later Mrs. Bounderby) the deprivation of pleasure is spiritually impoverishing. To the poor, for whom reality is not merely tedious and joyless but oppressive and painful, that deprivation is fatal.

> Utilitarian economists, skeletons of schoolmasters, Commissioners of Fact, genteel and used-up infidels, gabblers of many little dog's-eared creeds, the poor you will have always with you. Cultivate in them, while there is yet time, the utmost graces of the fancies and affections, to adorn their lives so much in need of ornament; or, in the day of your triumph, when romance is utterly driven out of their souls, and they and a bare existence stand face to face, Reality will take a wolfish turn, and make an end of you.[93]

· · ·

The attack on "Utilitarian economists, skeletons of schoolmasters, Commissioners of Fact" has exposed Dickens to the charge of being "philistine" and

---

*Although Dickens was fully aware of the utilitarian perversion of the idea of pleasure, he did not make a point of the perverse use of the word itself. Disraeli, however, did. In an early, little known tale, "The Voyage of Captain Popanilla," he waxed satiric over the process of reasoning by which the utilitarian deduced that "pleasure is not pleasant."

> He did not imagine that the most barefaced hireling of corruption could for a moment presume to maintain that there was any utility in pleasure. If there were no utility in pleasure, it was quite clear that pleasure could profit no one. If, therefore, it were unprofitable, it was injurious; because that which does not produce a profit is equivalent to a loss; therefore pleasure is a losing business; consequently pleasure is not pleasant.[91]

"unenlightened."[94] The utilitarians, we are reminded, were the progressives of their time; they tirelessly urged the importance of facts in order to bring about social reform, and they were zealous in promoting education to enable the poor to better themselves.* (Gradgrind's own children are subjected to exactly the same educational and emotional regimen as Sissy and Bitzer.) A more common complaint is that Dickens was too "bourgeois" to appreciate the magnitude of the social problem, the true plight of the industrial worker. Not understanding the problem, he was unable to suggest anything by way of remedy except the weakest palliatives, and refused to ally himself with the one realistic, progressive force available at the time, the trade unions.[96]

In the novel, trade unionism fares not much better than utilitarianism. Slackbridge, the union organizer, is a fitting adversary for Bounderby, the employer; they are equally disagreeable and hypocritical, selfish and obdurate. Slackbridge's influence on the workers is thoroughly pernicious, his demagogy undermining their native good sense. The hero, Stephen Blackpool, is a hero largely because of his refusal to join the union. For the rest he is not so much a hero as a victim, doomed by circumstances beyond his control: a drunken wife, an inexplicable promise that prevents him from joining the union and thus alienates him from his fellow workers, an employer who fires him for no good reason (instead of, one might think, promoting him for being a scab), a false accusation, and finally, the fatal accident (literally, an accident, a fall down an abandoned mine shaft on a dark night). His life, as he keeps saying, is "aw a muddle"—hardly the stuff of heroism, still less the stuff of which working class novels are normally made.

One of the flaws in the novel, which makes the book (as well as Stephen's life) something of a muddle, is the failure to explain his reason for not joining the union, except for a passing reference to a mysterious "promise." Critics have been at a loss to understand why Dickens deleted from both the serial parts and the volume a passage in the original manuscript (and in the corrected proofs) which would have made the plot more plausible and the book more effective as a social novel. Perhaps it was precisely for this reason, because the passage would have given the novel a social significance Dickens did not want to give it, that he chose to eliminate it, even at the cost of some obfuscation. The deleted passage refers to a gruesome accident in the factory in which the heroine's little sister has her arm torn off by a machine. Described in retrospect, the accident itself is less shocking than the negligence of the employer and the unconcern of the government.

---

*When the Secretary of the Department of Science and Art protested against this satire, Dickens placated him: "I often say to Mr. Gradgrind that there is reason and good intention in much that he does—in fact, in all that he does—but that he over-does it. Perhaps by dint of his going his way and my going mine, we shall meet at last."[95]

"Thou'st spokken o' thy little sister. There agen! Wi' her child arm tore off afore thy face." She turned her head aside, and put her hand up. "Where dost thou ever hear or read o' *us*—the like o' *us*—as being otherwise than onreasonable and cause o' trouble? Yet think o' that. Government gentlemen comes and makes report. Fend off the dangerous machinery, box it off, save life and limb; don't rend and tear human creeturs to bits in a Chris'en country! What follers? Owners sets up their throats, cries out, 'Onreasonable! Inconvenient! Troublesome!' Gets to Secretaries o' States wi' deputations, and nothing's done. When do *we* get there wi' *our* deputations, God help us! We are too much int'rested and nat'rally too far wrong t'have a right judgment. Happly we are; but what are they then? I' th' name o' th' muddle in which we are born and live and die, what are they then?" "Let such things be, Stephen. They only lead to hurt, let them be!" "I will, since thou tell'st me so. I will. I pass my promise."[97]

Had that passage been permitted to stand, it would have constituted a powerful indictment of laissez-faireism and would have weakened the case against trade unionism. But it would also have weakened the central theme of the book. By a kind of poetic irony, Stephen himself meets his death as the result of an accident, an unprotected mine shaft, "Old Hell Shaft," as it is known locally. As he lies there dying, he recalls the hundreds who have died in similar accidents and the vain appeals of the workers to the lawmakers "not to let their work be murder to 'em." "See how we die an' no need, one way an' another—in a muddle—every day!"[98] Stephen's accident, unlike the little girl's, occurs not in the factory but in the open fields, and not to an innocent child mangled by a machine but to a doomed man fated to die, as he himself says, "one way an' another." The "muddle" of his death is the muddle of his life, starting with his unfortunate marriage and going on to all the indignities, misunderstandings, and betrayals which finally destroy him. The "lettin alone" policy of the government is part of a larger problem, the indifference of his employer who fires him for no good reason, and the callousness of his co-workers who "send him to Coventry" when he ventures to differ from them.

If Stephen's role is not simply that of the oppressed worker, neither is Bounderby's that of the exploitative industrialist. Bounderby is, in fact, more often identified as a banker than as a factory owner, and he is never seen in his factory, only in his home and bank. Indeed, his one redeeming trait appears in his capacity as employer. He is dishonest and hypocritical in representing himself as a "self-made man," but it is a kind of democratic hypocrisy, a spurious claim of social equality. The only respect in which he professes to be different from his workers is the money he has acquired by his own efforts. And money, as Dickens's novels repeatedly suggest, is the least immutable of all class distinctions, far less divisive than speech, manners, education, or breeding—distinctions which Bounderby deliberately forgoes. When Stephen wants to consult Bounderby about his personal problems, he goes not to the factory or bank but to his home, and at a time when he knows Bounderby will be at lunch. Without an appointment, he knocks at the door, is announced by the servant, and is immediately ushered into the parlor where Bounderby is having his meal.* Whatever Bounderby's faults —he is a bad son, a bad husband, and a bad friend as well as a bad employer —they are the faults of character rather than class. He is obtuse, callous, willful, cruel, but he is not an "absentee" employer removed from his workers by an impassable barrier of class. On the contrary, it is precisely when he is most accessible to them, in his own parlor, discussing their personal problems, that his bad nature emerges most sharply.

At every point where the novel seems to falter in its purpose—the purpose later critics have assigned it, of being an "industrial" novel—it is in fact carrying out Dickens's purpose. Trade unionism is condemned on the same grounds as utilitarianism and laissez-faireism, because each of them threatens to undermine the already precarious personal relations which are the only basis for a decent society. Asked how he would set right the "muddle" of the strike, Stephen protests that it is not for him to say. " 'Tis them as is put ower me, and ower aw the rest of us. What do they tak upon themseln, Sir, if not to do 't?" When Bounderby explains how he proposes to settle the matter, by making an example of half a dozen union organizers and transporting them to penal colonies, Stephen replies that if a hundred Slackbridges were tied into sacks and sunk into the deepest ocean the problem will remain. So long as workers are treated "as so much Power, and reg'latin 'em as if they was figures in a soom [sum], or machines . . . wi'out souls to weary and souls to hope," so long as masters and workers are divided by a "black impassable world," the muddle will get worse.[99]

Poverty is only part of the muddle, and not the most important part. The "hard times" of the title do not signify the kind of hard times experienced by the silk weavers of Spitalfields, for example. The workers of Coketown are poor, but not acutely, intolerably poor. Their main problem is the unrelieved, grinding, hopeless nature of their work and lives. "Look how we live, an' wheer we live, an' in what numbers, an' by what chances, and wi' what sameness; and look how the mills is awlus a going, and how they never works us no nigher to onny dis'ant object—ceptin awlus, Death."[100] The question—the condition-of-England question as Dickens

*In *Mary Barton,* a worker seeking an infirmary order goes to the house of his employer and is brought into the library where he interrupts him at breakfast. Here too the employer is not a small master who is personally known and therefore accessible to his employees but the owner of a cotton mill, the largest, most impersonal kind of factory.

saw it—was not only one of material deprivation and physical disability but of moral and spiritual impoverishment, the emptiness and meaninglessness of a mechanical, impersonal, soulless existence. In this sense laissez faire, the policy of "letting alone," is a manifestation of the larger evil of utilitarianism. When Bounderby treats his workers as "figures in a soom, or machines," he is only following the model of Gradgrind addressing his pupils by number rather than name.

It is this conception of the social problem that integrates the themes of utilitarianism and political economy, as well as other parts of the plot which are often thought extraneous and distracting—the marital problems, for example, of Stephen Blackpool and Louisa Gradgrind. Louisa's first step on the road to salvation is her entrance into Stephen's home, when for the first time in her life she confronts an individual worker. She had known the workers as "crowds passing to and from their nests, like ants or beetles," as "something to be worked so much and paid so much . . . by laws of supply and demand," as something rising and falling "en masse" like the sea. But she had no more thought of "separating them into units, than of separating the sea itself into its component drops."[101] It is the discovery of them as real persons, as individuals, that finally makes her aware of her own individuality and of her spiritual and emotional impoverishment.* They are caught up in their domestic travails, as she is in hers. Their lives are differentiated and complicated by personal relations, emotions, frustrations, and tragedies which have little to do with their work in the factory and everything to do with the quality of their lives. These domestic and private problems, so far from being irrelevant to the social problem, are of its essence, for they remind the reader that the workers are not "merely" workers, not defined by their work, not reducible to numbers or machines.

The same message emerges from the trade union theme. Slackbridge, like Bounderby, sees the workers en masse, as a power to be used in the struggle against the employers, quite like the "steam power" they are to the employers. He appeals to them to rally around as "one united power" in

---

*Had John Stuart Mill's *Autobiography* been published at the time (a first draft was, in fact, written just then, but it was published, in a revised version, only posthumously), one might think that Dickens had "borrowed" the character of Louisa from Mill. For she suffered from the same emotional and esthetic deprivations as the young Mill, and for the same reasons, having been subjected to a rigorously utilitarian education that had no room for poetry or fancy, emotion or love. It is curious that Mill never referred to *Hard Times* in either his letters or his published writings. He had commented, most unfavorably, on *Bleak House,* published the previous year, complaining to his wife of Dickens's "vulgar impudence" in ridiculing the "rights of women"—a matter that particularly exercised him since he himself was then writing *The Subjection of Women.* [102] One might have expected him to be equally provoked by Dickens's views of utilitarianism and political economy, to say nothing of the parallel between Louisa's state and the "crisis" of his own youth, when he had felt himself reduced, by his education and upbringing, to "a stock or a stone," deprived of all feeling and sentiment, incapable of appreciating beauty, poetry, or nature.[103]

support of the union, the "United Aggregate Tribunal" (a name that might have been coined by Gradgrind himself—or by Bentham). Stephen alone refuses to join, not so much because he thinks a strike will be futile (although he does think that), as because of a private promise which he cannot explain but which is compelling to him precisely because it is private. Implicit in his refusal is his unwillingness to be intimidated or manipulated by Slackbridge any more than by Bounderby. Slackbridge's reprisal is exactly like Bounderby's. Instructing the workers that "private feelings must yield to the common cause," he orders them to condemn Stephen to a "life of solitude."[104] Bounderby then proceeds to dismiss Stephen, thus endorsing Slackbridge's judgment and carrying out his order.

> "You are such a waspish, raspish, ill-conditioned chap, you see," said Mr. Bounderby, "that even your own Union, the men who know you best, will have nothing to do with you. I never thought those fellows could be right in anything; but I tell you what! I so far go along with them for a novelty that *I*'ll have nothing to do with you either."[105]

Slackbridge and Bounderby are of a kind. Both think in terms of classes and masses instead of individuals and human beings. Both see the problem in mathematical and mechanical terms and seek solutions that are quantitative and mechanistic. Both talk the language of supply and demand, pounds and pence, force and power.

In an article published in *Household Words* at the same time *Hard Times* was being serialized there, an essay on the Preston strike that was the model for the strike in the novel, Dickens recounted an argument he had with a gentleman to whom he gave the name of Mr. Snapper. Proudly announcing himself a partisan of "Capital" against "Labour," Snapper called on Dickens to declare his sympathies. Dickens replied that he rejected those labels as he rejected all the abstractions of the political economists. The relations between employers and workers, like all other relations, had to have in them "something of feeling and sentiment; something of mutual explanation, forbearance, and consideration; something which is not to be found in Mr. McCulloch's dictionary, and is not exactly stateable in figures; otherwise those relations are wrong and rotten at the core and will never bear sound fruit."[106] This formulation of the social problem could as easily have appeared in *Hard Times* itself—or in Carlyle's *Chartism*. In the article, however, Dickens was able to make clear what was only intimated in the novel, that he was on the side of the workers although not of "Labour," and that he was not against unions as such (on the contrary, he insisted that the workers had the same right to organize as employers did), but that he was against the spirit and tactics of a Slackbridge, who compounded the evil rather than remedying it.

Today Dickens might be said to be "ambivalent" toward the working classes. But the duality implied in that word is ours, not his. From the perspective of a later time and a different mode of thought, we are inclined to applaud one side of Dickens, the Dickens who has the political economists demonstrate irrefutably that "the Good Samaritan was a Bad Economist," or the "national dustmen" in Parliament sift through mounds of Blue Books to prove that nothing has to be done, or the factory owners insist they will be ruined if they are obliged to do anything at all.

> They were ruined, when they were required to send labouring children to school; they were ruined when inspectors were appointed to look into their works; they were ruined, when such inspectors considered it doubtful whether they were quite justified in chopping people up with their machinery; they were utterly undone, when it was hinted that perhaps they need not always make quite so much smoke.[107]

On the other hand, we are apt to be embarrassed or dismayed by the Dickens who has Stephen protest that it is not for him but for "them as is put ower me" to resolve the muddle, and that what is needed is "the drawing nigh to fok, wi' kindness and patience an' cheery ways"; or makes Louisa determined to know her "humbler fellow-creatures" and "beautify their lives."[108] To the modern reader, these sentiments seem on a par with the "turtle soup and venison" that Bounderby takes to be the great passion of the workers.

To Dickens, it was all of a piece. If he criticized the "lettin alone" policy of Bounderby, it was because he believed the best interests of the workers lay in a society based on mutual trust, good will, and cooperation.* Today this gospel of social harmony seems suspiciously "pro-Capital," as Mr. Snapper would say. At the time the novel was widely interpreted as pro-Labor. The contemporary criticism of *Hard Times* was not that Dickens failed to make a good trade unionist out of Stephen Blackpool but that he made a "dramatic monster" out of Bounderby—a complaint shared by Ruskin, who was hardly well disposed to the Bounderbys of his world.[110] Other critics accused Dickens of being excessively partial to the workers and

---

*In a speech delivered at the time he began *Hard Times*, Dickens attributed to the Mechanics' Institutions his own views.

> It is in the fusion of different classes, without confusion; in the bringing together of employers and employed; in the creating of a better common understanding among those whose interests are identical, who depend upon each other, and who can never be in unnatural antagonism without deplorable results, that one of the chief principles of a Mechanics' Institution should consist.[109]

encouraging them in their unrealistic expectations (beer and skittles if not turtle soup and venison). Some read his gospel of harmony as an insidious way of fomenting social discontent: Macaulay charged him with fostering a "sullen socialism," Bagehot with cultivating a "sentimental radicalism," and Harriet Martineau with being a "humanity monger" and "pseudo-philanthropist."[111]

Toward the end of the century, criticism took a different turn. It was now Stephen Blackpool who was said to be unrepresentative of his class and Dickens who was ignorant of the plight of the industrial worker. George Gissing saw this as the main flaw of *Hard Times.*

> He shows us poor men who suffer under tyranny and who exclaim against the hardship of things; but never such a representative wage-earner as was then to be seen battling for bread and right. One reason is plain; Dickens did not know the north of England. With adequate knowledge of a manufacturing town, he could never have written so unconvincingly as in his book *Hard Times*—the opportunity for dealing with this subject. Stephen Blackpool represents nothing at all; he is a mere model of meekness, and his great misfortune is such as might befall any man anywhere, the curse of a drunken wife.[112]

To George Bernard Shaw, Slackbridge was a "mere figment of the middle-class imagination," the product of "pure middle-class ignorance." Dickens knew certain kinds of workers—servants, village artisans, the employees of small tradesmen. "But of the segregated factory populations of our purely industrial towns he knew no more than an observant professional man can pick up on a flying visit to Manchester."[113] The criticism may have been justified, although it came oddly from Gissing and Shaw, who knew little enough of the "representative wage-earner" or "segregated factory populations" of their own times, let alone of Dickens's.*

Whatever criticism Gissing and Shaw had of Dickens's treatment of industrial workers, they admired his portraits of the poor and his evident devotion to them. Gissing explained that he himself reread Dickens constantly (and wrote about him) so that he might better understand, and write about, the poor of his own time. "How the London poor should love Dickens," he observed, regretting that they no longer read him as much as they had.[115] Shaw too, for all his taunts about Dickens's "middle-class imagination" and "idealized Toryism," praised *Hard Times* as a composite of "Karl Marx, Carlyle, Ruskin, Morris, Carpenter," rising up "against civilization as against a disease." What he especially liked about the book

---

*They knew more, however, than the recent commentator who explained that Dickens's interest in "industrial England" came from his "having known and suffered factory life first-hand as a child" —as if pasting labels in a blacking warehouse in London had anything to do with "factory life" or "industrial England."[114]

was that Dickens attacked not this or that evil but "our entire social system," "the whole industrial order of the modern world." "Here you will find no more villains and heroes, but only oppressors and victims, oppressing and suffering in spite of themselves, driven by a huge machinery which grinds to pieces the people it should nourish and ennoble."[116]

Some later critics were less appreciative of Dickens's feeling for the poor and more intolerant of his deviation from the socialist orthodoxy. To George Orwell, Dickens was a "south of England man, and a cockney at that," who was "out of touch with the bulk of the oppressed masses, the industrial and agricultural labourers."[117] He conceded that Dickens went far beyond the exposure of particular evils. "Dickens at any rate never imagined that you can cure pimples by cutting them off. In every page of his work one can see a consciousness that society is wrong somewhere at the root." But because his conception of that root evil was "almost exclusively moral," he made no constructive suggestions for reform. He attacked the law, the government, the educational system, without proposing anything to put in their place. To be sure, it was not the business of the novelist or even of the satirist to suggest reforms. But in refusing to be constructive, Dickens failed to be sufficiently *"de*structive." He did not want the existing order to be overthrown, nor did he think it would make much difference if it were. For his target was "human nature" rather than the "economic system."

> There is not a line in the book that can properly be called Socialistic; indeed, its tendency if anything is pro-capitalist, because its whole moral is that capitalists ought to be kind, not that workers ought to be rebellious. . . . Bounderby is a bullying windbag and Gradgrind has been morally blinded, but if they were better men, the system would work well enough—that, all through, is the implication. And so far as social criticism goes, one can never extract much more from Dickens than this, unless one deliberately reads meanings into him. His whole "message" is one that at first glance looks like an enormous platitude: If men would behave decently the world would be decent.[118]

It is extraordinary to find, almost a century after the publication of *Hard Times,* that the issue remained what Dickens had made of it. Dickens's quarrel with Gradgrind and Bounderby had been that they reduced men to economic and material objects, "figures in a soom, or machines." Yet here was Orwell, like some latter-day political economist, criticizing Dickens for neglecting the economic and material basis of society. In making this point Orwell seriously distorted *Hard Times,* depriving the book not only of any claim to "social criticism" but of any intellectual substance. No serious contemporary critic misread the book as Orwell did, making Bounderby and Gradgrind deficient simply as individuals, the one a "bullying wind-bag," the other "morally blinded." No one else failed to see that their deficiencies were not trivial or idiosyncratic but were rooted in their ideas, indeed in a system of ideas, and that it was those ideas which prevented them from being "better men." Gradgrind did become better and Bounderby did not, precisely because the one was converted and the other remained an unreconstructed utilitarian. It is ironic that Orwell, himself so shrewd a recorder of the ideas of his time, so sensitive to ideas that were nothing less than moral principles, could so trivialize Dickens as to ignore the symbolic, ideological, moral meaning of Gradgrind and Bounderby. It is also odd to find him criticizing Dickens from the perspective of a socialism that was the mirror image of orthodox political economy, yet another version of economic man. The later Orwell, the Orwell of *1984* and *Animal Farm,* would surely have written a very different critique—or, it may be, an appreciation—of Dickens.

If Dickens failed to create "representative" workers, if he had a deficient sense of class and an exacerbated sense of morality, if he was not a socialist and did not think in terms of economic "systems," he was all the more representative of his own time and faithful to the reality of that time as most of his contemporaries, including a good many radicals, perceived it. There was, to be sure, a paucity of industrial workers among his poor, as there was also a paucity of agricultural laborers, miners, construction workers, handloom weavers, cobblers, bakers, and brewers. Dickens had not, after all, undertaken to write a conspectus of "The Laboring People of England in the Early Nineteenth Century." What did emerge from his novels was a multitude of poor people of varied conditions and dispositions who could not easily be accommodated in any class schema. Precisely because they were not members of a class but highly individualized characters—"characters," often, in the sense of eccentrics—they were inimitable and unforgettable. If the poor had ever been the "anonymous masses" some historians assume them to have been, they were assuredly not that once Dickens's novels had become the staples—"legs of mutton or loaves of bread," as Trollope said—of all classes of the population.[119]

In 1853 a Nonconformist minister told his flock: "There have been at work among us three great social agencies: the London City Mission; the novels of Mr. Dickens; the cholera."[120] It was a tribute Dickens would have appreciated. For it suggested that his novels had touched the lives of the poor as directly and forcefully as those other "agencies," not by reforming or classifying them, putting them in their proper place in the system, but by personalizing, individualizing, and dramatizing them. This was, perhaps, what Daniel Webster had in mind when, during Dickens's visit to America in 1842, he said that Dickens had done more to "ameliorate the condition of the English poor than all the statesmen Great Britain had sent into parliament."[121] What other reformers hoped to do by legislation, he did by a supreme act of moral imagination. He brought the poor into the forefront of the culture, and thus into the forefront of the consciousness and conscience of his own generation and generations to come.

XX

THE TWO NATIONS

After Dickens most novelists, certainly all the social novelists, are anti-climactic. Who now reads *Sybil* or *Coningsby, Mary Barton* or *North and South?* Except, of course, the social historian, who reads them as he would a parliamentary report on housing or a tract on the poor laws. This is not to say that these novels are without literary merit or entertainment value. But there is no doubt that their main interest is as social documents. Coming to their subjects from different directions, animated by different political and philosophical principles, written by people of different temperaments and backgrounds, they express ideas and assumptions about society and poverty which seem to transcend their differences.

If Dickens was quintessentially English, as was commonly said at the time, Disraeli was as conspicuously foreign. He did not himself forget, nor allow others to forget, his Jewish ancestry ("Hebraic race," as he proudly called it), and his name was often spelled, like his father's, "D'Israeli" (sometimes, though not always, invidiously). This alone would have been enough to make him an oddity in the political and social circles in which he traveled. But there was much else about him that was provocative. His brand of Toryism was as odious to the "backwoodsmen" of the party as to the "advanced" Peelites; and his idea of "Tory Democracy" was not at all what Sadler or Oastler meant by that label. The group he was associated with, "Young England" as it was grandly called, consisted of all of four Members of Parliament who deliberately flaunted their idiosyncrasies, as if to make an ideological statement in the cut of a waistcoat or the styling of hair. Disraeli himself seemed to go out of his way to court disfavor. As if his Jewishness were not affront enough, he paraded his dandyism, made no secret of his love affairs, and, perhaps most reprehensible, wrote novels—hardly the prescription for a young man trying to climb the "greasy pole" of the Tory Party.

Disraeli had enemies even among those who might have found his ideas

489

congenial—Carlyle, for example, who was no mean eccentric himself and who had much else in common with Disraeli. They shared the same enemies: utilitarians and economists, "constitution mongers" and reformers, liberals with a small "l" and with a capital "L." And they had some of the same heroes and ideals: a "natural" aristocracy that was as much a meritocracy as an aristocracy of birth; a reverence for work that made them as respectful of industry as of agriculture (*"Laborare est Orare,"* Carlyle wrote; *"Qui laborat, orat,"* Sybil said);[1] a social order in which the poor had basic human (though not political) rights and in which the rich assumed the social obligations commensurate with their privileges. Yet Carlyle heartily detested Disraeli, perhaps for no other reason than his being Jewish—"a superlative Hebrew conjurer," a "Pinchbeck-Hebrew, almost professedly a Son of Belial," a "cursed old Jew, not worth his weight in cold bacon."[2] Disraeli, perhaps knowing of Carlyle's feelings toward him, reciprocated by being cool and distant. Boasting that he had written about the "condition-of-the-people question" before it had been raised in Parliament, he implicitly challenged Carlyle's claim to priority. At a time when others were quoting Carlyle incessantly and praising him effusively, Disraeli rarely mentioned him either in public or in private, except for one occasion when, as prime minister, he offered Carlyle the Grand Cross of the Bath, only to be rebuffed. Yet it is difficult to believe that he had not read and been influenced by him. A passage from one of Disraeli's articles in *The Times* in 1838 is so redolent of Carlyle, in rhetoric and substance, as to verge on parody.

> Note ever, John, the difference between a true Nation-cry and a sham Nation-cry. Reform House of Commons, wise or unwise, true nation-cry; Reform House of Lords, sham nation-cry. Respecting the voice of the nation there can be no mistake; it sounds everywhere, in town and in country, streets and fields, lordly mansion, ten-pound tenement, unglazed hovel. Great chorus wherein all join, prince and peasant, farmer and factor, literate and illiterate, merchant and artisan, mariner and landlubber. The same thought stamped on the brain of everyone, from him who wears a coronet to him who drives a coster-monger's cart; same thought on the brain, same word on the tongue.[3]

Dickens was even more hostile to Disraeli, and with better reason. He had no nostalgia for "ye olde England," did not "love a lord," was not especially enamored of heroes, great men, or an aristocracy, however "natural," and had no great feeling for religion, whether of the Hebraic or high-Anglican variety. In *The Chimes,* published in November, 1844, six months after *Coningsby,* Dickens alternately satirized the utilitarian's "Facts and Figures, Facts and Figures," and the Tory's "Good Old Times, Good

Old Times." The story features a Member of Parliament, a self-styled "Poor Man's Friend and Father," who preaches the "Dignity of Labour" and whose paternalistic exertions on behalf of the poor consist of playing skittles with them and drinking their health every New Year's Day. His wife teaches "pinking and eyelet-holing" to the men and boys of the village and composes a ditty for them to sing while they work.

> Oh let us love our occupations,
> Bless the squire and his relations,
> Live upon our daily rations,
> And always know our proper stations.[4]*

Like most parodies, this was clever and unfair. While Dickens found much to deride in *Coningsby* (the proposal to revive the good old custom of dancing around the maypole) and much to take serious issue with (the argument against the repeal of the corn laws), there were other things in it that must have been congenial. Taper and Tadpole, the Tweedledum and Tweedledee of politics, who resolved the affairs of state at dinner parties and settled the vexing question of the malt tax while sipping claret, could have come straight out of the pages of Dickens's own novels, together with the statistical tables and dietary rules, the Poor Law Commissioners' rules and Sub-commissioners' reports, mockingly cited in praise of a "Spirit of the Age" that was truly a "Spirit of Utility."[6]

In *Coningsby*, published in 1844, the condition-of-England question was peripheral to the political theme of the novel; in *Sybil*, which appeared the following year, it was the dominant theme. Disraeli later said that he had not originally meant to put his ideas into fictional form but had decided to do so because it offered "the best chance of influencing opinion."[7] If the explanation was disingenuous—Disraeli was an old hand at fiction and took naturally to that form—it testifies to the social and even political importance attributed to novels at the time. Disraeli himself professed not to read novels —"When I want to read a novel, I write one"—and he once denied having read anything by Dickens except an "extract in a newspaper."[8] But he was extremely sensitive to intellectual and cultural (as to sartorial) fashions, and could hardly have been unaware of Dickens's work and popularity. (In

---

*The original draft of *The Chimes* contained even more pointed references to the Young Englanders, some of which Forster prevailed upon Dickens to remove. The "Good Old Times" speech was delivered by a "youngish sort of gentleman, in a white waistcoat":

> Restore . . . the Good Old Times, the Grand Old Times, the Great Old Times! Raise up this trodden worm into a man by the mysterious but certain quency (it always has been so) of Stained Glass Windows and Enormous Candlesticks. . . . Then his Regeneration is accomplished. Until then, Behold him![5]

Disraeli's last novel, *Endymion,* published in 1880, Dickens made a brief appearance under the name of "Gushy.") If Disraeli cherished the illusion that *Sybil* might do for the condition-of-England question what *Oliver Twist* had done for the New Poor Law, he was soon disabused. Neither *Sybil* nor *Coningsby* was serialized, each selling about 3,000 copies in the original three-volume edition, but both went through several editions, *Coningsby* five in as many years, Sybil three in as many months. While they did not reach a mass audience, in a small, influential circle they carried some weight, in part because they were taken as the manifesto of the Young Englanders.

Sybil was not the first "industrial" novel; Frances Trollope's *Michael Armstrong* preceded it by five years. But it received, and merited, far more attention than Mrs. Trollope's book, so that Disraeli could later take satisfaction in the knowledge that he had anticipated by several years the other important books in this genre: *Mary Barton* (1848), *Alton Locke* (1850), and *Hard Times* (1854). In a speech to his constituency before the publication of *Sybil,* Disraeli made a larger claim to priority, this time to the "condition of the people question." He had written about it, he said, before it had been discussed in Parliament, because he had long been convinced that "there was something rotten in the core of our social system." Fortunes were being amassed and Britain was becoming the most prosperous nation in the world at a time when the working classes, the creators of wealth, were "steeped in the most abject poverty and gradually sinking into the deepest degradation."[9] He did not say where he had written about this question and there is no evidence that he had done so to this effect; moreover, he claimed only to have written about it before it had been discussed in Parliament, not before others—Carlyle, most notably—had written about it.

If Disraeli could not plausibly claim priority over Carlyle on the condition-of-the-people question, he could take credit for popularizing the "two nations" metaphor, although not for inventing it.* That phrase appears as the subtitle of *Sybil,* and again in the much-quoted dialogue between Egremont, the good aristocrat (one is tempted to capitalize these

---

*In his "Memoir on Pauperism," in 1835, Tocqueville spoke of the poor law as breaking the link between the "two rival nations," the rich and the poor.[10] Half a dozen years later William Channing, the American Unitarian minister, wrote: "In most large cities there may be said to be two nations, understanding as little of one another, having as little intercourse, as if they lived in different lands."[11] A few months before *Sybil* was published, Engels finished the German manuscript of *The Condition of the Working Class in England,* in which he referred to the working class and the bourgeoisie as "two radically dissimilar nations, as unlike as difference of race could make them."[12] In *Sartor Resartus* (1833–34) Carlyle divided England into "two sects," the "dandies" and "drudges," who, he predicted (in anticipation of Marx), would one day divide England between them, "each recruiting itself from the intermediate ranks, till there be none left to enlist on either side."[13] Or one can carry the idea back to Plato's suggestion that in each city there are two cities "warring with each other, one of the poor, the other of the rich"—but within each of these, he added, there are very many cities.[14]

identifications, as in a morality play), and the "stranger," later identified as Stephen Morley, an Owenite. Egremont has just uttered the platitude:

> "Say what you like, our Queen reigns over the greatest nation that ever existed."
>
> "Which nation?" asked the younger stranger, "for she reigns over two."
>
> The stranger paused; Egremont was silent, but looked inquiringly.
>
> "Yes," resumed the younger stranger after a moment's interval. "Two nations; between whom there is no intercourse and no sympathy; who are as ignorant of each other's habits, thoughts, and feelings, as if they were dwellers in different zones, or inhabitants of different planets; who are formed by different breeding, are fed by a different food, are ordered by different manners, and are not governed by the same laws."
>
> "You speak of—" said Egremont, hesitatingly.
>
> "THE RICH AND THE POOR."[15]

In one sense the "two nations" metaphor is a variant of the "foreign country" image, the poor being the "other," the foreign nation. That foreignness is mitigated by the fact that the two nations, as Egremont points out, are ruled by the same queen and are part of the same realm. The word "nation" also endows the poor with a civic status, a weight and importance they do not have as "the poor"; however different they are from the rich, they are as much a "nation" as the rich. With that word, too, they cease being a peripheral group, a special class of the poor, and become the entire body of the poor, "THE PEOPLE," as they are more often referred to in the novel. In this sense, "nation" carries with it a Chartist connotation—the poor incorporated into the polity, the people politicized.

Yet the nation of the poor, it soon appears, is a most heterogeneous entity. There are the rural poor living in and around the market town of Marney, a "metropolis of agricultural labour"; the industrial poor, the factory workers in Mowbray, a mill town not far from Marney; the hand-loom weavers who continue to live in Mowbray but cannot make the transition to factory work (and who resent the fact that their children do); the coal miners in a nearby colliery town; and the "hell-cats" of Wodgate, ironmongers organized in the old master-apprentice system. Each of these groups has its distinctive character and each takes a jaundiced view of the others.

> "I pity them poor devils in the country," said Mick; "we got some of them at Collinson's, come from Suffolk, they say; what they call hagricultural labourers; a very queer lot indeed."
>
> "Ah! them's the himmigrants," said Caroline; "they're sold out

of slavery, and sent down by Pickford's van into the labour market to bring down our wages."[16]

The coal miners, themselves hardly a docile lot, caution Morley against venturing into "Hell-house Yard," as Wodgate is known to them. " 'Tayn't a journey for Christians," one miner says; "they're a very queer lot even in sunshine," contributes another; and a third warns him that they are "divils carnal," "no less than heathens."[17] Sybil and Morley may think of the poor as a nation united, but the workers themselves evidently do not.

It is interesting that Disraeli should have blunted the point of the "two nations" theme by making so much of the differences among the poor, and even more interesting that he should have described them as he did. One might have expected him to romanticize the rural poor in contrast to the urban poor. But quite the contrary: the agricultural laborers in *Sybil* are said to be in a worse state than the factory workers or even the coal miners—and are perceived as such by the workers and miners themselves. The housing and sanitary conditions in Marney are as bad as anything to be found in Mayhew's London or Engels's Manchester. The shock to the reader is all the greater because the scene opens in the usual pastoral mode with a picture of the undulating, wooded hills, the meadows, gardens, and streams surrounding the "rural town," and then turns to the center of the town where most of the agricultural laborers live: the cottages built of rubble with gaping chinks admitting blasts of wind, the humid, putrid thatch looking like the tops of dunghills and "exhaling malaria like all other decaying vegetable matter," the open drains and foul pits emitting disease and impregnating the very walls of the cottages. Here entire families may be found sleeping in a single room, freezing in the winter and suffocating in the summer, opening the door only to be met by the gaseous vapors of reeking dunghills.[18]

The mill town of Mowbray, by contrast, offers a relatively agreeable prospect, not beautiful but bustling and vital (except, of course, for the handloom weavers). The model factory outside of town has all the amenities of a miniature Utopia—good wages and working conditions, decent housing, a school and cultural activities. Even the not-so-model factories in town, where wages and conditions are far worse, pay the young workers enough to permit them to leave home and take lodgings for themselves (a practice much resented by their parents who are deprived of their earnings), to indulge themselves in an occasional evening of drink and entertainment at the "Temple of the Muses," and to join the local Mechanics' Institution, the "Shoddy Court Literary and Scientific Institute," which has fifty members and subscribes to three London papers, as well as the *Northern Star* and two copies of the *New Moral World*. The scene at the "Temple" (lively but "decorous") suggests that whatever grievances the young workers have about their jobs, they are pleased to be working in a town like Mowbray rather than in the country where, as one of them says, the laborers are "obliged to burn ricks to pass the time."[19]

Walter Gerard, Sybil's father and a militant Chartist, takes a more dire view of the condition of the workers.

> "There is more serfdom in England now than at any time since the Conquest. I speak of what passes under my daily eyes when I say, that those who labour can as little choose or change their masters now, as when they were born thralls. There are great bodies of the working classes of this country nearer the condition of brutes than they have been at any time since the Conquest. Indeed, I see nothing to distinguish them from brutes, except that their morals are inferior. Incest and infanticide are as common among them as among the lower animals.[20]

There is little in the novel to bear out this charge—not, at any rate, among the factory workers. Only among the ironmongers of Wodgate is there evidence of this kind of degradation. Like the Mint in *Jack Sheppard* and the den of thieves in *Oliver Twist,* Wodgate consists of a community of outcasts. In this case, however, the outcasts are not criminals but workers, and skilled workers at that, ironworkers whose products, we are assured, are sought after throughout England and even Europe. Thousands of people live in that town in something very like a state of nature; indeed, they are not so much people as "animals, unconscious, their minds a blank, and their worst actions only the impulse of a gross or savage instinct." They have no church or magistrate, no vestry or school, no public building or institution of any kind, not even a factory, for they cannot work together for the same reason they cannot tolerate any kind of public establishment. The industry is carried on by master workmen in their own houses, each master having unlimited power over his apprentices, a power more tyrannical and cruel than that of a slave owner in the colonies. Over this "aristocracy" there reigns one man, the governor of those who have no government—the "bishop," he is called, because, one of the workers explains, "as we have no church, we will have as good."[21]

This account of a class of workers so degraded as to be "unconscious of their degradation" is followed by Gerard's speech denouncing the "degradation of the people," the brutal condition of "great bodies of the working classes of this country." Yet the "hell-cats" of Wodgate are clearly not the "people" or "working classes" Gerard has in mind. In fact, it soon becomes evident that Gerard knows nothing of Wodgate and little enough even of the workers of Mowbray. He himself is employed in Trafford's model establishment outside of town, where, his daughter is pleased to report, "he labours among the woods and waters" instead of being "cooped up in a hot factory in a smoky street."[22]

Nor is Sybil more realistic about the people. Because she gives her name to the book (and because of the prophetic connotation of the name itself) one might think that she speaks for Disraeli when she takes her stand with "the Church and the people." But like her father and her friend Morley, she is as misguided as she is well intentioned, full of "phantoms" and "fallacious fancies," as Egremont tells her.[23] Her romantic image of a Golden Age when the English people had all the virtues to a superlative degree—they were "the truest, the freest, and the bravest, the best-natured and the best-looking, the happiest and most religious race upon the surface of this globe"—is as obviously fanciful as her apocalyptic view of the modern world "divided only between the oppressors and the oppressed," where to be "one of the people was to be miserable and innocent; one of the privileged, a luxurious tyrant."[24] Brought up in a convent with no experience of the real world, she lives in the rarefied atmosphere of her own moral indignation. In her hostility to industry and progress she has much in common with those retrograde and altogether unsympathetic aristocrats, Lord de Mowbray and Lord Marney, who regard factories as "enterprises for the canaille," and are "violent against railroads" because of their "dangerous tendency to equality."[25] Sidonia's rebuke to Coningsby might have been meant for Sybil as well: "The Age of Ruins is past. Have you seen Manchester?"[26]*

In this respect, his acceptance of industrialism, Stephen Morley, the Owenite, stands as a corrective to Sybil. Unlike Sybil, he wants to "create the future" rather than "recall the past." "The railways," he assures her, "will do as much for mankind as the monasteries did." His quarrel is not with the factory or the machine but with modern society. "There is no community in England; there is aggregation, but aggregation under circumstances which make it rather a dissociating than a uniting principle."[28] Large towns

*When Coningsby does visit Manchester, he finds it "as great a human exploit as Athens." His view of the cotton mill is as rhapsodic as the familiar pastoral idyll:

> He entered chambers vaster than are told of in Arabian fable, and peopled with habitants more wondrous than Afrite or Peri. For there he beheld, in long-continued ranks, those mysterious forms full of existence without life, that perform with facility, and in an instant, what man can fulfil only with difficulty and in days. A machine is a slave that neither brings nor bears degradation; it is a being endowed with the greatest degree of energy, and acting under the greatest degree of excitement, yet free at the same time from all passion and emotion. It is, therefore, not only a slave but a supernatural slave. And why should one say that the machine does not live? . . . Does not the spindle sing like a merry girl at her work, and the steam-engine roar in jolly chorus, like a strong artisan handling his lusty tools, and gaining a fair day's wages for a fair day's toil?[27]

exacerbate the problem, for there the density of population intensifies the struggle for existence, pitting man against man, neighbor against neighbor. This critique of a society too massive and at the same time too individualistic to allow for any genuine community seems plausible enough, until Morley proposes an alternative based on the Owenite "principle of association," which is so strenuously opposed to individualism it cannot even tolerate the institutions of home and family. In the present state of civilization, Morley announces, privacy and domesticity are obsolete. "Home is a barbarous idea; the method of a rude age; home is isolation; therefore anti-social. What we want is Community."[29]

If the Owenite solution appears worse than the problem itself, so does the Chartist solution, the idea that the social problem can be solved by giving the people political power. In his speech to the House of Commons opposing the Chartist Petition, Egremont declares himself in favor of the ends of Chartism but not its means, "the results of the Charter without the intervention of its machinery," social equity without political equality.[30] In the unmistakable voice of Young England he proclaims himself the champion of the "popular cause." The "rights of labour" are as sacred as those of property; the first duty of the statesman is the "social happiness of the millions."[31] The people, he tries to convince Sybil, are not ripe for power and perhaps never will be, but their rights can be secured and their condition alleviated by the "natural leaders of the People," enlightened aristocrats like himself who are attuned to modern civilization, sensitive to its problems, and prepared to fulfill their "social duties."[32]

Sybil (and perhaps the reader as well) remains unconvinced by this argument until the dramatic episode of the riot in which both her father and Morley, the proponents of Chartism and Owenism, are killed. While the riot serves to expose her illusions about the forces of good and evil, the righteous struggle of the poor against their tyrants, it is not meant to condemn all popular causes or to suggest that all working class actions necessarily end in violence. Disraeli goes out of his way to describe other such events sympathetically and even approvingly. The "monster meeting" protesting the arrest of Gerard has a "simple yet awful solemnity," the men, women, and children from the dissenting chapels, carrying flags, singing hymns, and clearly motivated by "high and earnest feelings."[33] Even the trade union initiation is appealing, in spite of the secret rites, masks, and mystic robes, and the awful oath binding the members to further the common cause by the "assassination of oppressive and tyrannical masters, or the demolition of all mills, works and shops that shall be deemed by us incorrigible."[34] And the account of the final riot is interrupted to describe an earlier demonstration in Lancashire where 2,000 workers had marched to the estate of the local squire to plead for food. In the absence of the squire they were greeted by his wife, who promised to give them a meal if they would wait patiently for the provisions to arrive. They did so, were properly fed, thanked the lady of the manor, and with her permission took a tour of the gardens, in the course of which not a single flower or fruit was plucked. (This idyllic scene carries the author's assurance that he can personally vouch for its truth.)[35]

Unfortunately, the demonstration at Mowbray is not led by those "gentle Lancashire insurgents." Nor is it led by the Chartist Gerard or the Owenite Morley, nor by the local trade unionists or factory workers, although it is initially supported by all of them. The leader is the "Bishop" of Wodgate, "The Liberator," as he is now called, who has been put up to it by a single Chartist agitator. His band of "hell-cats" march first through the mining town, ravaging, plundering, setting fires, and gathering up recruits (the miners, Morley explains, although better paid than the factory workers, are more brutal and violent). They then proceed to Mowbray, where they set out to destroy the model factory, on the theory, as the Chartist provocateur puts it, that Mr. Trafford, the philanthropic owner, is "a most inveterate capitalist, and would divert the minds of the people from the Five Points by allotting them gardens and giving them baths."[36] In *Barnaby Rudge,* it was the "very scum and refuse of London" that went on a rampage of destruction and violence, in the name of religion; in *Sybil,* it is the "hell-cats" of Wodgate, in the name of a Charter they do not begin to understand. As if to confirm the irrelevancy of the demonstration to any rational working class goal, the final scene of carnage takes place not in Mowbray or even in the model factory outside of town but in the muniment room of the castle, which contains the documents establishing Gerard as the legitimate Lord de Mowbray, and his daughter Sybil, no longer the "daughter" of the people but a proper spouse for Egremont, the new Earl of Marney.[37]

If there remain vestiges of the silver fork tradition in *Sybil,* it is because the aristocracy retains an important role in it. In a sense, *Sybil* is an upper class version of *Hard Times.* Where Dickens's solution to the social problem lay in an enlightened, humane, natural middle class—natural, as opposed to the utilitarians who tried to suppress all natural affections and instincts—Disraeli's lay in an enlightened, humane, natural aristocracy, an aristocracy of noble character and paternal purpose as well as title and estate. Dickens had contempt for that romantic idea of aristocracy, but not for the idea of paternalism itself. The Cheeryble brothers in *Nicholas Nickleby* would have found a kindred spirit in Mr. Trafford, agreeing with him that between employers and employed "there should be other ties than the payment and the receipt of wages."[38] And the young workers in *Sybil,* Devilsdust and Dandy Mick, would have been quite at home, under those names, as trade unionists in *Hard Times* (although they might not have enjoyed quite the same prospects—Dickens might have foreseen their future as successful businessmen, but not, as Disraeli did, as the progenitors of a "crop of members of Parliament and Peers of the realm").[39]

Finally what *Sybil* and *Hard Times* share, and what makes *Sybil* a social novel rather than a silver fork novel, is a sense of verisimilitude that spills over even into their melodramatic and satirical passages. Disraeli had a more hostile press than Dickens, reviewers taking the occasion to disparage his politics, character, race, and appearance. But even his critics paid tribute to his zeal as a social reporter, his attempt to seek out the best evidence on the condition-of-the-people question. Historians have since located the exact passages in *Sybil* which derive from various parliamentary reports: the Children's Employment Commission, the Select Committee on the Payment of Wages, the Midland Mining Commission, the Sanitary Commission.[40]* While contemporary reviewers did not have all these details, they were sufficiently impressed by Disraeli's use of such sources to speak of parts of his book as "transcripts" or "transcriptions" from the Blue Books. This was not always said in praise; one complaint was that whereas Dickens knew the poor intimately, personally, as real people, Disraeli knew them only from the "pages of parliamentary or statistical reports."[42] In fact Disraeli drew upon other sources as well: speeches in Parliament on the Ten Hours Bill, press accounts of the agitation against the New Poor Law, publications of the Chartists and the Anti-Corn Law League, and the private correspondence of the Chartist leader Feargus O'Connor. Having also visited several mill towns and depressed rural areas, he was able to claim, in the preface to *Sybil,* that his account of the condition of the people was generally based on "his own observation." That observation was obviously limited, and the Blue Books themselves, hardly a warrant of objectivity, were made less so by the inevitable process of selection and dramatization. Yet the preface and the reviews, by dwelling on the documentation, made the novel seem something like an exercise in what was later to be known as "social realism," which is all the more remarkable in view of the large part played in it by irony, fantasy, and, not least, ideology.†

*Disraeli was not the only novelist to exploit these reports. Mrs. Trollope's *Michael Armstrong* drew upon the Sadler Committee report of 1831–32 and the Factory Commission report of 1833. The picture of Wodgate in *Sybil* was indebted to the account of Willenhall in an appendix to the second report of the Children's Employment Commission of 1842–43. The author of that appendix was R. H. Horne, a friend of Dickens who was defending him, at just that time, against the charge of being a "low writer." It was not Horne, however, but the Benthamite reformer Southwood Smith who sent Dickens a copy of this report, which so deeply affected him that he considered writing a pamphlet to be called "An Appeal to the People of England, on behalf of the Poor Man's Child."[41] Dickens never wrote that pamphlet, but bits of "the Poor Man's Child" appeared in his other writings.

†All of this documentation did not prevent such boners as the young ironmonger of Wodgate who spoke of his master, in the unmistakable accents of Sam Weller, as "wery lib'ral too in the wittals."[43] Perhaps Weller was another of Disraeli's sources, in spite of his denial that he had ever read Dickens.

. . .

Disraeli's ideology has been a subject of much dispute among biographers and historians. How much of it was rhetoric, and how much substance? What did it entail by way of principle, and how did the principle translate into practice? How seriously did he intend it, and how much credence did others put in it? These questions have more to do with Disraeli the politician than with the novelist. In *Sybil,* the nature of the ideology is not in dispute, although its dramatic effectiveness may be. (One reviewer wondered whether the politician's objects were well served by the "mere novelist's tinsel.")[44] That ideology is communicated not only in the obviously didactic passages but in the very structure of the novel, the counterposition of high life and low life corresponding to the "two nations" of the title. The wonderfully satirical opening scene in the fashionable London gaming club (Crockford's, presumably) has a group of rich, blasé, effete young men chatting idly about the forthcoming Derby races, in the course of which one of them confesses that he rather likes bad wine because, you know, "one gets so bored with good wine."[45] Later, in the salons of the great houses, the ladies play at politics by extending or withholding invitations to their dinner parties, vainly attempting to extract information about the intentions of the Cabinet from their dim-witted companions who know even less than they.

The nation of the rich, however, turns out to be as little monolithic as the nation of the poor. Just as Carlyle's upper classes contained a toiling and an idle class, Master Workers and Non-Workers, so Disraeli's upper classes contained a responsible, compassionate, forward-looking class and a cynical, self-serving, retrograde one. Taper and Tadpole who make a game of politics, Lord de Mowbray who suspects the railroads of being dangerously egalitarian, Lord Marney who believes the New Poor Law to be the salvation of the country, have forfeited their right to rule by trivializing politics, rejecting modernity, and betraying their social responsibilities. But there are others of vision and integrity—a model aristocrat and a model industrialist, both, not by accident, younger sons who have combined the best of the old and new worlds. Mr. Trafford, the owner of the model factory, is the scion of an old, impoverished, landed family. Instead of idling away his life in genteel poverty, he has chosen to exploit those "new sources of wealth that were unknown to his ancestors," and to do so in the humane, paternalistic spirit of his ancestors. "With gentle blood in his veins, and old English feelings, he imbibed, at an early period of his career, a correct conception of the relations which should subsist between the employer and the employed. He felt that between them there should be other ties than the payment and the receipt of wages."[46] The sentiment might have come from Carlyle. But Mr. Trafford has evident advantages over Carlyle's self-made Captain of Industry. Carlyle could never explain why or how his Captain of Industry could succeed in rising above the "cash nexus" and establishing humane relations with his workers. Disraeli has a ready explanation at hand: it is Trafford's "gentle blood" and "old English feelings" that permit him to temper the new industrialism with the old paternalism. For Disraeli (as for Burke) blood and breeding may not be the necessary or sufficient conditions of virtue and wisdom, but they are the proximate and presumptive conditions.

The model employer produces appropriately model employees, happy, healthy, moral, intelligent. It is very like a utopia—not Sybil's medieval, religious utopia, nor Morley's communal one, nor Gerard's rural one, but a modern, secular, industrial one. Nor is it totally idyllic. Gerard is a militant Chartist in spite of the fact that he works for Trafford, and some of the workers in the other factories confess that they would have been bored at Trafford's and much prefer the less virtuous, less salubrious atmosphere of Mowbray.

The model industrialist, however, is something of an aside. The burden of the book is carried by the model aristocrat, Egremont—Mr. Egremont as he is in the beginning, the Earl of Marney at the end when he comes into an estate, the gossiping ladies estimate, equaled by only three peers in the kingdom. It is he who preaches the true social gospel: that "power has only one duty—to secure the social welfare of the PEOPLE." The people are not the repositories of power but the solemn responsibility of those entrusted with power, the "natural" aristocrats who are the "natural leaders of the People."[47] In refuting the medievalist, Chartist, and socialist solutions to the social problem, Egremont exposes the fallacies in their conceptions of the problem—and in their conceptions of the people, who are deemed problematic. His people are not the slavish, soured, stunted souls Sybil imagines them, nor the degraded brutes Gerard believes them to be, nor the isolated, embattled individuals Morley makes of them. Nor are the two nations, the RICH and the POOR, as implacably opposed to each other, as separated by an "utterly impassable" gulf, as they think.[48] That gulf, Egremont believes, can be bridged by meliorating the conditions of the poor and humanizing the relations of rich and poor—"not by levelling the Few," he tells Sybil, "but by elevating the Many."[49] Earlier a miner gave his version of the social problem: "Atween the poor man and the gentleman there never was no connection, and that's the wital mischief of this country."[50] Egremont's mission is to provide that "connection," thus restoring the unity of the two nations.

When Egremont makes his speech in Parliament endorsing the "results" of the Charter but not its "machinery," the clubmen do not know what to make of it.

"I think he must be going to turn radical," said the Warwickshire peer.

"Why, the whole speech was against radicalism," said Mr. Egerton.

"Ah, then he is going to turn Whig, I suppose."

"He is ultra anti-whig," said Egerton.

"Then what the deuce is he?" said Mr. Berners.

"Not a conservative certainly, for Lady St. Julians does nothing but abuse him."

"I suppose he is crotchety," suggested the Warwickshire noble.

"That speech of Egremont was the most really democratic speech that I ever read," said the grey-headed gentleman. . . . "I took him to mean, indeed it was the gist of the speech, that if you wished for a time to retain your political power, you could only effect your purpose by securing for the people greater social felicity."

"Well, that is sheer radicalism," said the Warwickshire peer; "pretending that the people can be better off than they are, is radicalism and nothing else."[51]

When Disraeli made his speech in Parliament, on July 12, 1839, endorsing the purpose of the Charter but not its mechanism, his colleagues did not know what to make of it. Like Egremont, Disraeli argued that the "social happiness" of the people depended not on their acquisition of "political rights" but on the security of their "civil rights," including the right to relief. Traditionally these rights had been assured by a ruling class that understood its own political power to be conditional upon the performance of its social duties. The middle classes enfranchised by the Reform Act did not understand this because they had no natural, neighborly relationship to the poor. Having attained power, they either denied the needs of the poor or, as in the case of the New Poor Law, transferred responsibility for those needs to a distant agency of the central government. Chartism was a protest against this irresponsible, alien idea of government, a protest tantamount to a "social insurrection" which the Whigs mistakenly took to be a "mere temporary ebullition." In that protest Disraeli proudly joined. "I am not ashamed to say, however much I disapprove of the Charter, I sympathize with Chartists."[52]

Three days after this debate in Parliament—Disraeli's Parliament, not Egremont's—there was a riot in Birmingham, which led the government to propose a bill for the establishment of a special police force. Of the 150 members of the House, Disraeli was one of three to vote against the bill, whereupon he was denounced by an Under-Secretary of State as an "advocate of riot and confusion." The following year he was in a minority of five opposing the severe punishments meted out to some of the Chartist leaders. Once again he called upon the aristocracy to assume its role as the natural leaders of the people and thus of the nation, "for the aristocracy and the labouring population form the nation." When a prominent radical praised him for his courageous action, he replied that a union between the Conservative Party and the "Radical masses" offered the only means by which the Empire could be preserved. "Their interests are identical; united they form the nation."[53]

Almost a century later the distinguished historian G. M. Young asked an elderly acquaintance, a "Gladstonian," why his generation was so distrustful of Disraeli. The answer surprised him. It was, his friend said, because of his "early Radicalism."[54] That answer would not have surprised the clubmen in *Sybil* or Disraeli himself. Nor would it have surprised the recent reviewer of several books on Disraeli who complained that the authors were not sufficiently appreciative of Disraeli's "revolutionary mind."[55] That comment carries some weight, coming as it does from Michael Foot, the leader of the Labour Party, for whom "revolutionary" is an unambiguous tribute.

Today Disraeli's version of Tory Radicalism may strike us as more Tory than radical. In his day "radical" was more often the operative word. What was radical about his Toryism was not his proposed solution to the social problem—the just and humane rule of a natural aristocracy—but his conception of the problem itself: the condition-of-the-people question, which was more than a question of poverty, which for him, as for Carlyle and Dickens, was a question of disposition as well as condition, of moral rights and duties, social obligations and "connections."

XXI

THE INDUSTRIAL POOR

A nineteenth century critic said that whereas Disraeli knew his subject, the condition of the people, as "a traveller knows the botany of a strange country," Mrs. Gaskell knew it as "an ardent naturalist knows the flora of his own neighborhood."[1] Elizabeth Gaskell's "neighborhood" was the country village in Cheshire sixteen miles from Manchester (a considerable distance in those days) where she spent her youth, and Manchester itself, where she lived as an adult. As a child making the rounds with her uncle, the local doctor, and as the wife of a Unitarian minister, she was as familiar with the daily lives of the poor as any middle class person could be—and as Disraeli never pretended to be.[2] Even after the success of *Mary Barton,* which brought her the acquaintance of Carlyle, Dickens, Thackeray, the Brontës, and other literary eminences, she remained worlds apart from Disraeli, geographically, socially, culturally, ideologically. Their novels were also worlds apart. Where he wrote social novels in the guise of silver fork novels, the scenes of lower class life alternating with high society and popular causes with parliamentary intrigues, her social novels were only once removed from domestic novels. Even her style was domesticated, less high-spirited and imaginative, lacking in the irony and wit, the flourish and fantasy that made his novels more entertaining if also less realistic. It is all the more remarkable, therefore, to find their diagnoses of the social problem so similar.

In *Sybil* it is the Owenite Stephen Morley who makes the memorable pronouncement about the "two nations." In *Mary Barton* it is the Chartist John Barton who complains of the gulf separating the "two worlds."

> Don't think to come over me with the old tale, that the rich know nothing of the trials of the poor. I say, if they don't know, they ought to know. We are their slaves as long as we can work; we pile up their fortunes with the sweat of our brows; and yet we are to live as separate as if we were in two worlds; ay, as separate as Dives and Lazarus, with a great gulf betwixt us.[3]

Although Disraeli had popularized that metaphor three years earlier, Mrs. Gaskell evidently came to it herself, for she seems not to have read *Sybil,* or, indeed, any of Disraeli's novels. Nor was the Chartist theme in her book inspired by the Chartist demonstration in the spring of 1848. *Mary Barton* was published several months after that event, but it had been completed by the end of 1847, so it was entirely fortuitous that the book, whose action revolved around the first Chartist convention of 1839, should have appeared after the fiasco of the last convention in 1848. What is even more curious is that the publisher, instead of capitalizing on its timeliness, delayed publication until October 1848, obliging the author to point out in the preface that it had been finished the year before and only received "confirmation" from the recent events on the Continent.[4]

The "two worlds" theme runs as a refrain throughout the novel, not only in the dialogue assigned to the characters but in the songs which preface each chapter and sometimes appear in the text as well. What the Blue Books were for Disraeli, the songs were for Gaskell—a testament of authenticity. A more compelling testament, in a sense, for the Blue Books were only secondary sources, statistics and reports drawn up by middle class officials, whereas the verses (like Reynolds's "histories") professed to speak in the native idiom of the poor, recounting their experiences and feelings in their own words and accents. The songs give this "Tale of Manchester Life" (as the subtitle has it) the appearance of something more than fiction, more even than a documentary, something very like a folktale. Gaskell was quite capable of summoning up moral passion and indignation in her own voice or in the voices of her characters. But she could never have been as unabashedly sentimental as the "Manchester Song" that opens, "How little can the rich man know / Of what the poor man feels," and concludes, "He [the rich man] never heard that maddening cry, 'Daddy a bit of bread!' "; or "The Oldham Weaver": "Oi'm a poor cotton-weyver, as mony as one knoowas, / Oi've nowt for t'yeat, an oi've woorn eawt my clooas"; or the poem by Samuel Bamford: "God help the poor, who, on this wintry morn, / Come forth from alleys dim and courts obscure."[5]

The songs, especially those in dialect, enhance the authenticity of the novel, as if giving witness to an existential reality the anonymous author was merely recording.* They also enhance the pathos, making it difficult to resist sympathizing and even identifying with the poor. When Gaskell wants to explain John Barton's reasons for becoming a Chartist, she does

---

*The painstaking rendition of the Lancashire dialect slows down the narrative and makes some of the dialogue almost incomprehensible. But it has the powerful effect of seeming to authenticate the characters and their opinions. Lest the reader have any doubt about the accuracy of the dialect, the fifth edition of *Mary Barton* appended two lectures by Mrs. Gaskell's husband, who had been responsible for the transliteration. The Lancashire dialect, he maintained, was closer to Chaucerian and Elizabethan English than to the modern "refined" language.

so by citing a poem: "What thoughtful heart can look into this gulf / That darkly yawns 'twixt rich and poor." She herself makes no secret of the fact that her own heart goes out to poor John Barton. He may be "wild and visionary" but his motives are honorable. Indeed, it is honorable to be visionary. "It shows a soul, a being not altogether sensual; a creature who looks forward for others, if not for himself."[6] Barton is visionary in the best sense, not at all the socialist or communist many suspect him of being.

> "You mean he was an Owenite; all for equality, and community of goods, and that kind of absurdity."
> "No, no! John Barton was no fool. No need to tell him that were all men equal to-night, some would get the start by rising an hour earlier tomorrow."[7]

If Barton is the hero of the novel—Gaskell's original title, *John Barton,* would have been more appropriate—his employer is by no means the villain.[8] Unlike Mr. Gradgrind and Mr. Bounderby, who are in the grip of a willfully perverse ideology, Mr. Carson is responding, however inadequately, to a real situation. Unless he lowers his costs, including the cost of labor, to meet foreign competition, his firm will go under and his workers will be unemployed rather than merely underpaid. "Distrust each other as they may, the employers and the employed must rise or fall together." The great mistake of the employers is that instead of making these facts known to their workers, they arrogantly stand on their right to pay whatever wages they like. And the workers, seeing the rich living in luxury while they are starving, determine to show their power and bring their masters to heel.

> So class distrusted class, and their want of mutual confidence wrought sorrow to both. The masters would not be bullied, and compelled to reveal why they felt it wisest and best to offer only such low wages; they would not be made to tell that they were even sacrificing capital to obtain a decisive victory over the continental manufacturers. And the workmen sat silent and stern with folded hands refusing to work for such pay. There was a strike in Manchester.[9]

. . .

"There was a strike in Manchester." To the Victorian reader that sentence was ominous, a signal of violence to come. And so it does, first in the workers' abuse of the "knob-sticks," the poor country weavers who flock into town looking for work and are waylaid by the strikers, beaten, and left lying half dead in the ditches. After witnessing a laborer blinded by vitriol thrown in his face, Barton swears he will have no part in such violence. But immediately afterward he commits himself to a more fatal act of violence when he takes the oath of fealty to his trade union and draws the marked paper that assigns him the task of assassinating his employer's son.

For most critics the assassination motif seriously vitiates the novel, converting what should have been a "representative" situation into an "exceptional" one, a "special case." Raymond Williams explains it as the "dramatization of the fear of violence which was widespread among the upper and middle classes at the time," a fear of what would happen if workers presumed to take matters into their own hands.[10] Others see it as an inability to confront the gravity of the class antagonism; when the issue is reduced to individual violence, it can be resolved by individual repentance and reconciliation. Here, as in other social novels, the plot is said to reflect the "limited social philosophies" of the authors, who are unable to see anything fundamentally wrong in the "social structure as a whole" and can only personalize the class conflict. The spectacle of violence thus has the effect of dissipating the problem and with it whatever sympathy may have been initially extended to the workers.[11]

There is some truth in these explanations, but not the whole truth. The violence that today seems gratuitous and contrived may not have seemed so at the time. If some scene of violence—a bloody strike, demonstration, riot, or murder—is as obligatory a part of the Victorian social novel as the sex scene in the modern novel, it may be because violence was so important a part of the social reality. (Early in the writing of *North and South,* Gaskell wrote to Dickens to ask whether he was planning to have a strike in *Hard Times,* which was then being serialized, and was relieved to hear that he was not.)[12] The burning of ricks and breaking of machines, the torchlight demonstrations and overturning of toll-booths, may not have aroused fears of revolution, but they did arouse and keep alive fears of violence. Murder, to be sure, was rare, but there was at least one notorious case in Manchester in 1831 similar to that in *Mary Barton,* an episode mentioned in several books written at the time and often referred to by later writers. Mrs. Gaskell denied having taken that as her model, although she remembered having heard about it and admitted that she might have been unconsciously influenced by it, as well as by "one or two similar cases at Glasgow."[13]*

The violence associated with strikes—with the very idea of a strike— reflected a conception of the social problem which made any kind of strike irrational and irrelevant. This conception of the problem was not as superficial as has been thought; indeed, it was precisely because these novelists took

---

*In *The Condition of the Working Class in England,* Engels spoke of the Manchester murder as unsolved, perhaps because he relied on the account in *The Manufacturing Population of England* by Peter Gaskell (no relation of Elizabeth Gaskell), which had been published in 1833 before the murderer was caught and tried. Peter Gaskell's book was a principal authority (and not only for this event) for important commission reports in the forties as well as for Engels, in spite of the fact that by then it was in many respects outdated.

so grave a view of the problem that they rejected the solutions represented by Slackbridge or Barton. Had they conceived of poverty as a problem of wages, hours, and working conditions, they might have been better disposed to unions and strikes which addressed just these issues. But theirs was the deeper problem of the two nations, the gulf between rich and poor that manifested itself not only in material deprivation but, as Gaskell said, in the more grievous "feeling of alienation."[14] In this view of the problem, the poor were not only poor—this they had always been, and, often, much poorer than they now were. What was new, or was perceived to be new, was the separation of the poor from the rest of society, as if their poverty disqualified them from membership in the larger human community, the one nation of Englishmen. To this problem neither strikes nor unions were the solution. In fact, they could only aggravate the problem by increasing the gulf between the classes, pitting them against each other, making their interests more irreconcilable and their common bonds of humanity more tenuous.

The problem, once again, was the one that had exercised Carlyle. One of the few literary references in *Mary Barton* was to "that worthy Professor Teufelsdreck, in *Sartor Resartus*."[15]* But Gaskell was more sensitive than Carlyle (or Dickens or Disraeli) to the practical problems of industry, and less hostile to the principles of political economy. Although they appreciated the importance and even the grandeur of industry and admired the enlightened, energetic entrepreneur, they were so busy reacting against what they took to be the mechanical, materialistic, inhuman precepts of political economy and utilitarianism that they could give no credence to the legitimate arguments of the economists. Gaskell, on the other hand, while professing to be ignorant of economic theory, was sufficiently familiar with the affairs of Manchester businessmen to have some respect for the basic principles, if not the entire philosophy, of political economy, and to try to reconcile those principles with the demands of morality and humanity.

That reconciliation is consummated toward the end of *Mary Barton* in a scene that the modern reader may find a disconcerting blend of sentimentality and ideology. On his deathbed John Barton confronts Harry Carson, his former employer whose son he has murdered. For the first time Carson appears to him not as "the enemy, the oppressor," a "being of another race," but as a poor, desolate old man mourning the death of his son.[17] Carson too is transformed by that encounter. While he cannot immediately bring

---

*Carlyle was one of the first to write Gaskell praising *Mary Barton* and identifying the author as a woman—"beautiful, cheerfully pious, social, clear and observant." Later the Carlyles and Gaskells met at dinner parties in London (occasionally at Dickens's house), and Carlyle was often a houseguest of the Gaskells in Manchester. Their friendship, however, did not prevent the acerbic Mrs. Carlyle from describing her as a "very kind cheery woman, but there is an atmosphere of moral dulness about her, as about all Socinian women."[16]

himself to forgive his son's murderer, after a feverish night of reflection and Gospel reading he returns to take the dying man in his arms and forgive him. He then asks two of Barton's friends to explain the tragedy. Barton, he is told, was "sadly put about to make great riches and great poverty square with Christ's Gospel." Not that he was an Owenite—"all for equality, and community of goods, and that kind of absurdity"; in fact, he had no care for material goods, still less for riches.

> "But what hurt him sore, and rankled in him as long as I knew him (and, sir, it rankles in many a poor man's heart far more than the want of any creature-comforts, and puts a sting into starvation itself), was that those who wore finer clothes, and eat better food, and had more money in their pockets, kept him at arm's length, and cared not whether his heart was sorry or glad; whether he was bound for heaven or hell. It seemed hard to him that a heap of gold should part him and his brother so far asunder. For he was a loving man before he grew mad with seeing such as he was slighted, as if Christ himself had not been poor. At one time, I've heard him say, he felt kindly towards every man, rich or poor, because he thought they were all men alike. But latterly he grew aggravated with the sorrows and suffering that he saw, and which he thought the masters might help if they would."[18]

Carson listens attentively and even sympathetically before putting his own case, the case of political economy, the natural laws of supply and demand which govern him as much as the workers. "We cannot regulate the demand for labour. No man or set of men can do it. It depends on events which God alone can control." One of the workers protests that if improvements in machinery throw men out of work, making "a man's life like a lottery," it must surely be part of God's plan that those He created happy and well off should relieve the suffering of those who were poor and miserable. Facts, Carson replies, have shown how undesirable relief is, how much better it is for every man to be independent and self-reliant. Facts, comes back the retort, are not "fixed quantities"; men's feelings and passions, weaknesses and strengths, are part of the problem, and these too are God-given. "Now, to my thinking, them that is strong in any of God's gifts is meant to help the weak,—be hanged to the facts!"[19]

So the dialogue goes on, both sides reasonable and honest, Carson making his case briefly and coolly, Job Legh, the worker, for all his protestations of ignorance, eloquently and persuasively. As they are about to part, Carson thanks him for his candor and regrets only that the masters do not have the power to remedy the situation. Job Legh then delivers himself of his final argument. It is not the want of power that is at issue but the "want of inclination." If only the employers had tried to find a remedy, that would have been enough; "we'd bear up like men through bad times." That effort alone, signifying that others are "caring for their sorrows," would have made all the difference, averting the strike and thus the murder.[20] Once Carson begins to understand this, he is moved to develop a new social philosophy which will make masters and men appreciate their common interests and bring them together for the common consideration of those interests. For this purpose it is necessary "to have educated workers, capable of judging, not mere machines of ignorant men; and to have them bound to their employers by the ties of respect and affection, not by mere money bargains alone; in short, to acknowledge the Spirit of Christ as the regulating law between both parties."[21]

The murder, then, is not a "special case," a willful act of violence introduced because the author knew no other way of resolving the problem. The murder of Carson's son may be understood as a response to the spiritual murder committed by the father, the murder of those natural feelings that should have bound him to his "fellow-creatures." It is the father who first broke the social compact expressed in "Christ's Gospel."[22] The killing of his son is an act of retribution—and perhaps something more than this, a reenactment, one suspects, from the repeated invocations of the name of Christ, of the murder of the Son of God.

This is not the way most commentators have interpreted it. To them the murder is a bit of trumpery, a pretext for an easy resolution and reconciliation—a "change of heart" solution to the social problem, as one critic contemptuously refers to it.[23] Yet the point of the novel is precisely the heartlessness not so much of the industrial system as of the philosophy of industrialism which makes the relations of masters and men dependent on "mere money bargains alone." In this sense Gaskell was more radical than the modern critic who believes the social problem more appropriately addressed by strikes or unions seeking better "money bargains." She was also more radical than the other social novelists of her own time who had less understanding of the economic imperatives behind those money bargains and were therefore more inclined to think of the masters as selfish, evil, or at the very least benighted. Mr. Carson is not a hypocritical egotist like Mr. Bounderby, nor a mindless prattler about facts and figures like Mr. Gradgrind, nor a petty exploiter like the firm of Shuffle and Screw in *Sybil*. He is thoughtful, dignified, honest, a worthy adversary for John Barton and Job Legh. When he talks about the need to compete with foreign manufacturers, it is not in the petulant spirit of the mill owners of Coketown who threaten "to pitch their property in the Atlantic" if they do not have things entirely their way. His is a genuine economic dilemma. He understands the grievances of the workers (he had been one himself), but he also understands the complexity of the problem. From the perspective of a socialist or a Marxist, his resolution of the problem appears contrived and inconsequential, an evasion of the class conflict and the structural crises of capitalism, a "personalized" solution providing for a "conciliation between the classes on terms put forward by exemplary employers."[24] At the time, however, that conciliation was no mean goal, especially when it required of those employers that they reconsider an ideology they had been taught to think of as embodying the very laws of nature, and admit to their counsels workers whose views they had never considered and whose judgments they had never valued.

In *North and South,* written six years later, the dialectic of conflict and conciliation works itself out in more complicated ways. Here it is not just a question of class pitted against class but of one culture against another, the industrial north against the rural south. The heroine carries the burden of this theme as she moves from the south to the north and experiences that enlargement of sympathy and sensibility which permits her to appreciate the crude virtues of industrialism, the kindness and candor that lie behind the brusque manners of rich and poor alike, the absence of social pretensions among the manufacturers in spite of their ostentatious display of wealth, and the independence of the workers in spite of their misery and discontent. Rural society appears to her more genteel and gracious but also less energetic and vital, more amiable in social relations but less democratic and less free.

The confrontation of north and south puts in a new perspective the earlier confrontation of capital and labor. For the vices of the north turn out to be mirror images of its virtues, reflections of the democratic spirit that animates the new industrial society. The servants in the north, Margaret Hale finds, are less accommodating, more impertinent than those in the south; but they are also less servile and more natural—better human beings if worse servants. And the factory workers, rough and bold by southern standards, have an "open, fearless manner" she can only admire. Her own servant, whom she has brought up with her from the south, finds it difficult to adjust to the new breed of workers. "Why master and you must always be asking the lower classes upstairs, since we came to Milton, I cannot understand. Folk at Helstone were never brought higher than the kitchen."[25]

The mill owners of Milton are also more democratic than the farmers and country gentlemen of Helstone. And they are so precisely when they are vaunting their wealth, for this is their only pretense to superiority. Early in their acquaintance, Thornton, the leading manufacturer of Milton, tells the newly arrived Hales something of his background. Not boastfully, as Bounderby might have done, but matter-of-factly he explains that his father died in very miserable circumstances and that he started his career as a poor shop-boy. Margaret's mother is shocked by this confession and later rebukes her husband (himself an impoverished clergyman) for exposing her to such an unseemly association. Margaret herself takes it in good part, as she does

Thornton's assertion that it is "one of the great beauties of our system, that a workingman may raise himself into the power and position of a master by his own exertions and behaviour." If this is a myth, as she suspects, it is an eminently democratic and agreeable one, for it makes success depend on virtues such as "prudent wisdom and good conduct," which are available to everyone, unlike breeding and cultivation, the characteristic virtues of the south, which are not.[26]

Thus it is the north, not in spite of but because of its newness and rawness, its concern for material acquisition and advancement, that offers a new mode of social conciliation. The strike in *North and South* is considerably less violent than that in *Mary Barton;* Thornton himself pronounces it a "respectable strike."[27] And the protagonists of this novel do not have to undergo the extreme experiences of those in *Mary Barton* in order to achieve either personal or social salvation. There is no murder, no deathbed scene, no spiritual conversion, no supreme effort of contrition and forgiveness. Thornton has only to lose his mill, not his son, to bring him to a better understanding of the workers, and the latter have only to suffer a trade depression to realize how thoroughly interdependent their interests are with those of their employers. If industrialism is the problem, it is also the solution to the problem. Margaret had an intimation of this earlier when she began to discover the attractiveness and virility of the industrialists.

> She liked the exultation in the sense of power which these Milton men had. It might be rather rampant in its display, and savour of boasting; but still they seemed to defy the old limits of possibility, in a kind of fine intoxication, caused by the recollection of what had been achieved, and what yet should be. If, in her cooler moments, she might not approve of their spirit in all things, still there was much to admire in their forgetfulness of themselves and the present, in their anticipated triumphs over all inanimate matter at some future time, which none of them should live to see.[28]

In the course of the novel, the trade depression and strike do much to subdue that spirit of "exultation." By the end the bankrupt Thornton is looking for a new position in which he modestly hopes to conduct "one or two experiments" to bring about a more intimate intercourse between workers and employers, a new relationship that would go beyond the "mere 'cash nexus.' " Asked whether such a relationship can prevent the recurrence of strikes, he admits that the most he expects is that they will no longer be the bitter, venomous affairs they had been. "A more hopeful man," he concludes, "might imagine that a closer and more genial intercourse between classes might do away with strikes. But I am not a hopeful man."[29] He is, in fact, being disarmingly modest. The idea that strikes can be an acceptable, even "respectable," part of the industrial scene is bolder than it sounds, as are his "one or two experiments" designed to involve the workers in the planning process and bring the two classes into "personal intercourse" by acquainting them with each other's "characters and persons, and even tricks of temper and modes of speech."[30] He proposes to go beyond the "cash nexus" while remaining within the system of industrial capitalism, to bridge the gulf between the two nations by diminishing the very real differences between them, differences of knowledge, custom, even—that most intractable of all class differences in England—"modes of speech."

North and South is the most "optimistic" of the social novels, not because it belittles the social problem but because it looks for its melioration within the framework of the same industrial order that created the problem. In this respect it signifies a return to the social vision of Adam Smith and a rejection of that of Malthus and Ricardo. Gaskell did not, to be sure, share Smith's confidence in the "invisible hand," the natural, automatic operation of a free economy which would assure the best interests of capitalists and laborers, producers and consumers. Like all the social novelists, she regarded the natural state of industry and commerce with some suspicion, just as she regarded any state of nature with suspicion. In that natural state, industry tended to be amoral and antisocial, subversive of traditional relationships and obligations. She went beyond the others, however, in sensing that industry was no longer in that natural, primitive state. Early in the novel, Thornton describes to Margaret the evolution of industry from the beginning of the century when the "cotton-lords" had wielded almost unlimited power and had exercised it tyrannically over customers as well as workers. Those days are over; now he stands hat in hand before customers and bargains on a more "evenly balanced" basis with workers.[31] By the end of the novel he is proposing to hasten that evolutionary process by actively engaging the workers in the planning of industry. If he no longer experiences that primitive, uninhibited sense of exultation, the feeling of unlimited power over nature, the "anticipated triumphs over all inanimate matters," he retains the vitality that permits him to remain in Milton in spite of his bankruptcy (unlike the characters in *Mary Barton* who emigrate to Canada, and in Kingsley's *Alton Locke* to America), and the confidence in industry that emboldens him to pursue his experiments.

North and South is also the most optimistic of the novels in its image of the industrial workers—more optimistic, indeed, than Adam Smith, who had feared that the division of labor, while promoting the material well-being of factory workers, would make them "as stupid and ignorant as it is possible for a human creature to become."[32] It is interesting that none of the social novelists, however bitter their indictment of industrialism on other counts, found it guilty of this particular charge. Whatever vestiges of rural idyll there were (and there were fewer than one might think), they had to do with the physical beauty of the countryside, the healthiness of country living (although Disraeli's portrait of Marney denied even this), the nostalgia for a simpler, more natural, more settled way of life. Compared with agricultural laborers, factory workers were often depicted as sickly, stunted, pale, unhappy, discontent. But mentally, intellectually, they were generally assumed to be more than a match for their "country bumpkin cousins."

The opening scene of *Mary Barton,* an outing of factory workers to the countryside outside of Manchester, is sometimes cited as an example of the idealization of country life, the pastoral scene providing a counterpoint to the grim factory town.[33] John Barton, lamenting the sickly condition of his wife, recalls how fresh and rosy-cheeked she was when she first came to Manchester from the country. On the previous page, however, the "fresh beauty" of the country girl is offset by the "deficiency of sense in her countenance, which is likewise characteristic of the rural inhabitants in comparison with the natives of the manufacturing towns." John Barton himself is such a native. Born and bred in Manchester with all the physical defects of the species, he is below the average in size and pale of complexion, but he has the "acuteness and intelligence of countenance, which has often been noticed in a manufacturing population."[34]

North and South conveys the same image of the factory workers— stunted, impoverished, embittered, but with an intellectual vitality that makes them worthy opponents (and potential collaborators) of their employers. Their vitality comes from precisely those conditions that are the cause for complaint—the congestion, noise, and tumult of the factory and the town. When Nicholas Higgins, the strike leader, tells Margaret that he is considering leaving his trade and going south to bring up his family in the dignity and comfort of the countryside, she disabuses him of that idyllic dream.

> You would not bear the dullness of the life; you don't know what it is; it would eat you away like rust. Those that have lived there all their lives, are used to soaking in the stagnant waters. They labour on from day to day, in the great solitude of steaming fields—never speaking or lifting up their poor, bent, downcast heads. The hard spadework robs their brain of life; the sameness of their toil deadens their imagination; they don't care to meet to talk over thoughts and speculations, even of the weakest, wildest kind, after their work is done; they go home brutishly tired, poor creatures! caring for nothing but food and rest. You could not stir them up into any companionship, which you get in a town as plentiful as the air you breathe, whether it be good or

bad—and that I don't know; but I do know, that you of all men are not one to bear a life among such labourers.[35]

This is an implicit refutation of the dire vision of factory life in that famous passage of the *Wealth of Nations,* and of the equally dire vision of urban life expressed by the Owenite Stephen Morley in *Sybil,* where the city appears as a teeming mass of individuals with no sense of community, an "aggregation" without "association."[36] Just as the factory workers in *Sybil* belie Morley's fears by happily congregating in the "Temple of the Muses" and the local Mechanics' Institution, talking, arguing, reading, and organizing themselves for the demonstration, so in *North and South* this communal side of urban life, the "companionship" that is as "plentiful as the air you breathe," emerges as one of the great advantages of the north over the south. This is the truly optimistic vision of Gaskell: not the "experiments" of Thornton to bring workers and employers closer together and thus bridge the gap between the two nations, but the image of workers who, however impoverished, are sufficiently alert and intelligent to bridge that gap by their own efforts. So far from being dehumanized by the machine and desocialized by the cash nexus, these workers are stimulated to meet, talk, think, and act—and strike, if they so desire. Technology and the division of labor are less fatal to the human spirit than the kind of "nature" from which these workers have escaped—the back-breaking toil in the fields and the isolated, stagnant life in the countryside.

Gaskell was not alone in coming to this conclusion. The myth of a Golden Age was widely perceived to be a myth. Certainly none of the great social novelists succumbed to the obvious temptation of idealizing rural life or seeking the restoration of a pre-industrial economy and society. Gaskell differed from the others only in focusing more intently on the industrial problem; she did not subsume it, as Dickens did, under the subject of utilitarianism, nor, as Disraeli did, under that of paternalism. Nor did she complicate the picture by the presence of all those Dickensian and Mayhewian characters who did not fit tidily into the industrial scene. Except for the occasional prostitute (like Mrs. Barton's sister—but even she left town), there were no street-folk, circus-folk, vagrants, paupers, criminals, or eccentrics in her novels. Milton, as its name suggests, was a pure mill town with a purely industrial working population. It was these workers Gaskell (and Thornton) so much admired and of whom they expected so much—workers whose lives were entirely circumscribed by the factory and town, who were totally dependent on the new technology and the new society created by it, who had not even the distractions of a circus or a Temple of the Muses to relieve the tedium of reality.

Gaskell would not have been opposed to a circus in Milton; indeed, she would have welcomed it. But she had no desperate need of it as Dickens had. And she had no need of it because Manchester (or its fictional equivalent) was no longer for her, as it still was for Dickens, a "shock city." Having lived in Manchester, she was not so disturbed by the noise and smoke of the town, the "crashing, smashing, tearing" of the machinery, as was the occasional visitor.[37] (Even Dickens, in his journalistic report on Manchester, was far less dramatic than in the fictional account of Coketown.) It was not that familiarity bred complacency; no one could justly accuse Gaskell of that. If she was optimistic about the future, about the possibility of an enlightened industrial order and a thriving industrial population, it was because she had come to realize that the present was not as deplorable as some thought, that industrialism was not as inhuman and soul-destroying, political economy as mean-spirited and unyielding, the class conflict as pervasive and devastating, nor the working classes as hopelessly demoralized and dehumanized. Her working classes, the workers of Milton, were resilient, assertive, independent, intelligent, entirely capable of taking direction of their lives and affairs. "There's granite in all these northern people," Margaret tells her father.[38]

There was poverty too, not the "natural" poverty inflicted by physical nature or an all too human nature, the poverty associated with bad harvests and famines, sickness and old age, improvidence and intemperance. The factory workers of Milton could not have been immune to this kind of misfortune, but this was not their grievance. The poverty they complained of seemed to them less natural, more arbitrary, than the perils of nature or the infirmities of body and soul. They resented the machines that appeared to cheapen the value of their labor and make them redundant—a "surplus population," as the political economists told them. And they were suspicious of laws of supply and demand, of trade depressions and foreign competition, which seemed always to work in their disfavor, impoverishing them far more than their employers. While Gaskell sympathized with their feelings, she was confident that they could be made to understand that their interests, as much as their employers', depended upon a proper exploitation of the machinery that enhanced the value of their labor and their purchasing power, and upon a proper respect for the imperatives of political economy which were neither as rigid nor as unjust as they thought. The situation as she presented it, as the enlightened workers and employers of Milton came to see it, was not at all the "muddle" it was for Stephen Blackpool. On the contrary, it was amenable to reason, good will, and, as Tocqueville would have said, self-interest "properly understood."

If for no other reason, this message may be found objectionable today because of its blandness, its careful trimming and balancing of the issues. At the time it was thought provocative and partisan, although readers disagreed on the nature of its partisanship. Herbert Spencer, himself a doctrinaire laissez-faireist, was annoyed with the author of *Mary Barton* (or authoress, as he had heard) for "torturing my feelings so needlessly"; but he thought it a most instructive book and hoped everyone would read it.[39] From the opposite ideological pole came the tribute of Thomas Carlyle, who also saw in it the fine hand of a woman, and praised it as a "real contribution (about the first real one) towards developing a huge subject."[40] To the radical worker, Samuel Bamford, it was a "sorrowfully beautiful production which few could contemplate with tearless eyes."[41] Mary Howitt, a Quaker with radical inclinations, reported that a silk manufacturer of Macclesfield, "a fat, jolly Conservative, whose people are emphatically *hands,*" denounced it as a "dangerous, bad book."[42] Gaskell herself had the impression that half the factory owners in Manchester were bitterly angry with her, and the other half (the better half, she thought) were buying the book for the local workers' libraries. "No one can feel more deeply than I how *wicked* it is to do anything to excite class against class; and the sin has been most unconscious if I have done so." But she did not believe she had done so; she had only tried to "represent the subject in the light in which some of the workmen certainly consider to be *true*"—which was not, she added, the "abstract absolute truth."[43]

Critics today are even more divided on the nature of the truth Gaskell tried to communicate, the truth as she herself saw it and as she thought the workers saw it. Whatever their other reservations, most radical commentators are inclined to commend her for representing the "real" working class, the industrial working class conscious of its "class-oneness," in contrast to those amorphous Dickensian "poor" whom Orwell and others found so unrepresentative and unsatisfactory. Nor is she praised only for her fictionally plausible working class characters and scenes. She is also credited with giving a historically "accurate" account of them, faithful to the details of their everyday life as well as their "characteristic feelings and responses." This accuracy, however, is not discerned in other aspects of her novels; the "exceptional" case of murder and the resolution of the social problem by "exemplary" employees are said to reflect her "middle class" ideology of humanitarianism, reformism, and class reconciliation. Thus radical critics judge the scenes evoking class consciousness and class conflict to be "successful," while those mitigating the conflict are dismissed as unrealistic.[44]

If the novels have an ideological bias, so, surely, has this critique. The historian may marvel at the confidence of the literary critic pronouncing upon the accuracy of details of everyday life and of "characteristic feelings and responses"—this purely on the basis of the novel itself. If Gaskell was so accurate in portraying the workers, why should it be supposed (short of deliberate dishonesty) that she was less accurate in portraying the employers, with whom she was obviously better acquainted? And if her resolution of the conflict is deemed "middle class," may it not be that the speeches of John Barton and his friends, so eloquently expressive of their working class consciousness, were themselves the product of her sympathetic and imaginative middle class consciousness? In fact her views of the social problem, however typical of the middle classes, were also typical of many spokesmen of the working classes. Here, as so often, "middle class" serves less as a class designation than as an ideological one, signifying any position that falls short of the degree of militancy and alienation the critic may deem appropriate.

Nor is the conservative critique more cogent: the idea that Gaskell, while commendably appreciative of economic realities, fell victim to the familiar fallacies about the impoverishment and misery of the working classes.[45] It may be true (the weight of the evidence suggests that it is true) that the standard of living of the working classes—on the average, in the aggregate, and over the whole of the period—improved as a result of industrialism, that social mobility increased, and that there was good reason to think that the improvement and mobility would continue. But it was also true that there was a widespread (although by no means universal) impression to the contrary, that in some sense—moral if not material, social if not economic—the condition of the working classes had deteriorated and the gulf between the two nations had become larger and more ominous. This impression was conveyed, in fiction as in reality, by scenes of misery and violence, exaggerated and exceptional to be sure, but capturing some part of the truth. If the novels seemed authentic to readers at the time, it was partly because they echoed the newspapers and magazines, parliamentary reports and sensationalistic exposés. Then, as always, it was not statistical averages and aggregates that shaped public opinion but individual cases and dramatic, often atypical, examples.

There is an important sense, then, in which the novels are authentic, even when they are ideologically biased and historically inaccurate. They are authentic in representing a point of view, Gaskell's, that was not as idiosyncratic or contrived as it may seem today, and in representing a view of the working classes, their conditions and dispositions, feelings and ideas, that appeared plausible at the time. Gaskell may have helped disseminate and perpetuate these views, but she did not invent them. And they gained in authenticity because, whatever one may think of them today, by comparison with the "sensation novel" they were notably unmelodramatic, realistic, even "domestic" in tone.

In fact, most of the social novelists had a more complicated view of the social reality than they are often credited with. They did not share the mythology and demonology of some of their contemporaries. They had no illusions about a merry old England before the age of the steam engine and railroad; if they found much to deplore in the present, they did not fall into the temptation of glorifying the past, still less seeking, as Cobbett did, to revive it. They regretted the loss of the peace, beauty, and simplicity of the countryside, but they were well aware of the less salubrious aspects of country life (the rural slum in Marney or, as Egremont reminded Gerard, the terrible pestilences in the old days). And while there were the usual set pieces about the noise, heat, and monotonous routine of the factory, the smoke, filth, congestion, and callousness of the town, there was also an acute sense of the vitality, intelligence, independence, and even communality generated by both factory and town. Raymond Williams complains that Gaskell evaded the social issue when she had her leading characters, at the end of *Mary Barton,* emigrate to Canada. But it is perhaps more significant that she did not have them return to the country; certainly in *North and South* the future of the characters, and their salvation, lay in the industrial north rather than in the rural south.[46] John Ruskin said that "Dickens was a pure modernist—a leader of the steam-whistle party par excellence. . . . His hero is essentially the ironmaster."[47] If that remark seems excessive, it is interesting that Ruskin could have thought of Dickens that way—and if Dickens, then surely Gaskell.

The issue in most of the novels was not, in fact, industrialism or capitalism but utilitarianism and political economy, or rather the ideas and attitudes generally associated with those doctrines, ideas and attitudes deemed fatal to the poor and crippling to the rich. They were thought dehumanizing because they reduced all human relationships to the "cash nexus," and demoralizing because they condemned individuals to an unremitting struggle for existence and classes to an unremitting struggle against each other. In that Benthamite, Malthusian, Ricardian universe, every good was purchased at great cost—at great cost to the individual who had to sacrifice beauty to utility, love to self-interest, tranquillity to economic security, and at great cost to other individuals with conflicting interests, needs, and wants. The result was a terrible disjunction between economics and morality, the individual and society, the rich and the poor.

If the conclusions of the novels are unsatisfactory, it is because the novelists were caught in an agonizing dilemma. They wanted the material, moral, and social benefits of technology and private enterprise, industrialism and capitalism; they saw in such an economy the means of alleviating poverty, broadening and enriching the lives of the poor, giving them opportunities for advancement, liberating them as individuals and elevating them as a class. But they were appalled by the ideas and values that seemed to be inextricably linked with such an economy, by what they regarded as a vulgar materialism and a ruthless individualism that were spiritually impoverishing, socially divisive, and morally repugnant. If there was any nostalgia for the past, it was for something very like Adam Smith's moral philosophy, although they would not have identified it as such: a philosophy designed to reconcile different kinds of goods, to harmonize the interests of individuals and classes, to bridge the gulf between rich and poor by stressing their common nature and making them both the beneficiaries of a free society and an expanding economy—to overcome, in short, that disjunction between economics and morality, the individual and society, the rich and the poor, which had become so grievous. That philosophy had been submerged for half a century or so, during which time the only support, the only legitimization, for an industrial, commercial, capitalist economy—the "industrial system," as it was called—seemed to be the dismal science of Malthus and Ricardo and the dismal philosophy of Bentham.

In the absence of an alternative ideology, the social novelists could only give voice to their moral outrage. Modern critics, radical and conservative alike, who find the novels ideologically jejune, are in this sense correct. What the novels expressed was not a coherent doctrine but a cry of protest, not a social ideology but an appeal to social consciousness and conscience. The *Athenaeum* said as much (ironically, in the language of political economy) in its review of *Sybil*.

> "Sybil" . . . is welcome, if taken as a sign of the times—a sign that the relations of rich and poor—the enlargement of the former's sympathies and the amelioration of the latter's misery,—are becoming matters of interest. Even if benevolence, and generosity, and liberality, are traded in (as the most simple cannot but suspect), the very fact that they are marketable, says something for the health and progress of Mankind.[48]

So too the *Westminster Review* on *Mary Barton*.

> It embodies the dominant feeling of our times—that the ignorance, destitution and vice which pervade and corrupt our society must be got rid of. The ability to point out how they are to be got rid of, is not the characteristic of this age. That will be the characteristic of the age that is coming.[49]

It is no criticism of the novelists, still less of the age, to say that the expression of moral concern, the enlargement of sympathies, the impulses of benevolence, generosity, and liberality, were a "sign of the times," even the "dominant feeling" of the times, but that they did not point the way to any positive philosophy or policy of reform; that such a philosophy and policy, capable of abolishing "ignorance, destitution, and vice," would have to await the "age that is coming." This was the legacy bequeathed by the early Victorians to the late Victorians—and by the late Victorians to all subsequent generations, including our own. Because ignorance, destitution, and vice are not so easily done away with, that legacy of social obligation carries with it a large burden of frustration and guilt. If we have still not discovered how to discharge that obligation, it was no small achievement of the early Victorians to have recognized the obligation itself. Indeed, it was something of a triumph of the moral imagination to have done so in the face of a powerful ideology that denied it and a powerful temptation to evade it, either by retreating to some pastoral idyll of a mythical past or some utopian idyll of a mythical future.

If the moral imagination found its most powerful expression in the literary imagination, it is not surprising that social consciousness was more highly developed than social ideology or social policy. Nor is it surprising that the poor, instead of being perceived en masse, as a collective working class, should emerge from the novels in all their variety and individuality. This was the real triumph of imagination, of the moral as well as literary imagination: to accord to the poor all the complexity of character and situation that had always been the prerogative of the rich. The best of the novelists complicated their stories the most, interweaving the public and private, the social and domestic, the misery of poverty and the tragedy of discord, the virtues and vices of the rich and the virtues and vices of the poor. It is sometimes said that the novelists moralized the poor, saw them through the lens of their own middle class morality. So they did. They moralized the poor just as they moralized the rich. If there were deserving poor, there were also deserving rich; if there were vicious, criminal poor, there were vicious, criminal rich; if the poor had their villains and heroes, and more who were something of both, so did the rich. To think it "middle class" to ascribe to the poor a moral identity that made them, in this respect at least, the peers of the rich, is a measure of how far we have come from the Victorians, how radically we have redefined the terms of moral discourse —and redefined them, perhaps, not entirely in the interests or to the credit of the poor.

EPILOGUE

"The mischievous ambiguity of the word *poor*"—if there was a single theme dominating the discussion of poverty in the early nineteenth century, it was this. The phrase appeared in the *Poor Law Report* of 1834.[1] But it had been anticipated almost forty years earlier by Edmund Burke when he objected to the "political canting language," the "puling jargon" of the expression "labouring poor."[2] The issue was not semantic; it went to the heart of the conception of poverty and the image of the poor, of the "social problem" as it was called, and of the social policies deemed appropriate to that problem.

Burke's objection was to the confusion of genres implied in "labouring poor," the confusion between those who worked for their subsistence and were properly known as "labouring people," and those who could not work and were dependent on charity or relief. It was for the latter, he insisted, that the word "poor" should be reserved—"for the sick and infirm, for orphan infancy, for languishing and decrepit old age."[3] The poor law reformers used other language to make the same point. By rigorously distinguishing, in theory and policy, between the "independent poor" and the "dependent," between "laborers" and "indigents" or "paupers," they hoped to eliminate the ambiguity that they thought had done so much mischief.

Both of them appealed to tradition to support their distinctions. But tradition told against them. What they took to be an unfortunate ambiguity had been the accepted and perfectly acceptable reality for centuries. It had not been an ambiguity for medieval churchmen who made the giving of alms to the poor—laboring or otherwise, "holy" or "unholy"—a sacred Christian duty. Nor for the Elizabethan statesmen who devised the system of public, compulsory relief known as the "poor laws," which were meant to provide for all the poor, including, in certain situations and under certain conditions, the "able-bodied poor." Nor for the justices of the peace who administered the laws of settlement, which gave every legal resident of a parish a claim upon that parish for relief in case of need. Nor for the mercantilists who devised ingenious means by which to convert the "idle poor" into the "industrious poor" for the greater benefit of the nation. Nor for the early Methodists who based their social gospel on the dictum, "The poor are the Christians." Nor for the philanthropists who founded scores of societies and institutions to minister to every kind of misfortune that could befall the poor. Nor for the poor themselves who assumed that they had a right to fair wages when they worked and to parish relief when they did not.

Nor was it an ambiguity for Adam Smith. Indeed, least of all was it an ambiguity for him. For Smith's "system of natural liberty" derived from his "moral philosophy," and that philosophy posited a continuum within the entire body of the poor and within the nation as a whole. He opposed the laws of settlement as a violation of liberty, a hindrance to mobility, and hence a grave impediment to the well-being of the poor. But he did not oppose the poor laws, and he favored state-subsidized education for the very poor. If he did not make an issue of pauperism it was because it was not a problem for him, the paupers being part of that large body of the poor who would benefit from a free, expanding, progressive economy, an economy that would generate a "universal opulence which extends itself to the lowest ranks of the people." Everyone was capable of functioning in that economy and everyone would profit from it, since nothing more was required than the simple, common, human attribute, "the propensity to truck, barter, and exchange."[4] This was a "low" view of human nature, but a democratic one, for it endowed everyone, from the lowest ranks to the highest, with the same "natural talents" and gave them the same stake in "natural liberty."

It was Malthus who made the idea of poverty "ambiguous"—fatally ambiguous, one might say—by raising the specter of a population constantly at the mercy of the food supply, and by condemning the poor to an eternal recurrence of "misery and vice." Smith's error, he said, was in assuming that an expanding industrial economy would create a direct correlation between the "wealth of nations" and the "happiness and comfort of the lower orders of society," an assumption decisively disproved by his own "principle of population," which established an inverse relationship between the two.[5] The growth of industry would indeed promote the wealth of the nation, but only at the expense of the welfare of the poor, for it would lead to an increase of population without a concomitant increase of food, thus aggravating the condition of those hardest pressed for subsistence. There was no way of ameliorating that condition since any relief given to paupers would lead to an increase of their numbers, a decrease of the food available for the entire body of the poor, and thus a greater degree of misery and vice.

Unlike Smith, then, Malthus opposed the poor laws. He also opposed, again unlike Smith, high wages, since they too would encourage the poor to have larger families. The idea of "moral restraint," introduced in the revised edition of the *Essay,* would have broken the cycle of a geometrically increasing population, an arithmetically increasing food supply, and a series of checks, all conducive to misery and vice, which kept the two in balance. But it could have done so only if Malthus repudiated the "principle of population," and this he was not prepared to do. The specter of Malthusianism, in its original, stark, unqualified, ineluctably tragic form, gripped the imagination of contemporaries for half a century, making even more fearful a period fraught with anxiety and insecurity.

With or without Malthus, it could be argued, the movement for the repeal or reform of the poor law would have come to a head. There is no doubt, however, that Malthusianism provided the "one thing needful," as Carlyle said, to undermine the old law: a theory which made that law not the solution to the problem of pauperism but a large part of the problem itself, a major cause of the pauperization and demoralization of the poor. Instead of abolishing the law, as Malthus advocated, the reformers decided to amend it. By separating pauper and poor, by giving relief to able-bodied paupers only in the workhouse and on the condition of "less-eligibility"—by creating, in effect, a pauper law rather than a poor law—they hoped to eliminate the "mischievous ambiguity" that had such unfortunate consequences.

The popular perception of the New Poor Law turned out to be quite the opposite. The "stigma" of pauperism, which was meant to differentiate the pauper from the poor, had the perverse effect of stigmatizing the entire body of the poor, thus reinforcing the very ambiguity the reformers had so strenuously tried to remove. The new ambiguity, however, was different from the old in one important respect. Where the old had assimilated the pauper into the body of the poor, the new unwittingly assimilated the poor into the class of the pauper. Ultimately, the new law may have had some of the salutary results the reformers had hoped for. By helping to break the cycle of dependency, by reducing the number of paupers and alleviating the burden on the economy, it may have improved the conditions of the laboring poor. More immediately, it seemed to pauperize the laboring poor, in spirit if not in fact. Perhaps it could not have been otherwise; at a time when pauper and poor were in the closest relationship, any stigma attaching to the one inevitably tainted the other as well.

That, at any rate, was how it appeared to a great many people who agreed on little else than this. The new law, Disraeli declared, announced to the world that in England "poverty is a crime."[6] The reformers had not, in fact, said or meant that; it was pauperism, not poverty, that they saw as the problem, and they saw it as a disease rather than a crime. To Disraeli, as to many traditional Tories, the cure for the disease was worse than the disease itself, for the new law jeopardized not only the paternalistic structure of society but the legitimacy of the social order, the ethos that bound rich and poor together in a "chain of connections." Carlyle denounced the old and the new law alike, the old for putting a "bounty on unthrift, idleness, bastardy and beer-drinking," the new as the epitome of the "pig philosophy" that reduced morality to utility and social relations to the "cash nexus."[7] Cobbett, on the other hand, defended the old law as an essential part of the "social contract" established at the time of the Reformation, and attacked the new law as a violation of that sacred undertaking, hence a subversion of the very foundations of society.

From the beginning the agitation against the New Poor Law merged with a variety of other issues: universal suffrage, child labor, female labor, safety conditions in factories and mines, sanitary conditions in the towns, the newspaper tax, the corn laws, the currency, national debt, temperance, taxation, education, emigration, machinery, private property, even the private family. Thus the controversies of the thirties and forties went beyond the issue of poverty or the condition-of-England question narrowly conceived, and raised the largest questions about property and equality, natural law and the social contract, the rights and duties of individuals, the obligations of society and the state. If there is any temptation to think of the early Victorians as complacent and insensitive, rigidly and predictably ideological, obsessed with material gain and private interest, the social and intellectual history of this period should put that misapprehension to rest.

What gave the question of poverty its urgency was not, as Engels thought, the fear of social revolution, of hordes of "dangerous classes" storming the citadels of property and power, but a profound sense of moral and social disarray. However poverty was viewed—as an inexorable fact of physical and human nature, as an unfortunate by-product of a particular law or institution, or as the fatal flaw of the entire system—it was seen as primarily, fundamentally, a moral problem. It was a moral problem for the poor and for society—for the poor as responsible moral agents, and for society as a legitimate moral order. Carlyle inveighed against the materialistic, mechanistic spirit of the age which sought simple solutions for complicated problems, "Morrison's pills" to cure all social ills. But those pills were intended to solve the moral and social as well as the material and economic ills of the poor. In their different ways, contemporaries sought to fill the moral vacuum created by Malthusianism, to "re-moralize" the poor by one or another means: a New Poor Law, which would remove the poor from the temptations and degradations of pauperism; or the restoration of the old Poor Law, which would legitimize relief and return the pauper to the community of the poor; or laissez-faireism, which would enhance the moral responsibility of the poor by making them free individuals in a free economy; or factory acts which would protect the most vulnerable of the poor, women and children, from the moral and physical debilitation of factory work; or sanitation acts which would shield the poor from the indignities and ravages of urban life; or a "new radicalism" which claimed for the poor the right to the full produce of their labor; or Chartism, which claimed for them the right to full membership in the polity.

A more dramatic challenge to the moral imagination came from those of the poor who were not so much a distinctive class as a distinctive "race," as Mayhew put it—a "culture," we would say today. Such were the street-folk, whose occupations and ways of life were so alien that they appeared to inhabit a "foreign," "unknown" country; or the "residuum," the refuse of humanity, who constituted a social problem in the same sense in which the refuse of the sewers (also called "residuum") was a sanitary problem; or the "ragged classes," whose "raggedness" infected their homes and lives as well as their attire; or the "dangerous classes," the criminals and outcasts, who were, as one commentator put it, "in the community, but neither *of* it, nor *from* it"—*in* the community of the poor physically, geographically, but not *of* it socially and morally, nor, some suspected, *from* it biologically.[8]

There had always been such marginal and "outcast" groups, but the growth of the large towns, and of the metropolis especially, had made them more conspicuous, if not more numerous. It is interesting that they became the center of attention at a time when their numbers were decreasing and the conditions of the working classes as a whole were improving. Perhaps it was for just this reason that Mayhew's "revelations" came as such a shock. When the ordinary poverty of the laboring poor became less problematic, the extraordinary, peculiar poverty of the street-folk and ragged classes, and the habitual, endemic criminality of the dangerous classes, became more problematic. To the mid-century Englishman basking in the glories of the Crystal Palace, the persistence of these types of poverty was a disquieting reminder of the limits of civilization. For they seemed to be caused not by the niggardliness of nature (famines or the disproportion of people and food), or the cyclical movements and maladjustments of the economy, or the technological revolution that threatened to create a "surplus population," but rather by the sheer recalcitrance of some human beings, the willful, perverse refusal to abide by the ethos that had stood so many other Englishmen in good stead. The street-folk were not simply poorer than other poor people; they were "peculiarly" poor, as Mayhew repeatedly said —peculiar in their habits and values, their attitudes toward work, play, family, sex, property, law, authority, religion. Mayhew spoke of their distinctive "moral physiognomy."[9] Today we might invoke the idea of a distinctive "culture of poverty," or, in the case of the dangerous classes, a "culture of criminality."

The moral imagination that was kindled by works like Mayhew's, by Royal Commission reports and journalistic exposés, by the debates over the Reform Act, New Poor Law, and Ten Hours Bill, was powerfully reinforced by the literary imagination. Indeed the two were intimately related, Carlyle inspiring Dickens and Dickens Mayhew (or vice versa, as some think), Disraeli drawing upon the Blue Books and Reynolds punctuating his Gothic novels with Chartist sermons. If the fiction, "low" and "high" alike, sensationalized the lowest types of poor (the Jack Sheppard and Fagin types), it also dramatized the "two nations" theme, the gulf between rich and poor that was said to be tearing society apart.

The problem of the two nations, for social critics as well as social novelists, was not so much a problem of poverty as such, not even of the gross inequality between rich and poor, but rather of the lack of "connection" between rich and poor, the "feeling of alienation."[10] This was the recurrent complaint: the sense that individuals and classes no longer felt responsible for each other, that human relations had been reduced to calculations of interest, that the only social reality was the "cash nexus." The problem, it was generally agreed, had been exacerbated by industrialism and urbanism, by conditions of work in the factories and life in the towns. But the novelists (like many of the radicals) were careful to dissociate themselves from anything resembling Luddism or socialism. Their quarrel was not with industrialism or capitalism but with utilitarianism and political economy, with the complex of ideas, attitudes, values, and practices epitomized by the dismal philosophy that de-humanized human beings and the dismal science that de-moralized social relations. They were less concerned with the condition-of-England question as we now understand it, the standard-of-living question, than with the moral and social condition of the poor. A good case was made out at the time that the standard of living of most of the working classes, during most of this period, was rising, and that this improvement was a direct consequence of the "industrial system." But this argument was largely irrelevant to those who thought that material conditions were less important than moral dispositions and social relations, and that in these respects the situation of the poor—and, indeed, of society as a whole—had deteriorated.

After the middle of the century, the sense of urgency began to abate, in part because the poor were visibly sharing in the moral as well as material progress of the nation, in part because the attitudes and ideologies that had seemed so threatening to them proved to be more humane and conciliatory in practice than in theory. Political economy, it was discovered, was less dogmatic than the first generation of Malthusians and Ricardians made it seem; Parliament was more amenable to social reforms and responsive to an aroused social conscience; and the economy was beginning to bear out the sanguine predictions of Adam Smith. As poverty—the normal poverty of the normal working classes—became less onerous and less problematic, the idea of poverty became normalized and "moralized." The stigma that had attached to poverty in the aftermath of the New Poor Law and in the turmoil of the thirties and forties gradually disappeared; whatever stigma remained was reserved for the dependent and the unrespectable poor, those who existed on the margins of society or were outcasts from society. The bulk of the poor, the "working classes" as they were increasingly called, were seen as respectable, deserving, worthy, endowed with the puritan virtues which had served the middle classes so well, and which were shortly to earn the working classes that coveted badge of respectability, the suffrage.

"When 'poverty' was rediscovered in the 1880s," E. P. Thompson has written, "few remembered that Mayhew had been there before."[11] The quotation marks around "poverty" suggest that what was "rediscovered" in the 1880s was very different from what Mayhew had discovered—that if few remembered he had been there before, it was for the good reason that he had not, in fact, been there.

In the sequel to this volume, the 1880s stand in dramatic contrast to the 1840s, a contrast all the more striking because on the surface the two decades seem so similar. In both cases economic depressions created social unrest among the working classes and a heightened social consciousness among the middle classes. In the forties that consciousness was largely channeled into legislative reforms, in the eighties into private philanthropies, institutions, and charities. One might have expected the reverse, that with the relaxation of laissez faire and the growth of the administrative agencies of the state, later generations would have been inclined to look to Parliament and the state for the solution of social problems. Perhaps it was the intensity of their zeal, a desire for personal commitment and sacrifice, which prompted so many high-minded men and women in the eighties to devote not only their money but their lives to good works. Or perhaps the appeal to Parliament had to wait until the "new" social problem was defined in such a way as to make it amenable to legislative action.

If any single event can be associated with the redefinition of that problem, it is the publication of Charles Booth's *Life and Labour of the People in London,* the first volume of which appeared in 1889 and subsequent volumes (seventeen in all) in the following fourteen years.[12] In 1886 (the year, as it happened, when Booth started his research), Sidney Webb wrote to the secretary of the Fabian Society: "Nothing in England is done without the consent of a small intellectual yet practical class in London not two thousand in number."[13] Charles Booth was a distinguished member of that class; the Booths were a prominent Liverpool shipping and trading family, and Mrs. Booth was a Macaulay and a cousin of Beatrice Potter (later Mrs. Sidney Webb). A Unitarian by birth and a Positivist by conviction, Booth was a perfect exemplar of what Beatrice Webb called the "Time-Spirit": the combination of public service and scientific faith which inspired that "small intellectual yet practical class."

The most highly publicized discovery of Booth's work was that 30.7 percent of the population of London was poor. The precision of that figure was as impressive as its magnitude; indeed, the precision seemed to authenticate the magnitude. Altogether, the study appeared to be a model of scientific objectivity. On the basis of a massive, meticulous, house-to-house survey, it established a "line of poverty" and differentiated various classes above and below that line. Contemporaries (and some historians) may be forgiven for thinking that the ambiguity which had so long befuddled the subject of poverty had finally been resolved. In fact a good deal of ambiguity remained. The income figures were often based on estimates rather than actual earnings, and the classes were described and even defined as much in moral as in economic terms. Booth made no secret of the fact that the "poor" were his "clients"; it was for their sake that he proposed to locate the "very poor" in industrial camps where they would be out of the way of the poor, not competing with them for jobs and not threatening their status. This was an extraordinary proposal for a laissez-faireist like Booth to make; he himself thought it tantamount to "state slavery."[14] In fact, it was an effort to do what the poor-law reformers had tried to do half a century earlier: to remove the able-bodied paupers from the society of the poor by confining them in workhouses.

If Booth's study was ambiguous in the sense that it was not as objective or precise as it professed to be, it was unambiguous in identifying the "poor" as his, and society's, "clients." These poor were distinguished on the one hand from the "very poor" (paupers, street-folk, the residuum), and on the other from the "comfortable" working classes who were above the "line of poverty." That line did not, contrary to most accounts, define poverty in purely economic terms. But it did make poverty problematic by defining everyone falling below that line—for whatever reason, moral or economic —as "poor."

The effect of this redefinition of poverty was profoundly moral. If earlier in the century the Malthusians and poor-law reformers had unwittingly "de-moralized" the poor by tainting them with the stigma of pauperism, toward the end of the century Booth (and a host of other philanthropists, reformers, socialists, and "social scientists," as they were beginning to be called) "re-moralized" the poor by focusing attention on a class that was poor but not pauperized, psychologically, morally, or culturally. This was very much like the old class of the deserving poor. But whereas earlier it had been assumed that the deserving poor were deserving because they were not a social problem and therefore did not require the assistance of society, now it was assumed that the deserving poor were a social problem requiring assistance precisely because they were deserving—and they did not become any the less worthy or respectable for receiving such assistance. This was the class that was the chief beneficiary of the major measures of social legislation of the early twentieth century, the Old Age Pensions Act of 1908 and the National Insurance Act of 1911.

The subsequent history of the idea of poverty has involved both a redefinition of poverty and a reformulation of the social problem. As a young Member of Parliament in 1920, Clement Attlee said that "Booth had dispelled forever the complacent assumption that the bulk of the people were able to keep themselves in tolerable comfort."[15] In fact Booth had confirmed just that assumption: if less than one-third of the people were below the line of poverty, more than two-thirds (including a large majority of the working classes) were above it—were, as Booth said, "in comfort." Attlee's misreading of Booth was prophetic, for it anticipated the welfare state he himself helped establish a quarter of a century later. The principle of the welfare state was to provide not relief but services; and not only to the poor or even the working classes but to everyone "across the board"; and not in accord with a "line of poverty" (not even the much elevated line of poverty devised by Seebohm Rowntree in his survey published in 1941), but of a standard of welfare; and not the minimum standard earlier proposed by the Webbs, but what the Labour Party manifesto of 1945 called an "optimum" standard.[16]

The concept of welfare might have displaced the idea of poverty, had it not been for the "rediscovery" of two older species of poverty: "pockets of poverty" among groups whose special needs were not satisfied by "across the board" services and who required "supplementary benefits" (a euphemism for relief), and a "culture of poverty" among those who proved to be as resistant to the ministrations of the welfare state as to any other kind of state. (It is perhaps no accident that Mayhew was reprinted at this time.) These, however, were peripheral groups and secondary problems. To restore the primacy and centrality of the idea of poverty, another redefinition was called for: poverty as "relative deprivation."[17] By that definition one-third, two-thirds, or any proportion of the people could fall into the category of the poor and be regarded as a "social problem."

That poverty is a relative concept is hardly a new discovery. Two centuries ago Adam Smith gave it its classic formulation: "By necessaries I understand, not only the commodities which are indispensably necessary for the support of life, but whatever the custom of the country renders it indecent for creditable people, even of the lowest order, to be without."[18] In a society like Smith's, which candidly recognized the existence and the legitimacy of different ranks, degrees, and orders, that relative concept had natural limits, limits established by the "custom of the country." Today the concept of relative deprivation has so thoroughly relativized the idea of poverty as to remove all limits, to make poverty so protean as to deprive it of form and shape. It is no longer a matter of raising the standard of "subsistence" or of extending the concept of "needs" to "felt needs"— "wants" as distinct from "needs." "Relative deprivation" has become whatever the social inquirer—not the "custom of the country" or the people who are the subject of inquiry—may regard as such. Thus the anthropologist Mary Douglas interprets poverty as "restriction of choice," while the sociologist Peter Townsend, in the most elaborate recent study of poverty, includes among his "indicators of poverty" the lack of hot breakfasts, of birthday parties, of holidays, and of the habit of dining out.[19]

The historian, contemplating this latest phase in the age-old controversy, may be tempted to review the data to find out what proportion of the people today would be judged poor by Booth's "line of poverty," or, conversely, what proportion of the people in Booth's time would be judged poor by Townsend's standard of deprivation. It is an interesting exercise, but not quite to the point. However striking that discrepancy may be, it does not take the full measure of the distance we have come. That distance cannot be measured quantitatively, in terms of a higher or lower standard of poverty, or the number or proportion of people designated as poor. The new measure is qualitatively, conceptually different from the old. As his critics have pointed out, Townsend's concept of relative deprivation measures not poverty but inequality. And not even inequality in the usual sense, defined by income, standard of living, or social status, but by differences of "styles of living." By such criteria the stigma of poverty may attach to any variation of habit, taste, preference, judgment, capacity, will, or character. It is not only a thoroughly relativistic idea; it is a thoroughly moralistic one. From the point of view of the "objective" social scientist, it is even regressive, for it makes of poverty once again a matter of manners and morals, of individual character and social ethos.

"The mischievous ambiguity of the word *poor*"—a century and a half after those words were penned, we may well find ourselves echoing that old complaint. Through all the stages of an industrial economy, from the "takeoff" to "mature," "late," and now "post" industrialism; through all the phases of an industrial society, from a vestigial paternalism, to laissez-faireism, to the "new liberalism" of social reform, to the welfare state; through all the vicissitudes of an expanding and contracting empire, of war and peace, depression and prosperity, the poor have remained with us and poverty has continued to be a "social problem."

Not, to be sure, the same poor, the same problem, or the same poverty. It is not a case of *Plus ça change, plus c'est la même chose.* Poverty today in England (and in America, Europe, or any advanced industrial country) is most decidedly not the same thing it was in the age of Smith and Malthus, Cobbett and Dickens. By any objective standard of income, condition, or status, the poor today in these countries are considerably better off, materially and socially, than they were then. Macaulay predicted that just as some of his own contemporaries located the Golden Age in a period which was anything but golden, when "noblemen were destitute of comforts the want of which would be intolerable to a modern footman," so Victorian England would appear to be a Golden Age to those who had far surpassed it.

> It may well be, in the twentieth century, that the peasant of Dorsetshire may think himself miserably paid with twenty shillings a week; that the carpenter at Greenwich may receive ten shillings a day; that labouring men may be as little used to dine without meat as they now are to eat rye bread; that sanitary police and medical discoveries may have added several years to the average length of human life, that numerous comforts and luxuries which are now unknown, or confined to a few, may be within the reach of every diligent and thrifty working man. And yet it may then be the mode to assert that the increase of wealth and the progress of science have benefitted the few at the expense of the many, and to talk of the reign of Queen Victoria as the time when England was truly merry England, when all classes were bound together by brotherly sympathy, when the rich did not grind the faces of the poor, and when the poor did not envy the splendour of the rich.[20]

Macaulay's errors are as instructive as his truths. He underestimated the rise of wages and of the standard of living, the improvement of sanitary conditions and the increase of longevity, the diffusion among the poor of comforts and luxuries once confined to the rich, and the invention of others not dreamed of by rich or poor. And he vastly overestimated the indulgence that the future would extend to the past. So far from early Victorian England being regarded as a "truly merry England," it is more often looked upon as a time of unmitigated misery and discontent, when the classes were divided by a great gulf of alienation, when the rich did indeed "grind the faces of the poor" and the poor envied and hated the rich. Yet there is a basic truth in his prediction. For the dissatisfaction that made his contemporaries think so ill of their own times is with us still. If it has not made us better disposed to Macaulay's age, neither has it made us better disposed to our own. Whatever progress has been charted on the graph of "progress and poverty," it is poverty that still strikes the eye and strikes at the heart. It is as if the modern sensibility can only register failure, not success, as if modernity has bequeathed to us a social conscience that is unappeasable and inconsolable.

If this is the bequest of modernity, it may be salutary to recall a past that was as complicated and varied as we know the present to be, when the best of intentions sometimes had the worst effects and unanticipated consequences were often more consequential than anticipated ones. Then, as now, solutions to the problem of poverty were inadequate to the problem itself, and not only for the obvious reasons—economic, technological, political, administrative—but because the problem itself was always changing. These changes reflected not only the new conditions of industrialism but also new modes of thought and sensibility. The industrial revolution was accompanied by a series of intellectual revolutions that were no less momentous: a new moral philosophy, a new political economy, a new social science, a new radicalism, a new Toryism. And with it all came a new moral imagination that could no longer take comfort in the ancient adage, "For ye have the poor always with you."

NOTES

The complete bibliographical information for each source appears in the first citation of that source in each chapter.

INTRODUCTION

1. James Boswell, *The Life of Samuel Johnson, LL.D.* (Chicago, 1952 [1st ed., 1791]), p. 182.

2. R. H. Tawney, *Religion and the Rise of Capitalism* (New York, 1947 [1st ed., 1926]), p. 222.

3. *The Rambler,* Sept. 18, 1750.

4. Benjamin Franklin, "On the Price of Corn, and Management of the Poor" (1766), and letter to Alexander Small (November 5, 1789), quoted by Howell V. Williams, "Benjamin Franklin and the Poor Laws," *Social Service Review,* 1944, pp. 79, 82.

5. Asa Briggs, "The Welfare State in Historical Perspective," *Archives européennes de sociologie,* 1961, p. 222.

6. As a result of the seminal work by Oliver MacDonagh ("The Nineteenth-Century Revolution in Government: A Reappraisal," *Historical Journal,* 1958, and *A Pattern of Government Growth, 1800–1860: The Passenger Acts and Their Enforcement* [London, 1961]), recent discussion has focused on the administrative capacity of the state. But the same analysis would apply to the legal, constitutional, and other factors which might have impeded or promoted particular "solutions."

7. R. G. Collingwood, *An Autobiography* (Oxford, 1970 [1st ed., 1939]), p. 110.

8. J. S. Mill, "Coleridge" (1840), *Essays on Politics and Culture,* ed. Gertrude Himmelfarb (New York, 1962), p. 121.

9. Laurence Veysey, "Intellectual History and the New Social History," in *New Directions in American Intellectual History,* ed. John Higham and Paul K. Conkin (Baltimore, 1979), p. 13.

10. On art, see, for example, John Barrell, *The Dark Side of the Landscape: The Rural Poor in English Painting, 1730–1840* (Cambridge, 1980); Francis D. Klingender, *Art and the Industrial Revolution* (New York, 1968); T. J. Edelstein, "They Sang 'The Song of the Shirt': The Visual Iconology of the Seamstress," *Victorian Studies,* 1980; Asa Briggs, *Iron Bridge to Crystal Palace: Impact and Images of the Industrial Revolution* (London, 1979).

11. Thomas Carlyle, *Chartism* (1839), in *English and Other Critical Essays* (London, Everyman ed., n.d.), p. 167.

12. This caution applies to the better known memoirs by, for example, William Lovett, Samuel Bamford, Thomas Cooper, and Alexander Somerville. For other memoirs or fragments of memoirs, see David

Vincent (ed.), *Testaments of Radicalism: Memoirs of Working Class Politicians 1790–1885* (London, 1977); Vincent (ed.), *Bread, Knowledge and Freedom: A Study of Nineteenth-Century Working Class Autobiography* (London, 1981); John Burnet (ed.), *Annals of Labour: Autobiographies of British Working-Class People, 1820–1920* (Bloomington, Ind., 1974) (published in London under the title *Useful Toil: Autobiographies of Working People from the 1820s to the 1920s*); Burnet (ed.), *Destiny Obscure: Autobiographies of Childhood, Education and Family from the 1820s to the 1920s* (London, 1982).

13. Most of the recent work on France has concentrated on the eighteenth century and earlier periods, e.g., Jeffry Kaplow, *The Names of Kings: The Parisian Laboring Poor in the Eighteenth Century* (New York, 1972); Olwen H. Hufton, *The Poor of Eighteenth-Century France, 1750–1789* (Oxford, 1974); Jean-Pierre Gutton, *La société et les pauvres: L'exemple de la généralité de Lyon, 1534–1789* (Paris, 1971); Gutton, *L'Etat et la mendicité dans la première moitié du XVIIIᵉ siècle: Auvergne, Beaujolais, Forex, Lyonnais* (Paris, 1973); Cissie C. Fairchilds, *Poverty and Charity in Aix-en-Provence, 1640–1789* (Baltimore, 1976); Alan Forrest, *The French Revolution and the Poor* (Oxford, 1980). Most of the recent works on America, like many of those on France, are local histories, e.g., Raymond A. Mohl, *Poverty in New York, 1783–1825* (New York, 1971); Nathan Irvin Huggins, *Protestants against Poverty: Boston's Charities, 1890–1900;* Eric H. Monkkonen, *The Dangerous Class: Crime and Poverty in Columbus, Ohio, 1860–1885* (Cambridge, Mass., 1975).

In one sense, local history works at cross-purposes with comparative history, provincializing rather than internationalizing, reducing rather than enlarging the scope of history. But within the national context, local history has successfully exploited the comparative method, comparing, for example, different cities or even different areas within a city. See, for example, John Foster, *Class Struggle and the Industrial Revolution: Early Industrial Capitalism in Three English Towns* (London, 1974); Gary B. Nash, *The Urban Crucible: Social Change, Political Con-* sciousness, and the Origins of the American Revolution (Cambridge, Mass., 1980) (on Boston, New York, and Philadelphia).

CHAPTER I

1. R. H. Tawney, *Religion and the Rise of Capitalism* (New York, 1947 [1st ed., 1926]), p. 19.

2. The quotation from the *Manifesto* is given here in the form in which it was quoted by Tawney, p. 223.

3. *Ibid.,* pp. 210, 223.

4. Lawrence Stone, introduction to R. H. Tawney, *The Agrarian Problem in the Sixteenth Century* (New York, 1967 [1st ed., 1912]), p. xi.

5. The Webbs have been most influential in perpetuating the view that relief in this period came under the heading of "The Framework of Repression." (Sidney and Beatrice Webb, *English Poor Law History* [London, 1927], Part I, p. 427.) For more balanced views, see Joyce Oldham Appleby, *Economic Thought and Ideology in Seventeenth-Century England* (Princeton, 1978); Dorothy Marshall, *The English Poor in the Eighteenth Century* (London, 1926); Marshall, *Dr. Johnson's London* (New York, 1968); M. Dorothy George, *London Life in the Eighteenth Century* (London, 1925); George, *England in Transition* (Penguin ed., London, 1953 [1st ed., 1931]); A. W. Coats, "Changing Attitudes to Labour in the Mid-eighteenth Century," *Economic History Review,* 1958; Coats, "Economic Thought and Poor Law Policy in the Eighteenth Century," *Economic History Review,* 1960; Coats, "Relief of Poverty, Attitudes to Labour, and Economic Change in England, 1660–1782," *International Review of Social History,* 1976. (See also below, p. 41.)

6. E. J. Hundert, "The Making of Homo Faber: John Locke Between Ideology and History," *Journal of the History of Ideas,* 1972, pp. 3–22; Maurice Cranston, *John Locke* (London, 1957), pp. 424–26.

7. Charles Wilson, *Economic History and the Historian* (New York, 1969), p. 77. (The title of Child's book varied from edition to edition.)

8. Daniel Defoe, *Works,* ed. John S. Keltie (Edinburgh, 1869), p. 544.

9. Great Britain. *The Statutes at Large from the Twelfth Year of King Charles II to the Last Year of King James II* (London, 1763), VIII, 94.

10. Wilson, *Economic History and the Historian,* p. 89. The estimates vary enormously, both among contemporaries and historians. For 1750, for example, the estimates of the poor rates range from £1,000,-000 to £3,500,000. (W. A. Speck, *Stability and Strife, England, 1714–1760* [Cambridge, Mass., 1977], p. 77.) The estimates of expenditures on private charities are even less reliable.

11. Appleby, p. 131.

12. Hundert, p. 7.

13. *English Historical Documents* (New York, 1953), VIII, 516–17. Other versions of the table differ from this since they are based on different manuscripts left by King. (E.g., George, *England in Transition,* pp. 150–51; Peter Mathias, *The First Industrial Nation: An Economic History of Britain, 1700–1914* [London, 1969], p. 24.) On the discrepancies among the various manuscripts, the flaws in King's statistics, and their interpretation, see Mathias, *First Industrial Nation,* pp. 25 ff; Mathias, "The Social Structure in the Eighteenth Century: A Calculation by Joseph Massie," *Economic History Review,* 1957, p. 32; G. S. Holmes, "Gregory King and the Social Structure of Pre-industrial England," *Transactions of the Royal Historical Society,* 1977.

14. Bernard Mandeville, *The Fable of the Bees,* ed. Philip Harth (London, 1970 [1st ed., 1723]), p. 294.

15. Tawney admitted that Mandeville's ideas about the poor were not "typical," but thought them "straws which show how the wind is blowing." (*Religion and the Rise of Capitalism,* p. 161.)

16. Mandeville, *Fable,* pp. 370, 208. (I have sometimes altered the capitalization, punctuation, and spelling so as not to distract from the natural reading of the text.)

17. *Ibid.,* p. 289. Mandeville himself claimed that the first edition of the *Fable* had been barely noticed by the press, and that it was only with the inclusion in the revised

edition of the "Essay on Charity and Charity-Schools" that the book acquired the notoriety it did.

18. The classic account of these schools does not use this expression nor convey this impression. (M. G. Jones, *The Charity School Movement: A Study of Eighteenth Century Puritanism in Action* [Cambridge, 1938].) But the concept appears in more recent studies, e.g., M. W. Flinn, "Social Theory and the Industrial Revolution," in *Social Theory and Economic Change,* ed. Tom Burns and S. B. Saul (London, 1967), pp. 14, 17; Richard Johnson, "Educational Policy and Social Control in Early Victorian England," *Past and Present,* 1970. For a critique of this theory applied to the Sunday schools, see Thomas Walter Laqueur, *Religion and Respectability: Sunday Schools and Working Class Culture, 1750–1850* (New Haven, 1976), pp. 187 ff. On the subject of social control in general, see Morris Janowitz, "Sociological Theory and Social Control," *American Journal of Sociology,* 1975; A. P. Donajgrodzki (ed.), *Social Control in Nineteenth Century Britain* (Totowa, N.J., 1977); review of Donajgrodzki by Martin J. Wiener, *Journal of Social History,* 1978; F. M. L. Thompson, "Social Control in Victorian Britain," *Economic History Review,* 1981; Alan Heesom, "The Coal Mines Act of 1842, Social Reform, and Social Control," *Historical Journal,* 1981. See pp. 41, 59–60, 178, 553 n. 2.

19. Mandeville, *Fable,* p. 283.

20. *Ibid.,* pp. 294–95.

21. *Ibid.,* p. 276.

22. Adam Smith, *Theory of Moral Sentiments* (7th ed., London, 1792 [1st ed., 1759]), II, 305.

23. Jacob Viner, *The Long View and the Short* (Glencoe, Ill., 1958), pp. 332–42. See also Nathan Rosenberg, "Mandeville and Laissez-Faire," *Journal of the History of Ideas,* 1963, pp. 183–96.

24. Tawney, *Religion and the Rise of Capitalism,* p. 161.

25. Max Weber, *The Protestant Ethic and the Spirit of Capitalism* (Chicago, n.d. [1st ed., 1904–05]), p. 95. For the later controversy on the nature of Methodism, see Elie Halévy, *England in 1815,* vol. I of *A History of the English People in the Nineteenth Century*

(London, 1960 [1st ed., 1913]), pp. 387 ff; J. L. and Barbara Hammond, *The Town Labourer, 1760–1832* (London, 1966 [1st ed., 1917]), pp. 258 ff; E. P. Thompson, *The Making of the English Working Class* (New York, 1964), pp. 350 ff; E. J. Hobsbawm, "Methodism and the Threat of Revolution in Britain," in *Labouring Men* (London, 1964), pp. 23–33; Gertrude Himmelfarb, "Postscript on the Halévy Thesis," in *Victorian Minds* (New York, 1968), pp. 292–99; J. D. Walsh, "Elie Halévy and the Birth of Methodism," *Transactions of the Royal Historical Society,* 1974; Robert F. Wearmouth, *Methodism and the Common People of the Eighteenth Century* (London, 1945); Wearmouth, *Methodism and the Working Class Movements, 1800–1850* (London, 1937); John Kent, *The Age of Disunity* (London, 1966); Michael Hill, *A Sociology of Religion* (New York, 1973), pp. 183 ff. An interesting philosophical (rather than historical) critique of the Weber thesis is by Leo Strauss, *Natural Right and History* (Chicago, 1953), pp. 59 ff. The most extensive recent study of Methodism, revising the "Halévy thesis" in some respects and reaffirming it in others, is Bernard Semmel, *The Methodist Revolution* (New York, 1973). Semmel has also translated and introduced an early essay by Halévy, *The Birth of Methodism in England* (Chicago, 1971 [1st ed., 1906]). This essay is strikingly different from Halévy's more familiar work, both because it deals with the early period of Methodism and because it offers a more economic, almost Marxist interpretation.

26. Quoted by Weber, p. 175.

27. John Wesley, *Works* (Grand Rapids, 1872), VI, 126, 136. This was the sermon cited by Tawney as a "conspicuous exception" to the "conventional ethics." (See above, p. 31.)

28. Wearmouth, *Methodism and the Common People,* pp. 207–08.

29. See J. H. Plumb, "The New World of Children in Eighteenth-Century England," *Past and Present,* 1975. Very little of this change of attitude is reflected in Ivy Pinchbeck and Margaret Hewitt, *Children in English Society* (2 vols., London, 1969–73).

30. J. D. Walsh, "Elie Halévy and the Birth of Methodism," *Transactions of the Royal Historical Society,* 1975, pp. 14–15.

31. W. J. Warner, *The Wesleyan Movement in the Industrial Revolution* (London, 1930), p. 163.

32. Semmel, *The Methodist Revolution,* p. 56.

33. Wearmouth, *Methodism and the Common People,* p. 229.

34. Semmel, *The Methodist Revolution,* p. 193.

35. Stuart Andrews, *Methodism and Society* (London, 1970), p. 46.

36. Mandeville, *Fable,* p. 329.

37. Francis Hutcheson, *An Inquiry into the Original of Our Ideas of Beauty and Virtue* (4th ed., London, 1738 [1st ed., 1725]), p. 181 (sect. 3, par. 8); *The Works of Jeremy Bentham,* ed. John Bowring (London, 1843), X, 46, 79–80, 567. Beccaria's *Essay on Crimes and Punishments* was first published in 1764 (translated in 1767), and Priestley's *Essay on Government* in 1768—both long after Hutcheson's work.

38. David Hume, *An Enquiry Concerning the Principles of Morals* (La Salle, 1938 [1st ed., 1751]), p. 67 (sect. 5, part 2).

39. William Maitland, *The History of London from Its Foundations by the Romans to the Present Time* (London, 1739), pp. 635, 800.

40. Maitland, *The History and Survey of London* (London, 1756), II, 764. (The title was changed for the second, two-volume edition.) Caroline Robbins makes the point that Scottish philosophers were more concerned with the condition of the poor than English philosophers at this time. (*The Eighteenth-Century Commonwealthman* [Cambridge, Mass., 1959], pp. 177 ff.) But if English philosophy was laggard, English philanthropy was not. For a list of philanthropic societies and institutions, see Ford K. Brown, *Fathers of the Victorians: The Age of Wilberforce* (Cambridge, 1961), pp. 329–40. On philanthropy in general, see David Owen, *English Philanthropy, 1660–1960* (Cambridge, Mass., 1964). An excellent monograph on one philanthropic institution is Ruth McClure, *Coram's Children: The London Foundling Hospital in the Eighteenth Century* (New Haven, 1981).

41. Jones, *The Charity School Movement,* p. 3.

42. George, *England in Transition*, p. 74.

43. Allan Bloom, introduction to Rousseau, *Emile, or On Education* (New York, 1979), pp. 18–20; Clifford Orwin, "Compassion," *The American Scholar*, 1980, p. 319. For Rousseau's use of the idea, see *Emile*, Book IV.

44. *The Life, Unpublished Letters and Philosophical Regimen of Anthony, Earl of Shaftesbury*, ed. Benjamin Rand (London, 1900), p. 158.

45. *Letters of Edmund Burke*, ed. Harold J. Laski (Oxford, 1922), pp. 303–04 (to the Chevalier de Rivarol, June 1, 1791).

46. George, *London Life*, p. 36.

47. Eveline Cruikshanks, *Hogarth's England* (London, 1957), p. 55.

48. Marshall, *Dr. Johnson's London*, p. 227; George Rudé, *The Crowd in History: A Study of Popular Disturbances in France and England, 1730–1848* (New York, 1964), p. 37.

49. George Rudé, *Paris and London in the Eighteenth Century: Studies in Popular Protest* (New York, 1971), p. 293; Henry Fielding, *The History of Tom Jones, A Foundling* (New York, 1950 [1st ed., 1749]), p. 25.

50. The classic study is Gustave Le Bon, *The Crowd: A Study of the Popular Mind* (Paris, 1895; Eng. trans. 1897). For the application of the term and concept to England, see Rudé, *Crowd in History*; E. P. Thompson, *Making of the English Working Class*, pp. 68 ff; Thompson, "The Moral Economy of the English Crowd in the Eighteenth Century," *Past and Present*, 1971. E. J. Hobsbawm has retained the contemporary term "mob" in the chapter, "The City Mob," *Primitive Rebels: Studies in Archaic Forms of Social Movement in the 19th and 20th Centuries* (Manchester, 1959).

51. Thompson, "Moral Economy," p. 79. Rudé shares the idea of a "moral economy," but stops short of the degree of politicization Thompson attaches to it. For a critique of Thompson's article, see A. W. Coats, "Contrary Moralities: Plebs, Paternalists and Political Economists," *Past and Present*, 1972, pp. 130–33.

52. Thompson, "Moral Economy," p. 88. In later writings Thompson has presented a less consensual view of eighteenth century society, in which paternalistic practices assumed the character of "theatre" and provoked a plebeian "counter-theatre" of oaths, bonfires, effigies, and obscenities. See "Patrician Society, Plebeian Culture," *Journal of Social History*, 1974; "Eighteenth-Century English Society: Class Struggle Without Class?" *Social History*, 1978. His *Whigs and Hunters: The Origins of the Black Act* (New York, 1975) is also more in accord with the class struggle model than with the paternalist one, although he does reject the Marxist idea that the "rule of law" was nothing more than the "superstructure" of capitalism, a device for the suppression of the proletariat.

53. On the concept of "take-off," see W. W. Rostow, *The Stages of Economic Growth: A Non-Communist Manifesto* (Cambridge, 1967), pp. 4 ff, and *Politics and the Stages of Growth* (Cambridge, 1971), pp. 54 ff. Rostow's analysis of this concept, and, even more, his chronology, have been much criticized. But the metaphor is useful and illuminating.

For a very different view of the "old society" from that presented by Thompson or Rudé, see Harold Perkin, *The Origins of Modern English Society, 1780–1880* (London, 1969), where pre-industrial society is portrayed as a "classless society" consisting of a "vertical hierarchy" made up of a multitude of "ranks," "degrees," and "orders"; or Peter Laslett, *The World We Have Lost* (London, 1965), where the concept of a "one-class" society expresses much the same idea. Linda Colley also complicates the picture of Tory "popularism" in "Eighteenth-Century English Radicalism Before Wilkes," *Transactions of the Royal Historical Society*, 1981.

54. Richard A. Cloward and Frances Fox Piven, *Regulating the Poor: The Functions of Public Welfare* (New York, 1972), p. 21; Fernand Braudel, *Capitalism and Material Life, 1400–1800*, trans. Miriam Kochan (New York, 1973 [1st ed., 1967]), p. 40 (italics in the original).

CHAPTER II

1. John Ruskin, *Fors Clavigera: Letters to the Workmen and Labourers of Great Britain* (1876), in *Works*, ed. E. T. Cook and Alex-

ander Wedderburn (London, 1907), XXVIII, 516, 764.

2. On the early history of the expression "laissez faire," see Dugald Stewart, *Biographical Memoir of Adam Smith* (New York, 1966 [1st ed., 1793]), p. 93, n. 1; August Oncken, *Die Maxime Laissez-faire et laissez-passer* (Bern, 1886); Edward R. Kittrell, " 'Laissez Faire' in English Classical Economics," *Journal of the History of Ideas*, 1966, pp. 610–20; Guy Routh, *The Origin of Economic Ideas* (New York, 1977), pp. 44–45.

3. Vernard Foley, "The Division of Labor in Plato and Smith," *History of Political Economy*, 1974, p. 242. (On Smith and Plato, see below, p. 54.) In his edition of the *Wealth of Nations* (London, 1904), Edwin Cannan cited Mandeville as the source of the expression (p. 3). But the passage quoted does not contain that phrase, and the illustration was watch-making rather than pin-making. In this general sense, dozens of other writers might be credited with it. On Chambers's *Cyclopaedia* (1728) and the *Encyclopédie* (vol. V, 1755), see Adam Smith, *Lectures on Jurisprudence*, ed. R. L. Meek, D. D. Raphael, and P. G. Stein (Oxford, 1978), p. 342, n. 18.

4. Adam Ferguson, *Essay on the History of Civil Society*, ed. Duncan Forbes (Edinburgh, 1966 [1st ed., 1767]), p. 181.

5. Stewart, p. 68. (In Smith's first year at Glasgow, 1751–52, he was Professor of Logic. His lectures on moral philosophy started in 1752, when he was transferred to that chair.)

6. Walter Bagehot, "Adam Smith as a Person" (1876), *Collected Works* (Cambridge, Mass., 1968), III, 93.

7. Joseph Schumpeter, *History of Economic Analysis*, ed. Elizabeth Boody Schumpeter (New York, 1974 [1st ed., 1954]), pp. 184–86.

8. Arnold Toynbee, *Lectures on the Industrial Revolution in England* (London, 1884 [delivered as lectures in 1881]). G. N. Clark traces the association of "industrial" and "revolution" to the early 1800s in France and the phrase itself to the French economist Jérôme-Adolphe Blanqui (not to be confused with the revolutionist Louis-Auguste Blanqui) in 1838, Friedrich Engels in 1845 *(Condition of the Working Class in England)*,

and John Stuart Mill in 1848 *(Principles of Political Economy)*. But it was Toynbee's work that popularized both the term and the idea. (Clark, *The Idea of the Industrial Revolution* [Glasgow, 1953].)

9. The best summary of this debate is C. P. Kindleberger, "The Historical Background: Adam Smith and the Industrial Revolution," in *The Market and the State: Essays in Honor of Adam Smith*, ed. Thomas Wilson and Andrew S. Skinner (Oxford, 1976), pp. 1–25. See the comments on this paper by Asa Briggs (pp. 25–33) and R. M. Hartwell (pp. 33–41).

10. Stewart, p. 52.

11. John Rae, *Life of Adam Smith* (London, 1895), p. 286.

12. Jacob H. Hollander, "The Founder of a School," in *Adam Smith, 1776–1926: Lectures to Commemorate the Sesquicentennial of the Publication of "The Wealth of Nations"* (New York, 1966 [1st ed., 1928]), p. 25; Rae, pp. 288–90.

13. John Millar in 1786, quoted by Asa Briggs in *The Market and the State*, p. 28.

14. Adam Smith, *An Inquiry into the Nature and Causes of the Wealth of Nations*, ed. Edwin Cannan (New York, 1937), pp. 11–14, 423, 651. The "invisible hand" metaphor also appears in a different context in the *Theory of Moral Sentiments* (7th ed., London, 1792 [1st ed., 1759]), I, 464.

15. One of the most effective statements of this view is Karl Polanyi, *The Great Transformation* (Boston, 1957 [1st ed., 1944]). A more sophisticated version has been advanced by E. P. Thompson, who describes the *Wealth of Nations* as an "anti-model" rather than a new model, the negation of the older, paternalist model. The new political economy, he argues, was "disinfested of intrusive moral imperatives," not because Smith and his colleagues were immoral or unconcerned with the public good, but because that was the objective consequence of their doctrine, regardless of their intentions. ("The Moral Economy of the English Crowd in the Eighteenth Century," *Past and Present*, 1971, pp. 89–90.)

16. *Moral Sentiments*, I, 146 ff.

17. August Oncken, "Das Adam Smith-Problem," *Zeitschrift für Sozialwissenschaft*, 1898. For recent statements and

reevaluations of this problem, see Ralph Anspach, "The Implications of the *Theory of Moral Sentiments* for Adam Smith's Economic Thought," *History of Political Economy*, 1972; Joseph Cropsey, "Adam Smith and Political Philosophy," in *Essays on Adam Smith*, ed. Andrew S. Skinner and Thomas Wilson (Oxford, 1975); D. D. Raphael, "The Impartial Spectator," *ibid.;* Thomas Wilson, "Sympathy and Self-Interest," in *The Market and the State;* Joseph Cropsey, "The Invisible Hand: Moral and Political Considerations," in *Adam Smith and Modern Political Economy*, ed. Gerald P. O'Driscoll, Jr. (Ames, Iowa, 1979); Richard Teichgraeber III, "Rethinking *Das Adam Smith Problem,*" *Journal of British Studies*, 1981.

18. *Moral Sentiments*, I, 47; II, 300, 305.

19. Jeremy Bentham, *The Handbook of Political Fallacies*, ed. Harold A. Larrabee (New York, 1962 [1st ed., 1824]), p. 230; *Works*, ed. John Bowring (London, 1838–43), XI, 72.

20. *Moral Sentiments*, I, 339.

21. *Ibid.*, II, 115.

22. The "design," as Smith described it in the seventh edition of *Moral Sentiments*, included his moral philosophy, political economy, and theory of jurisprudence. (I, vi–vii.)

23. Schumpeter, pp. 141, 182, 185.

24. *Wealth of Nations*, pp. 388–89, 424, 460, 463, 577.

25. *Ibid.*, pp. 98, 128, 250, 609.

26. *Ibid.*, p. 14.

27. *Ibid.*, p. 423.

28. *Ibid.*

29. *Ibid.*, p. 11.

30. *Ibid.*, pp. 78–79.

31. *Ibid.*, p. 248.

32. A. W. Coats, "Changing Attitudes to Labour in the Mid-eighteenth Century," *Economic History Review*, 1958, p. 39 (quoting Hume's *Political Discourses* of 1752).

33. Arthur Young, *The Farmer's Tour Through the East of England* (London, 1771), IV, 361.

34. Young, *A Six Months' Tour Through the North of England* (London, 1770), I, 196.

35. *Wealth of Nations*, p. 81.

36. *Ibid.*, pp. 82–83.

37. *Ibid.*, p. 81.

38. *Ibid.*, p. 11.

39. *Ibid.*, pp. 15–16.

40. *Ibid.*, p. 13.

41. *Ibid.*, pp. 248–49.

42. *Ibid.*, pp. 121–22.

43. For differing views of this subject, see Nathan Rosenberg, "Adam Smith on the Division of Labor: Two Views or One?" *Economica*, 1965; E. G. West, "The Political Economy of Alienation: Karl Marx and Adam Smith," *Oxford Economic Papers*, 1969; Robert L. Heilbroner, "The Paradox of Progress: Decline and Decay in the *Wealth of Nations,*" *Journal of the History of Ideas*, 1973 (reprinted in *Essays on Adam Smith*, ed. Andrew S. Skinner and Thomas Wilson [Oxford, 1975]); Robert Lamb, "Adam Smith's Concept of Alienation," *Oxford Economic Papers*, 1973; E. G. West, "Adam Smith and Alienation: A Rejoinder," *ibid.*, 1975.

44. Karl Marx, *Capital: A Critique of Political Economy*, ed. Friedrich Engels, rev. Ernest Untermann (New York, 1936), pp. 397–98.

45. *Wealth of Nations*, p. 734.

46. *Ibid.*, pp. 126–27.

47. *Ibid.*, p. 81. (See above, p. 52.)

48. *Ibid.*, pp. 8–9.

49. Robert Heilbroner, "The Paradox of Progress," *Journal of the History of Ideas*, 1973, p. 243.

50. On Smith and the Malthusian theory of population, see below, p. 109. See also Donald Winch, *Adam Smith's Politics: An Essay in Historiographic Revision* (Cambridge, 1978), pp. 143–44.

51. J. S. Mill, *Principles of Political Economy*, ed. J. M. Robson (Toronto, 1965 [1st ed., 1848]), II, 754.

52. *Wealth of Nations*, pp. 126–28.

53. *Ibid.*, p. 734.

54. *Ibid.*, pp. 736–38.

55. *Ibid.*, p. 737.

56. *Ibid.*, p. 740.

57. Mark Blaug, "The Economics of Education in English Classical Political Economy: A Re-examination," in *Essays on Adam Smith*, p. 572. Blaug does not, however, attach to "social control" the usual invidious implications. On social control, see pp. 29, 41, 178, and 553 n. 2.

58. M. G. Jones, *The Charity School*

Movement: A Study of Eighteenth Century Puritanism in Action (Cambridge, 1938), p. 159.

59. Joseph Cropsey, *Polity and Economy: An Interpretation of the Principles of Adam Smith* (The Hague, 1957); Cropsey, "Adam Smith," in *History of Political Philosophy*, ed. Leo Strauss and Joseph Cropsey (Chicago, 1963). See also essays cited in note 17.

60. The modification of the laissez faire stereotype goes back at least to Jacob Viner, "Adam Smith and Laissez-Faire," *Journal of Political Economy*, 1927. Among the more notable contributions to this revisionist interpretation are: Lionel Robbins, *The Theory of Economic Policy in English Classical Political Economy* (London, 1952); L. R. Sorenson, "Some Classical Economists, Laissez Faire, and the Factory Acts," *Journal of Economic History*, 1952; S. G. Checkland, "The Prescriptions of the Classical Economists," *Economica*, 1953; A. W. Coats, "Economic Thought and Poor Law Policy in the Eighteenth Century," *Economic History Review*, 1960; Coats, "The Classical Economists and the Labourer," in *Land, Labour and Population*, ed. E. L. Jones and G. E. Mingay (London, 1967); Coats (ed.), *The Classical Economists and Economic Policy* (London, 1971); Thomas Sowell, *Classical Economists Reconsidered* (Princeton, 1974); Nathan Rosenberg, "Adam Smith and Laissez-Faire Revisited," in *Adam Smith and Modern Political Economy*.

61. For example, Mark Blaug, *Economic Theory in Retrospect* (Homewood, Ill., 1968 [1st ed., 1962]), p. 51. Blaug's claim that Smith condemned the "Poor Laws in general" may rest on Smith's criticisms of trade corporations and assemblies, in the course of which he also criticized those regulations which made such assemblies necessary—the regulation, for example, "which enables those of the same trade to tax themselves in order to provide for their poor, their sick, their widows and orphans, [which] by giving them a common interest to manage, renders such assemblies necessary." (*Wealth of Nations*, p. 129.) But the poor rates were levied by the parish rather than by trades, and therefore did not come under Smith's stricture.

62. *Wealth of Nations*, p. 141.

63. *Ibid.*, pp. 777, 821, 683.
64. *Ibid.*, p. 142.
65. *Ibid.*, pp. 142, 66–67.
66. *Ibid.*, pp. 823, 248, 740.

CHAPTER III

1. A. V. Dicey, *Lectures on the Relation Between Law and Public Opinion in England During the Nineteenth Century* (London, 1962 [1st ed., 1905], pp. 126 ff. Dicey characterized this as the period of "Benthamism or individualism."

2. Except for F. M. Eden, in *The State of the Poor* (see below, pp. 75 ff.), the term "Speenhamland system" rarely appeared in the literature of the late eighteenth or early nineteenth centuries. See J. R. Poynter, *Society and Pauperism: English Ideas on Poor Relief, 1795–1834* (London, 1969), p. 78; Raymond G. Cowherd, *Political Economists and the English Poor Laws: A Historical Study of the Influence of Classical Economists on the Formation of Social Welfare Policy* (Athens, Ohio, 1977), p. 25, n. 45. On Speenhamland in the context of public relief in this period, see also A. W. Coats, "Economic Thought and Poor Law Policy in the Eighteenth Century," *Economic History Review*, 1960; R. G. Cowherd, "The Humanitarian Reform of the English Poor Laws from 1782 to 1815," *Proceedings of the American Philosophical Society*, 1960; Geoffrey W. Oxley, *Poor Relief in England and Wales, 1601–1834* (Newton Abbot, 1974); Peter Dunkley, "Paternalism, the Magistracy and Poor Relief in England, 1795–1834," *International Review of Social History*, 1979. Poynter's book is valuable for the whole of this period, especially for the lesser known theorists and polemicists.

3. Mark Blaug, "The Myth of the Old Poor Law and the Making of the New," *Journal of Economic History*, 1963; James Stephen Taylor, "The Mythology of the Old Poor Law," *ibid.*, 1969. See below, p. 154.

4. Kirk Willis speaks of the "considerable amount of scholarly attention this problem has received." ("The Role in Parliament of the Economic Ideas of Adam Smith, 1776–1800," *History of Political Economy*, 1979, p. 523.) But in the vast literature on Burke there are only a few brief articles on

the subject, and many full-length biographies do not so much as mention it, except for casual references to the friendship of Smith and Burke. None of the articles on the subject (mentioned in the footnotes below) seriously confronts Burke's view on economics with his views on society and politics.

5. Carl B. Cone, *Burke and the Nature of Politics: The Age of the American Revolution* (2 vols., Lexington, Ky., 1957–64), I, 326; Donald Barrington, "Edmund Burke as an Economist," *Economica,* 1954, pp. 252–58.

6. Burke, "Letter to a Noble Lord" (1796), *Works* (Bohn ed., London, 1909–12), V, 124.

7. Burke, *Reflections on the Revolution in France,* ed. Conor Cruise O'Brien (Pelican ed., London, 1968), pp. 173, 385 n. 66. On "mob" and "people," see above, p. 39, and below, pp. 299–300.

8. "Thoughts and Details on Scarcity," *Works,* V, 83–85.

9. *Ibid.,* pp. 89, 92, 109.

10. *Ibid.,* p. 89. It may have been passages such as this which persuaded C. R. Fay that this essay by Burke "clinches the doctrinal affinity with Adam Smith." (*The World of Adam Smith* [Cambridge, 1960], p. 20.)

11. *Works,* V, 107–08. (Italics in the original.)

12. *Ibid.,* p. 84.

13. "Letters on a Regicide Peace" (3rd letter, 1797), *Works,* V, 321–22.

14. *Reflections on the Revolution in France* (Dolphin ed., New York, 1961 [1st ed., 1790]), pp. 44–45, 89, 110; Letter to the Chevalier de Rivarol (June 1, 1791), *Letters of Edmund Burke,* ed. Harold J. Laski (Oxford, 1922), p. 300.

15. Letter to Captain Mercer (Feb. 26, 1790), *Letters,* pp. 286–87.

16. "Speech on . . . the Economical Reformation of the Civil and Other Establishments" (Feb. 11, 1780), *Works,* II, 83, 101.

17. "Speech on American Taxation" (April 19, 1774), *Works,* I, 432; *Reflections on the Revolution in France* (Dolphin ed.), p. 50.

18. "Thoughts and Details on Scarcity," *Works,* V, 89.

19. No serious commentary or biography of Burke fails to address this question.

Among the more provocative discussions are: Leo Strauss, *Natural Right and History* (Chicago, 1953); Cone, *Burke and the Nature of Politics;* Russell Kirk, *Edmund Burke: A Genius Reconsidered* (New York, 1967); Gertrude Himmelfarb, "Edmund Burke: The Hero as Politician, and the Politician as Philosopher," in *Victorian Minds* (New York, 1968); Frank O'Gorman, *Edmund Burke: His Political Philosophy* (Bloomington, Ind., 1973); and several works by Peter Stanlis, especially *Edmund Burke and the Natural Law* (Ann Arbor, Mich., 1958) and essays in *Modern Age* and *Studies in Burke and His Time.* Some commentators dismiss the "Burke-Smith problem" by suggesting that, while Burke sometimes presented himself as a disciple of Smith, he knew little and cared less about Smith's views. (See, for example, Cone, *Burke and the Nature of Politics,* II, 490; Willis, in *History of Political Economy,* 1979, pp. 523–24.)

20. "A Vindication of Natural Society," *Works,* I, 41–44.

21. Elie Halévy, *The Growth of Philosophic Radicalism,* trans. Mary Morris (Boston, 1955 [1st ed., 1901]), pp. 215–16. For an excellent discussion of Burke's essay and the misinterpretations to which it gave rise, see Stanlis, *Edmund Burke and the Natural Law,* pp. 125 ff.

22. C. B. Macpherson, *Burke* (New York, 1980), pp. 51 ff.

23. Macpherson, *The Political Theory of Possessive Individualism: Hobbes to Locke* (Oxford, 1962). For a critique of this thesis, see Isaiah Berlin, "Hobbes, Locke and Professor Macpherson," *Political Quarterly,* 1964.

24. Burke, *Reflections on the Revolution in France,* ed. Conor Cruise O'Brien (Pelican ed., London, 1968), p. 38.

25. John Rae, *Life of Adam Smith* (New York, 1965 [1st ed., 1895]), p. 405; John Ehrman, *The Younger Pitt: The Years of Acclaim* (New York, 1969), p. 512. Neither Ehrman nor Willis finds much concrete evidence of Smith's influence on Pitt's legislation, although, as Willis says, "Pitt read, knew, and admired Smith." (*History of Political Economy,* p. 534.) Bernard Semmel attributes Pitt's free trade policies to Josiah Tucker rather than Smith. (*The Rise of Free*

Trade Imperialism: Classical Political Economy, the Empire of Free Trade and Imperialism, 1750–1850 [Cambridge, 1970], pp. 30 ff.)

26. *Cobbett's Parliamentary Debates,* 32: 707 (Feb. 12, 1796).

27. Poynter, *Society and Pauperism,* p. 61; Harold Perkin, *The Origins of Modern English Society, 1780–1880* (London, 1969), p. 186; J. L. Hammond and Barbara Hammond, *The Village Labourer* (London, 1966 [1st ed., 1911]), p. 140. This was not the last attempt to enact a minimum wage; similar bills were introduced repeatedly, and with as little success, during the following decades.

28. *Cobbett's Parliamentary Debates,* 32: 709–10 (Feb. 12, 1796).

29. In a letter to Captain Woodford, Burke professed not to understand the purpose of Pitt's bill. "What relief do they [the poor] want except that which it will be difficult indeed to give to make men frugal or more industrious." He could only assume that Pitt was engaged in a contest for popularity with Fox. (*Correspondence of Edmund Burke,* ed. R. B. McDowell [Chicago, 1970], IX, 155 [Dec. 9, 1796].)

30. Jeremy Bentham, "Observations on the Poor Bill Introduced by the Right Honourable William Pitt," *Works,* ed. John Bowring (London, 1843), VIII, 443. For the discussion of *Pauper Management,* see below, pp. 78 ff.

31. Karl Marx, *Capital,* ed. Friedrich Engels, rev. Ernest Untermann (New York, 1936), p. 675.

32. Frederick Morton Eden, *The State of the Poor: or, an History of the Labouring Classes in England* (3 vols., London, 1797), I, 437–38, 447–48, 486–87.

33. *Ibid.,* pp. i, 2.

34. *Ibid.,* p. 57.

35. Arnold Toynbee, *Lectures on the Industrial Revolution in England* (Boston, 1956 [1st ed., 1884]), p. 69; Alfred Marshall, "Lectures on Progress and Poverty" (1883), reprinted in *Journal of Law and Economics,* 1969, p. 188. This goes beyond the thesis developed by Henry Maine in *Ancient Law* (1861), which traced the progression from custom to law, or status to contract.

36. Samuel Johnson, *A Dictionary of the English Language* (London, 1849 [1st ed., 1755]), p. 855. See also Eden, I, xix.

37. Johnson, p. 896. This was his first definition. The others had to do with metaphorical meanings of the word: "trifling," "paltry," "unhappy." The last of his definitions testified to the pervasive ambiguity of the word: "The *poor* [collectively]. Those who are in the lowest rank of the community; those who cannot subsist but by the charity of others; but it is sometimes used with laxity for any not rich."

38. Henry Fielding, *An Enquiry into the Causes of the Late Increase of Robbers* (1751), in *Works,* ed. James P. Browne (London, 1871), X, 400.

39. I. M. Rubinow, "Poverty," *Encyclopaedia of the Social Sciences,* XI, 286.

40. Patrick Colquhoun, *A Treatise on Indigence* (London, 1806), pp. 7–8.

41. Jeremy Bentham, *Outline of a Work Entitled Pauper Management Improved,* first published in 1798 in the *Annals of Agriculture* edited by Arthur Young, reprinted as a pamphlet in 1802 and 1812, and again in Bentham's *Works,* VIII, 369–437. The text in the *Works,* cited here, is identical with that in the *Annals.* For a more extensive account of this plan, see Gertrude Himmelfarb, "Bentham's Utopia: The National Charity Company," *Journal of British Studies,* 1970. A different view of it may be found in M. I. Zagday, "Bentham and the Poor Law," in *Jeremy Bentham and the Law,* ed. G. W. Keeton and G. Schwarzenberger (London, 1948).

42. Bentham, *Works,* IV, 39, 45. See also Gertrude Himmelfarb, "The Haunted House of Jeremy Bentham," in *Victorian Minds,* pp. 32–81.

43. *Works,* VIII, 369, 386. (The population estimate is in the Bentham Mss., University College, London, CLIIa, 146.)

44. *Works,* VIII, 386, 383, 369. (Here, and throughout, italics are in the original.)

45. Bentham Mss., CLIIIa, 21. On Colquhoun, see below, pp. 77–78.

46. *Works,* VIII, 398; Bentham Mss. CLIVb, 385. (The manuscripts sometimes express Bentham's views more forcefully and pithily than the published work, but the ideas are identical.)

47. *Works,* VIII, 397, 388.

48. Bentham Mss., CXXXIII, 17; CLIVa, 238; CLI, 157.

49. *Ibid.*, CLIVa, 181.

50. *Ibid.*, CLIIIa, 90, 107; CLIVb, 317.

51. *Works*, VIII, 388, 396, 397, 437; Bentham Mss. CLIIIa, 93.

52. *Works*, VIII, 437; Bentham Mss. CXXXIII, 94.

53. *Works*, VIII, 439, 362; Bentham Mss. CLI, 400.

54. *Works*, X, 212; XI, 97, 103.

55. Eden, I, v.

56. Bentham Mss. CLIIb, 335–36; CLI, 5; *Works*, VIII, 381.

57. Eden, I, 58–59.

58. Joseph Townsend, *A Dissertation on the Poor Laws* (London, 1787), p. 71.

59. 36 Geo. III c. 23.

60. Bentham, *Constitutional Code, Works*, IX, 441. For a more detailed account of Bentham and the New Poor Law, see Himmelfarb, *Journal of British Studies*, 1970, pp. 121–22. On the "workhouse test" and the other details of the New Poor Law, see below, Chapter VI.

61. See above, pp. 78 ff., and Poynter, pp. 201–02.

62. Colquhoun, *Treatise on Indigence*, pp. 89–90, 226, 229, 247.

63. Henry Collins, introduction to Thomas Paine, *Rights of Man* (Penguin ed., London, 1969), p. 37; Eric Foner, *Tom Paine and Revolutionary America* (New York, 1976), p. 218; Francis Canavan, "The Burke-Paine Controversy," *Political Science Reviewer*, 1976, p. 403; S. Maccoby, *English Radicalism, 1786–1832* (London, 1955), p. 53.

64. Thomas Paine, *Rights of Man* (Dolphin ed., New York, 1961), pp. 477, 481, 485. This edition, like so many others, is entitled *The Rights of Man*. The title under which it was originally issued, and reissued through innumerable editions during Paine's lifetime, was *Rights of Man*. The definite article first appeared in the edition of 1817, eight years after Paine's death.

65. *Ibid.*, pp. 490–91.

66. *Ibid.*, p. 480.

67. *Ibid.*, pp. 401, 315, 418, 429, 315, 396.

68. *Ibid.*, pp. 401–02, 461.

69. *Ibid.*, p. 511.

70. *Ibid.*, pp. 487, 485.

71. Adam Smith, *An Inquiry into the Nature and Causes of the Wealth of Nations*, ed. Edwin Cannan (New York, 1937), p. 777.

72. *Rights of Man*, pp. 448, 398, 400–01.

73. *Ibid.*, pp. 433, 398–400.

74. *Ibid.*, pp. 493–94, 462.

75. *Ibid.*, p. 482.

76. "Letter Addressed to the Addressers on the Late Proclamation" (1792), *Complete Writings*, ed. Philip Foner (New York, 1969), II, 478.

77. *Rights of Man*, pp. 396, 488.

78. Henry Collins, introduction to *Rights of Man*, p. 25; Eric Foner, *Tom Paine and Revolutionary America*, pp. 94, 157; Gwynn Williams, "Tom Paine," *New Society*, Aug. 6, 1970. See also Joseph Dorfman, *The Economic Mind in American Civilization, 1606–1865* (New York, 1947), I, 447 ff.

79. In the preface to the original French edition, Paine suggested that his pamphlet had been provoked by the "Conspiracy of the Equals." But the preface to the English edition later that year made it a rebuttal to a sermon by the Bishop of Llandaff, "The Wisdom and Goodness of God, in having made both Rich and Poor." Nowhere in the English edition did Paine mention Babeuf.

80. *Complete Writings*, ed. Philip Foner, I, 606, 611. (The date of the French edition is erroneously given here as 1796, perhaps because in the preface to the English edition Paine said that it had been written in the winter of 1795–96.)

81. *Ibid.*, p. 610.

82. *Ibid.*, p. 612.

83. *Ibid.*, p. 620.

84. *Ibid.*, p. 617. This sentence was omitted from the English edition.

85. *Ibid.*, p. 612, 617.

86. *Ibid.*, p. 621.

87. *Rights of Man*, p. 278.

88. Thomas Spence, *The Rights of Infants; . . . to which are added . . . Strictures on Paine's Agrarian Justice* (London, 1797), p. 3. Spence's *Rights of Man* first appeared in 1775, and William Ogilvie's *An Essay on the Right of Property in Land . . .* in 1781. Spence's pamphlet is often referred to as *Real Rights of Man*, which was the title given it by Max Beer in his *Pioneers of Land Reform* (London, 1920), perhaps to distinguish it from Paine's

work. It may have been Paine's usurpation of the title, and the enormous fame Paine achieved with it, that made Spence even more contemptuous of Paine than he might otherwise have been (although there were sufficient ideological reasons for his hostility).

89. Elie Halévy, *The Growth of Philosophic Radicalism,* p. 209. On Godwin, see below, pp. 102 ff., 236 ff.

90. David Freeman Hawke, *Paine* (New York, 1974), p. 328.

91. Moncure D. Conway, *The Life of Thomas Paine* (London, 1892), I, 346; Paine, *Writings,* ed. Philip Foner, I, 345, II, 910; Richard Altick, *The English Common Reader: A Social History of the Mass Reading Public, 1800–1900* (Chicago, 1957), p. 70.

92. *Rights of Man,* p. 407.

93. *Ibid.,* p. 454.

94. "Prospects on the Rubicon" (1787), *Writings,* II, 632; *Rights of Man,* p. 365.

95. Thomas Robert Malthus, *On Population,* ed. Gertrude Himmelfarb (Modern Library ed., New York, 1960), p. 517.

96. R. R. Fennessy, *Burke, Paine and the Rights of Man* (The Hague, 1963), p. 245 (quoting a letter by Lord Beauchamp to Burke, June 8, 1791).

97. Thomas Hardy, *Memoir* (London, 1832), p. 15.

98. *Rights of Man,* p. 462.

99. "Agrarian Justice," *Writings,* I, 617.

100. "Letter Addressed to the Addressers" (1792), *ibid.,* p. 506.

101. "A Serious Address to the People of Pennsylvania on the Present Situation of Their Affairs" (1778), *ibid.,* II, 287.

102. *Rights of Man,* p. 288. Shelley took it to mean the poor in his pseudonymous pamphlet, *We Pity the Plumage, But Forget the Dying Bird,* published in 1817.

103. E. P. Thompson, *The Making of the English Working Class* (New York, 1964), pp. 31, 90.

CHAPTER IV

1. For example, Joseph Schumpeter, *History of Economic Analysis,* ed. Elizabeth Boody Schumpeter (New York, 1974 [1st

ed., 1954]), p. 482; William Petersen, *Malthus* (Cambridge, Mass., 1979), p. 10. Mark Blaug finds "typical Smithian economic theory" in the *Essay* itself, in "the chapters on the Poor Laws, the Corn Laws, and the proper mixture of industry and agriculture in an economic system." (*Economic Theory in Retrospect* [rev. ed., Homewood, Ill., 1968], p. 90.)

2. Thomas Robert Malthus, *On Population,* ed. Gertrude Himmelfarb (Modern Library ed., New York, 1960), pp. 3–4. This edition includes the whole of the first edition and most of the last. All references, unless otherwise specified, are to this edition. For the full titles of the first and revised editions, see below, p. 114.

In the first edition Malthus acknowledged his indebtedness to Hume and Smith —not, however, for the principle of population as such but for the "principles on which it depends" (p. 7). The only name mentioned in connection with the principle of population was Robert Wallace. In the preface to the second edition he added the name of Richard Price to those from whom he had originally deduced his principle, and referred to others whose work he had evidently not known of: Benjamin Franklin, James Steuart, Arthur Young, and Joseph Townsend (pp. 147–48).

3. Elie Halévy, *The Growth of Philosophic Radicalism* (Boston, 1955 [1st ed., 1901–04]), p. 235. Extracts from this manuscript were first published in a review of Malthus's *Principles of Political Economy* by William Empson in the *Edinburgh Review,* 1837.

4. William Godwin, *The Enquirer* (London, 1823), p. 157.

5. C. Kegan Paul, *William Godwin: His Friends and Contemporaries* (London, 1876), I, 118. This remark is sometimes attributed to 1794, which would make it contemporaneous with the book. (George Woodcock, *William Godwin* [London, 1946], p. 100; F. E. L. Priestley [ed.], *Enquiry Concerning Political Justice and its Influence on Morals and Happiness* [Toronto, 1946], III, 101.) Both Woodcock and Priestley give Paul as their source, but Paul attributed it to a note evidently written in 1831. According to E. P. Thompson, Godwin's views reached

the working class public only after the wars, and then through the Notes to Shelley's *Queen Mab*. (*Making of the English Working Class* [New York, 1964], p. 98.) Pitt is reputed to have said that it was not necessary to proscribe Godwin's book, since it cost three guineas and was hardly likely to harm those "who had not three shillings to spare." (Paul, I, 80.)

6. Woodcock, p. 99.

7. Malthus cited the first edition of *Political Justice*, but almost all his quotations appeared in the later editions as well, and all his criticisms remained pertinent. Those commentators who minimize the changes in the later editions of *Political Justice* tend also to be those who minimize the utopian nature of Godwin's views: e.g., Woodcock; Priestley; and David Fleisher, *William Godwin: A Study in Liberalism* (London, 1951). The most recent biography makes more of the changes: Don Locke, *A Fantasy of Reason: The Life and Thought of William Godwin* (London, 1980). My own reading suggests that most of the changes were more rhetorical than substantive and that the radically utopian nature of the book survived all the editions.

8. *Political Justice*, ed. Priestley, I, 86. (Quoted by Malthus, p. 96.)

9. *Ibid.*, II, 520, 527–29.

10. *Ibid.*, II, 515–18.

11. *On Population*, p. 56.

12. *Ibid.*, p. 57.

13. *Ibid.*, p. 8.

14. *Ibid.*, pp. 8–9.

15. *Ibid.*, pp. 9–10.

16. *Ibid.*, p. 4.

17. *Ibid.*, p. 28.

18. *Ibid.*, p. 15.

19. *Ibid.*, pp. 74, 51–52, 34.

20. *Ibid.*, pp. 75, 136.

21. *Ibid.*, pp. 128–31.

22. *Ibid.*, pp. 129–35.

23. *Ibid.*, p. 100.

24. *Ibid.*, p. 108. In the beginning of the *Essay*, Malthus said that his argument depended on principles "explained in part by Hume, and more at large by Dr. Adam Smith" (p. 7). The main principle, of course, was free trade, although he departed even from that when he defended the corn laws.

25. *Ibid.*, p. 109.

26. *Ibid.*, pp. 120, 117.

27. *Wealth of Nations*, p. 70.

28. *Ibid.*, pp. 94–95.

29. John Rae, *Life of Adam Smith* (London, 1895), p. 400 (Smith to Eden, Dec. 22, 1785).

30. *On Population*, p. 122.

31. D. H. Monro, *Goodwin's Moral Philosophy* (Oxford, 1953), p. 83.

32. *On Population*, pp. 33–34.

33. *Ibid.*

34. *Ibid.*, p. 36.

35. *Ibid.*, p. 33.

36. *Ibid.*, p. 37.

37. *Ibid.*, p. 124.

38. *Ibid.*, p. 5.

39. *Ibid.*, pp. 124–25.

40. *Ibid.*, p. 149.

41. Paul, I, 321–25; Kenneth Smith, *The Malthusian Controversy* (London, 1951), p. 40.

42. *On Population*, p. 57.

43. Appendix to 5th ed. (1817), *Essay on Population* (New York, 1971), p. 512.

44. On "Neo-Malthusianism" and birth control, see J. A. Banks, *Prosperity and Parenthood: A Study of Family Planning among the Victorian Middle Classes* (London, 1954); J. A. and Olive Banks, *Feminism and Family Planning in Victorian England* (New York, 1964); N. E. Himes, "John Stuart Mill's Attitude toward Neo-Malthusianism," *Economic Journal*, 1929; Himes, "Bentham and the Genesis of Neo-Malthusianism," *Economic History*, 1937; Gertrude Himmelfarb, *On Liberty and Liberalism: The Case of John Stuart Mill* (New York, 1974), pp. 121 ff; William L. Langer, "The Origins of the Birth Control Movement in England in the Early Nineteenth Century," *Journal of Interdisciplinary History*, 1975.

45. *On Population*, p. 160.

46. *Ibid.*, p. 338.

47. *Ibid.*, p. 488.

48. *Ibid.*, p. 489.

49. For a discussion of Malthus's theological views, see Edmund N. Santurri, "Theodicy and Social Policy in Malthus' Thought," *Journal of the History of Ideas*, 1982; John M. Pullen, "Malthus' Theological Ideas and their Influence on his Principle of Population," *History of Political Economy*, 1981.

50. *On Population,* p. 487. (The quotation is the title of the chapter.)

51. *Ibid.,* pp. 495–96.

52. *Ibid.,* pp. 128, 131.

53. *Ibid.,* pp. 158–59.

54. *Ibid.,* pp. 4, 74, 34.

55. *Ibid.,* pp. 496, 498.

56. *Ibid.,* p. 469.

57. *Ibid.,* pp. 454–56.

58. Quoted by Patricia James, *Population Malthus: His Life and Times* (London, 1979), pp. 254, 262.

59. James, p. 312. Bernard Semmel has a more consistently physiocratic interpretation of Malthus. In some respects he finds Malthus to be even more physiocratic than the physiocrats—and more so in the revised edition of the *Essay* than the first. (*The Rise of Free Trade Imperialism: Classical Political Economy, the Empire of Free Trade and Imperialism, 1750–1850* [Cambridge, 1970], p. 52; Semmel, "Malthus: 'Physiocracy' and the Commercial System," *Economic History Review,* 1965.) Geoffrey Gilbert, on the other hand, presents a Malthus who is better disposed to industry. ("Economic Growth and the Poor in Malthus's *Essay on Population,*" *History of Political Economy,* 1980.)

60. *On Population,* p. 585.

61. *Ibid.,* pp. 74, 133.

62. *Ibid.,* pp. 497–98.

63. *Ibid.,* pp. 496.

64. *Ibid.,* pp. 367, 530. This is not quite the *"gradual* and *very gradual* abolition" he elsewhere made it out to be (p. 384, italics his).

65. *Ibid.,* p. 449.

66. *Ibid.,* p. 79.

67. For example, J. R. McCulloch, *The Principles of Political Economy* (London, 1870 [1st ed., 1825]), pp. 189–91; John Stuart Mill, *Principles of Political Economy* (Toronto, 1965 [1st ed., 1848]), pp. 947 ff. On Harriet Martineau, see below, pp. 168 ff.

68. *On Population,* p. 541.

69. *Ibid.,* p. 522.

70. *Ibid.,* p. 543.

71. *Ibid.,* pp. 584–85.

72. *Ibid.,* p. 593.

73. *Essay on Population* (London, 1903 [reprint of 2nd ed.]), p. 531.

74. Robert Southey, "State of the Poor" (1812), in *Essays, Moral and Political* (London, 1832), I, 93.

75. *On Population,* pp. 148–49, 590.

76. Nassau William Senior, *Two Lectures on Population* (London, 1829), pp. 56–57; Marian Bowley, *Nassau Senior and Classical Economics* (New York, 1967 [1st ed., 1937]), p. 121. (On Senior and Malthus, see below, pp. 157–58.)

77. Petersen, p. 48.

78. Southey, pp. 81–83.

79. James Bonar, *Malthus and His Work* (New York, 1924 [1st ed., 1885]), p. 1.

80. Friedrich Engels, "Outline of a Critique of Political Economy" (1844), in Karl Marx, *Economic and Philosophical Manuscripts of 1844* (London, 1958), p. 201.

81. William Cobbett, *Political Register,* May 8, 1819; Cobbett, *Advice to Young Men* (London, 1887 [1st ed., 1829]), p. 99.

82. Percy Bysshe Shelley, *A Philosophical View of Reform* (1819–20), in *Political Tracts of Wordsworth, Coleridge, and Shelley,* ed. R. J. White (Cambridge, 1953), p. 240.

83. Karl Marx, *Capital: A Critique of Political Economy,* trans. Samuel Moore and Edward Aveling (New York, 1936 [1st ed., 1867]), p. 676.

84. J. R. Poynter, *Society and Pauperism: English Ideas on Poor Relief, 1795–1834* (London, 1969), p. 168.

85. William Hazlitt, *Reply to the Essay on Population* (New York, 1967 [1st ed., 1807]), pp. 4, 127.

86. Dickens, "A Goblin's Story," *Works* (Philadelphia, 1843), IV, 41.

87. The original pamphlets were entitled *An Essay on Populousness* and *On the Possibility of Limiting Populousness.* The reprint bore the title: *The Book of Murder! A Vade-Mecum for the Commissioners and Guardians of the New Poor Law Throughout Great Britain and Ireland, being an exact reprint of The Infamous Essay on the Possibility of Limiting Populousness, by Marcus, One of the Three. With a Refutation of the Malthusian Doctrine* (London, 1839). "One of the Three" referred to the three Poor Law Commissioners. (See below, p. 349.)

88. William Hazlitt, *The Spirit of the Age* (Dolphin ed., New York, n.d. [1st ed., 1825]), p. 144.

89. Bonar, p. 364.

90. Walter Bagehot, "Malthus" (1880), *Collected Works* (London, 1978), XI, 331.

91. J. S. Mill, *Principles of Political Economy*, II, 353.

92. Bonar, p. 66.

93. Charles Darwin, *Life and Letters*, ed. Francis Darwin (London, 1887), II, 317 (Darwin to Charles Lyell, June 6, 1860).

94. Bonar, p. 85.

95. Bagehot, p. 341.

96. *On Population*, pp. 21, 190. (In the first edition, "struggle" was in the singular, in later editions in the plural.)

97. Darwin, *Origin of Species* (New York, 1909 [1st ed., 1859]), p. 528.

98. *On Population*, p. 63.

99. *Origin of Species*, p. 79.

100. Marx, *Briefwechsel* (June 18, 1862), in *Gesamtausgabe* (Berlin, 1930), Part 3, III, 77.

101. *Wealth of Nations*, p. 73.

102. Bonar, p. 41.

103. *Wealth of Nations*, p. 821.

104. *On Population*, pp. 21, 190.

105. J. M. Keynes, *Essays in Biography* (London, 1951 [1st ed., 1933]), p. 120. On Malthus and Ricardo, see below, p. 133.

CHAPTER V

1. Thomas Carlyle, *Latter-Day Pamphlets* (Feb. 1, 1850), *Works* (New York, 1897), XIII, 301.

2. There has been a spate of excellent monographs on economic thinking as reflected in Parliament and the press: Boyd Hilton, *Corn, Cash, Commerce: The Economic Policies of the Tory Government 1815–1830* (Oxford, 1977); Barry Gordon, *Political Economy in Parliament, 1819–1823* (New York, 1976); Gordon, *Economic Doctrine and Tory Liberalism, 1824–1830* (New York, 1980); Frank Fetter, "Economic Controversy in the British Reviews, 1802–1850," *Economica*, 1965; Fetter, "The Rise and Decline of Ricardian Economics," *History of Political Economy*, 1969; Fetter, *The Economist in Parliament, 1780–1868* (Durham, 1980); Kirk Willis, "The Role in Parliament of the Economic Ideas of Adam Smith, 1776–1800," *History of Political Economy*, 1979.

3. David Ricardo, *Principles of Political Economy and Taxation* (Penguin ed., London, 1971 [1st ed., 1817]), p. 121. For a less "pessimistic" interpretation of Ricardo, see Lionel Robbins, *The Theory of Economic Policy in English Classical Political Economy* (Philadelphia, 1978 [1st ed., 1952]); Maxine Berg, *The Machinery Question and the Making of Political Economy, 1815–1848* (Cambridge, 1980); Samuel Hollander, *The Economics of David Ricardo* (London, 1980). A more complicated and moderate view of Ricardianism is presented in two important works by Mark Blaug: *Ricardian Economics: A Historical Study* (New Haven, 1958), and *Economic Theory in Retrospect* (Homewood, Ill., 1962 [rev. ed., 1968]).

4. See the discussion of the "Ricardian socialists," pp. 236 ff.

5. The contemporary discussion of this question is dealt with throughout this volume. The debate among historians may be traced back to the 1830s with the controversy between Southey and Macaulay. It reemerged in the 1880s with Arnold Toynbee and Thorold Rogers versus Leone Levi and Robert Giffen; in the 1920s with J. L. and B. Hammond versus John Clapham; in the 1950s and '60s with E. J. Hobsbawm and E. P. Thompson versus T. S. Ashton and R. M. Hartwell. It has since become so voluminous one hardly knows where to start documenting it. Some important recent entrants into the field include Brian Inglis, *Poverty and the Industrial Revolution* (London, 1971); Malcolm I. Thomis, *The Town Labourer and the Industrial Revolution* (New York, 1974); Duncan Blythell, "The History of the Poor," *English Historical Review*, 1974; Blythell, *The Sweated Trades: Outwork in Nineteenth-Century Britain* (London, 1978); Arthur J. Taylor (ed.), *The Standard of Living in Britain in the Industrial Revolution* (New York, 1975); J. H. Treble, *Urban Poverty in Britain, 1830–1914* (New York, 1979); Peter Mathias, "Adam's Burden: Historical Diagnosis of Poverty," in *The Transformation of England: Essays in the Economic and Social History of England in the Eighteenth Century* (New York, 1979); Jeffrey G. Williamson, "Urban Disamenities, Dark Satanic

Mills, and the British Standard of Living Debate," *Journal of Economic History,* 1981.

6. See Duncan Blythell, *The Handloom Weavers: A Study in the English Cotton Industry During the Industrial Revolution* (Cambridge, 1969); Paul Richards, "The State and Early Industrial Capitalism: The Case of the Handloom Weavers," *Past and Present,* 1979.

7. Every serious work on this period has as its implicit theme "continuity and change." One of the most sensitive and thoughtful of these works, addressing the question most explicitly, is G. Kitson Clark, *The Making of Victorian England* (Cambridge, Mass., 1962).

8. David Landes, *The Unbound Prometheus: Technological Change and Industrial Development in Western Europe from 1750 to the Present* (Cambridge, 1969), p. 122.

9. Jacques Barzun, "The Imagination of the Real, or Ideas and Their Environment," in *Art, Politics and Will: Essays in Honor of Lionel Trilling,* ed. Quentin Anderson et al. (New York, 1977), p. 12.

10. William Wordsworth, "Tintern Abbey."

11. Wordsworth, "Proud Were Ye, Mountains" (1844), in *The Industrial Muse: The Industrial Revolution in English Poetry,* ed. Jeremy Warburg (London, 1958), p. 27.

12. Wordsworth, "Steamboats, Viaducts, and Railways" (1835), *ibid.,* p. 22.

13. *The Industrial Muse,* p. 28.

14. Ivy Pinchbeck, *Women Workers and the Industrial Revolution* (London, 1930), p. 232; Ivy Pinchbeck and Margaret Hewitt, *Children in English Society: From Tudor Times to the Eighteenth Century* (London, 1969), p. 311. For the problem of child labor in the later period, see Pinchbeck and Hewitt, *Children in English Society: From the Eighteenth Century to the Children Act of 1948* (London, 1973). A seminal study of the effect of industrialism on the family is Neil J. Smelser, *Social Change in the Industrial Revolution: An Application of Theory to the Lancashire Cotton Industry, 1770–1840* (Chicago, 1959).

15. Angela V. John, *By the Sweat of Their Brow: Women Workers at Victorian Coal Mines* (London, 1980), p. 25. See the *First Report to Her Majesty of the Commissioners for Inquiring into the Employment and Con-dition of Children in Mines and Manufactories* (London, 1842; repr. Shannon, 1968).

16. 3 Hansard 63:1335 (June 7, 1842).

CHAPTER VI

1. *Tocqueville and Beaumont on Social Reform,* ed. Seymour Drescher (New York, 1968), pp. 1–2. The "Memoir" was originally delivered to the Royal Academic Society of Cherbourg in 1835 and was printed in the proceedings of the Academy. Although it was known to some of Tocqueville's contemporaries, it was not included in Beaumont's edition of Tocqueville's collected works. It was reprinted in 1911, in the *Bulletin des sciences économiques et sociales du comité des travaux historiques et scientifiques,* and was translated only recently by Drescher. (See also Drescher, *Dilemmas of Democracy: Tocqueville and Modernization* [Pittsburgh, 1968].)

2. *Ibid.,* pp. 2, 10.

3. *Ibid.,* p. 10.

4. *Ibid.*

5. *Ibid.,* pp. 12, 14.

6. *Ibid.,* pp. 15–16.

7. *Ibid.,* p. 17.

8. *Ibid.,* pp. 18–20.

9. *Ibid.,* pp. 24–25.

10. Jean-Baptiste Say, *Cours complet d'économie politique* (1828), quoted by Drescher, *Dilemmas of Democracy,* pp. 109, 103.

11. Joseph Hamburger, *James Mill and the Art of Revolution* (New Haven, 1963).

12. Eric Hobsbawm and George Rudé assume that the New Poor Law "must have been influenced" by Swing, but admit that there is "no significant evidence for this connection." (*Captain Swing* [New York, 1968], p. 297.) Peter Dunkley argues for a more direct connection, by way of Senior especially. ("Whigs and Paupers: The Reform of the English Poor Laws, 1830–1834," *Journal of British Studies,* 1981, pp. 127–28.)

13. Eric Hobsbawm, *Industry and Empire* (Penguin ed., London, 1969), p. 106. For a very different interpretation of the Reform Act, see D. C. Moore, "The Other Face of Reform," *Victorian Studies,* 1961; Moore, "Concession or Cure: The Socio-

logical Premises of the First Reform Act," *Historical Journal*, 1966; Moore, *The Politics of Deference: A Study of the Mid-Nineteenth Century English Political System* (London, 1976).

14. Mark Blaug, "The Myth of the Old Poor Law and the Making of the New," *Journal of Economic History*, 1963; Blaug, "The Poor Law Report Reexamined," *ibid.*, 1964. For a critique of Blaug, see James Stephen Taylor, "The Mythology of the Old Poor Law," *ibid.*, 1969. Also see above, pp. 65–66.

15. R. H. Tawney, *Religion and the Rise of Capitalism* (Penguin ed., New York, 1947 [1st ed., 1926]), p. 225; Blaug, *Journal of Economic History*, 1963, p. 152.

16. Raymond G. Cowherd, *Political Economists and the English Poor Laws* (Athens, Ohio, 1977), p. 215. Bagehot's terms were "dignified" and "efficient." (*The English Constitution* [World's Classics ed., Oxford, 1952 (1st ed., 1867)], p. 4.)

17. S. E. Finer, *The Life and Times of Sir Edwin Chadwick* (New York, 1970 [1st ed., 1952]), p. 46; Marian Bowley, *Nassau Senior and Classical Economics* (New York, 1967 [1st ed., 1937]), p. 286. Both Chadwick and Senior left accounts of their intentions and actions: Chadwick, "Principles and Progress of the Poor Law Amendment Act," *Edinburgh Review*, 1836; Senior, "English Poor Laws," *ibid.*, 1841, reprinted in *Historical and Philosophical Essays* (London, 1865), vol. II.

18. J. R. Poynter is one of the few historians to make much of this, in his final chapter entitled "From Abolition to Amendment." (*Society and Pauperism: English Ideas on Poor Relief, 1795–1834* [London, 1969], pp. 295 ff.)

19. Patricia James, *Population Malthus: His Life and Times* (London, 1979), p. 395.

20. Senior, *A Letter to Lord Howick on a Legal Provision for the Irish Poor* (2nd ed., London, 1831), p. 14.

21. Senior, *Two Lectures on Population* (London, 1829), p. 35. Others were rediscovering, so to speak, Smith at about the same time. See, for example, Alexander H. Everett, *New Ideas on Population, with Remarks on the Theories of Malthus and Godwin* (1826), p. 26:

It is sufficiently notorious, that an increase of population on a given territory is followed immediately by a division of labour; which produces in its turn the invention of new machines, and improvement of methods in all the departments of industry, and a rapid progress in the various branches of art and science. The increase effected by these improvements in the productiveness of labour is obviously much greater in proportion than the increase of population, to which it is owing.

22. Senior, *Historical and Philosophical Essays*, II, 98.

23. In a private letter to the secretary to the Lord Chancellor, Chadwick explained why it was necessary to include in the report a passage arguing against the abolition of the poor laws. Such a statement was required to "keep to the windward of the humanity mongers," and also to make it clear that relief was proposed "as a matter of expediency and not as a matter of right." "Expediency" in this context was not the expediency of placating the poor but simply a denial of the theory that relief was a "right." (Anthony Brundage, *The Making of the New Poor Law: The Politics of Inquiry, Enactment and Implementation, 1832–1839* [New Brunswick, 1978], p. 37.)

24. *Report from his Majesty's Commissioners for Inquiring into the Administration and Practical Operation of the Poor Laws* (London, 1834), p. vi. A facsimile edition has been issued by the Irish University Press (1971). The page references below are to the original edition.

25. *Ibid.*, p. 29. (Italics here, and throughout, are in the original.)

26. *Ibid.*, p. 156.

27. *Ibid.*, pp. 72, 8.

28. Bowley, pp. 292–93 (citing Senior's manuscripts); Senior, *Historical and Philosophical Essays*, II, 48, 57.

29. Statute of Artificers, 5 Eliz. I, c. 4 (1563).

30. Bowley, *Senior*, p. 296.

31. *Report*, p. 127.

32. *Ibid.*

33. *Ibid.*, pp. 156, 28–29.

34. *Ibid.*, p. 29.

35. *Ibid.*, p. 40.

36. *Ibid.*, p. 49.

37. *Ibid.*, p. 144.

38. *Ibid.*, pp. 128, 147.

39. *Ibid.*, p. 127.

40. *Ibid.*, pp. 127, 123.

41. *Ibid.*, p. 129.

42. *Ibid.*, p. 148.

43. *Ibid.*, p. 151.

44. A. V. Dicey, *Lectures on the Relation Between Law and Public Opinion in England During the Nineteenth Century* (London, 1962 [1st ed., 1905]), p. 203.

45. The "administrative" thesis was launched by Oliver MacDonagh in "The Nineteenth-Century Revolution in Government: A Reappraisal," *Historical Journal*, 1958, and developed by him in *A Pattern of Government Growth, 1800–60: The Passenger Acts and their Enforcement* (London, 1961). It has been adapted to a variety of reforms by Roy M. MacLeod: "The Alkali Acts Administration, 1863–84: The Emergence of the Civil Scientist," *Victorian Studies*, 1965; "Social Policy and the 'Floating Population': The Administration of the Canal Boats Acts, 1877–1899," *Past and Present*, 1966; "Government and Resource Conservation: The Salmon Acts Administration, 1860–1886," *Journal of British Studies*, 1968. It has also provoked some criticism: e.g., Henry Parris, "The Nineteenth-Century Revolution in Government: A Reappraisal Reappraised," *Historical Journal*, 1960; Parris, *Constitutional Bureaucracy: The Development of British Central Administration Since the Eighteenth Century* (London, 1969); Jenifer Hart, "Nineteenth-Century Social Reform: A Tory Interpretation of History," *Past and Present*, 1965.

46. *Report*, p. 99.

47. For example, Mark Blaug, *Economic Theory in Retrospect* (Homewood, Ill., 1973 [1st ed., 1962]), p. 59.

48. Michael E. Rose, "Settlement, Removal and the New Poor Law," in *The New Poor Law in the Nineteenth Century*, ed. Derek Fraser (London, 1976), pp. 25 ff.

49. 3 Hansard 22:877–78 (Apr. 17, 1834).

50. The most comprehensive recent study of the transformation of the report into the law is Anthony Brundage, *The Mak-*

ing of the New Poor Law. On the actual operation of the New Poor Law, see Derek Fraser (ed.), *The New Poor Law in the Nineteenth Century;* and on the opposition to it, Nicholas C. Edsall, *The Anti–Poor Law Movement, 1834–44* (Manchester, 1971). References to monographic and periodical literature may be found in these works and in Ursula R. Q. Henriques, *Before the Welfare State: Social Administration in Early Industrial Britain* (London, 1979).

51. 3 Hansard 25:215 (July 21, 1834).

52. Harriet Martineau, *Illustrations of Political Economy* (9 vols., London, 1832–34), I, preface.

53. Joseph Schumpeter, *History of Economic Analysis*, ed. Elizabeth Boody Schumpeter (New York, 1974 [1st ed., 1954]), p. 477; T. B. Macaulay, "Milton" (1825), *Works*, ed. Lady Trevelyan (London, 1875), V, 4; Dorothy Lampen Thomson, *Adam Smith's Daughters* (New York, 1973), pp. 24–25.

54. Martineau, *Illustrations*, II, 119. (Cf. Malthus, *On Population* [New York, 1960], p. 530.)

55. *Ibid.*, p. 30.

56. *Ibid.*, pp. 39, 129.

57. Martineau, *A History of the Thirty Years' Peace, A.D. 1816–1846* (London, 1877 [1st ed., 1849]), II, 502. This was written in 1848, by which time Martineau had become less doctrinaire in her commitment to laissez faire. She defended, for example, laws limiting the hours of labor of women and children, although not of men. But she never wavered in her support of the New Poor Law. Robert K. Webb, *Harriet Martineau: A Radical Victorian* (New York, 1960), is a thoughtful and sympathetic but not sentimental account of a life and mind that were more complicated than might be thought.

58. J. S. Mill, "The Spirit of the Age" (1831), in *Essays on Politics and Culture*, ed. Gertrude Himmelfarb (New York, 1962), p. 3.

59. William Cobbett, *Political Register*, Sept. 13, 1834. The expression is also used by Disraeli in *Letters of Runnymede* (Boston, n.d. [1st ed., 1836]), p. 109.

60. J. S. Mill, *Autobiography*, ed. John Jacob Coss (New York, 1924 [1st ed., 1873]), p. 139. When Mill sent a copy of the book

to Carlyle, he did not acknowledge his part in it, although in an earlier letter to Carlyle he had mysteriously alluded to an essay by himself on Bentham which Carlyle would not be able to see. (Mill, *Earlier Letters, 1812–1848,* ed. Francis E. Mineka, *Collected Works* [Toronto, 1963], XII, 152, 184 [Apr. 11–12, Oct. 5, 1833].) Carlyle, evidently not recognizing Mill's fine hand, privately dismissed Bulwer's book as yet another example of the novelist's incorrigible "levity," his "bustling whisking agility and restlessness." (James Anthony Froude, *Thomas Carlyle: A History of the First Forty Years of His Life, 1795–1835* [London, 1882], II, 406.) In *Sartor Resartus* Carlyle attacked Bulwer as the archetype of the "fashionable" novelist, the "leading Teacher and Preacher" of the sect of the "Dandy." (Everyman ed., London, 1940 [1st ed., 1833–34], p. 209.) As it happened, *Sartor Resartus,* although written two years earlier, was published shortly after *England and the English,* which contained bitter satires of the Dandy in the portraits of "Lord Mute" and "Sir Paul Snarl."

61. Edward Lytton Bulwer, *England and the English,* ed. Standish Meacham (Chicago, 1970 [1st ed., 1833]), pp. 317–19.

62. *Ibid.,* pp. 72–73.

63. *Ibid.,* pp. 78–79.

64. *Ibid.,* pp. 83, 34.

65. *Ibid.,* pp. 34–35, 48.

66. *Ibid.,* p. 124.

67. *Ibid.,* pp. 124–26.

68. *Ibid.,* pp. 137, 141.

69. Jeremy Bentham, "Constitutional Code," *Works,* ed. John Bowring (London, 1843), IX, 119.

70. Bulwer, p. 140.

71. *Ibid.,* p. 398.

72. Schumpeter, p. 487.

73. Thomas Chalmers, *Tracts on Pauperism* (Glasgow, 1833 [reprint of speech delivered May 24, 1822]), p. 47. See also *On the Power, Wisdom and Goodness of God as Manifested in the Adaptation of External Nature to the Moral and Intellectual Constitution of Man* (1833). Robert K. Webb finds it a "historiographical scandal" that there is no adequate study of Chalmers. ("John Hamilton Thom: Intellect and Conscience in Liverpool," in *The View from the Pulpit: Victorian Ministers and Society,* ed. P. T. Phillips

[Toronto, 1978], p. 232.) For brief accounts, see Laurance James Saunders, *Scottish Democracy, 1815–1840: The Social and Intellectual Background* (Edinburgh, 1850); Poynter, pp. 234–47; Daniel F. Rué, "An Attempt at Systematic Reconstruction in the Theology of Thomas Chalmers," *Church History,* June 1979.

CHAPTER VII

1. See Nicholas C. Edsall, *The Anti-Poor Law Movement, 1834–44* (Manchester, 1971). Since it is customary to think of Evangelicals and Dissenters as carrying the burden of the moral and social conscience of the early Victorians, it is useful to be reminded of the role played by the Anglican clergy who were involved as guardians and magistrates in the administration of the poor law and who often used their authority to mitigate the rigor of the law. See G. Kitson Clark, *Churchmen and the Condition of England, 1832–1885: A Study in the Development of Social Ideas and Practice from the Old Regime to the Modern State* (London, 1973), pp. 36 ff., 156 ff. See also K. S. Inglis, *Churches and the Working Classes in Victorian England* (London, 1963). For the churches' involvement in another major social issue, see J. C. Gill, *The Ten Hours Parson: Christian Social Action in the 1830s* (London, 1959).

2. The "social control" thesis has been applied most systematically to the poor law by Anthony Brundage, *The Making of the New Poor Law: The Politics of Inquiry, Enactment, and Implementation, 1832–1839* (New Brunswick, 1978), pp. 182 ff. Social control in his sense means both the strengthening of the power of traditional authorities over their localities and of the rich over the poor. Peter Dunkley uses the term in a more neutral, less pejorative sense in "Paternalism, the Magistracy and Poor Relief in England, 1795–1834," *International Review of Social History,* 1979, pp. 373, 396. (See also above, pp. 29 with n. 18, 41, and 59 ff.)

3. Harriet Martineau, *Autobiography* (3rd ed., London, 1877), I, 223.

4. John Walter, *A Letter to the Electors of Berkshire* (London, 1834), pp. 36–37.

5. *The Times,* April 30, 1834; May 20, 1834.

6. *Ibid.,* April 30, 1834.

7. *Ibid.,* Feb. 25, May 2 and 20, June 20, 1834.

8. See above, pp. 122–23.

9. G. Poulett Scrope, "The New Poor Law," *Quarterly Review,* 1834, p. 234. The article is tentatively attributed to Scrope in the *Wellesley Index to Victorian Periodicals, 1824–1900,* ed. Walter E. Houghton (Toronto, 1966), I, 715.

10. *Quarterly Review,* 1834, p. 245.

11. *Ibid.,* p. 255.

12. *Ibid.,* p. 241.

13. *Ibid.,* pp. 241–42.

14. John Wilson, "On Poor's [sic] Laws and Their Introduction into Ireland," *Blackwood's Magazine,* 1833, pp. 815, 821. Even *Blackwood's* had an occasional article defending the New Poor Law and political economy.

15. W. F. Monypenny and G. E. Buckle, *The Life of Benjamin Disraeli, Earl of Beaconsfield* (London, 1929 [1st ed., 1910]), I, 224.

16. *Ibid.,* pp. 377–78.

17. 3 Hansard 49:248 (July 12, 1839). For Disraeli's views as expressed in his fiction, see below, chap. XX.

18. David Roberts, *Paternalism in Early Victorian England* (New Brunswick, N.J., 1979), p. 2 and *passim.*

19. Much of this discussion is based on Roberts, "How Cruel Was the Victorian Poor Law?" *Historical Journal,* 1963.

20. Charles Dickens, *The Adventures of Oliver Twist* (Oxford ed., n.d.), pp. 20–29.

21. Roberts, *Historical Journal,* p. 98.

22. *Ibid.,* pp. 101–07.

23. Ursula Henriques, "How Cruel Was the Victorian Poor Law?" *Historical Journal,* 1968, pp. 365–66. Henriques also maintains that the New Poor Law had been "devised to suit the pockets and prejudices of the 'middling classes' . . . and was part of a body of class legislation based on selfishness and class interests" (pp. 370–71). But this is not related to the rest of her thesis about cruelty; nor does she offer much evidence to support it.

24. Brundage, p. 160. The report came from two assistant commissioners writing to Nicholls, the commissioner.

25. George Crabbe, "The Village," quoted by Anne Digby, *Pauper Palaces* (London, 1978), p. 1.

26. Crabbe, "The Borough," *ibid.,* p. 2.

27. Brundage, "The Landed Interest and the New Poor Law: A Reappraisal of the Revolution in Government," *English Historical Review,* 1972; Brundage, *Making of the New Poor Law,* pp. 182 ff, and *passim;* Henriques, *Historical Journal,* pp. 368 ff.

28. *Poor Law Report,* p. 74.

CHAPTER VIII

1. James Anthony Froude, *Thomas Carlyle: A History of His Life in London, 1834–1881* (London, 1884), I, 174 (Jan. [n.d.] and Feb. 11, 1840).

2. *Tait's Edinburgh Magazine,* 1840, reprinted in *Thomas Carlyle: The Critical Heritage,* ed. Jules Paul Seigel (New York, 1971), pp. 164–66.

3. Philip Rosenberg claims that Carlyle's memory was at fault. Quoting another letter by Carlyle to Mill, Rosenberg interprets it as suggesting that, rather than Mill turning down the article, Carlyle simply decided not to write it at that time. (*The Seventh Hero: Thomas Carlyle and the Theory of Radical Activism* [Cambridge, Mass., 1974], p. 221, n. 4.)

4. Froude, I, 172 (Nov. 8, 1839).

5. *The Earlier Letters of John Stuart Mill, 1812–1848,* ed. Francis E. Mineka, *Collected Works* (Toronto, 1963), XIII, 414 (Mill to Carlyle, early Dec. 1839).

6. Froude, I, 173 (Dec. 1, 1839).

7. On five and six points, see below, p. 254.

8. Carlyle, *Chartism,* in *English and Other Critical Essays* (Everyman ed., London, n.d.), pp. 165–66.

9. *Ibid.,* pp. 165, 167.

10. *Ibid.,* pp. 168–73.

11. *Ibid.,* pp. 174–75.

12. *Ibid.,* p. 176.

13. *Ibid.,* pp. 175–77.

14. *Ibid.,* p. 177.

15. *Ibid.,* pp. 177–78.

16. *Ibid.*, pp. 178–79.

17. *Ibid.*, p. 179.

18. *Ibid.*, pp. 199–200.

19. *Ibid.*, pp. 203, 208.

20. *Ibid.*, p. 223.

21. Froude, I, 282 (Aug. 20, 1842); p. 286 (Feb. 23, 1843).

22. Grace J. Calder, *The Writing of "Past and Present": A Study of Carlyle's Manuscripts* (New Haven, 1949).

23. *Past and Present* (Everyman ed., n.d.), pp. 2, 4, 6.

24. *Ibid.*, pp. 18, 196, 254.

25. *Ibid.*, pp. 275–76, 181, 200, 261.

26. Hannah Arendt, *The Human Condition* (Chicago, 1958), pp. 79 ff. See below, p. 392.

27. *Ibid.*, pp. 189–99.

28. *Ibid.*, p. 199.

29. For example, Rosenberg, pp. 132–34; Michael Goldberg, *Carlyle and Dickens* (Athens, Ga., 1972), p. 39.

30. Rosenberg, pp. 27, 67, and *passim*.

31. *Past and Present*, pp. 188, 248, 265, 271.

32. *On Heroes, Hero-Worship, and the Heroic in History* (Everyman ed., n.d.), p. 240.

33. Froude, II, 2. For other contemporary labels, see reviews reprinted in *Thomas Carlyle: The Critical Heritage*, pp. 208 ff.

34. Karl Marx and Friedrich Engels, *Collected Works* (New York, 1975), III, 466.

35. *Ibid.*, IV, 579; *Werke* (Berlin, 1962), II, 502.

36. Ralph Waldo Emerson, in *The Dial* (1843), reprinted as introduction to *Past and Present* (Everyman ed.), p. x.

37. *The Life of Frederick Denison Maurice, Chiefly Told in His Own Letters* (London, 1884), I, 280 (Maurice to E. Strachey, Apr. 5, 1840).

38. Kathleen Tillotson, *Novels of the Eighteen-forties* (Oxford, 1965), pp. 150–51.

39. George Eliot, review of *Passages Selected from the Writings of Thomas Carlyle* in *Leader* (1855), repr. in *Thomas Carlyle: The Critical Heritage*, pp. 409–10.

40. *Letters of Matthew Arnold to Arthur Hugh Clough*, ed. H. F. Lowry (London, 1932), p. 111 (Sept. 23, 1849). For an account of Arnold's complicated feelings toward Carlyle, see Kathleen Tillotson, "Matthew Arnold and Carlyle," Warton Lecture on English Poetry, 1956.

41. Review in *Leader*, in *Thomas Carlyle: The Critical Heritage*, p. 410.

42. *Ibid.*

43. Quoted by John Mander, *Our German Cousins: Anglo-German Relations in the 19th and 20th Centuries* (London, 1974), p. 83.

44. George Levine, "The Use and Abuse of Carlylese," in *The Art of Victorian Prose*, ed. George Levine and William Madden (Oxford, 1968), p. 104 (quoting James in *The Century*, 1883). Thoreau went much further, praising Carlyle's style as a model of lucidity: "Not one obscure line, or halfline did he ever write. His meaning lies plain as the daylight. . . . He tells us only what he sees printed in largest English type upon the face of things. He utters substantial English thoughts in plainest English dialects." (*Thomas Carlyle: The Critical Heritage*, p. 280.)

45. Froude, *Thomas Carlyle: A History of the First Forty Years of his Life, 1795–1835* (London, 1882), I, 300.

46. John Morley, "Harriet Martineau" (1886), in *Nineteenth-Century Essays*, ed. Peter Stansky (Chicago, 1970), p. 246.

47. *On Heroes*, pp. 280–81.

48. *Communist Manifesto* (trans. Samuel Moore), in *Birth of the Communist Manifesto*, ed. Dirk J. Struik (New York, 1971), p. 91.

49. *Chartism*, p. 188.

50. Arnold Toynbee, "Industry and Democracy" (1881), in *Lectures on the Industrial Revolution in England, Popular Addresses, Notes and Other Fragments* (London, 1884), p. 193; J. M. Jefferson, "Industrialisation and Poverty: In Fact and Fiction," in *The Long Debate on Poverty*, ed. Arthur Seldon (London, 1972), p. 233; Patrick Brantlinger, *The Spirit of Reform: British Literature and Politics, 1832–1867* (Cambridge, Mass., 1977), p. 110.

51. *Past and Present*, pp. 286–87.

CHAPTER IX

1. *Political Register*, Sept. 13, 1834. (See above, p. 171.)

2. Thomas Carlyle, "Sir Walter Scott" (1838), in *Critical and Miscellaneous Essays* (London, n.d.), VI, 37.

3. *The Autobiography of William Cobbett: The Progress of a Plough-boy to a Seat in Parliament,* ed. William Reitzel (London, 1933), pp. 9–10.

4. *Register,* Nov. 11, 1817; Apr. 7, 1821.

5. *Ibid.,* Nov. 11, 1817.

6. *Ibid.,* Feb. 28, 1807.

7. *Ibid.,* Feb. 22, 1823.

8. *Autobiography,* p. 130 (Dec. 21, 1822).

9. *Ibid.,* p. 129.

10. *Register,* Nov. 30, 1816. (Italics here, as throughout, in the original.) On the question of manhood and universal suffrage, see below, pp. 233 and 265.

11. *Ibid.,* June 13, 1835.

12. *A Legacy to Labourers* (London, 1872 [1st ed., 1834]), p. 97.

13. *Ibid.,* pp. 104–05.

14. Cecil Driver, *Tory Radical: The Life of Richard Oastler* (Oxford, 1946), p. 284. (Italics in the original.)

15. Matthew Hale, *Tract Touching Provision for the Poor* (1683).

16. Jeremy Bentham, *A Fragment on Government* (1776).

17. *Register,* Aug. 18, 1827.

18. Bentham, *Works,* ed. John Bowring (London, 1843), XI, 68.

19. *Register,* Apr. 15, 1809; Nov. 2, 1816.

20. *Ibid.,* Apr. 15, 1809.

21. *Ibid.,* Nov. 1, 1817. Although Cobbett often quoted Burke, and sometimes in agreement, he also derided the "prostituted Burke" who took money from the government and was part of the hateful "Thing."

22. *Ibid.,* Apr. 2, 1831; Sept. 27, 1817.

23. *Tour in Scotland* (London, 1833), p. 55. See also *Rural Rides* (Penguin ed., London, 1979 [1st ed., 1830]), p. 100.

24. 3 Hansard 23:1337 (May 26, 1834).

25. G. K. Chesterton, *William Cobbett* (New York, 1926), p. 21.

26. *Register,* Nov. 20, 1824.

27. *Ibid.*

28. See above, p. 187.

29. *Tour in Scotland,* p. 208.

30. *Register,* Nov. 30, 1816.

31. *Ibid.*

32. *Rural Rides,* p. 117 (Aug. 1, 1823).

33. *Register,* Apr. 15, 1826; Dec. 25, 1830.

34. *Ibid.,* Feb. 8, 1806.

35. *Ibid.,* July 16, 1808. On his early Malthusianism, see *The Life and Letters of William Cobbett in England and America,* ed. Lewis Melville (London, 1912), I, 293 (Cobbett to George Hibbert, Dec. 29, 1805); Herman Ausubel, "William Cobbett and Malthusianism," *Journal of the History of Ideas,* 1952; Charles H. Kegel, "William Cobbett and Malthusianism," *ibid.,* 1958. It was much later, in 1819, that Cobbett made his famous comment on Malthus: "I have, during my life, detested many men; but never any one so much as you." (*Register,* May 8, 1819.)

36. *Advice to Young Men* (London, 1887 [1st ed., 1829]), p. 274 (par. 340).

37. *Ibid.,* p. 275 (par. 341). See below, pp. 266 ff and 301–02.

38. *Register,* July 12, 1834.

39. *Ibid.,* May 8, 1819.

40. *A Legacy to Labourers,* p. 95. (This is Cobbett's paraphrase of Montesquieu, not a direct quotation.)

41. *Register,* Nov. 15, 1823; Apr. 5, 1817; *Life and Letters of Cobbett,* I, 23 (May 1, 1823).

42. *Register,* Apr. 7, 14, 1821.

43. Cobbett, *Selections,* ed. A. M. D. Hughes (Oxford, 1951 [1st ed., 1923]), pp. 160–61 (excerpt from Cobbett's *Sermons,* 1821); *Register,* Sept. 14, 1833.

44. G. D. H. Cole, *The Life of William Cobbett* (London, 1924), pp. 304–05.

45. *Register,* Mar. 7, 1829.

46. *Advice to Young Men,* pp. 261–62 (par. 323).

47. *Autobiography,* 218–19. On this subject, see John W. Osborne, "William Cobbett and English Education in the Early Nineteenth Century," *History of Education Quarterly,* March 1964.

48. There is no mention of anti-Semitism in the whole of Cole's biography; "Jews" does not appear in the index, although there are some passing references to them in the text (in the chapter on *Rural Rides* written not by Cole but by F. E. Green). Nor does the subject appear in the volume of selections edited by G. D. H. and

Margaret Cole, *The Opinions of William Cobbett* (London, 1944); nor in the *Autobiography* edited by William Reitzel. G. K. Chesterton does mention Cobbett's hatred of Jews as a sign of his true Englishness, his feeling for the "traditions of the past and the instincts of the people" (p. 176). Cobbett's notes for a speech opposing the emancipation of the Jews contained such comments as: "Suppose it was proposed to us to admit a race of *cannibals* to these powers, should we have a right to do it? Jew has always been synonymous with *sharper, cheat, rogue*. This has been the case with no *other race* of mankind." His editor, Lewis Melville, prefaced these quotations with the comment that they "make amusing reading today, as his daughter Susan wrote after his death." (*Life and Letters,* I, 20–21.) The biographer John Osborne is a notable exception, dealing candidly and unapologetically with Cobbett's virulent anti-Semitism. (*William Cobbett: His Thought and His Times* [New Brunswick, 1966], pp. 33, 222–23.) The most recent biography (published after this chapter was written) gives relatively little weight to the subject, considering the length of the study; it occupies one sentence in the first volume and half a paragraph in the second, with some of the more damaging facts and quotations relegated to footnotes. (George Spater, *William Cobbett: The Poor Man's Friend* [Cambridge, 1982], pp. 199, 441, 590 n. 59, 591 ns. 73, 79.)

49. *Rural Rides,* pp. 34, 38, 119, and *passim.*

50. Osborne, p. 33.

51. *Register,* Mar. 12, 1811; Aug. 30, 1823. On the relationship between radicalism and abolitionism (or anti-abolitionism), see Seymour Drescher, "Cart Whip and Billy Roller: Antislavery and Reform Symbolism in Industrializing Britain," *Journal of Social History,* 1981.

52. See John W. Osborne, "William Cobbett's Role in the Catholic Emancipation Crisis, 1823–1829," *The Catholic Historical Review,* 1963.

53. *Rural Rides,* p. 109; *Life and Letters,* I, 20.

54. For circulation figures, see M. L. Pearl, *William Cobbett: A Bibliographical Ac-*

count *of His Life and Times* (Oxford, 1953).

55. *A Grammar of the English Language* (London, 1859 [1st ed., 1818], pp. 137–38 [pars. 247–48]).

56. The title of the first edition was *Advice to Young Men and (incidentally) to Young Women, in the Middle and Higher Ranks of Life.* Later editions abbreviated this, omitting the women or the ranks or both.

57. *Rural Rides,* p. 81. Cobbett got the figures wrong. He had the population increasing from 10,000,000 to 14,000,000; in fact the census of 1801 gave the population as almost 9,000,000 and that of 1821 as 12,000,000, an increase of 3,000,000. By 1831 the population had reached almost 14,000,000.

58. *Autobiography,* pp. 129–30, 143, 205.

59. Samuel Bamford, *Passages in the Life of a Radical* (London, 1844), p. 7.

60. William Hazlitt, *Table Talk* (1821), in *Collected Works,* ed. A. R. Waller and Arnold Glover (London, 1933), VIII, 50, 57.

61. Edward Lytton Bulwer, *England and the English,* ed. Standish Meacham (Chicago, 1970 [1st ed., 1833]), pp. 71–72.

62. Cole, p. 431.

63. Karl Marx, "Layard's Motion on the Ten Hours Bill" (1853), *Collected Works* (New York, 1979), XII, 189.

64. J. L. and Barbara Hammond, *The Village Labourer* (London, 1966 [1st ed., 1911]), pp. 233–34.

65. Cole, p. 12.

66. E. P. Thompson, *The Making of the English Working Class* (New York, 1964), pp. 746–62.

67. Chesterton, p. 196. For a review of Cobbett's historical reputation, see Martin J. Wiener, "The Changing Image of William Cobbett," *Journal of British Studies,* 1974.

68. See Osborne, *Cobbett,* p. 17.

69. *Register,* Aug. 2, 1817; Apr. 7, 1821.

CHAPTER X

1. T. Perronet Thompson, "Programme to the *Westminster Review*" (July 1830), in *Exercises, Political and Others* (Lon-

don, 1842), I, 269. This Colonel Thompson is not to be confused with the Owenite William Thompson who wrote a book in 1824 with the Benthamite title (but Owenite doctrine), *An Inquiry into the Principles of the Distribution of Wealth Most Conducive to Human Happiness.* T. Perronet Thompson was the part-owner, with Bentham, of the *Westminster Review.* It was he who wrote the reply to Macaulay's critique of Bentham which was attributed to Bentham himself until he disowned it. John Stuart Mill, who was then in his most anti-Benthamite phase, described Thompson as having "an understanding like a pin, going very far into a thing, but never covering a larger portion of it than the area of a pin's point." (*Earlier Letters of John Stuart Mill, 1812–1848,* ed. Francis Mineka, *Collected Works* [Toronto, 1963], XII, 127 [Mill to Carlyle, Oct. 22, 1832].)

2. Harriet Martineau, *A History of the Thirty Years' Peace, A.D. 1816–1846* (London, 1877 [1st ed., 1849]), I, 292.

3. Edward Lytton Bulwer, *England and the English,* ed. Standish Meacham (Chicago, 1970 [1st ed., 1833]), p. 388. Some of the varieties of radicalism in this period are discussed in Simon Maccoby, *English Radicalism, 1832–1852* (London, 1935). See also D. J. Rowe, "London Radicalism in the Era of the Great Reform Bill," in *London in the Age of Reform,* ed. John Stevenson (Oxford, 1977).

4. Patricia Hollis, *The Pauper Press: A Study in Working-Class Radicalism of the 1830s* (Oxford, 1970), pp. 8, 204, and *passim.* Another excellent book on the same subject, but with a different emphasis, is Joel H. Wiener, *The War of the Unstamped: The Movement to Repeal the British Newspaper Tax, 1830–1836* (Ithaca, 1969). See also Wiener, *A Descriptive Finding List of Unstamped British Periodicals, 1830–1836* (London, 1970).

5. The subtitle varied slightly from issue to issue, "powers," for example, sometimes appearing as "power." In 1834 it was changed to "A Weekly Paper for the People," the caption explaining that after three and a half years of persecution the recent trial of Hetherington had proved the paper to be "a strictly legal publication."

6. *Guardian,* Dec. 19, 1835. Hetherington's figures, like Cobbett's for the *Register,* are extremely unreliable. For other estimates of circulation figures see Hollis, *Pauper Press,* pp. 116–24; Wiener, *War of the Unstamped,* pp. 184–85; R. K. Webb, *The British Working Class Reader, 1790–1848: Literacy and Social Tension* (London, 1955), p. 61; Richard D. Altick, *The English Common Reader: A Social History of the Mass Reading Public, 1800–1900* (Chicago, 1957), p. 340.

7. Before O'Brien assumed the editorship in November 1832, the editor was Thomas Mayhew, Henry Mayhew's oldest brother. (See below, p. 312.)

8. Wiener, *War of the Unstamped,* pp. 22–24.

9. *Guardian,* Mar. 28, 1835. The expression "radical reform," used in this sense, was common in the late eighteenth century. For a discussion of universal and manhood suffrage, see below, p. 265.

10. *Ibid.,* Sept. 24, 1831.

11. *Ibid.,* Oct. 1, 1831. Here and elsewhere in this chapter, I have substituted capital initials for words and phrases that in the original were in upper case. In some instances where an entire passage was italicized, I have put it in roman type. The popular press used capitals and italics so freely that to transcribe the quotations in that form would give an undue emphasis to them. At no time have I italicized or capitalized a word that was not italicized or capitalized in the original.

12. *Ibid.,* Nov. 2, 1833.

13. *Ibid.,* Sept. 24, 1831; Oct. 22, 1831; Mar. 1, 1834.

14. *Ibid.,* Oct. 1, 1831; Aug. 20, 1831.

15. *Ibid.,* Jan. 26, 1833.

16. *Ibid.,* July 26, 1834.

17. *London Radicalism, 1830–1843: A Selection from the Papers of Francis Place,* ed. D. J. Rowe (London, 1970), p. 137 (Oct. 6, 1836); A. R. Schoyen, *The Chartist Challenge: A Portrait of George Julian Harney* (London, 1958), p. 7 (quoting Place Mss., Br. Mus., Add Mss. 27819).

18. *Guardian,* Sept. 28, 1833. The *Guardian* was replying to the article in the *Register* of Sept. 4, 1833. Yet Cobbett's reputation was such that after his death Hetherington and John Cleave (publisher of *Cleave's Weekly Police Gazette*) founded the Cobbett Club in London.

19. According to Halévy, Hodgskin never mentioned Godwin in his writings, although he was clearly influenced by him. (*Thomas Hodgskin,* ed. and trans. A. J. Taylor [London, 1956 (1st ed., 1904)], p. 31.) Neither of the books on the unstamped press, by Wiener and Hollis, mentions Godwin. E. P. Thompson, in his discussion of Hodgskin, suggests an oblique link between the two: "Hodgskin did not offer an alternative *system* (unless it was the supersession of all systems, in a Godwinian sense) and there is a sense in which he side-stepped the question of property rights." (*The Making of the English Working Class* [New York, 1964], p. 779.)

20. Thomas Hodgskin, *Labour Defended Against the Claims of Capital* (London, 1922 [1st ed., 1825]), p. 67; *Popular Political Economy* (London, 1827), pp. 265, 268.

21. Halévy, *Hodgskin,* p. 118 (quoting Hodgskin's *Natural and Artificial Right of Property*).

22. *Ibid.,* p. 171. Halévy may have exaggerated the continuity in Hodgskin's thought. There was a large difference between the defender of trade unionism in the twenties and the opponent of trade unionism in the fifties, or between the Chartist in the late thirties and the free trader of the late forties.

23. *Guardian,* Jan. 26, 1833. (This was a quotation from Godwin's *Political Justice.*)

24. Pierre Leroux, a follower of Saint-Simon, claimed to have been the first to use the word "socialist," in *Le Globe* in 1832. But it had appeared five years earlier in the Owenite journal, *Co-operative Magazine.* (See Arthur E. Bestor, Jr., "The Evolution of the Socialist Vocabulary," *Journal of the History of Ideas,* 1948; J. F. C. Harrison, *Quest for the New Moral World: Robert Owen and the Owenites in Britain and America* [New York, 1969], p. 45.)

25. Preface to the 1888 edition of the *Communist Manifesto,* in *Birth of the Communist Manifesto,* ed. Dirk J. Struik (New York, 1971), p. 136.

26. Harrison, p. 196.

27. *Guardian,* Sept. 22, 1832; Sept. 1, 1832.

28. *Ibid.*

29. *Ibid.,* Mar. 28, 1835.

30. *Ibid.*

31. *Ibid.*

32. Quoted in the *Guardian,* Nov. 7, 1835.

33. *Ibid.,* Oct. 1, 1831.

34. *Ibid.,* Nov. 7, 1835. In his *Last Will and Testament,* Hetherington said that he remained an Owenite at heart. It is likely that even at this time he was better disposed to Owenism than was O'Brien.

35. *Ibid.,* Mar. 21, 1835.

36. *Ibid.,* Dec. 3, 1831. It may be that this represented the view of Thomas Mayhew, who was then editing the paper. Yet even in this early period the rhetoric was sufficiently harsh.

37. *Ibid.,* Mar. 23, 1833.

38. *Ibid.,* Mar. 23, 1833; Aug. 17, 1833.

39. *Ibid.,* May 24, 1834.

40. *Ibid.,* Oct. 18, 1834.

41. *Ibid.*

42. *Ibid.,* Nov. 8, 1834.

43. *Ibid.,* Nov. 22, 1834.

44. *Ibid.,* Dec. 20, 1834.

45. *Ibid.,* Nov. 14, 1835.

46. *Ibid.,* Sept. 24, 1831.

47. The subtitle of *The Poor Man's Advocate* was: *A Full and Fearless Exposure of the Horrors and Abominations of the Factory System in England.* For the views of political economists, Tories, and radicals toward machinery and industrialism, see Maxine Berg, *The Machinery Question and the Making of Political Economy 1815–1848* (Cambridge, 1980).

48. Robert Owen, *Report to the County of Lanark* (Penguin ed., London, 1970 [1st ed., 1821]), p. 251. See also the quotations from his *Observations upon the Effect of the Manufacturing System* (1815) in the introduction to this edition, pp. 48–49. Although the *Report* was originally published in 1821, Owen never disavowed any part of it. Indeed, he reprinted it in 1832, at the very time that he was making his most ambitious overtures toward the working classes and trade unions, and he included it in the appendix to his autobiography published just before his death.

49. *Guardian,* May 5, 1832.

50. *Ibid.,* Sept. 5, 1835; Mar. 28, 1835; Mar. 30, 1833; Apr. 13, 1833.

51. *Ibid.,* Mar. 30, 1833.

52. *Ibid.,* July 6, 1833.

53. *Ibid.,* Nov. 2, 1833.

54. *Ibid.*, Dec. 7, 1833.

55. *Ibid.*, Dec. 14, 21, 28, 1833; Jan. 11, 1834.

56. *Ibid.*, Aug. 3, 1833; July 5, 1834.

57. *Ibid.*, Mar. 22, 1834; Nov. 2, 1833.

58. *Ibid.*, Apr. 21, 1832; Nov. 14, 1835.

59. *Ibid.*, Mar. 23, 1833; Feb. 1, 1834.

60. *Ibid.*, July 20, 1834; Feb. 1, 1834. This kind of anti-Semitism was endemic to the unstamped press, as it was to the culture in general. For examples from other papers, see Wiener, *War of the Unstamped*, pp. 152, 227. (See also above, pp. 222–23.)

61. *Ibid.*, Dec. 12, 1835.

62. *Ibid.*

63. *Ibid.*, Oct. 10, 1831.

64. *Ibid.*, Oct. 10, 1833.

65. Alfred Plummer claims that O'Brien anticipated the fundamental ideas of *Capital* and that Marx himself may have been partly inspired by him. But the evidence he cites is such that the same claim could be made for almost any socialist and most radicals. Plummer also points out that O'Brien was much taken with Babeuf; but this would place him in a very different tradition from that of Marx. (*Bronterre: A Political Biography of Bronterre O'Brien, 1804–1864* [Toronto, 1971], pp. 249 ff, 59.) I. Prothero, on the other hand, maintains that the originality of O'Brien's thought has been much exaggerated. ("Chartism, Early and Late," *Bulletin of the Society for the Study of Labour History,* 1972, p. 52.)

66. *Guardian,* Nov. 2, 1833.

67. "Labour Is the Source of Wealth" was the motto featured in the Declaration of the National Union of the Working Classes drawn up in 1831. (*Life and Struggles of William Lovett* [London, 1920 (1st ed., 1876)], p. 74.)

68. Hollis, p. 301.

CHAPTER XI

1. Thomas Carlyle, *Chartism,* in *English and Other Critical Essays* (Everyman ed., London, n.d.), p. 168. For the texts of the Charter, see Dorothy Thompson (ed.), *The Early Chartists* (London, 1971), p. 57; Simon Maccoby, *English Radicalism, 1832–1852* (London, 1935), p. 168.

2. J. L. and Barbara Hammond, *The Age of the Chartists, 1832–1854* (London, 1925). Max Beer used "Chartism" to refer to an even larger period, covering all the radical movements from 1825 to the early 1850s. (*A History of British Socialism* [London, 1940 (1st ed., 1919)], pp. 280–82.)

3. The situation within London was so complicated that it has lent itself to the most diverse interpretations, e.g., on the role of the London Working Men's Association in initiating and promoting Chartism, the social and ideological composition of London Chartism, the relations between London Chartism and the provincial associations, the relative importance of London Chartism itself. See Iorwerth Prothero, "Chartism in London," *Past and Present,* 1969; D. J. Rowe, "The Failure of London Chartism," *Historical Journal,* 1968. On differing interpretations of Chartism in general, see Henry Weisser, "Chartism and the Historians," *British Studies Monitor,* 1978. The most recent and comprehensive study appeared after this book went to press: David Goodway, *London Chartism, 1838–1848* (Cambridge, 1982).

4. Alexander Somerville, *The Autobiography of a Working Man,* ed. John Carswell (London, 1951 [1st ed., 1848]), pp. xiv–xv.

5. Patrick Brantlinger, *The Spirit of Reform: British Literature and Politics, 1832–1867* (Cambridge, Mass., 1977), p. 131. For differing estimates of the rhetoric and reality of violence, see F. C. Mather, *Public Order in the Age of the Chartists* (New York, 1967 [1st ed., 1959]); T. A. Critchley, *The Conquest of Violence: Order and Liberty in Britain* (New York, 1970); J. T. Ward, *Chartism* (New York, 1973); Malcolm Thomis and Peter Holt, *Threats of Revolution in Britain, 1798–1848* (London, 1977); John Stevenson and Roland Quinault (eds.), *Popular Protest and Public Order: Six Studies in British History, 1790–1920* (New York, 1975). G. Kitson Clark relates the vehemence of Chartist rhetoric to the rhetoric of romanticism, in "The Romantic Element—1830 to 1850," in *Studies in Social History: A Tribute to G. M. Trevelyan,* ed. J. H. Plumb (London, 1955), pp. 221 ff., 234 ff. (See below, p. 396.)

6. *Annual Register,* 1839 (London, 1840), pp. 304–05.

7. Cecil Driver, *Tory Radical: The Life of Richard Oastler* (Oxford, 1946), pp. 222, 289–90.

8. G. D. H. Cole, *Chartist Portraits* (London, 1965 [1st ed., 1941]), pp. 26, 80 ff.

9. Asa Briggs, "National Bearings," in *Chartist Studies,* ed. Briggs (London, 1959), p. 291. Sixteen local studies of Chartism, published since 1958, are included in the bibliography in David Jones, *Chartism and the Chartists* (London, 1975), p. 213. See also Henry Weisser, "The Local History of Chartism—A Bibliographical Essay," *British Studies Monitor,* 1973.

10. J. A. Epstein, "Feargus O'Connor and the Northern Star," *International Review of Social History,* 1976, p. 76. For a more conventional analysis of the influence of the *Northern Star,* see Donald Read, *Press and People, 1790–1850: Opinion in Three English Cities* (London, 1961).

11. The largest estimate, 60,000, comes from the Chartist Robert Lowery, quoted in *Life and Struggles of William Lovett in His Pursuit of Bread, Knowledge, and Freedom* (London, 1920 [1st ed., 1876]), p. 177. Other sources range from 40,000 to 50,000: J. F. C. Harrison, "Chartism in Leeds," in *Chartist Studies,* pp. 73–74; Richard D. Altick, *The English Common Reader: A Social History of the Mass Reading Public, 1800–1900* (Chicago, 1957), p. 393; Alfred Plummer, *Bronterre: A Political Biography of Bronterre O'Brien, 1804–1864* (Toronto, 1971), p. 85; Jones, p. 100; Epstein, pp. 69–70, 96–97.

12. Briggs, p. 292. See also Jones, p. 79.

13. Plummer, p. 154.

14. Lovett, p. 69.

15. For contrasting views of nineteenth century Methodism, see E. J. Hobsbawm, "Methodism and the Threat of Revolution in Britain," in *Labouring Men: Studies in the History of Labour* (London, 1964), 23 ff.; E. P. Thompson, *The Making of the English Working Class* (New York, 1964), pp. 350 ff. See also p. 537 n. 25.

16. Lovett, p. 94. (Italics in the original.)

17. *London Radicalism: 1830–1843; A Selection from the Papers of Francis Place,* ed. D. J. Rowe (London, 1970), p. 151.

18. Lovett, p. 95.

19. *Ibid.*

20. *Ibid.,* p. 94.

21. *London Radicalism,* p. 177.

22. Brian Harrison and Patricia Hollis, "Chartism, Liberalism and the Life of Robert Lowery," *English Historical Review,* 1967. The theory that class consciousness necessarily, by definition, implied a commitment to the class struggle, and ultimately to revolution, is an important part of E. P. Thompson's thesis about the pre-Chartist period. The same thesis applied to early Victorian England has been presented most forcibly by John Foster, *Class Struggle and the Industrial Revolution: Early Industrial Capitalism in Three English Towns* (London, 1974). For critiques of Thompson and Foster (and an implicit defense of Harrison and Hollis), see D. S. Gadian, "Class Consciousness in Oldham and Other North-west Industrial Towns, 1830–1850," *Historical Journal,* 1978; Craig Calhoun, *The Question of Class Struggle: Social Foundations of Popular Radicalism During the Industrial Revolution* (Chicago, 1982).

23. Briggs, p. 294.

24. *Ibid.*

25. Lovett, p. xiii.

26. Briggs, p. 299. See also Alexander Tyrrell, "Class Consciousness in Early Victorian Britain: Samuel Smiles, Leeds Politics, and the Self-Help Creed," *Journal of British Studies,* 1970.

27. S. G. Checkland, *The Rise of Industrial Society in England, 1815–1885* (London, 1964), p. 349.

28. Cole, p. 32.

29. J. T. Ward, *Chartism* (New York, 1973), p. 100. The wording varies slightly in different sources, e.g., Donald Read, "Chartism in Manchester," in *Chartist Studies,* p. 34; Cole, p. 74.

30. Cole, p. 193.

31. Dorothy Thompson, pp. 62 ff.

32. Ward, p. 85, quoting *Bronterre's National Reformer,* Jan. 15, 1837.

33. Dorothy Thompson, p. 89.

34. *Poor Man's Guardian,* July 26, 1834.

35. Mark Hovell, *The Chartist Movement,* ed. T. F. Tout (Manchester, 1959 [1st ed., 1918]), p. 236.

36. Dorothy Thompson, pp. 115 ff. On the issue of female suffrage among the

Chartists, see the tracts in Dorothy Thompson, pp. 89 ff; Lovett, p. 174; Lovett and John Collins, *Chartism: A New Organization of the People,* ed. Asa Briggs (New York, 1969 [1st ed., 1840]), pp. 61–63; Hovell, pp. 70, 206, 236. (See also above, p. 233.)

37. J. S. Mill, "Reorganization of the Reform Party" (1839), in *Essays on Politics and Culture,* ed. Gertrude Himmelfarb (New York, 1962), p. 303.

38. See above, p. 106.

39. For the implications of the Chartist vocabulary, see below, pp. 301 ff.

40. T. H. Marshall, "Citizenship and Social Class" (1949), in *Sociology at the Crossroads* (London, 1963).

41. Aristotle, *Politics,* Bk. I, ch. 2, 1253a; *Nicomachean Ethics,* Bk. I, ch. 7, 1097b.

CHAPTER XII

1. Friedrich Engels, *The Condition of the Working Class in England,* in Marx and Engels, *Collected Works* (New York, 1975), IV, 524. ("Must" was italicized in the original German edition but not in the English.) The edition cited here reproduces the English translation by Florence Wischnewetzky which had been supervised and approved by Engels for the American edition of 1887 and the English edition of 1892. A more recent edition edited by W. O. Henderson and W. H. Chaloner (Oxford, 1958) has a valuable introduction and notes, but the translation itself is less accurate than the earlier one. Unless otherwise indicated, all citations are to the *Collected Works.*

2. These questions have been most thoroughly addressed by Henderson and Chaloner in the introduction and notes to their edition of the *Condition.* The introduction has been criticized by E. J. Hobsbawm, "History and 'the Dark Satanic Mill,'" in *Labouring Men* (London, 1964).

3. Marx and Engels, *On Britain* (London, 1962), p. 17, 22.

4. On the reception of the book in Germany, see *Works,* IV, 701–02, n. 115; W. O. Henderson, *The Life of Friedrich Engels* (London, 1976), I, 61 ff.

5. It has been treated as a literary and psychoanalytic text by Steven Marcus, *Engels, Manchester, and the Working Class* (New York, 1974); and as a semiotic one by Karel Williams, *From Pauperism to Poverty* (London, 1981).

6. Henderson and Chaloner, xvi, xix.

7. Richard N. Hunt, *The Political Ideas of Marx and Engels* (Pittsburgh, 1974), I, 104 (letter to Berthold Auerbach, June 19, 1843).

8. Henderson, I, 20.

9. *Works,* II, 372 (Dec. 9, 1842).

10. *Ibid.,* p. 378 (Dec. 25, 1842).

11. Appendix to Marx, *Economic and Philosophic Manuscripts of 1844* (London, 1958), p. 175; *Works,* III, 429.

12. *Works,* III, 441.

13. *Ibid.,* p. 615 (n. 180).

14. *Ibid.,* p. 443.

15. Hunt, I, 115.

16. *On Britain,* p. 533 (Nov. 19, 1844).

17. *Works,* IV, 329–30, 394, 427, 502, 509, 512, 554.

18. *Ibid.,* pp. 374, 335.

19. Asa Briggs, *Victorian Cities* (New York, 1965), p. 92.

20. *Works,* II, 378.

21. *Ibid.,* IV, 361, 364. In the English edition, "intellectually" was changed to "physically."

22. *Ibid.,* pp. 411, 416. See also pp. 423–24.

23. *Ibid.,* p. 329. The reference is to Stirner's *Die Einzige und sein Eigentum,* published in 1845.

24. *Ibid.,* p. 418.

25. *Ibid.,* pp. 428, 407–08, 419.

26. *Ibid.,* p. 419.

27. *Ibid.,* p. 582.

28. *Ibid.,* pp. 329, 411, 416, 501, 506.

29. *Ibid.,* p. 298.

30. *Ibid.,* pp. 419–20.

31. *Ibid.,* pp. 437–41.

32. *Ibid.,* p. 420.

33. *Ibid.,* pp. 502–03, 425.

34. *Ibid.,* p. 386.

35. *Ibid.,* pp. 426–27.

36. *Ibid.,* p. 412.

37. *Communist Manifesto* in *Birth of the Communist Manifesto,* ed. Dirk J. Struik (New York, 1971), pp. 91–92.

38. *Works,* IV, 308.

39. *Ibid.,* pp. 308–09. The phrases "patriarchal relation" and "natural superior"

were not in quotation marks in the text, in either the original German or the later English edition. Elsewhere in the book, however, referring not to the landed aristocracy but to the bourgeoisie as the workers' "natural superiors," the expression was in quotation marks (in the German and English editions), with a footnote explaining that this was a "favourite expression of the manufacturers" (p. 376). It is also interesting that in the original German edition of the *Communist Manifesto* there were no quotation marks around "natural superiors"; those marks were added only in the English edition.

40. *Manifesto*, p. 94.

41. *Works*, IV, 309.

42. Henderson and Chaloner, p. xiv; Hobsbawm, pp. 115 ff.

43. *Works*, IV, 307, 309, 320. The German edition used the phrase *industrielle Revolution*. (*Werke* [Berlin, 1962], II, 237, 239.) See above, p. 44, and p. 540 n. 8.

44. *Works*, IV, 302.

45. *Ibid.*, pp. 419, 393, 567, 326, 467, 547.

46. *Ibid.*, p. 525.

47. There is some controversy about the extent to which Marx was influenced by Stein. See Robert C. Tucker, *Philosophy and Myth in Karl Marx* (Cambridge, 1961), pp. 115 ff.; Shlomo Avineri, *The Social and Political Thought of Karl Marx* (Cambridge, 1968), pp. 53 ff.; David McLellan, *Marx Before Marxism* (New York, 1970), pp. 156–57; McLellan, *Karl Marx: His Life and Thought* (New York, 1973), pp. 96–97. But the question here is not the large question of "influence" but simply the popularization of the term and concept of the "proletariat." Engels referred to both Stein and Proudhon in the articles he wrote while he was in England (e.g., *Works*, III, 388), and he also used the term "proletariat" at this time (*ibid.* II, 323; III, 379, 389). *The Holy Family*, written largely by Marx and published early in 1845, contained a long, not uncritical defense of Proudhon against the Bauers, and at least one reference to Stein. (In 1847 Marx bitterly attacked Proudhon in his *Misère de la philosophie*, the title a parody of Proudhon's *Philosophie de la misère*.)

48. *Works*, IV, 297, 302–04. The English edition hyphenates (here and through-

out) "working-classes" and "working-class." Since the German edition usually did not hyphenate them (not even in the English preface to the German edition), I have transcribed them without hyphens, except in the few instances where they were hyphenated in the German edition.

49. *Ibid.*, p. 307. The original German edition had "working class" in the first sentence of this opening paragraph and "proletariat" in the last two sentences.

50. *Ibid.*, p. 310. The last words were reversed in the German edition: *"proletarians* (working men)."

51. *Ibid.*, p. 320.

52. *Ibid.*, p. 562.

53. *Ibid.*, III, 266.

54. *Ibid.*, pp. xx–xxi.

55. Tucker, p. 115. This was not the "dangerous class" as the English understood that expression. See below, pp. 395 ff.

56. *Works*, III, 186–87.

57. *Ibid.*, IV, 36–37.

58. *Ibid.*, VI, 178.

59. *Birth of the Communist Manifesto*, p. 169.

60. Marcus, p. 256.

61. *German Ideology*, in *Works*, V, 49.

62. Marx and Engels, *Selected Correspondence*, 1846–1895, trans. Dona Torr (New York, 1942), p. 147 (Apr. 9, 1863); *Werke* (Berlin, 1964), XXX, 343.

CHAPTER XIII

1. Thomas Carlyle, *Sartor Resartus* (Everyman ed., London, n.d.), p. 54.

2. Asa Briggs, "The Language of 'Class' in Early Nineteenth-Century England," in *Essays in Labour History*, ed. Briggs and John Saville (New York, 1960), pp. 43 ff. See also Briggs, "Middle-Class Consciousness in English Politics, 1780–1846," *Past and Present*, 1956; Briggs, "The Language of 'Mass' and 'Masses' in Nineteenth-Century England," in *Ideology and the Labour Movement: Essays Presented to John Saville*, ed. David E. Martin and David Rubenstein (London, 1979); Raymond Williams, "Class," in *Keywords* (New York, 1976); R. S. Neale, "Class and Class-Consciousness in Early Nineteenth-Century En-

gland: Three Classes or Five?" *Victorian Studies*, 1968, repr. in *Class and Ideology in the Nineteenth Century* (London, 1972); Neale, *Class in English History* (Oxford, 1981); Harold Perkin, *The Origins of Modern English Society, 1780–1880* (London, 1969); R. J. Morris, *Class and Class Consciousness in the Industrial Revolution, 1780–1850* (London, 1979); George Watson, *The English Ideology: Studies in the Language of Victorian Politics* (London, 1973).

3. Perkin, pp. 176–77 and *passim*.

4. The *Oxford English Dictionary* gives one case of "a middle class of people" in 1766, in a letter written by the Queen of Denmark about England. But it is not clear whether this was a translation, and whether it signified "class" in the modern sense. (Supplement, vol. II [1976].)

5. Bruce Mazlish, *James and John Stuart Mill: Father and Son in the Nineteenth Century* (New York, 1975), pp. 369–72.

6. John Stuart Mill, *Principles of Political Economy, with Some of Their Applications to Social Philosophy*, ed. J. M. Robson (Toronto, 1965), p. 760. This variorum edition cites no instance of "lower classes" or "lower class" in any of the editions of this work.

7. George Rudé, *Wilkes and Liberty: A Social Study of 1763 to 1774* (Oxford, 1961), p. 26; E. P. Thompson, *The Making of the English Working Class* (London, 1964), p. 83.

8. Robert Owen, *A New View of Society and Report to the County of Lanark* (London, 1970), pp. 118, 129. See also pp. 131–32, 168, 193.

9. *Political Register*, Nov. 15, 1823.

10. Harriet Martineau, *A History of the Thirty Years' Peace, A.D. 1816–1846* (London, 1877 [1st ed., 1849]), I, 71.

11. Briggs, "Middle-Class Consciousness," *Past and Present*. "Class consciousness" is generally attributed to the English edition of Marx's *Capital* in 1887.

12. *Political Register*, Feb. 6, 1830.

13. D. C. Moore, "Concession or Cure: The Sociological Premises of the First Reform Act," *Historical Journal*, 1966; "The Other Face of Reform," *Victorian Studies*, 1961; *The Politics of Deference: A Study of the*

Mid-nineteenth Century English Political System (New York, 1976).

14. *Life and Struggles of William Lovett in His Pursuit of Bread, Knowledge, and Freedom* (London, 1920 [1st ed., 1876]), p. 95. (See above, p. 260.)

15. *Ibid*.

16. Adam Smith, *An Inquiry into the Nature and Causes of the Wealth of Nations*, ed. Edwin Cannan (New York, 1937), p. 639.

17. Chartist petition of 1842, *English Historical Documents* (New York, 1956), XII, 443.

18. See above, p. 197.

19. Williams, *Keywords*, p. 55. The earliest example given by the *Oxford English Dictionary* for "middle class" in the singular came from the *Examiner* in 1812. But Paine used it in the *Rights of Man* twenty years earlier. (Dolphin ed., New York, 1961, p. 487.) The adjectival form—"working-class association" or "middle-class suffrage"— gives the appearance of the singular, but it is a modifier, not a noun.

20. *Political Register*, Dec. 4, 1830; Feb. 6, 1830.

21. *London Radicalism: 1830–1843: A Selection from the Papers of Francis Place*, ed. D. J. Rowe (London, 1970), p. 215.

22. *Guardian*, Oct. 15, 1831; Nov. 2, 1833. There was at least one reference to "labouring class" (July 6, 1833). It is entirely possible that some instances of "working class" escaped me, but there cannot have been many such, at least not in the major editorials and articles.

23. *Ibid.*, Apr. 5, 1834.

24. See above, p. 283.

25. *Fabian Essays in Socialism*, ed. George Bernard Shaw (Dolphin ed., New York, n.d. [1st ed., 1889]), p. 59. Historians tend to make the opposite mistake, unwittingly transforming the contemporary plural form into the singular, e.g., Perkin, transcribing a quotation from Place cited by Graham Wallas, renders Place's "working classes" as "working class" (p. 235). On the other hand, Richard Hoggart, drawing upon his own working class experiences, uses the plural form in discussing the mid-twentieth century; see Chapter I, "Who

Are 'The Working Classes'?", *The Uses of Literacy: Aspects of Working-Class Life, with Special Reference to Publications and Entertainments* (London, 1957).

26. James Mill, *Essay on Government* (Library of Liberal Arts ed., New York, 1955), p. 89. "Middle rank" appears five times toward the end of the essay, the first time introduced as a "class." This essay, originally published in 1820 in the supplement to the *Encyclopaedia Britannica,* was reprinted throughout the twenties, the last time in a collection of Mill's essays in 1828.

27. *Guardian,* Mar. 23, 1833.

28. Most of these titles appear in Joel H. Wiener, *A Descriptive Finding List of Unstamped British Periodicals, 1830–1836* (London, 1970). Cobbett's *Poor Man's Friend* had the subtitle, *Companion for the Working Classes.* (This was not, properly speaking, a newspaper but a series of "letters.") "Conservative" (as in Hetherington's *'Destructive,' and Poor Man's Conservative,* later called *People's Conservative*) was probably not meant satirically but rather in the original meaning of "preservative" as opposed to "destructive." Satire was, however, common enough in other titles: *Twopenny Trash, Devil's Menagerie, London Policeman.*

29. Carl B. Cone, *The English Jacobins: Reformers in Late Eighteenth Century England* (New York, 1968), p. 126.

30. C. B. Macpherson, *The Political Theory of Possessive Individualism, Hobbes to Locke* (Oxford, 1962), pp. 194 ff.; Judith Richards, Lotte Mulligan, and John K. Graham, " 'Property' and 'People': Political Usages of Locke and Some Contemporaries," *Journal of the History of Ideas,* 1981.

31. Contemporaries were acutely aware of the several meanings attached to "people." See, for example, George Cornewall Lewis, *Remarks on the Use and Abuse of Some Political Terms* (London, 1832), pp. 118 ff.

32. Jeremy Bentham, *Works,* ed. John Bowring (London, 1838–43), IX, 97 (italics in original).

33. Ivor Jennings, *Party Politics* (Cambridge, 1960), I, xiii. For similar references see Cecil S. Emden, *The People and the Con-*

stitution (Oxford, 1959 [1st ed., 1933]), pp. 316 ff.

34. Edmund Burke, "An Appeal from the New to the Old Whigs" (1791), *Works* (London, 1909–12), III, 87.

35. "Letters on a Regicide Peace" (1796), *ibid.,* V, 190.

36. "Thoughts on the Cause of the Present Discontents" (1770), *ibid.,* I, 337.

37. "Remarks on the Policy of the Allies" (1793), *ibid.,* III, 423.

38. Emden, pp. 82–83.

39. Burke, "Letter on the Duration of Parliaments" (1780), *Works,* VI, 4.

40. "Thoughts on the Cause of the Present Discontents" (1770), *ibid.,* I, 369. (Italics in original.)

41. 3 Hansard 8:251 (House of Lords, Oct. 7, 1831).

42. John Campbell, *Lives of the Lord Chancellor and Keepers of the Great Seal of England* (London, 1869), VIII, 398. See also George Macaulay Trevelyan, *Lord Grey of the Reform Bill* (London, 1920), 308–09; Arthur Aspinall, *Lord Brougham and the Whig Party* (Manchester, 1927), p. 191; A. S. Turberville, *The House of Lords in the Age of Reform, 1784–1837* (London, 1958), p. 272.

43. *Guardian,* Oct. 15, 1831; Feb. 11, 1832; Mar. 31, 1832.

44. Paine, pp. 294–95.

45. Burke, *Reflections on the Revolution in France* (Dolphin ed., New York, 1961 [1st ed., 1790]), p. 81. On the "swinish multitude," see above, p. 67. See also the discussion of the "mob" or "crowd" in the eighteenth century (p. 39), and the "dangerous class" (pp. 285, 381 ff.).

46. J. S. Mill, "Civilization" (1836), in *Essays on Politics and Culture,* ed. Gertrude Himmelfarb (New York, 1962), p. 58.

47. Lovett, p. 94. For other references, see Asa Briggs, "The Language of 'Mass' and 'Masses'," in *Ideology and the Labour Movement,* pp. 62–83; Raymond Williams, *Keywords,* pp. 158–63.

48. Graham Wallas, *The Life of Francis Place, 1771–1854* (London, 1951 [1st ed., 1898]), p. 192.

49. *Class and Conflict in Nineteenth-Century England, 1815–1850,* ed. Patricia Hol-

lis (London, 1973), p. 80 (excerpt from *Pioneer*, June 28, 1834).

50. H. J. Hanham, *The Nineteenth-Century Constitution, 1815–1914: Documents and Commentary* (Cambridge, 1969), p. 270.

51. See above, p. 266. On the political status of paupers see T. H. Marshall, "Citizenship and Social Class," in *Sociology at the Crossroads* (London, 1963). Marshall argued that the minimal social rights remaining to the pauper after the passage of the New Poor Law had been purchased at the cost of his civil and political rights (p. 83).

52. See below, pp. 387 ff.

53. Briggs, "Language of 'Class'," in *Essays in Labour History*, p. 44.

54. John Foster, *Class Struggle and the Industrial Revolution: Early Industrial Capitalism in Three English Towns* (London, 1974), p. 4. Foster's is a more conventional, mechanical (rigorous, he would argue) application of the Marxist model than Thompson's.

55. See above, pp. 257–58.

56. E. J. Hobsbawm, "Class Consciousness in History," in *Aspects of History and Class Consciousness*, ed. I. Meszaros (London, 1971), p. 6.

57. Perkin, pp. 252 ff.; Neale, *Class and Ideology*, pp. 15 ff. Perkin has one working class, and Neale two—a "proletarian" class and a "deferential" one.

58. Hobsbawm, *The Age of Revolution, 1789–1848* (New York, 1964), p. 249.

59. Thompson, pp. 9, 275, and *passim*. For the dispute between Thompson and other English Marxists who insist upon a more "structuralist" definition of class, see the articles by Perry Anderson and Tom Nairn in *New Left Review*, 1963–64, and Thompson's reply, "The Peculiarities of the English," *The Socialist Register*, 1965, reprinted in Thompson, *The Poverty of Theory and Other Essays* (New York, 1978), pp. 245–301.

CHAPTER XIV

1. Percy Bysshe Shelley, "Peter Bell the Third," part 3, verse 1.

2. On the etymology of "rookery" see Thomas Beames, *The Rookeries of London: Past, Present, and Prospective* (London, 1852),

pp. 1–2. On the etymology of "slum" see H. J. Dyos, "The Slums of Victorian London," *Victorian Studies*, 1967, pp. 7–10; Anthony S. Wohl, *The Eternal Slum: Housing and Social Policy in Victorian London* (Montreal, 1977), p. 5. On the slums themselves, see Dyos, "Urban Transformation: A Note on the Objects of Street Improvement in Regency and Early Victorian London," *International Review of Local History*, 1957; Dyos and D. A. Reeder, "Slums and Suburbs," in *The Victorian City: Images and Realities*, ed. Dyos and Michael Wolff (London, 1973), I, 359 ff. Donald J. Olsen, *The Growth of Victorian London* (London, 1976), without focusing on the slum as such, helps put it in the perspective of the city as a whole.

3. This is the view of Francis Sheppard, *London, 1808–1870: The Infernal Wen* (Berkeley, 1971), pp. 158 ff. Sheppard quotes P. G. Hall, *The Industries of London since 1861* (London, 1962) in support of his position. This is in contrast to the more familiar view expressed in the census report of 1831: "In the appropriate application of the word manufacture, none of importance can be attributed to Middlesex . . . other than that of silk." (J. H. Clapham, *An Economic History of Modern Britain: The Early Railway Age, 1820–1850* [Cambridge, 1967 (1st ed., 1926)], pp. 67–68.)

4. Emile Durkheim, *The Division of Labor in Society*, trans. George Simpson (Glencoe, Ill., 1947 [1st ed., 1893]), pp. 257 ff. This concept is used (although not with particular reference to London) by J. A. Banks, "The Contagion of Numbers," in *The Victorian City*, I, 109.

5. Asa Briggs, *Victorian Cities* (New York, 1965), p. 321, quoting Benjamin Haydon's *Autobiography* (1841). When Henry Mayhew took a balloon trip in 1856 to observe from aloft "The Great World of London," he used the same metaphor, "dense canopy of smoke," to describe the scene. (Mayhew and John Binny, *The Criminal Prisons of London and Scenes of Prison Life* [London, 1968 (1st ed., 1862)], p. 9.)

6. B. I. Coleman (ed.), *The Idea of the City in Nineteenth-Century Britain* (London, 1973), p. 101 (extract from a sermon delivered in 1844).

7. Sheppard, p. 348.

8. Jean Jacques Rousseau, *Emile, or On Education,* trans. Allan Bloom (New York, 1979 [1st ed., 1762]), p. 59.

9. Robert Vaughan, *The Age of Great Cities, or Modern Society Viewed in Its Relation to Intelligence, Morals and Religion* (Shannon, 1971 [1st ed., 1843]), pp. 227–29.

10. Robert Southey, *Sir Thomas More: or, Colloquies on the Progress and Prospects of Society* (London, 1829), I, 108.

11. The quotation is from Rousseau, *La Nouvelle Héloïse,* part II, letter 27, in *Oeuvres complètes* (Pléiade ed., Dijon, 1964), II, 303.

12. Frederick Morton Eden, *The State of the Poor: or, an History of the Labouring Classes in England* (London, 1797), I, 58–59.

13. John L. and Barbara Hammond, *The Bleak Age* (London, 1934); E. Royston Pike, *"Golden Times": Human Documents of the Victorian Age* (New York, 1972). W. L. Burns, *The Age of Equipoise: A Study of the Mid-Victorian Generation* (London, 1964), proposes a more sober label for a period that was undeniably more stable and composed than the preceding decade.

14. The publication history is complicated and not entirely clear; see below, pp. 322, 568 n. 36. Unless otherwise noted, citations below are to the facsimile reprint, *London Labour and the London Poor,* ed. John D. Rosenberg (4 vols., New York, 1968). (For the full title and subtitles, see below, p. 322.)

15. The only full-length biography is Anne Humphreys, *Travels into the Poor Man's Country: The Work of Henry Mayhew* (Athens, Ga., 1977). Earlier biographical accounts are in the introductions to selections from his works edited by John L. Bradley, Stanley Rubinstein, and E. P. Thompson and Eileen Yeo. (See notes 18, 32, 37, 38, and 40.)

16. M. H. Spielmann, *The History of "Punch"* (London, 1895), p. 268.

17. An earlier *Punch in London* appeared in 1832, edited by Douglas Jerrold. *Punch* itself was frankly modeled on the French magazine *Charivari,* hence the *London Charivari* in its subtitle.

18. John L. Bradley, introduction to *Selections from "London Labour and the London Poor"* (London, 1965), p. xx.

19. The song inspired drawings and paintings as well as the obvious literary imitations. See T. J. Edelstein, "They Sang 'The Song of the Shirt': The Visual Iconology of the Seamstress," *Victorian Studies,* 1980.

20. *Fraser's Magazine,* Dec. 1849, p. 707.

21. *Chronicle,* Sept. 24, 1849.

22. *Ibid.,* Oct. 18, 1849.

23. *Ibid.,* Oct. 19, 1849.

24. "Pauper palaces" was a common expression for the workhouses. See above, pp. 187–88.

25. *Chronicle,* Oct. 19, 1849.

26. *Ibid.,* Oct. 23, 1849.

27. *Ibid.,* Oct. 26, 1849. (*London Labour,* III, 301.)

28. *Ibid.* See also Nov. 2, 1849. (*London Labour,* III, 312.)

29. *Ibid.,* Nov. 6, 1849.

30. H. Sutherland Edwards, *Personal Recollections* (London, 1900), p. 60.

31. *London Labour,* I, xvi.

32. *The Unknown Mayhew: Selections from the "Morning Chronicle," 1849–1850,* ed. E. P. Thompson and Eileen Yeo (London, 1971), pp. 45, 51, 55, 90–94, 478; Humpherys, pp. 39, 198 ff. On Reynolds, see below, p. 438.

33. The expression "labour aristocracy" used by historians today—e.g., E. J. Hobsbawm, "The Labour Aristocracy in Nineteenth-Century Britain," in *Labouring Men: Studies in the History of Labour* (London, 1964)—was of contemporary origin. In 1839 the Royal Commission *Report on the Constabulary* spoke of "skilled labourers, or an 'aristocracy' of skilled labourers." (*Report* [Irish University Press, Dublin, 1970], p. 84 [p. 70 of original ed.].) See also *London Labour,* I, 92.

34. *Chronicle,* Feb. 4, 1850; *Unknown Mayhew,* p. 35.

35. *Unknown Mayhew,* p. 38. This speech was delivered October 28, more than three weeks after his resignation. Yet during that time, and for another six weeks following the speech, the *Chronicle* continued to run articles from their "Special Correspondent" in London. The first three of these articles, on the transit workers, were certainly by Mayhew, having probably been written and paid for before his resignation; they were later included in *London Labour and the*

London Poor. Since none of the other eight articles was reprinted, not even those which were on subjects dealt with in those volumes, the likelihood is that they were not by Mayhew. (They may have been by his assistants using some of the material earlier collected by him.) Mayhew's editors have differed in their attribution of some or all of these articles to him, Thompson and Yeo reprinting four of them, Humpherys assigning two to him, and Bradley and Rosenberg differing in the total number of articles he contributed to the *Chronicle.*

36. It is generally said that two bound volumes were issued in 1851–52. Humpherys claims that only one volume appeared in 1851, and that the second was not published until 1861 (pp. 106–07). The Cambridge University Library has a two-volume edition cataloged as 1851–52. The first volume bears the date 1851 on the title page; the second has no proper title page and hence no date. It does, however, give every appearance of having been published in 1852, since it consists entirely of parts which had appeared by then: twenty-four parts of the regular series, plus a series on prostitution which ran concurrently with *London Labour* (on odd weeks from August 23, 1851, to February 7, 1852). The latter section (paginated separately) was prefaced by an introduction on "Those That Will Not Work," a "Classification of the Workers and Non-Workers of Great Britain," and some tables on population, criminality, and the like, all of which also appeared at this time. This last part of the original Volume II was included in Volume IV in the 1861–62 edition.

37. Included in the four-volume edition were parts published in 1856 under the title "The Great World of London." (See n. 5.) Dorothy George speaks of *The Criminal Prisons of London and Scenes of Prison Life* (1862) by Mayhew and John Binny as Volume V of *London Labour.* (Introduction to *The Street Trader's Lot: London: 1851,* ed. Stanley Rubinstein [London, 1947], p. xi.) But that volume was published separately and was not part of the four-volume edition of *London Labour.*

38. Volumes of selections include *The Street Trader's Lot,* ed. Rubinstein; *Mayhew's London,* ed. Peter Quennell (London, 1949);

Mayhew's Characters, ed. Quennell (London, 1951); *London's Underworld,* ed. Quennell (London, 1950); *Selections from "London Labour and the London Poor,"* ed. Bradley. The entire work has been reprinted by Dover Publications (New York, 1968).

39. *London Labour,* I, vi.

40. Thompson, "The Political Education of Henry Mayhew," *Victorian Studies,* 1967, p. 42. Thompson is here describing *London Labour,* not the *Morning Chronicle* articles.

41. *London Labour,* I, xv. (The preface was not part of the original pamphlets but was added when they were bound and issued as a volume in 1851.)

42. Humpherys, p. 24.

43. Within the articles on the street-folk there were occasional comments on the conventional trades—on the unemployed weavers, for example, who sometimes found their way to the docks. (*London Labour,* III, 301.) The only major exception was an article on cabinetmakers reprinted from the *Chronicle,* which appeared between the account of an "exhibitor of birds and mice" and a "doll's-eye maker." (III, 221–31.)

44. *Ibid.,* I, 1. The expression "wandering tribes" was often used at this time to refer to the vagrants who wandered through the countryside and passed through London. (See, for example, *Speeches of the Earl of Shaftesbury, upon Subjects Having Relation Chiefly to the Claims and Interests of the Labouring Class* [London, 1868], p. x.) But only Mayhew applied it to such London street-folk as street-performers, street-sellers, street-laborers, and the like. (For a recent account of the "wandering tribes" in a more literal sense, see Raphael Samuel, "Comers and Goers," in *The Victorian City,* I, 123–60.)

45. *Ibid.,* I, 2.

46. *Ibid.,* pp. 2–3.

47. *Ibid.,* pp. 7, 213–14.

48. *Ibid.,* pp. 6, 16, 24.

49. *Ibid.,* pp. 24, 477, 417.

50. *Chronicle,* May 25, 1850.

51. *London Labour,* I, 6.

52. *Ibid.,* pp. 22, 25.

53. *Ibid.,* p. 43.

54. *Ibid.,* pp. 477–9.

55. *Ibid.,* p. 101.

56. *Ibid.*, p. 101.

57. *Ibid.*, pp. 213–14.

58. *Ibid.*, p. 320.

59. *Ibid.*, pp. 320–21. (Italics in original.)

60. *Ibid.*, p. 322. Messrs. Moses and Nicol (sometimes spelled Nicoll) were the tailoring firms he had attacked in the *Chronicle*. (See above, p. 322.)

61. *Ibid.*, p. 323.

62. *Ibid.*, p. xv.

63. *Eclectic Review*, 1851, pp. 424–25.

64. *London Labour*, I, 104, 110, 466.

65. *Ibid.*, pp. 117–27.

66. *Ibid.*, p. 117.

67. *Ibid.*, p. 213.

68. *Ibid.*, II, 7.

69. *Ibid.*, pp. 136–48.

70. *Ibid.*, p. 152.

71. *Ibid.*, p. 155.

72. *Ibid.*, p. 172.

73. *Ibid.*, p. 147.

74. *Ibid.*, III, 233.

75. *Ibid.*, p. 283.

76. *Ibid.*, p. 301.

77. *Ibid.*, pp. 303, 307–08.

78. *Ibid.*, pp. 303, 310.

79. *Ibid.*, pp. 317–18.

80. *Ibid.*, pp. 368–70.

81. *Ibid.*, p. 371.

82. *Ibid.*, pp. 376–77, 397, 429.

83. *Ibid.*, p. 429.

84. *Ibid.*, pp. 397, 373, 376, 429, 377.

85. Mayhew also wrote part of the section on prostitution. All of his contributions to this volume date from 1851–52. Several paragraphs (IV, 34–35) reproduce portions of his first article in the *Morning Chronicle* series (Oct. 19, 1849) and of Vol. III of *London Labour* (pp. 429–30).

86. *Ibid.*, IV, 4, 9.

87. *Ibid.*, p. 1.

88. *Ibid.*, pp. 35–36.

89. *Ibid.*, p. 20.

90. Pamphlet cover, Mar. 29, 1851.

91. *London Labour*, II, 242–43.

92. *Ibid.*, pp. 243–44.

93. *Ibid.*, p. 252.

94. *Ibid.*, p. 264. (Italics in original.)

95. The covers were not included in the bound parts when they were issued as volumes. Some of this material was incorporated in a separate series issued under the title *Low Wages;* the four parts of this series were reissued as a separate pamphlet. (Citations to the covers are indicated by the dates of the pamphlets.)

96. Mar. 22, 1851.

97. Mar. 15, 1851.

98. July 5, 1851.

99. Apr. 19, 1851.

100. Mar. 29, 1851. Here Mayhew had Smith spending twelve years in that obscure Scottish village spinning out his fantasy. On July 19, 1851, he used the same image, but changed the number of years to fifteen.

101. Mar. 15, Sept. 27, and Feb. 15, 1851.

102. Talk by Mayhew reported in the *British Quarterly Review*, May 1850, p. 493.

103. Feb. 15, 1851.

104. Feb. 15, 1851; Sept. 27, 1851.

105. Sept. 13, 1851. (See also Feb. 15, 1851.) On Ikey Solomons, see below, pp. 429, 434, 459.

106. Feb. 8, 1851.

107. May 3, 1851.

108. July 19, 1851.

109. Feb. 8, 1851. (See also June 28, 1851.)

110. *Criminal Prisons*, p. 52.

111. *London Labour*, I, 6. This figure was repeated, II, 1.

112. *Ibid.*, II, 1.

113. *Ibid.*, III, 233.

114. *Ibid.* These figures (which first appeared in Mayhew's article in the *Morning Chronicle* on Dec. 21, 1849) correspond roughly to the 1841 census.

115. *Ibid.*, I, 4–5; II, 162.

116. *Ibid.*, I, viii (introduction by Rosenberg).

117. *Ibid.*, II, 464.

118. *Ibid.*, III, 429 (*Chronicle*, Oct. 19, 1849).

119. *Annals of the Royal Statistical Society, 1834–1934* (London, 1934), p. 22. (The Statistical Society was sometimes called the Statistical Society of London to distinguish it from the Statistical Society of Manchester, which had been formed the previous year. In 1887 the London organization became the Royal Statistical Society.)

120. *Quarterly Journal of the Statistical Society of London*, 1848, pp. 193–94. (Italics in original.) For the early history of statistics

as a discipline in England, see Frederic J. Mouat, "History of the Statistical Society," *Jubilee Volume of the Statistical Society* (London, 1885); M. J. Cullen, *The Statistical Movement in Early Victorian Britain: The Foundations of Empirical Social Research* (Sussex, 1975); Philip Abrams, *The Origins of British Sociology: 1834–1914* (Chicago, 1968); Asa Briggs, "The Human Aggregate," in *The Victorian City*, I, 83–104.

121. Thompson, *Victorian Studies*, 1967, p. 58. Yeo, on the other hand, makes Mayhew's errors a matter of faulty "proofreading." (*Unknown Mayhew*, p. 62.) Rosenberg finds him as "searingly accurate" as Engels and compares his data favorably to that of present-day government agencies. (*London Labour*, pp. v–vi.) J. T. R. Hughes judges his statistical evidence "usually objective and fairly sophisticated." ("Henry Mayhew's London," *Journal of Economic History*, 1969, p. 536.) James Bennett praises especially his mastery of "oral history" and "street-biography." (*Oral History and Delinquency: The Rhetoric of Criminology* [Chicago, 1981], pp. 11 ff.)

122. *London Labour*, I, xv.

123. F. B. Smith, "Mayhew's Convict," *Victorian Studies*, 1979, p. 440. The convict's story was in *London Labour*, III, 386–88.

124. Humpherys, p. 79. The quotations appeared on the covers of the parts dated Jan. 10 and 17, 1852. Compare with Carlyle's *Latter-Day Pamphlets*, in *Works* (New York, 1897 [1st ed., 1850]), p. 314; and *Chartism*, in *English and Other Critical Essays* (Everyman ed., London, n.d. [1st ed., 1839]), p. 237. On "Marcus," see above, pp. 125–26.

125. *Spectator*, Oct. 27, 1849, p. 1018.

126. *British Quarterly Review*, May 1850, p. 491.

127. Gordon Ray, *Thackeray: The Uses of Adversity, 1811–1846* (New York, 1955), p. 367. (Jerrold to Mrs. Cowden Clark, Feb. 22, 1850.)

128. *Punch*, Mar. 9, 1850, p. 93.

129. *Chronicle*, Dec. 18, 1849.

130. *Eclectic Review*, Oct. 1851, pp. 424–36.

131. *Athenaeum*, Nov. 15, 1851, pp. 1199–1201.

132. *Quarterly Review*, Sept. 1855, pp. 411–414.

133. *Edinburgh Review*, Apr. 1851, pp. 322–24. (Italics in original.) Mayhew was not explicitly mentioned in this article, but he was in an earlier issue, when Kingsley was taken to task for accepting uncritically Mayhew's account of the plight of the tailors. (Jan. 1851, p. 8.)

134. *Fraser's Magazine*, Jan. 1850, p. 8.

135. *British Quarterly Review*, May 1850, p. 494.

136. Thomas Hughes, prefatory memoir to *Alton Locke, Tailor and Poet* (London, 1884), p. xxxi (letter by Kingsley, Jan. 13, 1851).

137. *Cheap Clothes and Nasty*, in *Alton Locke*, p. lxiv. It was because of Mayhew's articles about the tailors in the *Chronicle* (Dec. 14, 18, 1849) that Kingsley could write to Ludlow later that month that Ludlow's "revelations" in *Fraser's* were all new to him "except about the tailors." (Kingsley, *His Letters, and Memories of His Life*, ed. Mrs. Kingsley [New York, 1900], I, 194 [Dec. 30, 1849]).

138. *Alton Locke*, p. 108.

139. Although the Jacob's Island scene was almost certainly suggested by Mayhew, Kingsley had taken the trouble to visit the area and had written movingly about it to his wife. (*Letters and Memories*, I, 191–92 [Oct. 24, 1849].) Mayhew's article had appeared just one month earlier.

140. Carlyle, *Latter-Day Pamphlets*, pp. 285–86 (Feb. 1, 1850).

141. *Economist*, Nov. 16, 1850, p. 1265. It may have been this episode that later provoked Mayhew to misquote and misrepresent Carlyle. (See above, p. 349.)

142. See below, pp. 468 ff., for a discussion of the personal and literary relationship between Mayhew and Dickens.

143. Mayhew's name does not appear in the memoirs or letters of such eminent Victorians as Dickens, Eliot, Gaskell, Disraeli, Mill—which does not mean that they had not read him or (as in Dickens's case) known him, but only that his work did not provoke comment.

144. The 13,000 figure is more accurate than most such estimates, since it was based on a lawsuit brought against Mayhew

at the time. (Humpherys, p. 24; Louis James, *Fiction for the Working Man, 1830–1850: A Study of the Literature Produced for the Working Classes in Early Victorian Urban England* [London, 1963], pp. 46, 52.) The *Morning Chronicle* circulation is more speculative. In 1854 it was estimated at about 2,500 but at the time Mayhew was writing his series it was known to be higher. It should also be remembered that some of the earlier *Chronicle* articles were reprinted or summarized in other journals. (H. R. Fox Bourne, *English Newspapers: Chapters in the History of Journalism* [London, 1887], II, 159.)

145. This is the selection edited by Thompson and Yeo. Another selection has been compiled by Anne Humpherys: *Voices of the Poor: Selections from the Morning Chronicle 'Labour and the Poor' (1849–1850)* (London, 1971). A complete edition of Mayhew's contributions to the *Chronicle* is *The Morning Chronicle Survey of Labour and the Poor: The Metropolitan Districts*, ed. P. E. Razzell (Sussex, 1980); this is the first of six projected volumes reprinting all the *Chronicle* articles, including those on the rural and industrial areas. There is also a selection from the rural and industrial series: *The Victorian Working Class: Selections from Letters to the Morning Chronicle*, ed. P. E. Razzell and R. W. Wainwright (London, 1973).

146. Patrick Brantlinger, *The Spirit of Reform: British Literature and Politics, 1832–1867* (Cambridge, Mass., 1977), p. 28.

147. *Report on the Sanitary Condition of the Labouring Population of Great Britain*, ed. M. W. Flinn (Edinburgh, 1965), p. 397. For Thackeray's remarks, see above, p. 350.

148. *Ibid.*, pp. 93–94, 112.

149. *Ibid.*, p. 397.

150. *Ibid.*, p. 202. This bit of evidence was taken from the *Poor Law Report*.

151. *Ibid.*, pp. 164–65.

152. S. E. Finer, *The Life and Times of Sir Edwin Chadwick* (New York, 1970 [1st ed., 1952], p. 300.

153. *Life and Struggles of William Lovett in his Pursuit of Bread, Knowledge, and Freedom* (London, 1920 [1st ed., 1876]), I, 80.

154. Alexander Welsh, *The City of Dickens* (Oxford, 1971), p. 17.

155. Finer, p. 209. A recent editor of the report disputes Finer's claim that it

created a sensation. It was not mentioned, John Duffy points out, in such journals as the *Edinburgh Review* or *Blackwood's Magazine*, and *The Times* referred to it belatedly and belittlingly. But Duffy admits that "there can be no question that it had a major impact on leading intellectual and political circles, nor that it enjoyed a wider distribution than any preceding governmental publication . . . , that Chadwick's findings proved a real shock to the English middle and upper classes, and that they made public health a major political issue for several years." (Introduction to selections from the *Sanitary Report* in *Social Welfare in Transition: Selected English Documents, 1834–1909*, ed. Roy Lubove [Pittsburgh, 1966], pp. 8–9.) Asa Briggs also points to some curious lacunae in the discussion of the sanitary issue. The *Annual Register*, for example, ignored the debates on the Public Health Bills in 1847 and 1848, although it devoted over 250 pages to the proceedings in Parliament in 1847 and almost 200 pages in 1848. (Briggs, "Public Opinion and Public Health in the Age of Chadwick" [lecture published by the Chadwick Trust, Nov. 1946], p. 28.)

156. Royston Lambert, *Sir John Simon, 1816–1904, and English Social Administration* (London, 1963), p. 137. *The Times* was referring to Eugène Sue's *Mysteries of Paris* and William Ainsworth's *Revelations of London*. (See below, p. 437.)

157. Asa Briggs, "Cholera and Society in the Nineteenth Century," *Past and Present*, 1961, p. 84.

158. *Ibid.*, p. 85.

159. "Cholera Gossip," *Fraser's Magazine*, Dec. 1849, p. 704.

160. *Economist*, Oct. 6, 1849, p. 1103.

161. See above, p. 340.

162. Thompson, introduction to *Unknown Mayhew*, p. 45; Bradley, introduction to *Selections*, p. xxix.

163. G. R. Porter, *The Progress of the Nation, in Its Various Social and Economic Relations, from the Beginning of the Nineteenth Century to Its Present Time* (London, 1836–43), I, preface; II, 38; III, 3; *Progress of the Nation* (one-volume ed., 1851), pp. 630 ff.

164. Thomas Babington Macaulay, *Works* (London, 1875), I, 333.

165. G. Otto Trevelyan, *The Life and*

Letters of Lord Macaulay (2-vol. ed., New York, 1875), II, 207–08. On the circulation of the volumes see Richard D. Altick, *The English Common Reader: A Social History of the Mass Reading Public, 1800–1900* (Chicago, 1957), pp. 238, 296.

166. Charles Kingsley, *Yeast: A Problem* (London, 1881), p. 97. (The novel first appeared serially in *Fraser's Magazine* in the autumn of 1848 and was published in volume form in 1851.)

167. Kingsley, *Letters and Memories,* I, 240.

168. C. R. Fay, *Palace of Industry, 1851: A Study of the Great Exhibition and Its Fruits* (Cambridge, 1951), p. 96 (quoting Hardy, *The Fiddler of the Reels*).

169. *"Golden Times": Human Documents of the Victorian Age,* ed. E. Royston Pike (New York, 1972), p. 43 (extract from *The Economist,* Feb. 1, 1851).

170. Asa Briggs, "The Crystal Palace and the Men of 1851," in *Victorian People: Some Reassessments of People, Institutions, Ideas and Events, 1851–1867* (London, 1954), p. 49.

171. *London Labour,* I, 10, 59.

172. Peter Quennell, *London's Underworld.*

173. Sheppard, *London,* p. 354 (quoting Francis Wey).

174. E. P. Thompson, "Time, Work-Discipline and Industrial Capitalism," *Past and Present,* 1967; N. N. Feltes, "To Saunter, to Hurry: Dickens, Time, and Industrial Capitalism," *Victorian Studies,* 1977.

175. Peter Mathias, *The First Industrial Nation: An Economic History of Britain, 1700–1914* (London, 1969), p. 264.

176. Thomas Walter Laqueur, *Religion and Respectability: Sunday Schools and Working Class Culture, 1780–1850* (New Haven, 1976), p. 218.

177. Oscar Lewis, *The Children of Sanchez: Autobiography of a Mexican Family* (New York, 1961). See also Lewis, *La Vida: A Puerto Rican Family in the Culture of Poverty* (New York, 1966). For a critical discussion of the concept of "culture of poverty," see *The Poor: A Culture of Poverty, or a Poverty of Culture?* ed. J. Alan Winter (Grand Rapids, Mich., 1971).

CHAPTER XV

1. Thomas Carlyle, *Chartism* (1839), in *English and Other Critical Essays* (Everyman ed., London, n.d.), pp. 182–83.

2. Friedrich Engels, *The Condition of the Working Class in England,* in Marx and Engels, *Collected Works* (New York, 1975), IV, 390, 368.

3. G. R. Porter, *The Progress of the Nation, in Its Various Social and Economic Relations, from the Beginning of the Nineteenth Century to Its Present Time* (London, 1838), II, 255–56.

4. See, for example, Mary Bayly, *Ragged Homes, and How to Mend Them* (1859); John Hollingshead, *Ragged London in 1861* (1861).

5. Alexander Somerville, *The Autobiography of a Working Man,* ed. John Carswell (London, 1951 [1st ed., 1848]), pp. 17 ff.

6. Ashley (Shaftesbury, as he later was) so dominated the movement that in the 1880s the Ragged School Union was renamed the Shaftesbury Society and Ragged School Union.

7. See M. G. Jones, *The Charity School Movement: A Study of Eighteenth Century Puritanism in Action* (Cambridge, 1938).

8. Bernard Mandeville, "An Essay on Charity, and Charity Schools" (1723), in *The Fable of the Bees,* ed. Phillip Harth (London, 1970), p. 288. See above, p. 29.

9. These are the more modest estimates of Thomas Walter Laqueur, *Religion and Respectability: Sunday Schools and Working Class Culture, 1780–1850* (New Haven, 1976), p. 44. Jones has as many as 250,000 in the Sunday schools by 1787 (p. 26). On the teaching of writing in the Sunday schools, see also W. R. Ward, *Religion and Society in England, 1790–1850* (London, 1972), pp. 136 ff.

10. Jones, p. 161.

11. Laqueur, p. 188. The quotation is from E. P. Thompson, "Time, Work-Discipline, and Industrial Capitalism," *Past and Present,* 1967, p. 84.

12. Engels, *Collected Works,* IV, 410.

13. On the question of literacy, see below, pp. 413–14, 578 n. 28.

14. *Quarterly Review,* Dec. 1846,

quoted by Mayhew, *Morning Chronicle,* March 19, 1850.

15. "The Charities and Poor of London," *Quarterly Review,* Sept. 1855, p. 436.

16. J. Wesley Bready, *Lord Shaftesbury and Social and Industrial Progress* (London, 1926), p. 161.

17. *Ibid.,* p. 143.

18. *Quarterly Review,* Dec. 1846, quoted by Mayhew, *Chronicle,* Mar. 19, 1850.

19. *Speeches of the Earl of Shaftesbury, upon Subjects Having Relation Chiefly to the Claims and Interests of the Labouring Class* (London, 1868), p. 191. See also his speech in the House of Commons on June 6, 1848, *ibid.,* pp. 227 ff.

20. G. F. A. Best, *Shaftesbury* (London, 1964), p. 114; Mayhew, *London Labour,* III, 430–39.

21. Dickens parodied a ragged school in *Our Mutual Friend* and published mildly critical but basically approving articles about them in *Household Words.* See John Forster, *Life of Charles Dickens* (London, n.d.), I, 194; Philip Collins, *Dickens and Education* (London, 1964), pp. 86–93; Collins, "Dickens and Ragged Schools," *Dickensian,* 1959, pp. 94–109.

22. Ashley, *Quarterly Review,* Dec. 1846.

23. *The Pleasures of Peacock,* ed. Ben Ray Redman (New York, 1947), p. 373. (This scene was called to my attention by Patrick Brantlinger, *The Spirit of Reform: British Literature and Politics, 1832–1867* [Cambridge, Mass., 1977], pp. 21–22.) *Crotchet Castle* was published in 1831 and therefore predates the ragged schools; one of its targets was the Society for the Diffusion of Useful Knowledge, the "Steam Intellect Society," as Peacock called it. A few years later, Disraeli spoke sarcastically of "the march of intellect and the spirit of the age." (*The Letters of Runnymede* [Boston, n.d. (1st ed., 1836)], p. 109 [letter XIII].)

24. *Chronicle,* Mar. 19, 25, 1850.

25. *Ibid.,* Apr. 25, 1850.

26. *Ibid.,* Mar. 25, Apr. 25, 1850. Perhaps because these articles were so unflattering, to the ragged classes as well as the ragged schools, they were not included in *London Labour.* The only allusion to the subject was a single paragraph quoting an anonymous informant who judged them to have done more harm than good (I, 316). E. P. Thompson suggests that some of Mayhew's hostility to the ragged schools was prompted by his distaste for Evangelical reformers and his resentment at Ashley's having taken over the cause of the slop tailors. ("The Political Education of Henry Mayhew," *Victorian Studies,* 1967, p. 52.) This may well be true. But it is also true that Mayhew had always been suspicious of the presumed correlation between literacy and morality. Anne Humpherys points out that in 1842 he wrote a tract, *What to Teach and How to Teach It,* in which he exposed, as the title of the first chapter put it, "The Fallacy of the Supposed Connexion Between Reading and Writing, and Morality and Intelligence." (*Travels into the Poor Man's Country: The Work of Henry Mayhew* [Athens, Ga., 1977], p. 57.) That "fallacy" worked both ways: it implied that the illiterate were not necessarily immoral, and also that the immoral were not necessarily illiterate.

27. Donald J. Olsen, *The Growth of Victorian London* (London, 1976), pp. 17 ff. The quotation is from G. A. Sala, *Gaslight and Daylight* (1859).

28. *Nineteenth-Century Crime in England: Prevention and Punishment,* ed. J. J. Tobias (New York, 1972), p. 46.

29. Mary Carpenter, *Reformatory Schools, for the Children of the Perishing and Dangerous Classes, and for Juvenile Offenders* (London, 1968 [1st ed., 1851]), pp. 2–3. (Punctuation slightly altered, italics in original.)

30. *Ibid.,* p. 38.

31. *Ibid.,* pp. 347–48.

32. *Ibid.,* p. 73.

33. Bready, p. 133.

34. J. Estlin Carpenter, *The Life and Work of Mary Carpenter* (London, 1879), p. 125 (Carpenter to Mrs. Follen, Feb. 17, 1849). See also Jo Manton, *Mary Carpenter and the Children of the Streets* (London, 1976); Ivy Pinchbeck and Margaret Hewitt, *Children in English Society: From the Eighteenth Century to the Children Act of 1948* (London, 1973), pp. 431 ff.

35. Henry Mayhew and John Binny, *The Criminal Prisons of London and Scenes of*

Prison Life (London, 1862), p. 84. This view is in direct contrast to that of Eric H. Monkkonen, *The Dangerous Class: Crime and Poverty in Columbus, Ohio, 1860–1885* (Cambridge, Mass., 1975). Defining the "dangerous class" as "rural criminals, urban criminals, rural paupers, urban paupers, and tramps," Monkkonen maintains that it blended with the "normal population," so that the differences between the "dangerous class" and the other classes were more of degree than of kind. And since over one-quarter of the county population had no property, "distinctions between the bottom fourth of society and the paupers are hazy, to say the least" (pp. 4–5). An Englishman would have been astonished at the affluence of a county in which three-quarters of the population had some property, and still more astonished that anyone without property should have been regarded as almost indistinguishable from a pauper. Much of Monkkonen's thesis depends upon the equation of propertylessness (or poverty) with pauperism, and thus with the dangerous class. "Nineteenth century observers," he remarks, "often lumped criminals together with poor people" (p. 73). As evidence he quotes Charles Loring Brace, *The Dangerous Classes of New York* (1872), who spoke of "great masses of destitute, miserable, and criminal persons" hidden "beneath the surface of New York" who were ready for revolutionary outbreak at any moment (Brace, p. 29). But it was not "poor people" (who must have been perfectly visible on the surface) whom Brace lumped together with criminals, but the "destitute" and the "miserable."

36. Edward Lytton Bulwer, *England and the English,* ed. Standish Meacham (Chicago, 1970 [1st ed., 1833]), pp. 130–31.

37. *First Report of the Commissioners Appointed to Inquire as to the Best Means of Establishing an Efficient Constabulary Force in the Counties of England and Wales* (1839), p. 11.

38. Carpenter, *Reformatory Schools,* p. 239.

39. J. J. Tobias, *Urban Crime in Victorian England* (New York, 1972), p. 208. (This book was originally published in 1967 under the title *Crime and Industrial Society in the Nineteenth Century.*)

40. Donald Rumbelow, *I Spy Blue: The Police and Crime in the City of London from Elizabeth I to Victoria* (London, 1971), 170 (quoting *The Times,* Mar. 8, 1848).

41. W. A. Miles, *Poverty, Mendicity and Crime; or, The Facts, Examinations, etc. upon Which the [Constabulary] Report Was Founded* (London, 1839), p. 87.

42. Tobias, p. 207; Gertrude Himmelfarb, "The Haunted House of Jeremy Bentham," in *Victorian Minds* (New York, 1968), pp. 58 ff.

43. M. Heather Tomlinson, " 'Prison Palaces': A Re-appraisal of Early Victorian Prisons, 1835–77," *Bulletin of the Institute of Historical Research,* 1978, pp. 60–71.

44. Carpenter, p. 72.

45. *Constabulary Report,* p. 67.

46. G. R. Porter, *Progress of the Nation* (1851 ed.), p. 633. Modern authorities also disagree, Leon Radzinowicz maintaining that crime had increased in the first half of the century, and Tobias that it had decreased. (Tobias, p. 127; Radzinowicz, *Ideology and Crime: A Study of Crime in Its Social and Historical Context* [London, 1966], p. 60. See also David Philips, *Crime and Authority in Victorian England: The Black Country, 1835–1860* [London, 1977].)

47. Thomas Plint, *Crime in England, Its Relation, Character, and Extent, as Developed from 1801 to 1848* (New York, 1974 [1st ed., 1851]), pp. 26–27, 144, 148–49.

48. For example, Samuel Bamford, *Passages in the Life of a Radical* (London, 1844); "Autobiography of a Navvy" (1861), in *Annals of Labour: Autobiographies of British Working-Class People, 1820–1920,* ed. John Burnett (Bloomington, Ind., 1974), pp. 55 ff.; "When I Was a Child," by an old potter (on 1839–42), *ibid.,* pp. 297 ff. See also Martha Vicinus, *The Industrial Muse: A Study of Nineteenth Century British Working-Class Literature* (New York, 1974), pp. 176 ff. The evils of drink were a perennial theme of the unstamped radical papers (e.g., *Poor Man's Guardian,* Nov. 12, 1831; July 14, 1832; Apr. 5, 1834), and even more of the Chartist press, the temperance advocates being well represented in the *Northern Star* and other papers. The Select Committee on the Inquiry into Drunkenness (1834) also helped focus attention on this issue.

49. Tobias, p. 179.

50. Brian Harrison, *Drink and the Victorians: The Temperance Question in England, 1815–1872* (Pittsburgh, 1971), pp. 69–70 and *passim*.

51. Plint, pp. 153, 120, 146.

52. *Ibid.*, p. 153.

53. *Ibid.*, p. 146.

54. *Birth of the Communist Manifesto*, ed. Dirk J. Struik (New York, 1971), p. 100.

55. *The Red Republican*, Nov. 16, 1850, p. 171. This translation, by Helen Macfarlane, was reprinted in two American journals in 1871 (*The World*, Sept. 21, and *Woodhull and Claflin's Weekly*, Dec. 30), and in book form in two editions published by the anarchists, the first in New York in 1883 and the second in London in 1886. Almost all later English and American editions used the authoritative translation of 1888 by Samuel Moore (who also translated *Das Kapital*). One of the few exceptions is a translation by Eden and Cedar Paul for the edition prepared by D. Ryazanoff (New York, 1963); this translated *Lumpenproletariat* as "the slum proletariat." French editions have translated it as *le proletariat de la canaille, la canaille,* or *la voyoucratie.*

56. See above, p. 285.

57. Hegel, *Philosophy of Right*, trans. T. M. Knox (Oxford, 1942), pp. 150, 277 (paragraphs 244–45, additions 148–49).

58. Max Stirner (né Johann Caspar Schmidt), *Der Einzige und sein Eigentum* (Leipzig, 1882 [1st ed., 1844]), pp. 121, 143–44; *The Ego and His Own*, trans. S. T. Byington (London, 1912), pp. 154–55, 184. My translations generally agree with the English edition except for *Lump* and its variations, which Byington translates as "ragamuffin," "ragamuffinhood," etc. Since these terms have a juvenile connotation, I prefer "ragged," which is the more literal translation and conforms to English usage at the time. Although Stirner has recently been the subject of two English studies, neither has commented on his use of *Lump* nor on its relation to Marx's *Lumpenproletariat*. See John Carroll, *Break-out from the Crystal Palace: The Anarcho-psychological Critique: Stirner, Nietzsche, Dostoyevsky* (London, 1974); R. W. K. Paterson, *The Nihilistic Egoist: Max Stirner* (London, 1971). For a more adequate

discussion of this subject, see Hans G. Helms, *Die Ideologie der anonymen Gesellschaft: Max Stirners "Einziger" und der Fortschritt des demokratischen Selbstbewusstseins vom Vormärz bis zur Bundesrepublik* (Cologne, 1966).

59. Paterson, p. 81.

60. The expression "primitive rebels" is E. J. Hobsbawm's, although he does not relate it to Stirner and some of his subjects do not fit the Stirner model. (*Primitive Rebels: Studies in Archaic Forms of Social Movement in the 19th and 20th Centuries* [Manchester, 1959].)

61. *German Ideology,* in Marx and Engels, *Collected Works,* V, 201–02, 338.

62. *Ibid.*, p. 226 n.

63. The only biography of Weitling in English, by Carl Wittke, *The Utopian Communist: A Biography of Wilhelm Weitling, Nineteenth-Century Reformer* (Baton Rouge, 1950), makes no mention of the "thieving proletariat" or other apocalyptic aspects of Weitling's thought. In his pioneering study of the Young Hegelians, Sidney Hook mentions him only once in passing, and the index identifies him as "Weitling, social reformer." (*From Hegel to Marx* [Ann Arbor, 1966 (1st ed., 1950)], p. 335.) David McLellan, in the foreword to the translation of Weitling's *The Poor Sinner's Gospel* (trans. Dinah Livingstone, London, 1969), emphasizes his "New Christianity" doctrine. Among those who do refer to his more violent ideas are James Joll, *The Anarchists* (New York, 1966), p. 56, and Richard N. Hunt, *The Political Ideas of Marx and Engels* (Pittsburgh, 1974), I, 153–54. The biography by Waltraud Seidel-Hoppner, written from a decidedly Marxist point of view (it chastises Weitling for being "petty bourgeois"), does discuss his idea of the lumpenproletariat and the role he assigned them in the revolution (*Wilhelm Weitling: Der erste deutsche Theoretiker und Agitator des Kommunismus* [Berlin, 1961].)

64. Wilhelm Weitling, *Garantien der Harmonie und Freiheit*, ed. Franz Mehring (Berlin, 1908), p. 235.

65. Marx and Engels, *Collected Works,* III, 401–03, 413 (*New Moral World,* Nov. 18, 1843; Jan. 20, 1844).

66. It is ironic that Bakunin's translation of the *Manifesto* into Russian in 1869 (a

translation published in Switzerland) should have been a turning point in the history of that document, for that translation inspired a spate of other translations and editions in the following years.

67. Marx, *The Revolutions of 1848*, ed. David Fernbach (New York, 1974), pp. 176, 180–81 (*Neue Rheinische Zeitung*, Nov. 7, 12, 1848).

68. *The Class Struggles in France*, in *Collected Works*, X, 62.

69. *The Peasant War in Germany* (1870), in Marx, *Selected Works*, ed. V. Adoratsky (New York, 1939), II, 539.

70. Marx and Engels, *Collected Works*, VI, 246–47 (*Deutsche-Brüsseler Zeitung*, Sept. 12, 1847). See also above, p. 280.

71. Stirner, *Ego and His Own*, p. 160.

72. Hannah Arendt, *The Human Condition* (Chicago, 1958), pp. 79 ff. (See above, p. 197.)

73. Radzinowicz, pp. 39–42.

74. Quoted by Louis Chevalier, *Laboring Classes and Dangerous Classes in Paris During the First Half of the Nineteenth Century*, trans. Frank Jellinek (New York, 1973 [1st ed., 1958]), p. 144. These are accurate translations from the French, *pauvres* consistently translated as "poor," *paupérisme* as "pauperism," *les misérables* as "the destitute." (*Classes laborieuses et classes dangereuses à Paris pendant la première moitié du XIXe siècle* [Paris, 1958], pp. 159, 162–63.)

75. Chevalier, *Laboring Classes*, pp. 141–42.

76. *Ibid.*, pp. 364–65.

77. *The Earlier Letters of John Stuart Mill, 1812–1848*, ed. Francis E. Mineka, *Collected Works* (Toronto, 1963), XIII, 736 (Mill to Sue, May[?] 1848).

78. Marx, *Economic and Philosophic Manuscripts of 1844* (London, 1958), pp. 34–35; *Collected Works*, III, 194–96 (*Vorwärts*, Aug. 7–10, 1834); *ibid.*, pp. 415–16 (*New Moral World*, Feb. 3, 1844); *Holy Family, ibid.*, IV, 19 ff.

79. Chevalier, p. 134.

80. *Ibid.*, pp. 2, 27. Chevalier's book has been criticized as disorganized and repetitive, impressionistic and statistically weak. And some of its theses have been disputed— the "uprootedness" thesis, for example, which holds that crimes and riots were largely the work of immigrants to the city uprooted from their traditional occupations and milieus. (For a summary of this controversy, see George Rudé, *Debate on Europe, 1815–1850* [New York, 1972], pp. 81–87.) The charge that he was overly impressionistic, relying upon literary rather than statistical evidence, overlooks the fact that part of his argument concerns the opinions contemporaries had about the social reality, opinions which are not quantifiable.

81. *Ibid.*, p. 364.

82. William L. Langer, *Political and Social Upheaval, 1832–1852* (New York, 1969), p. 337.

83. T. A. Critchley, *The Conquest of Violence: Order and Liberty in Britain* (New York, 1970), pp. 1–2. (See pp. 256, 558 n. 5.)

84. E. P. Thompson, *The Making of the English Working Class* (New York, 1964), p. 814.

85. Mayhew, *London Labour*, I, 20–22; II, 5.

86. Plint, p. 146.

87. Walter Bagehot, *Works*, ed. Mrs. Russell Barrington (London, 1915), X, 394.

88. See, for example, Laqueur, *Religion and Respectability*; Peter Bailey, " 'Will the Real Bill Banks Please Stand Up?' Towards a Role Analysis of Mid-Victorian Working-Class Respectability," *Journal of Social History*, 1979; Trygve R. Tholfsen, *Working Class Radicalism in Mid-Victorian England* (New York, 1977); Iorwerth Prothero, *Artisans and Politics in Early Nineteenth Century London: John Gast and His Times* (London, 1979); Harrison, *Drink and the Victorians*, pp. 367 ff. The older view of respectability as a purely middle class phenomenon is expressed by Walter E. Houghton, *The Victorian Frame of Mind, 1830–1870* (New Haven, 1957), pp. 184 ff., where "respectability" is subsumed under "the commercial spirit" and equated with wealth, the implication being that only the rich were truly respectable.

CHAPTER XVI

1. Lionel Trilling, "Manners, Morals, and the Novel" (1947), in *The Liberal Imagination: Essays on Literature and Society* (New

York, 1950), p. 206. The most fashionable schools of literary criticism today, including structuralism and deconstructionism, eschew any reference to a historical reality; to them this enterprise must appear naïve and old-fashioned. (See below, p. 454.)

2. William O. Aydelotte, "The England of Marx and Mill as Reflected in Fiction," *Journal of Economic History*, 1948 (supplement), p. 43.

3. J. Michael Jefferson, "Industrialisation and Poverty: In Fact and Fiction," in *The Long Debate on Poverty: Eight Essays on Industrialisation and 'The Condition of England'*, ed. Arthur Seldon (London, 1972), pp. 189–238. See also Humphry House, *The Dickens World* (Oxford, 1941), pp. 18 ff; W. H. Chaloner, "Mrs. Trollope and the Early Factory System," *Victorian Studies*, 1960.

4. This assumption is so prevalent it is almost invidious to single out any examples. If it seems especially intrusive in Sheila M. Smith, *The Other Nation: The Poor in English Novels of the 1840s and 1850s* (Oxford, 1980, e.g., pp. 167, 258), it is because the book is otherwise so full of valuable material. (See also below, p. 410.)

5. See above, pp. 350 ff. See also reviews quoted by Louis James, *Fiction for the Working Man, 1830–1850: A Study of the Literature Produced for the Working Classes in Early Victorian Urban England* (London, 1963), p. 1; Keith Hollingsworth, *The Newgate Novel, 1830–1847: Butler, Ainsworth, Dickens, and Thackeray* (Detroit, 1963), p. 127; P. J. Keating, *The Working Classes in Victorian Fiction* (London, 1971), p. 37; Kathleen Tillotson, *Novels of the Eighteen-Forties* (Oxford, 1965 [1st ed., 1954]), p. 79. The novelists themselves frequently made use of these metaphors: e.g., G. W. M. Reynolds, *The Mysteries of London* (London, 1845), I, 75.

6. Raymond Williams, *Culture and Society, 1780–1950* (New York, 1966 [1st ed., 1958]), pp. 87 ff; Arnold Kettle, "The Early Victorian Social-Problem Novel," in *From Dickens to Hardy* (vol. VI of *Pelican Guide to English Literature*, London, 1958), pp. 169 ff. The pioneer study of the "social novel" is Louis Cazamian, *The Social Novel in England, 1830–1850: Dickens, Disraeli, Mrs. Gaskell, Kingsley*, trans. Martin Fido (London, 1973 [1st French ed., 1903]). In addition to works cited in notes 4 and 5, see Margaret Dalziel, *Popular Fiction One Hundred Years Ago: An Unexplored Tract of Literary History* (London, 1957); Ivanka Kovacevic, *Fact into Fiction: English Literature and the Industrial Scene, 1750–1850* (Leicester, 1975); Igor Webb, *From Custom to Capital: The English Novel and the Industrial Revolution* (Ithaca, 1981).

7. Less well known, even in their day, were such novels as Charlotte Elizabeth Tonna's *Helen Fleetwood* (1839–40), or Richard Henry Horne's *The Dreamer and the Worker* (1851). Other, better known works, such as George Eliot's *Felix Holt* (1866), do not fall into this period.

8. Igor Webb, p. 9.

9. Tillotson, p. 235, quoting W. C. Roscoe, in *National Review*, Jan. 1856.

10. *The Letters and Private Papers of William Makepeace Thackeray*, ed. Gordon N. Ray (Cambridge, Mass., 1945), II, 772 (quoting David Masson, (*North British Review*, May 1847).

11. F. R. Leavis, *The Great Tradition* (London, 1948). Raymond Williams uses the term "selective tradition" to describe that small part of literature which enters the canon, in distinction to the bulk of the "recorded culture" of any period and the still larger body of the "lived culture." (*The Long Revolution* [New York, 1961], pp. 49 ff.) It is interesting that Williams himself, in his earlier, more influential book, *Culture and Society*, confined his study of the "industrial novel" entirely to the familiar social novels admitted to the "selective tradition." Even in *The Long Revolution*, where he mentions some of the more popular novels, he does not discuss them at any length.

12. Martha Vicinus, *The Industrial Muse: A Study of Nineteenth Century British Working-Class Literature* (New York, 1974), p. 1.

13. See M. W. Rose, *The Silver-Fork School* (London, 1936).

14. James, p. 103 (quoting Mrs. Kentish, *The Maid of the Village; or, the Farmer's Daughter* [1847]).

15. Charles Knight, *Popular History of England* (London, 1852–62), VIII, 478.

16. Richard D. Altick, *The English Common Reader: A Social History of the Mass*

Reading Public 1800–1900 (Chicago, 1957), p. 346.

17. John Forster, *The Life of Charles Dickens* (3-vol. ed., London, 1872–74), I, vi.

18. *Charles Kingsley: His Letters and Memories of His Life,* ed. Mrs. Kingsley (1-vol. ed., London, 1888), pp. 65–66.

19. Henry Mayhew, *London Labour and the London Poor* (New York, 1968 [1st ed., 1861–62]), I, 26. This was probably a reference to Reynolds's *Mysteries of the Court of London.* (See below, p. 435.)

20. Ernest Jones, *Notes to the People* (New York, 1968 [1st ed., 1852]), p. 515.

21. Vicinus, p. 124.

22. Jones, p. 514. Another novel, *The Secret,* by the Chartist Thomas Frost has the familiar changeling and seduction themes, the only twist being the marriage of the upper class girl (who has been brought up as a working class girl) to a Chartist, and the marriage of the working class girl (brought up as an aristocrat) to a duke.

23. Friedrich Engels, *The Condition of the Working Class in England,* in Marx and Engels, *Collected Works* (New York, 1975), IV, 528.

24. Amy Cruse, *The Victorians and Their Reading* (Boston, 1935), p. 127. (This was published in England as *The Victorians and Their Books.*)

25. Altick, pp. 252–53.

26. Mayhew, I, 26.

27. James, p. 46.

28. This was the estimate of R. K. Webb in his seminal essay, "The Victorian Reading Public," in *From Dickens to Hardy,* pp. 213–14. After much research on his part and others, it remains the consensus of most historians today. On the variety of schools available to the poor, see above pp. 372 ff. On the subject of literacy, see Webb, "Working Class Readers in Victorian England," *English Historical Review,* 1950; Webb, *The British Working Class Reader, 1790–1848: Literacy and Social Tension* (London, 1955); Lawrence Stone, "Literacy and Education in England, 1640–1900," *Past and Present,* 1969; Michael Sanderson, "Literacy and Social Mobility in the Industrial Revolution in England," *ibid.,* 1972; Thomas Laqueur, "Literacy and Social Mobility in the Industrial Revolution in England," *ibid.,* 1974; Sanderson, "Literacy and

Social Mobility in the Industrial Revolution in England: A Rejoinder," *ibid.,* 1974; E. G. West, *Education and the State* (London, 1965); West, *Education and the Industrial Revolution* (London, 1975); West, "Literacy and the Industrial Revolution," *Economic History Review,* 1978; Carlo M. Cipolla, *Literacy and Development in the West* (London, 1969); David Levine, "Illiteracy and Family Life during the First Industrial Revolution," *Journal of Social History,* 1980; Harvey J. Graff, *The Literacy Myth: Literacy and Social Structure in the Nineteenth-Century City* (New York, 1979).

29. John W. Dodds, *The Age of Paradox: A Biography of England 1841–1851* (London, 1953), p. 130; George H. Ford, *Dickens and his Readers: Aspects of Novel-Criticism since 1836* (Princeton, 1955), p. 78.

30. Q. D. Leavis, p. 310, n. 94 (quoting *Reynolds' Miscellany,* 1846).

31. For sales figures, see James, pp. 40 ff.; Cruse, p. 124; Altick, p. 382; Walter C. Phillips, *Dickens, Reade, and Collins: Sensation Novelists: A Study in the Condition and Theories of Novel Writing in Victorian England* (New York, 1962 [1st ed., 1919]), p. 3.

32. Williams, *Long Revolution,* p. 55.

33. Michael Sadleir, *Collecting "Yellow-backs" (Victorian Railway Fiction)* (London, 1938).

34. Mayhew, I, 25.

35. See also Celina Fox, "The Development of Social Reportage in English Periodical Illustration During the 1840s and Early 1850s," *Past and Present,* 1977.

36. Frederic Harrison, *The Creed of a Layman* (New York, 1907), pp. 6–7.

37. Thackeray, "George Cruikshank" (1840), *The Works of William Makepeace Thackeray,* ed. Lady Ritchie (New York, 1968 [1st ed., 1910–11]), XXIII, 447.

38. J. Hillis Miller, "The Fiction of Realism: *Sketches by Boz, Oliver Twist,* and Cruikshank's Illustrations," in *Charles Dickens and George Cruikshank* (Los Angeles, 1971), p. 44.

39. On the dispute generated by these claims, see John Forster, *The Life of Charles Dickens* (2-vol. ed., London, n.d. [1st ed., 1872–74]), I, 63n., II, 19 ff.; Blanchard Jerrold, *The Life of George Cruikshank: In Two Epochs* (London, 1883), pp. 139 ff.

40. Dickens, *The Posthumous Papers of the Pickwick Club edited by Boz* (Oxford ed., London, n.d.), pp. 7 ff.; Forster, I, 40 ff. There is a vast literature on Dickens and his illustrators: e.g., F. G. Kitton, *Dickens and His Illustrators* (London, 1899); John Harvey, *Victorian Novelists and Their Illustrators* (New York, 1970); F. R. and Q. D. Leavis, *Dickens the Novelist* (New Brunswick, 1979 [1st ed., 1970]), pp. 332 ff.; Jane R. Cohen, " 'All-of-a-Twist': The Relationship of George Cruikshank and Charles Dickens," *Harvard Library Bulletin*, 1969; *Graphic Works of George Cruikshank*, ed. Richard A. Vogler (New York, 1979); David Borowitz, "George Cruikshank: Mirror of an Age," in *Charles Dickens and George Cruikshank* (Los Angeles, 1971); Jonathan E. Hill, "Cruikshank, Ainsworth, and Tableau Illustration," *Victorian Studies*, 1980.

41. Miller, p. 50.

42. Israel Solomons, "Satirical and Political Prints on the Jews' Naturalisation Bill, 1753," *Transactions of the Jewish Historical Society of England*, 1908–10; Thomas Whipple Perry, *Public Opinion, Propaganda, and Politics in Eighteenth-Century England: A Study of the Jew Bill of 1753* (Cambridge, Mass., 1962).

43. R. J. Cruikshank, *Roaring Century, 1846–1946* (London, 1946), p. 201.

CHAPTER XVII

1. S. M. Ellis, *William Harrison Ainsworth and his Friends* (London, 1911), I, 73. On Ainsworth, see also the privately printed memoir by W. E. A. Axon, *William Harrison Ainsworth* (London, 1902); Richard Maxwell, "City Life and the Novel: Hugo, Ainsworth, Dickens," *Comparative Literature*, 1978.

2. Edgar Johnson, *Charles Dickens: His Tragedy and Triumph* (Boston, 1952), I, 158.

3. Ellis, I, 254. Several "flash" dictionaries appeared in the first half of the century, some of them appended to perfectly respectable books. *Poverty, Mendicity, and Crime*, by W. A. Miles (London, 1839), a commentary on the Report on the Constabulary, included a "Dictionary of the Flash or Cant Language, Known to Every

Thief and Beggar," compiled by H. Brandon.

4. Ainsworth, *Jack Sheppard* (London, n.d.), pp. 302–03.

5. *Ibid.*, p. 75.

6. *Ibid.*, pp. 102–03.

7. *Ibid.*, p. 166.

8. *Ibid.*, pp. 246, 13.

9. *Ibid.*, p. 176.

10. *Ibid.*, p. 388.

11. Ellis, I, 374–75.

12. *Ibid.*, p. 328 (Ainsworth to James Crossley, May 29, 1837).

13. Henry Mayhew, *London Labour and the London Poor* (New York, 1968), IV, 301. (This section was written by John Binny.)

14. *The Letters and Private Papers of William Makepeace Thackeray*, ed. Gordon N. Ray (Cambridge, Mass., 1945), I, 395 (Dec. 1–2, 1839).

15. Keith Hollingsworth, *The Newgate Novel, 1830–1847: Butler, Ainsworth, Dickens, and Thackeray* (Detroit, 1963), pp. 145–47.

16. *Athenaeum*, Oct. 26, 1839, pp. 803–05.

17. *Examiner*, Nov. 3, 1839, pp. 691–93.

18. *Ibid.*, June 28, 1840.

19. Thackeray, *Letters*, I, 198 (May 6, 1832).

20. *Ibid.*, p. 432 (March 1840).

21. Hollingsworth, pp. 158–59. The same charges were made in an article attributed (at least in part) to Thackeray which appeared in the same issue of *Fraser's*, and in a review in *The Times* the following year of a new edition of Fielding, which gave Thackeray the opportunity to explain why *Jack Sheppard* was "infinitely more immoral" than anything Fielding ever wrote.

22. Ellis, I, 376.

23. *Ibid.*, pp. 375–79; Hollingsworth, pp. 144–45. The favorable notices cited in these books appeared over the course of years and did not have the impact of the more hostile reviews at the time of publication.

24. *Athenaeum*, Oct. 26, 1839, p. 803.

25. *Jack Sheppard*, p. 166.

26. *Ibid.*, p. 281.

27. *Ibid.*, p. 277.

28. Hollingsworth, p. 69.

29. *Ibid.*, p. 66.

30. *Fraser's Magazine,* Feb. 1840, pp. 228, 243.

31. On Mayhew's "Ikey Solomons," see above, p. 344, on Thackeray's, p. 429, and on Dickens's Fagin, below, p. 459. The Fagin type, so pervasive in the fiction and nonfiction of the time, has been the subject of much historical inquiry and speculation: e.g., Lauriant Lane, "Dickens's Archetypal Jew," *Proceedings of the Modern Language Association,* 1958; J. J. Tobias, *Prince of Fences: The Life and Crimes of Ikey Solomons* (London, 1975).

CHAPTER XVIII

1. Keith Hollingsworth, *The Newgate Novel, 1830–1847: Butler, Ainsworth, Dickens, and Thackeray* (Detroit, 1963), p. 161 (quoting Thackeray's review of Fielding, 1840).

2. It is as a Chartist rather than a writer that Reynolds is largely remembered in the *Dictionary of National Biography.* Some reference works do not mention him at all, e.g., the *Columbia Encyclopedia* and the bibliography, *The Victorians and After, 1830–1914,* ed. Edith Batho and Bonamy Dobrée (New York, 1938). There is no full-scale biography or study but there are valuable discussions and information in Montague Summers, *A Gothic Bibliography* (New York, 1964); Louis James, *Fiction for the Working Man, 1830–1850: A Study of the Literature Produced for the Working Classes in Early Victorian Urban England* (London, 1963); Margaret Dalziel, *Popular Fiction One Hundred Years Ago: An Unexplored Tract of Literary History* (London, 1957); and Hollingsworth. Neither Raymond Williams, *Culture and Society, 1780–1950* (New York, 1958), nor Amy Cruse, *The Victorians and Their Reading* (Boston, 1935), mentions him at all.

3. Richard D. Altick, *The English Common Reader: A Social History of the Mass Reading Public, 1800–1900* (Chicago, 1957), p. 394. The complete title of the *Miscellany—Reynolds's Miscellany of Romance, General Interest, Science and Art*—suggests its scope, in contrast to *Reynolds's Weekly Newspaper,* subtitled, "Journal of Democratic Progress and General Intelligence."

4. S. M. Ellis, *William Harrison Ains-worth and His Friends* (London, 1911), I, 360. On Reynolds and Dickens, see below, p. 457.

5. James, p. 41. The bound volumes of *The Mysteries of London* comprise 4 series in 8 large, double-column volumes. The first four volumes, appearing from 1845 to 1848, were written by Reynolds and the rest by other writers. The sequel, *The Mysteries of the Court of London,* was even more popular and ran even longer (to 1856). In its entirety the work was estimated as the equivalent of 48 average novels. The books were frequently reissued, a uniform (but not complete) edition in 42 volumes appearing in 1884–85 and a 6-volume "deluxe" American edition in 1900.

6. Henry Mayhew, *London Labour and the London Poor* (New York, 1968), I, 25.

7. Altick, p. 352, n. 6.

8. See above, p. 421. Only several parts of the *Revelations of London* appeared in 1846. Almost twenty years later, Ainsworth hastily completed it and published it under the title *Auriol, or the Elixir of Life.* (See Richard Maxwell, "City Life and the Novel: Hugo, Ainsworth, Dickens," *Comparative Literature,* 1978.)

9. Eugène Sue, *The Mysteries of Paris* (London, 1845), I, 1.

10. Reynolds, *The Mysteries of London* (London, 1845–48), I, 2–3.

11. *Ibid.,* pp. 1–2.

12. *Ibid.,* p. 43.

13. *Ibid.,* p. 44.

14. *Ibid.,* p. 45.

15. *Ibid.,* p. 51.

16. *Ibid.,* p. 55.

17. *Ibid.,* p. 54.

18. *Ibid.,* pp. 415–16.

19. *Ibid.,* pp. 179–80.

20. *Ibid.,* p. 151.

21. *Ibid.,* p. 324.

22. *Ibid.,* p. 61.

23. *Ibid.,* p. 114. (Italics in original.)

24. *Ibid.,* p. 203.

25. *Ibid.,* p. 101.

26. *Ibid.,* pp. 99–100.

27. *Ibid.,* pp. 303, 310.

28. *Ibid.,* p. 301.

29. *Ibid.,* p. 202.

30. *Ibid.,* p. 203.

31. *Ibid.,* pp. 204–05.

32. See above, p. 337.

33. *Mysteries of London*, I, 353–56.

34. *Ibid.*, p. 167.

35. *Ibid.*

36. *Ibid.*, p. 371.

37. *Ibid.*, p. 179.

38. *Ibid.*, p. 70.

39. *Ibid.*, IV, 416.

40. *Ibid.* There was a real Prince of Castelcicala (1763–1832), a Neapolitan diplomat who distinguished himself by refusing to represent his court in Paris during the French Revolution, and later by refusing to accept the constitution of Naples. He lived in London for many years, sometimes as ambassador, sometimes in exile.

41. *Ibid.*, I, 70.

42. Dalziel, p. 141.

43. James, pp. 166–67.

44. Dalziel, p. 142; James, p. 166.

45. Q. D. Leavis, *Fiction and the Reading Public* (London, 1932), pp. 175–77.

46. John Stuart Mill, *On Liberty* (Everyman ed., London, 1940), pp. 68, 119–20. See Gertrude Himmelfarb, *On Liberty and Liberalism: The Case of John Stuart Mill* (New York, 1974).

CHAPTER XIX

1. *Dickens: The Critical Heritage*, ed. Philip Collins (New York, 1971), p. 476.

2. Philip Collins, "The Significance of Dickens's Periodicals," *Review of English Literature*, 1961, pp. 62–63. Collins is the author of several books and innumerable articles which are models of historical scholarship, e.g., *Dickens and Crime* (London, 1962) and *Dickens and Education* (London, 1964). Other historians and critics have focused on other social issues, e.g., Norris Pope, *Dickens and Charity* (London, 1978). See also Collins, "A Dickens Bibliography," in *The New Cambridge Bibliography of English Literature*, ed. George Watson (Cambridge, 1969).

3. An early, moderate example of this mode of criticism is J. Hillis Miller, *Charles Dickens: The World of His Novels* (Cambridge, Mass., 1958).

4. Lionel Trilling, "Little Dorrit," in *The Opposing Self: Nine Essays in Criticism* (London, 1955), p. 52. On symbol-hunting

in *Our Mutual Friend* and *The Waste Land,* see Trilling, "The Dickens of Our Day," in *A Gathering of Fugitives* (Boston, 1956), pp. 42–43. Philip Collins traces the emergence in literary criticism of the symbol of the prison in "Little Dorrit: The Prison and the Critics," *Times Literary Supplement,* Apr. 18, 1980.

5. Robert L. Patten, "The Sale of Dickens's Work," in *Dickens: The Critical Heritage,* pp. 617–20. See also Patten, *Dickens and His Publishers* (New York, 1978); Richard D. Altick, *The English Common Reader: A Social History of the Mass Reading Public 1800–1900* (Chicago, 1957); Edgar Johnson, *Charles Dickens: His Tragedy and Triumph* (Boston, 1952); George H. Ford, *Dickens and His Readers: Aspects of Novel-Criticism Since 1836* (Princeton, 1955).

6. *Dickens: The Critical Heritage,* p. 324; Collins, *Dickens and Education,* p. 221.

7. *Dickens: The Critical Heritage,* p. 64.

8. Henry Mayhew, *London Labour and the London Poor* (New York, 1968), I, 250.

9. Ford, p. 79.

10. Walter Bagehot, "Charles Dickens" (1858), in *Literary Studies* (London, 1898), II, 128.

11. *Dickens: The Critical Heritage,* pp. 502, 93.

12. *Dictionary of National Biography* (London, 1888), V, 935.

13. Montague Summers, *A Gothic Bibliography* (New York, 1964), pp. 14–15; Louis James, *Fiction for the Working Man, 1830–1850: A Study of the Literature Produced for the Working Classes in Early Victorian Urban England* (London, 1963), pp. 46, 62.

14. James, p. 60.

15. R. H. Horne defended Dickens against this criticism in *A New Spirit of the Age* (New York, 1844), p. 18.

16. Q. D. Leavis, *Fiction and the Reading Public* (New York, 1965 [1st ed., 1932]), pp. 153, 157–58; F. R. Leavis and Q. D. Leavis, *Dickens the Novelist* (New Brunswick, 1979 [1st ed., 1970]), pp. 111 ff.

17. *Dickens: The Critical Heritage,* p. 284. See also Richard C. Maxwell, Jr., "G. W. M. Reynolds, Dickens, and the Mysteries of London," *Nineteenth-Century Fiction,* 1977.

18. John Ruskin, "Fiction, Fair and

Foul" (1880), *Works,* ed. E. T. Cook and Alexander Wedderburn (London, 1908), XXXIV, 276–77.

19. *Uncollected Writings from Household Words, 1850–59,* ed. Harry Stone (Bloomington, Ind., 1968), I, 13 (March 30, 1850).

20. *The Girlhood of Queen Victoria: A Selection from Her Diaries, 1832–40,* ed. Viscount Esher (London, 1912), II, 86 (Dec. 30, 1838).

21. *Ibid.*

22. Keith Hollingsworth, *The Newgate Novel, 1830–1847: Butler, Ainsworth, Dickens, and Thackeray* (Detroit, 1963), p. 159 (quoting the original edition of *Catherine*).

23. Quoted by Sheila M. Smith, *The Other Nation: The Poor in English Novels of the 1840s and 1850s* (Oxford, 1980), p. 59.

24. Horne, p. 18.

25. Steven Marcus, *Dickens: From Pickwick to Dombey* (New York, 1965), p. 359. John Bayley also associates Oliver and Fagin: "That the two worlds are one in the mind appears even in Cruikshank's drawings, where Oliver often has a distinct look of Fagin." (*Dickens and the Twentieth Century,* ed. John Gross and Gabriel Pearson [Toronto, 1962], p. 52.)

26. *David Copperfield* (Modern Library ed., New York, n.d. [1st ed., 1849–50]), p. 172.

27. *Oliver Twist* (Oxford ed., London, n.d. [1st ed., 1837–38]), p. 81.

28. *Ibid.,* pp. 179, 182.

29. Marcus, p. 67. This part of Marcus's analysis is at variance with his equation of Oliver and Fagin, the pauper and the criminal. Refuting Thackeray's charge that Dickens tended to confuse virtue and vice, Marcus insists that, on the contrary, he kept them so sharply demarcated that "goodness and wickedness seem to live in quite separate regions where commerce with each other is at best minimal."

30. *Oliver Twist,* p. 29.

31. George Orwell, "Charles Dickens" (1940), in *The Collected Essays, Journalism and Letters of George Orwell,* ed. Sonia Orwell and Ian Argus (New York, 1968), I, 429–41.

32. *The Posthumous Papers of the Pick-*

wick Club (Oxford ed., London, n.d. [1st ed., 1836–37]), p. 208.

33. *Ibid.,* p. 267.

34. Orwell, p. 440.

35. *Ibid.,* p. 415.

36. George Gissing, *Charles Dickens, A Critical Study* (New York, 1966 [1st ed., 1898]), p. 243.

37. Louis Cazamian, *The Social Novel in England, 1830–1850: Dickens, Disraeli, Mrs. Gaskell, Kingsley,* trans. Martin Fido (London, 1973 [1st Fr. ed., 1903]), pp. 155–57. Other critics have made the same point, Richard Aldington, for example, claiming that Dickens's "really sympathetic characters all come from the middle and lower middle classes." (*Four English Portraits* [London, 1948], p. 150.)

38. Peter Mathias, *The First Industrial Nation: An Economic History of Britain, 1700–1914* (London, 1969), p. 219.

39. *The Old Curiosity Shop* (Oxford ed., London, n.d. [1st ed., 1840–41]), p. 371.

40. *David Copperfield,* p. 13.

41. *Ibid.,* p. 147.

42. *Ibid.,* p. 36.

43. Orwell, p. 415.

44. *David Copperfield,* p. 37.

45. Cazamian, p. 155.

46. *Dickens: The Critical Heritage,* p. 153. See also below, p. 472.

47. *A Christmas Carol* (New York, 1939 [1st ed., 1843]), pp. 121, 129.

48. *David Copperfield,* p. 31.

49. *Dombey and Son* (Oxford ed., London, n.d. [1st ed., 1846–48]), p. 268.

50. *Bleak House* (Oxford ed., London, n.d. [1st ed., 1852–53]), pp. 390, 560.

51. *Old Curiosity Shop,* p. 111.

52. *Bleak House,* pp. 54, 58.

53. *Dickens: The Critical Heritage,* p. 444. For a more favorable estimate by Ruskin, see "Fiction, Fair and Foul," *Works,* XXXIV, 277.

54. Francis Sheppard, *London 1808–1870: The Infernal Wen* (Berkeley, 1971), p. 282.

55. *Our Mutual Friend* (Modern Library ed., New York, 1960 [1st ed., 1864–65]), p. 6.

56. Harland S. Nelson, "Dickens's *Our Mutual Friend* and Henry Mayhew's *London Labour and the London Poor,*" *Nineteenth-*

Century Fiction, 1965; Harvey Peter Sucksmith, "Dickens and Mayhew: A Further
Note," ibid., 1969; Richard J. Dunn, "Dickens and Mayhew Once More," ibid., 1970;
Q. D. Leavis, Dickens the Novelist, pp. 184–
86; Anne Humpherys, Travels into the Poor
Man's Country: The Work of Henry Mayhew
(Athens, Ga., 1977), pp. 178 ff. Humpherys
finds no evidence of "direct influence," but
claims that "internal evidence does suggest
that Dickens might have drawn on Mayhew's work for his own." She also points out
that Dickens might have had good reason to
conceal any indebtedness to Mayhew. His
Household Words was a rival to the Morning
Chronicle, and his differences with Douglas
Jerrold, Mayhew's father-in-law, on the
issue of capital punishment might have led to
a coolness toward Mayhew. (See above, p.
355.)

57. Oliver Twist, p. 460.
58. The Dickens Critics, ed. George H.
Ford and Lauriat Lane, Jr. (Ithaca, N.Y.,
1966 [1st ed., 1961]), p. 50.
59. Nelson, pp. 215 ff.
60. Dunn, pp. 348, 352.
61. London Labour, II, 24–25; Sketches
by Boz (Oxford ed., London, n.d. [1st ed.,
1836]), pp. 220–23 (scene 21).
62. Sucksmith, pp. 345, 349.
63. "The Prisoner's Van" (not reprinted in Sketches by Boz), quoted by J.
Hillis Miller, "The Fiction of Realism:
Sketches by Boz, Oliver Twist, and Cruikshank's Illustrations," in Charles Dickens and
George Cruikshank (Los Angeles, 1971), p. 3.
64. Dombey and Son, pp. 43–44.
65. Ibid., pp. 98 ff.
66. London Labour, IV, 281–82.
67. Oliver Twist, preface, p. 8; David
Copperfield, p. 179. On Dickens and London,
see F. S. Schwarzbach, Dickens and the City
(London, 1979); Alexander Welsh, The City
of Dickens (Oxford, 1971); Christopher Hibbert, "Dickens's London," in Charles Dickens
1812–1870: A Centennial Volume, ed. E. W. F.
Tomlin (New York, 1969), pp. 73–99;
Philip Collins, "Dickens and London," in
The Victorian City: Images and Realities, ed.
H. J. Dyos and Michael Wolff (London,
1973), II, 537–57; Raymond Williams, The
Country and the City (New York, 1973), pp.
153–64.

68. Dickens: The Critical Heritage, p.
81.
69. Pickwick Papers, p. 576.
70. Dickens: The Critical Heritage, pp.
60, 52–53.
71. Ibid., p. 36.
72. Pickwick Papers, pp. 675–76.
73. Marcus, p. 17.
74. Dickens: The Critical Heritage, p.
37.
75. Ibid., p. 38.
76. See above, p. 455.
77. Dickens: The Critical Heritage, p.
34.
78. For example, Blackwood's Magazine, Apr. 1855; Westminster Review, Oct.
1854, quoted by Joseph Butwin, "Hard
Times: The News and the Novel," Nineteenth-Century Fiction, 1977, p. 186.
79. John Forster, The Life of Charles
Dickens (2-vol. ed., London, n.d. [1st ed.,
1872–74]), II, 85 (Jan. 20, 1854).
80. Hard Times, ed. George Ford and
Sylvere Monod (New York, 1966 [1st ed.,
1854]), p. 227 (July 13, 1854). This edition has
notes and appendices relating to the novel.
81. See Sheila Smith, p. 78; Bernard
Semmel, Jamaican Blood and Victorian Conscience (Boston, 1963), pp. 114 ff.; Michael
Goldberg, "From Bentham to Carlyle:
Dickens' Political Development," Journal of
the History of Ideas, 1972.
82. Hard Times, p. 1.
83. Ibid., p. 11.
84. Ibid., p. 17.
85. Ibid.
86. Ibid., pp. 9, 15, 26–27, 179, 275.
87. Ibid., p. 23.
88. Ibid., p. 27.
89. James Anthony Froude, Thomas
Carlyle: A History of His Life in London,
1834–1881 (London, 1884), II, 420 (Nov. 5,
1873).
90. To some historians, the circus
would represent yet another form of "social
control"—the "bread and circus" phenomenon. For such an analysis applied to the fair,
see Hugh Cunningham, "The Metropolitan
Fairs: A Case Study of the Social Control of
Leisure," in Social Control in Nineteenth Century Britain, ed. A. P. Donajgrodzki (London, 1977). (Sketches of Boz contains a piece
on Astley's circus, but it is almost entirely

concerned with the audience and hangers-on rather than the performers.)

91. Benjamin Disraeli, *Popanilla and Other Tales,* ed. Philip Guedalla (London, 1926), p. 15.

92. *Hard Times,* p. 2.

93. *Ibid.,* p. 125.

94. K. J. Fielding, "Charles Dickens and the Department of Practical Art," *Modern Language Review,* 1953; John Holloway, "*Hard Times:* A History and a Criticism," in *Dickens and the Twentieth Century,* pp. 163 ff.; Monroe Engel, *The Maturity of Dickens* (Cambridge, Mass., 1959), pp. 171 ff. This criticism has been rebutted by Robin Gilmour, "The Gradgrind School: Political Economy in the Classroom," *Victorian Studies,* 1967. See also Gilmour, "Dickens and the Self-Help Idea," in *The Victorians and Social Protest,* ed. J. Butt and I. F. Clarke (Devon, 1973).

95. *Hard Times,* p. 276 (Dickens to Henry Cole, June 17, 1854).

96. Holloway, pp. 166 ff.; G. D. Klingopulos, "Notes on the Victorian Scene," in *From Dickens to Hardy* (vol. VI of *Pelican Guide to English Literature,* London, 1958), p. 44; Ivanka Kovacevic, *Fact into Fiction: English Literature and the Industrial Scene, 1750–1850* (Leicester, 1975), pp. 114 ff.; Dingle Foot, introduction to Oxford ed. of *Hard Times* (1955), pp. xii ff.

97. *Hard Times,* p. 252. *Household Words* ran several articles on mutilations and deaths resulting from unprotected machinery, e.g., "Ground in the Mill," "Fencing with Humanity," "Death's Ciphering Book." See also Butwin, pp. 166 ff., for an account of an actual episode similar to that alluded to in this deleted passage.

98. *Hard Times,* pp. 206–07.

99. *Ibid.,* pp. 115–16.

100. *Ibid.,* p. 114. The original manuscript also included the phrase, "an' wi'out a thing to grace our lives" (p. 258). This was deleted on the proofs, perhaps because it was too fanciful a thought to assign to Stephen. But the idea does appear at the very end of the book, when Louisa is given the role of bringing "imaginative graces and delights" to the workers' lives, thus mitigating the effects of "machinery and reality" (p. 226).

101. *Ibid.,* pp. 120–21.

102. *The Later Letters of John Stuart Mill, 1849–1873,* ed. Francis E. Mineka and Dwight N. Lindley (Toronto, 1972), I, 190 (March 20, 1854).

103. Mill, *Autobiography,* ed. John Jacob Coss (New York, 1924), p. 99. One commentator on Mill who denies the similarities between Mill's situation and Louisa's also belittles the "crisis" episode in the *Autobiography* and Mill's own account of the emotional and esthetic effects of utilitarianism. (Alan Ryan, *J. S. Mill* [London, 1974], pp. 23 ff.)

104. *Hard Times,* p. 110.

105. *Ibid.,* p. 116.

106. *Ibid.,* p. 288.

107. *Ibid.,* pp. 164, 84.

108. *Ibid.,* pp. 115–16, 266.

109. *Ibid.,* p. 272 (Dec. 30, 1853). See also K. J. Fielding and Anne Smith, "*Hard Times* and the Factory Controversy: Dickens vs. Harriet Martineau," *Nineteenth Century Fiction,* 1970.

110. Forster, II, 86.

111. G. Otto Trevelyan, *The Life and Letters of Lord Macaulay* (New York, 1875), II, 320 (Aug. 12, 1854); Bagehot, *Literary Studies,* p. 157; *Dickens: The Critical Heritage,* p. 304.

112. Gissing, p. 242.

113. *The Dickens Critics,* pp. 127–28.

114. Charles Shapiro, "Afterword" to New American Library ed. of *Hard Times* (New York, 1961), p. 294.

115. *The Dickens Critics,* p. 171.

116. *Ibid.,* pp. 127–29.

117. Orwell, p. 434.

118. *Ibid.,* pp. 416–17.

119. See above, p. 455.

120. G. M. Young, *Victorian England: Portrait of an Age* (New York, 1954 [1st ed., 1936]), p. 89. In *Early Victorian England, 1830–1865,* ed. G. M. Young (London, 1934), II, 4 n., the minister is identified as Baldwin Brown.

121. Forster, I, 129.

CHAPTER XX

1. Carlyle, *Past and Present* (Everyman ed., London, 1912 [1st ed., 1843]), p.

197; Disraeli, *Sybil, or the Two Nations* (London, 1970 [1st ed., 1845]), p. 286.

2. William Flavelle Monypenny and George Earle Buckle, *The Life of Benjamin Disraeli, Earl of Beaconsfield* (London, 1929 [1st ed., 1910–20]), I, 866; II, 698; Lawrence and Elisabeth Hanson, *Necessary Evil: The Life of Jane Welsh Carlyle* (New York, 1952), p. 413 (quoting Carlyle's notebook, Feb. 28, 1852). For other evidence of Carlyle's anti-Semitism, see James Anthony Froude, *Thomas Carlyle: A History of His Life in London, 1834–1881* (London, 1884), II, 449.

3. Quoted by Morris Edmund Speare, *The Political Novel: Its Development in England and in America* (New York, 1966 [1st ed., 1924]), pp. 165–66.

4. Dickens, "The Chimes," in *Christmas Books* (Oxford, 1954), pp. 100, 106–07.

5. Michael Slater, "Dickens's Tracts for the Times," in *Dickens 1970: Centenary Essays,* ed. Michael Slater (London, 1970), p. 110.

6. *Coningsby, or, The New Generation* (London, 1870 [1st ed., 1844]), p. 134.

7. *Ibid.,* pp. vii–viii (preface to the 5th ed.).

8. Robert Blake, *Disraeli* (London, 1966), p. 191; Monypenny and Buckle, I, 1496 (Sept. 16, 1857).

9. Monypenny and Buckle, I, 629 (Aug. 31, 1844). His biographers suggest that he was alluding to "The Voyage of Captain Popanilla," published in 1828, which would have given him priority over Carlyle. But while that story was a biting satire on utilitarianism and political economy, it did not address itself specifically to the condition-of-the-people question; nor did it use that expression.

10. *Tocqueville and Beaumont on Social Reform,* ed. Seymour Drescher (New York, 1968), p. 18. (See above, p. 150.)

11. Asa Briggs, "The Language of 'Class' in Early Nineteenth-Century England," in *Essays in Labour History,* ed. A. Briggs and J. Saville (New York, 1960), p. 48.

12. Marx and Engels, *Collected Works* (New York, 1975), IV, 419–20. In the German edition of 1892, Engels noted that Disraeli had expressed a similar idea about the same time in *Sybil.*

13. Carlyle, *Sartor Resartus* (Everyman ed., London, 1908), pp. 214–15.

14. Plato, *The Republic,* Book IV, 423a.

15. *Sybil,* pp. 76–77. There was a well-known Lord Egremont, George O'Brien Wyndham, the third Earl of Egremont, a rich eccentric and a generous patron of agriculture and the arts who was mentioned in Cobbett's *Rural Rides.* (Penguin ed., London, 1967, p. 119.) This Lord Egremont died in 1837. Disraeli's character, it should be noted, is Mr., not Lord, Egremont; when he succeeds to the title, it is as the Earl of Marney.

16. *Sybil,* p. 112.

17. *Ibid.,* pp. 167–68.

18. *Ibid.,* pp. 60–62.

19. *Ibid.,* p. 116.

20. *Ibid.,* p. 198.

21. *Ibid.,* pp. 163–65.

22. *Ibid.,* p. 203.

23. *Ibid.,* pp. 204, 335, 319.

24. *Ibid.,* pp. 143, 335.

25. *Ibid.,* pp. 144, 118.

26. *Coningsby,* p. 115.

27. *Ibid.,* pp. 154–55.

28. *Sybil,* pp. 194, 96, 74–75.

29. *Ibid.,* pp. 95, 223.

30. *Ibid.,* p. 326.

31. *Ibid.,* p. 337.

32. *Ibid.,* pp. 319–20.

33. *Ibid.,* pp. 392–93.

34. *Ibid.,* p. 255.

35. *Ibid.,* p. 436.

36. *Ibid.,* p. 457.

37. *Ibid.,* p. 144.

38. *Ibid.,* p. 209.

39. *Ibid.,* p. 487.

40. Sheila Smith, "Willenhall and Wodgate: Disraeli's Use of Blue Book Evidence," *Review of English Studies,* 1962; Smith, *The Other Nation: The Poor in English Novels of the 1840s and 1850s* (Oxford, 1980), pp. 70 ff., 118 ff., and *passim;* Martin Fido, "The Treatment of Rural Distress in Disraeli's *Sybil,*" *Yearbook of English Studies,* 1975; Fido, " 'From His Own Observation': Sources of Working Class Passages in Disraeli's 'Sybil,' " *Modern Language Review,* 1977; Patrick Brantlinger, "Bluebooks, the Social Organism, and the Victorian Novel," *Criticism,* 1972.

41. *Letters of Charles Dickens*, ed. M. House and G. Storey (Oxford, 1974), III, 459 (March 6, 1843).

42. *Athenaeum*, May 17, 1845. See also *Douglas Jerrold's Shilling Magazine*, June 1845; Leslie Stephen, "Mr. Disraeli's Novels," *Fortnightly Review*, Oct. 1874.

43. *Sybil*, p. 192. The *Westminster Review* (1845) commented on the "Cockneyisms or Americanisms" Disraeli put into the mouths of his provincial workers. (See also Smith, p. 139.)

44. *Athenaeum*, May 17, 1845.

45. *Sybil*, p. 3.

46. *Ibid.*, pp. 208–09.

47. *Ibid.*, pp. 315, 320.

48. *Ibid.*, p. 284.

49. *Ibid.*, p. 340.

50. *Ibid.*, p. 166.

51. *Ibid.*, pp. 325–26.

52. 3 Hansard 49:246–52 (July 12, 1839).

53. Monypenny and Buckle, I, 483, 486.

54. G. M. Young, Review of Harold Beeley's *Disraeli* (1936), in *Victorian Essays* (London, 1962), p. 162.

55. Michael Foot, "The Tory as Hero," *Times Literary Supplement*, Apr. 18, 1980.

CHAPTER XXI

1. Kathleen Tillotson, *Novels of the Eighteen-Forties* (Oxford, 1965 [1st ed., 1954]), p. 208 (quoting *Fortnightly Review*, 1878).

2. Her father, William Stevenson, was widowed when she was one, and continued to live in London while she lived with her mother's family in Knutsford. He too had been a Unitarian minister near Manchester before his marriage, but had given up that vocation (because he did not believe it right to be paid for preaching the Gospel) in order to become first a farmer, then a university coach and writer in Edinburgh, then the Keeper of the Records at the Treasury, a sinecure that required his residence in London. It was there that Elizabeth was born in 1810. There has been a spate of full-length studies of Mrs. Gaskell recently, among

them, Winifred Gérin, *Elizabeth Gaskell* (Oxford, 1976); Wendy A. Craik, *Elizabeth Gaskell and the English Provincial Novel* (London, 1975); Coral Lansbury, *Elizabeth Gaskell: The Novel of Social Crisis* (London, 1975); Enid L. Duthie, *The Themes of Elizabeth Gaskell* (London, 1980); Angus Easson, *Elizabeth Gaskell* (London, 1979).

3. *Mary Barton: A Tale of Manchester Life* (Everyman ed., London, 1969 [1st ed., 1848]), p. 9. (Subsequent citations, except where otherwise noted, are to this edition.)

4. *Mary Barton*, in *The Works of Mrs. Gaskell* (New York, 1972), I, lxxxi. On the delay in publication, see *The Letters of Mrs. Gaskell*, ed. J. A. V. Chapple and Arthur Pollard (Cambridge, Mass., 1967), pp. 55 ff.

5. *Mary Barton*, pp. 52, 32, 104. Sheila Smith suggests that the text of "The Oldham Weaver" quoted by Mrs. Gaskell is a watered-down version of the original, which was more militant and bitter. Smith speculates that the singer from whom Gaskell took down the song probably gave her a "gentler version out of respect for her and her station in life." (*The Other Nation: The Poor in English Novels of the 1840s and 1850s* [Oxford, 1980], p. 201.) It may be that there were several versions circulating at the time and that Gaskell's was neither doctored by her nor toned down by her informant.

6. *Mary Barton*, pp. 158–60.

7. *Ibid.*, p. 363.

8. In the same letter in which Gaskell defended her original title (her publisher persuaded her to change it to *Mary Barton*), she spoke of John Barton as "my hero, *the* person with whom all my sympathies went, with whom I tried to identify myself at the time." (*Letters*, p. 74 [to Mrs. Greg, March (?) 1849].)

9. *Mary Barton*, pp. 161–62.

10. Raymond Williams, *Culture and Society, 1780–1950* (New York, 1966 [1st ed., 1958]), p. 90.

11. John Lucas, "Mrs. Gaskell and Brotherhood," in *Tradition and Tolerance in Nineteenth-Century Fiction*, ed. David Howard et al. (New York, 1967), p. 173; P. J. Keating, *The Working Classes in Victorian Fiction* (London, 1971), pp. 227 ff.; John Gross, review of Arthur Pollard, *Mrs. Gaskell, New York Review of Books*, Dec. 29,

1966. Arnold Kettle, although basically agreeing with this criticism (he speaks of Gaskell's "pious desire to mediate"), gives her credit for transcending the "limitations of her conscious outlook." ("The Early Victorian Social-Problem Novel," in *From Dickens to Hardy [Pelican Guide to English Literature,* London, 1958], VI, 181.) Tillotson's account is notably free of this criticism; for her the murder is an integral, unproblematic part of the novel (pp. 204 ff.).

12. *Letters,* p. 281 (Apr. 23, 1854).

13. *Ibid.,* p. 196 (Aug. 16, 1852).

14. *Mary Barton,* p. 78.

15. *Ibid.,* p. 172. Gaskell anglicized the professor's name. Carlyle's professor was "Teufelsdröckh."

16. Gérin, pp. 89–90 (Nov. 8, 1848); Lawrence and Elisabeth Hanson, *Necessary Evil: The Life of Jane Welsh Carlyle* (New York, 1952), p. 407 (Sept. 7, 1851).

17. *Mary Barton,* pp. 345–46.

18. *Ibid.,* p. 363.

19. *Ibid.,* pp. 363–64.

20. *Ibid.,* p. 365.

21. *Ibid.,* pp. 366–67.

22. *Ibid.,* pp. 365, 362.

23. Keating, pp. 228 ff.

24. *Ibid.,* p. 233; Lucas, p. 173.

25. *North and South* (London, 1951 [1st ed., 1855]), pp. 75, 303.

26. *Ibid.,* pp. 87–88.

27. *Ibid.,* p. 333.

28. *Ibid.,* p. 166.

29. *Ibid.,* pp. 427–28.

30. *Ibid.,* p. 428.

31. *Ibid.,* p. 87.

32. See above, pp. 55–56.

33. For example, Arthur Pollard, *Mrs. Gaskell: Novelist and Biographer* (Cambridge, Mass., 1965), pp. 44–45.

34. *Mary Barton,* pp. 4–7.

35. *North and South,* pp. 304–05.

36. See above, p. 496.

37. Dickens, *Hard Times* (New York, 1966 [1st ed., 1854]), p. 53.

38. *North and South,* p. 307.

39. Herbert Spencer, *An Autobiography* (London, 1904), I, 350.

40. Gérin, pp. 89–90.

41. Amy Cruse, *The Victorians and Their Reading* (Boston, 1935), p. 144.

42. *Ibid.*

43. Gaskell, *Letters,* p. 68 (Jan. 1, 1849); p. 67 (late 1848).

44. Williams, pp. 87 ff.; Keating, pp. 6–8; Kettle, pp. 178, 181; Martha Vicinus, *The Industrial Muse: A Study of Nineteenth Century British Working-Class Literature* (New York, 1974), p. 126. Williams is more respectful than the others of Gaskell's intentions, and they all tend to be more respectful of *Mary Barton* than of *North and South.*

45. J. M. Jefferson, "Industrialisation and Poverty: In Fact and Fiction," in *The Long Debate on Poverty: Eight Essays on Industrialisation and 'The Condition of England,'* ed. Arthur Seldon (London, 1972), pp. 199 ff.

46. Williams, p. 91. Perhaps this is why the social novelists do not figure prominently in Williams's *The Country and the City* (New York, 1973). The one novelist who does, Dickens, is properly represented as a great lover of London.

47. Philip Collins, "Dickens and Industrialism," *Studies in English Literature,* 1980, p. 654.

48. *Athenaeum,* May 17, 1845.

49. Tillotson, p. 206 (quoting *Westminster Review,* April 1849).

EPILOGUE

1. *Report from His Majesty's Commissioners for Inquiring into the Administration and Practical Operation of the Poor Laws* (London, 1834), p. 156.

2. Burke, "Thoughts and Details on Scarcity" (1795), *Works* (Bohn ed., London, 1909–12), V, 84; "Letters on a Regicide Peace" (1797), *ibid.,* p. 321.

3. *Ibid.,* p. 321.

4. Smith, *An Inquiry into the Nature and Causes of the Wealth of Nations,* ed. Edwin Cannan (New York, 1937 [1st ed., 1776]), pp. 11–16.

5. Malthus, *On Population,* ed. Gertrude Himmelfarb (New York, 1960 [1st ed., 1798]), p. 109.

6. W. F. Monypenny and G. E. Buckle, *The Life of Benjamin Disraeli, Earl of Beaconsfield* (London, 1929 [1st ed., 1910]), I, 378.

7. Carlyle, *Chartism,* in *English and Other Critical Essays* (Everyman ed., London, n.d.), p. 17.

8. Thomas Plint, *Crime in England, Its Relation, Character, and Extent, as Developed from 1801 to 1848* (New York, 1974 [1st ed., 1851]), p. 153.

9. *Morning Chronicle,* May 25, 1850.

10. See above, pp. 220, 501, 508.

11. E. P. Thompson, "The Political Education of Henry Mayhew," *Victorian Studies,* 1967, p. 43.

12. The first volume, published in 1889, was entitled *Life and Labour of the People* and was entirely on East London. The second volume, which appeared two years later under the title *Labour and Life of the People,* was on the whole of London. In 1892–93 these two volumes were reissued (revised and rearranged) in a four-volume edition under the title *Life and Labour of the People in London.* This title was retained for the rest of the work, with the first four volumes subtitled "Poverty Series."

13. Norman and Jeanne MacKenzie, *The Fabians* (New York, 1977), p. 62.

14. Booth, I, 166, 177.

15. T. S. Simey and M. B. Simey, *Charles Booth: Social Scientist* (Oxford, 1960), p. 261, n. 5.

16. Seebohm Rowntree's *Poverty and Progress: A Second Social Survey of York* (London, 1941) was a sequel to his earlier study of York, *Poverty: A Study of Town Life* (London, 1901). The argument for a "national minimum" appeared in Sidney and Beatrice Webb, *The Break-up of the Poor Law: Being Part One of the Minority Report of the Poor Law Commission* (London, 1909).

17. The first systematic use of this concept was by W. G. Runciman, *Relative Deprivation and Social Justice* (Berkeley, 1966). Runciman did not relativize the idea as thoroughly as Peter Townsend and others were to do.

18. Smith, p. 821.

19. Mary Douglas, "Relative Poverty—Relative Communication," in *Traditions of Social Policy: Essays in Honour of Violet Butler,* ed. A. H. Halsey (Oxford, 1976); Peter Townsend, *Poverty in the United Kingdom: A Survey of Household Resources and Standards of Living* (London, 1979).

20. Thomas Babington Macaulay, *The History of England from the Accession of James II,* in *Works* (London, 1875), I, 333.

INDEX

Gertrude Himmelfarb is Distinguished Professor of History at the Graduate School of the City University of New York. She has received fellowships from the Guggenheim Foundation, the Rockefeller Foundation, the National Endowment for the Humanities, and the Woodrow Wilson International Center, among others. Her previous books include *Lord Acton: A Study in Conscience and Politics*, *Darwin and the Darwinian Revolution*, *On Liberty and Liberalism: The Case of John Stuart Mill*, and *Victorian Minds*, which was nominated for a National Book Award in 1968. Miss Himmelfarb has also edited works by Acton, Malthus, and Mill.

A NOTE ON THE TYPE

The text of this book was set in film in a typeface named Bembo. The roman is a copy of a letter cut for the celebrated Venetian printer Aldus Manutius by Francesco Griffo. It was first used in Cardinal Bembo's DE AETNA of 1495—hence the name of the revival. Griffo's type is now generally recognized, thanks to the research of Stanley Morison, to be the first of the old-face group of types. The companion italic is an adaptation of the chancery script type designed by the Roman calligrapher and printer Lodovico degli Arrighi, called Vincentino, and used by him during the 1520's.

Composed by The Haddon Craftsmen, Inc.,
Scranton, Pennsylvania.
Printed and bound by Murray Printing Company,
Westford, Massachusetts.

Design by Judith Henry